T0180014

Lecture Notes in Computer Science 13210

More information about this series at https://link.springer.com/bookseries/558

Oliver Hohlfeld · Giovane Moura ·
Cristel Pelsser (Eds.)

Passive and Active Measurement

23rd International Conference, PAM 2022
Virtual Event, March 28–30, 2022
Proceedings

 Springer

Editors
Oliver Hohlfeld 🆔
Brandenburg University of Technology
Cottbus, Germany

Giovane Moura 🆔
SIDN Labs - TU Delft
Arnhem, The Netherlands

Cristel Pelsser 🆔
ICube - University of Strasbourg
Illkirch, France

ISSN 0302-9743   ISSN 1611-3349   (electronic)
Lecture Notes in Computer Science
ISBN 978-3-030-98784-8   ISBN 978-3-030-98785-5   (eBook)
https://doi.org/10.1007/978-3-030-98785-5

This Springer imprint is published by the registered company Springer Nature Switzerland AG
The registered company address is: Gewerbestrasse 11, 6330 Cham, Switzerland

Preface

We are excited to present the proceedings of the 23rd annual Passive and Active Measurement (PAM) conference. After more than two decades, PAM continues to provide an essential venue for emerging and early-stage research in network measurements – work that seeks to better understand complex, real-world networked systems and offer critical empirical foundations and support to network research. In light of a still ongoing global COVID-19 pandemic, this 23rd edition of PAM was held as a virtual (online) conference during March 28–30, 2022. This year's edition benefited from experiences gathered by measuring the partcipants' feedback from PAM 2020 and PAM 2021, both held online.

This year's proceedings demonstrate the importance and extent to which measurements permeate systems – from protocols to performance to security. In total, we received 62 double-blind submissions from authors representing 47 unique institutions, of which the Technical Program Committee (TPC) selected 30 for publication – on a par with last year's published papers. A novelty this year was the possibility of submitting long papers. We received 30 long submissions, out of which half were accepted. We thus reached the same acceptance rate for long and short submissions. We paid particular attention to the TPC composition, intending to have it as broadly representative as possible, including both junior and senior researchers. We are indebted to the hard-working TPC members, who ensured that each paper received four reviews and carried out a lively (and in several cases spirited) online discussion to arrive at the final program. TPC members were asked to provide constructive feedback, bearing in mind PAM's focus and goals that recognize promising early work and reproducibility effort. For PAM 2022 we once again implemented a Review Task Force (RTF), following the model used by USENIX Security and ACM IMC. The RTF included senior, experienced researchers from the community, who are also great mentors. The engagement of such a group ensured that all the TPC's feedback met high standards of technical correctness, specific critiques, and a positive, constructive tone. To ensure the quality of the program and equanimity of the presented results, 18 papers were assigned a shepherd from the TPC members who reviewed the paper. We are delighted with the final set of 30 papers and hope the readers find them as valuable and provocative as we do.

We would be remiss not to thank the Steering Committee for helping organize the conference. We thank SIDN for being the hosting institution. We thank Marco Davids as Web chair, Moritz Müller as Registration chair, and Caspar Schutijser as Video chair, along with all the volunteers who helped run the online sessions. We also thank the legal team at SIDN (Maarten Simon, Karin Vink, and April Löwe) who helped us navigate the Dutch and European privacy laws. Last but not least, we thank all the researchers who have made PAM such an exciting and essential conference for all these years.

March 2022   Oliver Hohlfeld
                                                                             Giovane Moura
                                                                             Cristel Pelsser

Organization

General Chair

Giovane C. M. Moura   SIDN Labs/TU Delft, The Netherlands

Program Committee Chairs

Oliver Hohlfeld   Brandenburg University of Technology, Germany
Cristel Pelsser   University of Strasbourg, France

Web Chair

Marco Davids   SIDN Labs, The Netherlands

Registration Chair

Moritz Müller   SIDN Labs/University of Twente, The Netherlands

Steering Committee

Marinho P. Barcellos   University of Waikato, New Zealand
Fabian E. Bustamante   Northwestern University, USA
Anja Feldmann   Max Planck Institute for Informatics, Germany
Jelena Mirkovic   University of Southern California, USA
Michalis Faloutsos   University of California, USA
Steve Uhlig   Queen Mary University of London, UK

Program Committee

Abhishta Abhishta   University of Twente, The Netherlands
Alan (Zaoxing) Liu   Boston University, USA
Alessandro Finamore   Huawei Technologies, France
Alessio Botta   University of Napoli Federico II, Italy
Alexander Gamero-Garrido   Northeastern University, USA
Amreesh Phokeer   ISOC, Mauritius
Anja Feldmann   MPI, Germany
Anna Brunström   KAU, Sweden
Anna Sperotto   University of Twente, The Netherlands
Anubhavnidhi   ByteDance, USA
   Abhashkumar
Aqsa Kashaf   Carnegie Mellon University, USA

Arani Bhattacharya	Indraprastha Institute of Information Technology (IIIT) Delhi, India
Benoit Donnet	University of Liège, Belgium
Carlos Ganan	ICANN, The Netherlands
Chadi Barakat	Université Côte d'Azur/Inria, France
Diana Andreea Popescu	Amazon Web Services, UK
Esteban Carisimo	Northwestern University, USA
Fabian Bustamante	Northwestern University, USA
Gareth Tyson	Queen Mary University of London, UK
Georgios Smaragdakis	TU Delft, The Netherlands
Ioana Livadariu	SimulaMet, Norway
Johan Mazel	ANSSI, France
Juan Tapiador	Universidad Carlos III de Madrid, Spain
Kensuke Fukuda	NII, Japan
Kevin Vermeulen	Columbia University, USA
Kittipat Apicharttrisorn	Carnegie Mellon University, USA
Kyle Schomp	Akamai, USA
Lianjie Cao	Hewlett Packard Labs, USA
Liz Izhikevich	Stanford University, USA
Luca Vassio	Politecnico di Torino, Italy
Maciej Korczyński	Grenoble Alps University, France
Marcel Flores	Edgecast, USA
Mark Allman	ICSI, USA
Marwan Fayed	Cloudflare, UK
Matteo Varvello	Nokia Bell Labs, USA
Matthew Luckie	University of Waikato, New Zealand
Matthias Wählisch	Freie Universität Berlin, Germany
Mattijs Jonker	University of Twente, The Netherlands
Maurizio Naldi	LUMSA University, Italy
Moritz Müller	SIDN/University of Twente, The Netherlands
Niklas Carlsson	Linköping University, Sweden
Olaf Maennel	Tallinn University of Technology, Estonia
Oliver Gasser	Max Planck Institute for Informatics, Germany
Owezarski Philippe	LAAS-CNRS, France
Ram Durairajan	University of Oregon, USA
Ramakrishna Padmanabhan	CAIDA/UC San Diego, USA
Randy Bush	IIJ, Japan/Arrcus, USA
Ricky K. P. Mok	CAIDA/UC San Diego, USA
Robert Beverly	NPS, USA
Roland van Rijswijk-Deij	University of Twente, The Netherlands
Romain Fontugne	IIJ, Japan
Ryo Nakamura	University of Tokyo, Japan
Sandrine Vaton	IMT Atlantique, France
Shuai Hao	Old Dominion University, USA
Soheil Abbasloo	University of Toronto, Canada
Solange Rito Lima	University of Minho, Portugal

Srdjan Matic	IMDEA Networks Institute, Spain
Stephen McQuistin	University of Glasgow, UK
Stephen Strowes	Fastly, UK
Suranga Seneviratne	University of Sydney, Australia
Tatsuya Mori	Waseda University, Japan
Thomas Krenc	NPS, USA
Tijay Chung	Virginia Tech, USA
Tobias Fiebig	TU Delft, The Netherlands
Vaibhav Bajpai	TU Munich, Germany
Vasileios Giotsas	Lancaster University, UK
Yang Chen	Fudan University, China
Youngjoon Won	Hanyang University, Korea
Zachary Bischof	CAIDA/UC San Diego, USA
Zili Meng	Tsinghua University, China

External Reviewers

| Stefanie Roos | TU Delft, The Netherlands |
| Oğuzhan Ersoy | TU Delft, The Netherlands |

Contents

DNS and Routing

Routing II

Internet Applications

Security

LogoMotive: Detecting Logos on Websites to Identify Online Scams - A TLD Case Study

Thijs van den Hout[1(✉)], Thymen Wabeke[1], Giovane C. M. Moura[1,2], and Cristian Hesselman[1,3]

[1] SIDN Labs, Arnhem, The Netherlands
{thijs.vandenhout,thymen.wabeke,giovane.moura,cristian.hesselman}@sidn.nl
[2] TU Delft, Delft, The Netherlands
[3] University of Twente, Enschede, The Netherlands

Abstract. Logos give a website a familiar feel and promote trust. Scammers take advantage of that by using well-known organizations' logos on malicious websites. Unsuspecting Internet users see these logos and think they are looking at a government website or legitimate webshop, when it is a phishing site, a counterfeit webshop, or a site set up to spread misinformation. We present the largest logo detection study on websites to date. We analyze 6.2M domain names from the Netherlands' country-code top-level domain .nl, in two case studies to detect logo misuse for two organizations: the Dutch national government and *Thuiswinkel Waarborg*, an organization that issues certified webshop trust marks. We show how we can detect phishing, spear phishing, dormant phishing attacks, and brand misuse. To that end, we developed `LogoMotive`, an application that crawls domain names, generates screenshots, and detects logos using supervised machine learning. `LogoMotive` is operational in the .nl registry, and it is generalizable to detect any other logo in any DNS zone to help identify abuse.

1 Introduction

A logo is a critical element of the visual identity of an organization. They influence people's perception of an organization [47], and help people to identify the associated company quickly. In the *real world*, organizations are typically very keen to protect their corporate identity (and their logo's use), by using brand protection methods [61].

The same is true for unauthorized *online* use of corporate logos: phishing attacks, for example, often attempt to impersonate organizations and use their logos both in e-mails and on webpages [1,29] while counterfeit luxury goods webshops perform trademark infringement by misusing the original brand's logos [58,59].

Besides phishing and trademark infringement, logos can also be misused in *government impersonation scams* [13,15,16], in which fraudsters attempt to impersonate governments to perform a series of crimes: "extortion, tax fraud, social security fraud, asking for donations, lenient punishment, waiver of fines, and so on" [16]. Government impersonation ultimately undermines the government's own authority to enforce laws and policies [16].

This paper focuses on identifying various types of online abuse and scams that rely on logo misuse. We do so by detecting logos on all websites in the .nl zone and continuously monitoring newly registered domain names, providing brand owners' abuse analysts with a complete overview of their logo's use online. With this point of view, various forms of abuse can be detected, including phishing, spear phishing, trademark infringement, misinformation, and more. To that end, we present LogoMotive (Sect. 2), an application that employs deep-learning for logo detection on websites' screenshots. LogoMotive crawls a domain, generates screenshots, detects logos in these screenshots and provides analysts with a web dashboard for annotation. Our system is designed to have operational impact, which means that we want to prevent LogoMotive from making autonomous decisions about domain names – ultimately protecting domains from being mislabeled and their potential consequences, such as being suspended or removed from the DNS zone. Therefore we decided to follow the human-in-the-loop principle [38]. This means we leave the assessment of whether a website abuses a logo to human analysts and do not automatically classify websites.

We present two cases studies, in which we apply LogoMotive to the 6.2M domains present in the .nl DNS zone – the country-code top-level domain (ccTLD) of the Netherlands. As such, ours is the largest research on logo detection on websites to date (the largest study before us analyzed 350k websites [29]).

In the first case study, we partner with the Dutch national government to detect government impersonation scams. In the second case study, we team up with *Thuiswinkel Waarborg*, a widely recognized trust mark certificate issuer for webshops in the Netherlands, to identify false claims of trust mark membership. We detected over 10k domain names containing the logo in both studies, which were all annotated manually by human abuse analysts at the respective organizations.

We make the following contributions: first, we show that logo detection is a powerful method to detect phishing, spear phishing, and potential phishing attacks in government impersonation scams (Sect. 3.1): we detect 168 instances of government logo misuse, 6 were active phishing domains, which attempted to commit online identity theft and bank credential theft, targeting the citizens of the Netherlands. These phishing websites were removed from the .nl zone after the usual legal due diligence.

LogoMotive is a powerful tool because it detects abuse usually missed by the traditional blocklist or HTML-based detection methods. Furthermore, it is more broadly applicable than finding phishing attacks only; it provides a complete overview of a logo's (mis)use in a DNS zone. Optionally, users can choose to monitor only newly registered websites with LogoMotive, which greatly reduces the amount of manual work over analyzing the entire .nl zone. In our experiments, we found that most malicious use of logos is found in recently registered domain names.

Our second contribution is to document the presence of "dormant" phishing websites (Sect. 3.2): government typo-squatted domains, which employ HTTP redirects [14] to forward users to the *legitimate* government website. While seemly innocuous, these websites might do so to leverage search engine optimization to increase the number of visitors [59], and could, at their will, replace the HTTP redirect by an actual phishing website, potentially compromising their visitors. Typo-squad detection systems are insufficient since they rely on a predetermined list of domain names on which variants are based. We found 9 cases of dormant phishing websites and 2 cases of dormant spear phishing attacks (targeted at very specific government agencies). Some of these typo-squat domains had MX records [34] – which specify e-mail servers – indicating that phishing e-mails can be sent from these very suspicious domains. Worse, these malicious domains websites would *redirect* users to the *legitimate* government website, which could give a false sense of legitimacy to these suspicious domains, increasing the chances of spear phishing success.

Our third contribution is to show that logo detection can be successfully used to detect fake claims of trust mark certification (Sect. 4): we detect 208 domain names leading to webshops that falsely claimed to be certified by the trust mark organization by displaying their logo, thereby misleading consumers. The trust mark organization requested these websites to remove the logo.

`LogoMotive`, our tool, is operational and has been active in the `.nl` zone for the last 8 months for both use cases here presented. We show operational impact by removing phishing websites before users can be compromised and displaying its broad applicability in finding online logo abuse. `LogoMotive` can be applied to any DNS zone and easily trained to support different logos. Hence, we make `LogoMotive`'s source code available upon request for academic purposes on https://logomotive.sidnlabs.nl, and actively promote deployment by peer registries such that `LogoMotive` can be used to find abuse in other DNS zones besides `.nl`.

2   LogoMotive

Next we present `LogoMotive`, the application that we have developed to perform logo recognition on websites. It has three main modules, as shown in the lower part of Fig. 1: *Crawler*, which takes a list of domain names as input and generates screenshots from their webpages, *Logo Detector*, which applies a deep learning algorithm to detect logos on those screenshots, and the *Dashboard*, which is used by abuse analysts who are responsible for labeling the results.

`LogoMotive` detects the presence of logos on websites, but it is not designed to automatically determine if the logo is used legitimately or not – for that, we rely on manual validation. Analysts evaluate each domain name on which their respective logo was detected. Our case studies in Sect. 3 and Sect. 4 show how analysts evaluated more than 20k domain names from the `.nl` zone.

We also add other requirements for `LogoMotive`: It must be accurate enough to limit the number of false positives and stay manageable by human analysts.

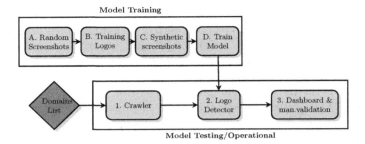

Fig. 1. `LogoMotive` architecture: model training (upper part) and operational part (lower part).

It should also be scalable, *i.e.,* able to be used to analyze DNS zones of different sizes in reasonable time, and adaptable, meaning it should be possible to detect new logos with ease.

2.1 LogoMotive Modules

Crawler: As shown in Fig. 1, the Crawler module takes a list of domain names as input and crawls the homepage of their websites (if available), following any redirects. For each website, it generates 1024×1024 pixels screenshots: two semi-overlapping from the page header towards the footer and, if not yet captured, two semi-overlapping screenshots from the footer (bottom) of the page up. We focus on the header and footer of websites, where logos are typically placed, reducing the search space for screenshots, especially on very long webpages. In our experiments, the crawler module generates 2.7 screenshots per website on average; in 65%, the first two screenshots of the header already cover all the homepage's display area.

To implement this module, we use Selenium hub [53], an automated, programmable browser that allows running multiple browser sessions in parallel. We run this module in Docker containers to easily deploy our crawler and up or down scale the number of browser nodes. Instead of downloading all image resources, we take screenshots to make sure we analyze the webpages as a regular user would see it. Furthermore, images might be hidden in CSS or SVG paths, and logos could be embedded in a larger image, thereby escaping detection.

Performance: our code is parallelized, and with 15 browser nodes, we are able to crawl 5.2 domain names per second (19k/hour) on a 12-CPU 64 GB memory machine.

Logo Detector: To detect logos on the screenshots of websites, we employ YOLO [45], which is a supervised machine learning (deep learning) algorithm designed to perform object detection.

Why YOLO: there is a large number of object detection algorithms that could be used for image recognition, such as Single Shot Multibox Detector [30], Fast(er)

Fig. 2. YOLO detects the government logo on a website.

R-CNN [46], or static feature-extraction and matching models using for example SIFT [31], SURF [3], or ORB [49]. We chose YOLO because recent comparison studies have shown YOLO outperforms other deep learning models in terms of inference speed, and in many cases also accuracy [51,54]. It is also easy and relatively fast to train, which is important for the scalability of LogoMotive. Because we do not change any significant details in the training or deployment of the detection model, we trust the existing comparison studies in making our choice. In our experiments, we found that the static detection methods using feature description matching perform worse than YOLO since it is not accelerated by a GPU. Also, it struggles with detection if multiple logos are shown on a page, and requires to be applied separately for each logo class we wish to detect.

How YOLO Works: YOLO is a one-stage detection model, which means it is trained to do bounding box regression and classification at the same time, making it faster than two-stage counterparts such as Faster R-CNN [54]. YOLO is a supervised machine learning model which is trained on images that contain the to-be-detected objects (logos in our case), and a list of coordinates and dimensions that describe bounding boxes around the objects, with their corresponding class labels.

At inference time, YOLO first divides the input image into multiple grids of a varying number of cells, each of which predicts several bounding boxes, as well as the class label and confidence scores of each detection. We show an example in Fig. 2. We crawl a random website and YOLO detects the logo on it. The output is the corner coordinates of the bounding boxes that describe where logos are found on the image, together with the logo class, and confidence scores (ranging from 0 to 1), which indicate how certain the model is of its detections.

Overlapping detections are filtered out by a process called nonmaximal suppression, which discards the results with lower confidences, keeping only the detections with the highest confidence.

Performance: In our setup (12-CPU/64 GB RAM machine), we use an Nvidia GeForce RTX 2080Ti for training YOLO, which is designed to leverage GPUs.

Table 1. Datasets used for `LogoMotive` training and validation.

	Value
Crawled random domains	25,000
Screenshots generated	64,893
Synthetic training samples	100,000
training set	95,000
validation set	5,000

In this setup, we can evaluate 50 screenshots per second. We use the YOLOv5 open-source python implementation by Ultralytics [57].

Scalability: YOLO can successfully be trained to detect many classes at once, e.g. the Objects365 dataset [52], which contains 365 object classes. This indicates YOLO will not be a bottleneck in the scalability of `LogoMotive`, as more logos are to be detected.

Dashboard: The last component is a web dashboard, on which analysts manually evaluate the logo detection results. It lists the domain names, the screenshots on which logos were detected, and metadata such as registration information to aid in the labeling. It allows the analysts to classify each detection, and label the use of logos on the websites as malicious or legitimate. This can later be used to follow up on the results with the appropriate measures. We host a dashboard for each class of logos we detect, meaning only relevant results are shown on each dashboard. We include a screenshot of the analysis pop-up on the dashboard in Appendix Sect. A.

Scalability: Abuse analysts at the brand owner's organization analyze the webpages on which their logo was found. This means that as `LogoMotive` is scaled to detect more logos, the workload of any particular analyst does not increase. The dashboard is a dockerized web application that can easily be scaled up.

2.2   Model Training

As a supervised learning algorithm, YOLO requires *labeled* data to be trained, so it can learn to recognize logos.

Generating labeled datasets for the training of object detection models is a very time-intensive task when performed manually. To avoid that, we generate a synthetic training dataset, a common practice in the training of various object detection models [12,56]. We generate the synthetic training datasets by (i) crawling 25k random `.nl` domain names with our crawler module, resulting in 64k screenshots, and (ii) overlaying the logos we wish to detect at random locations on these screenshots.

We randomly augment the logos by changing aspects such as scale, opacity, color, blur, occlusion, and others, such that the model becomes robust against the various appearances of logos on websites. Additionally, the augmentations make the detector robust against simple adversarial attacks. We create 100k training samples with this process, which is sufficient to train our model to convergence, meaning the mean average precision does not increase further. We use 95% (95k) as training samples, and the remaining 5% for validation (5k), see Table 1. The validation set is used during training to monitor the generalizability of the model and to spot issues such as model overfitting. We generate 100K training samples in a little over 30 min using our method. This allows us to train the model on any logos we want to detect with minimal effort.

YOLO can be trained to detect multiple logos at once, so we do not need to train a separate detection model for each logo. We generate the synthetic training data with all the logos we wish to detect, resulting in a single dataset with screenshots that each contain one or more logos that should be detected. When more logos are to be detected, we can simply regenerate the training data including the new logos, and retrain the model, making this process scalable in practice.

The detection model was trained in 50 iterations over the whole training set, using the Adam optimizer [24], after which we found the model converged.

2.3 Model Tuning

YOLO assigns a confidence score to each logo it detects, as shown in Fig. 2. We can choose a confidence threshold to reduce the number of false positives. Detections with a confidence score lower than the confidence threshold are discarded. Tweaking the confidence threshold thus changes the trade-off between the model's precision and recall evaluation metrics. Precision is the fraction of detected domain names that indeed display the logo. Recall is the fraction of domain names that display the logo that we successfully detected. A high confidence threshold means we discard more detections, which leads to lower recall, but a higher precision.

The results of the logo detection module are manually analyzed and labeled on the web dashboard (Sect. A) by abuse analysts. Manual annotation of these results is a time-intensive task, so we would like to limit the number of false positive-samples the analysts must go through. Experimentally we found that a confidence threshold of 0.8 results in a precision of 90%, which is sufficient to still allow analysts to manually classify the results without overwhelming them. Given this confidence threshold, LogoMotive still finds logos that are visually altered by for example changing colors, stretching, and changing details. Logos that are altered beyond the point of recognition will not instill trust in the visitors and are therefore not a threat in the scope of this research.

2.4 Model Evaluation

In practice, we cannot determine the recall performance of our model in the entire .nl zone, because we do not have the ground truth of all .nl-websites. To evaluate the recall of our model, we generated a test set with the two logos of

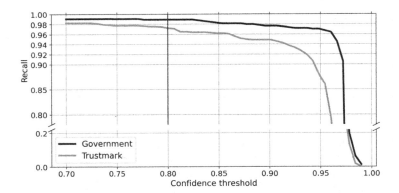

Fig. 3. Recall performance of LogoMotive at confidence thresholds. The vertical line denotes our chosen threshold.

the institutions we collaborate with: the logo of the Dutch national government, and the logo of *Thuiswinkel Waarborg*.

Dataset Generation: We used our crawler module to take screenshots of 1271 domain names from the government's website portfolio, 1300 domain names from the trust mark's member list, and 1300 random domain names from the .nl-zone, which generally do not include either logo. We manually annotated the screenshots generated by the crawler module to determine which logos are shown on the crawled websites. Our manual annotation resulted in a test set with 635 domain names showing a website with the Dutch national government logo, 962 with the *Thuiswinkel Waarborg* logo, and 2096 showing neither logo.

We then applied our logo detection model on this test set to compute the recall of our algorithm at various confidence thresholds. The results are shown in Fig. 3.

Using our default confidence threshold of 0.8, we obtain precision scores of 0.986 and 0.983 and recall scores of 0.989 and 0.968 for the government logo and trust mark logo respectively. This indicates that the model misses very few logos in the .nl zone. The small difference in recall between logos represents the difficulty of detecting a particular logo. Generally speaking, the more distinct features a logo contains, the easier it is to detect.

Note that the precision in this set is higher than it would be in the entire .nl zone, because this evaluation set contains a larger fraction of screenshots with a logo. The precision in practice is around 90% in the entire .nl zone at a confidence threshold of 80%, according to the manual annotation of the results in our use cases.

3 Government Impersonation Case Study

After training our model to detect logos, we apply it to detect Dutch national government impersonation scams in the .nl zone, which is the primary TLD used by the national government. We apply `LogoMotive` in two modes. In the first mode (Sect. 3.1), we evaluate monthly snapshots of the entire zone. To detect short-lived scams, we also apply the model in the live mode, in which we evaluate every newly registered domain name (Sect. 3.2).

3.1 Full Zone Evaluation

Data Collection: Using the Crawler module (Sect. 2.1), we obtain screenshots from websites in the entire `.nl` zone. For this case study, we report 5 full passes on the `.nl` zone (covering March to July 2021). Table 2 shows our datasets.

Table 2. Datasets for government impersonation case study (2021).

	March	April	May	June	July
Domains	6.02M	6.18M	6.19M	6.20M	6.20M
Domains without websites	3.75M	3.53M	3.28M	3.30M	3.56M
Domains with websites	2.27M	2.65M	2.91M	2.90M	2.64M
unchanged websites	–	750K	744K	985K	873K
changed/new websites	–	1.90M	2.17M	1.92M	1.77M
Domains processed	2.27M	1.90M	2.17M	1.92M	1.77M

Reducing Search Space: The `.nl` zone has over 6.2M domain names. `.nl` crawls its entire zone monthly using DMAP [62]; another crawler tool that collects metadata of `.nl`-websites. We use this metadata to reduce our search space by removing domain names that do not host a webpage, show an empty page or give HTTP errors. As shown in Table 2, this allows us to go from 6.02M domain names to 2.27M domains on which we generate screenshots, for March. For April through July, we can further reduce the number of domain names the Crawler visits by excluding websites that have not changed compared to the previous visit, which we identify by analyzing the hash of the webpage.

Results: The "Full-Zone" column in Table 3 shows the results (we explain the "Newly-Registered" column in Sect. 3.2). In total, `LogoMotive` detected 12.8K domain names, 11.7K of which indeed displayed the government logo (91% precision). Given `LogoMotive` only detects the presence (or absence) of the government logo, we need to rely on manual inspection of these domains to determine if they are malicious or not. Abuse analysts at the Dutch national government manually went through the 12.8K results and categorized all of them. The analysts deal with domain name abuse daily and by working for the government they are in the best position to determine whether or not their logo is used maliciously or legitimately. Due to the time-intensive nature of the annotation work, each result is labeled by one analyst, which restricts us from comparing results between analysts.

Table 3. Manual validation results for government impersonation case study.

Label	Full-Zone	Newly-Registered
Total	12862 (100.00%)	53
Without gov. logo (FP)	1164 (9.05%)	0 (0.00%)
With gov. logo (TP)	11698 (90.95%)	53 (100.0%)
Benign	10595 (82.37%)	32 (60.38%)
Government impersonation	151 (1.17%)	17 (32.09%)
Phishing	3 (0.02%)	3 (5.66%)
Potential threat	73 (0.57%)	9 (16.98%)
Other (false endorsements, satire, etc.)	75 (0.58%)	5 (9.43%)
Government domains	952 (7.40%)	4 (7.55%)
In portfolio	636 (4.94%)	2 (0.00%)
Not in portfolio	316 (2.46%)	2 (3.77%)
Added	109 (0.85%)	1 (1.89%)
Pending	207 (1.61%)	1 (1.89%)

The most critical category covers government impersonation. We found 151 domains in this category, of which 3 were phishing domains. Two of them were phishing websites mimicking the National Tax Authority (Belastingdienst) of the Netherlands, and the other one was a phishing website related to the national online authentication system (DigiD). The average age of these domains was 15 d upon detection. This shows that LogoMotive can help to pick up scams that have not been reported to blocklists yet. Shorter-lived attacks may be detected quicker by continuously scanning the zone. This is why we look specifically at new registrations in Sect. 3.2.

The government impersonation category also contains 73 domain names that are a potential threat. This includes domains that return an HTTP redirect to a legitimate government domain but are registered by a third party who has no connection with the government. This includes suspicious names, such as a domain containing the terms 'vaccination' and 'appointment' which redirected to the official government website (coronatest.nl), the website on which Dutch citizens can plan an appointment for a COVID-19 test.

Domain Name Popularity: we estimate, indirectly, how popular these government impersonation scams are compared to legitimate government websites. To do that, we use Authoritative DNS server logs. Authoritative DNS servers are a type of DNS server that knows the contents of a zone from memory [22]. DNS resolvers, such as Google Public DNS [17] and the default configurations in user devices, ultimately ask the authoritative servers for records in their zones.

As the .nl operator, we have access to historical authoritative DNS traffic of two of the three authoritative servers. We collect this data and store it in ENTRADA [63], our open-source Hadoop-based database from which we can query this data. Although we do not receive every DNS query because of caching [35,36], this still provides an indication of how popular the domains are.

We compare the average number of daily queries for the 73 potentially malicious domain names and the 952 legitimate government domain names, as

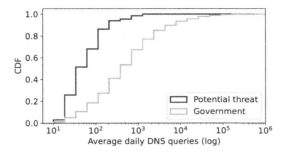

Fig. 4. CDF of average daily DNS queries seen at .nl authoritative nameservers.

observed by our authoritative name servers in the 7 days before annotation. (We choose one week given the known weekly and diurnal patterns of Internet traffic [44]).

Figure 4 shows the results for average daily DNS queries across these two groups in a cumulative distribution function (CDF). The fraction of domain names on the y-axis receives at most the number of DNS queries on the x-axis. It shows that potentially malicious domains receive fewer queries ($\mu = 132.8, \sigma = 239.0$) than government domains ($\mu = 5566.2, \sigma = 30724.2$). However, there are some potentially malicious domains that are popular. For instance, the suspicious COVID-19-related domain name receives 1% of the queries received by the official coronatest.nl. Although 1% may seem small, it still represents a large number of users given the popularity of the official domain name during the pandemic.

Domain Registration Data: We also manually inspected the registration data of domain names that are a potential threat. As the registry for .nl, we store the registrant information when a domain is registered. This data appears valid and legitimate for most of these domains, similar to what we see in normal registrations.

Domain Age: we show in Fig. 5 the CDF of the domain age per group. We see that the potential threat domain names are newer than government domains: 80% of the government domains are at least 2 years old, whereas only 20% of the potential threat domains are two years old.

This raises the question of whether attackers build a reputation with the seemingly legitimate domain name, and later on, launch an attack. Attackers may, at any time, direct users to a scam or send e-mails that appear to be from the government. We observe that 49% of the suspicious domain names published MX records on the day of labeling and could potentially send malicious e-mails that appear to be sent from a government domain.

75 domain names fall into the category *other* under government impersonation. This category comprises dubious applications of the government logo, such as false testimonials or endorsements, visually altered logos, and satirical websites. Analysts discussed these cases with the government's communication department who in some cases asked the webmaster to remove the logo or be

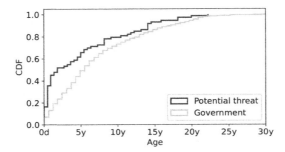

Fig. 5. CDF of domain age.

more clear in the relation with the government. Notably, `LogoMotive` could even detect highly visually altered variants of the government logo.

Most domains on which the logo was found fall into the *benign* category, *i.e.*, websites that are not directly related to the government but make use of the logo legitimately. For example, these include news websites and companies using the government logo in a testimonial.

The last category includes government websites. We detected 636 known government websites but also discovered 316 legitimate government domain names that were not listed in the website portfolio of the Dutch national government. 109 of these discovered domains could be added to the portfolio directly and 207 cases are still pending investigation at the time of writing. Asking the analysts about this, we found that the reason for this is that different branches of government such as ministries, government agencies, and regulators often use their own registrar instead of the national government registrar. This is against the government policy for registering domains and has several drawbacks. As opposed to existing abuse detection methods, `LogoMotive` can find unknown domain names that are not malicious.

Domains outside the government portfolio are a latent risk, for example, because they can expire and be re-registered by a third party, *e.g.*, a domain drop-catcher [26], who are specialized in registering the domain names within seconds after they become available. This has happened before and led to data breaches at the police and a health organization in the Netherlands [40,41]. This resulted in sensitive information such as arrest warrants and the health records of thousands of children reaching journalists.

Security Standards Adoption: the Dutch national government has committed to adopting security protocols on their domain names, and monitors the adoption rate of the websites in their domain name portfolio. These security protocols include DNSSEC [2], which adds authenticity and integrity to DNS using cryptographic algorithms, and DMARC [25], which adds authenticity to mail servers and provides domain owners with a way of advertising their legitimate e-mail servers using DNS. Domains *not* in the government portfolio cannot be monitored on the adoption of these standards, and may therefore unknowingly be insecure.

Table 4. DNSSEC and DMARC adoption in Dutch national government domain names.

| | Government Domains | |
	In portfolio	Not in portfolio
Total		
with DNSSEC	623 (98%)	230 (74%)
without DNSSEC	13 (2%)	79 (26%)
with DMARC	584 (92%)	126 (41%)
without DMARC	52 (8%)	183 (59%)

We evaluate DMARC and DNSSEC adoption in these two categories of domains using our crawler DMAP [62]. .nl-websites. Table 4 shows the results (our crawler missed data for 7 domains that are not in the portfolio). We see that the adoption of DNSSEC and DMARC is prevalent in the monitored government websites. The unmonitored domains have lower adoption rates for both DNSSEC and DMARC, meaning that for those domain names users are not protected against DNS and e-mail spoofing.

Summary: LogoMotive's evaluation of the entire .nl zone allowed to detect 3 phishing domains, 73 domains that could become malicious, and 75 other embodiments of government impersonation. An unexpected finding was that we also discovered legitimate domain names that communicate on behalf of the government, but were not included in the government's portfolio, which could become a security threat. LogoMotive helps in detecting such threats.

3.2   Live Registration Monitoring

Given phishing domains tend to be short-lived [4], we applied LogoMotive to domains right after their registration, to detect potential scams faster.

Data Collection: For this case study, we continuously process every domain added to the .nl zone for two months (Aug. 15th to Oct. 15th, 2021). For each domain added to the zone, we ran the LogoMotive pipeline every 3 h for 15 days after the registration date We only generate *new* screenshots if the page contents changed. In total, we analyzed 134.4k domains, and 44.4k eventually had a webpage.

Results: We apply LogoMotive to detect the government logos on these 44.4k domains, and found 53 domains with the government logo on their website. Similar to the full zone scans, the government analysts also validated these results.

The "Newly-Registered" column in Table 3 shows the results. First, there were no false positives – so every detected domain indeed displayed the logo of the government. We then use the same categories from Sect. 3.1 to further classify these domains. 33 domains (62%) were labeled as benign and 4 (7.55%) as government domains, but 16 (30.19%) domains were government impersonation scams.

Phishing Domains: from the 16 impersonation scams domains, we found 3 phishing websites. Their target group comprised all citizens of the Netherlands. Two impersonated the National Tax Authority – they presented the website visitors with a tax penalty warning, and request the users to proceed with the payment. The other phishing domain attempt to obtain citizens' online identification credentials, by impersonating the national online authentication system (DigiD). We found that 2 of these 3 domains were present in Netcraft's [32] blocklist, a popular phishing URL provider, which collects phishing URLs from reports by volunteers that run their toolbar. This suggests that `LogoMotive` complements existing techniques. Upon detection and evaluation, these domains were ultimately removed from the `.nl` zone, after the required legal procedures.

Potential Threats: further, the analysts classified 9 domains as potential threats. They all follow the same pattern: they typo-squat a legitimate government domain, but instead of directing web users to a malicious scam page, they redirect users to the *legitimate* government website, using HTTP redirects. We expect this is a strategy to build up a domain reputation with users, and, once popular enough, use the domain name to host a phishing website. Three of these domains also published MX records, which means they could potentially be used to send e-mails that appear to be sent by the national government. These domains were also removed after the evaluation.

Dormant Spear Phishing: 2 of the potential threats are likely dormant spear phishing attacks. 1 of these redirected to a specialized branch of the government that is likely not known by the general public. This domain name also published MX records which pointed to a mail server that is often used in shady activities, according to our abuse analysts. The other dormant spear phishing attack redirected to a service that is only intended for government employees. These domain names could become a serious threat because compromising a national-level agency could have severe implications. For example, the United States has documented cases of spear phishing against various government agencies [9]. Given that spear phishing is harder to detect, they tend to not appear on lists like Netcraft – indicating that our method is complementary to existing techniques. These malicious domain names were removed from the zone.

Summary: `LogoMotive`'s live monitoring of the `.nl` zone allowed us to detect 3 phishing domains and 9 potential threats. 2 of these threats were targeted at very specialized branches of the Dutch national government. `LogoMotive` can find scams that have not yet been reported to blocklists.

4   Trustmark Abuse Case Study

Background: *Thuiswinkel Waarborg* is an organization that certifies online webshops to show visitors which shops are secure, trustworthy, and honest. They evaluate whether webshops meet certain legal, security and financial stability requirements, for example, the shop must offer lawful return policies and pay after delivery options.

The *Thuiswinkel Waarborg* logo is widely recognized in the Netherlands, by more than 90% of the population [33]. The consumers association in the Netherlands (*Consumentenbond*) also recommends this trust mark [10]. This suggests that consumers are more likely to trust a webshop having the *Thuiswinkel Waarborg* logo on it, and therefore, be more likely to shop on these certified webshops. As a consequence, online shops have an incentive to obtain the trust mark legitimately, or to *abuse* it.

Data Collection. As in Sect. 3.1, we apply `LogoMotive` to evaluate the entire .nl zone from 2021-06-24 until 2021-09-27 and detect webpages that contain *Thuiswinkel Waarborg*'s logo. We use the member list of *Thuiswinkel Waarborg* to automatically label domain names specified by members as benign. The certified members are required to include the *Thuiswinkel Waarborg* logo on their websites, which should link to a page on the *Thuiswinkel Waarborg* website where the certificate details can be verified. For example, for which shop *Thuiswinkel Waarborg* has issued the certificate, and which of the shop's domain names may use it. We check whether the webpages we detect publish a hyperlink to a valid *Thuiswinkel Waarborg* certificate and if the detected domain matches with the certificate's domain we also automatically label it as benign.

Logo Detection and Validation. Table 5 shows `LogoMotive` results: it found 10,669 domain names with the logo of *Thuiswinkel Waarborg*. To validate our results, we shared them with analysts at *Thuiswinkel Waarborg* using `LogoMotive`'s dashboard, who manually labeled the domain names from 2021-09-23 until 2021-12-16.

We also add a column with unique URLs, because we observe that webshops often register multiple domain names, where one is used as the primary domain and the others serve an HTTP redirect forwarding users to the primary domain. This strategy of using multiple outlets is probably done for search engine optimization (SEO) and/or marketing purposes.

From the set of 10,669 domains names, 5582 (52.32%) were automatically labeled as benign because they belong to certified webshops and show the correct certificate, so they did not require manual annotation. 83 domains (0.78%) did not show the trust mark at the time of inspection. The remaining 10,586 (99.22%) indeed showed the trust mark logo.

The *Thuiswinkel Waarborg* analysts then classified each domain with the trust mark into subcategories. The majority of the domains fall in the *benign* category, *i.e.,* certified webshops and a few other domains, for instance, the website of *Thuiswinkel Waarborg* itself and those of events they organized.

The second category is trust mark abuse. This category contains 208 domains of webshops that have the *Thuiswinkel Waarborg* trust mark, while they are not a member. These shops are unlikely to meet the requirements that *Thuiswinkel Waarborg* members must meet and therefore pose a risk to consumers who are likely not aware of this deception.

Table 5. Manual validation results for trust mark abuse case study.

Label	Domains	Unique-URLs
Total	10669	3890
Without trust mark	83 (0.78%)	64 (1.65%)
With trust mark	10586 (99.22%)	3826 (98.35%)
Benign	10324 (96.77%)	3691 (94.88%)
Trustmark abuse	208 (1.95%)	106 (2.72%)
Discovered	54 (0.51%)	29 (0.75%)

Action Taken: Thuiswinkel Waarborg contacted the companies behind the abusive domains with the request to remove the trust mark. *Thuiswinkel Waarborg* may take legal actions if this request is not responded to. At the time of writing, 104 of the 208 (50%) of domains that abused the *Thuiswinkel Waarborg* trust mark have removed it from their website.

Domains Profile: We manually analyzed a sample of the 208 domains, and most of them seem to be legitimate shops, with rich and well-designed websites, and some even mention a valid Chamber of Commerce number, which in the Netherlands indicates that it is an existing business.

Domain Age: Next we look into the average age of the domain names in both groups. Figure 6 shows that, for both groups, the domains are relatively old: half of the domains are at least 11 years old (benign) and the trust mark abuse are least 6 years old. That is very different from phishing, in which domains tend to be short-lived (Sect. 3.2).

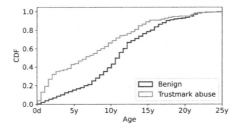

Fig. 6. Age of benign and trust mark abuse webshops.

Reasons for Trust Mark Misuse: feedback from *Thuiswinkel Waarborg* analysts confirms that webshops that misuse the trust mark are not necessarily malicious. They hypothesize that these webshops misuse the logo to improve sales, and avoid obtaining their own certificates from *Thuiswinkel Waarborg* either due to the costs involved and/or the legal and financial requirements they have to meet to obtain the certification.

Domains Popularity: We indirectly measure the popularity of these domains by analyzing incoming DNS queries for the `.nl` authoritative DNS server, as we did in Sect. 3.1. For each domain name, we compute the number of average daily queries and unique IP addresses of resolvers we observed one week before the annotation date. While the number of queries and resolvers do not correspond to the number of unique visitors (due to caching at DNS resolvers), it indicates how popular a domain name is.

Figure 7 shows the average number of daily DNS queries for the 151 trust mark abuse and 9659 benign domains, and Fig. 8 shows the average daily number of resolvers. Differently from the government impersonation case (Sect. 3.1), we see that both classes of domains have a similar number of queries *and* resolvers. The fraction of domains receiving over 1k queries per day is in the same range (14.0% for benign and 12.5% for trust mark misuse).

In addition, 3.6% (367 domains) of the benign domains receive more than 10k queries compared to 1.4% (3 domains) with trust mark misuse. This shows that domains that misuse the trademark are also very popular (not necessarily because of the trademark misuse), which is different from the government impersonation case.

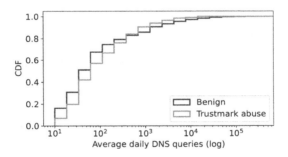

Fig. 7. Cumulative distribution function on the average number of daily DNS queries.

The last category contains 54 domain names of *Thuiswinkel Waarborg* members that were previously unknown to *Thuiswinkel Waarborg*. Analysts found that these domains belong to a certified *Thuiswinkel Waarborg* member, but the domain itself was not specified by the member. Similar to the discovered domains of the Dutch national government, these domains are a lurking risk, because *Thuiswinkel Waarborg* was unable to monitor whether those domains comply with the rules and standards imposed by the organization.

Summary: `LogoMotive` evaluation of the entire `.nl` zone allowed to detect 208 domains that abuse the *Thuiswinkel Waarborg* trust mark. We show that these domains have a long life cycle (6.8 years) and attract as many visitors as certified *Thuiswinkel Waarborg* webshops.

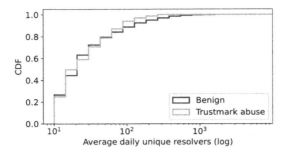

Fig. 8. Cumulative distribution function on the average number of daily unique resolvers.

5   Related Work

Phishing Detection: phishing detection is a very active research field *e.g.*, [4,11, 29,43]. Most previous research focus on textual features such as URLs [27,39,50], or HTML content [28,43,48]. We, on the other hand, rely on visual features on a page, namely logos, to detect phishing and other malicious content involving logo abuse.

Single feature: we design `LogoMotive` to detect logos, and rely on human validation to determine if there is abuse or not. Therefore, we did not explicitly design it to detect phishing or other types of malicious websites. `LogoMotive` is a broadly applicable tool for any organization aiming to protect its brand from online abuse. Given we are interested only in logo detection, we refrain from using textual features, such as registrant details, to make no assumption about the usage of logos. We can in future research combine the output from `LogoMotive` to phishing detection systems.

Visual features have been used for the detection of phishing in previous research. [66] Uses the global visual similarity of a target page to a suspicious page, combined with the existence of the target logo, to detect phishing sites. [1] detect phishing websites by comparing websites to a profile of trusted websites' appearances, which is created using text features, as well as logos which are detected using SIFT, a method for image matching. They apply their method on 1000 phishing sites from the Phishtank dataset and 200 legitimate sites from the Alexa top sites. [60] also uses SIFT image matching to find logos on pages and use a browser plugin to warn users if a logo is found on an unauthorized page.

Logo Detection: logo detection is a subset of object detection, for which various methods exist and have been applied in previous related research. Deterministic feature extraction and matching methods using SIFT [31] and SURF [3] have been employed to detect logos on websites by [1,60]. [5] use features of Histogram of Oriented Gradients to obtain a visual representation of phishing target brand logos. We found these methods to perform inadequately for our purpose, and instead use a machine learning object detection method. Recently, deep learning object detection models are used to detect logos on websites. [29,64] use Faster R-CNN to detect the identity logo and input text fields [29]. Our approach applies YOLO version 5 to detect logos on screenshots of .nl webpages, because of its fast inference speed.

Phishing Detection with Logos: logo recognition has been previously used to detect phishing websites. [7,8,29,65] all detect logos on webpages and attempt to match the logo's brand identity to an organization. Next, they use this information to determine if a website is a phishing site by comparing the domain name with the organization's known URLs, for example, if the Amazon logo is found, whether the domain name matches amazon.com or not. Their underlying assumption is that the relationship between the logo and domain name is exclusive, implying that logos may only be used legitimately on a select set of domain names. We, however, show in Sect. 3 that the government logo can legitimately be used on domain names that do not belong to the government. Another example is credit card company logos, which are often placed on e-commerce websites, which simply use these payment services. In contrast, our work does not assume any relationship between a logo and a company in the detection process: it simply detect logos, and it is up to to the brand owners to further label the classification results. In certain cases, we can prioritize results or automatically label a subset of the results, for example, if a logo may only be used on specific websites.

The most recent related study is Phishpedia [29]. This study aimed to detect phishing pages using logo detection, while our goal is much wider: we want to detect all websites containing a particular logo, which exposes many kinds of logo (mis)use, including phishing. This difference is reflected in multiple aspects. First, Phishpedia detects the most prominent logo (identity logo) using Faster-RCNN, while we detect all logos on a webpage using YOLO. Second, Phishpedia also identifies whether webpages contain text fields. This information is not relevant for our use case, because LogoMotive does not solely detect phishing websites. Third, Phishpedia compares the URL with a white-list of brand URLs. If a webpage contains a brand's identity logo, a text input field, and its URL is not white-listed, it is marked as phishing. In contrast, LogoMotive does not automatically make decisions about the websites it finds but facilitates abuse analysts in determining the motive with which their logo is used. Finally, Phishpedia is evaluated on a set of 30K phishing websites obtained from the OpenPhish database. LogoMotive is deployed in the .nl zone and is evaluated in two case studies, showing operational impact.

It is difficult to compare the accuracy of LogoMotive to any existing work, given that our proposed system employs the human-in-the-loop principle. LogoMotive is used by abuse analysts of various companies to help detect online abuse of their logo. Comparing it to phishing detection methods falls short of the broader applicability of LogoMotive. However, the phishing domain names we detected were not yet reported to blocklists, indicating that LogoMotive can be used to detect phishing websites more quickly than existing methods.

Dataset Size: [8] evaluate their results on a dataset consisting of 1140 web-pages. [29] apply their method on the OpenPhish service for six months, in total accumulating 350K phishing URLs. After crawling and filtering out empty and legitimate pages, they end up with 29,496 phishing websites used in their evaluations. They use 29,951 benign webpages from the top-ranked Alexa dataset to evaluate their detection method. [7] evaluate their method on 400 phishing websites from the popular PhishTank database and 50 legitimate websites from Alexa. [65] use a dataset of 726 webpages containing both phishing and legit webpages. We evaluate our contributions on the .nl zone, consisting of over 6.2 million domain names. Moreover, `LogoMotive` is operational in the .nl DNS zone. In addition, we generate a ground-truth dataset of over 20K manually annotated domain names with the logos detected for our use cases. This dataset can be used for future research on abuse detection, including the automatic prioritization of `LogoMotive`'s results.

Recently, phishing kit detection has risen in popularity [4,11,42]. Phishing kits are purchasable, easily deployable phishing site templates. [4] study phishing in the wild by detecting the use of such phishing kits. They apply their method to the TLS Transparancy Logs Project [18] and find 1,363 phishing domains targeted at a Dutch audience. They also found that phishing sites are very short-lived, with a median up-time of merely 24 h. This supports our findings; we found few phishing domains when crawling the entire .nl DNS zone, but found more abuse when monitoring new domain name registrations live.

Spear Phishing Detection: Spear phishing detection has previously been based on e-mail and textual analysis [19,55]. Our system is not focused on spear phishing per se, but it has proved useful in detecting them and filling a void where phishing blocklists fail to cover.

Fake Webshop Detection: fake webshop detection and counterfeit luxury goods detection has been also done in the past [58,59]. In both cases, while logos were mentioned, logo detection was not employed. Both studies found a very large set of webpages selling counterfeit goods. Our case study with *Thuiswinkel Waarborg* (Sect. 4) differs from them because we find a smaller set of domains that misuse the trust mark, but they are legitimate webshops that have been active for many years but still mislead visitors.

6   Legal, Ethical, and Privacy Considerations

Legal Considerations: In this study, we first obtained legal permission from SIDN, the .nl registry, as well as from both institutions in the case studies. We established a data-sharing agreement between SIDN and both the Dutch national government and *Thuiswinkel Waarborg*, so the metadata associated with the detected domains could be shared through the dashboard (Sect. 2.1) for the analysts to evaluate and label the results. These agreements conform to both EU and Dutch [6,20] legislation. Because the .nl zonefile is not publicly available, we cannot share the list of domain names analyzed in the presented case studies.

Ethical Considerations: Object detection, which we employ for the detection of logos, is a field in artificial intelligence that raises several ethical, privacy, and legal concerns. We address them by training our model solely to detect the logos of organizations on the screenshots of public .nl websites. Therefore, it has no notion of other concepts or objects of which the automatic detection could raise ethical and legal issues, such as persons, faces, or race [21,23,37], and thus cannot be used for these purposes.

The goal of this study was to determine the feasibility of logo detection in detecting scams and trust mark misuse – both ultimately affect real users. By helping to detect and remove such scams, we help protect Internet users by preventing those scams to take place; our use case partners support this claim. We chose these two use cases because they directly affect real Internet users. Finally, LogoMotive operates based on the "human in the loop" principle [38]. This means it cannot make autonomous decisions about domain names like removing them from the zone, and always requires human input. We meet this requirement by presenting the results on a dashboard that helps human abuse analysts to assess suspect domain names.

Privacy Considerations: In this study, all data analysis and measurements were conducted by SIDN employees. Only the manual validation and annotation of logo detection results was carried out by analysts at the Dutch national government and *Thuiswinkel Waarborg*, and in that regard, we minimized the data shared with these organizations – restricting it only to screenshots and metadata of the domains on which logos were found. This way of working was approved by our Data Protection Officer. In addition, we have developed a publicly available data privacy framework [6] with our legal department that conforms to both EU and Dutch [6,20] legislation. This framework has been applied for this study and the resulting privacy policy is monitored by a privacy board that oversees SIDN Labs' research.

7   Conclusions and Future Work

Logos are widely used on websites, with both benign and malicious intentions. We proposed LogoMotive, a system that detects logos on .nl-websites and provides analysts with insights into their logo's (mis)use. LogoMotive outperforms existing logo detection methods with high recall values over 97% and its unique flexibility due to our automatic and dynamic training method. Our vantage point as manager of the .nl ccTLD zone allowed us to detect logos, and by extension phishing, trust mark misuse, and other malicious logo use, in 6.2M domain names.

We evaluate LogoMotive in two use cases. In a use case with the Dutch national government, we detect and annotate 11.6K domain names that display the government logo, In total, we found 6 phishing domains, 82 potential future threats including dormant phishing attacks, and 80 cases of another misuse of the government logo. We also evaluated `LogoMotive` with a renowned Dutch certified webshop trust mark. Webshops require certification and must comply with strict rules and standards regarding security and consumer protection before they may display the logo on their website. Unauthorized use of the trust mark is, per definition, misleading visitors. `LogoMotive` found close to 10K domain names leading to 3253 unique websites that display the trust mark's logo. 151 of these webshops unjustly displayed the logo and received a cease and desist letter from *Thuiswinkel Waarborg*.

Our work has an operational impact: the government acted upon 168 embodiments of impersonation and 104 trust mark misuse websites removed their logos. It also allowed for the Dutch government to detect and include government websites that were registered outside the official regulations, and, this way, mitigate the risks associated with domain expiration and lack of security standards adoption – namely DNSSEC and DMARC.

`LogoMotive` has proven a useful system and will be deployed in production at SIDN. In future research, we could use the ground truth data resulting from the two use cases in further efforts to automatically detect malicious websites. We intend to combine its results with phishing-tailored detection systems. Furthermore, in the future, we can explore whether existing data sources allow us to prioritize the websites on which a logo is found based on their likeliness to be malicious. Automatic classification or prioritization of the logo detection results would require a use case-specific approach because the definition of misuse varies between logos. We currently focus on the home page of websites, because traversing websites' internal pages in the entire zone is not feasible. In future work, we can explore if it is feasible to traverse internal pages of recently registered domain names, where most abuse is found.

Acknowledgments. We thank very much the manual validation and annotation work carried by the anonymous analysts at the Dutch national government and *Thuiswinkel Waarborg*, for more than 10k domain names. We would also like to thank our colleagues at SIDN for reviewing and indirectly contributing to this study.

SIDN was partly funded by the European Union's Horizon 2020 Research and Innovation programme under Grant Agreement No 830927 (https://cordis.europa.eu/project/id/830927). Project website: https://www.concordia-h2020.eu/.

A   Appendix: LogoMotive Dashboard

(See Fig. 9).

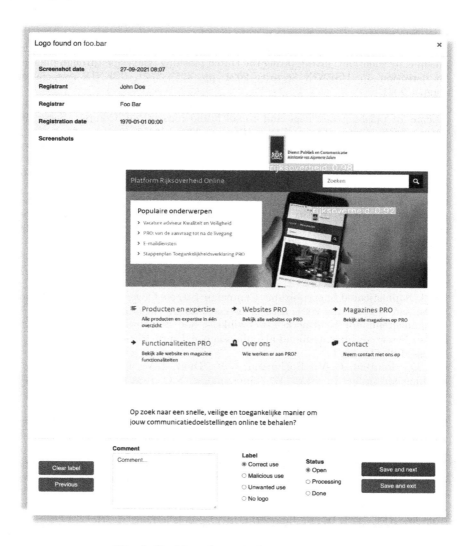

Fig. 9. Dashboard annotation pop-up screen

References

1. Afroz, S., Greenstadt, R.: PhishZoo: detecting phishing websites by looking at them. In: 2011 IEEE Fifth International Conference on Semantic Computing. IEEE, September 2011. https://doi.org/10.1109/icsc.2011.52

2. Arends, R., Austein, R., Larson, M., Massey, D., Rose, S.: DNS Security Introduction and Requirements. RFC 4033, IETF, March 2005. http://tools.ietf.org/rfc/rfc4033.txt
3. Bay, H., Ess, A., Tuytelaars, T., Gool, L.V.: Speeded-up robust features (SURF). Comput. Vis. Image Underst. **110**(3), 346–359 (2008). https://doi.org/10.1016/j.cviu.2007.09.014
4. Bijmans, H., Booij, T., Schwedersky, A., Nedgabat, A., van Wegberg, R.: Catching phishers by their bait: investigating the Dutch phishing landscape through phishing kit detection. In: USENIX Security 2021, pp. 3757–3774. USENIX Association, August 2021
5. Bozkir, A.S., Aydos, M.: LogoSENSE: a companion HOG based logo detection scheme for phishing web page and e-mail brand recognition. Comput. Secur. **95**, 101855 (2020). https://doi.org/10.1016/j.cose.2020.101855
6. Hesselman, C., Jansen, J., Wullink, M., Vink, K., Simon, M.: A privacy framework for DNS big data applications. Technical report, SIDN (2014). https://www.sidnlabs.nl/downloads/yBW6hBoaSZe4m6GJc_0b7w/2211058ab6330c7f3788141ea19d3db7/SIDN_Labs_Privacyraamwerk_Position_Paper_V1.4_ENG.pdf
7. Chang, E.H., Chiew, K.L., Sze, S.N., Tiong, W.K.: Phishing detection via identification of website identity. In: 2013 International Conference on IT Convergence and Security (ICITCS). IEEE, December 2013. https://doi.org/10.1109/icitcs.2013.6717870
8. Chiew, K.L., Chang, E.H., Sze, S.N., Tiong, W.K.: Utilisation of website logo for phishing detection. Comput. Secur. **54**, 16–26 (2015). https://doi.org/10.1016/j.cose.2015.07.006
9. CISA: Sophisticated Spearphishing Campaign Targets Government Organizations, IGOs, and NGOs, May 2021. https://us-cert.cisa.gov/ncas/alerts/aa21-148a
10. Consumentenbond: Keurmerken webwinkels: hoe betrouwbaar zijn ze? (2019). https://www.consumentenbond.nl/online-kopen/keurmerken-webwinkels. Accessed 20 Oct 2021
11. Cui, Q., Jourdan, G.-V., Bochmann, G.V., Onut, I.-V.: Proactive detection of phishing kit traffic. In: Sako, K., Tippenhauer, N.O. (eds.) ACNS 2021. LNCS, vol. 12727, pp. 257–286. Springer, Cham (2021). https://doi.org/10.1007/978-3-030-78375-4_11
12. Eggert, C., Winschel, A., Lienhart, R.: On the benefit of synthetic data for company logo detection. In: Proceedings of the 23rd ACM International Conference on Multimedia. ACM, October 2015. https://doi.org/10.1145/2733373.2806407
13. FBI: FBI Warns Public to Beware of Government Impersonation Scams, April 2021. https://www.fbi.gov/contact-us/field-offices/boston/news/press-releases/fbi-warns-public-to-beware-of-government-impersonation-scams
14. Fielding, R., Reschke, J.: Hypertext Transfer Protocol (HTTP/1.1): Semantics and Content. RFC 7231, IETF, June 2014. http://tools.ietf.org/rfc/rfc7231.txt
15. FTC: How To Avoid a Government Impersonator Scam, April 2021. https://www.consumer.ftc.gov/articles/how-avoid-government-impersonator-scam
16. Goel, R.K.: Masquerading the government: drivers of government impersonation fraud. Public Finan. Rev. **49**(4), 548–572 (2021)
17. Google: Google Public DNS (2021). https://developers.google.com/speed/public-dns/
18. Google Inc.: Certificate transparency. https://certificate.transparency.dev/
19. Han, Y., Shen, Y.: Accurate spear phishing campaign attribution and early detection. In: Proceedings of the 31st Annual ACM Symposium on Applied Computing. ACM, April 2016. https://doi.org/10.1145/2851613.2851801

20. Hesselman, C., Moura, G.C., Schmidt, R.D.O., Toet, C.: Increasing DNS security and stability through a control plane for top-level domain operators. IEEE Commun. Mag. **55**(1), 197–203 (2017). https://doi.org/10.1109/mcom.2017.1600521cm
21. Hill, K.: The Secretive Company That Might End Privacy as We Know It, January 2020. https://www.nytimes.com/2020/01/18/technology/clearview-privacy-facial-recognition.html
22. Hoffman, P., Sullivan, A., Fujiwara, K.: DNS Terminology. RFC 8499, IETF, November 2018. http://tools.ietf.org/rfc/rfc8499.txt
23. Introna, L.D.: Disclosive ethics and information technology: disclosing facial recognition systems. Ethics Inf. Technol. **7**(2), 75–86 (2005). https://doi.org/10.1007/s10676-005-4583-2
24. Kingma, D.P., Ba, J.: Adam: a method for stochastic optimization (2017)
25. Kucherawy, M., Zwicky, E.: Domain-based Message Authentication, Reporting, and Conformance (DMARC). RFC 7489, IETF, March 2015. http://tools.ietf.org/rfc/rfc7489.txt
26. Lauinger, T., Buyukkayhan, A.S., Chaabane, A., Robertson, W., Kirda, E.: From deletion to re-registration in zero seconds. In: Proceedings of the Internet Measurement Conference 2018. ACM, October 2018. https://doi.org/10.1145/3278532.3278560
27. Le, A., Markopoulou, A., Faloutsos, M.: PhishDef: URL names say it all. In: 2011 Proceedings IEEE INFOCOM. IEEE, April 2011. https://doi.org/10.1109/infcom.2011.5934995
28. Li, Y., Yang, Z., Chen, X., Yuan, H., Liu, W.: A stacking model using URL and HTML features for phishing webpage detection. Futur. Gener. Comput. Syst. **94**, 27–39 (2019). https://doi.org/10.1016/j.future.2018.11.004
29. Lin, Y., et al.: Phishpedia: a hybrid deep learning based approach to visually identify phishing webpages. In: 30th USENIX Security Symposium (USENIX Security 2021) (2021)
30. Liu, W., et al.: SSD: single shot multibox detector. In: Leibe, B., Matas, J., Sebe, N., Welling, M. (eds.) ECCV 2016. LNCS, vol. 9905, pp. 21–37. Springer, Cham (2016). https://doi.org/10.1007/978-3-319-46448-0_2
31. Lowe, D.G.: Distinctive image features from scale-invariant keypoints. Int. J. Comput. Vis. **60**(2), 91–110 (2004). https://doi.org/10.1023/b:visi.0000029664.99615.94
32. Netcraft Ltd.: Netcraft, 10 October 2021. https://www.netcraft.com/
33. Markt, A.C.: Onderzoek naar de kennis, houding en gedrag van consumenten ten aanzien van keurmerken (2016). https://web.archive.org/web/20180420203000/www.thuiswinkel.org/data/uploads/publication/ACM_en_GfK_onderzoek_keurmerken_2016.pdf. Accessed 20 Oct 2021
34. Mockapetris, P.: Domain names - implementation and specification. RFC 1035, IETF, November 1987. http://tools.ietf.org/rfc/rfc1035.txt
35. Moura, G.C.M., Heidemann, J., Müller, M., de O. Schmidt, R., Davids, M.: When the dike breaks. In: Proceedings of the Internet Measurement Conference 2018. ACM, October 2018. https://doi.org/10.1145/3278532.3278534
36. Moura, G.C.M., Heidemann, J., de O. Schmidt, R., Hardaker, W.: Cache me if you can. In: Proceedings of the Internet Measurement Conference. ACM, October 2019. https://doi.org/10.1145/3355369.3355568
37. Mozurl, P.: One Month, 500,000 Face Scans: How China Is Using A.I. to Profile a Minority, April 2019. https://www.nytimes.com/2019/04/14/technology/china-surveillance-artificial-intelligence-racial-profiling.html

38. Munro, R.: Human-in-the-Loop Machine Learning. Manning Publications, New York, October 2021
39. Nguyen, L.A.T., To, B.L., Nguyen, H.K., Nguyen, M.H.: A novel approach for phishing detection using URL-based heuristic. In: 2014 International Conference on Computing, Management and Telecommunications (ComManTel), pp. 298–303. IEEE (2014)
40. Nieuws, R.: Politiegeheimen op straat door verlopen mailadressen (2017). https://www.rtlnieuws.nl/nieuws/nederland/artikel/240411/politiegeheimen-op-straat-door-verlopen-mailadressen. Accessed 15 Oct 2021
41. Nieuws, R.: Groot datalek bij jeugdzorg: dossiers duizenden kwetsbare kinderen gelekt (2019). https://www.rtlnieuws.nl/tech/artikel/4672826/jeugdzorg-datalek-dossiers-kinderen-utrecht-email. Accessed 15 Oct 2021
42. Oest, A., Safei, Y., Doupe, A., Ahn, G.J., Wardman, B., Warner, G.: Inside a phisher's mind: understanding the anti-phishing ecosystem through phishing kit analysis. In: 2018 APWG Symposium on Electronic Crime Research (eCrime). IEEE, May 2018. https://doi.org/10.1109/ecrime.2018.8376206
43. Opara, C., Wei, B., Chen, Y.: HTMLPhish: enabling phishing web page detection by applying deep learning techniques on HTML analysis. In: 2020 International Joint Conference on Neural Networks (IJCNN). IEEE, July 2020. https://doi.org/10.1109/ijcnn48605.2020.9207707
44. Quan, L., Heidemann, J., Pradkin, Y.: When the internet sleeps. In: Proceedings of the 2014 Conference on Internet Measurement Conference. ACM, November 2014. https://doi.org/10.1145/2663716.2663721
45. Redmon, J., Divvala, S., Girshick, R., Farhadi, A.: You only look once: unified, real-time object detection. In: 2016 IEEE Conference on Computer Vision and Pattern Recognition (CVPR). IEEE, June 2016. https://doi.org/10.1109/cvpr.2016.91
46. Ren, S., He, K., Girshick, R., Sun, J.: Faster R-CNN: towards real-time object detection with region proposal networks. IEEE Trans. Pattern Anal. Mach. Intell. 39(6), 1137–1149 (2017). https://doi.org/10.1109/tpami.2016.2577031
47. van Riel, C.B., van den Ban, A.: The added value of corporate logos - an empirical study. Eur. J. Mark. 35(3/4), 428–440 (2001). https://doi.org/10.1108/03090560110382093
48. Roopak, S., Thomas, T.: A novel phishing page detection mechanism using HTML source code comparison and cosine similarity. In: 2014 Fourth International Conference on Advances in Computing and Communications. IEEE, August 2014. https://doi.org/10.1109/icacc.2014.47
49. Rublee, E., Rabaud, V., Konolige, K., Bradski, G.: ORB: an efficient alternative to SIFT or SURF. In: 2011 International Conference on Computer Vision. IEEE, November 2011. https://doi.org/10.1109/iccv.2011.6126544
50. Sahingoz, O.K., Buber, E., Demir, O., Diri, B.: Machine learning based phishing detection from URLs. Expert Syst. Appl. 117, 345–357 (2019)
51. Sanchez, S.A., Romero, H.J., Morales, A.D.: A review: comparison of performance metrics of pretrained models for object detection using the TensorFlow framework. In: IOP Conference Series: Materials Science and Engineering, vol. 844, p. 012024, June 2020. https://doi.org/10.1088/1757-899x/844/1/012024
52. Shao, S., et al.: Objects365: a large-scale, high-quality dataset for object detection. In: 2019 IEEE/CVF International Conference on Computer Vision (ICCV). IEEE, October 2019. https://doi.org/10.1109/iccv.2019.00852
53. Software Freedom Conservancy: Selenium hub. https://hub.docker.com/r/selenium/hub/tags

54. Srivastava, S., Divekar, A.V., Anilkumar, C., Naik, I., Kulkarni, V., Pattabiraman, V.: Comparative analysis of deep learning image detection algorithms. J. Big Data **8**(1), 1–27 (2021). https://doi.org/10.1186/s40537-021-00434-w
55. Stringhini, G., Thonnard, O.: That ain't you: blocking spearphishing through behavioral modelling. In: Almgren, M., Gulisano, V., Maggi, F. (eds.) DIMVA 2015. LNCS, vol. 9148, pp. 78–97. Springer, Cham (2015). https://doi.org/10.1007/978-3-319-20550-2_5
56. Su, H., Zhu, X., Gong, S.: Deep learning logo detection with data expansion by synthesising context. In: 2017 IEEE Winter Conference on Applications of Computer Vision (WACV). IEEE, March 2017. https://doi.org/10.1109/wacv.2017.65
57. Ultralytics: Yolov5. https://github.com/ultralytics/yolov5
58. Wabeke, T., Moura, G.C.M., Franken, N., Hesselman, C.: Counterfighting counterfeit: detecting and taking down fraudulent webshops at a ccTLD. In: Sperotto, A., Dainotti, A., Stiller, B. (eds.) PAM 2020. LNCS, vol. 12048, pp. 158–174. Springer, Cham (2020). https://doi.org/10.1007/978-3-030-44081-7_10
59. Wang, D.Y., et al.: Search + seizure. In: Proceedings of the 2014 Conference on Internet Measurement Conference. ACM, November 2014. https://doi.org/10.1145/2663716.2663738
60. Wang, G., et al.: Verilogo: proactive phishing detection via logo recognition. Department of Computer Science and Engineering, University of California (2011)
61. Wilson, J.M., Grammich, C.A.: Brand protection across the enterprise: toward a total-business solution. Bus. Horiz. **63**(3), 363–376 (2020). https://doi.org/10.1016/j.bushor.2020.02.002
62. Wullink, M., Moura, G.C.M., Hesselman, C.: DMAP: automating domain name ecosystem measurements and applications. In: 2018 Network Traffic Measurement and Analysis Conference (TMA). IEEE, June 2018. https://doi.org/10.23919/tma.2018.8506521
63. Wullink, M., Moura, G.C.M., Muller, M., Hesselman, C.: ENTRADA: a high-performance network traffic data streaming warehouse. In: NOMS 2016–2016 IEEE/IFIP Network Operations and Management Symposium. IEEE, April 2016. https://doi.org/10.1109/noms.2016.7502925
64. Yao, W., Ding, Y., Li, X.: Deep learning for phishing detection. In: ISPA/IUCC/BDCloud/SocialCom/SustainCom. IEEE, December 2018. https://doi.org/10.1109/bdcloud.2018.00099
65. Yao, W., Ding, Y., Li, X.: LogoPhish: a new two-dimensional code phishing attack detection method. In: ISPA/IUCC/BDCloud/SocialCom/SustainCom. IEEE, December 2018. https://doi.org/10.1109/bdcloud.2018.00045
66. Zhou, Y., Zhang, Y., Xiao, J., Wang, Y., Lin, W.: Visual similarity based anti-phishing with the combination of local and global features. In: 2014 IEEE 13th International Conference on Trust, Security and Privacy in Computing and Communications, pp. 189–196. IEEE (2014)

Early Detection of Spam Domains
with Passive DNS and SPF

Simon Fernandez[(✉)], Maciej Korczyński, and Andrzej Duda

Univ. Grenoble Alpes, CNRS, Grenoble INP, LIG, 38000 Grenoble, France
{simon.fernandez,maciej.korczynski,andrzej.duda}@univ-grenoble-alpes.fr

Abstract. Spam domains are sources of unsolicited mails and one of
the primary vehicles for fraud and malicious activities such as phishing
campaigns or malware distribution. Spam domain detection is a race: as
soon as the spam mails are sent, taking down the domain or blacklisting
it is of relative use, as spammers have to register a new domain for their
next campaign. To prevent malicious actors from sending mails, we need
to detect them as fast as possible and, ideally, even before the campaign
is launched.

In this paper, using near-real-time passive DNS data from Farsight
Security, we monitor the DNS traffic of newly registered domains and
the contents of their `TXT` records, in particular, the configuration of the
Sender Policy Framework, an anti-spoofing protocol for domain names
and the first line of defense against devastating Business Email Compromise scams. Because spammers and benign domains have different SPF
rules and different traffic profiles, we build a new method to detect spam
domains using features collected from passive DNS traffic.

Using the SPF configuration and the traffic to the `TXT` records of a
domain, we accurately detect a significant proportion of spam domains
with a low false positives rate demonstrating its potential in real-world
deployments. Our classification scheme can detect spam domains before
they send any mail, using only a single DNS query and later on, it can
refine its classification by monitoring more traffic to the domain name.

Keywords: Spam detection · SPF · Passive DNS · Machine learning

1 Introduction

For years, malicious mails have been representing a significant technical, economic, and social threat. Besides increasing communication costs and clogging
up mailboxes, malicious mails may cause considerable harm by luring a user into
following links to phishing or malware distribution sites.

Typically, malicious actors run campaigns with instant generation of a large
number of mails. Hence, their detection is a race: if we want to prevent their malicious activity, we need to detect spam domain names as soon as possible, blacklist
and block them (at the registration level). Once the campaign is over, domain
blacklisting is less effective because the recipients have already received mails.

O. Hohlfeld et al. (Eds.): PAM 2022, LNCS 13210, pp. 30–49, 2022.
https://doi.org/10.1007/978-3-030-98785-5_2

Early detection of spam domains that generate malicious mails is challenging. One of the approaches is to leverage the Domain Name System (DNS) that maps domain names to resource records that contain data like IP addresses. We can use DNS traffic and domain name characteristics to compute features for training and running machine learning detection algorithms, even if malicious actors may try to hide their traces and activities, and avoid domain takedown [12,30]. The main difference between various algorithms is the set of features used to train and run classifiers. The features mainly belong to four categories: i) lexical: domain names, randomness of characters, or similarity to brand names [1,3,5,19,22,23, 34], ii) domain and IP address popularity: reputation systems based on diversity, origin of queries, or past malicious activity [1,2,9,16,23,24,31], iii) DNS traffic: number of queries, their intensity, burst detection, or behavior changes [5,24], and iv) WHOIS: domain registration patterns [9,23,27].

In this paper, we propose a scheme for early detection of spam domains, even before they send a single mail to a victim. It is based on the domain SPF (Sender Policy Framework) rules and traffic to the TXT records containing them.

SPF rules are means for detecting forged sender addresses—they form the first line of defense in the case of, for instance, Business Email Compromise scams that represented over $1.8 billion USD of losses in 2020 [6]. As malicious actors generally use newly registered domains for sending mails, they also configure the SPF rules for their domains to increase their reputation and thus avoid proactive detection. We have discovered that the content of the SPF rules and traffic to the TXT records containing them are different for malicious and benign domains. We have used these features to design a domain classifier algorithm that can quickly detect spam domains based on passive DNS traffic monitoring [8]. With low false positive rate and high true positive rate, our scheme can improve existing real-time systems for detecting and proactively blocking spam domains using passive DNS data.

The rest of the paper is organized as follows. Section 2 provides background on SPF and spam campaigns. Section 3 presents the proposed scheme. Sections 4 and 5 introduce the classification algorithms and present their results. We discuss other related approaches in Sect. 6 and Sect. 7 concludes the paper.

2 Background

In this section, we describe the SPF protocol and the mail delivery process, highlighting the steps during which we gather features to detect malicious activity.

2.1 Sender Policy Framework (SPF)

The Sender Policy Framework (SPF) [17] is a protocol used to prevent domain (mail) spoofing. Figure 1 presents the procedure for sending mails and SPF verification. Alice (sender) sends a benign mail to Bob (receiver). Mallory (attacker) wants to send a mail that impersonates Alice to Bob. Mallory and Alice use their respective servers (`mallory.com` and `alice.com`) to send mails.

An effective anti-spoofing mechanism needs to differentiate the Mallory message from the benign Alice mail. The current first lines of defense to protect users from spoofed mails include SPF [17], DKIM [20], and DMARC [21]. SPF

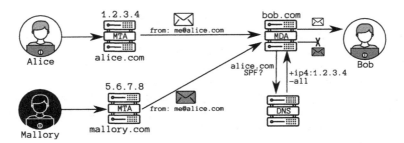

Fig. 1. Sending mails with SPF verification.

is a set of text-form rules in TXT DNS resource records specifying a list of servers allowed to send mails on behalf of a specific domain. During mail delivery over the SMTP protocol, the recipient server authenticates the sender Mail Transfer Agent (MTA) by comparing the given MAIL FROM (or HELO) identity and the sender IP address with the content of the published SPF record.

In our example, the Mail Delivery Agent (MDA) on the Bob's server queries the DNS for a TXT record of the sending domain (alice.com). This record contains the SPF rule of alice.com and specifies which IP addresses can send mails on behalf of this domain. The mail from Alice comes from a whitelisted server, so it gets delivered. The Mallory's server was not whitelisted, so the (spoofed) mail is rejected.

A valid SPF version 1 record string must begin with v=spf1 followed by other SPF entries with the following structure: <qualifier><mechanism>[:<target>]. The mail sender is matched with the <mechanism>:<target> part; the output is determined by the <qualifier>. Four types of <qualifier> are possible: PASS (+) (the default mechanism), NEUTRAL (~), SOFTFAIL (?), FAIL (-). The most common SFP mechanisms are the following:

ip4, ip6– the sender IP address matches the predefined IP address or the sub-network prefix,
a, mx– the domain has an A (or MX) record that resolves to the sender IP address,
ptr– a verified reverse DNS query on the sender IP address matches the sending domain (not recommended by RFC 7208 [17] since April 2014),
exists– the domain has an A record,
include– use the rules of another domain,
all– the default mechanism that always matches.

To illustrate the operation of SPF rules, let us consider the following configuration for example.com domain: v=spf1 a ip4:192.0.2.0/24 -all where the A record (example.com A 198.51.100.1) is stored in DNS. The SPF rule states that only a host with the IP address of 198.51.100.1 (the a mechanism) or machines in the 192.0.2.0/24 subnetwork (the ip4 mechanism) are permitted senders, all others are forbidden (the -all mechanism).

2.2 Life Cycle of a Spam Campaign

Most spam campaigns follow the same life cycle presented below.

Domain Registration. As most mail hosting companies deploy tools to prevent their users from sending spam, malicious actors need to register their own domains to send spam. To run multiple campaigns, spammers usually register domains in bulk [10]. Once the domains are registered, spammers configure zone files and fill the corresponding resource records in the DNS.

Configuration of Anti-spoofing Mechanisms. To use SPF, DMARC, or DKIM, each domain must have a TXT resource record describing which hosts can send a mail on their behalf and deploying keys to authenticate the sender. Even if DMARC is still not widely used, many benign domains deploy SPF [7, 26, 28]. Thus, a mail from a domain without SPF configuration is likely to be flagged as spam (especially when combined with other indicators of malicious intent). To appear as benign as possible, spammers fill in at least the SPF rule in the TXT record. Our scheme extracts most of the features for detecting spam at this step because the SPF records of spam domains are generally different from the configurations of benign domains and even if a given domain has not yet sent a single mail, we can access its SPF rules and detect suspicious configurations. The SPF rules can be actively fetched by sending a TXT query to the domain (e.g., newly registered), but to avoid active scanning, we have chosen to use passive DNS to analyze TXT requests. In every detected spam campaign, we observe at least one TXT query that may originate from a spammer testing its infrastructure.

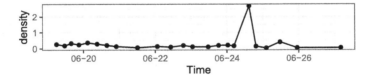

Fig. 2. Density of DNS TXT traffic to a spam domain (`promotechmail.online`)

Spam Campaign. When a mail server receives a mail, it tries to resolve the TXT record of the sending domain to get its SPF rule and checks for possible sender forgery. During a spam campaign, spammers send mails to many servers across the world. At the beginning of a campaign, the (validating) mail servers will all try to retrieve the TXT DNS record of the sender domain almost at the same time. Therefore, we expect to observe a surge in queries for TXT records. Figure 2 presents traffic density (corresponding to the number of DNS queries over time, defined precisely later) to a spam domain detected during our study. The burst in the number of queries during a time window of less than 24 h, then traffic dropping and never rising again is the typical profile of spammers.

Detection, Blacklisting, and Cleanup. When spam mails reach the targets, security experts and spam detection algorithms parsing the mail content and its headers flag the sending domain as a spamming source and may report it to domain blacklists like SpamHaus [32] or SURBL [33]. When a domain appears on a blacklist, mail servers will likely drop mails from it. Future spam campaigns from this domain will be unsuccessful, so it becomes useless for spammers. Hosting services may also suspend the sending server whereas domain registrars may take down the spam domain as it often violates their terms of service and is considered as DNS abuse [4,19]. Once the domain is blacklisted (or taken down), spammers may just acquire another one and repeat the previous steps.

When looking for spammers, timing is the key: the sooner we detect a spamming domain, the fewer mails it can send, and if an algorithm only detects a spam mail upon reception, it means that the campaign has started and reached some of the targets. This observation was the motivation for our scheme for early detection of spamming domains even before the start of a spam campaign.

3   Scheme for Early Detection of Spam

In this section, we present the proposed scheme. It takes advantage of passive DNS data to obtain the SPF rules for a given domain and the frequency of the queries to retrieve them.

3.1   Data Source: Passive DNS

Passive DNS consists of monitoring DNS traffic by *sensors* usually deployed above recursive resolvers to monitor queries between a local resolver and authoritative name servers [35]. Locally observed queries are aggregated into feeds available for analyses. In this work, we have used the near-real-time Farsight SIE Passive DNS channel 207 [8] to obtain DNS traffic data for the TXT records and SPF rules for each domain. We extract the following fields: the queried domain, the record type, the answer from the authoritative server, a time window, and the number of times a given query was observed during the time window.

To be effective, the scheme must analyze unencrypted DNS traffic. Therefore, it is not suitable when using the DNS over TLS (DoT) [13] or DNS over HTTPS (DoH) [11] standards that encrypt user DNS queries to prevent eavesdropping of domain names. To monitor such traffic, the scheme would have to be implemented, e.g., in public recursive resolvers providing DoT or DoH services.

3.2   Features Based on SPF Rules

The SPF configuration for a given domain is stored in the TXT record of the domain. Since most mail hosting services provide a default SPF records for their customers, many domains share the same SPF rules. Nevertheless, some domains use custom SPF rules that whitelist specific servers. We have focused on the similarities of domains: two domains that use the same custom SPF rules and whitelist the same IP addresses are likely to be managed by the same entity. Therefore, if one domain starts sending spam, it is reasonable to consider that the domains sharing the same SPF rules are likely to be (future) spammers.

We have analyzed the SPF configuration of spam and benign domains to see if they differ (we later discuss ground truth data in Sect. 4.1). Figure 3 shows that benign and spam domains do not necessarily use the same rules. For example, benign domains more frequently use the +include mechanism while spammers +ptr.

We presume that legitimate domains, hosted by major mail hosting providers, are more likely to have default configurations with the +include mechanism to indicate that a particular third party (e.g., a mail server of the provider) is authorized to send mails on behalf of all domains (e.g., in a shared hosting environment). Spam domains may use custom mail servers instead, thus they are more likely to whitelist the IP addresses of their servers with, for instance, the +ip4 mechanism. We suspect that in some cases spammers may not want to reveal the IP addresses of hosts sending spam. Therefore, they may use the +all mechanism (that accepts mails from all hosts) relatively more than legitimate domains whose administrators are concerned about rejecting spam mails from unauthorized host. Finally, the +ptr mechanism is marked as "do not use" since April 2014 by RFC 7208 [17]. Major hosting providers seem to follow this recommendation, but individual spammers may not have changed their practices and continue to use this outdated but still supported mechanism.

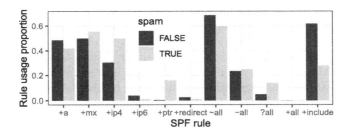

Fig. 3. Usage proportion of SPF rules for benign and spamming domains

For each domain, we compute the number of occurrences of each mechanism in its rule to generate the set of SPF features. Because not all possible combinations of qualifiers and mechanisms are actually used, we have selected the sets of qualifiers and mechanisms that appear in more than 0.1% of domains to avoid overfitting, which leaves us the ones presented in Fig. 3.

3.3   Graph Analysis of SPF Rules

Some SPF rules point to an IP address or a subnetwork prefix (like ip4 and ip6) and some point to domain names (like include and sometimes a and mx). We build the relationship graph between domains and IP ranges as shown in Fig. 4. For example, the edge between node A (a.org) and node B (b.com) reflects the fact that node B has an SPF rule that points to node A. The edge between b.com and 192.0.2.1 represents the fact that this IP address is used in the +ip4 rule in the b.com SPF configuration.

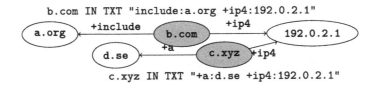

Fig. 4. Example of a relationship graph derived from SPF rules (Color figure online)

This graph is built and updated in near real time: nodes and edges are added when domains with SPF data appear in the passive DNS feed, and spam domains (marked in red in Fig. 4) are added or deleted from blacklists (SpamHaus and SURBL in our scheme). Thus, over time, the graph becomes more complete, providing more precise relationships and features for domain classification.

We have analyzed different structures in the graph built from our dataset and detected distinctive patterns. Figure 5 shows three examples of the observed structure types to illustrate some typical SPF configuration relationship graphs for spam domains. Red nodes represent spamming domains and white nodes correspond to the targets of their SPF rules. Figure 5a shows the pattern in which multiple spam domains share the same configuration: they have a rule targeting the same IPv6 network (these domains are likely to be managed by the same entity). Figure 5b presents spam domains that have an include mechanism that points to the same domain and exactly three other custom targets that no other domain uses (this is the case when domains are hosted by a hosting provider that provides an SPF configuration for inclusion by its clients). Finally, many spam domains have rules like in Fig. 5c in which a domain has a single target (a custom IP address) that no other domain uses.

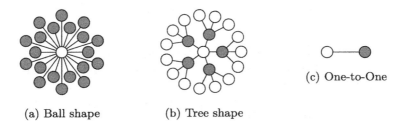

(a) Ball shape   (b) Tree shape   (c) One-to-One

Fig. 5. SPF relation graph for spam domains (Color figure online)

The study of these structures can highlight potential spam domains. In our dataset, we found structures like in Fig. 5a or Fig. 5b in which dozens of domains used the same rule and the majority of them appeared on spam blacklists. As such, it is reasonable to assume that the remaining domains are likely to have not yet been detected or are not yet active spam domains.

To detect the structures indicating spam domains, we have defined two unique features describing the properties of domains in the relationship graph.

Toxicity. We define the *toxicity* of a node as the proportion of its neighbors that are flagged as spam in the graph, or 1 if the domain itself is flagged as spam. With this metric, SPF targets used by known spammers get a high value of *toxicity*. To detect the domains that use rules with high *toxicity* targets, we compute the *Max Neighbor Toxicity*: the maximum *toxicity* amongst all the targets of a domain. This way, if a domain has a target mainly used by spammers, its *Max Neighbor Toxicity* is high.

Neighbor Degree. For each node, we look at the degrees of its neighbors: is it connected to highly used domains and IP addresses? Or, is it using custom targets that no other domain uses? We expect spamming domains to more likely use custom targets that no other domains use (with a small degree in the graph) like in Fig. 5c, compared to benign domains that would use the default configurations of the hosting service and share the same targets as many other domains (with a high degree in the graph).

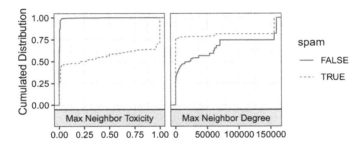

Fig. 6. Cumulative distributions of Max Neighbor Toxicity and Max Neighbor Degree for spamming and benign domains.

Figure 6 shows that the expected differences of *Max Neighbor Toxicity* and *Max Neighbor Degree* between spammers and benign domains match our hypothesis: spammers are more likely to use targets shared by some other spammers and are more likely to use custom targets with low degrees in the graph.

3.4   Time Analysis of Traffic to DNS TXT Records

When a domain starts a spam campaign, we expect multiple servers to query DNS for the TXT record of the sender domain to check its SPF configuration. Therefore, we can observe an unusual number of queries related to the (newly registered) domain. The passive DNS feed we use contains aggregated queries over a given time window: when a DNS query is detected by a sensor, it is inserted in an aggregation buffer with the insertion timestamp. The subsequent identical queries only increase a counter in the buffer. When the buffer is full, the oldest inserted queries are flushed out, yielding an aggregated message with the query, the answer from the authoritative server, and three extra fields: `time_first`, `time_last`, and `count` meaning that the query was seen `count` times during the time window from `time_first` to `time_last`.

From these aggregated messages, we compute the traffic density by dividing the number of queries (in the `count` field) by the window duration, and then, dividing this value by the time between the end of the window and the end of the previous window to take into account the time windows in which there is no traffic. The resulting formula is the following:

$$density(i) = \frac{\texttt{count}}{\texttt{time\_last} - \texttt{time\_first}} \times \frac{1}{message\_end(i) - message\_end(i-1)}$$

For a more in-depth definition of the density and an explanation on how we handled overlapping windows, see Appendix A.

Max Variation. To detect large variations in density, we compute the *Max Variation* feature defined as the maximum density variation during 24 h. Domains with a slowly increasing traffic have a low *Max Variation* and those with a spike in the number of TXT queries, a high *Max Variation*. We compute two versions of this feature: i) the *Global Max Variation*, using the same time steps to compare all domains and ii) the *Local Max Variation* in which a custom time step is computed for each domain. See Appendix A for more details about the difference between these features.

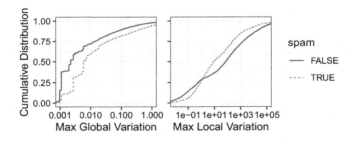

Fig. 7. Cumulative distribution of Max Variation (log scale x-axis)

Figure 7 presents the cumulative distribution of the two features. As expected, we observe that spam domains have a relatively higher *Max Global Variation* when all domains share the same time steps.

However, when we look at the *Max Local Variation*, we observe that benign domains tend to have a higher variation. The distributions are different because this feature is close to the average density variation: domains with a lot of traffic variation and small windows will have a higher *Local Variation*, whereas spam domains with almost no traffic except for a few spikes will have a lower *Local Variation* due to long periods of inactivity before a spike.

4 Classifiers

In this section, we present the classifiers used for the detection of spam based on the proposed features.

4.1 Ground Truth

We have taken the precaution of carefully selecting the domains in our ground truth. We recorded four months (between May and August 2021) of passive DNS traffic to TXT records from Farsight Security [8]. Because most spam domains are newly registered and discarded as soon as they are blacklisted, we only considered newly registered domains. From the ICANN Central Zone Data Service (CZDS) [14], we have built a list of new domains by computing the difference between consecutive versions of each generic Top Level Domain (gTLD) zone files. Appendix C provides the general statistics of the collected dataset.

Using SURBL [33] and SpamHaus [32] spam blacklists, we have identified all domains (in near-real time) in our database flagged by one of these sources. Spam blacklists are not perfect and sometimes they may flag benign domains as spam. Therefore, to obtain reliable ground truth, we added an extra layer of verification: a domain is labeled as

- **benign** if it has not been blacklisted and has been active during the entire period of the study (and has a valid A and NS records), or
- **malicious** if it was blacklisted by SURLB or SpamHaus and was taken down.

With these criteria, our ground truth dataset contained 37,832 non-spam and 2,392 spam domains.

4.2 Classifier

For spam detection, it is crucial to keep the True Negative[1] Rate (TPR) as high as possible to avoid flagging benign domains as spam. Once a True Negative Rate of at least 99% is achieved, we maximize the True Positive[2] Rate (TPR) to detect as many spam domains as possible. To compare classification results we use true negative and true positive rates, and the F1-score as described in Appendix B. We explored multiple classifiers and parameters with Weka [36], then implemented two of them with the scikit-learn [29] Python library, for better benchmarking. Two classifiers that performed the best are:

C4.5 or J48: a decision tree able to describe non-linear relations between features. It highlights complex conditional relations between features.
Random Forest: a set of multiple decision trees with a voting system to combine their results. Its drawback is low explainability.

---

[1] True Negative: non-spam domain correctly classified as such.
[2] True Positive: spam domain correctly classified as malicious.

Table 1. Features used by the classifiers

Category	Feature	Outcome
SPF Rules	Number of...	
	+all, +mx, +ptr, -all	Malicious
	+a, +include, +redirect, ~all	Benign
	+ip4, +ip6, ?all	Mixed[a]
SPF Graph	Max Neighbor Degree	Benign
	Max Neighbor Toxicity	Malicious
Time Analysis	Max Global Variation	Malicious
	Max Local Variation	Benign

[a]Depends on how many times the rule is present in the configuration

We use the k-fold cross-validation technique with k set to 5 (see Appendix B for more information). The number of spam domains in our ground truth dataset represents less than 10% of all domains. The decision tree algorithms are not suitable for classification problems with a skewed class distribution. Therefore, we have used a standard class weight algorithm for processing imbalanced data [37] implemented in the scikit-learn Python library [29].

Table 1 summarizes the features used by the classifiers and whether they indicate maliciousness or benignness of the domain.

5   Classification Results

We evaluate the efficiency of the classifiers with two sets of features: i) the *static* set without the time analysis features (Max Variation) and ii) the *static + dynamic* set that includes both static and the time analysis features. We have distinguished between the sets because even if the efficiency is lower without the time analysis features, we can get the static features (SPF configuration and graph properties) from a single TXT query to the target domain allowing for a rapid detection of most spam domains. Then, we can refine the classification by adding the time based features that are more robust against evasion techniques but require more time to detect spam domains.

5.1   Performance Evaluation

Figure 8 compares the Receiver Operating Characteristic (ROC) curves of each classifier for two sets of features (to see better the differences in performance, we zoom into high values of TPR). When training the classifiers, we change the weight of the spam class to change the reward of accurately finding a spam domain. If the spam class weight is low, the classifier will be less likely to risk

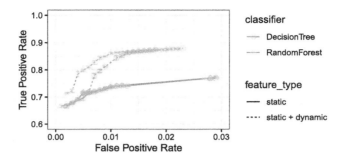

Fig. 8. ROC curve for different classifiers on two sets of features

getting a false positive. On the contrary, if the spam class weight is high, the classifier gets higher reward if it accurately flags a spam domain. Therefore, the classifier will "take more risks", reducing its TNR to increase TPR. If we require the False Positive Rate (benign domains flagged as spam) under 1%, the Random Forest is the best algorithm reaching a True Positive Rate of 74% using only the static set and 85% once we add the time analysis features.

Figure 9 illustrates how long we need to monitor a domain so that the classifiers reach their best efficiency. Over time, we observe traffic to each domain and the time analysis features get more precise (until one week), which improves classification. Both classifiers reach almost the best detection performance (computed as the F1-score) after observing a domain for one day.

5.2   Detection Time

The static results (labeled as 0H in Fig. 9) show the efficiency of the scheme when a single TXT request is observed. In this case, the classifier has no time properties of the traffic and only uses the static features (SPF Rules and SPF Graph). We can replace passive detection of SPF Rules with active DNS scans (assuming we have a list of newly registered domain names, which is generally the case for legacy and new gTLDs but not for the vast majority of ccTLD [4,18]): by actively querying the TXT records of new domains and classifying them based on their SPF configuration and formed relationships. Then, over time, as we passively observe traffic to the domain records, the performance of the classifier improves achieving very good results after 30 min (F1-score of 0.83) of monitoring (with Random Forest) in comparison with the F1-score of 0.86 after one day.

Using only static features, we compared the spam domain detection speed of our scheme with two commercial blacklists (SpamHaus and SURBL). In Fig. 10, we plotted the time elapsed between the detection by our scheme and the appearance of domains in the blacklists (with an hourly granularity). We limited the graph to 50 h, but considerable number of domains only appear in the commercial

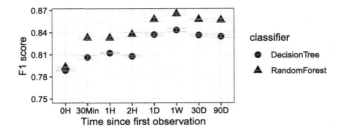

Fig. 9. F1-score of classifiers after the first appearance of each domain

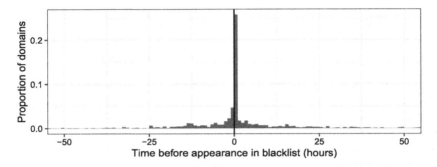

Fig. 10. Time before detected spam domains appear in commercial blacklists

blacklists weeks after we detect them. Positive values mean that our scheme was faster: for 70% of the detected spam domains, our scheme was faster than the commercial blacklists. However, 26% of the domains detected by our scheme appear in the commercial blacklists in the following hour, whereas 30% of the domains are detected more than 24 h in advance. The negative values represent domain names where our scheme was slower than the commercial blacklists: 30% of the domains were already in the blacklists when they were observed in our passive DNS feed for the first time and classified as spam.

5.3   Feature Importance

The importance of each feature was computed by looking at how selective the feature was in the Random Forest classifier [29]. The importance of each feature and each category is described in Table 2. It is not a surprise that the Maximum Neighbor Toxicity is by far the most important feature: a domain whitelisting the same IP addresses and domains as a known spamming domain is very likely to be managed by spammers. The most important SPF rule for classification is `+ptr`: as we discussed in Sect. 3.2, this rule is almost never used by benign domains (following the RFC 7208 recommendations). Lastly, the Global Max Variation is the most important dynamic feature: massive increases in the number of queries to a domain is a distinctive trait of spamming domains, as presented in Sect. 2.2, but this feature is only useful after the start of the spam campaign.

Table 2. Importance of each feature for the Random Forest classifier

Feature	Importance
SPF Graph features	**0.574515**
neighbor_max_toxicity	0.463689
neighbor_max_degree	0.110826
SPF Rules features	**0.232846**
+ptr	0.100481
+a	0.029005
+ip4	0.028789
+mx	0.021006
+include	0.017561
?all	0.013728
~all	0.011522
Other rules	<0.01
Time Analysis features	**0.192638**
global_max_variation_24h	0.122167
local_max_variation_24h	0.036828
global_max_triggers_24h	0.022380
local_max_triggers_24h	0.011263

6 Related Work

The four main categories of features used to detect malicious domains are the following: i) Lexical: domain name, randomness of characters, or similarity to brand names [1,5,22,23,27], ii) Domain and IP address popularity: reputation systems based on diversity, origin of queries, or past malicious activity [1,2,9,23,27,31], iii) DNS traffic: number of queries, intensity, burst detection, behavior changes [5,24], iv) WHOIS (domain registration data): who registered a given domain[3], when, and at which registrar [9,23,27]. Other methods develop specific features extracted from the content of mails: size of the mail, links, or redirections [25,27]. With the selected features, machine learning algorithms classify malicious and benign domains.

With respect to the methods that work on passive data such as Exposure [5] that need some time to detect abnormal or malicious patterns, we focus on

---

[3] Not available after the introduction of the General Data Protection Regulation (GDPR) and the ICANN Temporary Specification [15].

early detection of spam domains. Exposure for instance, needs around a week of observation before possible detection, while we achieve a F1-score of 79% based on a single DNS query. Our scheme can be applied at early stages of a domain life cycle: using passive (or active) DNS, we can obtain SPF rules for newly registered domains and classify them immediately, or wait until we detect TXT queries to that domain and refine the classification using hard-to-evade temporal features.

Other methods generally try to detect abnormal or malicious patterns at later phases of the domain life cycle. Schemes based on content or long period traffic analysis may reach high efficiency but generally cannot run before or at the beginning of an attack. Schemes using lexical and popularity features can run preemptively but may have reduced efficiency, compared to dynamic schemes.

Our scheme may complement other approaches that aim at detecting spam during other phases in the life cycle of spam campaigns and other algorithms that rely on a variety of different features.

7   Conclusion

In this paper, we have proposed a new scheme for early detection of spam domains based on the content of domain SPF rules and traffic to the TXT records containing them. With this set of features, our best classifier detects 85% of spam domains while keeping a False Positive Rate under 1%. The detection results are remarkable given that the classification only uses the content of the domain SPF rules and their relationships, and hard to evade features based on DNS traffic. The performance of the classifiers stays high, even if they are only given the static features that can be gathered from a single TXT query (observed passively or actively queried).

With a single request to the TXT record, we detect 75% of the spam domains, possibly before the start of the spam campaign. Thus, our scheme brings important speed of reaction: we can detect spammers with good performance even before any mail is sent and before a spike in the DNS traffic. To evaluate the efficiency of the proposed approach based on passive DNS, we did not combine the proposed features with other ones used in previous work like domain registration patterns [9,23,27]. In practical deployments, the classification can be improved by adding other features based on, e.g., the content of potentially malicious mails or the lexical patterns of the domain names.

The features used in our scheme yield promising results, so adding them to existing spam detection systems will increase their performance without large computation overhead as SPF data can easily be extracted from near-real-time passive DNS feeds already used in some schemes.

Acknowledgement. We thank Paul Vixie and Joe St Sauver (Farsight Security), the reviewers, our shepherd, and Sourena Maroofi for their valuable and constructive feedback. We thank Farsight Security for providing access to the passive DNS traffic as well as SpamHaus and SURBL for the spam blacklists. This work was partially supported by the Grenoble Alpes Cybersecurity Institute under contract ANR-15-IDEX-02 and by the DiNS project under contract ANR-19-CE25-0009-01.

Appendix

A Density Computation

Comparing the time windows of multiple domains in passive DNS data is a complex task: each window has a different size and we have no information on how the queries are spread inside it.

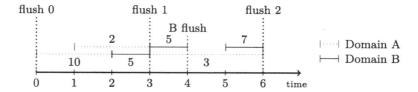

Fig. 11. Computation of traffic density from Passive DNS messages

The query density of multiple domains can only be compared if they are computed the same way, over the same time period. If a period starts or ends in the middle of a domain time window, we need to make an assumption about how the queries are spread inside the time window, to determine how many queries are inside the time period. However, we do not have such information so a period can only start and end at a timestamp that it is not included in any time window. We call those usable timestamps *flushes*. Then, the query density of a domain between two flushes is computed by measuring the time during which the domain was active, the total time between the flushes and the number of queries. For example, in Fig. 11, between flush 0 and 1, Domain A has a `count` (total number of queries) of 12 and an `active_time` (total time covered by time windows) of 3, and Domain B has a `count` of 5, and an `active_time` of 1. If $flush(i)$ is the timestamp of the i-th flush, we define the density at time i as:

$$density(i) = \frac{count}{active\_time} \times \frac{1}{flush(i+1) - flush(i)}.$$

The first fraction represents the density of requests in the aggregated time window. The second fraction normalizes this value by the size of the flush window so that all domains have a comparable density, as the flushes are not evenly spread. Therefore, $density(0)$ for domain A is $12/3 \times 1/3 = 4/3$ and $5/1 \times 1/3 = 5/3$ for domain B.

For the *Max Global Variation*, the *flushes* are computed using the time windows of all domains in our ground truth (the numbered flushes in Fig. 11). This results in fewer *flushes* but the traffic density between different domains can be compared (as they all use the same time steps). The *Max Local Variation* of a domain is computed using only the time windows of this domain to compute the *flushes* (numbered *flushes* plus domain *flushes* in Fig. 11). The *Local Max*

Variation uses more time steps so the density is more precise, but these time steps are different for each domain and have a tendency to reduce the detection of sudden bursts following a long inactivity window.

B   Classifier Metrics and Algorithms

The performance of each classifier is measured with three metrics:

F1-score: $\frac{2TP}{2TP+FP+FN}$, with TP, FP and FN being respectively the number of True Positives, False Positives, False Negatives

True Positive Rate (TPR): $\frac{TP}{TP+FN}$: proportion of spam domains accurately flagged as spam.

True Negative Rate (TNR): $\frac{TN}{TN+FP}$: proportion of benign domains accurately flagged as benign.

To calculate performance metrics, we use the k-fold technique: the whole ground truth dataset is split in 5 equal parts. We select one fold for testing and train the model using the $k-1$ remaining folds. We repeat this process for each fold. Each metric is the average of the five iterations.

C   Dataset Statistics

Table 3 shows the number of queries and unique domains at each data collection and analysis stage. The first step captures DNS TXT queries to newly registered domain names observed in the passive DNS feed. The next step retains only the TXT queries that contain valid SPF data. Then, we build ground truth with the approach described in Sect. 4.1.

Table 3. Number of queries and unique domains in the dataset at different stages

Stage	Queries	Unique domains	Spam domains
1. Traffic to new domains	399M	14M	0.8%
2. SPF traffic	36M	1.4M	1.5%
3. Ground truth	26M	40,224	5.9%

D   Classification Results

Table 4 shows the results of the Random Forest classifier using static and dynamic features (SPF Rules, SPF Graph and Time Analysis features). It corresponds to the model from Fig. 8 with a TPR of 0.717 and FPR of 0.006. The second and third columns (Spam and Benign) represent how commercial blacklists (SpamHaus and SURBL) classified the domains (ground truth data),

Table 4. Classification results for the Random Forest classifier on the ground truth dataset.

Our method	Blacklists		
	Spam	Benign	**Total**
Spam	TP = 1 716	FP = 210	**1 926**
Benign	FN = 676	TN = 37 622	**38 298**
Total	**2 392**	**37 832**	**40 224**
	TPR	**TNR**	**F1-score**
	71.7%	99.4%	79.5%

whereas the second and third row represent how our system classified the same domains. For example, in the table we can note that 676 domains were classified as Benign by our classifier, but they appear in the commercial blacklists—this represents the number of False Negatives (FN). The second part of the table shows the metrics used to evaluate our classifier (TPR, TNR, and F1-score) as described in Appendix B.

References

1. Antonakakis, M., Perdisci, R., Dagon, D., Lee, W., Feamster, N.: Building a dynamic reputation system for DNS. In: USENIX Security (2010)
2. Antonakakis, M., Perdisci, R., Lee, W., Vasiloglou, N., Dagon, D.: Detecting malware domains at the upper DNS hierarchy. In: USENIX Security (2011)
3. Antonakakis, M., et al.: From throw-away traffic to bots: detecting the rise of DGA-based malware. In: USENIX Security (2012)
4. Bayer, J., et al.: Study on Domain Name System (DNS) Abuse Appendix 1 - Technical Report. Technical report (2022). https://doi.org/10.2759/473317
5. Bilge, L., Sen, S., Balzarotti, D., Kirda, E., Kruegel, C.: Exposure: a passive DNS analysis service to detect and report malicious domains. ACM Trans. Inf. Syst. Secur. 16(4), 1–28 (2014)
6. Crime Complaint Center (IC3), FBI: Internet Crime Report (2020). https://www.ic3.gov/Media/PDF/AnnualReport/2020_IC3Report.pdf
7. Deccio, C.T., et al.: Measuring email sender validation in the wild. In: CoNEXT. ACM (2021)
8. Farsight Inc.: Farsight SIE. https://www.farsightsecurity.com/solutions/security-information-exchange/
9. Hao, S., Kantchelian, A., Miller, B., Paxson, V., Feamster, N.: PREDATOR: proactive recognition and elimination of domain abuse at time-of-registration. In: ACM CCS (2016)
10. Hao, S., et al.: Understanding the domain registration behavior of spammers. In: IMC (2013)
11. Hoffman, P.E., McManus, P.: DNS Queries over HTTPS (DoH) (2018). https://doi.org/10.17487/RFC8484. https://datatracker.ietf.org/doc/rfc8484
12. Holz, T., Gorecki, C., Rieck, K., Freiling, F.C.: Measuring and detecting fast-flux service networks. In: NDSS (2008)

13. Hu, Z., Zhu, L., Heidemann, J., Mankin, A., Wessels, D., Hoffman, P.E.: Specification for DNS over Transport Layer Security (TLS) (2016). https://datatracker.ietf.org/doc/rfc7858
14. ICANN: ICANN: Centralized Zone Data Service. http://czds.icann.org/
15. ICANN: Temporary Specification for gTLD Registration Data, May 2018. https://www.icann.org/resources/pages/gtld-registration-data-specs-en
16. Kheir, N., Tran, F., Caron, P., Deschamps, N.: Mentor: positive DNS reputation to skim-off benign domains in botnet C&C blacklists. In: Cuppens-Boulahia, N., Cuppens, F., Jajodia, S., Abou El Kalam, A., Sans, T. (eds.) SEC 2014. IAICT, vol. 428, pp. 1–14. Springer, Heidelberg (2014). https://doi.org/10.1007/978-3-642-55415-5_1
17. Kitterman, S.: Sender Policy Framework (SPF) for Authorizing Use of Domains in Email, Version 1 (2014). https://datatracker.ietf.org/doc/rfc7208
18. Korczyński, M., Tajalizadehkhoob, S., Noroozian, A., Wullink, M., Hesselman, C., Van Eeten, M.: Reputation metrics design to improve intermediary incentives for security of TLDs. In: IEEE EuroS&P (2017)
19. Korczyński, M., et al.: Cybercrime after the sunrise: a statistical analysis of DNS abuse in new gTLDs. In: ACM AsiaCCS (2018)
20. Kucherawy, M., Crocker, D., Hansen, T.: DomainKeys Identified Mail (DKIM) Signatures (2011). https://doi.org/10.17487/RFC6376. https://datatracker.ietf.org/doc/rfc6376
21. Kucherawy, M., Zwicky, E.: Domain-based Message Authentication, Reporting, and Conformance (DMARC) (2015). https://datatracker.ietf.org/doc/rfc7489
22. Le Pochat, V., Van Goethem, T., Joosen, W.: A Smörgåsbord of typos: exploring international keyboard layout typosquatting. In: IEEE SPW (2019)
23. Le Pochat, V., et al.: A practical approach for taking down avalanche botnets under real-world constraints. In: NDSS (2020)
24. Lison, P., Mavroeidis, V.: Neural reputation models learned from passive DNS data. In: 2017 IEEE International Conference on Big Data (2017)
25. Marchal, S., Armano, G., Grondahl, T., Saari, K., Singh, N., Asokan, N.: Off-the-hook: an efficient and usable client-side phishing prevention application. IEEE Trans. Comput. **66**(10), 1717–1733 (2017)
26. Maroofi, S., Korczyński, M., Duda, A.: From defensive registration to subdomain protection: evaluation of email anti-spoofing schemes for high-profile domains. In: TMA (2020)
27. Maroofi, S., Korczyński, M., Hesselman, C., Ampeau, B., Duda, A.: COMAR: classification of compromised versus maliciously registered domains. In: IEEE EuroS&P, pp. 607–623 (2020)
28. Maroofi, S., Korczyński, M., Hölzel, A., Duda, A.: Adoption of email anti-spoofing schemes: a large scale analysis. IEEE Trans. Netw. Serv. Manag. **18**(3), 3184–3196 (2021)
29. Pedregosa, F., et al.: Scikit-learn: machine learning in Python. J. Mach. Learn. Res. **12**, 2825–2830 (2011)
30. Perdisci, R., Corona, I., Dagon, D., Lee, W.: Detecting malicious flux service networks through passive analysis of recursive DNS traces. In: ACSAC (2009)
31. Pochat, V.L., van Goethem, T., Tajalizadehkhoob, S., Korczynski, M., Joosen, W.: Tranco: a research-oriented top sites ranking hardened against manipulation. Network and Distributed System Security Symposium, NDSS (2019). https://www.ndss-symposium.org/ndss-paper/tranco-a-research-oriented-top-sites-ranking-hardened-against-manipulation/

32. SpamHaus: The SpamHaus Project. https://www.spamhaus.org
33. SURBL: SURBL - URI reputation data. http://www.surbl.org
34. Wang, W., Shirley, K.: Breaking Bad: Detecting Malicious Domains Using Word Segmentation (2015). http://arxiv.org/abs/1506.04111
35. Weimer, F.: Passive DNS Replication. https://www.first.org/conference/2005/papers/florian-weimer-paper-1.pdf
36. Weka 3: Machine Learning Software in Java. https://www.cs.waikato.ac.nz/ml/weka/
37. Zhu, M., et al.: Class weights random forest algorithm for processing class imbalanced medical data. IEEE Access **6**, 4641–4652 (2018)

Changing of the Guards: Certificate and Public Key Management on the Internet

Carl Magnus Bruhner[1], Oscar Linnarsson[1], Matus Nemec[1], Martin Arlitt[2], and Niklas Carlsson[1(✉)]

[1] Linköping University, Linköping, Sweden
carbr307@student.liu.se, niklas.carlsson@liu.se
[2] University of Calgary, Calgary, Canada

Abstract. Certificates are the foundation of secure communication over the internet. However, not all certificates are created and managed in a consistent manner and the certificate authorities (CAs) issuing certificates achieve different levels of trust. Furthermore, user trust in public keys, certificates, and CAs can quickly change. Combined with the expectation of 24/7 encrypted access to websites, this quickly evolving landscape has made careful certificate management both an important and challenging problem. In this paper, we first present a novel server-side characterization of the certificate replacement (CR) relationships in the wild, including the reuse of public keys. Our data-driven CR analysis captures management biases, highlights a lack of industry standards for replacement policies, and features successful example cases and trends. Based on the characterization results we then propose an efficient solution to an important revocation problem that currently leaves web users vulnerable long after a certificate has been revoked.

1 Introduction

Aided by several initiatives (e.g., [1,16,68]), the last decade saw a major shift from non-encrypted to encrypted web traffic. Today, most websites use HTTPS [9,14,37] and other TLS-based protocols (e.g., QUIC [48]) to deliver their content. These protocols rely heavily on X.509 certificates. At a high-level, before a secure and trusted connection can be established, the server must present the client with a valid X.509 certificate that maps the server's public key to the server's domain and that has been issued (and signed) by a recognized Certification Authority (CA) that is *trusted* by the client. Since users expect 24/7 secure access to trusted services, it is therefore important that the servers present clients with a valid and trusted certificate. This has made careful certificate management an important problem.

Careful certificate management is also a challenging problem, as not all certificates are created and managed in the same way. From a domain administrator perspective, there are many issues to consider. For example, there are many issuing CAs and certificate types with different issuing processes and costs, the trust

O. Hohlfeld et al. (Eds.): PAM 2022, LNCS 13210, pp. 50–80, 2022.
https://doi.org/10.1007/978-3-030-98785-5_3

and usage of different CAs is changing over time, different services have different security requirements, and the trust in individual keys may quickly change.

To complicate the situation, for a number of reasons [76] modern browsers do not perform sufficient revocation checks [28] to protect users against man-in-the-middle attacks made possible by compromised keys even after they have been revoked by the domain owner and its CA [55]. While Chrome and Firefox browsers periodically (e.g., with software updates) push a proprietary set of revocations to their users [41,59], the frequency and size of such revocation sets leave clients vulnerable long after most compromised certificates have been revoked. The situation appears most pressing for mobile browsers. For example, Liu et al. [55] found that not a single native mobile browser on iOS, Android, or Windows Phones checks the revocation status of certificates. Finally, regardless of the choices made by the websites and CAs to address these challenges, websites (with the help of the CAs) need to make sure that they always can present their clients with valid and trusted certificates.

In this paper, we (1) present a novel server-side characterization of the certificate replacement (CR) relationships observed in practice, which provides insights into biases in how services manage their certificates; (2) examine the subset of CRs that reuse the same key when a certificate is replaced; and (3) demonstrate how targeted modifications to how CRs with reused keys are handled can reduce the reliance of revocation checks and solve this revocation problem.

Our analysis is based on data extracted from all biweekly scans of port 443 (Oct. 30, 2013 to Jul. 13, 2020) done within Rapid7's Project Sonar [2]. After presenting our methodology (Sect. 2), we characterize the full set of CRs (Sect. 3) that highlights positive trends and behaviors. For this analysis, we use misman-agement indicators and study how much safety margin servers use (e.g., in terms of validity period overlap), differences in the timing of validity periods and when certificate changes actually are observed, and whether there are replacement differences based on validity type, key reuse, CA changes, and CA selection.

Our characterization demonstrates and highlights the effects of a lack of general industry standards for replacement policies [38]. This includes, for example, a clear discrepancy in the overlap patterns between the top-issuing CAs, dividing those having automated renewal/replacement support and those dependent on manual effort. However, despite several of the CAs issuing cheaper domain validated (DV) certificates with shorter validity periods using common validity-period overlaps, the least gaps (defined as CRs in which the validity periods of the replaced and replacing certificates are non-overlapping) and early/late usage of certificates are still associated with more expensive certificates using extended validation (EV). Positive trends include a decreasing fraction of CRs with gaps, and a decreasing fraction of certificates being observed in use before they are valid or after they have expired. We also observe that the decision to change CAs often is associated with gaps, but that the decision to reuse keys is not.

The later parts of the paper look closer at two particularly interesting aspects identified in the dataset and motivated by our findings, respectively. First, we study the subset of CRs in which the same key is reused by the replacing certificate. Here, we also examine the "replacement chains" that are formed when the same key is reused for a series of consecutive CRs in which the replacing certificate of CR i is the replaced certificate in CR $i + 1$ of the series. Throughout the paper, we call such a CR and chain a *Same Key CR* (SKCR) and an *SKCR chain*, respectively. Our analysis highlights big differences in how customers of different CAs reuse keys. While the customers of three CAs (Sectigo, GlobalSign, Go Daddy) had higher than 65% key reuse, the customers of several other CAs (e.g., Google, cPanel, Amazon, Microsoft) typically did not appear to reuse keys. Encouragingly, the three CAs with the most key reuse achieved substantially fewer gaps when reusing keys than when not reusing keys. However, while SKCRs make up only 14% of Let's Encrypt's customers' CRs, they present the perhaps most interesting use case. For example, by combining longer key-reuse chains with consistent issuing of 90-day certificates with 30-day overlaps, their customers achieve high relative key utilization (e.g., aggregated lifetime compared to aggregate validity period over the certificate making up the reuse chains) without having to frequently replace the public keys used on their servers.

Finally, motivated by the effectiveness and potential of some of the observed automation solutions and trends, we outline a new way (Sect. 5) to address the currently open revocation problem discussed above. Our solution framework is based on observations highlighted in the paper, takes some current trends to the extreme, and combines the use of short-lived three-phase certificates (modification of an idea by Rivest [66]). It also introduces the new concept of parent-child certificate relationships and new simple management rules. The framework ensures efficient use of certificates in such a way that it does not need to increase how frequently servers change their public keys or how frequently certificates must be logged in Certificate Transparency (CT) logs [50]. Using our CR datasets, we also demonstrate and quantify the reduced overhead that these efficiencies of our approach would provide when some set of CAs select to reduce their certificate lifetimes using our approach rather than naively.

In summary, the paper provides both new insights into the status of current HTTPS certificate management (Sect. 3), including the reuse of keys (Sect. 4), and novel solutions to improve certificate management and to address the currently unresolved revocation problem so far unsatisfactorily handled by browsers (Sect. 5).

2   Analysis Methodology

Rapid7 Dataset: We used two certificate datasets [3] from Project Sonar [2]. These datasets consist of biweekly scans of the IPv4 address space, collected using Rapid7's extensions [4] of ZMap [35]. First, we used all HTTPS _certs files between 2013-10-30 and 2020-07-13 to extract the full Privacy-Enhanced Mail (PEM) [44,54] encoded certificates and their SHA-1 fingerprints. Second, for our observation-based statistics, we used the corresponding _hosts files collected for port 443 to determine at what IP addresses and time these certificates were observed (using the SHA-1 fingerprints for mapping between the files).

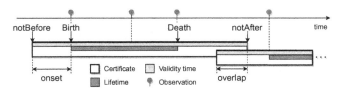

Fig. 1. Replacement relation between two certificates. (Color figure online)

Identifying and Extracting CR Relationships: Using the above datasets, we identify certificate replacement (CR) relationships. Here, we define a CR to exist between a pair of certificates under the following conditions. (1) The two certificates were observed at the same IP address (and port number). (2) The two subjectCN either matched perfectly or matched after following three wildcard rules: wildcards are only allowed to be used at the lowest domain level, at the third domain level and down, and only one wildcard is allowed per match. (3) The validity period of the *replacing* certificate must begin later than the beginning of the validity period of the *replaced* certificate and must extend past the end of the validity of the replaced certificate. Figure 1 shows a toy example with overlapping validity periods (green color) and the first certificate of the CR only were observed during three scans (first three red markers). Here, the *validity period* is defined as the time between the notBefore and notAfter values in the certificate, and following the terminology used by Chung et al. [29], the *lifetime* is defined as the time period between the first scan when a certificate is observed (referred to as its *birth*) and the last scan it is observed (referred to as its *death*).

In addition to extracting information about the individual certificates and different metrics related to their relative validity periods (e.g., the *overlap* in Fig. 1), we also extract information regarding when the two certificates were seen in use. Of particular interest here are cases when the servers present their certificates *before* the validity period has started or *after* it has expired.

Multi-step CR Identification and Extraction: We performed a series of processing steps to create an aggregated dataset including all CR relationships.

- **Step 1 (parse + process certificates):** Using a Node.js library *node-forge*[1] and OpenSSL (when node-forge was unable to parse a certificate) we extracted data from the certificates, including (1) certificate identifiers and basic information, (2) issuer and subject identifiers, (3) CA status and chain info (e.g., we determined whether the subject is a CA and whether it is self-signed, self-issued, or signed by third party), (4) validity period, (5) verification type (determined based on the Object Identifiers (OIDs) [5,7]), and (6) public key properties.
- **Steps 2+3 (extract birth and death):** We next identify the *birth* and *death* of each certificate, respectively. In these steps, the output files were

---

[1] Available at: https://www.npmjs.com/package/node-forge/v/0.9.0.

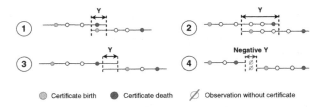

Fig. 2. Certificate replacement search order.

sorted based on the first birth (step 2) and last death (step 3). We also keep track of IP addresses and the number of observations.

- **Step 4 (extract CR relations):** CRs were identified one certificate at a time based on each certificate's birth. For each certificate, we search backwards in time from its time of death (increasing overlap); stopping as soon as we find a matching CR. If no such CR is found, we instead search for births forward in time (decreasing overlaps) until either such CR is found or no CR can be identified for the certificate. (Fig. 2 illustrates the search order.) For every match, the precision difference between the subjectCN is stored, indicating if it was an exact match, if it is more precise, or if it is less precise. To allow wildcard certificates to be replaced by multiple certificates, a wildcard certificate is considered for multiple matches if it has the same birth date as the first found CR.

- **Step 5 (identify SKCR chains):** Finally, we used the SHA1 hashes of the *replaced* and *replacing* certificate of each CR in which the two certificates contained the same public key (i.e., an SKCR relationship) to identify chains of SKCRs. Starting from the base case of a single SKCR, which has a chain length of one, we search for additional CRs for which the *replaced* certificate was the *replacing* certificate of the most recent SKCR. The chaining was repeated until ether a new public key was used in the chain, or until no matching CR could be found.

Our analysis mostly focuses on the outputs from steps 4 and 5.

Limitations: Like most internet measurements, the Rapid7 dataset has its limitations. First, the biweekly scans limit how fine a granularity we can consider for CRs. Second, Project Sonar only tries each IP address once during a scan. While many certificates are seen across many IPs, this could potentially introduce biases against certificates of services with few servers or that are further away from the scanners. Third, the dataset does not capture how many real users download each certificate or how popular the services using the certificates are. Here, we treat all certificates observed in the Rapid7 datasets equally. Fourth, the Rapid7 dataset misses many certificates that may be found in CT logs [78]. While this may cause us to miss some certificates that may be of interest, the Rapid7 dataset has the advantage that it allows us to measure when a certificate was used (not only what its intended validity period is) and helps focus on certificates actually observed in the wild.

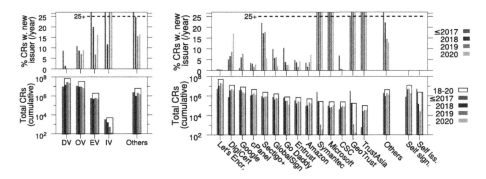

Fig. 3. Total number of certificate replacements (bottom panes) and the fractions of these for which the second certificate had a new issuer (top panes). The ranking of CAs are shown based on the certificates from the last three years (2018–2020) shown using combined boxes around those years.

Fifth, some HTTPS servers listen on ports other than 443. The addition of scans of non-443 ports could have increased the observed lifetimes of some certificates. However, the majority of HTTPS servers use port 443. Sixth, long-lived certificates can bias the CRs observed in the beginning of the measurement period and CRs with large gaps may be missed towards the end. Given current validation period and overlap distributions, these biases should have limited impact on the set of CRs identified between 2016–2019. Despite these limitations, we believe our analysis provides an insightful glimpse into HTTPS certificate and public key management on the Internet over the past seven years.

Finally, we acknowledge that our paper would benefit from a measure of how often security incidents exploited revoked certificates. For example, such a measure would enable a risk assessment and help determine the ideal validity period of a certificate. However, to the best of our knowledge, such a measurement has not been published and is out of scope of our paper.

3   Certificate Replacement Analysis

In total, we observed 217,221,681 unique certificates and identified 129,382,646 CRs. After filtering out self-issued and self-signed certificates, the number of CRs reduced to 108,751,863. (21.4 million CRs for the set ≤2017, 22.8 million for 2018, 35.9 million for 2019, and 28.6 million for 2020 (Jan-Jun).)

3.1   Certificate Selection Characterization

Not all certificates are created and managed in the same way. For example, different CAs offer different trust, issuing processes, and costs, and there are several validation types. Different websites therefore make different choices, and some may change CAs. Figure 3 summarizes the most common certificate choices in the last few years. The bottom panes show the total number of CRs per certificate type and issuer, and the top panes show the fraction of those CRs that changed issuer. Throughout the paper we label CRs using the characteristics of the replaced certificate and say that the issuer has changed whenever the issuer's common name (issuerCN) is different. For the per-CA breakdown we rank the CAs based on the number of CRs between 2018–2020 (shown as combined bars in the plot) and only show results for CAs with at least 100,000 CRs and for which the majority of the certificates are approved by the major browser vendor's trust stores. When interpreting these plots, it is important to note that a CR represents a successful certificate replacement.

For the analysis in this paper, we omit self-signed and self-issued certificates. Prior works have shown that these certificates are responsible for the majority of invalid certificates in the dataset [29]. To illustrate how big a portion of the CRs that these two certificate types represent we include them in the right-hand panes here, but exclude them from all other analysis (including the results shown in the left-hand panes). Here it is important to note that the majority of the studied certificates are issued by the top-CA.

Certificate Types and Issuer Changes: There are big differences in the issuance requirements of different validity types. Domain Validated (DV) certificates have the least requirements and Extended Validation (EV) certificates the most rigorous (and time consuming) requirements [7]. Organization Validated (OV) and Individual Validation (IV) certificates fall between the two, adding somewhat to the requirements (and costs) of DVs [5]. DV certificates is the dominating certificate type in the dataset. Customers using DV certificates seldomly change issuer. A key reason for the higher issuer change rates of the other types is likely customers switching to cheaper services (e.g., free DV certificates). Two contributing factors for users having moved away from EV certificates during this period may be (1) the introduction of Let's Encrypt's free and easy-to-use DV certificates and (2) several major browsers (e.g., Safari, Chrome, Firefox) ending or announcing the ending of user interfaces displaying EV certificates differently than DV certificates. Both these aspects are expected to have reduced the incentive to spend extra money/effort for EV certificates.

Selected CAs and Their Retention Rates: For the per-CA breakdown, we rank CAs based on CRs between 2018–2020 and only show results for CAs with at least 100,000 CRs and for which the majority of the certificates are approved by the major browser vendors' trust stores (e.g., Apple, Microsoft, Mozilla/NSS). With these root stores having been responsible for most TLS user agents [56] at the time the dataset was collected (and before Chrome released their own root store in Dec. 2020 [6]) and all of them having significant overlaps in their root selections [45], we expect these CAs to have very good end-user reach. Both Symantec and GeoTrust have had very few CRs the last two years (purple+orange bars in bottom-right pane of Fig. 3). This is also reflected by the high rate of new issuers associated with CRs involving these two CAs (constantly above 25% for all four time buckets). Domains leaving Symantec is perhaps not surprising given that Google over this time period implemented a plan

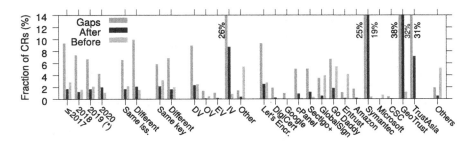

Fig. 4. Fraction of CRs with *gaps* or for which the first certificate was presented *after* it had expired or *before* it became valid. Only 2019 CRs are used here (with exception for the three categories "2020", "2018" and "≤2017" to the left).

to distrust Symantec [65]. Microsoft and TrustAsia have also seen high issuer churn over this time period. Of the dominant CAs, Let's Encrypt has the lowest change rate, suggesting that they have a high customer retention rate. DigiCert's change rate is increasing over time, while Google, Sectigo (formerly Comodo), and GlobalSign were able to improve their retention rates in 2020.

3.2 Analysis Using Mismanagement Indicators

Changing a certificate (or CA) is not always seamless. We next look closer at potential mismanagement indicators, including CRs with *gaps* between the validity periods of the two certificates in the CR, and the certificates that are used either *after* their expiry or *before* their validity period started. These results are summarized in Fig. 4. For this and all later figures, all results are based only on the CRs from 2019 (the most recent complete year of data we have; marked "*"), unless a different year is indicated (labeled "≤2017", "2018" or "2020"), and we use the same order of the CAs as provided by the rankings in Fig. 3.

Decreasing Fraction of Gaps: There has been a clear improvement over time. For example, since CRs including 2017 (9.34% gapped), the fraction of CRs with a gap has steadily decreased and was more than halved by 2020 (4.26%). This suggests that servers may be becoming better at replacing their certificates on time. One possible explanation is that Chrome and other browsers increasingly inform and/or block users from accessing websites that do not meet current HTTPS standards and practices, incentivizing websites to be compliant.

Changing CA More Frequently Results in Gaps: We have observed a disproportionate fraction of gaps associated with issuer changes. This may in part be due to some administrators leaving updates until it is too late. We have also found that the first certificate in a CR with overlapping validity periods typically is used for the better part of the overlap period, suggesting that server administrators may not be in a rush to switch to the replacement certificate or that they do not always get access to them right away, even when the certificate has an overlapping validity period.

Reuse of Keys: At an aggregate level, the reuse of keys does not appear to change the fraction of CR gaps, post-usage of expired certificates, or the pre-usage of not-yet valid certificates. Sect. 4 analyzes this case further.

CRs with EV and OV Certificates Have the Fewest Gaps: The CRs with the fewest-to-most gaps are: EV, OV, DV, and IV. This suggests that services that pay extra for EV (and OV) certificates indeed manage to ensure that they have fewer CR gaps than organizations that use cheaper DV certificates. This could potentially be due to differences in operational support between such websites. As IV usage is becoming increasingly rare, people may find fewer reasons to keep them up-to-date. Furthermore, with the use of timestamped code, code-signing certificates can be used for validation also after expiration [67].

Management Indicators Differ Substantially Across CAs: First, there is a big difference between the CAs with the largest fraction of gapped (bad) and overlapping (good) CRs. Like for validation types, the largest fraction of gapped CRs is associated with the CAs with the lowest retention rates and decreasing usage: Symantec (25%), GeoTrust (38%), and TrustAsia (32%). As expected, these three CAs also have the largest fraction of certificates used after their expiry date. We also observed 9.3% gaps associated with the free DV certificates issued by Let's Encrypt. In contrast, CRs with certificates issued by Microsoft (0.08%), CSC (0.4%), Google (1.0%), Entrust (1.1%), Amazon (1.7%), and DigiCert (1.9%) are much less likely to have gaps. The relatively low fraction of gaps suggests a significant level of automation and/or better process for certificate replacements. Second, we have observed a substantially higher fraction of certificate observations timestamped *before* they were valid when issued by four (different) CAs: Go Daddy (5.4%), Entrust (4.2%), GlobalSign (3.3%), and Let's Encrypt (2.8%). While the exact fraction of certificates observed early may be inflated by the granularity and accuracy of our *birth* estimates, the significant differences between the CAs are substantial and shows that some CAs may use significantly bigger safety margins than others to ensure that some clients (with clock offsets, for example) does not invalidate an okay certificate. Careful certificate management include both using sufficient overlap in the validity periods and deciding when to switch from using one certificate of a CR to the next.

The above differences may also be an indication that different classes of organizations are more likely to choose certain CAs. For example, one would expect significant differences in the fraction of gaps between organizations that depend on HTTPS for their business and those that simply want a web presence. The latter likely lack either the incentives or the means to prevent problems like gaps. Our results also suggest that organizations that are looking to switch CAs (possibly due to cost) are likely to contribute to yet additional one-time gaps.

EV and OV Certificates are More Carefully Managed: Similar to gapped CRs, the fraction of certificates that are used after or before their validity period is much smaller for OV and EV certificates than for DV certificates. This again shows that organizations employing such certificates indeed appear to manage their certificates more carefully.

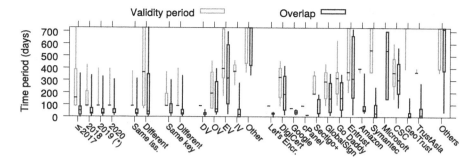

Fig. 5. Validity periods and CR overlaps. For each CR category, we show the 10-percentile (bottom marker), 25-percentile (bottom of box), median (middle/black marker), 75-percentile (top of box), and 90-percentile (top marker). Only 2019 CRs are used here (with exception for the three categories "2020", "2018" and "≤2017" to the left).

3.3   Overlap Analysis

Overlapping validity periods are typically used to protect against service outages. To better understand the safety margins used in practice, we next compare and contrast the overlaps of different CR sets. Figure 5 shows a box-and-whisker plot of the CR overlaps and the validity periods, for different categories of CRs.

Decreasing Overlaps: Regardless of which percentile we consider, overlaps have decreased over time. This observation is both interesting and encouraging, when considered in combination with our earlier observation that the fraction of gapped CRs has reduced substantially over the same period.

The above reductions have been achieved at the same time that the validation periods themselves have been reduced. The reduction in validity periods is particularly clear when considering the fraction of long-lived certificates (e.g., see 90-percentile values in Fig. 5) that have been pushed away by new regulations and best practices such as the CA/Browser Forum Baseline Requirements (BR) [5]. This trend towards shorter validity periods is expected to continue. As an example, in March 2020, Apple decided to reduce the maximum allowed lifetime of certificates in its root policy to 398 days (previously 825 days) for certificates issued starting September 2020 [12,31]. Chrome (June), Mozilla (July) and the BR (July) have since followed suit [25,40,81].

Gap Issues with Older (long-lived) Certificates: There is a disproportionate fraction of gaps associated with instances where old long-lived certificates expire. One possible explanation is that without automated solutions, the use of long-lived certificates increases the chance that a customer forgets to renew the certificate in time. While we expect CAs using automated issuance to be more likely to use short-lived certificates and provide/support automated certificate replacement solutions for their customers, we could only see a weak correlation between the CAs with longer validation periods and those with more gaps,

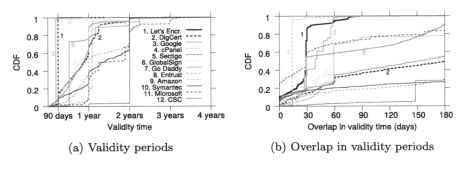

(a) Validity periods   (b) Overlap in validity periods

Fig. 6. CDFs for the 12 most frequently observed CAs. (Based on CRs in 2019.) (Color figure online)

when excluding Let's Encrypt. Instead, Let's Encrypt had a surprising number of gaps. We expect this to have more to do with the domains that select to use free certificates than the service provided by Let's Encrypt. However, more work is needed to confirm the underlying reasons for the above observations.

Subject vs Issuer Dominated Overlap Decisions: Clearly, all subjects have some control over the certificate overlaps: first the size of the validity period overlaps and second the specific date and time when to replace a certificate (and a key). Subjects can also decide if and when to change their issuing CA. However, the variation in these overlaps and decisions differ substantially depending on which issuing CA the subject uses. For example, the CAs with longer validity times have higher variability in the overlap distribution relative to CRs with certificates issued by CAs with shorter validity periods. One possible explanation is that the overlap of short-validity certificates is influenced more by the issuer than the subject, whereas the overlap with long-validity certificates appears influenced more by the subject. We again do not see any major differences when conditioning on whether the key is reused in the certificates.

DV Certificates Use Shorter Validity Periods and Overlaps than OV and EV Certificates: The validity periods are shorter for DV certificates regardless of whether Let's Encrypt certificates are included or excluded. While the average statistic (not shown) increases from 103 to 187 days when excluding Let's Encrypt, these values are still lower than for OV (241 days) and EV (461 days). One reason is that DV certificates typically use a faster validation process, simplifying use of short-lived certificates. Interestingly, DV certificates typically also use much shorter overlaps (safety margin). For example, the EV certificates have a median overlap of 317 days compared to 29 days for DV certificates.

Distinguishing Features of CAs: There are big differences in the validity periods and the overlaps. For example, Let's Encrypt, Google, and cPanel always use 90-day validity periods; services using their certificates have fairly specific overlaps for the majority of their CRs (typically 15 or 30 days). In contrast, most of the other CAs use much longer validity periods and their customers use both larger and much more diverse overlaps.

To better understand the distinct behaviors observed for the customers of different CAs, Fig. 6 shows the empirical cumulative distribution function (CDF) of the validity periods and CR overlaps observed in 2019 for each of the top-12 CAs in our dataset. To improve readability, the top-6 are shown with distinct color coding and enumeration, the CAs with ranks 7–9 are shown in green, and the CAs with ranks 10–12 are shown in yellow.

Increasing Validity Periods with Decreasing Rank: While there are exceptions, we note a clear shift in the CDFs based on the CA ranks. The three CAs with the shortest validity periods (left-most CDFs in Fig. 6) are roughly followed by the three CAs with ranks 2, 5 and 6, which are followed by the three CAs with ranks 7–9 (green curves), which finally are followed by the CAs with ranks 9–12 (yellow curves). This is in part due to some of the top-ranked CAs now offering attractive low-cost certificates with simple, automated validation checks and shorter validity periods. These distribution examples also show that many of the less popular CAs have had to make relatively bigger changes to comply with the recently imposed 398-day limit.

Automated Replacement Solutions: Some of the CAs have a clear "knee" in their overlap distributions. This behavior appears to be due to default values used in automated processes simplifying certificate management. For example, the two CAs with the most significant knee are cPanel (rank 4) and Let's Encrypt (rank 1). These CAs typically have an overlap of 15 and 30 days, respectively.

Both Let's Encrypt and cPanel automate some of their certificate services with the recently standardized Automatic Certificate Management Environment (ACME) [9,17]. Let's Encrypt, for instance, has created its own automation tool Certbot as an ACME agent [75]. The cPanel system also issues other certificates, and almost one out of five Let's Encrypt certificates are issued using cPanel [9].

Other CAs with sharp (although smaller) knees in the overlap distribution are Google (multiple steps), Sectigo (30 days), Amazon (60 days), Microsoft (30 days), and CSC (148 days). This suggests that websites using these services also use automated certificate replacement processes to a significant degree.

4   Reuse of Keys

There is a cost associated with mapping subjects to keys. Unless a key has been compromised, in some cases it may therefore be desirable to keep using the same key when issuing a new certificate. For example, servers do not have to replace their private keys and the CA could potentially simplify the domain validation process somewhat knowing that the domain already is in possession of the key. We call a CR where the public key is reused a Same Key CR (SKCR). The fraction of SKCRs is increasing and are today responsible for roughly 13% of all CRs. We next look closer at the SKCRs and the SKCR chains formed when a key is reused for consecutive replacements.

4.1   High-Level SKCR Analysis

Figure 7 shows the fraction of CRs that reuse the same key (black bars), and the fraction of those that have *gaps* (purple bars). As a reference point, we also include the overall fraction of gaps for each category (× markers). These reference point values are the same that were reported in Fig. 4.

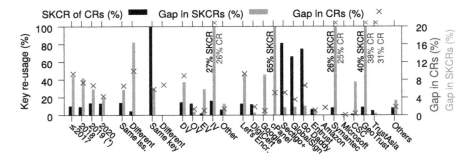

Fig. 7. Fraction of CRs that are SKCRs and have *gaps*. Only 2019 CRs are used here (with exception for the 3 categories "2020", "2018", "≤2017" to the left).

Small Difference or Reduced Fraction of Gaps: In most cases, reusing a key has limited effect on the results. We have only seen a few cases when services reusing keys have more gaps: the issuer changes, the certificate is of type EV, and (at a first glance) the first certificate in a CR was issued by certain CAs.

However, these cases can be explained by a change in CA (the characteristic most likely resulting in a gap). For example, the three CAs (Google, cPanel, CSC) with noticeable higher fraction of SKCR gaps (i.e., higher purple bars than × markers), as well as Amazon, have very small key reuse (black bars). It appears that these CAs typically do not allow reuse of keys. Instead, these rare cases are associated with a customer re-using their key with a different CA. (Google, cPanel, and Amazon has less than 0.003% reuse and CSC 0.6%.)

Three CAs with High Key Reuse and Fewer Gaps: The customers of three CAs have higher than 65% key reuse: Sectigo (81%), GlobalSign (66%), and Go Daddy (75%). The highest reuse among the other CAs is less than 13%. Interestingly, these three CAs (together with DigiCert and Trust Asia) also achieved less gaps when reusing a key (shorter purple bars than × markers). We believe that the reuse of keys is part of the operational practices of these CAs and may simplify the validation process as well as the key and certificate management process of the customers. In Sect. 5 we expand on this observation and show how key reuse can be used as a building block in an improved certificate management system.

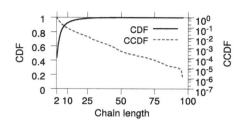

Fig. 8. Chain length distributions.

Fig. 9. Aggregate validity of SKCRs (one CDF per chain length)

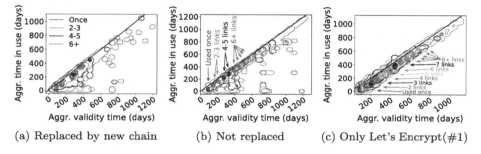

(a) Replaced by new chain   (b) Not replaced   (c) Only Let's Encrypt(#1)

Fig. 10. Aggregate validity period vs aggregate observed use for SKCR chains. (Color figure online)

4.2 SKCR-Chain Analysis

Let us next consider the *SKCR chains* formed when the same key is reused for a series of SKCRs (numbered from first to last) in which the replacing certificate in SKCR i is the certificate being replaced in SKCR $i + 1$ of the series.

Short Chains are Common: We have found that most chains are short (e.g., CDF in Fig. 8 shows that 80% of the chains of lengths at least two are no longer than five) and that the tail of the chain-length distribution has exponential characteristics (e.g., straight-line CCDF behavior on linear-log scale).

Long Chains are Dominated by Automated Services: Figure 9 shows the CDFs of the aggregate validity periods, when merging the validity periods of all certificates associated with an SKCR chain. When interpreting this figure, note that the single certificate line roughly captures the overall validity period distribution across all certificates. For example, as shown in Figs. 5 and 6, most certificates have a validity period of 90 days (Let's Encrypt, Google, cPanel) or around either one or two years (most other top-CAs). While we see some chains of length two (pink line) that clearly include long-lived certificates (e.g., steps around 1 year and 2 years), close to 40% of the chains with length 2 (pink line) have an aggregate validity period of 150 days (90+60), matching our previous observation that most of the Let's Encrypt certificates have a validity of 90 days

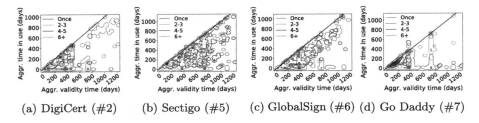

(a) DigiCert (#2)   (b) Sectigo (#5)   (c) GlobalSign (#6) (d) Go Daddy (#7)

Fig. 11. CA-based comparison of the validity vs. use as aggregated over all certificates in certificate-replacement chains. (Rank in parenthesis.)

and an overlap of 30 days. For chain lengths of three, the higher age steps have almost disappeared, and the aggregate duration instead appears to be dominated by Let's Encrypt chains. This is seen by the consecutive CDFs being shifted by roughly 60 days up-to a chain length of 10 certificates. The 11+ curve includes a mix of longer chain lengths (mapped to different CAs) and therefore has a somewhat different general shape, without any distinct steps.

Keys Used in Chains are Typically Used for Close to the Full Aggregate Validity Period: Figure 10 shows contour plots of the aggregate validity period versus (vs) the aggregate observed use for certificate-replacement chains of different replacement lengths. For easier visualization, we use contour plots. These plots are based on data between 2017-01-02 and 2020-07-13 and are generated using a matrix granularity of 5 days (meaning that any point falling within any of the 5 × 5 possible day combinations would add to the same counter), outliers are removed using a threshold of 0.15% of the total observations, and we have applied a Gaussian smoothing with a smoothing constant (sigma) of 2, where the smoothing can be seen as us simply taking the sum across twice as many buckets when doing a regional summation. We separate results based on whether the chain is eventually replaced by a new chain (Fig. 10(a)), which uses a different key, or whether no additional certificate replacement is observed (Fig. 10(b)). While we observe more variations in both use and validation periods for the second case, the general characteristics and observations are the same for both cases. First, the largest volumes (peaks or ridges in the plots) are observed just under the diagonal, suggesting that the observed use typically spans almost the full aggregate validity period. This shows that the websites typically make good use of the aggregate validity period. Second, we the shortest chains (red) have the largest portion of points well below the diagonal.

Behavior Varies Noticeably by CA: Looking closer at individual CAs, Let's Encrypt has the most interesting behavior. Figure 10(c) shows how it nicely stacks up longer and longer chains along the diagonal. As discussed above, this is desirable and demonstrates good use of the aggregated validity periods. This shift comes from Let's Encrypt customers consistently using a validity period of 90 days and often using an overlap of approximately 30 days.

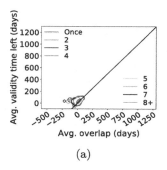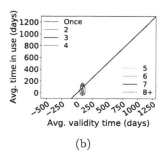

(a)   (b)

Fig. 12. Replacement timing for Let's Encrypt (rank #1), measured using (a) the average overlap vs the average validity left for the certificates in CR chains and (b) the average validity vs. use for certificates in CR chains.

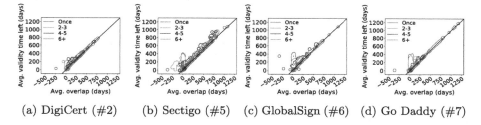

(a) DigiCert (#2)   (b) Sectigo (#5)   (c) GlobalSign (#6)   (d) Go Daddy (#7)

Fig. 13. Example CA-based comparison of the replacement timing as measured using the average overlap vs the average validity left for the certificates in certificate-replacement chains. (Rank in parenthesis.)

CA-Based Comparisons: Figure 11 shows the aggregated validity period vs. the aggregated use (over all certificates in the SKCR chains) for the other four CAs with key reuse of at least 12% in 2019. As a reminder, Let's Encrypt and DigiCert had just over 12% SKCRs and the other three CAs shown (Sectigo, GlobalSign, and GoDaddy) all had over 65% SKCRs. (Keys from certificates by Google and cPanel, with ranks 3 and 4, respectively, only were reused in $4.7 \cdot 10^{-6}$ and $1.2 \cdot 10^{-5}$ of their respective CRs.) For the customers of the other CAs we observe much more diverse behaviors. For these other CAs, many chains are also only observed for a small portion of the aggregate validity period (i.e., areas well below the diagonal). While four CAs have clear singularities in the aggregate validity period (e.g., around the 1-year and 2-year marks), their diversity differs substantially. Both DigiCert and GoDaddy primarily appear to have aggregated validity period of a year, suggesting that they limit the reuse and often have significant overlap in their SKCRs. In contrast, both Sectigo and GlobalSign has much more diversity in their SKCR chains (both with regards to aggregate validity period and aggregate usage period). For all four of these later CAs, we again see a shift towards the diagonal as the chains become longer.

Let's Encrypt Highly Automated: As we have seen, Let's Encrypt's highly automated services stand out in many ways. Another way to highlight this is shown in Figs. 12(a) and 13. Here, we compare the replacement timing, measured using the average overlap (based on validity periods) versus the average of the validity left for the first certificate of each SKCR in the SKCR chains when the replaced certificate is last observed. Again, Let's Encrypt displays a highly distinct pattern, as all CRs in the SKCR chains are equally treated. In particular, the validity periods are always 90 days and Let's Encrypt appears to aim to use a 30-day overlap, regardless of whether a key is re-used or not.

Replacement Certificates Typically Used Close to the Time They Become Valid: For all five CAs, the replacement certificates are typically being seen in use soon after they have become valid. This is seen by almost all points falling along (or slightly above) the diagonal in Fig. 13. However, exactly as we observed for the full set of CRs (Fig. 6(b)), compared with Let's Encrypt, the overlaps of the other four CAs are much more diverse and are therefore spread much more evenly along the diagonal. Yet, these results clearly show that certificates typically are replaced almost immediately even when there are large overlaps. While this may suggest that the old certificates in some cases are invalidated prematurely (especially in the case they are replaced with a certificate of the same key), it should be noted that websites or CAs may select to change certificates prematurely for other reasons (e.g., to add/remove domains or subdomains that can use the key).

5   Towards Short-Lived Certificates

Motivated by the success of recent automation systems (observed in prior sections), in this section we present a *data-driven case study* that take current trends of the validity periods and reuse of keys (characterized in prior sections) to the extreme. After presenting the problem and highlighting current trends, we first sketch out a solution that combines several new ideas to address the revocation problem that currently leaves all web users vulnerable to man-in-the-middle attacks on most compromised keys long after a certificate has been revoked. Second, we demonstrate the effectiveness of our solution using the different subsets of the CRs identified and characterized in the previous sections as baselines.

5.1   Motivation

Revocation problem: While we have shown that some CAs (e.g., Let's Encrypt, Google, cPanel) mostly issue certificates with roughly 90-day validity periods, even these validity periods can leave users vulnerable to attacks for a long time period. One reason for this is that most browsers (especially mobile browsers) do not sufficiently verify whether an X.509 certificate has been revoked or not [55]. While, as discussed in the introduction, Chrome and Firefox browsers periodically push a by-them-selected set of revocations to their users [41,59], the frequency and size of these revocation sets still leave users of most revoked (leaf) certificates vulnerable long after the compromised certificates have been revoked.

A Case for Shorter Validity Periods: One way to address the lack of revocation checks is to use short-lived certificates. This is not new [62,71,76]. One reason this idea has not been widely adopted is due to the lack of automation in past systems (e.g., wide-scale automation was first implemented and deployed by Let's Encrypt [9]), but also due to the significant increase in the number of certificates that would need to be handled.

Current Status: We have seen several success stories of automated solutions, including the effectiveness of Let's Encrypt's automated solutions. In addition, our results show that Let's Encrypt allows its customers to effectively reuse the same key over multiple certificates in a resource effective way.

Overhead Tradeoffs: There are important security-overhead tradeoffs to consider with short-lived certificates. On one hand, short validity periods reduce the attacker's time window and the potential impact of a compromised key. However, its use also increases the issuance and replacement overheads, and puts much tighter and less flexible timing requirements on certificate replacements.

It is easy to see how automation can help resolve timing issues in the certificate distribution between CAs and their customers. However, there still are significant overheads associated with the subject-key verification during issuance and it is unclear how Certificate Transparency (CT) logs [42,50,69] would handle the increased submission rates resulting from use of short-lived certificates. For example, while splitting a log into several logs may offset the load that a single log would observe, it does not reduce the combined load of the logs. To provide similar response times, for example, the combined set of resources of such solution would hence still need to scale with the load.

The primary purpose of CT is to provide public immutable records that help detect maliciously or mistakenly issued certificates. Since 2018, Chrome and Apple require all newly issued certificates to be included in CT logs [13,63]. These are public, auditable, append-only logs that at submission return a Signed Certificate Timestamps (SCTs) that the servers can then deliver with their certificates so to prove that the certificate has been logged. However, CT logs do not log revocations and do not protect from misuse of a revoked certificate.

Without new methods to reduce the overheads associated with short-lived certificates, it is unlikely that short-lived, CA-issued certificates with validity periods of one or a few days will see extended use in the near future.

5.2 Parent-Child Certs: Limiting the Cost of Short-Lived Certificates

We next propose a novel approach to address the above tradeoff so as to achieve the advantages of short-lived certificates while keeping the overheads low for CAs. Our approach makes use of three key observations.

First, and most importantly, we note that significant overhead savings can be achieved by decoupling the subject-key verification done by CAs and their issuance of certificates confirming the validity of these pairings. Such decoupling allows CAs to easily create many short-lived certificates that reuse the same key without requiring new domain validation checks. As long as the owner of a key does not report to the CA that the key has been compromised, the CA can continue to generate short-lived certificates with that key.

Second, when using short-lived certificates, it is important to have a fallback mechanism when a certificate is not replaced in time. A key observation here is that the current Online Certificate Status Protocol (OCSP) [39] solutions provide an excellent fallback mechanism (that can be called upon at such instances). OCSP is already implemented by all CAs and the server load is primarily determined by the request volume, not by the number of certificates with tracked status. (Memory and disk to keep track of certificates are not expected to be bottlenecks for an individual CA.)

Third, with today's high CT compliance, the load of CT logs would be proportional to the rate that new certificates are issued. As a naive implementation of short-lived certificates would result in a huge increase in the issuance rate of new certificates (e.g., Fig. 15, discussed later in this section), this could result in a very high load also at CT logs. To address this issue, we introduce the concept of *parent* and *child* certificates. This concept would enable the CAs to submit a *parent* certificate to the CT logs as a means to obtain a special SCT that can be used as inclusion proof for all issued *child* certificates that use the same subject-key mapping and for which the validity period t is a subset of the parent's validity period T (i.e., $t \subseteq T$).

The idea of logging a *parent* on behalf of its *child* certificates is inspired by the use of pre-certificates in current CT systems [51]. Pre-certificates are created and logged prior to certificate issuance in order to obtain an SCT for the certificate, but include a critical *poison extension* that ensures that it can not be validated by a client.

By only logging *parent* certificates, the CAs can help keep the load on CT logs low even when issuing many more *child* certificates. An alternative idea of how to effectively obtain an SCT for a larger set of certificates (in our case a set of child certificates) is to introduce specific log entries into CT logs [36], where several short-lived certificates can be contained in one CT entry. Our solution would work with this approach too.

Motivated by these three key observations, we propose an approach inspired by the general ideas of a three-phased certificate, first presented by Rivest in 1998 [66]. In contrast to regular certificates (as used today), which only have two phases: probable (check revocation status) and expired, Rivest suggested that certificates should have three phases: *guaranteed, probable, expired*. The idea is to make checking revocation status unnecessary during the first (guaranteed) phase and only check in the second (probable) phase. To combine the first two observations, we extend Rivest's idea to separate the key generation and validation process from the certificate generation process. To do this: (1) *Parent*

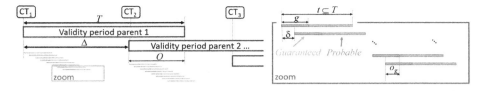

Fig. 14. Parent-child issuance overview. Left-hand side shows *parent* certificates logged in CT. Right-hand side zooms in on a few overlapping *child* certificates.

certificates with a validity period T are issued and submitted to CT logs every Δ days with an overlap of $O = T - \Delta$ days. (2) *Child* certificates are issued every $\delta \ll \Delta$ days with an overlap of $o_g = g - \delta$ days in the *guaranteed* phases, where g is the duration of the *guaranteed* phase. (3) Revocations are handled by (i) requiring OCSP checks of *child* certificates after g days and (ii) asking the CA to stop generating/releasing new *child* certificates based on that key. Figure 14 provides an overview of the issuance and logging process.

Note that a client would only need to perform OCSP calls when a child certificate is not replaced with another child certificate within time g or when a certificate actually is compromised. In both cases, the client would perform the OCSP checks as soon as the guaranteed period g has expired. At this time, a client would be informed whether the certificate (and its parent certificate) has been revoked.

Browser Discussion: With our solution, the *parent* should not sign the *child*. Instead, the *child* certificate's is expected to use a validity period $t \subseteq T$ that is a subset of its parent's validity period T. Non-CT enabled browsers can treat the certificate independently, while CT-enabled browsers implementing our solution can use the special shared SCTs to validate that the subject-key mapping has been logged in a similar manner as with SCTs based on regular pre-certificates.

Another interesting browser-related aspect is the browser-side usage of OCSP checks. Here, our solution is designed such that OCSP only is used as a fallback mechanism during the *probable* phase. This design choice is motivated by similar reasons (e.g., privacy, performance, etc.) as why Chrome today does not perform OCSP checks [76]. By avoiding the use of OCSP checks for any certificate in the *guaranteed* phase we incentivize CAs and servers to properly manage their certificates so that they always can present a certificate in its *guaranteed* phase. Any performance penalties (which can be sever if enforcing strict OCSP checks), for example, are only endured when a certificate already should have been replaced by a new child certificate. While Chrome currently does not perform OCSP checks, other browsers do. Furthermore, all CAs operate active OCSP servers that provide (mostly) good response rate for status checks of all their issued certificates up to the expiry time of each individual certificate (and beyond) [46]. Implementing such fallback mechanism is therefore expected to be trivial for all browsers. Also, as long as the servers properly maintain their certificates, the browsers should never need to make any OCSP checks.

Parameter Discussion: We next briefly discuss the best parameter choices in the context of prior research and best practices. For part of this discussion, we refer to the CA/Browser Forum Baseline Requirements (BR). These BR are shaped in a democratic process of CAs and browser vendors, where both the browser vendors and the CAs have a strong interest in security while keeping costs low. Today, the BR has a central role in the governance of CAs [19]. For example, non-compliance has been used as an argument for root removal [57], and the major root programs require CAs to comply with the BR [70].

The guaranteed period determines the worst-case response time to a revocation. The intention is to allow organizations to choose their own guaranteed period based on their individual risk assessment. However, for the CAs to comply with the BR, they must revoke certificates within 24 h in some serious cases (e.g., key compromise) and within 5 days for less critical cases [24,26]. Therefore, the revocation mechanism would remain a part of the system. Furthermore, using a *guaranteed* period g of 24 h is expected to provide as good protection as achieved by a conservative client always performing revocation checks and better protection than the current status-quo of not doing revocation checks. Motivated by OCSP responses being cached for 4 days on average [74], others have suggested that similar guarantees as OCSP can be achieved using certificates with a 4-day validity period [76]. Based on these observations, we foresee that a good selection for the *guaranteed* period g may vary between 1-to-4 days.

Currently, the CA/Browser EV Guidelines suggest that EV certificates should be valid for up to a year [7]. Given this and the measured average frequency that different CAs currently issue certificates, we suggest that new keys are generated, CAs perform re-validation checks of such subject-key mappings, and that the *parent* certificates are submitted to CT logs accordingly (i.e., $\Delta < T$ is less than a year). During this period, new *child* certificates (reusing this key) are then generated every δ days. To ensure overlapping *guaranteed* phases and avoid unnecessary OCSP checks, we suggest using $\delta < g$.

Finally, we note that the validity periods of the *child* certificates can be much longer than g, as long as the browsers commit to OCSP lookups during the *probable* phase.

This approach ensures that domains that always maintain an up-to-date certificate in the *guaranteed* phase can provide services to their clients without any performance penalty. We propose that browsers only penalize the domains that do not provide up-to-date certs (i.e., that are in the *probable* phase).

Deployment Incentives and Challenges: Like past successful changes to the certificate management practices (e.g., CAs becoming CT compliant and 398-day compliant), new solutions must be easy to deploy and/or driven by demand/pressure from users and browser vendors. First, assuming that browsers would demand CA compliance, we believe that our solution easily can be deployed by CAs to meet such expectations. Second, there already is interest in shorter certificate lifetimes. For example, Let's Encrypt publicly expressed interest in shorter lifetimes than the 90-day validity periods used today [8], which was selected to "allow plenty of time for manual renewal if necessary".

Third, our solution allows individual CAs to use different parameters and safety margins based on the level of automation that they can provide each customer. Since different safety margins have different security-performance tradeoffs, some CAs are likely to compete based on the level of automation that they can provide. This could drive the demand of good implementations compatible with our framework.

Finally, there are other subtle policy decisions that browsers can do to incentivize CAs and servers to implement and properly maintain up-to-date child certificates. For example, consider again our use of OCSP checks as a potential fallback mechanism during the *probable* phase. While they initially could use a safe-fail policy here (to limit performance implications of slow OCSP responses), it is foreseeable that some may eventually (in the long term) push for strict OCSP checks for any certificate that is not within its (short initial) *guaranteed* phase, regardless of whether it is a child certificate or a regular certificate. This would incentivize servers to both use our *child-parent* approach and to make sure that they always can present an up-to-date child certificate. Ideally all servers would eventually try to maintain up-to-date child certificates and OCSP checks would only be needed when a server fails to do so (of legit or non-legit reasons).

5.3   Data-Driven Overhead Analysis

In this section we examine the overhead associated with different high-level certificate management solutions.

For this analysis, we assume that the overhead is proportional to the issuance rate of certificates that require (1) the validation of subject-key mappings and (2) the submission of new certificates to CT logs. Both overheads are important since the subject-key validation process can be both time consuming and costly, and since many CT logs already contain more than a billion certificates and the log sizes are quickly growing [73].

To illustrate the value of *parent* certificates, we present a simple model that captures the relative increase in the number of certificates (parent or traditional) that must be issued for a set of domains when the validity period is reduced.

Model: Consider the set of certificates $\mathcal{N}$ currently used by a large set of servers. Let T and O denote the average validity time and overlap, respectively. Assuming the system is in steady state, we can then use Little's law to obtain the average rate λ that new certificates must be generated as: $\lambda = N/(T-O)$, where $T > O$ and $N = |\mathcal{N}|$. The relative increase in the issuance rate can now be calculated as: $(T_{old} - O_{old})/(T_{new} - O_{new})$, where the subscripts capture change.

Baseline Comparisons: Figure 15 illustrates the effect that certificate lifetimes can have on the issuance rate. For this discussion, we normalize all numbers relative to two basic baselines. In particular, we show the relative increase in the number of subject-key validations and CT submissions of when using a few different example management policies relative to the corresponding overhead when using these two baselines, as a function of the selected validity period when

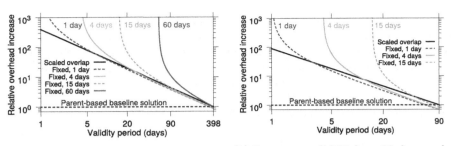

(a) Basecase: valid 398 days, 60-day overlap   (b) Base case: valid 90 days, 30-day overlap

Fig. 15. Relative increase in the number of subject-key validations and CT submissions of selected management policies compared to two baselines.

Table 1. Increase in overhead for different CAs using short-lived certificates without the proposed technique. We show results for different average inter-issuance intervals $\Delta = T_{new} - O_{new}$, measured in days. The columns to the left are based on the CAs' current median values for T_{old} and O_{old}. The columns to the right are based on the observed distributions of T_{old} and O_{old} for each CR of a CA.

	Based on median values						Based on full distribution					
	60	20	10	5	2	1	60	20	10	5	2	1
Let's Encrypt	1.02	3.05	6.10	12.20	30.50	61.00	1.05	3.14	6.28	12.56	31.39	62.78
DigiCert	2.32	6.95	13.90	27.80	69.50	139.00	1.59	4.76	9.52	19.04	47.60	95.19
Google	0.52	1.55	3.10	6.20	15.50	31.00	0.52	1.57	3.15	6.29	15.73	31.45
cPanel	1.27	3.80	7.60	15.20	38.00	76.00	1.35	4.06	8.12	16.23	40.58	81.16
Sectigo/Comodo	2.68	8.05	16.10	32.20	80.50	161.00	2.72	8.16	16.32	32.63	81.59	163.17
GlobalSign	2.32	6.95	13.90	27.80	69.50	139.00	1.87	5.60	11.21	22.42	56.04	112.08
Go Daddy	2.72	8.15	16.30	32.60	81.50	163.00	2.22	6.65	13.30	26.61	66.51	133.03

using the different example policies. Fig. 15(a) shows the relative (multiplicative) increase when we start with an average validity time of 398 days and an average overlap of 60 days, and then reduce the lifetimes in different manners. Figure 15(b) shows the corresponding statistics when we start with an average validity period of 90 days and an average overlap of 30 days. The first default scenario corresponds to changes relative to the most commonly used certificates and overlaps used by Amazon and the second case corresponds to what subjects using Let's Encrypt usually use. In both cases, we include results for the case when the overlap is scaled proportionally to the validity period, the cases when a fixed overlap (e.g., 1, 4, 15, or 60 days) always is used (regardless of validity period), and for our proposed method. Here, we assume that *parent* certificates are issued with a similar frequency and overlap as in the baseline systems. For this solution, the *validity time* (on the x-axis) corresponds to the frequency that *child* certificates are generated (by CA) and used (by servers). Again, the overhead associated with these actions is very small compared to the overhead of validating a subject-key pairing and submitting *parent* certificates to CT logs.

The first scenario (Fig. 15(a)) illustrates that a CA reducing its validity period from 398 days to 90 days using normal means would increase its issuance overhead by more than a factor of four (i.e., >300%), and that further reductions to a 5-day validity period with a 1-day overlap would increase overhead by a factor of 84.5 (or 8,350%). In contrast, our parent-based solutions can be used with even shorter *guaranteed* periods without increasing the number of subject-key verifications or CT-log submissions. This clearly demonstrates the effectiveness of our approach. When comparing against the second baseline (Fig. 15(b)) of 90-day certificates (e.g., currently used by Let's Encrypt) we still see significant reductions in overhead. For example, with a validity period of 5-days and a 1-day overlap, we would see a factor 15 (or 1,400%) difference and for organizations that would want daily certificates the overhead would be 90x (8,900%) higher than the *parent* certificate approach.

Measurement-Based CA Comparisons: To put the above changes in perspective we first refer back to the CDFs of the most popular CAs validity periods and current overlaps (Fig. 6). With all CAs having a median value well above one of these two base cases, our approach would hence consistently result in substantial improvements in overhead compared to the naïve approaches when using short-lived certificates.

We next quantify the improvements for individual CAs. Table 1 shows the relative overhead increases that the top-7 CAs (including the five for which we observed key re-usage) would see when changing to use different example certificate update intervals (listed in the second row and measured in days). This corresponds to $\Delta_{new} = T_{new} - O_{new}$. Here, we calculate the increases in two ways: (1) The columns to the left are based on the CAs' current median values for T_{old} and O_{old}. (2) The columns to the right are based on the actual distributions of T_{old} and O_{old} values, as observed for CRs associated with each CA. Note that the increase is substantial when we get down to update intervals of less than a week. For example, with an update interval of 5 days (e.g., a 7-day certificate with a 2-day overlap) all CAs except Google would need to submit 12–33 times as many certificates to CT logs as they do now, and if updating certificates on a daily basis (potentially still with bigger overlap) the overhead increase would be 61–163 times current loads. The lower overheads for Google are due to them already using substantially shorter update intervals than the other CAs (e.g., median of (70–39) days compared to (90–29) days for Let's Encrypt).

In comparison, using our approach a CA could easily use the same certificate update interval for their parent certificates as they do now (i.e., $\Delta = T_{old} - O_{old}$), or perhaps more likely even increase it. If they increase the update interval for parent certificates, the improvements would be even greater with our approach than suggested here. For example, we expect updates of parent certificates to be significantly less frequent than the 41 days used by Google on average at the moment. By creating and submitting new using parent certificates less frequently, CAs could hence easily reduce the number of CT submissions and subject-to-key checks they perform at the same time as the lifetime of their child certificates can be reduced substantially.

Finally, there are many validity-overlap pairings that result in the same update intervals. The best overlap is expected to be both website dependent and depend on how strictly browsers would enforce OCSP checks (suggested as a fallback mechanism during the *probable* phase). Differences are also expected between CAs. Again, the relatively bigger overlaps used by Google compared to Let's Encrypt was a contributing factor to their shorter update intervals.

6   Related Work

Wide-Area Certificate Scanning: Fast internet-scale certificate measurements using systems and tools such as ZMap [35] and Censys [33] have enabled researchers to quickly scan large IP address spaces to collect and analyze large volumes of certificates. Researchers have studied the certificates collected using such tools (e.g., Rapid7 and Censys) and the certificates found in public CT logs [42,50,69] to characterize the certificate landscape [78], analyze how well CAs construct certificates [47], study the popularity of cryptographic libraries [61], label devices [11], and a wide range of other purposes. Others have considered the effect of location [79] or discussed how to best adapt the scanning solutions for the much larger IPv6 address space [60].

Certificate Management: Complicated issuance and certificate management processes are believed to have slowed down the original HTTPS deployment [20]. Let's Encrypt addressed many of these issues through the introduction of Certbot and other automated processes [9,75]. However, there are still many issues yet to address, including frequent errors in the CAs' issuance processes [47]. Kumar et al. [47] developed a certificate linter (ZLint), quantified the compliance of the CA/Browser Forum's baseline requirements and RFC 5280 [22]. While there has been a drastic reduction in the fraction of certificates with errors, errors are still frequent [47]. Acer et al. [10] used client-side reports from within Chrome to analyze the main causes of certificate errors, and found that almost all date errors are caused by expired certificates.

Others have proposed extensions to the ACME protocol. For example, Borghol et al. [23] presents a related mitigation technique to better protect against domain takeover attacks for trust-based domain-validation services. Their solution introduces an additional issuance challenge (for trusted re-issuance) that easily can be solved by domains that are currently in possession of the private key associated with a trusted certificate that has been previously issued for the domain.

Certificate Replacements: Most papers on certificate replacement consider the reissuing and revoking of certificates during mass-revocation events related to Heartbleed [34,82] or the case when invalid certificates are replaced by other invalid certificates [29]. These studies suggested that the top sites were quicker at revoking certificates and addressing the Heartbleed vulnerabilities than less popular sites [34] and that sites that did not do this immediately were very slow to do so [34,82]. None of these works considered replacement relationships under normal circumstances, the primary focus in this paper. Mirian [58] finds that popular websites are more likely to be proactive in their certificate renewal than less popular websites. In parallel work, Omolola et al. [64] evaluated how reactive administrators utilizing automation for reissuing certificates were in the event of the Let's Encrypt mass-revocation event (Apr. 2020). They found that 28% successfully reissued their certificates manually within a week—around three times better than the result a week after the Heartbleed bug. They focus on Let's Encrypt certificates found in CT logs and do not consider key reusage or when replacements occur on the servers.

Revocation Problems: Browsers have traditionally performed revocation checks using the Online Certificate Status Protocol (OCSP) [39] or Certificate Revocation Lists (CRLs) [22]. However, due to several security, privacy, and performance issues many browser vendors today do not utilize these protocols [28,55].

One area of broad research interest is better ways to revoke certificates. While the goal is the same as OCSP and CRLs, the paths taken differ substantially between solution approaches [30,32,49,72]. Proposals include more efficient push-based protocols and compact forms to convey which certificates have been revoked [49,72] and the caching/sharing of revocation statuses [32]. Others have considered if the world is ready for OCSP Must-Staple and hard-fail policies [30].

Short-Lived Certificates: Other solutions to the above problem include the use of short-lived certificates [62,71,76], proxy certificates [28,77,80], and the use of different delegation schemes [15,18,21,27,43,52,53]. Conceptually, the idea to use shorter validity periods is simple. Unlike our work, previous works on short-lived certificates did not reuse keys. As we previously noted, just shortening the validity period would result in a big overhead for CAs and CT logs. An interesting alternative way to obtains SCTs for the child certificates may be to combine our idea with that of utilizing special log entries for a collection of short-lived certificates [36]. However, such hybrid scheme may require some extra care in how to best ensure that child certificates are not leaked ahead of time and would still benefit from key reusage and the rest of our proposal.

Both proxy certificates and delegation schemes typically are designed to allow a third party to serve content on behalf of a domain owner without giving them access to the private key of the domain owner. Chuat et al. [28] present a nice survey and high-level comparison of the above approaches, in which they also make a case for the use of short-lived proxy certificates. While proxy certificates [28] and delegated credentials [15,43] (and similar approaches) help reduce the number of servers that keep long-lived certificates, they do not address the actual problem of speeding up revocations when revocations are needed.

7   Conclusion

This paper first presents a novel server-side characterization of the CR relationships in the wild, including the reuse of public keys. Second, it proposes and demonstrates a simple way to combine parent-child certificate relationships and three-phase certificate handling to reduce the reliance of revocation checks.

Our data-driven CR analysis captures management biases, including the influence that the services offered by different CAs may have on the timing of replacements, safety margins, certificate violations (e.g., early/late usage), and whether the public key is reused. The results highlight a lack of industry standards for replacement policies [38]. Interestingly, the top-CAs using shorter validity periods often also use more common (default) overlaps and their customers achieve more consistent/predictable lifetime characteristics.

Having said that, we observe the smallest fraction of gaps and early/late usage for the more expensive (and longer-lived) EV certificates. Another interesting observation is that the three CAs (Sectigo, GlobalSign, Go Daddy) with highest key reuse (>65%) all achieved substantially less gaps when reusing keys than when not reusing keys. While they do not have as high key reuse, Let's Encrypt nicely demonstrates how key-reuse chains can help customers achieve good key utilization.

Finally, motivated by the effectiveness and potential of some of the observed automation solutions and trends, we present a new way to address an important revocation problem currently leaving web users highly vulnerable to man-in-the-middle attacks of compromised keys. Our solution takes some current trends to the extreme and combines the use of short-lived three-phase certificates, the introduction of the concept of parent-child certificate relationships, and some simple management rules. The solution addresses the important revocation problem without needing to increase the frequency of subject-key validations and CT log submissions.

Interesting future work includes the collection and analysis of more fine-grained datasets, comparisons with alternative data sources (e.g., CT logs) to obtain a more complete picture of the certificate replacement landscape, performing additional analyses to understand other characteristics (such as relationship of current characteristics to domain popularity), and the implementation and testing of the proposed solution.

Acknowledgment. This work was supported by the Swedish Research Council (VR) and the Wallenberg AI, Autonomous Systems and Software Program (WASP) funded by the Knut and Alice Wallenberg Foundation.

References

1. Marking HTTP as Non-secure. https://www.chromium.org/Home/chromium-security/marking-http-as-non-secure
2. Project Sonar. https://www.rapid7.com/research/project-sonar/
3. SSL Certificates - Rapid7 Open Data. https://opendata.rapid7.com/sonar.ssl/
4. Scanning All the Things (2013). https://blog.rapid7.com/2013/09/26/internet-wide-probing-rapid7-sonar/
5. Baseline Requirements for the Issuance and Management of Publicly-Trusted Certificates (2020). https://cabforum.org/wp-content/uploads/CA-Browser-Forum-BR-1.7.0.pdf
6. Chrome root program (2020). https://www.chromium.org/Home/chromium-security/root-ca-policy

7. Guidelines for the Issuance and Management of Extended Validation Certificates (2020). https://cabforum.org/wp-content/uploads/CA-Browser-Forum-EV-Guidelines-v1.7.2.pdf
8. Aas, J.: Why ninety-day lifetimes for certificates? (2015). https://letsencrypt.org/2015/11/09/why-90-days.html
9. Aas, J., et al.: Let's encrypt: an automated certificate authority to encrypt the entire web. In: Proceedings of the ACM CCS (2019)
10. Acer, M.E., et al.: Where the wild warnings are: root causes of Chrome HTTPS certificate errors. In: Proceedings of the ACM CCS (2017)
11. Antonakakis, M., et al.: Understanding the Mirai botnet. In: Proceedings of the USENIX Security (2017)
12. Apple: About upcoming limits on trusted certificates, March 2020. https://support.apple.com/en-us/HT211025. Accessed Jan 2021
13. Apple: Apple's Certificate Transparency policy (2020). https://support.apple.com/en-us/HT205280. Accessed Jan 2020
14. Bano, S., et al.: Scanning the internet for liveness. SIGCOMM Comput. Commun. Rev. (2), 2–9 (2018)
15. Barnes, R., Iyengar, S., Sullivan, N., Rescorla, E.: Delegated Credentials for TLS. Internet Draft, June 2020. https://tools.ietf.org/html/draft-ietf-tls-subcerts-09
16. Barnes, R.: Deprecating Non-Secure HTTP (2015). https://blog.mozilla.org/security/2015/04/30/deprecating-non-secure-http/
17. Barnes, R., Hoffman-Andrews, J., McCarney, D., Kasten, J.: Automatic Certificate Management Environment (ACME). RFC 8555, March 2019
18. Basin, D., Cremers, C., Kim, T.H.J., Perrig, A., Sasse, R., Szalachowski, P.: Design, analysis, and implementation of ARPKI: an attack-resilient public-key infrastructure. IEEE Trans. Dependable Secure Comput. **15**(3), 393–408 (2016)
19. Berkowsky, J.A., Hayajneh, T.: Security issues with certificate authorities. In: Proceedings of the IEEE UEMCON (2017)
20. Bernhard, M., Sharman, J., Acemyan, C.Z., Kortum, P., Wallach, D.S., Halderman, J.A.: On the usability of HTTPS deployment. In: Proceedings of the CHI (2019)
21. Bhargavan, K., Boureanu, I., Fouque, P.A., Onete, C., Richard, B.: Content delivery over TLS: a cryptographic analysis of keyless SSL. In: Proceedings of the IEEE Euro S&P (2017)
22. Boeyen, S., Santesson, S., Polk, T., Housley, R., Farrell, S., Cooper, D.: Internet X.509 Public Key Infrastructure Certificate and Certificate Revocation List (CRL) Profile. RFC 5280, RFC Editor, May 2008
23. Borgolte, K., Fiebig, T., Hao, S., Kruegel, C., Vigna, G.: Cloud strife: mitigating the security risks of domain-validated certificates (2018)
24. CA/Browser Forum: Ballot SC6 - revocation timeline extension (2018). https://cabforum.org/2018/09/14/ballot-sc6-revocation-timeline-extension
25. CA/Browser Forum: Ballot SC 31: Browser alignment (2020). https://cabforum.org/2020/07/16/ballot-sc31-browser-alignment/
26. CA/Browser Forum: Baseline requirements documents (2021). https://cabforum.org/baseline-requirements-documents/
27. Cangialosi, F., et al.: Measurement and analysis of private key sharing in the https ecosystem. In: Proceedings of the ACM CCS (2016)
28. Chuat, L., Abdou, A., Sasse, R., Sprenger, C., Basin, D., Perrig, A.: SoK: delegation and revocation, the missing links in the web's chain of trust. In: Proceedings of the IEEE Euro S&P (2020)
29. Chung, T., et al.: Measuring and applying invalid SSL certificates: the silent majority. In: Proceedings of the IMC (2016)

30. Chung, T., et al.: Is the web ready for OCSP must-staple? In: Proceedings of the IMC (2018)
31. Cimpanu, C.: Apple strong-arms entire CA industry into one-year certificate lifespans, June 2020. https://www.zdnet.com/article/apple-strong-arms-entire-ca-industry-into-one-year-certificate-lifespans/. Accessed Jan 2021
32. Dickinson, L., Smith, T., Seamons, K.: Leveraging locality of reference for certificate revocation. In: Proceedings of the ACSAC (2019)
33. Durumeric, Z., Adrian, D., Mirian, A., Bailey, M., Halderman, J.A.: A search engine backed by internet-wide scanning. In: Proceedings of the ACM CCS (2015)
34. Durumeric, Z., et al.: The matter of heartbleed. In: Proceedings of the IMC (2014)
35. Durumeric, Z., Wustrow, E., Halderman, J.A.: ZMap: fast internet-wide scanning and its security applications. In: Proceedings of the USENIX Security (2013)
36. Eskandarian, S., Messeri, E., Bonneau, J., Boneh, D.: Certificate transparency with privacy, vol. 2017, pp. 329–344 (2017). https://doi.org/10.1515/popets-2017-0052
37. Felt, A.P., Barnes, R., King, A., Palmer, C., Bentzel, C., Tabriz, P.: Measuring HTTPS adoption on the web. In: Proceedings of the USENIX Security (2017)
38. Fu, P., Li, Z., Xiong, G., Cao, Z., Kang, C.: SSL/TLS security exploration through X.509 certificate's life cycle measurement. In: Proceedings of the IEEE ISCC (2018)
39. Galperin, S., Adams, D.C., Myers, M., Ankney, R., Malpani, A.N.: X.509 Internet Public Key Infrastructure Online Certificate Status Protocol - OCSP. RFC 2560, RFC Editor, March 1999
40. Google: Certificate lifetimes (2020). https://chromium.googlesource.com/chromium/src/+/master/net/docs/certificate_lifetimes.md. Accessed Jan 2021
41. Google: CRLSets (The Chromium Projects) (2020). https://dev.chromium.org/Home/chromium-security/crlsets
42. Gustafsson, J., Overier, G., Arlitt, M., Carlsson, N.: A first look at the CT landscape: certificate transparency logs in practice. In: Kaafar, M.A., Uhlig, S., Amann, J. (eds.) PAM 2017. LNCS, vol. 10176, pp. 87–99. Springer, Cham (2017). https://doi.org/10.1007/978-3-319-54328-4_7
43. Guzman, A., Nekritz, K., Iyengar, S.: Delegated credentials: improving the security of TLS certificates. Facebook blog, November 2019. https://engineering.fb.com/2019/11/01/security/delegated-credentials/
44. Josefsson, S., Leonard, S.: Textual Encodings of PKIX, PKCS, and CMS Structures. RFC 7468, April 2015
45. Korzhitskii, N., Carlsson, N.: Characterizing the root landscape of certificate transparency logs. In: Proceedings of the IFIP Networking (2020)
46. Korzhitskii, N., Carlsson, N.: Revocation statuses on the internet. In: Hohlfeld, O., Lutu, A., Levin, D. (eds.) PAM 2021. LNCS, vol. 12671, pp. 175–191. Springer, Cham (2021). https://doi.org/10.1007/978-3-030-72582-2_11
47. Kumar, D., et al.: Tracking certificate misissuance in the wild. In: Proceedings of the IEEE S&P (2018)
48. Langley, A., et al.: The QUIC transport protocol: design and internet-scale deployment. In: Proceedings of the ACM SIGCOMM (2017)
49. Larisch, J., Choffnes, D., Levin, D., Maggs, B.M., Mislove, A., Wilson, C.: CRLite: a scalable system for pushing all TLS revocations to all browsers. In: Proceedings of the IEEE S&P (2017)
50. Laurie, B.: Certificate transparency. Commun. ACM **57**(10), 40–46 (2014)
51. Laurie, B., Langley, A., Kasper, E.: Certificate Transparency. RFC 6962 (2013)
52. Lesniewski-Laas, C., Kaashoek, M.F.: SSL splitting: securely serving data from untrusted caches. Comput. Netw. **48**(5), 763–779 (2005)

53. Liang, J., Jiang, J., Duan, H., Li, K., Wan, T., Wu, J.: When https meets CDN: a case of authentication in delegated service. In: Proceedings of the IEEE S&P (2014)
54. Linn, J.: Privacy Enhancement for Internet Electronic Mail: Part I: Message Encryption and Authentication Procedures. RFC 1421, February 1993
55. Liu, Y., et al.: An end-to-end measurement of certificate revocation in the web's PKI. In: Proceedings of the IMC (2015)
56. Ma, Z., Austgen, J., Mason, J., Durumeric, Z., Bailey, M.: Tracing your roots: exploring the TLS trust anchor ecosystem. In: Proceedings of the IMC (2021)
57. Markham, G.: Mailing list: Mozilla dev.sec.policy: Procert decision (2017). https:// groups.google.com/g/mozilla.dev.security.policy/c/Ymrpsm7s5_I
58. Mirian, A., Thompson, C., Savage, S., Voelker, G.M., Felt, A.P.: HTTPS adoption in the longtail. Technical report, Google and UC San Diego (2018). https:// research.google/pubs/pub49037/
59. Mozilla: OneCRL (CA/Revocation Checking in Firefox) (2020). https://wiki. mozilla.org/CA:RevocationPlan#OneCRL
60. Murdock, A., Li, F., Bramsen, P., Durumeric, Z., Paxson, V.: Target generation for internet-wide IPv6 scanning. In: Proceedings of the IMC (2017)
61. Nemec, M., Klinec, D., Svenda, P., Sekan, P., Matyas, V.: Measuring popularity of cryptographic libraries in internet-wide scans. In: Proceedings of the ACSAC (2017)
62. Nir, Y., Fossati, T., Sheffer, Y., Eckert, T.: Considerations for using short term certificates. Technical report/Internet-Draft, March 2018. https://tools.ietf.org/ id/draft-nir-saag-star-01.html
63. O'Brien, D.: Certificate Transparency Enforcement in Chrome and CT Day in London (2018). https://groups.google.com/a/chromium.org/d/msg/ct-policy/ Qqr59r6yn1A/2t0bWblZBgAJ. Accessed Jan 2020
64. Omolola, O., Roberts, R., Ashiq, M.I., Chung, T., Levin, D., Mislove, A.: Measurement and analysis of automated certificate reissuance. In: Hohlfeld, O., Lutu, A., Levin, D. (eds.) PAM 2021. LNCS, vol. 12671, pp. 161–174. Springer, Cham (2021). https://doi.org/10.1007/978-3-030-72582-2_10
65. O'Brien, D., Sleevi, R., Whalley, A.: Chrome's plan to distrust symantec certificates. Google Security Blog, September 2017. https://security.googleblog.com/ 2017/09/chromes-plan-to-distrust-symantec.html
66. Rivest, R.L.: Can we eliminate certificate revocation lists? In: Hirchfeld, R. (ed.) FC 1998. LNCS, vol. 1465, pp. 178–183. Springer, Heidelberg (1998). https://doi. org/10.1007/BFb0055482
67. Sander, R.: What is a code signing certificate? how does it work? IEEE Computer Society (2021). https://www.computer.org/publications/tech-news/trends/what-is-a-code-signing-certificate
68. Schechter, E.: A secure web is here to stay (2018). https://security.googleblog.com/ 2018/02/a-secure-web-is-here-to-stay.html
69. Scheitle, Q., et al.: The rise of certificate transparency and its implications on the internet ecosystem. In: Proceedings of the IMC (2018)
70. Serrano, N., Hadan, H., Camp, L.J.: A complete study of PKI (PKI's known incidents). Available at SSRN 3425554 (2019)
71. Sheffer, Y., Lopez, D., de Dios, O.G., Perales, A.P., Fossati, T.: Support for short-term, automatically renewed (STAR) certificates in the automated certificate management environment (ACME). RFC 8739, March 2020
72. Smith, T., Dickinson, L., Seamons, K.: Let's revoke: scalable global certificate revocation. In: Proceedings of the NDSS (2020)

73. Spotter, C.: Certificate transparency log growth (2021). https://sslmate.com/labs/ct_growth/. Accessed Jan 2021
74. Stark, E., Huang, L.S., Israni, D., Jackson, C., Boneh, D.: The case for prefetching and prevalidating TLS server certificates. In: Proceedings of the NDSS (2012)
75. Tiefenau, C., von Zezschwitz, E., Häring, M., Krombholz, K., Smith, M.: A usability evaluation of let's encrypt and certbot: usable security done right. In: Proceedings of the ACM CCS (2019)
76. Topalovic, E., Saeta, B., Huang, L.S., Jackson, C., Boneh, D.: Towards short-lived certificates. In: Proceedings of the IEEE W2SP (2012)
77. Tuecke, S., Welch, V., Engert, D., Pearlman, L., Thompson, M.: Internet X.509 public key infrastructure (PKI) proxy certificate profile. RFC 3820 (2004)
78. VanderSloot, B., Amann, J., Bernhard, M., Durumeric, Z., Bailey, M., Halderman, J.A.: Towards a complete view of the certificate ecosystem. In: Proceedings of the IMC (2016)
79. Wan, G., et al.: On the origin of scanning: the impact of location on internet-wide scans. In: Proceedings of the IMC (2020)
80. Welch, V., et al.: X. 509 proxy certificates for dynamic delegation. In: Proceedings of the Annual PKI R&D Workshop (2004)
81. Wilson, B.: Reducing TLS Certificate Lifespans to 398 Days. Mozilla Security Blog, July 2020. https://blog.mozilla.org/security/2020/07/09/reducing-tls-certificate-lifespans-to-398-days/. Accessed Jan 2021
82. Zhang, L., et al.: Analysis of SSL certificate reissues and revocations in the wake of heartbleed. In: Proceedings of the IMC (2014)

Web

Design and Implementation of Web-Based Speed Test Analysis Tool Kit

Rui Yang[1]([✉]), Ricky K. P. Mok[2], Shuohan Wu[3], Xiapu Luo[3], Hongyu Zou[4], and Weichao Li[5]

[1] ETH Zürich, Zürich, Switzerland
[2] CAIDA/UC San Diego, San Diego, USA
[3] The Hong Kong Polytechnic University, Hung Hom, Hong Kong
[4] UC San Diego, San Diego, USA
[5] Peng Cheng Laboratory, Shenzhen, China

Abstract. Web-based speed tests are popular among end-users for measuring their network performance. Thousands of measurement servers have been deployed in diverse geographical and network locations to serve users worldwide. However, most speed tests have opaque methodologies, which makes it difficult for researchers to interpret their highly aggregated test results, let alone leverage them for various studies.

In this paper, we propose WebTestKit, a unified and configurable framework for facilitating automatic test execution and cross-layer analysis of test results for five major web-based speed test platforms. Capturing only packet headers of traffic traces, WebTestKit performs in-depth analysis by carefully extracting HTTP and timing information from test runs. Our testbed experiments showed WebTestKit is lightweight and accurate in interpreting encrypted measurement traffic. We applied WebTestKit to compare the use of HTTP requests across speed tests and investigate the root causes for impeding the accuracy of latency measurements, which play a vital role in test server selection and throughput estimation.

1 Introduction

Internet surfers often use web-based speed tests to measure their access bandwidth, diagnose slow residential broadband connections [27], and validate the ISP-advertised speed [12,38]. A few such testing platforms make the collected data and source code publicly available (e.g. M-Lab NDT [20]), which researchers have leveraged for various studies including evaluating video streaming and cloud platform performance [8,21], measuring Internet latency [13], and inferring network congestion [1,35,42]. On the contrary, commercial speed tests (e.g., `fast.com`), serving millions of users across the world, have much more diverse server deployment than open-source ones. As of October 2021, there have been over 38 billion tests conducted by Ookla [23], a popular speed test which deploys tens of thousands of test servers worldwide. Meanwhile, video content providers

O. Hohlfeld et al. (Eds.): PAM 2022, LNCS 13210, pp. 83–96, 2022.
https://doi.org/10.1007/978-3-030-98785-5_4

including Netflix and Hulu advise users to run speed tests using their custom platforms [16, 22] which host their servers in video delivery networks.

Despite their popularity and resources, unfortunately, it is still very hard for the research community to effectively utilize these proprietary tests. First, most speed tests offer only a web interface that selects a default test server for users, which makes automatic and configurable test execution burdensome. Second, despite the overhead introduced by different layers (e.g. the browser itself) and environmental dynamics (e.g. network congestion), these platforms report only few simple metrics (e.g. download/upload throughput). Without data providing the necessary context, diagnosing the root causes of performance degradation is very difficult. Finally, even though the measurement traffic is dummy data, speed tests run over HTTPS, preventing observation of HTTP transactions directly from packet captures. This opacity presents challenges for understanding speed tests since correlating the HTTP transactions with timings of the corresponding packets is essential for comprehensively analyzing speed test results (e.g. mapping TCP congestion behavior to underlying test methodologies).

To bridge this gap, we propose WebTestKit, a lightweight framework which enables automatic execution and in-depth analysis of web-based speed tests. WebTestKit has three design goals: (i) provides a unified and configurable interface for executing reproducible tests across multiple platforms, (ii) captures test data extensively from multiple layers in a lightweight manner, and (iii) conducts cross-layer analysis to provide a comprehensive view of the speed test results.

We implemented a prototype of WebTestKit to achieve our goals. The key idea of WebTestKit is to keep our framework lightweight and still allow an in-depth analysis of test results with high accuracy. To achieve this, we (i) minimized overhead by capturing only packet headers of measurement traffic and (ii) developed a packet matching algorithm to locate HTTP messages in encrypted traffic without decrypting them. We used a headless Chromium browser to automate the execution of five major web-based speed tests: Ookla Speedtest [24], Comcast Xfinity test [7], Netflix Fast.com [9], CloudFlare speed test [6], and speedof.me [2]. We crawled the full server lists by exploiting RESTful APIs used on Ookla and Xfinity test websites. When conducting measurements, WebTestKit allows users to select specific servers from these server lists.

Our testbed experiments showed that WebTestKit has a significantly lower impact on measurements compared to capturing full-size packets. WebTestKit is also accurate in inferring the locations of HTTP messages in packet traces, allowing us to extract many timing information from the encrypted traffic.

We demonstrated the capability and usability of WebTestKit with three use cases. We studied the behavior of different speed tests (Sect. 6.1) and found that the number and size of HTTP requests/responses were largely different between tests. Some tests sent thousands of small requests, increasing the load of the client. We discovered that preflighted requests were often unintentionally triggered, generating additional network overhead. We also used WebTestKit in the wild to run Xfinity speed test from Google Cloud (GCP) for two weeks (Sect. 6.2). We found high round-trip time (RTT) variances reported by the test due to the plausible glitches in the web interface. We compared the accuracy of two sets of JavaScript APIs that speed tests commonly used for RTT measurements. We found that the measurements using XMLHttpRequest API suffered from at least 2.3 ms error, compared to the RTTs captured by `tcpdump`.

2   Related Work

In this section, we first survey work on speed test tools and then, explore the studies on evaluating their performance and accuracy.

Speed Test Tools. Most commercial web-based speed tests [2,7,9,20,24] are flooding-based which use one or multiple parallel TCP connections to saturate the access link. However, these tools could incur high costs including excessive data transfer. Probe-optimized tools like Spruce [33] and IGI/PTR [15] employ the Probe Gap Model which sends back-to-back packet pairs to estimate the available bandwidth with the packet pair dispersion. There are also some tools using the Path Rate Model (e.g., Pathload [17] and Pathchirp [28]) which sends packet trains at different sending rates to self-induce congestion at the bottleneck. Unfortunately, these tools are highly sensitive to different network dynamics (e.g. packet loss), often leading to non-negligible inaccuracies especially in high-speed networks. Recently, FastBTS [43] used a statistical sampling framework to probe elastic bandwidth for high-speed wide-area networks, with significantly reduced data usage and test duration. CLASP [21] leveraged speed tests to perform throughput measurements from the cloud. Murakami [19] supports running automated speed test measurements and collecting test results. It also provides a configurable interface for recurring jobs. Instead of building new speed test tools, WebTestKit focuses on analyzing the existing web-based speed tests that are most popular among end-users.

Speed Test Evaluation. Goga and Teixeira [11] compared the accuracy of flooding-based methods [28,33] and probe-optimized tools [15,17,33] for measuring residential broadband performance from home gateways. Sundaresan *et al.* [34] conducted experiments to determine the number of parallel TCP flows required to accurately perform throughput measurements using the BISMark platform. Li *et al.* [18] evaluated three commonly used browser-based delay measurement methods, and found that the socket-based approach incurred smaller overhead than the HTTP-based one. Feamster and Livingood [10] and Bauer *et al.* [4] identified potential issues in various speed test platforms for measuring Gigabit broadband networks (e.g. the selected off-net measurement servers). Yang *et al.* [43] evaluated the accuracy of eight representative speed tests. However, different from WebTestKit, they did not perform any further analysis of test data to infer causes of inaccuracies.

3   Web-Based Speed Test Platforms

Web-based speed test platforms conduct bulk data transfers over HTTP(S)/ TCP [25] to measure the bandwidth of the bottleneck link by saturating it

with TCP flows. The bottleneck link is commonly the "last mile"—the access
link between the client and the Internet. In this scenario, the ideal location of
the server is as close as possible to the client to minimize the latency. TCP
throughput has a well-understood inverse relationship with latency [26]—the
longer the latency across a path, the lower the throughput, all other factors being
equal. As broadband access speeds increase, low latencies from test servers to
clients ensure that measurement flows can saturate the bottleneck link [3].

Table 1. Comparison of HTTP-based speed test platforms.

Platform	# of Servers	Network(s)	Server Selection	# of TCP flows[‡]
Ookla [24]	>12,000	Various ISPs	Latency, IP Geolocation	6
Xfinity [7]	78[†]	Comcast	IP Geolocation	18
Fast.com [9]	Unknown	Netflix	Latency, IP Geolocation	11
SpeedOf.Me [2]	88	Verizon Edgecast	Anycast	1
Cloudflare [6]	Unknown	Cloudflare CDN	Anycast	1

[‡]: Speed test platforms may adapt the number of connections used depending on the
type and speed of connections. We evaluated the tests in a wired Gigabit network.
[†]: These Xfinity servers were distributed in 29 locations in the United States.

Table 1 summarizes the properties of HTTP-based speed test platforms
that WebTestKit supports. The scale of deployment and network coverage
largely varies across platforms. Ookla speedtest has deployed the largest number
(>12 000) of measurement servers around the world. These servers are hosted
by ISPs, web-hosting companies, and cloud services. Other speed test platforms
host servers only within their own networks or CDNs. Speed test platforms
employ different methods to select test servers for users. Ookla first selects 10
servers nearest to the user based on IP geolocation and uses the one with the
lowest round-trip time from the user. CDN-based speed tests share the same
catchment functions as their host CDNs to divert users. All the platforms,
except `speedof.me`, use HTTP/1.1 over TLS to perform throughput measurements. Three of the platforms establish multiple concurrent TCP connections to
saturate the bottleneck. Although `speedof.me` adopts HTTP/2, it sequentially
downloads/uploads web objects without invoking the multiplexing mechanism.

Some of these speed tests do offer a command-line interface (CLI) [29–31].
Though convenient for automating tests, these CLIs cannot capture multiple-
layer information (e.g. browser-layer), which is essential for correctly interpreting
measurements and performing further analysis.

4   Design of WebTestKit

In this section, we discuss the design objectives of WebTestKit (Sect. 4.1), then
its components (Sect. 4.2) and implementation (Sect. 4.3).

4.1   Design Objectives

The main challenge of building a tool to leverage the many web-based speed tests for various research studies, lies in designing a framework that extensively collects and provides in-depth analysis of test data, while keeping it lightweight and easy to use. Specifically, we have the three following design objectives.

A Unified and Configurable Interface. Our first design objective is to provide users with a unified and configurable interface for automatically executing all web-based speed tests we support. This objective is two-fold: *(i)* a unified interface to improve usability and repeatability of these platforms which allows fair comparison among them, and *(ii)* a configurable interface to support measurement server selection which effectively exploits the resources of speed tests.

Lightweight and Extensive Data Collection. Our second design objective is to enrich metrics we collect to allow correct interpretation of measurements. Due to the run-time dynamics of speed tests, collecting information to monitor the local environment, browser, and network traffic is essential for in-depth analysis of network quality and possible sources of measurements inaccuracies. Lightweight data collection also necessary mitigates potential interference with actual speed test measurements.

In-depth Cross-layer Analysis. Our third design objective, closely related to the second, is to perform cross-layer analysis of collected data. We aim at providing a comprehensive and in-depth view across different layers in the system.

4.2   Components of WebTestKit

With the three design objectives in mind, we propose WebTestKit, a lightweight framework for automating speed tests with different configurations and providing in-depth analysis of test results. WebTestKit consists of three modules:

1. *Measurement server exploration module* discovers available measurement servers in speed test infrastructures. Of the five platforms listed in Table 1, Xfinity and Ookla speed tests support manual selection of measurement servers. However, their full lists of servers are not publicly available like M-Lab. To allow adjustably configuring the targeted servers for different needs, WebTestKit first identifies RESTful APIs that the web interface uses to query measurement servers by observing the associated HTTP transactions, and then uses these RESTful APIs to retrieve measurement server information including hostnames, IP addresses, and physical locations. As of October 2021, WebTestKit found 78 and 12 149 test servers in Xfinity and Ookla platforms, respectively.

2. *Test execution module* integrates a suite of tools to automate the execution of speed tests and capture data from different layers. The main challenge is to minimize the interference of data collection with throughput measurements. Our key insight is to capture only headers of measurement packets to minimize overhead. We show (Sect. 5.1) that this module is lightweight and has minimal impact on the throughput measurements.

For all speed test platforms we support, WebTestKit provides a command-line interface for programmably visiting and executing tests. To guarantee that our results are identical to a user manually running the test with a Chromium browser, we used an actual browser to render and interact with the speed test platforms. Given a speed test platform and the measurement configurations (e.g. target server), the interface will interact with the web page by clicking the 'Start' button, selecting measurement options, detecting the completion of the test, and capturing the results displayed on the page.

In the browser, WebTestKit uses the performance trace function [37] to reveal the resource timing API information [39] and event information received by JavaScript `XMLHttpRequest` API [41]. We could have obtained such information by capturing two types of internal messages (`devtools .timeline` and `blink.user_timing`). However, a recent update in Chrome (and Chromium) [14] removed visibility of pre-flight HTTP `OPTIONS` requests from performance trace. Having only partial visibility of HTTP transactions could easily cause inaccuracies in matching the corresponding packets. Therefore, we employed Chrome's NetLog [36], which provides network layer information including TCP source ports and the data transmission progress of *all* HTTP flows at the socket level.

At the packet level, WebTestKit captures the first 100 bytes of packets which include the headers. It also collects CPU and memory usage of the end host every second during the execution of tests using `SoMeta` [32].

3. Analysis module performs analysis of data collected in *Test execution module* to generate an in-depth view of all HTTP transactions from application level to packet level. WebTestKit conducts its analysis in a three-step fashion: *(i)* identifies URLs for measurement flows, *(ii)* extracts information for HTTP transactions, and *(iii)* locates HTTP messages in encrypted packet traces.

The module first identifies URLs of RESTful APIs or web objects corresponding to download/upload tests by response/request sizes and crafts platform-specific regular expressions to match URLs. Then, it uses the NetLog trace to filter HTTP transactions associated with measurement flows.

The second step is to extract events from NetLog and performance traces to obtain timing information observed by the browser and JavaScript, respectively. Since both traces have limited documentation, to correctly interpret the traces, we used visualization tools (e.g., NetLog viewer [5] and `about:tracing` tool [37]). For each HTTP transaction in the measurement flows, WebTestKit extracts the send/arrival times of HTTP requests/responses, and the sending/receiving progress events of downloading/uploading large objects.

Finally, we developed a packet matching algorithm to locate HTTP messages in encrypted traffic. This step is the key for our analysis because lacking visibility of HTTP messages at the packet level will make an in-depth analysis almost impossible. For example, without such visibility, we cannot quantify the overhead posed by different layers from timing information of measurement traffic. Although we could export SSL keys from the browser to decrypt the traffic, this approach requires us to capture full-size packets, posing significant overhead.

To make WebTestKit lightweight but capable of performing an in-depth analysis, we only capture packet headers and then locate packets containing HTTP messages by referring to the information extracted from NetLog (e.g. sequence number, payload size). This task is challenging due to the use of HTTP persistent connections and TLS encryption. An HTTP persistent connection reuses a single TCP connection for multiple HTTP transactions. We used HTTP request/response sizes to separate consecutive HTTP transactions in the same TCP flow. However, we could not directly apply the HTTP request/response sizes obtained from NetLog to infer the total packet payload sizes, because TLS encryption induces an overhead of 20–40 bytes to TLS records to include the TLS Record header and padding bytes. The size of overhead depends on the cipher suite negotiated in the TLS Handshake process.

Our packet-matching algorithm is designed to tackle these two challenges. The algorithm first calculates the TLS overhead by identifying the first HTTP request packet in the first measurement flow. Because all test platforms initially perform latency or download tests using HTTP GET, the HTTP request is small and should fit in one packet. Therefore, the difference between the size of the HTTP header and the TCP payload size is the TLS overhead, S_{tls}. We assume the overhead is constant across different flows in the same experiment since the same cipher suite is used.

After the algorithm identifies the TLS overhead, it locates the end of the POST requests/GET responses, by estimating the size of the messages after TLS encryption using $S_{body} + S_{tls} \times N_{prog}$, where S_{body} is the message body size of the HTTP request/response, and N_{prog} is the number of progress update events of HTTP transactions in NetLog. For HTTP POST requests, N_{prog} is equal to the number of TLS records, which allows us to accurately calculate the size of requests after TLS encryption. However, as the network socket aggregates incoming response packets spanning multiple TLS records before passing data to the browser, the number of update events is fewer than of TLS records, implying an underestimation of the post-encrypted data size. To this end, the algorithm determines to have found the end of GET responses when it observes any outgoing data packet after receiving the expected amount of data (indicating the next HTTP request) or the end of TCP connection.

4.3   Implementation

Our implementation of WebTestKit[1] consists of $\approx 2k$ lines of JavaScript code and $\approx 10k$ lines of Golang code. For test execution and data collection, it uses `puppeteer`, a node.js library, to control a headless Chromium browser to programmably execute speed tests. It uses `tcpdump` to capture measurement packets, and `SoMeta` [32] to collect CPU and memory usage information on the end host.

5   Testbed Evaluation

We set up a semi-controlled testbed to examine the resource consumption of WebTestKit in four configurations and its impact on throughput measurements

---

[1] Available at https://github.com/CAIDA/webtestkit.

(Sect. 5.1), and the accuracy of the analysis module in matching packets to HTTP transactions in measurement flows (Sect. 5.2).

We performed two sets of experiments using *(i)* a server (Intel E3-Xeon 1270, 32 GB RAM, 1 Gbps Ethernet, Ubuntu 20.04), and *(ii)* a virtual machine (VM) allocated with 2 vCPU and 8 GB RAM set up on this server to simulate a client with low computational power. We performed speed tests with the five platforms listed in Table 1 using WebTestKit. For consistency, Ookla tests used a server hosted by 13D.net in Hong Kong, and Xfinity speed tests used servers in Seattle, WA. We configured four scenarios in WebTestKit, denoted with $(snaplen, D/N)$, where *snaplen* is the snapshot length used in `tcpdump` (disabled when $snaplen = 0$), and D/N represents disabling/enabling NetLog. We ran each speed test in each scenario 50 times in the VM.

5.1   Resource Overhead of WebTestKit

We studied resource usage and its impact on measurements results under different configurations of WebTestKit. Figure 1a and 1b show box-and-whisker plots of CPU idle rate and reported download throughput of Ookla speed tests in the VM, respectively. As expected, the control case (0,D) consumed the least CPU resource. By default, WebTestKit adopted the leftmost scenario (100,N) in the figures, which consumed 4.2% more CPU time in median than that of (0,D), but 1.5% less than (65535,N), which captures full-size packets. Comparing scenarios (100,N) and (100,D), we found that enabling NetLog slightly increased the median CPU usage by 2.4%. The download throughput followed a similar pattern to the CPU idle rate. Capturing full-size packets had the lowest median throughput (507 Mbps), 41 Mbps lower than the (100, N) scenario. Our results showed that compared to full-size packet capture, the default configuration of WebTestKit had a significantly lower impact on the throughput measurement.

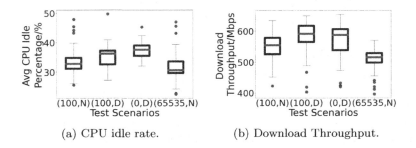

(a) CPU idle rate.   (b) Download Throughput.

Fig. 1. Box-and-whisker plots for Ookla test results under four configurations.

5.2   Accuracy of Analysis Module

We evaluated the accuracy of the analysis module in identifying HTTP transactions in encrypted packets. We used data collected in test scenario (65535,N) in our testbed experiments from the server, so that we could decrypt the traffic to reveal HTTP messages as ground truth. We compared the packet sequence numbers of HTTP request and response headers inferred by our analysis module and the actual ones observed in the decrypted traffic. We define *Request/Response matching accuracy* ($= \frac{\text{\# of correctly located HTTP requests/responses}}{\text{Total \# of HTTP requests/responses}}$) to quantify the accuracy of our packet matching algorithm.

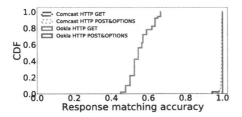
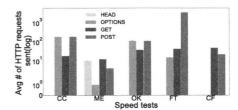

Fig. 2. Accuracy of the packet matching algorithm for HTTP responses

Fig. 3. The number of different HTTP requests for five speed tests

We examined our results in Ookla and Xfinity speed tests, because we could select the same servers in repeated trials. We found that WebTestKit achieved 100% matching accuracy in locating all HTTP requests. Figure 2 shows CDFs of the response matching accuracy over 50 runs. We obtained very high accuracy here as well, except the HTTP GET responses in Ookla tests, where the median accuracy was 54.5%. The reason is that the Ookla server sent a TLS new session ticket packet to the client right after receiving the probing GET requests. We cannot easily distinguish this type of control packet from HTTP headers based on the information in the TLS record protocol header. We found that these mismatches had minimal impact on analyzing measurements. First, all these incorrectly inferred HTTP responses were for latency measurements before the actual download throughput tests, which had only a header indicating 200 OK status. Second, the send times of the TLS packets were close to those of the send HTTP response headers. Specifically, these TLS packets were only 3 or 4 packets ahead of the actual HTTP responses.

6   Use Cases

We present three use cases of WebTestKit: *(i)* characterizing the types and sizes of HTTP transactions of 5 speed test platforms (Sect. 6.1), *(ii)* diagnosing high variances in latency measurements (Sect. 6.2), *(iii)* and evaluating the inaccuracy in latency measurement using HTTP request-response time (Sect. 6.3).

6.1   Characterizing Speed Tests with HTTP Transactions

Without access to the source code, speed tests' methodologies remain opaque. We used WebTestKit to characterize their implementations. We ran five speed tests – Xfinity (CC), SpeedOf.Me (ME), Ookla (OK), Fast.com (FT), and Cloudflare (CF) – 20 times with default settings in a workstation connected to a 1 Gbps campus network. Figure 3 shows the average number of each type of HTTP request elicited by the tests. All tests sent 10–50 HTTP GET requests to measure downlink throughput. Meanwhile, Xfinity, Ookla, and Fast.com sent hundreds to thousands of HTTP POST requests, mainly for uplink throughput tests. Except for CloudFlare, all tests sent many HTTP OPTIONS requests. These requests were the preflighted requests to enforce the cross-origin resource sharing policy (CORS) in browsers [40]. The test servers in these four tests were in different domains from the web interface, which triggered a preflighted request for every new URIs to the test servers. Although small, these requests still consumed network bandwidth and delayed the sending of POST requests.

Figure 4 shows two histograms of response sizes of HTTP GET and request sizes of HTTP POST for the five platforms. Over 80% of web objects downloaded by Fast.com were either 2KB (20.15%) or 24 MB (63%). Xfinity's download objects sizes were between 53 MB and 78 MB and the download test often did not finish due to time limit expiration. SpeedOf.Me used the largest web object (128 MB) among all tests. 35% of GET requests from Ookla tests had the response size of only 300B and 79% of GET requests from Cloudflare tests had the response size <1 MB. All uplink tests had more consistent choices in POST request sizes than GET response sizes. We found that the POST requests sent by Fast.com were either very small (98% were 480Bytes) or very large (0.9% were >26 MB). High variances between numbers and sizes of HTTP transactions for different platforms might lead to inaccuracies in various network environments [10].

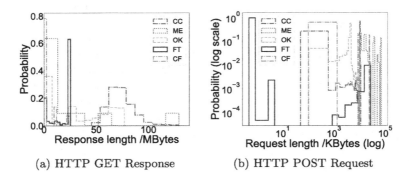

(a) HTTP GET Response   (b) HTTP POST Request

Fig. 4. The distribution of HTTP object sizes for the five speed tests.

6.2   Variances in RTT Measurements

To observe RTT variances, we conducted analysis on the data collected using CLASP [21], which performed hourly tests from a VM in Google Cloud us-west1 to the nearest Xfinity speed test servers in Seattle, WA for two weeks (Jul 7–15, 2020). Because Xfinity by default selected servers in Little Rock, AR, we had WebTestKit instead configure the server location to Seattle, WA. Xfinity speed

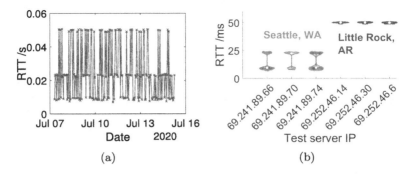

(a)   (b)

Fig. 5. Hourly Xfinity measurements from GCP us-west1 to test servers in Seattle, WA. (a) RTTs fluctuated throughout the measurement period. (b) 25.7% of tests reported high RTTs (>50 ms) still used the default servers in Little Rock, AR, ignoring our selection.

test sent ten persistent HTTP GET requests consecutively and reported the minimum HTTP request-response time as the RTT.

RTTs largely varied between 10–55 ms throughout the time period (Fig. 5a). The screen capture WebTestKit recorded after each test confirmed that the script correctly selected the server location. However, WebTestKit revealed that the measurements reporting high RTTs did not use the correct servers. Figure 5b shows the distributions of the RTTs reported by each test according to the test servers' IP. We used the server information crawled from the test platform to locate the servers. Each location had three test servers in the same /24 subnet. The left-/right-three servers were located in Seattle/Little Rock, respectively. The RTTs to servers in Little Rock were above 50 ms, while the RTTs to Seattle servers showed a bimodal distribution with peaks at 9 ms and 23 ms, possibly due to an asymmetric reverse path (Comcast → GCP).

The high RTT variations were partially due to Xfinity speed test failing to switch to the selected servers even when specified in the webpage. We reported this issue to Comcast for further investigation. This example illustrates WebTestKit's capability to diagnose problems with speed test implementations.

6.3 Accuracy of RTT Measurements

Web-based speed tests often use HTTP request-response times (HRTs) to estimate RTTs, an important factor for server selection and throughput estimation. The packet matching algorithm allows WebTestKit to estimate HRTs from packet traces. Meanwhile, JavaScript-based test clients could use two APIs to measure HRTs: `XMLHttpRequest` (XHR) [41] and Resource Timing APIs (RET) [39], which both could introduce overhead to measurement results from browser rendering and system function calls. To evaluate the accuracies of these two APIs, WebTestKit records timing information from both in execution and compares them with the derived HRTs.

We analyzed the HRTs in our Xfinity speed test measurements (Sect. 6.2). We obtained three HRTs for the ith HTTP transactions used for latency measurements with XHR (T_X^i), RET (T_R^i), and packet traces (T_P^i). We then computed the differences between two of the HRTs, $\Delta_{B-A}^i (= T_B^i - T_A^i. \forall A, B \subset \{X, R, P\})$. Blue, cyan, and purple bars in Fig. 6 represent the probability of different values of Δ_{X-R}, Δ_{R-P}, and Δ_{X-P}, respectively. We found XHR performed much worse than RET. The minimum value of Δ_{R-P} and Δ_{X-P} were 0.59 ms and 2.3 ms, respectively, indicating the unavoidable inflation in HRTs. 66.4%/83.1% of $\Delta_{R-P}/\Delta_{X-P}$ was less than 1 ms/10 ms, respectively. Even though RET was much more accurate than XHR, we found 10% of Δ_{R-P} were higher than 28 ms.

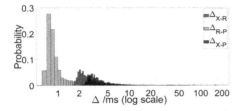

Fig. 6. Normalized histograms of HRT differences, Δ, between T_X, T_R, and T_P.

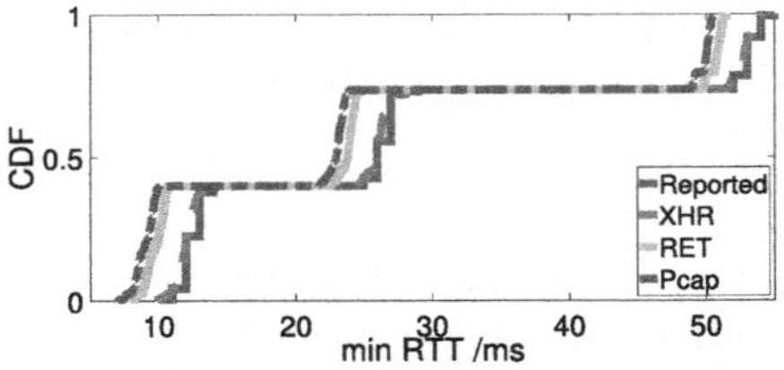

Fig. 7. CDFs of reported latency and minimum RTTs obtained from different layers.

We studied the impact of the HRT inaccuracy on the final measurement results. We selected the minimum HRTs measured with XHR, RET, and packet trace (Pcap) in each test. Figure 7 shows the CDFs of the minimum RTTs and the reported latency. Xfinity speed test used the XHR method to measure RTTs. Therefore, the reported values were almost identical to the XHR values, except for the rounding errors. The RTTs derived using RET and packet trace were consistently lower than the XHR RTT values by around 2 and 2.9 ms, respectively, consistent with our results in Fig. 6. As the RTT between the VM and test servers in Seattle was low (The lowest RTT was 7.01 ms/7.93 ms/10.0 ms measured by packet trace/RET/XHR), the error rate in RET/XHR was over 13%/30%, respectively. We concluded that using XHR to measure RTTs resulted in inflated values. Applying a minimum filter to measurements did not mitigate this error.

7   Conclusion

We presented WebTestKit, a unified and configurable framework for automating speed tests and performing cross-layer analysis of test results. Our evaluation showed WebTestKit was lightweight and accurate in interpreting encrypted traffic. We used WebTestKit to characterize the behavior of five major speed tests and identify a large number of preflighted requests, generating additional network overhead. We discovered high variances in RTT measurements of Xfinity speed test, caused by inconsistency between web interface and test servers.

Acknowledgment. We thank anonymous reviewers for their valuable comments. This work was supported by the Key-Area Research and Development Program of Guangdong Province (No. 2020B010164001), NSF CNS-2028506, NSF OAC-1724853, Comcast Innovation Fund, and Google Cloud credit grant.

References

1. Ookla open datasets. https://registry.opendata.aws/speedtest-global-performance/
2. Speedof.me. https://speedof.me
3. Bauer, S., Clark, D., Lehr, W.: Understanding broadband speed measurements. In: Proceedings of the TPRC (2010)
4. Bauer, S., Lehr, W., Mou, M.: Improving the measurement and analysis of gigabit broadband networks. Technical report, Massachusetts Institute of Technology (2016)
5. Chromium. Netlog viewer. https://netlog-viewer.appspot.com/
6. CloudFlare. Cloudflare speed test. https://speed.cloudflare.com
7. Comcast. Xfinity speed test. http://speedtest.xfinity.com
8. Doan, T.V., Bajpai, V., Crawford, S.: A longitudinal view of Netflix: content delivery over IPv6 and content cache deployments. In: Proceedings of the IEEE INFOCOM (2020)
9. Fast.com. Internet speed test. https://fast.com
10. Feamster, N., Livingood, J.: Measuring internet speed. Commun. ACM **63**(12), 72–80 (2020)
11. Goga, O., Teixeira, R.: Speed measurements of residential internet access. In: Taft, N., Ricciato, F. (eds.) PAM 2012. LNCS, vol. 7192, pp. 168–178. Springer, Heidelberg (2012). https://doi.org/10.1007/978-3-642-28537-0_17
12. Haselton, T.: CNBC tech guide: how to make sure you're getting the internet speeds you pay for (2018). https://www.cnbc.com/2018/08/17/how-to-check-internet-speed.html
13. Høiland-Jørgensen, T., Ahlgren, B., Hurtig, P., Brunstrom, A.: Measuring latency variation in the internet. In: Proceedings of the ACM CoNEXT (2016)
14. HTTP Toolkit. Chrome 79+ no longer shows preflight CORS requests. https://httptoolkit.tech/blog/chrome-79-doesnt-show-cors-preflight/
15. Hu, N., Steenkiste, P.: Evaluation and characterization of available bandwidth probing techniques. IEEE J. Sel. A. Commun. **21**(6), 879–894 (2006)
16. Hulu. Hulu help center: Test your internet connection. https://help.hulu.com/s/article/speed-test?language=en_US
17. Jain, M., Dovrolis, C.: End-to-end available bandwidth: measurement methodology, dynamics, and relation with TCP throughput. IEEE/ACM Trans. Netw. **11**(4), 537–549 (2003)
18. Li, W., Mok, R., Chang, R., Fok, W.: Appraising the delay accuracy in browser-based network measurement. In: Proceedings of the ACM/USENIX IMC (2013)
19. M Lab. Murakami. https://www.measurementlab.net/blog/murakami/. Accessed 15 July 2021

20. M-Lab. NDT (network diagnostic tool). https://www.measurementlab.net/tests/ndt/
21. Mok, R.K., Zou, H., Yang, R., Koch, T., Katz-Bassett, E., Claffy, K.: Measuring the network performance of Google Cloud platform. In: ACM IMC, Virtual Event (2021)
22. Netflix. Netflix help center: Internet connection speed recommendations. https://help.netflix.com/en/node/306
23. Ookla. About ookla. http://www.speedtest.net/en/about
24. Ookla. Speedtest. http://www.speedtest.net
25. Ookla. How does the test itself work? How is the result calculated? (2012). https://support.speedtest.net/hc/en-us/articles/203845400-How-does-the-test-itself-work-How-is-the-result-calculated-
26. Padhye, J., Firoiu, V., Towsley, D.F., Kurose, J.F.: Modeling TCP reno performance: a simple model and its empirical validation. IEEE/ACM Trans. Netw. **8**, 133–145 (2000)
27. Philip, A.: Slow internet? how to figure out if it's your problem or your service provider's. https://www.azcentral.com/story/news/local/arizona-investigations/2018/09/06/your-internet-slow-heres-how-figure-out-whos-fault/1058007002/
28. Ribeiro, V.J., Riedi, R.H., Baraniuk, R.G., Navratil, J., Cottrell, L.: pathChirp: efficient available bandwidth estimation for network paths (2003)
29. Sivel. Cloudflare-cli. https://github.com/KNawm/speed-cloudflare-cli
30. Sivel. Fast-cli. https://github.com/sindresorhus/fast-cli
31. Sivel. Speedtest-cli. https://github.com/sivel/speedtest-cli
32. Sommers, J., Durairajan, R., Barford, P.: Automatic metadata generation for active measurement. In: Proceedings of the ACM IMC (2017)
33. Strauss, J., Katabi, D., Kaashoek, F.: A measurement study of available bandwidth estimation tools. In: Proceedings of the ACM IMC (2013)
34. Sundaresan, S., de Donato, W., Feamster, N., Teixeira, R., Crawford, S., Pescapé, A.: Broadband Internet performance: a view from the gateway. In: Proceedings of the ACM SIGCOMM (2011)
35. Sundaresan, S., Lee, D., Deng, X., Feng, Y., Dhamdhere, A.: Challenges in inferring internet congestion using throughput measurements. In: Proceedings of the ACM IMC (2017)
36. The Chromium Projects. NetLog: Chrome's network logging system. https://www.chromium.org/developers/design-documents/network-stack/netlog
37. The Chromium Projects. The trace event profiling tool. https://www.chromium.org/developers/how-tos/trace-event-profiling-tool
38. The Office of the New York State Attorney General. Are you getting the internet speeds you are paying for? https://ag.ny.gov/SpeedTest
39. W3C. Resource Timing Level 2. https://www.w3.org/TR/resource-timing-2/. Accessed 26 June 2021
40. M. web docs. Cross-origin resource sharing (cors). https://developer.mozilla.org/en-US/docs/Web/HTTP/CORS#Preflighted_requests. Accessed 23 Feb 2019
41. WHATWG. XMLHttpRequest Living Standard. https://xhr.spec.whatwg.org
42. Xu, D., et al.: Understanding operational 5G: a first measurement study on its coverage, performance and energy consumption. In: ACM SIGCOMM, Virtual Event, NY, USA (2020)
43. Yang, X., et al.: Fast and light bandwidth testing for internet users. In: USENIX NSDI, Virtual Event (2021)

BatteryLab: A Collaborative Platform for Power Monitoring

https://batterylab.dev

Matteo Varvello[1][✉], Kleomenis Katevas[2], Mihai Plesa[3], Hamed Haddadi[3], Fabian Bustamante[4], and Ben Livshits[5]

[1] Bell Labs Nokia, Holmdel, USA
matteo.varvello@nokia.com
[2] Telefonica Research, Madrid, Spain
kleomenis.katevas@telefonica.com
[3] Brave Software, Santa Clara, USA
{mplesa,hhaddadi}@brave.com
[4] Northwestern University, Evanston, USA
fabianb@cs.northwestern.edu
[5] Imperial College London, London, UK
b.livshits@imperial.ac.uk

Abstract. Advances in cloud computing have simplified the way that both software development and testing are performed. This is not true for battery testing for which state of the art test-beds simply consist of one phone attached to a power meter. These test-beds have limited resources, access, and are overall hard to maintain; for these reasons, they often sit idle with no experiment to run. In this paper, we propose to *share* existing battery testbeds and transform them into *vantage points* of BatteryLab, a power monitoring platform offering heterogeneous devices and testing conditions. We have achieved this vision with a combination of hardware and software which allow to augment existing battery test-beds with remote capabilities. BatteryLab currently counts three vantage points, one in Europe and two in the US, hosting three Android devices and one iPhone 7. We benchmark BatteryLab with respect to the accuracy of its battery readings, system performance, and platform heterogeneity. Next, we demonstrate how measurements can be run atop of BatteryLab by developing the "Web Power Monitor" (WPM), a tool which can measure website power consumption at scale. We released WPM and used it to report on the energy consumption of Alexa's top 1,000 websites across 3 locations and 4 devices (both Android and iOS).

Keywords: Battery · Test-bed · Performance · Android · iOS

1 Introduction

Power consumption is a growing concern in the mobile industry, ranging from mobile phone users, operating system vendors, and app developers. To accurately measure a device power consumption, two options are currently available:

© The Author(s), under exclusive license to Springer Nature Switzerland AG 2022
O. Hohlfeld et al. (Eds.): PAM 2022, LNCS 13210, pp. 97–121, 2022.
https://doi.org/10.1007/978-3-030-98785-5_5

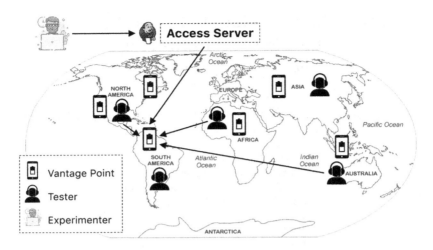

Fig. 1. Distributed architecture of BatteryLab.

software-based measurements, which rely on battery readings from the device, and *hardware-based* measurements which leverage an external power monitor connected to a device battery. Software-based power measurements are easy to use, but lack the accuracy and granularity an experimenter might require [15,38]. Few startups [20,27] offer, for a price, improvements upon the accuracy of software-based power measurements by relying on few devices for which they have performed heavy "calibration" (their secret sauce). Hardware-based power measurements are accurate, fine-grained, but quite cumbersome to setup.

For years, researchers have been building home-grown test-beds for hardware-based power measurements, consisting of an Android device connected to a high-frequency power monitor [13,14,21,40]. This required expertise in hardware setup and writing code when automation is needed – code which is unfortunately never shared with the community. Such closed-source test-beds have limited accessibility, e.g., requiring physical access to the devices, and shareability, even among members of the same group. This became clear during the COVID-19 pandemic: remote desktop tools like VNC came to the rescue, but often the only solution was to move that precious test-bed at home.

In this paper we challenge the assumption that such battery test-beds need to be "local" and propose *BatteryLab*, a cooperative platform for battery measurements. We envision BatteryLab as a cooperative platform where members contribute hardware resources (e.g., some phones and a power monitor) in exchange for access to the resources contributed by other platform members. Nevertheless, the hardware/software suite we have built and open sourced [25] can also be used "locally", i.e., augmenting an existing battery test-bed with scheduling and remote control capabilities. The following contributions are the founding blocks of BatteryLab:

Automation for Hardware-Based Power Measurements. BatteryLab comes with an intrinsic automation requirement. For example, an *experimenter* from Europe needs to be able to activate a power meter connected to a phone in the US. To make this possible, we have designed *vantage points* as the above local test-beds enhanced with a lightweight *controller* such as a Raspberry Pi [34]. The controller runs BatteryLab's software suite which realizes "remote power testing", e.g., from activating a device's battery bypass to enabling remote control of the device via the experimenter's browser.

A Library for Android and iOS Automation. While the Android Debugging Bridge (ADB) is a powerful tool to automate Android devices, an equivalent does not exist for iOS. BatteryLab builds atop of ADB to offer seamless automation of Android devices. For iOS, we have built and open-sourced a Python library which maps commands like touch, swipe, and text input to a (virtual) Bluetooth keyboard and mouse. To the best of our knowledge, we are the first to provide automation of any third party app on actual iOS devices (i.e., other than simulators as in [6,36]). Even commercial products for iOS, such as TeamViewer [39] or the recent SharePlay [7] of iOS 15, can only provide remote screen sharing.

Usability Testing for Power Measurements. BatteryLab allows an experimenter to interact with a real device via its browser. This feature is paramount for debugging automation scripts, but also a key enabler of *usability testing*, or battery measurements coupled with actual device interactions from real users.

Deployment at Three Research Institutions. BatteryLab currently has three vantage points, two in the US and one in Europe (with more vantage points going live soon) and hosts a range of Android devices and an iOS device (iPhone 7).

We evaluate BatteryLab on battery readings accuracy, system performance, and platform heterogeneity. To illustrate the value and ease-of-use of BatteryLab, we have also built the "Web Power Monitor" (WPM), a service which measures the power consumption of websites loaded via a test browser running at any BatteryLab's device. With a handful of lines of code, WPM allowed us to conduct the largest scale measurement study of energy consumption on the Web, encompassing Alexa's top 1,000 websites measured from four devices and two operating systems. We have released WPM as a web application integrated with BatteryLab which offers such testing capabilities to the public, in real time. This paper extends our previously published work [44] in many ways:

- We add support for device automation also to Apple iOS by exploiting the Bluetooth HID and AirPlay services.
- We deploy BatteryLab at three research institutions and benchmark its performance including, among others, a comparison with software-based battery measurements.
- We open source BatteryLab's code for "local" use, and BatteryLab as a testbed for battery measurements.

- We develop and release WPM, a tool for measuring website power consumption at scale; we further use WPM to measure the energy consumption of Alexa's top 1,000 websites across 3 locations and 4 devices.
- We explore support for usability testing via "action replay", a mechanism to automatically build app automation scripts based on human inputs.

2   BATTERYLAB Architecture

This section presents the design and implementation details of BatteryLab (see Fig. 1). Our current iteration focuses on mobile devices, but the architecture is flexible and can be extended to other devices, e.g., laptops and IoT devices.

BatteryLab consists of a centralized *access server* that remotely manages a number of nodes or *vantage points*. Each of these vantage points, hosted by universities or research organizations around the world, includes a number of test devices (a phone/tablet connected to a power monitor) where experiments are carried out. BatteryLab members (*experimenters*) gain access to test devices via the access server, where they can request time slots to deploy automated scripts and/or remote control of the device. Once granted, remote device control can be shared with *testers*, whose task is to manually interact with a device, e.g., scroll and search for items on a shopping application. Testers are either volunteers, e.g., recruited via email or social media, or paid, recruited via crowdsourcing websites like Mechanical Turk [3].

In the remainder of this section, we describe BatteryLab's main components in detail. Next, we focus on BatteryLab's automation capabilities and on the procedure for new members to join the platform.

2.1   Access Server

The main role of the access server is to manage the vantage points and schedule experiments on them based on experimenters' requests. We built the access server atop of the Jenkins [22] continuous integration system which is free, open-source, portable (written in Java) and backed by an active and large community. Jenkins enables end-to-end test pipelines while supporting multiple users and concurrent timed sessions.

BatteryLab's access server runs in the cloud (Amazon AWS) which enables further scaling and cost optimization. Vantage points have to be added explicitly and pre-approved in multiple ways (IP lockdown, security groups). Experimenters need to authenticate and be authorized to access the web console of the access server, which is only available over HTTPS. The access server communicates with the vantage points via SSH. New BatteryLab members grant SSH access from the server to the vantage point's controller via public key and IP white-listing (Sect. 3.4).

Experimenters access vantage points via the access server, where they can create *jobs* to automate their tests. Jobs are programmed using a combination of BatteryLab's Python API (Table 1), e.g., for user-friendly device selection

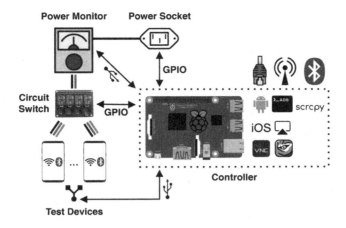

Fig. 2. Vantage point design.

and interaction with the power meter, and code specific to each test. Only the experimenters who have been granted access to the platform can create, edit, or run jobs and every pipeline change has to be approved by an administrator. This is done via a role-based authorization matrix.

After the initial setup, the access server dispatches queued jobs based on the experimenter constraints, e.g., target device, connectivity, or network location, and BatteryLab constraints. For example, no concurrent jobs are allowed at the same vantage point since the power monitor can only be associated with one device at a time and isolation is required for accurate power measurements. By default, the access server collects logs from the power meter which are made available for several days within the job's workspace. Android logs (e.g., `logcat` and `dumpsys`) can be requested via the `execute_command` API for the supported devices (Table 1).

2.2 Vantage Point

Figure 2 shows a graphical overview of a BatteryLab's vantage point with its main components: controller, power monitor, test devices, circuit switch, and power socket.

Controller – This is a Linux-based machine responsible for managing the vantage point. This machine is equipped with both Ethernet, WiFi and Bluetooth connectivity, a USB controller with a series of available USB ports, as well as with an external General-Purpose Input/Output (GPIO) interface. We use the popular Raspberry Pi 3B+ [34] running Raspberry Pi OS (Buster, September 2019) that meets these requirements at an affordable price.

The controller's primary role is to manage connectivity with test devices. Each device connects to the controller's USB port, WiFi access point (configured in NAT or Bridge mode), and Bluetooth, based on automation needs (see

Sect. 3.2). USB is used to power each testing device when not connected to the power monitor and to instrument Android devices via the Android Debugging Bridge [19] (ADB), when needed. WiFi provides Internet access to all devices and extend ADB automation and device mirroring to Android devices without incurring the extra USB current, which interferes with the power monitoring procedure. (De)activation of USB ports is realized using uhubctl [43]. Bluetooth is used to realize automation across OSes (Android and iOS) and connectivity (WiFi and cellular).

The second role of the controller is to provide *device mirroring*, i.e., remote control of device under test. We use VNC (tigervnc [41]) to enable remote access to the controller, and noVNC [31], an HTML VNC library and application, to provide easy access to a VNC session via a browser without additional software required at the experimenter/tester. We then *mirror* the test device within the noVNC/VNC session and limit access to only this visual element. In Android, this is achieved using scrcpy [18], a screen mirroring utility which runs atop of ADB for devices running API 21 (Android $\geq$ 5.0). In iOS, we utilize AirPlay Screen Mirroring [8] using RPiPlay [17], an AirPlay mirroring server for devices running iOS $\geq$ 9.0.

We have also built a graphical user interface (GUI) around the default noVNC client. The GUI consists of an *interactive area* where a device screen is mirrored (bottom of the figure) while a user (experimenter or tester) can remotely mouse-control the physical device, and a *toolbar* that occupies the top part of the GUI and implements a convenient subset of BatteryLab's API (see Table 1).

Power Monitor – This is a power metering hardware capable of measuring the current consumed by a test device in high sampling rate. BatteryLab currently supports the Monsoon HV [29], a power monitor with a voltage range of 0.8V to 13.5V and up to 6A continuous current sampled at 5 KHz. The Monsoon HV is controlled using its Python API [30]. Other power monitors can be supported, granted that they offer APIs to be integrated with BatteryLab's software suite.

Test Device(s) – It is an Android or iOS device (phone or tablet) that can be connected to a power monitor using a battery bypass modification (i.e., isolate the battery power circuit and provide power via the power monitor). While devices with removable batteries are easier to setup, more complex configurations (e.g., all iOS and recent Android devices) are also supported by doing the battery bypass modification at the battery controller level.

Circuit Switch – This is a relay-based circuit with multiple channels that lies between the test devices and the power monitor. The circuit switch is connected to the controller's GPIO interface and all relays can be controlled via software from the controller. Each relay uses the device's voltage (+) terminal as an input, and programmatically switches between the battery's voltage terminal and the power monitor's Vout connector. Ground (-) connector is permanently connected to all devices' Ground terminals.

This circuit switch has three main tasks. First, it allows to switch between a direct connection between the phone and its battery, and the "battery bypass"—

Table 1. BatteryLab's core API.

API	Description	Parameters
list_nodes	List matching vantage points	label, state
list_devices	List identifiers of test devices	vantage_point
device_mirroring	Activate device mirroring	device_id
power_monitor	Toggle Monsoon power state	state (on/off)
set_voltage	Set target voltage	voltage_val
start_monitor	Start battery measurement	device_id, duration
stop_monitor	Stop battery measurement	-
batt_switch	(De)activate battery	device_id
execute_command	Execute a command on device	device_id, command, automation

which implies disconnecting the battery and connecting to the power monitor. This is required to allow the power monitor to measure the current consumed during an experiment. Second, it allows BatteryLab to concurrently support multiple test devices without having to manually move cables around. Third, it allows to programmatically switch the power meter on and off.

Power Socket – This is a relay-based power socket that allows the controller to turn the Monsoon on and off, when needed. It connects to the controller via the GPIO port, and it is controlled by our Python API.

3   Using BatteryLab

In the following paragraphs we illustrate the use of BatteryLab's API, discuss its support of test automation, and the generation of automation scripts from human input. We close the section with a description of the steps needed to join BatteryLab.

3.1   API Usage

Experimenter jobs are interleaved with "control" jobs which manage the vantage points, e.g., they update BatteryLab wildcard certificates (Sect. 3.4) and ensure that the power meter is not active when not needed (for safety reasons). We here present some of these jobs as examples of BatteryLab's API usage. We have chosen the set of jobs that are also used by the application we have built atop of BatteryLab (Sect. 5). Note that these jobs effectively *extend* the API available to BatteryLab's experimenters; these are not listed in Table 1 which focuses only on core API.

NODE_SETUP – The goal of this job/API is to prepare a vantage point for power measurements on a device d. This implies activating the power meter (power_monitor), offering the voltage that d requires (set_voltage) and activating the relay to realize d's battery bypass (batt_switch). The job continues by verifying that WiFi is properly working, eventually switching frequency based on the device characteristics—with 5 GHz preferred, when available. Based on the device and the requested automation (see Sect. 3.2), the job continues by either activating ADB over WiFi or the Bluetooth HID service. Finally, USB connection is interrupted—to avoid noise on the power measurements—and device mirroring is activated, if needed (device_mirroring).

DEVICE_SETUP – The goal of this job/API is to prepare a device d such that "noise" on the upcoming power measurement is minimized. We have identified several best practices which help in doing so and we offer them as an API. Nevertheless, the experimenter is the ultimate decision maker and can either ignore or further improve on these operations. The job starts by disabling notifications, set the device in airplane mode with WiFi only activated—unless a mobile connection is needed and available—and close all background apps. Next, the job ensures that the device is not using automatic brightness and further sets the brightness to a default value or a requested one. The last step is important since the variation in ambient light can impact the outcome of a measurement.

CLEANUP – The goal of this job/API is to ensure that a vantage point is in a "safe" state. This implies turning off the power meter if no testing job is undergoing and removing any eventual battery bypass. Finally, USB connectivity is re-enabled which ensures that the device's battery get charged. This job further proceeds removing installed apps which were not used in the last seven days, with the goal to avoid overloading testing devices.

REFRESH – The goal of this job/API is to verify reachability of vantage points and devices therein. The information collected is used to populate a JSON file which enhances Jenkins data past sites reachability via SSH. This job currently runs across the whole platform every 30 min.

3.2   Android/iOS Automation Library

BatteryLab provides a Python library—which we open-sourced together with the BatteryLab's code—that greatly simplifies test automation on both Android and iOS. At high level, the library offers APIs like input(tap, x, y) which map to several underlying automation mechanisms, each with its own set of advantages and limitations. The library automatically switches to an automation solution based on the experiment needs, e.g., device and connectivity, hiding unnecessary complexity to the experimenter.

Android Debugging Protocol (Android) – ADB [19] is a powerful tool/ protocol to control an Android device. Commands can be sent over USB, WiFi, or Bluetooth. While USB guarantees highest reliability, it interferes with the power monitor due to the power required to activate the USB micro-controller at the device. Accordingly, BatteryLab's automation library uses ADB over USB *whenever* the power monitor is not used, e.g., when installing an app or cleaning a device, while resorting to WiFi (or Bluetooth) for all other automations. Note that using WiFi implies not being able to run experiments leveraging the mobile network. However, these experiments are possible leveraging Bluetooth tethering, when available.

Bluetooth HID Service (iOS/Android) – Automating third-party apps in iOS is challenging due to the lack of ADB-like API. Even commercial solutions like TeamViewer [39] or the new SharePlay [7] of iOS 15 limit their iOS offering to remote screen viewing only. The only solution to control an iOS device without physical access requires using a wireless keyboard and mouse. We exploit this feature to map commands like touch, swipe and text input into (virtual) mouse and keyboard actions.

Specifically, we virtualize the mouse and keyboard by designing a Human Interface Device (HID) service [11] atop of BlueZ Bluetooth Protocol Stack [12] v5.43. The controller broadcasts a custom Combo Keyboard/Pointing HID service (i.e., HIDDeviceSubclass: 0xC0 [11]) which enables a connection to previously paired test devices over Bluetooth. The automation library translates keyboard keystrokes, mouse clicks and gestures into USB HID Usage Reports [42] that simulate user actions to the controlled device (e.g., locate an app, launch it, and interact with it). While we exploit this automation strategy for iOS only, the approach is generic and can be used across all devices which support the Bluetooth HID profile for both mouse and keyboard (i.e., Android v8.0+ and iOS v13.0+).

3.3   Action Replay

Regardless of the automation mechanism used, building automation scripts for mobile devices is a time consuming task [24,32,35]. Device mirroring offers a unique opportunity to speed up the generation of such automation scripts in BatteryLab. The key idea is to record an experimenter/tester clicks, mouse, keyboard input, and use them to generate an automation script.

We have thus modified noVNC – precisely `mouse.js` and `keyboard.js` – to POST the collected user input to the controller's web application (see Sect. 2.2) where the device being mirrored is hosted. The web application collects the user input and map it to APIs from the above automation library, which translates into, for example, an ADB command such as `tap` or `swipe`. When screen coordinates are involved, e.g., for a `tap` command, the actual coordinates are derived by offsetting the coordinates recorded in noVNC as a function of the size of the VNC screen and the actual device size. Under the assumption that an application GUI is similar across platforms, the human-generated automation script at a given device could be re-used for other devices.

3.4 How to Join?

Joining BatteryLab is straightforward and consists of three steps. First, the vantage point needs to be physically built as described in Fig. 2. At this point, the controller (Raspberry Pi) should also be flashed with the latest Raspberry Pi OS image along with some standard setup as described in the associated tutorial [9]. Second, the network where the controller is connected (via Ethernet) needs to be configured to allow the controller to be reachable at the following configurable ports: 2222 (SSH, access server only)[1], 8080 (web application for GUI and action/replay). Third, a BatteryLab account should be created for the new member. This involves downloading the access server's public key—to be authorized at the controller—and uploading a human readable identifier for the vantage point (e.g., node1), and its current public IP address. This information is used by the access server to add a new entry in BatteryLab's DNS (e.g., node1.batterylab.dev)—provided by Amazon Route53 [5]—and verify that SSH access to the new vantage point is now granted. Since the whole BatteryLab traffic is encrypted, a wildcard letsencrypt [23] certificate is distributed to new members by the access server, which also manages its renewal and distribution, when needed.

The next step consists of installing BatteryLab's software at the controller. This step is realized automatically by BatteryLab's access server and it is the first job to be deployed at the new vantage point. At high level, this consists in the following operations. First, the OS is updated. Next, common security practices are enforced: 1) install fail2ban which neutralizes popular brute-force attacks over SSH, and 2) disable password authentication for SSH. Next, BatteryLab code is pulled from its open source repository [25] along with all packages and software needed. Code is compiled, where needed, and packages are installed. Then, the controller is turned into an "access point" where the test devices will connect to. By default, the access point spins a new SSID (BatteryLab) with a pre-set password operating on 2.4 GHz. However, BatteryLab automatically switches to 5 GHz for devices that support it. This "switch" is required since the Raspberry Pi does not mount two WiFi antennas and thus both frequencies cannot be active at the same time.

Next, several crontab entries are added. At reboot and every 30 min, a task monitors the controller's public IP address and update its entry at BatteryLab's DNS. At reboot, the GPIO pins used by BatteryLab are set as "output" and the IP rules needed by the controller to act as an access point are restored. The next step consists in setting up device mirroring, i.e., VNC password and wildcard certificate used by both noVNC and the web application. This setup job also learns useful information about the devices connected: ADB identifier (if available), screen resolution, IP address, etc. This information is reported to the access server to further populate the JSON file maintained by the REFRESH job/API. Last but not least, several tests are run to verify: 1) Monsoon connectivity, 2) device connectivity, 3) circuit relay stability, 4) device mirroring.

---

[1] The SSH agent at the node also needs to be configured accordingly. An iptable rule should be added to limit access to the access server only.

Table 2. BatteryLab test-bed composition.

	J7DUO	IPHONE7	SMJ337A	LMX210
Vendor	Samsung	Apple	Samsung	LG
OS	Android 9.0	iOS 13.2.3	Android 8.0.0	Android 7.1.2
Location	United Kingdom	United Kingdom	New Jersey	Illinois
CPU Info	Octa-core (2x2.2 GHz Cortex-A73, 6x1.6 GHz	Quad-core 2.34 GHz Apple A10 Fusion	Quad-core 1.4 GHz Cortex-A53	Quad-core 1.4 GHz Cortex-A53
Memory	4 GB	2 GB	2 GB	2 GB
Battery	3,000 mAh	1,960 mAh	2,600 mAh	2,500 mAh

BatteryLab currently counts three vantage points located in the UK, New Jersey, and Illinois, with a total of three Android devices and one iPhone 7. Table 2 provides detailed information of the devices currently available to the public via BatteryLab. At the time of writing, three other organizations are in the process of setting up a BatteryLab vantage point.

4 Benchmarking

This section benchmarks BatteryLab. We first evaluate its *accuracy* in reporting battery measurements. We then evaluate its *performance* with respect to CPU, memory, and responsiveness of its device mirroring mechanism. We then investigate BatteryLab's *heterogeneity* and the feasibility of usability testing when coupled with power monitoring.

4.1 Accuracy

Compared to a classic *local* setup for device performance measurements, BatteryLab introduces some hardware (circuit relay) and software (device mirroring) components that can impact the *accuracy* of the measurements. We devised an experiment where we compare three scenarios. First, a *direct* scenario consisting of the Monsoon power meter, the testing device, and the Raspberry Pi to instrument the power meter. For this setup, we strictly followed Monsoon indications [29] in terms of cable type and length, and connectors to be used. Next we evaluate a *relay* scenario, where the relay circuit is introduced to enable BatteryLab's programmable switching between battery bypass and regular battery operation (see Sect. 2.2). Finally, a *mirroring* scenario where the device screen is mirrored to an open noVNC session. While the relay is always "required" for BatteryLab to properly function, device mirroring is only required for usability testing. Since we currently do not fully support usability testing for iOS (see Sect. 2.1), we here only focus on Android.

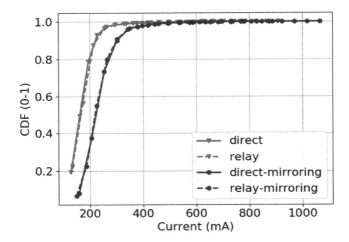

Fig. 3. CDF of current drawn (direct, relay, direct-mirroring, relay-mirroring).

Figure 3 shows the Cumulative Distribution Function (CDF) of the current consumed in each of the above scenarios during a 5 min test. For completeness, we also consider a *direct-mirroring* scenario where the device is directly connected to Monsoon and device mirroring is active. During the test, we play an MPEG4 video pre-loaded on the SD card of the device (J7DUO, UK). The rationale is to force the device mirroring mechanism to constantly update as new frames are initiated. The figure shows negligible difference between the "direct" and "relay" scenarios, regardless of the device mirroring status being active or not. A larger gap (median current grows from 160 to 220 mA) appears with device mirroring. This is because of the background process responsible for screencasting to the controller which causes additional CPU usage on the device (∼15%). At the end of this section, we investigate a more challenging usability testing scenario along with a potential solution to minimize the additional power consumption caused by device mirroring.

A related question is: *what is the accuracy that BatteryLab offers compared to software measurements?* Having verified that BatteryLab is as accurate as a local setup, and granted that hardware-based battery measurements are the "ground truth", the question is really how accurate are software-based battery measurements? While this question is out of scope for this paper, it has to be noted that Android software-based battery readings can be realized in Battery-Lab via ADB[2]. With respect to iOS, while some high level *energy usage* reports are available—reporting battery consumption every second on an arbitrary 0 to 20 scale—they are currently unavailable to BatteryLab since they require a developer-enabled macOS.

---

[2] Either using Android bug-report files or with `adb shell cat sys/class/power_supply/*/uevent`.

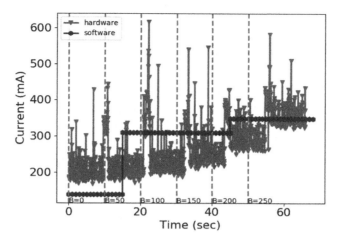

Fig. 4. Current over time under variable screen brightness (B) from 0 to 250, Android's max value. Software versus hardware measurements (LMX210).

We find that pure software measurements are *enough* to identify trends in measured current, but have limited overall accuracy and granularity, e.g., a 30 s reporting frequency across all our Android devices. As an example, Fig. 4 shows the time evolution of the current measured via BatteryLab (hardware) and software while increasing the screen brightness from minimum (0) to maximum (250) by 50 units over 60 s, as indicated by the vertical dashed lines. This plot shows that pure software measurements are *enough* to identify trends, but have limited overall accuracy and granularity – while the plot refers to the LMX210, we measured a similar reporting frequency (30 s) across all Android devices.

To further investigate the reporting frequency, we have performed the same test also on Samsung's Remote Test Lab [37].[3] We find a 10 s reporting frequency on Samsung Galaxy S5 (Android 6) and S7 (Android 8), and 30 s on S8 and S9 (Android 9). When repeating the same tests on newer models, we find that the reported sampling rate improves to a mean of 2.23 s ($\pm$1.65) for Google Pixel 3a (Android 12), 0.66 ($\pm$0.24) for Google Pixel 4 (Android 12) and 0.60 ($\pm$0.25) for Google Pixel 5. The sampling rate was unaffected from different configurations (screen on, off, or streaming a HD video). Note that internal battery readings can be enhanced with additional data (e.g., cpu, screen usage), alongside device calibration, to achieve higher accuracy, as discussed in [15].

4.2 System Performance

Next, we benchmark overall BatteryLab performance. We start by evaluating the CPU utilization at the controller. Figure 5 shows the CDF of the CPU utilization during the previous experiments (when a relay was used) with active and inactive device mirroring, respectively. When device mirroring is inactive, the controller is

---

[3] These tests were not possible on AWS Device Farm [4] due to lack of ADB access.

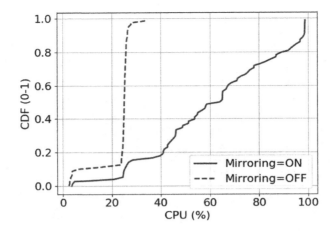

Fig. 5. CDF of CPU consumption at the controller (Raspberry Pi 3B+)

mostly underloaded, i.e., constant CPU utilization at 25%. This load is caused by the communication with the power meter to pull battery readings at the highest frequency (5 kHz). With device mirroring, the median load increases to ~75%. Further, in 10% of the measurements the load is quite high and over 95%.

Device mirroring only impacts the CPU usage. The impact on memory consumption is minimal (extra 6%, on average). Overall, memory does not appear to be an issue given less than 20% utilization of the Raspberry Pi's 1 GB. The networking demand is also minimal, with just 32 MB of upload traffic for a ~7 min test (due to device mirroring). Note that we set `scrcpy`'s video encoding (H.264) rate to 1 Mbps, which produces an upper bound of about 50 MB. The lower value depends on extra compression provided by `noVNC`.

Finally, we investigate the "responsiveness" of device mirroring. We call *latency* the time between when an action is requested (either via automation or a click in the browser), and when the consequence of this action is displayed back in the browser, after being executed on the device. This depends on a number of factors like network latency (between the browser and the test device), the load on the device and/or the controller, and software optimizations. We estimate such latency by recording audio (44,100 Hz) and video (60 fps) while interacting with the device via the browser. We then manually annotated the video using ELAN multimedia annotator software [46] and compute the latency as the time between a mouse click (identified via sound) and the first frame with a visual change in the app. We repeat this test 40 times while co-located with the vantage point (1 ms network latency) and measure an average latency of 350 (±80) ms.

4.3 Devices and Locations

BatteryLab's distributed nature is both a *feature* and a *necessity*. It is a feature since it allows battery measurements under diverse device and network

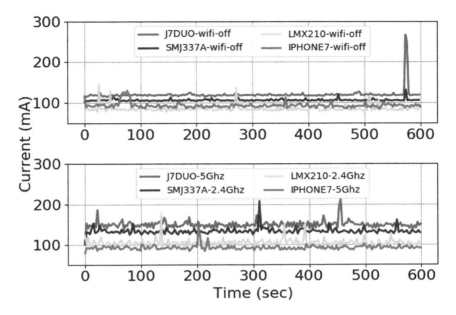

Fig. 6. Time evolution of current usage per device at rest (WiFi off and on).

conditions which is, to the best of our knowledge, a first for research and development in this space. It is a necessity since it is the way in which the platform can scale without incurring high costs. We here explore the impact of such diversity on battery measurements.

Figure 6 displays the evolution over time (600 s) of the current used by each BatteryLab device at "rest", i.e., displaying the default phone desktop after having run BatteryLab's API DEVICE_SETUP (Sect. 2.1) to ensure equivalent device settings. We further differentiate between the case when WiFi was active or not. For Android, regardless of WiFi settings, the figure shows that the J7DUO consumes the most, while the LMX210 consumes the least – about 25% less (270 vs 359 J over 600 s). Overall, the similar results in the case without WiFi suggest that the difference between the device is intrinsic of the device configurations, e.g., more power-hungry hardware and different Android versions with potential vendor customization. Understanding the event responsible of the variations shown in Fig. 6 is out of the scope of this analysis. It is worth noticing some correlations between peaks suggesting vendor specific operations, e.g., the peak around 580 s for the J7DUO and SMJ337A, both Samsung devices. The IPHONE7 consumes the least when considering active WiFi, while the LMX210 consumes the least in absence of WiFi. The take away of this analysis is that BatteryLab's devices (and locations) have the potential to offer a large set of heterogeneous conditions for the experimenters to test with.

Next, we compare the performance of the *same* device at different locations. Since we do not have such testing condition, we emulate the presence of one

Table 3. ProtonVPN statistics.

Speedtest server (Kms)	Download (Mbps)	Upload (Mbps)	Latency (ms)
South Africa Johannesburg (3.21)	6.26	9.77	222.04
China Hong Kong (4.86)	7.64	7.77	286.32
Japan Bunkyo (2.21)	9.68	7.76	239.38
Brazil Sao Paulo (8.84)	9.75	8.82	235.05
CA, USA Santa Clara (7.99)	10.63	14.87	215.16

device (J7DUO) at different locations via a VPN. We use a basic subscription to ProtonVPN [33] set up at the controller. Table 3 summarizes five locations we choose, along with network measurements from SpeedTest (upload and download bandwidth, latency). VPN vantage points are sorted by download bandwidth, with the South Africa node being the slowest and the California node being the fastest. Since the SpeedTest server is always within 10 km from each VPN node, the latency here reported is mostly representative of the network path between the vantage point and the VPN node.

Next, we leverage WPM (see Sect. 5) to investigate the battery consumption of Chrome in comparison to a new privacy-preserving browser (Brave). We assume a simple workload where each browser is instrumented to sequentially load 10 popular news websites. After a URL is entered, the automation script waits 6 s – emulating a typical page load time (PLT) – and then interact with the page by executing multiple "scroll up" and "scroll down" operations.

Figure 7 shows the average energy consumption (J) over 5 runs (standard deviation as errorbars) per VPN location and browser. The figure does not show significant differences among the battery measurements at different network location. For example, while the available bandwidth almost doubles between South Africa and California, the average discharge variation stays between standard deviation bounds. This is encouraging for experiments where BatteryLab's distributed nature is a *necessity* and its noise should be minimized.

Figure 7 also shows an interesting trend when comparing Brave and Chrome when tested via the Japanese VPN node. In this case, Brave's energy consumption is in line with the other nodes, while Chrome's is minimized. This is due to a significant (20%) drop in bandwidth usage by Chrome, due to a systematic reduction in the overall size of ads shown in Japan. This is an interesting result for experiments where BatteryLab's distributed nature is a *feature*.

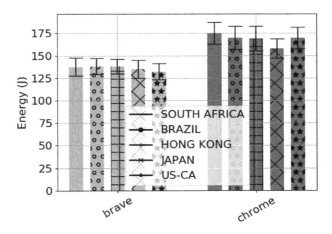

Fig. 7. Brave and Chrome energy consumption measured through VPN tunnels.

4.4 Usability Testing

The above analysis indicates that the extra (CPU) cost of device mirroring can invalidate the power measurements reading. Accordingly, our recommendation is to only leverage device mirroring when debugging an application over BatteryLab, but then disable it during the actual power measurements. This is not possible in case of usability testing where, by definition, a remote tester requires access to a device.

"Action replay" (see Sect. 3.3) is a potential solution to this limitation. The intuition is that a usability test can be split in two parts. First, the tester performs the required test while action replay is used to record her actions. Then, the tester's actions are replayed without the extra cost associated with device mirroring. While this approach provides, in theory, better accuracy, record and replay of human actions is challenging.

Figure 8 shows current measured over time at SMJ337A when a human interacts with the news workload in Brave (*action* curve), versus a bot generated by the action replay tool (*replay* curve). The figure shows overall lower current usage in the replay case versus the action case, resulting in an overall lower energy consumption: 345 versus 399 J over 380 s. The figure also shows high correlation between the two curves, suggesting accurate replay. Nevertheless, the overall error for energy estimation is fairly low (about 10%) and overall constant, similar to what suggested by Fig. 3 and now confirmed in a more challenging scenario.

Record and replay of human actions is generally challenging. Not all applications behave equally between successive runs. For example, in our testing scenario, a webpage could suddenly slow down and the replay might fail to click on an article that was not loaded yet. This opens up a potential interesting research area of building ML-driven tools for app testing based on human input,

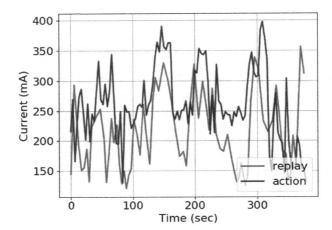

Fig. 8. Evolution over time of current (mA) measured during "action" (one human interacting with 10 news websites in sequence) and "replay" (a bot reproducing human activity).

as previously discussed in [2]. This is currently out of the scope of this work, but pairing such research with device behavior monitoring is an interesting avenue for future work.

5   The Web Power Monitor

There is an increasing interest in understanding the power drawn by modern websites and browsers [13,14,40], especially on smartphones due to inherent battery constraints. Although different, these studies share a *scalability* limitation: 1) they most target a single Android device, 2) they only test 100 websites or less accessed from a single location. This is because of the intrinsic limitations of the test-bed used which BatteryLab aims at solving. In the following, we present the "Web Power Monitor" (WPM), a BatteryLab application which enable large scale measurements of energy consumption in the Web. WPM currently powers a Web service [10] which offers such testing capabilities to the public, in real time.

5.1   Design and Implementation

Back-end – This is a Jenkins job whose goal is to report on the power consumed by a webpage when loaded on a BatteryLab device via a desired browser. Algorithm 1 shows the pseudocode describing such job; for simplicity, we omit the part of the job that takes care to identify *where* this test should run, i.e., either a specific device or a vantage point. As a first step (L1), the job prepares the vantage point by calling NODE_SETUP (see Sect. 3.1) which activates power monitoring and device mirroring, if requested. Next, the device is prepared for the test using DEVICE_SETUP (L2), also described in Sect. 3.1.

Algorithm 1: Pseudocode for WPM's backend.

Input: Device *device*, URLs to be tested *url_list*, Browser *browser*, Number
of repetitions *reps*, Power flag *power*, Visual flag *visual*, Automation
automation

Output: JSON file with performance metrics

1 *node_status* ← NODE_SETUP(*power*, *visual*)
2 *device_status* ← DEVICE_SETUP(*device*)
3 **for** *r* ← 0 **to** *reps* **do**
4 │ BROWSER_SETUP(*device*, *browser*)
5 │ RUN_TEST(*device*, *browser*, *url_list*, *automation*)
6 **end**
7 *device_status* ← CLEANUP(*device*)

Next is BROWSER_SETUP (L3), where the browser is i) installed (if needed), ii) cleaned (cache and configuration files), and iii) freshly started, e.g., Chrome requires to go through an onboarding process when launched for the first time. This function is equivalent to what an experimenter would have to design for a local experiment, with the caveat that it has to be tested on a range of devices. BatteryLab further simplifies this task for an experimenter via the "action replay" module (see Sect. 3.3) which generates automation scripts from human input collected via BatteryLab's browser interface.

The next step is RUN_TEST (L5) where a list of URLs (*url_list*) is tested. The experimenter defines how URLs should be loaded, e.g., sequentially in a new tab. The experimenter also controls whether to perform a *simple load*, i.e., load the page for a fixed amount of time, or interact with each page, e.g., scroll the page up and down multiple times for a certain duration. Finally, CLEANUP (see Sect. 3.1) is invoked to restore the node state (e.g., turn off the power meter) and, if needed, expose the collected data to the front-end.

Front-end – This is inspired by webpagetest [45], a tool for measuring webpage load times. Similarly, WPM offers a simple Web interface where a visitor can choose the URL to test, the browser, the device (along with *where* this device is located in the world) and which test to run. Power measurements are always collected, while visual access to the device needs to be explicitly requested. If so, the front-end alerts the user that this condition might impact the absolute value of the measurements, as discussed in Sect. 4.

Once the requested test is submitted, the user is presented with a page showing the progress of the experiment. If visual access was requested, as DEVICE_SETUP is completed, an iframe is activated on the page to show the requested device in real time. At the end of RUN_TEST, several plots are shown on screen such as CPU and current consumption during the test. We invite the interested reader to try out WPM at [10].

Front-end information (locations, devices, and browsers available) is maintained by the REFRESH job (see Sect. 3.1) and then retrieved as a JSON file via an

Table 4. WPM's measurement study versus previous works.

Study	OSes	Devices	Websites	Locations
[40]	Android	1	25	1
[14]	Android	1	80	1
[13]	Android	1*	100	1
WPM	Android/iOS	4	715	3

AJAX call. Similarly, the status of the experiment is pulled over time to switch between showing the remote device or results, when available.

5.2 Results

We used WPM to study the power consumption of Alexa's top 1,000 websites from 3 Android devices (NJ, IL, and UK) and one iPhone 7 (UK). We assume a simple load, where each page is loaded for up to 30 s. We load each page 3 times (with browser cache cleanup in between), and then report on the median for each metric. We synchronize experiments at the different locations using a 2 min fixed duration. The iOS test was not synchronized (one day delay) since only one testing device can be measured at a time per location.

To limit the scope (and duration) of this test, we only experiment with a single browser. We choose Brave, rather than Chrome as done in related work, since its ad-blocking feature offers a more consistent browsing experience location-wise (see Fig. 7) which in turn implies offering a similar workload to the different devices. We invite the interest reader to leverage WPM's online service to compare the energy consumption of different browsers.

Table 4 summarizes the scale of this measurement in comparison with related work. We use Alexa's top 1,000 list from Nov. 2019 as an input. Out of the 1,000 websites we filtered 49 URLs potentially associated with adult websites—to avoid downloading and showing inappropriate content at our participating institutions—and 83 URLs associated with multiple top-level domains, e.g., `google.it` and `google.fr`. In the latter case, we kept the most popular domain according to Alexa, i.e., mostly the `.com` domain. Before the full experiment, we quickly tested the remainder URLs via a simple GET of the landing page. We find that 57 URLs had problems related with their certificate, 38 URLs timed out (30 s) and 58 URLs responded with some error code, 403 (Forbidden) and 503 (Service Unavailable) being the most popular errors. In the end, we are left with 715 active URLs.

We start by validating the assumption that Brave's ad-blocking helps in offering a similar workload to each device, irrespective of its location. Figure 9 shows the CDF of the bandwidth consumed across websites when accessed from the three different device/locations. Overall, the figure confirms our assumption showing minimal difference between the four CDFs. Note that some variations are still possible because of, for instance, OS-specific differences, geo-located

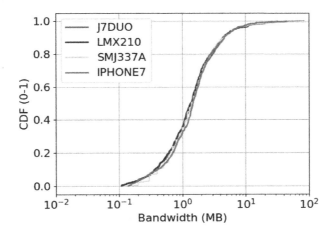

Fig. 9. CDF of bandwidth consumption.

content, or consent forms that tend to be more prevalent in Europe due to the General Data Protection Regulation (GDPR) [16].

Figure 10 shows the CDF of the energy (J) consumed across websites, measured on each device. The J7DUO is by far the most power hungry device consuming, on average, 50% more energy than both Android and the iOS devices— a trend that has previously been observed during benchmarking (see Fig. 6). A more similar trend is instead shared by the other devices, with most websites (~80%) consuming between 10 and 20 J. The main differences can be observed in the tail of the distributions (10–20%) where the results start to diverge.

For completeness, we also analyze the CPU utilization during the test. We focus on Android only since, due to OS restrictions, it was not possible to obtain the CPU traces. We sample the CPU utilization every 3 s during each website load and report the 25th, 50th, and 75th percentile, respectively. Figure 10 summarizes this analysis as boxplots (across websites) for each percentile and device. An intuitive way to read this plot is to consider that low CPU values (25th percentile) refer to times before and after the CPU load, while the high CPU values (75th percentile) refer to times when the webpage was loaded. We observe that LMX210 and SMJ33, despite mounting similar hardware (see Table 2), exhibit different CPU usages, with SMJ33 spending overall more time at higher CPU utilization. The reason behind this are manifold, e.g., different OS versions and vendors. As expected, J7DUO suffers from less CPU pressure thank to its overall higher resources.

To conclude, BatteryLab allows to measure websites power consumption (and more) at unprecedented scale, in term of number of websites, devices, and network conditions. This opens up a new set of interesting research questions that we hope will appeal to the broader research community.

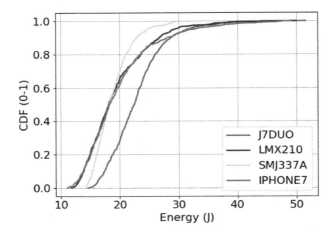

Fig. 10. CDF of power consumption.

6   Related Work

Several commercial products—such as AWS Device Farm [4], Microsoft App-Center [26], and Samsung Remote Test Labs [37]—could leverage BatteryLab's ideas to match our capabilities in a paid/centralized fashion. The same is true for startups like GreenSpector [20] and Mobile Enerlytics [27], which offer software-based battery testing on few devices.

In the research world, MONROE [1] is the only measurement platform sharing some similarities with BatteryLab. This is a platform for experimentation in operational mobile networks in Europe. MONROE currently has presence in 4 countries with 150 *nodes*, which are ad-hoc hardware configurations [28] designed for cellular measurements. BatteryLab is an orthogonal measurement platform to MONROE since it targets commercial devices (Android and iOS) and fine-grained battery measurements. The latter requires specific instrumentation (bulky power meters) that cannot be easily added to MONROE nodes, especially the mobile ones. Nevertheless, we are exploring BattOr [38], a portable power meter, to enhance BatteryLab with mobility support.

Last but not least, BatteryLab offers full access to test devices via a regular browser. This feature was inspired by [2], where the authors build a platform to grant access to an Android emulator via the browser to "crowdsource" human inputs for mobile apps. We leverage the same concept but also further extend it to actual devices and not emulators only. Further, remote access is just one tool in BatteryLab's toolbox and not our main contribution (Fig. 11).

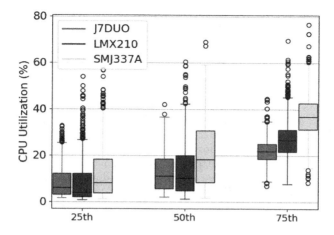

Fig. 11. Boxplot with percentiles of CPU usage.

7   Conclusion

This paper has presented BatteryLab, a collaborative platform for high-accuracy battery measurements where members contribute hardware resources (e.g., some phones and a power monitor) in exchange for access to the resources contributed by other platform members. To achieve this, we have built a complete prototyping suite which enables *remote power testing* for both Android and iOS devices. By releasing our code and setup, we invite the community to join BatteryLab, or at least we offer to eliminate the frustration associated with building "yet-another" home-grown performance measurement test-bed.

BatteryLab currently counts three vantage points, one in Europe and two in the US, hosting overall three Android devices and one iPhone 7. We evaluated BatteryLab with respect to its accuracy of battery readings, system performance, and platform heterogeneity. We show that BatteryLab's hardware and software have, for the most part, no impact on the accuracy of battery readings – when compared with a "local" setup. This is not true when visual remote access to the device is required, e.g., for *usability* testing. However, BatteryLab allows to "record and replay" usability tests which still offer accurate readings.

Towards the end of the paper, we also demonstrated how to design and run large scale measurements via BatteryLab. As an example, we have conducted, to the best of our knowledge, the largest scale measurement study of energy consumption on the Web, encompassing Alexa's top 1,000 websites measured from four devices on both Android and iOS. We have further released a web application integrated with BatteryLab which allows to measure the power consumption of a website, in real time.

Acknowledgment. This work was partially supported by the EPSRC Databox and DADA grants (EP/N028260/1, EP/R03351X/1).

References

1. Alay, Ö., et al.: Experience: an open platform for experimentation with commercial mobile broadband networks. In: Proceedings of the ACM MobiCom (2017)
2. Almeida, M., et al.: Chimp: crowdsourcing human inputs for mobile phones. In: Proceedings of the WWW (2018)
3. Amazon Inc.: Amazon Mechanical Turk (2022). https://www.mturk.com/
4. Amazon Inc.: AWS Device Farm (2022). https://aws.amazon.com/device-farm/
5. Amazon Inc.: Route 53 DNS (2022). https://aws.amazon.com/route53/
6. Appetize: Run native mobile apps in your browser (2022). https://appetize.io/
7. Apple Inc.: SharePlay (2021). https://developer.apple.com/shareplay/
8. Apple Inc.: How to AirPlay video and mirror your device's screen (2022). https://support.apple.com/HT204289
9. BatteryLab: Batterylab tutorial for new members (2022). https://batterylab.dev/tutorial/blab-tutorial.pdf
10. BatteryLab: The Web power monitor (2022). https://batterylab.dev/test-website.html
11. Bluetooth SIG Inc: Human Interface Device (HID) Profile (2022). https://www.bluetooth.com/specifications/profiles-overview/
12. BlueZ Project: BlueZ: Official Linux Bluetooth protocol stack (2022). http://www.bluez.org
13. Bui, D.H., Liu, Y., Kim, H., Shin, I., Zhao, F.: Rethinking energy-performance trade-off in mobile web page loading. In: Proceedings of the ACM MobiCom (2015)
14. Cao, Y., Nejati, J., Wajahat, M., Balasubramanian, A., Gandhi, A.: Deconstructing the energy consumption of the mobile page load. In: Proceedings of the ACM on Measurement and Analysis of Computing Systems, vol. 1, no. 1, pp. 6:1–6:25 (2017)
15. Chen, X., Ding, N., Jindal, A., Hu, Y.C., Gupta, M., Vannithamby, R.: Smartphone energy drain in the wild: analysis and implications. In: Proceedings of the ACM SIGMETRICS (2015)
16. Data protection: Rules for the protection of personal data inside and outside the EU (2022). https://ec.europa.eu/info/law/law-topic/data-protection_en
17. Florian Draschbacher: RPiPlay - An open-source AirPlay mirroring server for the Raspberry Pi (2022). https://github.com/FD-/RPiPlay
18. Genymobile: Display and control your Android device (2022). https://github.com/Genymobile/scrcpy
19. Google Inc.: Android Debug Bridge (2022). https://developer.android.com/studio/command-line/adb
20. Greenspector: Test in the cloud with real mobile devices (2022). https://greenspector.com/en/
21. Hwang, C., et al.: Raven: perception-aware optimization of power consumption for mobile games. In: Proceedings of the ACM MobiCom (2017)
22. Jenkins: The leading open source automation server (2022). https://jenkins.io/
23. Let's Encrypt: A a free, automated, and open Certificate Authority (2022). https://letsencrypt.org
24. Leung, C., Ren, J., Choffnes, D., Wilson, C.: Should you use the app for that?: comparing the privacy implications of app- and web-based online services. In: Proceedings of the ACM IMC (2016)
25. Varvello, M., Katevas, K.: BatteryLab Source Code (2022). https://github.com/svarvel/batterylab

26. Microsoft, Visual Studio: App Center is mission control for apps (2022). https://appcenter.ms/sign-in
27. Mobile Enerlytics: The Leader in Automated App Testing Innovations to Reduce Battery Drain (2022). http://mobileenerlytics.com/
28. MONROE - H2022-ICT-11-2014: Measuring Mobile Broadband Networks in Europe (2022). https://www.monroe-project.eu/wp-content/uploads/2017/12/Deliverable-D2.2-Node-Deployment.pdf
29. Monsoon Solutions Inc.: High voltage power monitor (2022). https://www.msoon.com
30. Monsoon Solutions Inc.: Monsoon Power Monitor Python Library (2022). https://github.com/msoon/PyMonsoon
31. noVNC: A VNC client JavaScript library as well as an application built on top of that library (2022). https://novnc.com
32. Onwuzurike, L., De Cristofaro, E.: Danger is my middle name: experimenting with SSL vulnerabilities in Android apps. In: WiSec (2015)
33. ProtonVPN: High-speed Swiss VPN that safeguards your privacy (2022). https://protonvpn.com/
34. Raspberry Pi: Raspberry Pi 3 Model B+ (2022). https://www.raspberrypi.org/products/raspberry-pi-3-model-b-plus/
35. Ren, J., Rao, A., Lindorfer, M., Legout, A., Choffnes, D.: Recon: revealing and controlling PII leaks in mobile network traffic. In: MobiSys (2016)
36. RunThatApp: Enjoy Mobile Apps In The Browser (2022). https://runthatapp.com
37. Samsung: Remote Test Lab (2022). https://developer.samsung.com/remote-test-lab
38. Schulman, A., Schmid, T., Dutta, P., Spring, N.: Phone power monitoring with battor. In: Proceedings of the ACM MobiCom (2011)
39. TeamViewer GmbH.: TeamViewer (2022). https://www.teamviewer.com/
40. Thiagarajan, N., Aggarwal, G., Nicoara, A., Boneh, D., Singh, J.P.: Who killed my battery?: analyzing mobile browser energy consumption. In: Proceedings of WWW (2012)
41. TigerVNC: A high-performance, platform-neutral implementation of VNC (Virtual Network Computing) (2022). https://tigervnc.org
42. USB Implementers' Forum: Universal Serial Bus HID Usage Tables (2022). https://www.usb.org/document-library/hid-usage-tables-112
43. Mikhailov, V.: uhubctl - USB hub per-port power control (2022). https://github.com/mvp/uhubctl
44. Varvello, M., Katevas, K., Plesa, M., Haddadi, H., Livshits, B.: Batterylab, a distributed power monitoring platform for mobile devices. In: HotNets (2019)
45. Webpagetest: Test website performance (2022). https://www.webpagetest.org/
46. Wittenburg, P., Brugman, H., Russel, A., Klassmann, A., Sloetjes, H.: Elan: a professional framework for multimodality research. In: LREC, vol. 2006 (2006)

GPS-Based Geolocation of Consumer IP Addresses

James Saxon$^{(\boxtimes)}$ and Nick Feamster

University of Chicago, Chicago, IL 60637, USA
{jsaxon,feamster}@uchicago.edu

Abstract. This paper uses two commercial datasets of IP addresses from smartphones, geolocated through the Global Positioning System (GPS), to characterize the geography of IP addresses from mobile and broadband ISPs. Datasets that geolocate IP addresses based on GPS offer superlative accuracy and precision for IP geolocation and thus provide an unprecedented opportunity to understand both the accuracy of existing geolocation databases as well as other properties of IP addresses, such as mobility and churn. We focus our analysis on three large cities in the United States.

After evaluating the accuracy of existing geolocation databases, we analyze the circumstances under which IP geolocation databases may be more or less accurate. Within our sample, we find that geolocation databases are more accurate on fixed-line than mobile networks, that IP addresses on university networks can be more accurately located than those from consumer or business networks, and that often the paid versions of these databases are not significantly more accurate than the free versions. Addresses on /24 subnets that are geographically concentrated are geolocated more accurately. We then characterize how quickly /24 subnets associated with fixed-line networks change geographic locations, and how long residential broadband ISP subscribers retain individual IP addresses. We find, generally, that most IP address assignments are stable over two months, although stability does vary across ISPs. Finally, we evaluate the suitability of existing IP geolocation databases for understanding Internet access and performance in human populations within specific geographies and demographics. Although the median accuracy of IP geolocation is better than 3 km in some contexts – fixed-line connections in New York City, for instance – we conclude that relying on IP geolocation databases to understand Internet access in densely populated regions such as cities is premature.

1 Introduction

IP geolocation is a longstanding problem in computer networking, with both an active academic research and a wide array of commercial solutions and applications. IP geolocation is used for a variety of purposes, including mapping clients to nearby content delivery network (CDN) replicas, personalization of search results and advertising, and customization of content (e.g., weather or language

O. Hohlfeld et al. (Eds.): PAM 2022, LNCS 13210, pp. 122–151, 2022.
https://doi.org/10.1007/978-3-030-98785-5_6

localization). In a legal context, IP geolocation is used for digital rights management (e.g., geographic licensing restrictions), compliance with the laws and regulations of a region or country (e.g., gambling, sales taxes, privacy regulations), and to assist with law enforcement (e.g., determining jurisdictions or collecting evidence). In security contexts, government and commercial entities use it for counter-terrorism, attack attribution, monitoring access to private networks, and detecting potential fraud. It facilitates operations and site reliability (e.g., monitoring packet loss from a location), and informs infrastructure investments by both industry and policymakers [2,9,12,19,25,29]. Computer science researchers also use IP geolocation to study the properties and evolution of the network itself, such as the structure and graph parameters of networks [6,28].

Increasingly, IP geolocation is being used to address various problems in *policy and social science* that entail drawing inferences about various demographics and geographies based on inferred locations of IP addresses. Social scientists have noted the potential to use "big data" as a lens on human behaviors and interactions [18], and as modern society is increasingly mediated through the Internet, many of our interactions are associated with IP addresses. Server logs and speed measurements, for instance, show who accesses resources and the quality of their connections. This allows aggregate statistics or time trends. But associating these behaviors and network conditions with human populations ultimately requires a way to map IP addresses to physical locations. A natural approach would be to use IP geolocation with census tract-scale precision to link IP addresses to physical locations. In this paper, we leverage reference locations of unprecedented geographic precision to evaluate whether free and paid IP geolocation databases can achieve this level of accuracy in large cities in the United States. We also extend past work by analyzing the determinants of IP geolocation accuracy – the IP addresses for which geolocation is or is not reliable. We then interpret these findings with a view towards social research, describing *who* gets lost from a naïve reliance on IP geolocation, and what the consequences might be for academic or policy analysis.

The accuracy of IP geolocation databases has practical implications for the answers to a wide range of social and public policy questions. One area of particular timeliness is that of the so-called "digital divide." Calls for digital equity and inclusion, already urgent, have reached a fever pitch during the COVID-19 pandemic. Prominent studies of broadband performance from Microsoft and M-Lab rely on IP geolocation to associate Internet throughput and latencies with zip codes [17,24]. Ganelin and Chuang studied whether or not geolocation databases could reliably indicate socioeconomic status of MOOC registrants with known physical addresses. That study ultimately concluded, as will we, that answering such questions based on existing IP geolocation databases is premature [7].

We revisit this problem now, due both to its practical implications, and thanks to the availability of two highly-accurate and large-scale groundtruth datasets of GPS-located IP addresses. These datasets, from Unacast and Ookla® Speedtest Intelligence®, afford us a view of consumer behaviors on both fixed-line and mobile networks, that is markedly different from the geolocation targets used in past work.

Table 1. Main findings, with pointers to sections.

§	Main findings
4.1	GPS reports are a credible groundtruth of IP locations
4.2	MaxMind's GeoIP2 service provides the lowest median error among tested services and cities: 2.62 km on fixed-line addresses in NYC
5.1	IP geolocation performs better on fixed-line consumer networks and universities, and worse on mobile broadband and businesses
5.2	The physical size of subnets is correlated with the accuracy with which they are IP geolocated
5.3	On the two-month time-scale, the median fixed-line /24 IPv4 subnet in US cities moves less than 1 km
5.4	Churn of individual IP addresses on fixed-line networks in major US cities takes months
6	Access modalities – mobiled vs fixed – differ between demographic groups. Even on fixed-line networks, relying on IP geolocation to identify neighborhoods would lead to biased results

Table 1 lists our main findings. The rest of this paper is organized as follows. Section 2 discusses related work in IP geolocation, both in research and in commercial product offerings. Section 3 describes the datasets that we use for the analysis in this paper. Section 4 evaluates the quality of the datasets that we are using, in particular exploring the suitability of using GPS data as a "ground truth" for evaluating IP geolocation databases. Section 5 presents the result of our study, including findings about the circumstances under which IP geolocation is more or less accurate. In Sect. 6, we interpret and extend our results in the context of research on human populations and privacy. We conclude in Sect. 7.

2   Related Work

Past work on IP geolocation generally takes three approaches, as outlined by Padmanabhan and Subramanian [23]. Their IP Geolocation work, IP2Geo, compared the complementary strengths of active latency measurements (GeoPing), active traceroutes paired with DNS hints (GeoTrack), and static databases of outside information (GeoCluster). Each of these approaches has evolved. Padmanabhan and Subramanian concluded that database-driven methods held the greatest promise. Commercial products have accordingly built databases with proprietary methods that include registry information, outside data, and active methods. On the other hand, academic work has tended to focus on active and DNS-based measurements.

IP Geolocation Methods. Starting with DNS, Spring et al. developed techniques in their Rocketfuel project to map infrastructure (i.e., routers) to physical locations. A significant contribution was to optimize traceroute targets to minimize redundancy and ensure that each path will traverse its target ISP [28], although their use of the DNS to geolocate routers was pioneering at the time. Their subsequent approach to DNS hint identification was largely manual – "browsing through the list of router names" – but the resultant undns tool has proven influential and enduring. Freedman et al. extended undns' coverage [6]. These projects were driven by questions about properties of the network, specifically the topology of large ISPs and the efficiency of block assignments in BGP routing tables. More recently, Dan et al. [2] attempted to enumerate all possible DNS city name hints and finalize location decisions with machine learning. Like IP2Geo, the authors relied on a large dataset from Microsoft for their ground truth, although the ground truth data was from Bing instead of Hotmail.

In the latency-based space, Gueye et al. [12] and Katz-Bassett et al. [15] introduced constraint-based geolocation (CBG) and topology-based geolocation (TBG). CBG is essentially the intersection of several latency-derived distance buffers, while TPG also localizes intermediate hosts so that targets can be constrained by their relation to passive landmarks rather than just active probes. Subsequently, Octant incorporated both positive *and negative* constraints (the IP address is *not* within a certain radius) [30].

In addition to this "geometric" approach are several statistical strategies. Eriksson and colleagues, developed first a Bayesian approach and then a likelihood-driven choice among possibilities with the CBG-derived regions [3,4]. Other work presents strategies using kernel density and maximum likelihood estimation [1,31]. It is also possible to constrain location from the covariance matrix of latency measurements with locations.

Notable in Eriksson's Bayesian work is the insight that outside information can help constrain or inform geolocation. They used population as a measure of places' importance, as have later researchers [2]. Other forms of information help as well. In trace-based work reminiscent of TPG, Wang et al. performed extensive webscraping and analysis to identify and confirm businesses with locally-hosted sites that they could "enlist" as passive landmarks. They used those landmarks to identify the locations of routers near the geolocation target [29].

Scalability has long been a limitation of active measurements. Since locations are most-constrained by the closest locations, Hu et al. developed methods to prioritize measurements from nearby hosts, effectively by localizing avatars from subnets [13]. Alternatively, Li et al. "flip" the standard infrastructure of active geolocation with GeoGet: the targets to be localized measure the latency themselves, through javascript, rather than generating pings through an API [19]. This reduces the number of servers and traffic required, and it is also helpful since clients' devices or networks may fail to respond to pings or complete traceroutes.

Evaluating Commercial Services. These advances notwithstanding, commercial geolocation tends to be implemented through databases, which are inexpensive to distribute and can aggregate historical observations across many sources. The leading services—MaxMind, IP2Location, Akamai, or NetAcuity—all use proprietary methods. A number of papers assess the performance of these databases, comparing with the preceding active methods [11], points-of-presence paired with routing tables from a large ISP [25], DNS lookups paired with ground truth rules from domain operators [8], from RIPE ATLAS built-in measurements, or PlanetLab nodes, or against each other, sometimes with a majority logic applied. The databases are themselves often taken as the ground truth for latency-based measurements often with a sort of majority logic. Shavitt and Zilberman employ that strategy in evaluating the databases themselves, but also focus on *consistency* among addresses determined to share a point-of-presence, based on an earlier algorithm [5,27]. Similarly, Huffaker et al. assess the agreement of country determinations and distances from a centroid, from majority votes (supplemented by PlanetLab ground-truth and limited round-trip time measurements) [14].

On the whole, both the formal literature and "popular wisdom" paint a fairly pessimistic picture of geolocation performance. Research studies from about ten years ago assessed median accuracy of these services at 25 km in Western Europe and 100 km in the United States. On the commercial side, Poese et al. quote median accuracies between tens and hundreds of kilometers for MaxMind and IP2Location [25]. Other early works present distributions with ranges between hundreds or thousands of kilometers [27]. Gharaibeh et al. present results for routers in particular, with median accuracies between 10 km for NetAcuity and 1,000 km for IP2Location, on either extreme of the free and paid versions of MaxMind. More recently, Dan et al. presented medians between 10 and 30 km, depending on the sample and service. [2] They present results in 10 km bins and do not differentiate performance at the very bottom of the range.

Studies of How Internet Infrastructure Affects Geolocation Accuracy. A persistent though somewhat more subtle current of the literature has explored the physical structure of the Internet and its relation to geolocation accuracy. Padmanabhan and Subramanian anticipated the interplay between network infrastructure and geolocation accuracy in 2001 [23]. They noted the impact of the geographical concentration of AOL's login nodes on accuracy, and showed that clusters of addresses that were physically larger were associated with poorer performance for the GeoCluster (database) method. This point was echoed in 2007 by Gueye et al. [11] Similarly, Freedman et al. measured the physical scale of autonomous systems. Later, Gharaibeh et al. probed the common assumption of databases that /24 subnets are co-located [11] Those papers show that systems, subnets, and IP prefixes advertised by the Border Gateway Protocol (BGP) can span large physical distances. In this paper, we seek to extend this work, aiming to identify the circumstances when they are large or small. Huffaker et al. characterized accuracy according to carriers' network role; we extend that line of exploration in this research, exploring how accuracy varies between commercial ISPs, large companies, and universities. We categorize addresses by "Doing-Business As" names reported in IP address registries; to our knowledge, such a characterization is unprecedented, at least in the current era where mobile devices are significantly more prevalent than they were a decade ago.

In addition to work on IP address *locations*, our data also shed light on the persistence of dynamically assigned IP addresses, itself an active area of analysis. Recent works have used RIPE Atlas probes [16,21], javascript-based user monitoring by a large CDN [22], and browser extensions [20] to study address retention times. Times range from nearly-ephemeral on mobile networks, to many months for fixed-line connections in the North America. The retention times we observe are broadly consistent with previous findings for North America.

Finally, our project is informed by recent work on Carrier-Grade Network Address Translation (CG-NAT). CG-NATs are increasingly common across all ISPs, but almost ubiquitous on mobile carriers [26]. Since we geolocate public IP addresses, it stands to reason that the geolocation accuracy of devices behind a CG-NAT cannot be more precise than the basic spatial scale over which a public address is used. Nevertheless, the physical extent of CG-NATs' structures have not been studied. Public IP addresses could map to limited geographic locations like antennas, or to larger ones like cities.

How this Paper Extends Past Work. Past work that evaluates IP geolocation accuracy has tended to rely either on active measurements of somewhat coarse precision, or on a fairly consistent set of (unrepresentative) benchmarks: specifically, PlanetLab sites and university clusters. The dataset we rely on for this paper of course has its own peculiarities—it is a non-random sample of mobile devices— but this view from the access network, including mobile devices, is critical and distinctive from past studies. It is a large sample, indicative of realistic consumer geolocation targets in major cities in the United States. The Global Positioning System (GPS) has long served as a counterpoint to IP geolocation, both as a benchmark of accuracy and as an analog in multilateration. Historically, its deployment and use for Internet measurement felt impossibly far off [3,4,15], but the future has now arrived.

This paper complements and extends previous work as a result of its large sample of consumer smartphone locations on diverse networks. The primary dataset was provided by Unacast; we confirm our basic findings with a smaller, Chicago-only sample of GPS-located Speedtest® data from Ookla®. Similar datasets are readily available for commercial applications and academic research. We exploit this sample to understand how IP geolocation accuracy varies by geography, carrier, mode of access, and other factors. In contrast to previous work, which has tended to question the overall reliability of geolocation even at country-level accuracy, we find that it works fairly well in predictable and well-defined contexts. Nevertheless, the imperfect accuracy and context-specific performance still currently constrain the applicability of IP geolocation for studying Internet access by human populations.

3   The Data

This paper relies on two commercial datasets with GPS-tagged IP addresses to analyze the geography of consumer IP addresses. We also evaluate and analyze the performance of databases for IP geolocation from two popular, commercial services: IP2Location and MaxMind from the same time periods. Table 2 lists the datasets that we use, and Fig. 1 illustrates how these datasets are joined and augmented in our analysis.

Table 2. Data sources: geographic and temporal coverage, and data volumes (for GPS data only).

	Geography	Date	Location reports
Unacast Clusters	NYC, Chi., Phl	Aug-Oct 2020	248M
	+ 40 mi buffer	Apr 2021	9.5M
Speedtest Intelligence	Chicago Region	2020	4M
MaxMind Free	Global	Aug 2020	–
	Global	Apr 2021	–
MaxMind Paid	North America	Apr 2021	–
IP2Location Free	Global	Aug 2020	–
	Global	Apr 2021	–
IP2Location Paid	Global	Apr 2021	–

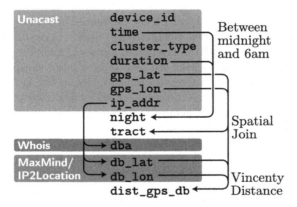

Fig. 1. Simplified illustration of the data augmentation process, for Unacast data. The fundamental data consist of device identifiers, times, locations, and IP addresses. Clusters (see text) are also labelled by type, for instance, TRAVEL or LONG_AREA_DWELL. The time and duration are used to construct a flag for night-time clusters. The IP address is used with the ARIN whois resource to construct Doing Business As (DBA) names, and database-defined locations are retrieved from up to four databases by MaxMind and IP2Location. Vincenty distances are calculated between database and GPS locations

The GPS data were delivered anonymized and remain so. The data were collected in accordance with local laws and opt-out policies (GDPR), and analyzed with approval from our university's Institutional Review Board (IRB). The IRB approved analysis of reconstructed "home locations" for earlier work, but emphasized the sensitivity of doing so. For that reason, we avoided geographic analysis of individual devices in this project, and proxied "residence" simply as activities recorded at night.

3.1   Unacast GPS Smartphone Locations

The primary dataset used for the analysis is from Unacast, a location intelligence firm. This dataset contains GPS locations reported by mobile devices, along with timestamps and unique, anonymous identifiers. Unacast aggregates multiple location data streams from other firms; they perform extensive data validation, de-duplication, and processing on those streams. The exact applications that generate locations are not provided. The share of data reporting IANA reserved or private addresses is low, at 0.5%, and the share of addresses associated with foreign Internet registries totals just 0.2% (mostly RIPE, breakdown shown in the Appendix). The traffic observed in the Unacast dataset is overwhelmingly IPv4, at 99.6%.

We were provided with data for three major cities in the United States: New York, Chicago, and Philadelphia. Data were drawn from a 40 mile buffer of each city's boundaries; this large buffer encompasses both urban and rural populations. Two samples were provided in time. The first was from August–October 2020. A second, shorter period from April 2021 was provided to align with licenses for paid geolocation databases, allowing us to evaluate the accuracy of those services. As discussed below, the IP address from which a physical location is reported is recorded for about half of clusters in the 2020 sample, although this falls to just 15% in the 2021 sample. Data are used only when they contain an IP address, and the full dataset thus offers IP addresses recorded at over 248 million locations. Of course, individual IP addresses may be reported many times.

The data also report an estimate of the GPS-based location accuracy; the median reported accuracy is 17 meters on the 2020 sample and 11 meters on the 2021 sample. A small fraction of data (1.7%) are recorded with four or fewer decimal points of coordinate precision, corresponding to a physical distance of about 10 m. We exclude these data from subsequent analyses, along with location reports with estimated accuracy worse than 50 m. We also exclude the small fraction of addresses associated with private IP ranges and foreign NICs. These requirements do change the "Universe" of data included in the analyses that follow, and may impact CDFs.

Location Clustering and Classifications. Each line of data represents a *cluster* of location reports, called *bumps*. Clusters are built by combining bumps from an individual device that are close in both time and space, using Unacast's proprietary algorithm. That algorithm uses machine learning to account for variation in physical scale among locations: a mall is larger than a coffee shop or a home. Clusters are labelled according to their durations, which are also reported. Locations recorded during movement are labelled as TRAVEL. See the Appendix for a listing of cluster frequencies. This clustering reduces the data volume by a factor of 20 while retaining most of the information. Just as important, Unacast's data licenses with *its* suppliers often preclude re-licensing the raw, un-clustered data.

The clustering entails some subtlety: a single physical location and IP address is reported per cluster, and thus the centroid of a TRAVEL cluster may not exactly coincide with the moment that the reported IP address was used. Indeed, the physical location of a consumer IP address is often not fixed; for instance, consumers can roam freely through their home while connected to their Wi-Fi. In practice, individual IP addresses are recorded at many physical locations—and these locations may be close or distant from each other.

Flagging Night-time Activity. We augment the provided data in several ways, illustrated in Fig. 1. As a means of selecting residential location reports, we flag clusters generated at night. Night-time clusters are those for which the period between the first and last bumps extends into the hours between midnight to 6am of any day. These clusters represent just 4.7% of clusters but 26% of bumps. Only 18% of devices have at least one night-time cluster, but those devices generate the vast majority of the data: 80% of clusters and 88% of bumps. In short, weighted by data volume, most devices have observations at times when they can reasonably be assumed to be at home. For the set of devices with night-time clusters, the ratio of devices to the population of the study region is about one device for every 20 people.

Identifying ISPs. To investigate the determinants of geolocation accuracy, we also identify ISPs. Each address is associated with its /24 subnet, whose organization is retrieved from the ARIN whois registry, on September 1 2020, or April 25 2021. If the prefix size of the associated CIDR block exceeds 24 on IPv4 or 48 on IPv6, we follow whois' link to the "parent" network. This strategy is similar in intent to an ASN lookup, and we include an ASN-based breakdown of ISPs in the Appendix. The whois look-up differs in practice primarily in superior coverage of the Department of Defense NIC and wireless carriers (AT&T and T-Mobile), especially for the RouteViews databases from August 2020. Further, the ASN lookup also "fractures" organizations like small city governments or businesses from their providers. We associate large and common organizations with standardized "Doing Business As" (DBA) names, taking particular care to capture the major ISPs in each market (Comcast, Charter, etc.). We separate AT&T's and Verizon's mobile broadband from their fixed offerings based on the words "Mobility" or "Wireless" in the organization name. This may not be a perfect division: "Verizon Business" and "AT&T Services" may include mobile offerings, but examining the ASN tables suggests this is not their primary use. It is worth noting that the sample is dominated by locations recorded while connected through mobile providers: there are ten times as many locations on AT&T mobile than AT&T fixed-line services, and more than five times as many on Verizon mobile than Verizon fixed-line. However, as we will separate addresses by ISP, this sample volume effect is largely "partitioned out." Ultimately, each address is associated with a single DBA name for analysis.

These procedures also identify large companies and institutions, in particular, universities. We flag addresses from universities with at least ten thousand students, and Fortune 100 companies. University clusters are "classic" targets for academic work on geolocation, since they have meaningful and well-known locations, but they are not representative of the consumer space. We exclude ISPs, including Google, from the Fortune 100 set. We tabulate IANA special use and non-ARIN addresses, as checks on the underlying data, but exclude these from subsequent analysis.

3.2 Geolocated Ookla Speedtest Data

In addition to the data from Unacast, we have obtained Speedtest data from Ookla. The data are for tests performed on smartphones, again with locations from GPS. This dataset is substantially smaller, and is limited in geographic extent to the counties surrounding Chicago. We appeal to these data as a cross-check of the Unacast data that, though more voluminous, were not designed for this work.

We have received over 4 million individual Speedtest measurements for 2020, though only 270 thousand match the period of the study (August 2020). Unlike Unacast data, each location comes from a single moment in time (it is not a cluster). On the other hand, the Speedtest data include only the first three bytes of the IP address, due to privacy restrictions. We rely on Ookla's coding of Internet Service Providers.

3.3 Geolocation Databases and Distances

We obtain the free versions of the MaxMind and IP2Location databases, for August 1, 2020. We also acquire both the free and paid versions of these databases from April 26, 2021. The NetAcuity and Akamai geolocation services, which are much more expensive, are not included in this work. Using these databases, we geolocate IP addresses from the GPS sample. Per the license, this is done only for the months of GPS data matching the databases (August 2020 and April 2021). A recent review showed that MaxMind is by far the most-used database in the academic literature. It also found that databases change non-negligibly over short periods and emphasized that precision with respect to dates is imperative [10].

We then measure the Vincenty distance (on the ellipsoid of Earth) from each IP-geolocated point to the location recorded by the GPS-enabled device. For most of what follows, we take the centroids of the GPS clusters as the "ground truth" and call the entire distance the "accuracy" or "error." Since the database providers acknowledge their limited resolution and in certain cases quantify it accurately, this language is perhaps unfair: it is different for a database to acknowledge a location as unknown or indeterminate (as in reserved, private addresses) than to be "wrong" about the location. Moreover, the GPS data themselves do have some limitations, noted below. Semantics aside, the balance of this work tabulates distances with respect to the ground truth and seeks to explain their heterogeneity.

4 Evaluating Data Quality

Before coming to questions about the properties of consumer IP addresses, we analyze the quality of our data. We first explore the consistency of the GPS-based location data we obtain from Unacast and Ookla by comparing the data against each other, with respect to geolocation databases.

4.1 Are GPS Data a Credible Ground Truth of IP Address Locations?

The accuracy of IP geolocation is central to Unacast's core business, and the company dedicates enormous resources to validating and maintaining their incoming data streams. While GPS data from smartphones is generally understood to be accurate, datasets from smartphone-based services do often incorporate additional data to assist with locating devices in circumstances where GPS does not work (e.g., indoors). Thus, while we expect these GPS-based datasets to be reasonably accurate in general, it behooves us to explore the quality of these datasets before proceeding with other questions. Since we aim to use these datasets as "ground truth", this analysis may seem a bit circular. Our strategy is to compare the *consistency* of IP geolocation results for different GPS contexts and across independent GPS samples (Unacast and Ookla). Of course, this analysis does not exclude the possibility of systematic errors arising in *both* GPS datasets, or across all datasets, but given the lack of further ground truths, we are left with consistency checks.

Direct cross-checks of IP addresses' locations between the two samples are not possible, because the Ookla data report /24 subnets rather than unique addresses. Many IP addresses are recorded at multiple physical locations, and in general a different set of addresses may be reported per subnet, in the two samples. Notwithstanding, the distance *can* be calculated between the medioids (the median of the x and y directions) observed for a subnet, in the two datasets. We do this for fixed-line providers in Chicago, on subnets with at least 10 distinct addresses and 10 distinct devices in the Unacast sample. If we weight subnets by the geometric mean of the number of observations in the two samples, the distance between their medioids is less than 2.5 km for 58% of subnets and less than 5 km for 83% of subnets.

Evaluating Cluster Types. The correspondence between GPS coordinates and the physical location of its IP address may not be perfect. For example, we expect that the clustering procedures could affect the "compatibility" of the IP address and GPS location. Further, if a GPS location is recorded when no network is available, it may be subsequently *reported* at a different physical location where an IP address can be obtained. We would expect these effects to be most severe for TRAVEL clusters, as previously discussed. The flip side of this argument is that navigation applications are more likely to be active during TRAVEL. These apps record location more frequently, which could *improve* accuracy.

To evaluate the effects of imperfect knowledge of locations, stemming from these effects, we contrast TRAVEL clusters with others. We will show below that geolocation performance differs by network. Obviously, it is easier to "travel" when connected to a mobile than fixed-line network. We therefore focus this

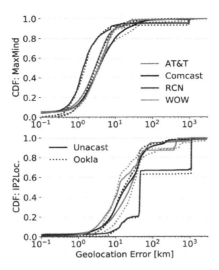

Fig. 2. Geolocation error of GPS location targets in Chicago, on both Unacast and Ookla Speedtest Intelligence® data, (Based on the authors' analysis of Ookla® Speedtest Intelligence® data for August 2020 in Chicago. Ookla trademarks used under license and reprinted with permission.) using the free versions of the MaxMind and IP2Location databases for August 2020.

check on a single, mobile network: AT&T Mobility. We do observe that accuracy is worse for travel than non-travel data, but the difference at the median is only about 2.5%, for either IP2Location or MaxMind. As can be seen in the Appendix, the cumulative distribution functions for travel and non-travel clusters are fairly close across their entire domain.

Analysis of Independent Samples. To further validate the GPS data, we contrast data from Unacast with Ookla, for fixed-line broadband ISPs, in Chicago and August 2020, where both datasets are available and aligned with the free versions of the geolocation databases. Figure 2 shows these results: the CDF of location reports as a function of geolocation accuracy. MaxMind performs somewhat better on Comcast addresses from the Ookla dataset than the Unacast data, and somewhat worse on AT&T; RCN and WOW! are very consistent. Discrepancies are somewhat larger on IP2Location as is comparative performance by the two databases.

One notable feature in the 2020 Unacast dataset is a small but non-negligible share of the data with IP geolocation "error" *very* close to zero. Depending on the ISP, that share is 4–5% of the fixed-line locations on MaxMind and 1–2% of those on IP2Location. On close inspection, these appear to be locations reported by applications *relying on the IP Geolocation services themselves*, rather than true GPS coordinates. For example, these ultra- "accurate" locations are not at residences, as one might expect for fixed-line ISPs, but in parks, as is MaxMind's practice for default locations [16, 20]. The share of "too-close" locations is smaller

Table 3. Quantiles of accuracy in kilometers, for each database and city.

Quantiles	New York				Chicago				Philadelphia			
	MaxMind		IP2Loc.		MaxMind		IP2Loc.		MaxMind		IP2Loc.	
	Paid	Free	Paid	Free	Paid	Free	Paid	Free	Paid	Free	Paid	Free
0.10	0.7	0.8	3.0	3.0	1.0	1.0	4.6	4.7	1.1	1.2	4.2	4.2
0.25	1.4	1.5	6.1	6.1	1.8	1.9	9.8	9.9	2.1	2.3	9.0	9.0
0.50	2.6	2.8	12.0	12.1	3.3	3.6	24.0	24.3	4.0	4.3	20.9	21.0
0.75	5.0	5.5	30.1	30.5	6.4	7.1	45.6	45.7	7.6	8.2	39.6	39.7
0.90	9.7	11.0	61.8	63.0	13.0	16.1	196.4	202.9	13.5	15.0	78.3	78.8

on the 2021 clusters; however, the IP address field is populated for a lower share of those data.

However, the basic features of Fig. 2 are consistent in the completely separate sample from Ookla, which does not exhibit this feature.

4.2 Which Database Provides the Lowest Error in Location?

The practical question is which database to use, and how well it should be expected to perform. This analysis, uniquely, is performed using the April 2021 sample from Unacast, for which the paid geolocation databases were licensed. Since Sect. 5.1 will show that geolocation on mobile broadband is very poor, this analysis focusses on fixed-line broadband.

The short answer is that MaxMind's paid database, GeoIP2, provides the best accuracy, in terms of geolocation error on all quantiles. The traditional way of reporting this is the median error, which is 2.62 km in New York City, 3.31 km in Chicago, and 4.02 km in Philadelphia. Other quantiles and the other three databases are shown in Table 3. Figure 3 shows the distribution of distances by city and database. We use "city" to refer to the city itself along with the 40-mile buffer around it. Because the distance from Staten Island to North Philadelphia is only 46 miles, some data are included in the curves for both New York and Philadelphia.

Although the paid databases are more accurate in each city and at every quantile, the relative improvements in accuracy are modest. An important limitation of this particular study is our focus on urban areas in the United States. In particular, we do not test accuracy of these databases outside of major metro areas, and global or national performance may of course be different. Nonetheless, it would be possible to perform the analysis we have presented in this section for other datasets, if and when they are made available.

5 The Geography of Consumer Subnets

We now turn from an initial assessment of the dataset and databases, to measurements of the geography of the underlying networks.

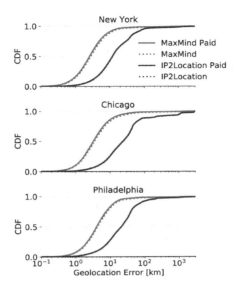

Fig. 3. Cumulative distribution function by geolocation database and city. Colors reference databases, and line styles denote paid and free versions. (Color figure online)

5.1 Under What Circumstances are IP Geolocation Databases Accurate?

The basic results of Sect. 4.2 mask extreme but unsurprising heterogeneity. Figure 3 already shows that geolocation performs better in New York than Chicago, and better in Chicago than Philadelphia. But the largest source of heterogeneity stems from providers, which deploy different physical infrastructures (and serve different cities). This entire section relies entirely on the free databases.

Fixed-Line and Mobile Networks. Figure 4 shows accuracies observed in New York, Chicago, and Philadelphia for major broadband carriers in each market. Again the CDF is the share of location reports. In the best cases, such as either RCN or Comcast on MaxMind in Chicago, the median error is less than 5 km. In each city/database pair, the accuracy is good for fixed broadband and poor for any mobile broadband. This Figure, and others in the main text, rely on ISP classification via whois, as described in Sect. 3.1. A version of this Figure based on an IP addresses' ASNs, is included in the appendix, and is very consistent.

In Chicago, MaxMind is more accurate with fixed-line (AT&T, RCN, WOW, and Comcast) than on mobile (AT&T Mobile, T-Mobile, Sprint, Verizon Mobile) carriers. (IP2Location performs poorly with RCN.) Similarly in New York, Charter, Cablevision, Comcast and Verizon are better localized than AT&T Mobile, Sprint, T-Mobile, and Verizon Mobile; and in Philadelphia, geolocation is more accurate on Comcast than Verizon, T-Mobile, AT&T Mobile, or Verizon Mobile.

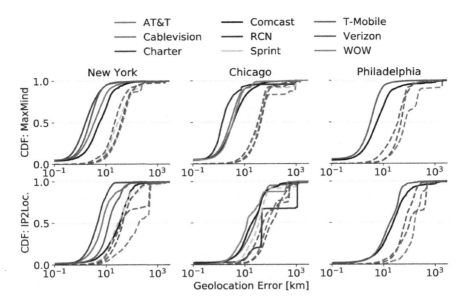

Fig. 4. Geolocation performance by city, database provider, and ISP. Free versions of the database are used in each case. ISPs are shown by their "brand" colors, according to the whois database, which leaves the Sprint and T-Mobile networks distinguishable. Fixed-line networks are denoted by solid lines while mobile networks shown by dashed lines. (Color figure online)

Quantitatively, the share of Comcast data in New York that MaxMind's free service locates within 10 km of the GPS location is 67%. At the other extreme, 87% of T-Mobile location reports from the New York region are IP geolocated to just two distinct locations representing New York itself and Newark; 98% are assigned either to those two, or to one of six other locations in Philadelphia (3), Providence, Boston, and Washington. As a result, only 18% of devices are assigned within 10 km of their true location. In fairness, it must be emphasized that MaxMind does not *claim* to assign these devices within 10 km: almost all of the T-Mobile addresses assigned to the New York and Newark locations are in the 200 km accuracy class.

This basic dichotomy between mobile and fixed broadband is apparent even within ISPs. AT&T offers both services in Chicago, and the CDFs for its fixed-line and mobile services are widely separated. The individual /24 subnets with the largest geolocation errors all belong to the AT&T Mobility organization. In New York and Philadelphia, AT&T only operates mobile networks, and this is reflected in those cumulative distributions. The observation that mobile and fixed-line networks differ may appear obvious once stated, but it need not have been true. Mobile carriers could have constructed networks and CG-NATs with a fixed set of public IP addresses at each antenna. That does not appear to be what they did.

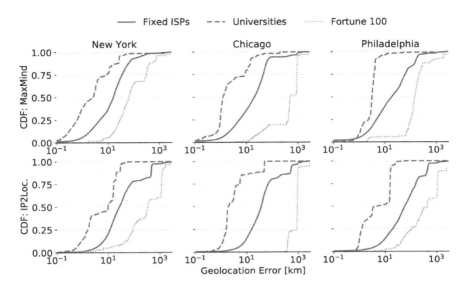

Fig. 5. Geolocation performance on consumer ISPs, contrasted with large universities and Fortune 100 companies.

Universities, Businesses, and Consumer Networks. Before continuing, we also contrast geolocation performance on consumer fixed-broadband, with large universities and companies. We include universities with at least ten thousand students, and Fortune 100 companies other than ISPs. Again, we note that we are implicitly studying the Wi-Fi access points that these institutions operate and which their employees, students, and clients connect to via mobile devices, rather than wired connections or fixed infrastructures of servers. Universities are a classic target in the academic literature on geolocation, but Fig. 5 shows that they are in general more-accurately geolocated than either consumer ISPs or companies. This is not surprising: they have large, physically-concentrated networks, with registration addresses clearly spelled out in ARIN records. In most cases, median geolocation error on MaxMind (free) is less than 2 km, though a few institutes – DePaul in Chicago and the City University of New York – are mislocated by upwards of 10 km. Note that the nominal sample period is August 2020, when students – and indeed many staff and faculty – were not on campus, due to both summer vacation and the coronavirus pandemic.

Figures 3, 4 and 5 suggest that for a substantial share of traffic, IP geolocation is quite accurate. However, this does not do us much good unless those locations can be identified in advance. It is already clear that the picture is rosier with fixed broadband. Those data can be easily identified, either via a `whois` look-up or (in some cases) through the geolocation databases themselves. But mobile and fixed is not the only lever. MaxMind is able to perform better on RCN than on Comcast in Chicago, and better on Charter or Cablevision than Comcast in New York. How are we to identify localizable blocks of addresses?

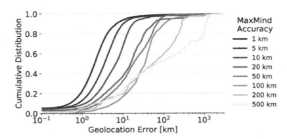

Fig. 6. Cumulative distribution of geolocation accuracy on the MaxMind database, by quoted accuracy bin.

We highlight two additional methods. MaxMind's database provides an "accuracy" field that successfully identifies the precision of entries. Figure 6 shows the CDF for successive bins of claimed accuracy on the free database. In the most precise bin, accuracy of "1 km," the median device in Chicago is geolocated just 2.0 km from the GPS-based location. The "error" with respect to the ground-truth degrades in-line with quoted accuracy, though there is enormous spread in the least-precise, 500 km bin. It is thus *possible* to identify accurately-located addresses – MaxMind does it. But this leaves an open question: *why* are those addresses well or ill-located?

That brings us to the second method. Our hypothesis is that if /24 subnets are geographically localized – small – then addresses within them are more-likely to be accurately geolocated. If they are large, then precise locations would require finer, address-level data. The question can then be re-posed: what is the physical scale of /24 subnets, and is subnet scale in fact correlated with geolocation accuracy?

5.2   What is the Geographic Scale of /24 Subnets?

What are the physical and network properties of accurately-located subnets? In this section, we analyze /24 subnets; in high density cities, where all 255 client addresses *could* credibly be assigned in a small area like a city block. Are they? We require that subnets have at least 10 devices and 10 distinct IP addresses, and focus on a single, fixed network – Comcast. Between the three cities, Comcast has over twenty thousand /24 subnets satisfying these cuts; it carries over 40% of the fixed-line traffic that we observe.

Constructing a Physical Scale. To quantify whether or not a subnet is localized, we define a characteristic physical scale. Many subnets have some outliers, perhaps with locations reported after the fact. To mitigate the impact of these outliers, we must first identify them. We compute the medioid of locations in the subnet, defined in this case simply as the median of the x and y coordinates in a projected (flat) geometry (EPSG 2163). We then measure individual locations' distances from that medioid. We select a configurable fraction f of the data that is "closest" by that measure. For that subset of the data, we calculate the convex

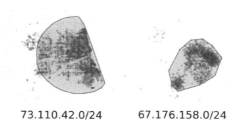

73.110.42.0/24   67.176.158.0/24

Fig. 7. Illustration of the procedure defining the physical scale of /24 subnets, for one dispersed and one well-localized subnet in Chicago. Convex hulls wrap around $f = 0.9$ of the points within the subnet. The "scale" is the square root of this area. The linear scale on the right-hand side (67.176.158.0/24) is a factor of 8 larger than on the right-hand side. Gaussian noise has been added to the locations for illustrative purposes only.

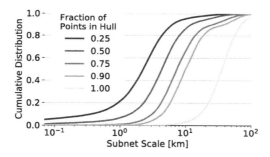

Fig. 8. Cumulative density of subnets' distance scale as derived from the convex hull of locations, as described in the text.

hull. If $f = 1$, then the convex hull covers all locations recorded on the subnet; if $f = 1/2$, it covers the half of points closest to the medioid. Finally we take the area of the convex hull, and "convert" this area to a distance by taking its square root. That square root defines the length scale of the subnet. Figure 7 illustrates this procedure for two subnets. (To preserve anonymity, random noise has been added to the individual points in the illustration.)

Figure 8 shows this distance scale for /24 subnets with at least 10 devices and addresses, for several choices of f. By construction, the scale is smaller or larger when outliers are more or less suppressed, respectively. Setting $f = 0.5$ results in a median subnet scale of 4.3 km, and $f = 0.9$ leads to a scale of 9.9 km. However, the proportion of subnets with scales exceeding 10 km is small for any choice of $f < 0.9$.

The Relationship of Physical Scale and Accuracy. Armed with this scale, we return to the earlier question: when can *addresses* be accurately located? Discarding locations with geolocation error over 100 km, the correlation is 0.69 between the $f = 0.75$ scale of /24 subnets and mean address geolocation error, for

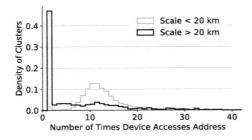

Fig. 9. The number of times a single device visits a single IP address on the subnet (weighted by visits). On subnets with scale greater than 20 km ($f = 0.75$), nearly half of visits device/IP pairs are unique.

MaxMind Free (GeoLite). However, that correlation is only 0.30 on IP2Location, which has worse performance overall. We thus confirm the hypothesis that localization and localizability are related, though strictly speaking, this analysis is not causal.

Still, this analysis has delayed but not *answered* the question; it suggests that geolocation fails on fixed-line addresses when their /24 subnets are geographically dispersed, but this in turn raises the issue of why these disperse subnets exist at all. Comcast has /24 subnets that are spatially concentrated and others that are disperse. Are disperse ones used differently?

We hypothesize that the spatially-concentrated subnets are nearly static whereas large ones provide a reserve of "ephemeral" addresses – perhaps for devices awaiting assignment of a long-term address. A client assigned to an "ephemeral" address would be unlikely to fall on that same address again, whereas a "sticky" address granted to a home network would be used repeatedly. The relevant variable is thus the number of times that a single client is observed at each IP address (weighted by visits). Figure 9 confirms the hypothesis: for subnets with scale greater than 20 km ($f = 0.75$) nearly half of visitors to an IP address visit exactly once.

This behavior is reproduced on Charter, Cablevision, and RCN. It is true to a lesser extent on AT&T, in the sense that devices register far fewer locations on addresses from physically-disperse subnets than on concentrated ones, but the mode at a single visit is not present. Verizon and WOW do not reproduce this behavior.

5.3   How Persistent are the Physical Locations of /24 Subnets?

Geolocation providers are quick to point out that databases evolve continuously. Clearly, the physical infrastructure of the Internet evolves over time, but how quickly do subnets actually move? Because mobile networks subnets are already physically very large, and addresses on them are not accurately located, we focus this analysis on fixed-line broadband.

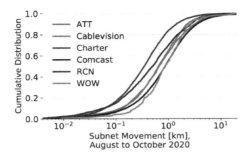

Fig. 10. Distance moved by the medioids of /24 subnet on fixed-line networks, over a two-month period from August to October 2020.

The Movement of Subnets. Figure 10 presents the physical distance between the medioids of individual /24 subnets, as constructed in August and October 2020. As in Sect. 5.2, the medioid is the median of the x and y coordinates. To enter into this figure, subnets must have at least ten unique devices and ten unique addresses in each month. We consider only fixed-line broadband carriers, for this exercise.

On each network considered, the median /24 subnet moves less than a kilometer; There is some inherent variability in our construction of the medioid as the "location" of the subnet in each period, and the Figure shows the difference of these two "noisy" measurements. We thus suspect that this overstates movement. In short, we conclude that on this time scale, subnet locations are quite stable.

Is the Sample Biased? A substantial threat to this analysis is sample composition: by requiring 10 devices and 10 addresses, the subnet *must* be observed in New York, Chicago, or Philadelphia in both months, to enter the sample at all. However, it does not seem to be the case that subnets are moving out of sample. Of the subnets satisfying the cuts in August, 92% also pass them in October (vice versa, 96%). If we raise the thresholds to enter the sample, requiring 20 devices and 20 addresses, 95% of /24 subnets passing these cuts in August also show up with at least 10 devices in October (vice versa, 98%). Raising the thresholds yet further to 50 devices and 50 addresses, the persistence from August to October exceeds 99% (vice versa, 98%).

5.4   How Long Does a Consumer Connection Retain an IP Address?

The analyses above show that IP addresses identify physical locations at the level of 2 km, under the best circumstances. On its own, the IP address clearly does not identify individuals.

Of course, physical locations – geographic coordinates – are not the only way in which IP addresses identify people. Linked to log-ins or other online behaviors, IP addresses can be used to track users over time even without cookies

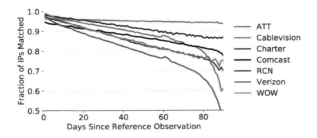

Fig. 11. Persistence of IP addresses. The Figure shows the share of night-time clusters on a single ISP and device, separated by d days, for which the IP addresses are equal on both clusters. Note that for visual clarity, the y axis begins at 0.5 instead of 0.

or fingerprinting (or as a component of a fingerprint). If the IP address is static for a long time, it easier to link online behaviors. A critical concern is thus *how long* fixed-line IP addresses remain with a single household.

Defining Churn. We define *churn* as the likelihood of a device returning to the same IP address on an ISP, after a delay of d days. The denominator includes every pair of night-time connections by a single device to one ISP, d days apart. We select night-time activity, to focus on periods when devices can be reasonably assumed "at home." The numerator is the number of those pairs for which the two nights' connections are on the same IP address. Stated less formally: if I see a device on Monday night ($d = 0$) and again on the same ISP Tuesday night ($d = 1$), what are the chances that it will be on the same IP address? What about next Monday ($d = 7$)?

Since the sample selection is somewhat peculiar – devices are necessarily recorded on fixed-line broadband on multiple nights – one should take some care in interpreting these results. This consideration is particularly acute at the maximum of the range, since there are fewer opportunities for a device to be observed 80 days apart (just 10) let alone 90 (just 1). This perhaps explains the drop-off on the right-hand side.

Rates of Change, Over Two Months. Figure 11 shows the persistence of IP-addresses on fixed-line broadband ISPs. It is clear that devices "leave" individual IP addresses gradually, but at different rates on different ISPs. After one month, more than 90% of devices observed reconnecting to AT&T, RCN, and Cablevision do so on the same IP address. After two months, more than three-quarters of devices return to the same IP address, for all major ISPs in the three cities shown.

6   Can IP Geolocation Databases be Used to Study Internet Access?

At this stage, we would usually turn to a general discussion of findings. Here, we focus our discussion and extend our results, according to the question that originally motivated our work: assessing the potential for using IP-referenced data in *social science* research on Internet access. *Where* and *for what demographic groups* is geolocation accurate? Can *IP geography* enable *Internet demography*? To make this query concrete, imagine a study of the "homework gap" – (in)equity in access to digital resources for education – based solely on server logs from a site like Wikipedia. If we observe frequencies of use by IP subnet *alone*, can we infer what groups do and do not access the site?

General Considerations. This question is non-trivial, since it confronts the correlations of population density and demographics with geolocation accuracy, along with the spatial patterns of connection modality (mobile vs fixed). Cities have smaller subnets simply because they have higher density of people and devices. They also tend to have larger minority populations. This alone leads to a correlation between geolocation accuracy with demographics or disadvantage. For Chicago and its buffer, the correlation between tract median geolocation error on MaxMind (free) and population density is -0.09 ($p < 0.0001$); in turn, population density is correlated with log median household income ($r = -0.18$, $p < 10^{-10}$). Both of these are small but significant. The flip side of better accuracy at higher density is that distance precision *has* to improve in dense environments, to associate activity with the right population. It's easier to "jump" over many people when they are close together.

Accuracy also varies *within* the city, due to heterogeneity in the fraction of people on mobile vs fixed broadband. There are two reasons for this. People use mobile devices (1) when they are on the go, or (2) because they do not have access to a fixed broadband connection at home. That means that devices in the present sample observed in city centers appear to have "inaccurate" IP geolocation, simply because the device users are more-likely on mobile on the way to or at work. On the other hand, populations without fixed broadband access are unlikely to be accurately IP geolocated, even in their home neighborhood.

As a final consideration before proceeding, one must not confound "unknown" addresses with "mis-located" ones. For example, if a default database location for T-Mobile addresses sits in a particular neighborhood, that neighborhood will appear to have "accurate" geolocation, even though the locations are not known any better than elsewhere. Performance will appear to "degrade" radially, with distance from the default location. Since the default locations are usually in or near cities, that would (*ceteris paribus*) give a false impression that IP addresses in cities (or near the center of the United States, for instance) are accurately-located.

Differences in Access Modality by Demographic Group. Returning to the data, Fig. 12 presents the proportion of the night-time clusters in each tract of Chicago, that are on fixed and mobile broadband. Note that the data are inherently mobile devices with GPS chips; this does not include laptops, for instance. This classifies AT&T, Comcast, WOW, and RCN, as fixed-line providers, and T-Mobile, Sprint, Verizon, and AT&T Mobile as mobile. For those familiar with Chicago, the results are no surprise: the proportion of night-time pings on mobile networks is lower on the wealthier North Side of the city than on the West

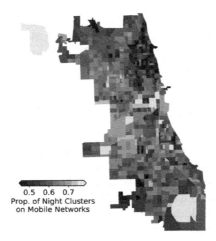

Fig. 12. Proportion of night-time clusters in Chicago recorded on mobile networks.

or South Sides. Indeed, our eyes do not deceive us: the tract level correlation between this constructed variable and share of households with a broadband contract as reported to the Census is -0.25. The correlation between the proportion of night-time pings on mobile networks and the proportion of a neighborhood that is Hispanic is 0.23 (both $p < 10^{-10}$). In other words, connection type is correlated with demographic factors and broadband adoption. This would be reflected in geolocation accuracy. In practice, this means that limiting analyses of Internet activity to accurately-located, fixed-line IP addresses would disproportionately drop traffic from lower-income and minority populations.

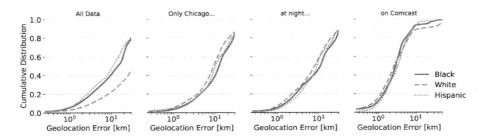

Fig. 13. Cumulative distribution of geolocation error for tracts with white, Black, and Hispanic super-majorities. The first panel presents all data, while the second through fourth restrict to Chicago, Chicago at night, and Chicago at night on Comcast.

The Influences of Density, Demographics, and Modality on IP Geolocation Accuracy. Figure 13 offers an alternative view of this effect, disentangling the countervailing forces of density, demographics, and access modality.

It displays the CDF geolocation accuracy in hyper-segregated neighborhoods of Chicago – ones where two-thirds of residents are white (only), Black (alone or in combination with other races), or Hispanic (of any race). These classifications are made based on data from the US Census' American Community Survey (ACS). Moving from left to right, we begin from the full dataset and layer the cumulative requirements of devices in Chicago proper (not the 40 mile buffer), at night (that is, likely at home), and on Comcast (i.e., on a single, fixed broadband network). The CDF shows the share of location reports. The first plot shows an enormous difference between geolocation in "white" tracts and other segregated tracts – geolocation performs much worse. This effect appears to have more to do with density than race: it reverses when focusing on the City of Chicago, and zeroing in on a single network, the performance lines up quite closely. The exception is at the very high end (above 10 km and 90% of the CDF), where there is apparently an error for locations reported from "white" tracts. About 80% of points are within 5 km of the true location, for all three categories of neighborhood.

Attenuation Bias, from Reliance on Mis-Attributed IP Addresses. The analyses of device modalities above suggest that IP geolocation databases' ability to attribute online behaviors to populations will tend to fail more often for disadvantaged groups. Still, if we were to persist, what errors might we expect to "accrue," by moving an observation from its GPS-based location to the IP-based location? In essence, this question pits the scale of geolocation accuracy against the physical scale of demographic segregation. If IP geolocation moves a point among communities with similar demographics, the error does not directly bias results.

This illustrative analysis is limited to fixed-broadband data from Comcast, where geolocation has a chance of succeeding. Figure 14 presents the log median household income as it would be imputed from a MaxMind look-up, against the true median household income of the neighborhood (Census tract). This results in an unsurprising regression to the mean: as is the usual case with measurement error, the slope is simply attenuated. This suggests that even for fixed broadband, efforts to use IP address alone to "link" online behaviors with human populations are inadvisable at this physical scale. They will in general yield estimates whose magnitudes are biased down. In other words, measurements of "who uses what" that rely on IP geolocation will tend to *understate* differential access. This is consistent with Ganelin and Chuang's work on the socioeconomic status of MOOC registrants. They found that using IP geolocation to identify users' neighborhoods led to underestimates of inequity in adoption [7].

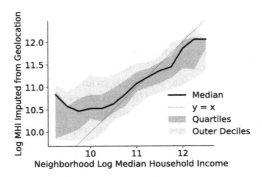

Fig. 14. Quantiles of neighborhood log median household income as "imputed" from MaxMind geolocation (y) as a function of the true neighborhood value (x).

7 Conclusion

Using a large sample of GPS-based smartphone locations this paper has quantified the performance of commercial geolocation databases in New York, Chicago, and Philadelphia. The precision of this analysis far outstrips past work. The analysis has demonstrated significant heterogeneity in geolocation accuracy. The median error for MaxMind's free service is well less than 10 km on fixed commercial broadband networks and at Universities. On mobile networks, IP geolocation is not accurate below the city level. While we consider that consumer devices in large cities in the United States represents a particularly useful vantage point, our conclusions concerning database accuracy and network structure are necessarily limited to the setting that we have observed.

Our analysis has also sought to explain *why* some addresses are accurately located whereas others are not. The physical size of/24 subnets is strongly correlated with accuracy. Geographically disperse/24's appear to be used for "ephemeral" addresses, which clients do not use repeatedly.

Finally, we have contextualized these findings for applications to research on human populations. Both the present data and existing surveys show that disadvantaged populations are less likely to use a fixed broadband subscription at home. Traffic originating from mobile broadband networks cannot be accurately attributed to a neighborhood-level geography, and dropping this traffic altogether would disproportionately remove from analysis the traffic associated with poorer populations. Focussing on the fixed-line context where geolocation is more reliable, the accuracy is still inadequate for associating online activities with real-world geographies and demographics.

From a privacy perspective, a single IP address does not identify an individual, but it both localizes private networks and provides an "index" through time that may be used to aggregate other indirect identifiers. We have shown that the time for IP reassignment of fixed-line broadband consumers varies by ISP, but is typically on the order of months.

A   Additional Plots and Tables

See Tables 4, 5 and Figs. 15, 16.

Table 4. Proportion of bumps and clusters according to the classification type assigned by Unacast (cf Sect. 3.1).

Cluster class	Bumps	Clusters
Long Area Dwell	0.382	0.079
Travel	0.322	0.264
Area Dwell	0.193	0.173
Short Area Dwell	0.074	0.290
Potential Area Dwell	0.025	0.127
Ping	0.003	0.066
Large Variance	0.001	0.000
Moving	0.000	0.000
Split	0.000	0.000

Table 5. Proportion of clusters with IP addresses in foreign Internet registries (cf Sect. 3.1).

NIC	Frac.
AFRINIC	0.00011
APNIC	0.00015
LACNIC	0.00016
RIPE	0.00169

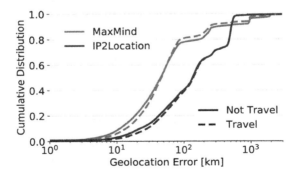

Fig. 15. Empirical cumulative distribution of geolocation accuracy, for travel and non-travel clusters on AT&T's mobile network, as evaluated on the free versions of the MaxMind and IP2Location databases (cf Sect. 4.1).

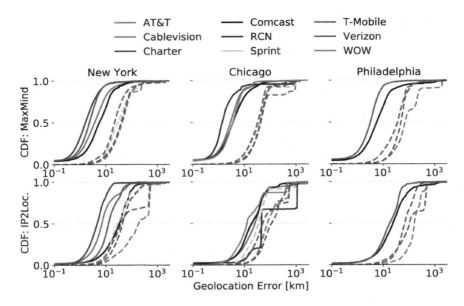

Fig. 16. Geolocation performance by city, database provider, and ISP. The Figure is identical to Fig. 4 of the text, except that ISPs are identified by ASN instead of via whois. ASNs associated with each ISP are listed in Table 6. Free versions of the database are used in each case. ISPs are shown by their "brand" colors, according to the whois database, which leaves the Sprint and T-Mobile networks distinguishable. Fixed-line networks are denoted by solid lines while mobile networks shown by dashed lines. (Color figure online)

Table 6. Autonomous systems asssociated with each ISP, for the data within the study region. This listing is a categorization of the ASNs seen most-frequently in the data. It is not expected to be an exhaustive listing of all ASes corresponding to the ISPs, even in the New York, Chicago, and Philadelphia regions. ASNs are ordered by the number of /24 subnets observed in the data.

ISP	ASNs
AT&T	7018, 2386, 6389, 2686, 4473, 4466, 797, 6431, 17225, 17227
AT&T Mobile	20057
Cablevision	6128, 13490, 32953, 14638, 19720
Charter	12271, 10796, 20115, 11351, 11426, 33363, 20001, 11427, 33588, 14065, 7843, 17359, 16787
Comcast	7922, 33491, 33659, 33287, 7016, 33657, 33651, 7725, 7015, 20214, 33661, 395980, 33652, 396019, 396021
RCN	6079
Sprint	10507, 1239
T-Mobile	21928
Verizon	701, 2828, 23148, 15133, 11486, 12079
Verizon Mobile	22394, 6256, 6167
WOW!	12083, 11693

References

1. Arif, M.J., Karunasekera, S., Kulkarni, S., Gunatilaka, A., Ristic, B.: Internet host geolocation using maximum likelihood estimation technique. In: 24th IEEE International Conference on Advanced Information Networking and Applications, pp. 422–429. IEEE, Perth (2010)
2. Dan, O., Parikh, V., Davison, B.D.: IP geolocation through reverse DNS. CoRR abs/1811.04288, pp. 1–10 (2018)
3. Eriksson, B., Barford, P., Maggs, B., Nowak, R.: Posit: a lightweight approach for IP geolocation. SIGMETRICS Perform. Eval. Rev. **40**(2), 2–11 (2012). https://doi.org/10.1145/2381056.2381058
4. Eriksson, B., Barford, P., Sommers, J., Nowak, R.: A learning-based approach for IP geolocation. In: Krishnamurthy, A., Plattner, B. (eds.) PAM 2010. LNCS, vol. 6032, pp. 171–180. Springer, Heidelberg (2010). https://doi.org/10.1007/978-3-642-12334-4_18
5. Feldman, D., Shavitt, Y., Zilberman, N.: A structural approach for pop geo-location. Comput. Netw. **56**(3), 1029–1040 (2012). https://doi.org/10.1016/j.comnet.2011.10.029. http://www.sciencedirect.com/science/article/pii/S1389128611004191
6. Freedman, M.J., Vutukuru, M., Feamster, N., Balakrishnan, H.: Geographic locality of IP prefixes. In: 5th ACM SIGCOMM Conference on Internet Measurement, IMC '05, pp. 153–158. USENIX Association, USA (2005). https://doi.org/10.5555/1251086.1251099
7. Ganelin, D., Chuang, I.: IP geolocation underestimates regressive economic patterns in MOOC usage. In: 11th International Conference on Education Technology and Computers, pp. 268–272. Association for Computing Machinery, New York City (2019). https://doi.org/10.1145/3369255.3369301
8. Gharaibeh, M., Shah, A., Huffaker, B., Zhang, H., Ensafi, R., Papadopoulos, C.: A look at router geolocation in public and commercial databases. In: Internet Measurement Conference, IMC '17, pp. 463–469. Association for Computing Machinery, New York (2017). https://doi.org/10.1145/3131365.3131380
9. Gill, P., Ganjali, Y., Wong, B., Lie, D.: Dude, where's that IP? circumventing measurement-based IP geolocation. In: 19th USENIX Conference on Security, USENIX Security'10, p. 16. USENIX Association, USA (2010). https://doi.org/10.5555/1929820.1929842
10. Gouel, M., Vermeulen, K., Beverly, R., Fourmaux, O., Friedman, T.: IP geolocation database stability and implications for network research. In: Proceedings of the Network Traffic Measurement and Analysis (TMA) Conference. Online (2021). https://www.cmand.org/papers/geostable-tma21.pdf
11. Gueye, B., Uhlig, S., Fdida, S.: Investigating the imprecision of IP block-based geolocation. In: Uhlig, S., Papagiannaki, K., Bonaventure, O. (eds.) PAM 2007. LNCS, vol. 4427, pp. 237–240. Springer, Heidelberg (2007). https://doi.org/10.1007/978-3-540-71617-4_26
12. Gueye, B., Ziviani, A., Crovella, M., Fdida, S.: Constraint-based geolocation of internet hosts. IEEE/ACM Trans. Netw. **14**(6), 1219–1232 (2006). https://doi.org/10.1109/TNET.2006.886332
13. Hu, Z., Heidemann, J., Pradkin, Y.: Towards geolocation of millions of IP addresses. In: Internet Measurement Conference, IMC '12, pp. 123–130. Association for Computing Machinery, New York (2012). https://doi.org/10.1145/2398776.2398790

14. Huffaker, B., Fomenkov, M.: kc claffy: geocompare: a comparison of public and commercial geolocation databases. Technical report, Cooperative Association for Internet Data Analysis (CAIDA), San Diego, CA (2011). https://www.caida.org/publications/papers/2011/geocompare-tr/
15. Katz-Bassett, E., John, J.P., Krishnamurthy, A., Wetherall, D., Anderson, T., Chawathe, Y.: Towards IP geolocation using delay and topology measurements. In: 6th ACM SIGCOMM Conference on Internet Measurement, IMC '06, pp. 71–84. Association for Computing Machinery, New York (2006). https://doi.org/10.1145/1177080.1177090
16. Komosny, D., Rehman, S.U.: Survival analysis and prediction model of IP address assignment duration. IEEE Access **8**, 162507–162515 (2020). https://doi.org/10.1109/ACCESS.2020.3021760
17. Lab, M.: M-lab visualizations (2021). https://www.measurementlab.net/visualizations/
18. Lazer, D.: Computational social science. Science **323**(5915), 721–723 (2009). https://doi.org/10.1126/science.1167742
19. Li, D., et al.: IP-geolocation mapping for moderately connected internet regions. IEEE Trans. Parallel Distrib. Syst. **24**(2), 381–391 (2013). https://doi.org/10.1109/TPDS.2012.136
20. Mishra, V., Laperdrix, P., Vastel, A., Rudametkin, W., Rouvoy, R., Lopatka, M.: Don't count me out: On the relevance of IP address in the tracking ecosystem. In: Proceedings of The Web Conference 2020, WWW '20, pp. 808–815. Association for Computing Machinery, New York (2020). https://doi.org/10.1145/3366423.3380161
21. Padmanabhan, R., Dhamdhere, A., Aben, E., Claffy, k., Spring, N.: Reasons dynamic addresses change. In: Proceedings of the 2016 Internet Measurement Conference, IMC '16, pp. 183–198. Association for Computing Machinery, New York (2016). https://doi.org/10.1145/2987443.2987461
22. Padmanabhan, R., Rula, J.P., Richter, P., Strowes, S.D., Dainotti, A.: DynamIPs: analyzing address assignment practices in ipv4 and ipv6. In: Proceedings of the 16th International Conference on Emerging Networking EXperiments and Technologies, CoNEXT '20, Association pp. 55–70. Association for Computing Machinery, New York (2020). https://doi.org/10.1145/3386367.3431314
23. Padmanabhan, V.N., Subramanian, L.: An investigation of geographic mapping techniques for internet hosts. In: Conference on Applications, Technologies, Architectures, and Protocols for Computer Communications. SIGCOMM '01, pp. 173–185. Association for Computing Machinery, New York (2001). https://doi.org/10.1145/383059.383073
24. Pereira, M., Kim, A., Allen, J., White, K., Ferres, J.L., Dodhia, R.: U.S. broadband coverage data set: a differentially private data release, pp. 1–7 (2021)
25. Poese, I., Uhlig, S., Kaafar, M.A., Donnet, B., Gueye, B.: IP geolocation databases: unreliable? SIGCOMM Comput. Commun. Rev. **41**(2), 53–56 (2011). https://doi.org/10.1145/1971162.1971171
26. Richter, P., et al.: A multi-perspective analysis of carrier-grade NAT deployment. In: Proceedings of the 2016 Internet Measurement Conference, IMC '16, pp. 215–229. Association for Computing Machinery, New York (2016). https://doi.org/10.1145/2987443.2987474
27. Shavitt, Y., Zilberman, N.: A geolocation databases study. IEEE J. Sel. Areas Commun. **29**(10), 2044–2056 (2011). https://doi.org/10.1109/JSAC.2011.111214

28. Spring, N., Mahajan, R., Wetherall, D.: Measuring ISP topologies with Rocket-fuel. In: Conference on Applications, Technologies, Architectures, and Protocols for Computer Communications, SIGCOMM '02, pp. 133–145. Association for Computing Machinery, New York (2002). https://doi.org/10.1145/633025.633039
29. Wang, Y., Burgener, D., Flores, M., Kuzmanovic, A., Huang, C.: Towards street-level client-independent IP geolocation. In: 8th USENIX Conference on Networked Systems Design and Implementation, NSDI'11, USA, pp. 365–379 (2011). https://doi.org/10.5555/1972457.1972494
30. Wong, B., Stoyanov, I.: Octant: a comprehensive framework for the geolocalization of internet hosts. In: 4th USENIX Symposium on Networked Systems Design & Implementation (NSDI 07), pp. 313–326. USENIX Association, Cambridge (2007). https://www.usenix.org/conference/nsdi-07/octant-comprehensive-framework-geolocalization-internet-hosts
31. Youn, I., Mark, B.L., Richards, D.: Statistical geolocation of internet hosts. In: 18th International Conference on Computer Communications and Networks, pp. 1–6. IEEE, San Francisco (2009). https://doi.org/10.1109/ICCCN.2009.5235373

Performance

Jitterbug: A New Framework
for Jitter-Based Congestion Inference

Esteban Carisimo[1]([✉]), Ricky K. P. Mok[2][iD], David D. Clark[3], and K. C. Claffy[2]

[1] Northwestern University, Evanston, USA
esteban.carisimo@northwestern.edu
[2] CAIDA, UC San Diego, San Diego, USA
{cskpmok,kc}@caida.org
[3] MIT, Cambridge, USA
ddc@csail.mit.edu

Abstract. We investigate a novel approach to the use of jitter to infer network congestion using data collected by probes in access networks. We discovered a set of features in jitter and *jitter dispersion* —a jitter-derived time series we define in this paper—time series that are characteristic of periods of congestion. We leverage these concepts to create a jitter-based congestion inference framework that we call *Jitterbug*. We apply Jitterbug's capabilities to a wide range of traffic scenarios and discover that Jitterbug can correctly identify both recurrent and one-off congestion events. We validate Jitterbug inferences against state-of-the-art autocorrelation-based inferences of recurrent congestion. We find that the two approaches have strong congruity in their inferences, but Jitterbug holds promise for detecting one-off as well as recurrent congestion. We identify several future directions for this research including leveraging ML/AI techniques to optimize performance and accuracy of this approach in operational settings.

1 Introduction

The general notion of network congestion – demand exceeds capacity for network (link capacity or router buffer) resources – is widespread on the Internet, and an inherent property of traditional TCP dynamics. A TCP connection endpoint induces congestion to infer its appropriate sending rate, increasing this rate until it fails to receive acknowledgement of receipt of a packet by the other endpoint, i.e., infers congestion based on packet loss [19]. More recent attempts to improve TCP's congestion control algorithms rely on increased latency rather than packet loss as a signal of congestion [7,8,22,35].

Outside of protocol dynamics, latency and loss are still the fundamental metrics used to detect episodes of network congestion, or more generally path anomalies that degrade performance [12–15,17,30]. Although researchers have developed autocorrelation techniques to infer persistent recurrent patterns congestion [12], the challenge of detecting one-off episodes of congestion in traffic data remains an open problem after 30 years of Internet evolution. One-off episodes of congestion

O. Hohlfeld et al. (Eds.): PAM 2022, LNCS 13210, pp. 155–179, 2022.
https://doi.org/10.1007/978-3-030-98785-5_7

have many causes, including traffic management transitions, router operating system overheads, network configuration errors, flash crowds (e.g., software releases), and DDoS attacks. Inferring congestion from these phenomenological events is still an open challenge for the research network community.

We propose a new framework – Jitterbug – to use jitter and other metrics derived from round-trip-time (RTT) measurements to infer congestion. RTT measurements alone are often insufficient to infer congestion episodes, but we found that jitter-related metrics can distinguish congestion from other path anomalies, e.g., route changes. Specifically, we identify a correlation between periods of elevated latency (minimum RTT) and changes in the profile of jitter signatures – *jitter dispersion* – during congestion episodes. Relying on this concept, we develop a new framework that allows us to extend interdomain congestion inferences from recurrent patterns to one-off congestion events, i.e., discern recurrent from one-time congestion events. Using data collected between 2017 and 2020, this novel approach obtains similar results to state-of-the-art autocorrelation-based methods [12], but overcomes the limitation of the autocorrelation methods that can only detect recurrent periodic patterns of congestion. We find that Jitterbug introduces a promising approach to detect one-off congestion events. Our contributions are:

1. We identified a set of features in jitter and jitter dispersion time series, including a change of regime or transitory increase of the jitter dispersion, that characterize periods of congestion.
2. We used these features to develop and implement Jitterbug, a new jitter-based congestion inference method that combines pre-existing approaches to change point detection with information embedded in jitter signals.
3. We applied the Jitterbug framework to a wide range of challenging traffic scenarios, and explain its inferences.
4. We compare Jitterbug congestion inferences to the state-of-the-art autocorrelation-based methods [12], finding strong consistency in autocorrelation-applicable scenarios, i.e., for recurrent periodic congestion.
5. We release the source of code of Jitterbug[1].

The rest of the paper is structured as follows. We provide context by describing the latency model (Sect. 2.1) and jitter signatures in multiple real-world examples (Sect. 2.2). Leveraging these concepts, Sect. 3 describes Jitterbug and its components in detail. Section 4 describes the dataset we use to *(i)* investigate Jitterbug congestion inferences in different scenarios (Sect. 5), and *(ii)* cross-validate Jitterbug congestion inferences against other methods (Sect. 6). Section 7 summarizes lessons we learned during our study. Section 8 provides an extensive list of related work and Sect. 9 discusses open challenges in congestion inference. Finally, Sect. 10 offers concluding thoughts.

2   Background on RTT and Jitter Signatures

To provide context, we describe the latency model (Sect. 2.1) and four typical signatures we extract from RTTs and jitter (Sect. 2.2).

---

[1] Jitterbug repository: https://github.com/estcarisimo/jitterbug.

2.1   Latency Model

Round-trip time (RTT) in end-to-end measurements comprises both deterministic and random components. Equation (1) depicts the components of RTT between source (u) and destination (v) for a packet traversing a total of H hops in the round-trip path [21].

$$RTT(u,v) = d_{icmp} + \sum_{i=0}^{H}(d_s(i) + d_{prop}(i) + d_q(i) + d_{proc}(i)), \qquad (1)$$

where d_{icmp} is the processing delay of ICMP messages in routers. d_s, d_{prop}, and d_{proc} represent delay induced by serialization, propagation, and packet processing, respectively. These deterministic components do not depend on traffic volume or link utilization. In contrast, d_{icmp} and d_q are random variables and contribute RTT variance, because their values depend on router CPU utilization and queue size of network interfaces when packets arrive. Prior work [12,23] has shown that RTT correlates with bottleneck link utilization, indicating that the queuing delay is the dominant factor in delay variation. Delay jitter, also referred to as jitter or IP packet delay variation [10], is the absolute difference between the current RTT value and the reference value of the previous time episode (i.e., $J_T = RTT(u,v)_T - RTT(u,v)_{T-1}$), where T is the current time episode. In this work we develop and evaluate a framework for using simple RTT and jitter-based metrics to classify path anomalies.

2.2   Analyzing RTT and Jitter Signatures in Congested Links

We use four real-world examples to illustrate the challenges and opportunities of using RTT and jitter to detect and identify path anomalies (Fig. 1). We focus on three properties of RTT and jitter to characterize the nature of path anomalies: *periodicity, amplitude, variability*.

Periodicity captures events that recur at a fixed frequency and duration, such as diurnal variations.

Amplitude measures the degree of changes in RTTs from the baseline. During network congestion events, probe packets are more likely to experience queuing delay. The elevation of RTTs reflects the queue size in the bottleneck link.

Variability refers to the stability of RTTs during the elevated periods, which allows us to discern congestion from other path anomalies such as a route change.

Figure 1 shows four examples of two-week RTT and jitter time series measured from four vantage points in the U.S. to four router interfaces on the far-side[2] of interdomain links. Two examples (Fig. 1a and 1b) show periodic inflation

---

[2] We referred as *near* and *far* sides to consecutive IP pairs in a traceroute path following the convention defined by Luckie *et al.* [23].

in RTTs (blue/orange curves), indicating recurring congestion events. However, the jitter amplitude (green curve) in Fig. 1b, is much lower than that of Fig. 1a, consistent with a smaller queue size in the bottleneck link. Previous use of autocorrelation methods have shown that such persistent diurnal elevations in RTT at the far-side of an interdomain are evidence of interdomain congestion [12]. In contrast, the two cases in Fig. 1c and 1d are one-off events. The interesting difference is that in Fig. 1d the jitter increases as the RTT baseline jumps from 20 ms to 40 ms. In contrast, in Fig. 1c the jitter remains stable throughout. We suspect that this latter scenario was a route change event rather than congestion.

Although many different approaches to RTT change point detection could partition these time series into intervals, an approach solely based on RTTs would fail to distinguish congestion from other path anomalies such as route changes. The RTT signal is simply too noisy. This example shows that evaluating changes in jitter can enable us to differentiate these scenarios and thus we should consider jitter as a metric for characterizing path anomalies.

We next introduce our framework to support systematic analysis and classification of type of path anomalies with three properties that we extract from RTT and jitter time series data.

3   Jitterbug: Jitter-Based Congestion Inference

Figure 2 shows the building blocks of our framework, which combines change point detection algorithms (Sect. 3.2) with simultaneous analysis of minimum RTT and jitter time series obtained from latency measurements. The change point detection algorithm splits RTT timeseries into *candidate* time intervals that might suffer from congestion. The next step of the framework is to analyze the jitter in each time interval to classify candidate intervals as congestion events or other path anomalies. We infer congestion based on the three elements we observed in Sect. 2.2: changes in baseline RTT, increase of jitter amplitude, and increase of jitter dispersion during a phase transition. We developed two different statistical methods for this analysis– *(i) KS-test method*, and *(ii) jitter dispersion method (JD)*. The first combines detection of changes on RTT latency baseline with the Kolmogorov-Smirnov (KS) test to detect changes in the jitter time series. The *jitter dispersion method (JD)* detects a jitter dispersion increase that correlates with a baseline RTT increases as a signal of congestion. The common goal of both methods is to objectively capture the signatures in the jitter signals. This section describes the role of each element of the Jitterbug framework in detail. We designed Jitterbug to support different RTT data sources, and have applied it to measurements collected by Ark CAIDA and RIPE Atlas. The current implementation uses a 5-min and 15-min granularity for RTT measurements and the aggregated minimum RTT time-series, respectively.

3.1   Signal Filtering

Jitterbug congestion inferences use three signals: *(i) min* RTT time series, *(ii)* jitter, and *(iii)* jitter dispersion. As we saw in Sect. 2.2, raw RTTs can be too

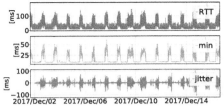

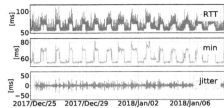

(a) Recurring congestion event. RTTs and jitter increase during congestion episodes.

(b) Recurring congestion event. Jitter does not significantly increase during elevated RTT periods, likely due to small buffer size in the bottleneck router.

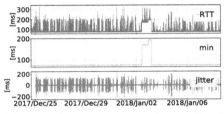

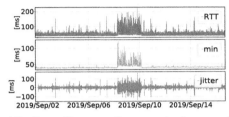

(c) One-off non-congestion event on Jan 2. Jitter remained stable in face of inflated RTT.

(d) One-off congestion event. Increased varibility in jitter indicates the occurance of congestion.

Fig. 1. Typical examples of network events. The raw timeseries (top figures) is the raw RTT data with 5-min resolution. We aggregate the raw data into 15-min buckets with the minimum function to filter noise (middle figures). We compute jitter using the 15-min aggregated data to quantify variability in RTTs (bottom figures). (Color figure online)

noisy to yield meaningful signatures. We first aggregate the raw RTT data by selecting the minimum value in each 15-min time interval (*min* time series). The signal filtering module then computes the jitter using both the *raw RTT* and *min* time series to produce *jitter* and *j-min* time series, respectively.

We use two additional filters to better capture the variability in *j-min*. First, we apply the *Moving IQR filter* to the *j-min* time series, which computes the inter-quartile range (IQR) of a sliding window of 150 min (10 jitter samples). We define as jitter dispersion to the operation of computing the moving IQR to a jitter signal.

We then compute the 5-sample moving average of the resultant time series as the *jitter dispersion* time series to mitigate the impact of short-term latency spikes. Fig. 3 shows the correlation between the *min* RTT time series and the *jitter dispersion* of previous examples (Fig. 1). Correlation between the two time series in Fig. 3c) is low. We believe that the shift of baseline RTT corresponds to a route change that increased the propagation delay, which is a deterministic component that induces low variance to RTTs.

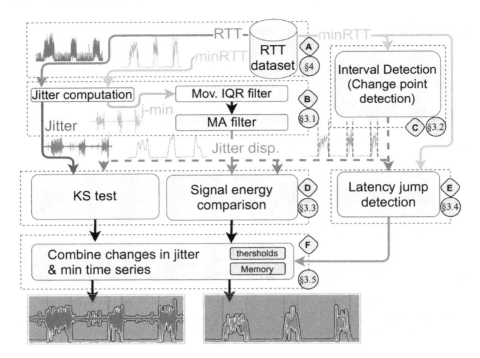

Fig. 2. The Jitterbug framework comprises: (A) data acquisition (B) signal filtering (C) detection of intervals of elevated latency (D) detection of changes of state of jitter and jitter dispersion signals (E) detection of increments of the min time series (F) correlation of changes in jitter state with increments of changes of state in jitter signals.

3.2   Detection of Period of Elevated Latency

Identifying time intervals with elevated RTTs. is a fundamental step of the congestion inference process since the subsequent modules examine these periods to determine if latency elevations were caused by increases of traffic loads. Our framework can accommodate any change point detection algorithm that can segment time intervals based on changes in RTTs. As proof of concept, we use two state-of-the-art change point detection algorithms—Bayesian Change Point (BCP) Detection or Hidden Markov Models (HMM)—to process the *min* time series. We have not yet had the opportunity to test these methods on a large variety of data sources, so we provide both alternatives to let Jitterbug users select which is more effective for their data source. We believe these two algorithms can complement each other in circumstance where one fails to cover all change points in a signal. In Sect. 5.8, we test both algorithms with challenging latency signatures and show how all periods of elevated latency are captured by at least one of the methods.

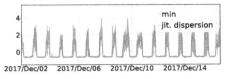

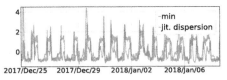

(a) Recurring congestion event. There is a correlation between periods of elevated latency and the growth of jitter dispersion.

(b) Recurring congestion event. Jitter dispersion transitorily increases at the beginning of periods of elevated latency

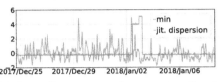

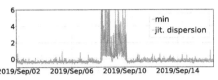

(c) One-off non-congestion event on Jan 2, with no correlation between signals.

(d) One-off congestion event, with a positive correlation between the *min* and jitter dispersion time series.

Fig. 3. *min RTT* (orange) and jitter dispersion (purple) time series. We normalized the values using standard score for this visualization; normalization is not necessary in actual computation. In a) and d), these two signals are strongly correlated during period of congestion. In b), jitter dispersion has a transitory increase at the beginning of the period of elevated latency. c) (no apparent congestion) shows no correlation between these signals, which is consistent with a route change that increased RTT. (Color figure online)

- **Bayesian Change Point (BCP)**: We chose an offline BCP algorithm[3] proposed by Xuan *et al.* [36]. We experimented with other popular change point detection algorithms (e.g., Change finder [11] and ATDK LevelShift [6]) and found that BCP was the most effective at detecting boundaries of intervals with RTT latency measurements in our data.
- **Hidden Markov Models (HMM)**: We selected an implementation designed to identify different discrete states in RTT latency time series, by combining Hidden Markov Models (HMM) with Hierarchical Dirichlet Process (HDP) [27]. HMM also yields boundaries for each state (or level) in the time series, and in our case, consecutive RTT latency samples typically belong to the same state for long periods of times.

3.3 Examination of Jitter Signals

Jitterbug uses two approaches to examine changes in jitter and jitter dispersion time series during periods of elevated latency (Module (D) in Fig. 2): *(i) KS-test method* (using the jitter time series), and *(ii) Jitter dispersion method* (using

---

[3] Implementation of Xuan *et al.* change point detection algorithm: https://github.com/hildensia/bayesian_changepoint_detection.

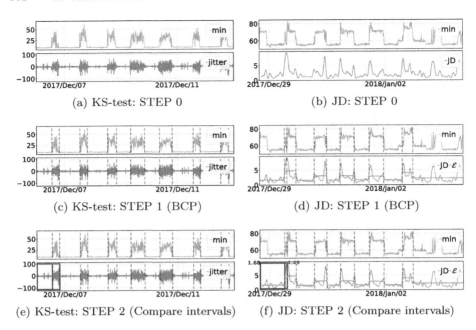

(a) KS-test: STEP 0   (b) JD: STEP 0

(c) KS-test: STEP 1 (BCP)   (d) JD: STEP 1 (BCP)

(e) KS-test: STEP 2 (Compare intervals)   (f) JD: STEP 2 (Compare intervals)

Fig. 4. Steps of KS-test (left) and jitter dispersion (right) congestion inference methods. In both methods, Jitterbug uses the *min* time series to identify the beginning and end of periods of elevated latency (c and d). Using these boundaries, both methods look for changes in jitter signals in adjacent intervals. To detect these changes, KS-test computes the Kolmogorov-Smirnov test on adjacent jitter samples (e); the jitter dispersion method (f) compares the mean value of the jitter dispersion signal ($\mathcal{E}$).

the jitter dispersion time series). Both methods rely on boundaries previously identified by the Interval Detection Module (Module (C) in Fig. 2). Figure 4 describes the input time series of each method, how they use change points detected by Interval Detection Module and how they detect changes in jitter signals.

KS-Test Method. This method examines changes in the jitter time series (Fig. 4a). Using the change points extracted from the minimum time series by the Interval Detection Module (Fig. 4c), Jitterbug detects a change of regime in jitter time series during periods of elevated latency. Our hypothesis is that a trace switched into a different congestion state if there is a change point in the minimum time series and, at the same time, the jitter changes to a different regime. To identify such a regime, Jitterbug applies the Kolmogorov-Smirnov (KS) test to jitter samples in partitions before and after the change point (Fig. 4e). In case the jitter samples in the partition before the change point have a different distribution from the following partition, the KS test will reject the null hypothesis ($\alpha = 0.05$) meaning both samples were not generated by the same random process. To verify that the result of the KS test is not an artifact due to the change point detection method, we apply the KS test to two random samples in the same interval. For this validation test, we expect the KS test does not reject the null hypothesis, which means there is no evidence to conclude that samples within the same partition belong to different jitter regimes. We repeat this process for all pairs of adjacent partitions.

Jitter Dispersion Method. The input to this method is the jitter dispersion time series that we pre-computed in Sect. 3.1 (Fig. 4b). Similar to the KS-test method, this method uses change points extracted from the minimum time series by the Interval Detection Module (Fig. 4c), as boundaries between periods of elevated latency (Fig. 4d). We assume when the elevation of latency is caused by congestion, then the jitter dispersion increases, either transitorily at the beginning (phase transition) or throughout the period (Sect. 3.1).

In both cases, during a period of congestion the average jitter dispersion is larger than that of congestion-free periods. If the mean value of the jitter dispersion between consecutive periods (Fig. 4f) increases, we consider this period as congested. We repeat this inference process for all pairs of adjacent partitions.

3.4   Latency Jump Detection

Jitterbug assumes that *a period of congestion is a period of elevated latency* that manifests the growth of routers' buffers occupancy. In the Latency Jump Detection module (Module (E) in Fig. 2) Jitterbug uses the *min* time series and the intervals identified by the Interval Detection Module (Module (C) in Fig. 2) to detect latency increments. This modules flags a candidate *period of congestion* if it detects in that period an increment of the mean value of the *min* time series compared to its predecesor.

3.5   Combine Changes in Jitter and Minimum Time Series

Jitterbug classifies a *period of congestion* (Module F in Fig. 2) if adjacent intervals meet two conditions: *(i)* an increase in the RTT latency baseline *(ii)* an increase in the jitter amplitude (transitory or generalized). Jitterbug combines the results obtained by the Latency Jump Detection module with KS-test and Jitter dispersion methods. Jitterbug assumes that a period of elevated latency was generated by an increase in routers buffer occupancy if the KS-test or jitter dispersion method detected changes in the jitter signals during that interval.

To increase the accuracy of these Jitterbug inferences in challenging scenarios, and to allow users to calibrate inferences with their tolerance values, Jitterbug includes two *additional features*: *(i)* congestion inference thresholds, and *(ii)* memory.

- **Congestion inference thresholds.** To increase confidence of Jitterbug congestion inferences, we include *congestion inference thresholds* when we compare the mean value of the minimum RTT time series of consecutive intervals.

Table 1. Description of the near- and far-side ASes in the evaluation dataset. We use measurements collected from 13 Ark monitors hosted in 6 U.S. ISP to 18 far-side ASes (7 Content Providers and 11 Access/Transit networks) and 49 far-IP addresses. This data collection comprises 1.7M raw RTT samples collected between 2017 and 2020. for 1290 unique combinations of <day, VP, far IP>.

near-side ASes		far-side ASes	
# VPs	ISPs	#ASes (# addr.)	far ASname
13	COMCAST, Verizon, AT&T, CenturyLink, Charter, Cox	18 (49)	COMCAST (AS7922), Netflix (AS2906), NTT (AS2914), Level3 (AS3356), PCCW (AS3491), KT (AS4766), Telstra (AS4637), TATA (AS6453), China Telecom (AS4134), Zayo (AS6461), Cloudflare (AS13335), Charter (AS7843), XO (AS2828), Edgecast (AS15133), Google (AS15169), Amazon (AS16509), Akamai (AS20940), Facebook (AS32934)

We also include a Jitter dispersion threshold (JD threshold) in the jitter dispersion method when we compare changes in the mean value of the signal in adjacent intervals. The values we use for this research are 0.25ms and 0.5ms thresholds for jitter dispersion and baseline, respectively, as we found in the evaluation dataset (see Sect. 4) that min and jitter dispersion fluctuations tend to be below these values during periods of no suspected congestion. These parameters allow us to reduce false positives and false negatives in Jitterbug congestion inferences.

– **Memory**. To reduce errors in congestion inferences as a result of false positives in the change point detection process, we include the concept of *memory*. In some cases, change point detection algorithms identify path anomalies within periods of congestion (e.g., route change during a congestion episode) or a false positive. Under these circumstances, our congestion detection methodology would not detect any change, either transitory or permanent in the jitter, and it would label the next interval as a *period of no congestion*. However, the congestion status has not changed between these adjacent intervals. To overcome this limitation, we include a rule called *memory* that assumes that *a period of congestion has not finished if in the following interval the mean value of the minimum RTT does not decrease*. For example, for two given adjacent intervals I_1 and I_2, we will label I_2 as *a period of congestion* if we also labeled I_1 as *a period of congestion* and $mean(minRTT(I_2)) \geq mean(minRTT(I_1))$.

4   Dataset

We focus on congestion at interdomain links which requires identification of IP addresses of intedomain routers' interfaces. MANIC [2] uses *bdrmap* [24] to infer the IP addresses of all interdomain links visible from the Autonomous System hosting a CAIDA Ark [1] vantage point (VP). *bdrmap* returns pairs of near- and far-side IP addresses of an interdomain link, and a set of prefixes reachable through a path containing those near- and far-side IP addresses. We use the data API of the MANIC platform [2] to obtain longitudinal RTT measurements from Ark's VPs to the far-side interface of interdomain links using the Time-Series Latency Probing (TSLP) method [23]. Each VP runs TSLP measurements every 5 min using ICMP TTL-limited packet probes to all near- and far-side pairs to collect RTT samples between the VP and IP addresses on the near and far side of interdomain links. Furthermore, the MANIC platform labels interdomain links that might have congestion events using an autocorrelation-based method [12], which is effective in locating recurring congestion events that significantly inflate the RTTs. We will use these inferences as cross-validation (Sect. 6.2).

We demonstrate our methodologies by inferring congestion from 13 VPs in 6 U.S. ISPs to 18 far ASes and 49 far-IP addresses, as it is shown in Table 1. This dataset covers a total of 1290 unique combinations of <day, VP, far IP> and contains 1.7M raw RTT samples collected between 2017 and 2020.

5   Results

We present our results of Jitterbug congestion inferences in the scenarios we introduced in Sect. 2.2, which map to the taxonomy in Fig. 5. Specifically, we show Jitterbug congestion inferences for periodic signals of large (Sect. 5.1) and small (Sect. 5.2) amplitude as well as for one-off periods of elevated latency (Sect. 5.3 and 5.4). We further investigate Jitterbug congestion inference in hybrid scenarios with one-off events in the middle of repetitive periods of elevated latency (Sect. 5.5). We also study the impact of *memory* (Sect. 5.6) and the *JD threshold* (Sect. 5.7) in the accuracy of Jitterbug congestion inferences. Finally, we investigate how errors in detecting change points impact in Jitterbug congestion inference (Sect. 5.8).

5.1   Scenario 1: Recurrent Period of Elevated Latency with Large Amplitude Signals

Both methodologies labeled every recurrent period of elevated latency as a period of congestion (Fig. 6). We suppose that the accuracy of the congestion inferences is partially due to the small of contribution of other random factors since we observe small variability in the baseline during periods of non-elevated latency. The profile of the minimum time series indicates a small contribution of other random components, which create slight fluctuations during periods of non-elevated latency. In addition, the size of this router buffer amplifies the range of the raw, min and jitter time series (in some cases over 100ms) which simplifies the task of identifying periods of high jitter fluctuations.

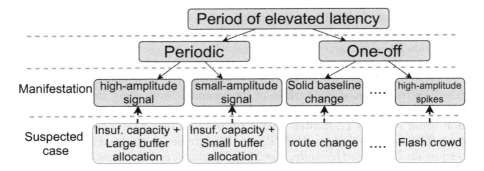

Fig. 5. Hierarchical classification of characteristics of elevated latency. We classify periods of elevated latency as either *periodic* (left branch) or *one-off* (right branch). Recurrent latency with a consistent period (periodic) suggests an underprovisioned link. A one-off episode of elevated latency can have many causes, e.g., bufferbloat, flash crowd, misconfiguration, route change.

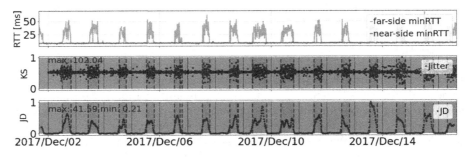

Fig. 6. KS-test (middle plot) and Jitter dispersion (lower plot) congestion inferences for a periodic high-amplitude signal. In this case, both methods label every recurrent period of elevated latency as periods of congestion. Red-filled intervals indicate periods of congestion. (Color figure online)

5.2   Scenario 2: Recurrent Period of Elevated Latency with Small Amplitude Signals

Figure 7 shows that only the jitter dispersion method labels periods of elevated latency as periods of congestion. We believe that the stability in the jitter time series at periods of elevated latency impedes the KS-test method's inferences. This jitter stability may be due to small buffers (differences between peak and valley values is 30 ms) or traffic engineering on the far side network, which in this case is a large Content Provider. On the other hand, the high amplitude of the phase transitions in the jitter dispersion time series allows the JD method to detect differences in the mean value of this signal during periods of elevated latency. We note that the change point detection module is not capable of detecting period of elevated latency between January 1, 2018 and January

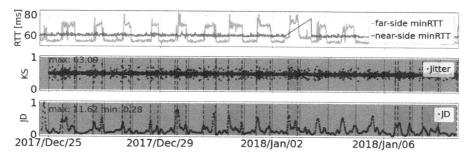

Fig. 7. KS-test and Jitter dispersion congestion inferences for a periodic small-amplitude signal. Only the jitter dispersion method infers congestion from this recurrent pattern, which we speculate relates to small buffers that keep jitter itself relatively stable. Remarkably, the change point detection algorithm was not able to capture some periods of elevated latency. Red-filled intervals indicate periods of congestion. (Color figure online)

3, 2018. (The slightly smoother transition during this period trace could have hindered the accuracy of the change point detection algorithm.)

5.3 Scenario 3: One-Off Period of Elevated Latency with No Congestion

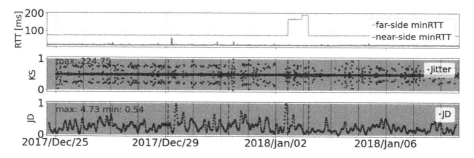

Fig. 8. KS-test and Jitter dispersion congestion inferences for a one-off event suspected as a route change. Inferences for this case indicate no congestion. Red-filled intervals indicate periods of congestion. (Color figure online)

Figure 8 shows an example in which neither method infers congestion. In this case, we do not observe any change in either the jitter time series or the jitter dispersion either before or after the period of elevated latency. We suppose that this period corresponds to a route change based on the stability of the jitter time series and the clean profile of the min time series during the transition. Since there is no simultaneous increase in near-side RTT (orange curve in Fig. 8 top panel), we believe that a route changed in the reverse path from the far-side router.

5.4   Scenario 4: One-Off Period of Elevated Latency with Congestion

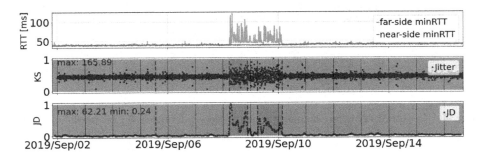

Fig. 9. KS-test and Jitter dispersion congestion inferences for a one-off congestion event. In this case, both methods infer congestion during periods of elevated latency. Red-filled intervals indicate periods of congestion. (Color figure online)

(Figure 9) Congestion inferences from both methods partially agree on classifying this one-time episode of high amplitude latency spikes as a period of congestion. Detection of multiple change points, and the fact that the period in between has slightly smaller mean value in the min time series, generate that the period of congestion inferred is smaller than the actual period of elevated latency.

5.5   Scenario 5: One-Off Event During Recurrent Periods of Elevated Latency

The biggest challenge for latency-based congestion detection is to distinguish congestion-induced elevated latency from other path anomalies, such as a route change. Figure 10 shows two examples of KS-test and jitter dispersion congestion inferences when route changes occur in the middle of recurrent periods of elevated latency. In these cases, we confirm that the events occurring on March 20, 2017 at 12pm (Fig. 10a) and on April 20, 2017 before midnight (Fig. 10b) are route changes in the internal network of the ISP since the near- (orange) and far-side (blue) *min* time series detect an elevation simultaneously. As we expected for a route change, these events do not show any change in jitter signals. Our method used the jitter dispersion metric to correctly rule out a candidate congestion period as a route change (rather than congestion), due to low jitter dispersion which we know is not strongly correlated with congestion dynamics. This example illustrates the importance of jitter dynamics in detection of network congestion events.

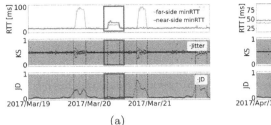 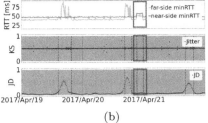

(a)   (b)

Fig. 10. Two examples of suspected route changes in the middle of recurrent periods of elevated latency. Neither method inferred any congestion. Red-filled intervals indicate periods of congestion. (Color figure online)

5.6   Scenario 6: Change Point Detection Over-Detects Change Points

We use an additional set of examples to investigate how the *memory* feature compensates for weaknesses in change point detection algorithms, specifically when algorithms are over-sensitive and create too many intervals.

Figure 11 shows examples of how *memory* improves the accuracy of congestion inferences in different circumstances. Figure 11a and 11b shows how *memory* increases the accuracy of congestion inferences in the presence of over-partitioned periods of elevated latency. While this feature increases the number of intervals labeled as periods of congestion in the presence of multiple change points, it is not able to fix all of them. Figure 11c and 11d show how *memory* extends the inferred period of congestion where there is a legitimate change point during this period. These figures show a persistent increase in the minimum RTT baseline, which we suspect was due to a route change during a period of congestion. We assume that the lack of RTT measurements below that baseline corresponds to speed-of-light constraints induced by the more circuitous path used during the period of congestion.

5.7   Scenario 7: Adjusting JD Threshold to Minimize False Positives

Figure 12 shows examples of how one can adjust the JD threshold to minimize false positives in congestion inferences. Figure 12a and 12b compare congestion inferences using JD thresholds of 0.25 ms and 0.5 ms, respectively. In this example, the jitter dispersion ranges from 0.26 to 92.64 ms, showing a flat curve for most of the period and a one-off event that generates a large spike. Due to the flatness of the curve we selected two thresholds close to the baseline jitter dispersion values (D+0.25 and D+0.5 ms), and inferred a period of congestion if jitter dispersion exceeded these thresholds, which in this case means the jitter dispersion doubled or tripled. We found that our first threshold (0.25) was too sensitive, since a small perturbation in jitter dispersion, in addition to a false positive inference from the change point algorithm, generated a false positive congestion inference.

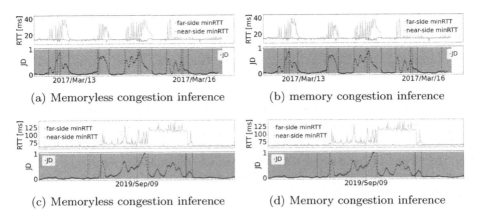

(a) Memoryless congestion inference   (b) memory congestion inference

(c) Memoryless congestion inference   (d) Memory congestion inference

Fig. 11. Examples of how the *memory* feature improves accuracy of congestion inferences in the presence of over-partitioned intervals and other path anomalies. a) and b) display how *memory* maximizes congestion inferences in scenarios where change point detection algorithms overfit detection, breaking the time series into too many intervals. c) and d) show another example of how *memory* can inform congestion inference when a route change occurs within a period of congestion. Red-filled intervals indicate periods of congestion. (Color figure online)

5.8   Scenario 8: False Negatives in Change Point Detection

One desired characteristic of a change point detection algorithm is the ability to precisely detect the beginning and ending points (all of them) of *all* periods elevated latency. In practice this is not possible for every time series, and in our case the lack of change points hinder the accuracy of congestion inferences. We use additional examples to investigate the accuracy of the change point detection algorithms we included in Jitterbug.

Figure 13 shows two pairs of examples where the precision of Interval Detection varies depending on the algorithm being applied and the traffic scenario: BCP is more precise that HMM (Fig. 13a and 13b) and HMM is more precise than BCP (Fig. 13c and 13d)). Figure 13a shows a scenario where HMM misses several consecutive change points, creating a prolonged period that does not precisely capture the periods of congestion in that measurement. For the same scenario, Fig. 13b shows that BCP correctly infers those periods of congestion. Conversely, Fig. 13c shows a scenario in which HMM is more accurate than BCP at detecting change points (Fig. 13d).

6   Comparative Evaluation of Jitterbug

The current version of Jitterbug allows users to infer congestion using 4 different configurations by changing: *(i)* the change point detection algorithm (BCP or HMM, see Sect. 3.2), or *(ii)* the congestion inference method (KS-test or jitter dispersion, see Sect. 3.3). In this section we compare Jitterbug inferences

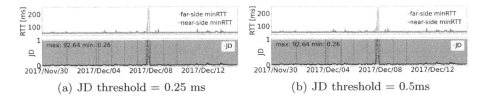

(a) JD threshold = 0.25 ms   (b) JD threshold = 0.5ms

Fig. 12. Adjusting the JD threshold can mitigate false positive in congestion inferences. a) shows that a too-sensitive threshold can yield errors even in the presence of a flat jitter dispersion time series. b) shows how small adjustments in this threshold can mitigate false positive congestion inferences. Red-filled intervals indicate periods of congestion. (Color figure online)

for each configuration, first comparing the KS-test and JD methods to each other (Sect. 6.1), and cross-validated with the state-of-the-art congestion detection methods [12] (Sect. 6.2).

6.1 Comparing Inferences of KS-Test and JD Methods

Table 2 compares congestion inferences of KS-test and jitter dispersion methods for the same interval using different change point detection alternatives (BCP on the left hand-side and HMM on the right hand-side). The results show no significant variations related to the change point detection used for the inferences. KS-test and jitter dispersion indicate the same congestion status for most intervals since the fraction of intervals equally labelled is 0.67 (128/192) and 0.64 (129/201) when using BCP and HMM, respectively. The jitter dispersion method tends to label more intervals as *period of congestion* than the KS-test method where the fraction of intervals considered as *periods of congestion* only by jitter dispersion is 0.29 (56/192) and 0.32 (63/201) for BCP and HMM, respectively. The KS-test method labels fewer intervals as *period of congestion* since this method only detects a narrow type of congestion signature in which congestion implies a change in jitter regime. For instance, when random components of latency are more significant than queueing delay, this noise limits the ability of KS-test to detect a change in the jitter regime. In addition, we found that the KS-test is unable to detect congestion generating changes of jitter regimes when a bottleneck router buffer is small. We suspect that small buffers do not allow us to observe jitter fluctuations to classify them as a change of jitter regime. Active traffic engineering strategies could keep jitter within a certain band. Despite that the KS-test method effectively infers congestion for a narrow type of congestion signature, we have included this method for its simplicity to detect congestion in cases with a large signal-to-noise ratio.

6.2 Comparing Inferences with Cross-Validation Data

We validate KS-test and jitter dispersion congestion inferences using CAIDA's autocorrelation-based congestion inferences as cross-validation data. In the pres-

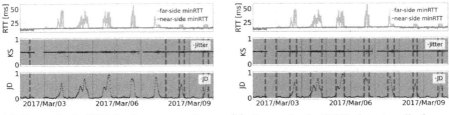

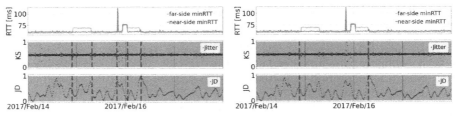

(a) Example A: HMM misses some change points

(b) Example A: BCP detects all change points

(c) Example B: HMM detects more change points than BCP (Fig. 13d)

(d) Example B: BCP misses some change points

Fig. 13. Two pairs of examples showing the limitations of change point detection algorithms to detect *all* change points (vertical dashed lines). a) shows an example where HMM is not able to capture some change points in contrast to BCP that detects all of them (b). c) shows an example where HMM is a more accurate than BCP at detecting change points (d) Red-filled intervals indicate periods of congestion. (Color figure online)

ence of recurrent congestion, CAIDA's congestion inferences count the number of 15-min intervals with elevated latency. Using this schema, CAIDA's congestion inferences report the daily congestion severity of a link with a variable that ranges from 0 to 96[4]. We use Jitterbug outputs to generate the same daily estimations.

Figure 14 shows how close are the daily congestion estimations of Jitterbug and CAIDA's congestion inference data. We also compared estimations with a maximum difference of 10% (in number of congested 15-min intervals), and the fraction of days that agree to within this 10% margin rises to 76–80% depending on the combination (80% for JD method using BCP). The most prominent discrepancies in this evaluation corresponds to two categories: *(i)* Jitterbug false positive inferences in periods with no congestion, and *(ii)* one-off congestion events detected by Jitterbug but not present in CAIDA's congestion inference data since CAIDA's method only attempts to infer recurrent (periodic) congestion episodes.

---

[4] One day has 96 periods of 15 min.

Table 2. Fraction (and total number) of (dis)agreements for different methodologies. The bar on top means a scenario with no congestion.

	BCP			HMM		
	$\overline{C_{KS}}$	C_{KS}	**SUM**	$\overline{C_{KS}}$	C_{KS}	**SUM**
$\overline{C_{JD}}$	0.43 (82)	0.04 (8)	0.47 (90)	0.39 (80)	0.04 (9)	0.43 (89)
C_{JD}	0.29 (56)	0.24 (46)	0.53 (92)	0.31 (63)	0.24 (49)	0.57 (112)
SUM	0.72 (138)	0.28 (54)	**192**	0.70 (143)	0.28 (58)	**201**

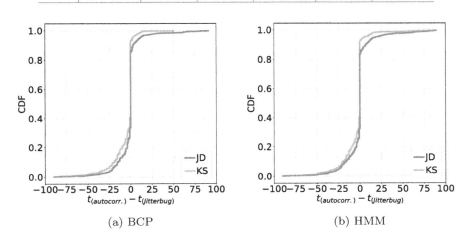

(a) BCP   (b) HMM

Fig. 14. Cumulative distribution function of the differences between the estimated daily time of congestion by autocorrelation-based methods and Jitterbug. These methods show remarkable similarity: 52% of days show no difference in inference regardless of change point detection method or congestion-detection method (KS vs JD).

7   Lessons Learned

In this section we enumerate important aspects we have identified for jitter-based congestion inference.

1. **Jitter and jitter dispersion signatures provide meaningful information to identify congestion events as periods of elevated latency.** We found that periods of congestion manifest in RTT latency measurements not only as periods of elevated latency, but also changes in jitter (and jitter-derived signals) time series.
2. **Jitter signals allowed us to discard periods of elevated latency generated by other path anomalies, e.g., route changes.** Including jitter-based analysis in the detection of congestion events allowed us to differentiate congestion events from other path anomalies. In non-congestion-related events, jitter and jitter dispersion time series tend *not* to change during periods of elevated latency.

3. **Period of elevated latency only to the far-side does not necessarily mean congestion**. We noticed that the simultaneous periods of elevated latency to near- and far-sides suggest a route change in the internal network of the ISP but a period of elevated latency to the far-side only does not necessarily indicate congestion. Although in many cases a period of elevated latency to the far-side only indicates a growth in the buffer occupancy of the interdomain link, this event could also suggest a route change only in the reverse path from the far-side router. We use jitter and jitter dispersion to identify traces with elevations only to the far-side router but not corresponding to congestion events.

4. **Shallower increments of RTT values when a link transitions to a period of congestion tend to affect jitter signatures too**. We observed a negative correlation between the increment of RTT values during periods of congestion and the visibility of changes in jitter signatures. We suppose this decrement in the contrast of RTT latency values between periods of elevated latency and other periods is related to the size of router buffers. We speculate that modern recommendations to keep buffers small [5] will likely affect jitter time series.

5. **The contribution of other random components of RTT latency can reveal congestion dynamics** . Some traces contain random contributions that mask queueing delay fluctuations in the jitter time series during periods of elevated latency. Although this is not a widespread phenomenon, it could compromise Jitterbug's ability to infer congestion, especially with the KS-test method.

6. **Limitations of change point detection methodologies to detect *all* periods of elevated latency**. None of the change point detection algorithms we examined could identify all change points in the *min* time series in our data. There is a wide variety of signal profiles in RTT latency measurements and several types of congestion signatures, including periods of elevated latency with flat, smooth and spiky signatures. We suppose that change point detection algorithms may not be able to capture change points for all types of signatures in this large set of profiles. To be able to identify *all* periods of elevated latency is crucial since the accuracy of Jitterbug congestion inferences mostly relies on detecting these intervals.

7. **Change point detection is expensive**. The BCP and HMM methods required significant time to execute on the 15-day traces we analyzed for this study, typically between 60 and 90 seconds. Optimizing performance of these methods will be critical for operational utility.

8. **The KS-test method only captures a limited type of congestion event signature**. But it is a simple and clean congestion inference approach, cost-effective for many scenarios beyond those we studied, and can inform further research in this area.

8   Related Work

Inferring Network Congestion with RTT Measurements. Previous research efforts focused on interdomain congestion inference leveraging from recurrent periods of elevated latency [12,23]. To generate these inferences, these works relied on a set of CAIDA's (Ark) [1] to run RTT latency measurements to all visible IP-level interconnection links [24]. Time Series Latency Probes (TSLP) [12,23] is the result of these latency measurement campaigns. An autocorrelation method is apply to traces on the TSLP data collection to find multiday repetition of elevated delays around the same times, i.e., driven by diurnal demand. However, this method to detect congestion requires some level of manual inspection. With a similar approach, Fontugne *et al.* [15] proposed a latency-based methodology to detect congestion in last-mile access networks. They used RIPE Atlas probes to run traceroute measurements campaigns and inferred congestion applying a methodology to detect latency deviations.

Anomaly Detection on Network Paths. RTT time series has been also used to detect a wide range of network events, such as path anomalies [13,14] and route changes [17,30].

Change Point Detection. Change Point Detection algorithms aim to detect *change point detection* (also known as time series segmentation) as abrupt changes in a sequence of observations (e.g., a time series) to divide a sequence into a finite number of non-overlapping partitions [3]. These algorithms are typically based on mathematical or machine learning models [3,4,11,31,36]. Another study found that some unsupervised anomaly detection tools for change point are notably time consuming [32]. Even though these methods are effective in capturing change points in the time series [9], event classification still requires human inspection.

Mathematical Approaches for Congestion Detection. Another type of studies brought sophisticated mathematical and statistical concepts to investigate congestion events. Mouchet *et al.* [27] proposed to use Hidden Markov Models (HMM) to identify different states in RTT latency time series, however, these states correspond to different latency values and do not report discriminate events caused by different types of events (e.g., route change vs congestion event). More recently, Spang *et al.* [34] proposed to use A/B tests in TCP lab measurements to generate unbiased evaluations of TCP Congestion Control Algorithms (CCA). However, the applicability of this approach relies on the assumption on independent traffic flows, which in practice may be compromised by the synchronization of TCP flow and short-lived TCP transfers. In addition, engineers typically used more pragmatic evaluations to test the impact of their changes.

9   Open Challenges

Other approaches not covered in this paper may be useful to extract information embedded in jitter signals. Early in this project we proposed and tested at least other four different approaches to jitter-based congestion inference. One aimed to capture the jitter variability at the beginning of a period, and another applied the same concept of the KS-test method but using j-min (definition in Sect. 3.1) instead. A third alternative used anomaly detection techniques to detect changes in jitter volatility. The fourth alternative used parametric models, including Normal and Levy-Stable distributions, to fit jitter behavior. These alternative approaches are promising and it is worth exploring them as part of future work.

In the future we also expect fluctuations of queueing delay to become more challenging to distinguish in RTT latency measurements as a consequence of smaller router buffers following modern buffer sizing recommendations [5,16]. Jitterbug central assumption is that *a period of congestion is a period of elevated latency*, however, if latency signatures show imperceptible queueing delays, this may comprise the accuracy of change point detection algorithms to detect periods of elevated latency. In addition, the rise of delay-sensitive real-time applications (e.g., videocalls, online gaming, etc.) could also incentivize the reduction of router buffer sizes. We observed (Sect. 2.2) a correlation between jitter signatures and buffer sizes and recognize that smaller buffer sizes could impede Jitterbug congestion inferences.

More demanding requirements of jitter-sensitive applications (e.g. live video streaming) could also modify traffic patterns and latency signatures. Today's HTTP-based video delivery relies on playback modulation to mitigate jitter impact on video flow [28,29]. However, in the future, real-time video broadcasting may requiere shorter playback jitters—and consequently dedicated traffic engineering strategies—that could modify the shape of the jitter curve and thus Jitterbug inferences.

Foreseeable changes in the foundational protocols of the TCP/IP stack could modify traffic dynamics and the nature of latency signatures. New latency-based Congestion Control Algorithms could modify latency signatures and buffer occupancy. The rollout of QUIC [8,18,22,33] could spread new features in the network potentially reshaping the nature of traffic dynamics. For example, QUIC proposes to aggregate and multiplex multiple short-lived web data transfers—typically run in parallel per-resource TCP sessions [8]—into a single transport-layer protocol session.

We expect that future work from ML/AI communities develop more cost-effective change point detection tools. The growing necessity of monitoring large-scale time series databases to generate (near) real-time anomaly detection is likely to be the driver of optimization in this space [32]. We expect that in the coming years we are going to count with more rapid and optimized supervised and unsupervised anomaly detection algorithms to detect change points.

10   Conclusions and Future work

In this paper we proposed Jitterbug, a novel framework to infer network congestion combining pre-existing approaches with information embedded in jitter signals. We found that jitter allowed us to expand congestion inference beyond scenarios of recurrent congestion patterns, such as one-time congestion events. We discovered that jitter (and jitter-derived signals) time series is useful to discriminate periods of elevated latency caused by congestion from route changes.

We have also learned about the various challenges of inferring network congestion with RTT latency measurements. The vastly heterogeneous structure of the network is reflected in diverse latency signatures showing large and short buffer sizes, remarkable presence of randomness unrelated from congestion events, etc. We have also learned about limitations of change point detection algorithms in detecting all beginning and ending points of periods of elevated latency as well as the time required to obtain results from these algorithms.

Applying Jitterbug to the cases in our dataset, we obtained similar results to recent autocorrelation methods [12]. However, in contrast to that method, which is based on the repetitiveness of the signal and uses information of near- and far-side RTT latency measurements, Jitterbug is fully based on far-side RTT latency measurements and does not rely on repetitiveness to discern the congestion status of a period.

We hope that this work will encourage studies focused on network congestion inference, jitter analysis and change point detection algorithms. In the future, we would like to investigate how sampling rates (higher and lower) affect congestion inferences and profiles of RTT latency signatures. For example, studies in financial time series have found that the distribution of assets returns vary depending on the scaling factor (i.e. time elapsed between samples) [20,25], we would like to investigate if this also happens on jitter time series. We are also interested in studying whether we could develop purely jitter-based congestion inference methods. Another topic that we would like to investigate is if inter-packet delay in back-to-back measurements, for example using FAST probing tool [26], could allow us to infer congestion.

Acknowledgement. We thank the anonymous reviewers for their insightful comments, and Maxime Mouchet for providing an implementation of the HMM algorithm. We would like to thank Fabian Bustamante (Northwestern University) for coming up with the original term *Jitterbug* to name this paper. This work was partly funded by research grants DARPA HR00112020014, NSF OAC-1724853 and NSF CNS-1925729.

References

1. Archipelago measurement infrastructure updates. https://catalog.caida.org/details/media/2011_archipelago. Accessed 30 Sept 2021
2. Manic. https://catalog.caida.org/details/software/manic. Accessed 13 Oct 2021
3. Adams, R.P., MacKay, D.J.: Bayesian online changepoint detection. arXiv preprint arXiv:0710.3742 (2007)
4. Aminikhanghahi, S., Cook, D.J.: A survey of methods for time series change point detection. Knowl. Inf. Syst. **51**(2), 339–367 (2016). https://doi.org/10.1007/s10115-016-0987-z
5. Appenzeller, G., Keslassy, I., McKeown, N.: Sizing router buffers. ACM SIGCOMM Comput. Commun. Rev. **34**(4), 281–292 (2004)

6. ARUNO: ADTK Detectors (2021). https://arundo-adtk.readthedocs-hosted.com/en/stable/api/detectors.html

7. Cardwell, N., Cheng, Y., Gunn, C.S., Yeganeh, S.H., Jacobson, V.: BBR: congestion-based congestion control: measuring bottleneck bandwidth and round-trip propagation time. Queue **14**(5), 20–53 (2016)

8. Carlucci, G., De Cicco, L., Mascolo, S.: HTTP over UDP: an experimental investigation of QUIC. In: Proceedings of the 30th Annual ACM Symposium on Applied Computing, pp. 609–614 (2015)

9. Davisson, L., Jakovleski, J., Ngo, N., Pham, C., Sommers, J.: Reassessing the constancy of end-to-end internet latency. In: Proceedings of IFIP TMA (2021)

10. Demichelis, C., Chimento, P.: RFC 3393: IP packet delay variation metric for IP performance metrics (IPPM) (2002). https://datatracker.ietf.org/doc/html/rfc3393

11. Desobry, F., Davy, M., Doncarli, C.: An online kernel change detection algorithm. IEEE Trans. Signal Process. **53**(8), 2961–2974 (2005)

12. Dhamdhere, A., et al.: Inferring persistent interdomain congestion. In: Proceedings of the 2018 Conference of the ACM Special Interest Group on Data Communication, pp. 1–15 (2018)

13. Fontugne, R., Mazel, J., Fukuda, K.: An empirical mixture model for large-scale RTT measurements. In: Proceedings of IEEE INFOCOM (2015)

14. Fontugne, R., Pelsser, C., Aben, E., Bush, R.: Pinpointing delay and forwarding anomalies using large-scale traceroute measurements. In: Proceedings of ACM Internet Measurement Conference (2017). https://doi.org/10.1145/3131365.3131384

15. Fontugne, R., Shah, A., Cho, K.: Persistent last-mile congestion: not so uncommon. In: Proceedings of the ACM Internet Measurement Conference, pp. 420–427 (2020)

16. Gettys, J.: Bufferbloat: dark buffers in the internet. IEEE Internet Comput. **15**(3), 96–96 (2011)

17. Iodice, M., Candela, M., Battista, G.D.: Periodic path changes in RIPE Atlas. IEEE Access **7**, 65518–65526 (2019). https://doi.org/10.1109/access.2019.2917804

18. Iyengar, J., Thomson, M. (eds.): QUIC: a UDP-based multiplexed and secure transport. RFC 9000 (Proposed Standard) (2021). https://doi.org/10.17487/RFC9000. https://www.rfc-editor.org/rfc/rfc9000.txt

19. Jacobson, V.: Congestion avoidance and control. ACM SIGCOMM Comput. Commun. Rev. **18**(4), 314–329 (1988)

20. Jaroszewicz, S., Mariani, M.C., Ferraro, M.: Long correlations and truncated levy walks applied to the study Latin-American market indices. Physica A **355**(2–4), 461–474 (2005)

21. Laki, S., Mátray, P., Hága, P., Csabai, I., Vattay, G.: A detailed path-latency model for router geolocation. In: EAI Tridentcom. IEEE (2009). https://doi.org/10.1109/tridentcom.2009.4976258

22. Langley, A., et al.: The QUIC transport protocol: design and internet-scale deployment. In: Proceedings of the Conference of the ACM Special Interest Group on Data Communication, pp. 183–196 (2017)

23. Luckie, M., Dhamdhere, A., Clark, D., Huffaker, B., Claffy, K.: Challenges in inferring internet interdomain congestion. In: Proceedings of the 2014 Conference on Internet Measurement Conference, pp. 15–22 (2014)

24. Luckie, M., Dhamdhere, A., Huffaker, B., Clark, D., Claffy, K.: Bdrmap: inference of borders between IP networks. In: Proceedings of the 2016 Internet Measurement Conference, pp. 381–396 (2016)

25. Mantegna, R.N., Stanley, H.E.: Econophysics: scaling and its breakdown in finance. J. Stat. Phys. **89**(1), 469–479 (1997)
26. Marder, A., Claffy, K.C., Snoeren, A.C.: Inferring cloud interconnections: validation, geolocation, and routing behavior. In: Hohlfeld, O., Lutu, A., Levin, D. (eds.) PAM 2021. LNCS, vol. 12671, pp. 230–246. Springer, Cham (2021). https://doi.org/10.1007/978-3-030-72582-2_14
27. Mouchet, M., Vaton, S., Chonavel, T., Aben, E., Den Hertog, J.: Large-scale characterization and segmentation of internet path delays with infinite HMMs. IEEE Access **8**, 16771–16784 (2020)
28. Mustafa, I.B., Nadeem, T.: Dynamic traffic shaping technique for http adaptive video streaming using software defined networks. In: 2015 12th Annual IEEE International Conference on Sensing, Communication, and Networking (SECON), pp. 178–180. IEEE (2015)
29. Pu, W., Zou, Z., Chen, C.W.: Video adaptation proxy for wireless dynamic adaptive streaming over HTTP. In: 2012 19th International Packet Video Workshop (PV), pp. 65–70. IEEE (2012)
30. Pucha, H., Zhang, Y., Mao, Z.M., Hu, Y.C.: Understanding network delay changes caused by routing events. ACM SIGMETRICS Perform. Eval. Rev. **35**(1), 73–84 (2007). https://doi.org/10.1145/1269899.1254891
31. Punskaya, E., Andrieu, C., Doucet, A., Fitzgerald, W.J.: Bayesian curve fitting using MCMC with applications to signal segmentation. IEEE Trans. Signal Process. **50**(3), 747–758 (2002)
32. Ren, H., et al.: Time-series anomaly detection service at Microsoft. In: Proceedings of the 25th ACM SIGKDD International Conference on Knowledge Discovery & Data Mining, pp. 3009–3017 (2019)
33. Rüth, J., Poese, I., Dietzel, C., Hohlfeld, O.: A first look at QUIC in the wild. In: Beverly, R., Smaragdakis, G., Feldmann, A. (eds.) PAM 2018. LNCS, vol. 10771, pp. 255–268. Springer, Cham (2018). https://doi.org/10.1007/978-3-319-76481-8_19
34. Spang, B., Hannan, V., Kunamalla, S., Huang, T.Y., McKeown, N., Johari, R.: Unbiased experiments in congested networks. arXiv preprint arXiv:2110.00118 (2021)
35. Turkovic, B., Kuipers, F.A., Uhlig, S.: Interactions between congestion control algorithms. In: 2019 Network Traffic Measurement and Analysis Conference (TMA), pp. 161–168. IEEE (2019)
36. Xuan, X., Murphy, K.: Modeling changing dependency structure in multivariate time series. In: Proceedings of the 24th International Conference on Machine Learning, pp. 1055–1062 (2007)

Can 5G mmWave Support Multi-user AR?

Moinak Ghoshal[1(✉)], Pranab Dash[2], Zhaoning Kong[2], Qiang Xu[2],
Y. Charlie Hu[2], Dimitrios Koutsonikolas[1], and Yuanjie Li[3]

[1] Northeastern University, Boston, USA
{ghoshal.m,d.koutsonikolas}@northeastern.edu
[2] Purdue University, West Lafayette, USA
{dashp,kong102,xu1201,ychu}@purdue.edu
[3] Tsinghua University, Beijing, China

Abstract. Augmented Reality (AR) has been widely hailed as a representative of ultra-high bandwidth and ultra-low latency apps that will be enabled by 5G networks. While single-user AR can perform AR tasks locally on the mobile device, multi-user AR apps, which allow multiple users to interact within the same physical space, critically rely on the cellular network to support user interactions. However, a recent study showed that multi-user AR apps can experience very high end-to-end latency when running over LTE, rendering user interaction practically infeasible. In this paper, we study whether 5G mmWave, which promises significant bandwidth and latency improvements over LTE, can support multi-user AR by conducting an in-depth measurement study of the same popular multi-user AR app over both LTE and 5G mmWave.

Our measurement and analysis show that: (1) The E2E AR latency over LTE is significantly lower compared to the values reported in the previous study. However, it still remains too high for practical user interaction. (2) 5G mmWave brings no benefits to multi-user AR apps. (3) While 5G mmWave reduces the latency of the uplink visual data transmission, there are other components of the AR app that are independent of the network technology and account for a significant fraction of the E2E latency. (4) The app drains 66% more network energy, which translates to 28% higher total energy over 5G mmWave compared to over LTE.

1 Introduction

Augmented Reality (AR) promises unprecedented interactive and immersive experiences to users by augmenting physical objects in the real world with computer-generated perceptual information. As such, a complete AR app often needs to perform several challenging tasks to understand and interact with the physical environment, such as pose estimation or object detection [1].

While single-user AR can potentially perform AR tasks locally on the mobile device [9], *multi-user AR apps*, also known as networked AR apps, which allow multiple users to interact within the same physical space, critically rely on the cellular network and often a cloud server to support user interactions. Further,

O. Hohlfeld et al. (Eds.): PAM 2022, LNCS 13210, pp. 180–196, 2022.
https://doi.org/10.1007/978-3-030-98785-5_8

to provide high-quality, interactive experience, such networked AR apps need to perform the needed AR tasks (e.g. pose estimation and synchronization to the same physical environment) at very low latency, which places high uplink bandwidth demand on the wireless network. It is because of this stringent network requirement that networked AR has been widely viewed as one of the "killer" apps for 5G [10,29,38], e.g., in the AT&T and Microsoft alliance as well as the Verizon and AWS alliance to showcase 5G edge computing solutions [11,39].

Previously, Apicharttrisorn *et al.* conducted an in-depth measurement study [8] of a popular two-user app that performs the most basic multi-user interaction, i.e., displaying an object, to study whether LTE can support the needed QoE of multi-user AR. That study showed that the latency from the moment a user (host) places a virtual object in the physical environment to the moment a second user (resolver) sees that object in their screen is 12.5 s in the median case and can be as high as 26 s over LTE, which renders the most basic user interaction in multi-user AR apps practically infeasible.

5G mmWave is being rapidly deployed by all major mobile operators promising ultra-high bandwidth and lower latency compared to 4G LTE. As an example, Table 1 shows the uplink and downlink TCP throughput (measured with iperf3), the end-to-end (E2E) round trip latency (measured with ping), and the RAN latency (approximated as the round trip latency to the first hop router) between a mobile device and a Google Cloud server. We observe that 5G mmWave offers 16x higher downlink throughput and 3.4x higher uplink throughput compared to LTE while it reduces the RAN (E2E) latency by 56% (42%).

Table 1. Throughput and Latency comparison over 5G mmWave and LTE.

	Throughput (Mbps)		Latency (ms)	
	Downlink	Uplink	RAN	E2E
5G	1715 ± 57	152 ± 6	14 ± 2	25 ± 4
LTE	110 ± 17	44 ± 8	32 ± 5	43 ± 4

Driven by these initial observations, in this paper we revisit the previous feasibility study of multi-user AR over cellular networks by conducting an in-depth measurement study of the same popular multi-user AR app side-by-side over both LTE and 5G mmWave. Our dataset is publicly available [2]. Our study tries to answer two key questions: (1) Can 5G mmWave provide much better support for multi-user interactions in AR compared to LTE to the extent that real-time multi-user interaction becomes feasible? (2) Does multi-user AR drain significantly more energy under 5G compared to under LTE?

The main findings of our study are as follows: (1) The E2E latency over LTE is significantly lower (by 6.6 s) compared to the values reported in [8], however, it remains too high for real-time multi-user AR apps. (2) 5G mmWave does not reduce the E2E latency of the AR app compared to LTE in spite of its much higher bandwidth and lower RTT. (3) While 5G mmWave yields a small reduction to the latency of the uplink visual data transmission, there are other components of the AR app that contribute significantly to the E2E latency regardless of the underlying cellular technology. In addition, we discovered a new

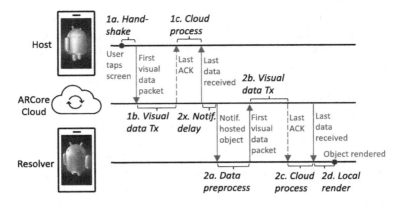

Fig. 1. Cloud-based multi-user AR.

latency component between the cloud and the resolver, which was not reported in [8], and is often a major contributor to the E2E latency. (4) The app drains on average 66% more network energy over 5G mmWave compared to over LTE. Since the network energy accounts for about 32% of the total energy, such high network energy difference translates into smaller (but still significant) difference in the total app energy drain, by 23% on the host and 43% on the resolver.

2 Background and Related Work

2.1 Multi-user AR

Current mobile AR systems like Google ARCore [4], Apple ARKit [3], and Microsoft Hololens [6] use SLAM to construct a 3D coordinate structure of the physical world and get an estimation of the user's location and orientation (pose). The users first need to share their coordinates to create a common and consistent real-world coordinate system. Once a virtual object is placed on the screen, SLAM is run to get an estimation of the device's current pose and the real-world coordinate features, and objects in the user's field of view are rendered on the screen. Popular multi-user AR apps on the market, enabled by Google ARCore, Apple ARKit, or Microsoft Hololens offload most of the computations to cloud servers to reduce the workload on the phones. In the following, we briefly describe the workflow of such applications, shown in Fig. 1.

The host initiates a connection with a cloud based Firebase [5] database by creating a room ID (R). The resolver uses the same room ID and waits for incoming connections from the host via the cloud. After an object is placed on the host's screen, the following events take place.

1. Hosting device: (a) Device Handshakes. The host places an object and two connections to Google Cloud are instantiated for object positioning. **(b) Visual Data Transmission.** The host sends the real world visual information about the overlaid virtual object to the cloud. **(c) Cloud Processing.** The cloud processes the host's visual data. It sends back the SLAM-computed world frame to the host and notifies the resolver to start the resolution process.

2. Resolving device:(a) Cloud Connection Initiation. The Firebase notifies the resolver to start a connection with the Google Cloud instance. The resolver scans the world frames through camera and pre-processes the data. **(b) Data Transmission.** On getting notified by the cloud, the resolver uploads its visual data to the cloud. **(c) Cloud Processing.** The cloud, on receiving the resolver's frames, tries to match them against the host's SLAM-computed data, estimates the pose of the resolver in the world frame and send its back to the resolver. If the cloud processing fails (e.g., because the environment lacks visual features, such as high contrast edges, colors, etc.), the cloud asks the resolver to upload new visual data. Hence, this process might involve multiple rounds of communication and cloud processing. In the following, we include only the first round of communication in the data transmission delay (2b), while any additional rounds of communication are included in the cloud processing delay (2c). **(d) Object Rendering.** The resolver uses the data from the cloud to estimate the virtual object's pose and display it on its screen.

We note that there may be an additional delay before the notification of the hosted object is received by the resolver, denoted as **2x: Notification delay** in Fig. 1. This delay was not reported in [8], but it is often a major contributor to the E2E latency in our experiments.

2.2 Related Work

Multi-user AR. Unlike single-user AR (e.g., [9,12,22,31]), there have been very few works on multi-user AR. A few works [30,32,44] focus on application layer sharing while our work focuses on the impact of the cellular network in multi-user AR performance. In contrast to [8], which studies multi-user AR performance over LTE, our work is the first to our best knowledge to study the performance and energy consumption of multi-user AR over 5G mmWave. A few recent works study edge-assisted [34] or P2P-based [33] multi-user AR. In contrast, our work focuses on cloud-assisted multi-user AR, which is the default approach in most popular AR apps on the market.

5G mmWave Performance. A few recent studies focus on early-stage 5G mmWave performance and its impact on downlink-oriented mobile apps (web browsing and video streaming) [24–26]. To our best knowledge, there is no other work studying the impact of 5G mmWave on multi-user AR, which has very different application and communication features compared to web browsing or video streaming.

3   Methodology

Multi-user AR Application. Google's Cloud Anchor API [4] forms the foundation for most of the cloud-based, multi-user AR Android apps today. We used

Table 2. 5G mmWave Uplink throughput for different operators and cities.

Operator and City	Throughput (Mbps)
Verizon, Boston	152 ± 6
Verizon, Chicago	47 ± 15
Verizon, Indianapolis	43 ± 5
AT&T, Indianapolis	150 ± 50

Google's popular multi-user application, Cloud Anchor, which was also used in [8]. The application lets a user place a virtual object on a real-world surface while another user can view it.

Devices. We used two Google Pixel 5 phones for our experiments. For the measurements involving the LTE network, we disabled the 5G radio through the phone's settings.

5G Carrier and Location. We conducted uplink throughput measurements in three different cities over two different cellular operators (Table 2). Based on these measurements, we selected Boston and Verizon for our experiments in this work, as that was the combination that provided the highest throughput. We used Verizon's NSA-based 5G service that provides mmWave coverage over the 28/39 GHz frequency bands (n260/261).

Experimental Methodology. We conducted our experiments near the downtown of Boston, at two different locations. At each location, we stood 80 ft away from the base station (BS); we confirmed via SpeedTest measurements that this distance yielded the maximum possible uplink throughput. The experiments at each location spanned a 1-week period. All measurements were done at day time, from 9 am to 5 pm. For 5G mmWave, we consider two cases – when the users face towards the BS and when they face away from the BS; in the later case, their bodies block the Line of Sight (LOS) between the BS and the UE.

Measurement Tools. To extract the end to end latency of the AR app, we modified the app to log the Unix timestamps and captured packets with timestamps via tcpdump. We also extracted low-level, signalling messages using MobileInsight [20].

4 Performance of Multi-user AR

We begin our study by comparing the E2E latency of the AR app over LTE and 5G mmWave in Sect. 4.1 and then study the individual app components in Sect. 4.2–4.5. Finally, in Sect. 4.6, we study the impact of two optimizations, which were shown in [8] to improve the latency over LTE networks. Figure 2 plots the E2E latency as well as the latency of the individual components over 20 runs.

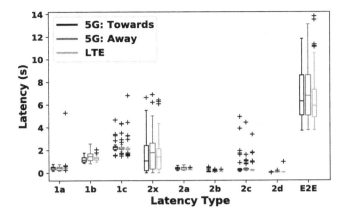

Fig. 2. Multi-user AR latency breakdown.

4.1   End to End Performance

From Fig. 2, we make the following observations: (i) The E2E latency over LTE is significantly lower compared to the numbers reported in [8]. The median (maximum) latency is 5.9 s (14 s) vs. 12.5 s (27 s) in [8]). We conjecture that this reduction may be due to different levels of congestion in the LTE network and the cloud and/or technological advances in the LTE network and the UEs. However, the latency remains unacceptably high and severely impacts the user QoE. (ii) 5G mmWave, when the user faces the BS, *reduces the worst-case E2E latency* by more than 2 s. However, surprisingly, *the median latency and the 75-th percentile over 5G mmWave are higher than over LTE by 0.4 s and 1.4 s, respectively*, despite the much higher speeds and lower RTTs brought by 5G mmWave compared to LTE (Table 1). (iii) Self-blockage has minimal impact on the performance of the multi-user AR app, increasing the median E2E latency by about 0.5 s and the 75-th percentile by about 0.2 s. (v) Similar to the results in [8], the key contributors of the E2E latency are on the hosting side for both 5G mmWave and LTE. Together, the handshakes (1a), the visual data transmission (1b), and the cloud processing (1c) account for about 60% of the E2E latency over both 5G mMWave and 64% over LTE. In contrast, the resolving side components (2a - 2d) contribute together only 12% of the median E2E latency.

Overall, 5G mmWave brings practically no improvements to the performance of multi-user AR apps. In the following, we take a closer look at the latency of the individual app components and try to uncover the root causes of this surprising result and the factors that prevent 5G mmWave to unleash its potential.

4.2   Latency 2x: Resolver Notification

In our experiments, we often observed a substantial delay between the last data packet sent by the cloud to the host and the moment the notification from the cloud of a new hosted object is received by the resolver. In Fig. 2, we observe that this delay, which we call 2x and was not reported in [8], varies from under 100 ms to as high as 7 s, and can be a significant contributor to the E2E latency over both LTE and 5G mmWave, accounting for about 16%, 26% and 23% of the E2E latency in the median case for 5G-towards (1.05 s), 5G-away (1.77 s) and LTE (1.4 s), respectively.

To understand the root cause of this delay, we set up a proxy between the cloud server and the resolver UE. The proxy is a server on Google Cloud, and is connected to the resolver UE through an L2TP tunnel. We synchronized the proxy and the two UEs using NTP and used tcpdump to capture and analyze packet traces on both sides. By comparing timestamps, we further broke down the 2x latency into two parts: between the last data packet sent by the cloud to the host and the moment the notification from the cloud is received by the proxy (2x_1) and between the moment the notification is received by the proxy and the moment the notification is finally received by the resolver (2x_2).

We found that 2x_1 is always short (about 100 ms), suggesting that the load on the server has minimal impact on the total 2x latency. Hence, the main contributor to the 2x latency is 2x_2 (varying from a few about 100 ms to more than 6 s) and the the root cause of the high 2x latency lies somewhere on the path from the proxy to the UE. We further found that every time the 2x latency was higher than a few 100 s of ms, there was a TCP retransmission of the notification packet from the server. In contrast, no retransmission was observed for the cases when 2x_2 was comparable to 2x_1. Since the TCP retransmission packet was always received by the proxy within 100 ms and retransmissions over the wireless link (at the MAC and RLC layers) are unlikely to cause a delay of several seconds, we conjecture that the root cause of the high 2x latency lies in the cellular packet core network and the various middlebox (NATs, firewalls) policies implemented by the operator, which have been shown to often have a significant impact on E2E TCP performance [40].

4.3   Latency 1a and 2a: Connection Handshakes

In [8], it was shown that TCP connection handshakes between the app and the cloud take 3 s on average on the hosting side (1a), contributing significantly to the E2E latency, while the handshakes and data pre-processing on the resolving side (2a) finish in less than 1 s. In contrast, Fig. 2 shows that the 1a latency in our experiments is significantly reduced over both 5G mmWave and LTE and is similar to the 2a latency (below 1 s), with the exception of 1 run over LTE that experienced a 2a latency higher than 5.5 s.

One would expect the 1a and 2a latencies to be lower over 5G mmWave compared to over LTE, as 5G mmWave has lower RTTs (Table 1). However, a closer look at these latencies (Fig. 3) shows that this is not the case. While the minimum values of 1a and 2a are indeed lower over 5G mmWave, the 75-th percentiles and maximum values are higher. Analyzing the root cause of this result is difficult, as each of these delays consists of multiple components (e.g., 1a involves tapping the screen, an optional DNS transaction, a TCP handshake

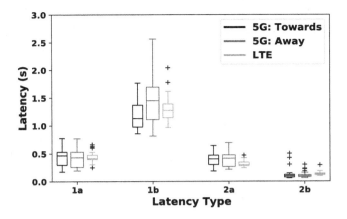

Fig. 3. Closer look at latencies 1a, 1b, 2a, 2b.

with the cloud, and a TLS handshake) and the delay of each component might affect other delays. For example, we found that when the TCP handshake is preceded by a DNS transaction, the time to complete the TCP handshake is half over 5G mmWave compared to over LTE (~20 ms vs. ~40 ms), whereas in the absence of a DNS transaction it is higher (~220 ms vs. ~170 ms), possibly due to different promotion delays (e.g., the delay for the radio to switch from the idle state to the connected state) in 5G and LTE. Since the contribution of both 1a and 2a to the E2E latency is minimal over both cellular networks, we do not further study these latencies.

4.4   Latency 1c and 2c: Cloud Processing

Figure 2 shows that the latency of the cloud processing of the host data (1c) is 2.2 s in the median case over both 5G mmWave and LTE, although there are a few outliers as high as 7.5 s, which we attribute to temporary server overloads. This value is significantly lower than the value reported in [8] (5 s), as the cloud technology has evolved over the past 2 years, but remains high, contributing about 30–35% to the E2E latency. In contrast, the cloud processing latency on the resolving side (2c) is in general negligible (200–400 ms), similar to what was reported in [8]. However, there are outlier values that can be as high as 5.5 s. We found that these outliers are due to multiple rounds of communication and processing when the cloud processing fails and requests the resolver to upload new visual data, as we explained in Fig. 1. One such example is shown in Fig. 4. After the first chunk of visual data upload (0–0.07 s), the cloud processing fails, and the resolver uploads another chunk of visual data (0.89–0.95 s), which the cloud processes successfully. We also observe that the cloud processing delay is much longer in the case of a failure (the first cloud processing delay in Fig. 4 takes 0.82 s while the second one takes only 0.16 s).

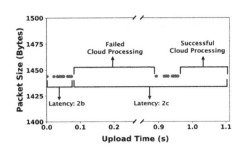

Fig. 4. Visual data re-uploaded by resolver as cloud processing failed in the first attempt.

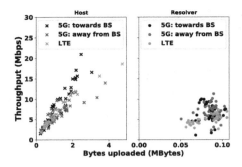

Fig. 5. Throughput as a function of uploaded bytes.

4.5   Latency 1b and 2b: Uplink Data Communication

In [8], the average 1b latency was found to be 10 s over a public LTE network. In contrast, our measurements in Fig. 2 show that the 1b latency over LTE is much lower, with a median value of 1.27 s and a maximum value of 2.04 s, which explain the large drop in the LTE E2E latency compared to the values reported in [8]. Hence, unlike the results reported in [8], 1b is no longer the primary contributor to the E2E latency over LTE, although its contribution still remains significant. On the other hand, the contribution of the 2b latency on the resolving side remains negligible.

Figure 2 shows that 5G mmWave reduces both 1b and 2b latency when the user faces towards the BS, as expected due to its higher bandwidth and lower RTTs. However, the improvement is very small – 0.14 s and 0.27 s, in the median case, for 1b and 2b, respectively. Self-blockage increases the 1b latency to 1.44 s (vs. 1.13 s in the absence of blockage) in the median case and to 2.6 s (vs. 1.77 s) in the worst case, but no impact on the resolving side.

To understand why 5G mmWave has minimal impact on the uplink transmission latency in spite of the much higher uplink bandwidth compared to LTE, we show in Fig. 5 scatterplots of the uplink throughput vs. the uploaded bytes on the hosting and resolving side for each of the 40 runs. We observe that the data transfer size on both sides is very small – up to 5 MB on the hosting side and up to 0.11 MB on the resolving side, similar to the numbers reported in [8]. The small data transfer sizes explain the small improvement in the uplink data communication latency brought by 5G mmWave compared to LTE. The data uploads always finish before TCP exits the slow start phase, preventing it from taking advantage of the much higher available bandwidth offered by 5G mmWave. This is clearly shown in Fig. 5, where we observe very low throughput values (at most 22 Mbps on the host side and 12 Mbps on the resolver side), which are similar over 5G mmWave and LTE, especially for data transfer sizes up to 2 MB.

Figure 5 further shows that facing away from the BS results in a small throughput reduction compared to facing towards the BS and to LTE for transfer sizes larger than 2 MB. This result appears to contradict recent studies reporting that the user orientation has a significant impact on 5G mmWave performance. The reason for the small observed throughput (and latency) degradation in our experiments is again the very small data transfer sizes, which prevent TCP from exit-

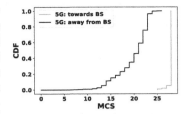

Fig. 6. 5G mmWave MCS.

ing slow start. Figure 6, which plots the CDF of the modulation and coding scheme (MCS) values collected by MobileInsight every 5 ms, further corroborates this claim. The MCS values are much lower when the user faces away from the BS compared to when the user faces towards the BS, confirming that self-blockage deteriorates significantly the link quality. However, this large degradation of the link quality is perceived to a much lesser degree by the multi-user AR app, due to the very low application layer throughput.

4.6   AR Design Optimizations

In this section, we study two optimizations that were proposed in [8] to reduce the uplink data transmission latency (1b and 2b) over LTE networks.

Packet Size Adaptation. In scenarios when the RAN is congested, large IP packet sizes can experience heavier segmentation at the Radio Link Control (RLC) layer, which can increase the per-packet RLC latency and subsequently, the TCP RTT, and adversely impact the growth of the TCP window during an AR upload burst. While smaller IP packets can help address this issue, they increase the network overhead. In [8], it was shown that a TCP Maximum Segment Size (MSS) of 650 bytes can increase throughput by 62% and reduce the RAN latency by 37% compared to the default MSS.

We experimented with the same three MSS values used in [8]: 400 bytes, 650 bytes, and default (1356 bytes). We conducted 10 runs with each MSS over 5G mmWave with the user facing towards the BS. The results are shown in Fig. 7.

We observe that changing the MSS has a minimal impact over of 5G mmWave networks. On the hosting side, all three MSS values result in roughly the same median latency. On the resolving side, the default MSS results in a slightly lower median latency than the other two values but in a slightly higher worst case latency. We conjecture that the minimal impact of the MSS on the 1b and 2b latency is due to the fact that 5G mmWave deployments are still at their infancy and they are unlikely to be congested, unlike LTE networks. To test the impact of this optimization in a congested network, we repeated the experiment with a third phone sending backlogged UDP traffic to a cloud server. Figure 7 shows that in a congested network, the smallest MSS (400 bytes) results in a

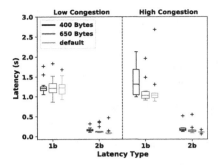
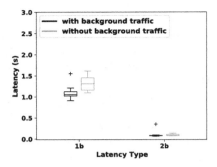

Fig. 7. Data transmission latency with varying MSS.

Fig. 8. Data transmission latency with background ICMP traffic.

much higher latency, especially in the case of 1b, similar to what was observed in [8]. However, the other two MSS values still yield similar latency.

Small Background Traffic. Every time the application starts sending a new uplink data burst, the UE has to request resources from the BS. The BS is initially unaware of the uplink sending buffer, and may allocate a small uplink grant for the UE, causing RLC segmentation and increasing the per-packet RAN latency. In order to make the BS aware of the UE's uplink buffer during an AR session, the authors in [8] proposed to generate small amounts of background uplink traffic, using ICMP packets during an AR session. To examine the effectiveness of this optimization over 5G mmWave, we conducted 10 runs with and without ICMP traffic with the user facing towards the BS. Figure 8 shows that this optimization is effective over 5G mmWave, bringing a significant reduction to the 1b latency on the hosting side. The median latency reduces from 1.31 s (without ICMP traffic) to 1.05 s (with ICMP traffic). The 2b latency is also reduced but the reduction is much smaller compared to the 1b latency due to the much smaller transfer sizes. However, since the contribution of the 1b and 2b latencies to the E2E latency is small (Sect. 4.5), this optimization has a small impact on the E2E latency.

Summary. Overall, in spite of the much higher bandwidth and lower RTT over LTE, 5G mmWave brings no benefits to multi-user AR apps. Although 5G mmWave brings a small reduction to the visual data transmission latency and certain optimizations that were proposed over LTE networks are equally effective over 5G networks and can further reduce this latency, there are other major contributors to the E2E AR latency (resolver notification, cloud processing), which are independent of the underlying cellular network technology. As a result, the E2E latency over 5G mmWave remains too high to enable practical user interaction in multi-user AR apps.

5   Energy Consumption

In this section, we compare the power draw and energy drain of both the host and the resolver in running the AR app over LTE and 5G mmWave.

5.1   Methodology

The AR app uses five power-hungry phone components: CPU, GPU, Camera, Display, and the cellular NIC. We use the utilization-based power models [13] for mobile devices, which have been widely used [14,16,18,19,27,36,37,41–43] to model the instantaneous power draw of the CPU and the GPU. In a nutshell, such a model derives the correlation between the utilization of a phone component in each of its power states, and the resulting power draw using carefully designed micro-benchmarks. To use such a model, the CPU and GPU usage are logged during app execution using Linux event trace [21] and afterwards fed into the power model as input to estimate the per-component power draw during the app execution. For the OLED display, we used the piece-wise OLED model recently proposed in [15], which decomposes the RGB color space into $16 \times 16 \times 16$ subgrids and derives accurate pixel power model for each subgrid using liner regression to achieve low OLED power prediction error of no more than 4.6% on four recent generations of phones. We developed a program by modifying the Android "screenrecord" program to record the screen during the app execution and applied the OLED display power model from [15] for the Pixel 5 phone used in our study to estimate the OLED display power. Finally, we model the camera power draw as a constant [13]. Since the LTE/5G NIC power drain is known to be sensitive to external conditions such as the signal strength [17], practical power models based on regression on observed throughput [19,26] are coarse-grained, and the app does not use other power-hungry phone components such as the hardware decoder, we instead directly measure the instantaneous device power using the built-in power sensor via the Linux power supply class [7] and subtract from it the power drawn by CPU, GPU, Camera, and OLED display to derive the power draw by the cellular NIC.

We adopted the above power modeling methodology for three reasons. (1) We needed to measure component-wise power draw to compute the network power draw by the AR app from the total power. SnapDragon Profiler, Monsoon Power Monitor [23], or BattOR [35] can only provide the total power consumption, as they do not provide power counters for the individual components. (2) Using power modeling eases experimentation, as attaching a Monsoon power monitor to a phone would require dismantling and instrumenting the device, which would be difficult for field experiments. (3) The power models themselves are benchmarked against the Monsoon power monitor, making them reasonably accurate. For example, we used the OLED display model from [15], which has error less than 5% for Pixel 5 on average, and the CPU and GPU models use the Linux event trace to estimate the power consumption with very high resolution.

5.2 Results

Figure 9 shows the average (over 5 runs) energy drain by the host and the resolver during the AR app execution and the breakdown into 7 app phases, over 5G mmWave (facing towards the BS) and LTE. We make the following observations.

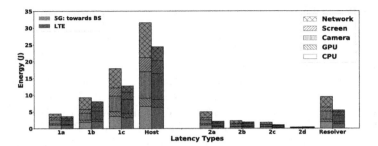

Fig. 9. Energy breakdown

Host vs. Resolver. Overall the app drains much more total energy on the host than on the resolver, by 70% (31 J vs. 9 J) and 80% (24 J vs. 5 J), over 5G and LTE, respectively. This happens as the 3 phases 1a, 1b, and 1c on the host drain significantly higher energy than the later 4 phases (2a – 2d) on the resolver.

Total Energy Comparison. On the host, the app drains 23% more total energy when running over 5G compared to running over LTE. The energy breakdown by phone components shows that the major contributor to the difference is the network energy, which over 5G is 60% higher than over LTE. Similarly, on the resolver, the app drains 43% more total energy when running over 5G compared to running over LTE, although the absolute difference is much smaller compared to on the host side. The major difference again comes from the network energy drain, which over 5G is significantly higher than over LTE, by 83%.

Per-app Phase Comparison. To understand where the energy difference happens in the different phases of the app, we look at the energy breakdown by app phases. Figure 9 shows that on the host side higher energy drain over 5G compared to over LTE happens in all app phases, by 18%, 14% and 29% in phases 1a, 1b, and 1c, respectively. Hence, the energy difference within each phase mainly comes from network energy, which is 41%, 56% and 68% higher under phases 1a, 1b, and 1c, respectively, over 5G than over LTE. Similarly, on the resolver side, the major contribution to the higher energy drain over 5G compared to over LTE also comes from all app phases, by 42%, 18% and 43% in phases 2a, 2b, and 2c, respectively. Again, the energy difference within each phase mainly comes from network energy, which is 88%, 77%, and 77% higher under phases 2a, 2b, and 2c, respectively, over 5G than over LTE.

Power Comparison. Figure 10 shows a timeline of the instantaneous device and network power consumption for one representative run over 5G mmWave and LTE. In each timeline, we use different colors to denote the different app phases.

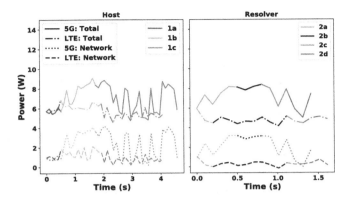

Fig. 10. Power timeline.

We make the following observations: (1) The total instantaneous device power consumption is higher during phase 1b on the host side over both 5G mmWave and LTE and during phase 2b on the resolver side over 5G mmWave – the two phases where we primarily have network activity (the device power over LTE on the resolver side is largely constant over all four phases, due to low network activity and the low power draw of the LTE NIC). (2) The network power draw is non-zero in phases 1a, 1c, 2a, 2c, 2d, in spite of minimal network activity during those phases due to the well-known tail power state in cellular networks. (3) The network power draw fluctuates largely over time, especially over 5G mmWave. In contrast, the power for all other device components remains largely constant over time. For example, for CPU, even though the average utilization in phase 1a (578%) is higher than in phase 1c (535%), the average power difference is just 108 mW. This is because the app utilizes almost exclusively the LITTLE cores, and the difference in utilization does not get translated to significant power difference. Hence, the fluctuations of the network power contribute to the large fluctuations of the device power consumption observed in Fig. 10.

In summary, our detailed energy drain analysis shows that, as expected [26], the app drains significantly higher network energy under 5G compared to under LTE. Since the network energy accounts for about 32% of the total energy, such significant network energy difference translates into smaller difference in the total app energy drain, by 23% on the host and 43% on the resolver.

6 Conclusion

In this paper, we studied whether 5G mmWave can support multi-user AR by conducting an in-depth measurement study of a popular multi-user AR app over both LTE and 5G mmWave. Our measurements showed that, in spite of the much higher bandwidth and lower RTT, 5G mmWave results in only a small reduction to the visual data transmission latency due to the small data burst sizes, which do not allow TCP to exit slow start and take full advantage of the higher bandwidth. A potential approach to addressing this issue is to leverage TCP splitting [28], and maintain a persistent TCP connection with a very large window between an edge server and the cloud, while the UE establishes a TCP connection to the edge server. We also found that an optimization that was proposed over LTE networks can also be effective over 5G networks and can further reduce the data transmission latency. However, other major contributors to the E2E AR latency keep it in the order of several seconds, rendering user interaction practically infeasible. Since some of these factors (e.g., cloud processing) are independent of the underlying cellular network, one may have to consider more drastic changes to the design of multi-user AR apps, e.g., moving the cloud services to the edge [34] – a rapidly increasing trend among both content providers and cellular operators [11,39] – or shifting from a client-server to a P2P paradigm [33]. Additionally, there is a need for cellular operators to revisit the middlebox policies in their packet core networks, which can also have an adverse impact on multi-user AR performance. Finally, our energy analysis showed that the app drains 66% more network energy over 5G mmWave compared to over LTE, which translates into 23% and 43% higher total energy on the host and the resolver, respectively, showing that 5G mmWave networks are not currently optimized to efficiently support this type of apps.

Acknowledgement. We thank our shepherd Arani Bhattacharya and the anonymous reviewers for their helpful comments. This work was supported in part by NSF grant 2112778-CNS.

References

1. Fundamental concepts of ARCore (2021). https://developers.google.com/ar/discover/concepts
2. Dataset: Can 5G mmWave support Multi-User AR? (2022). https://github.com/NUWiNS/pam2022-5G-mmwave-multi-user-ar-data
3. Apple ARKit: Creating a Multiuser AR Experience (Online). https://developer.apple.com/documentation/arkit/creating_a_multiuser_ar_experience
4. Google Cloud Anchor (Online). https://developers.google.com/ar/develop/java/cloud-anchors/overview-android
5. Google Firebase (Online). https://firebase.google.com/
6. Microsoft Hololens 2 (Online). https://www.microsoft.com/en-us/hololens
7. Android kernel's linux power supply class. https://android.googlesource.com/kernel/common/+/refs/heads/android-4.14-p/Documentation/power/power_supply_class.txt
8. Apicharttrisorn, K., et al.: Characterization of multi-user augmented reality over cellular networks. In: Proceedings of IEEE SECON (2020)
9. Apicharttrisorn, K., Ran, X., Chen, J., Krishnamurthy, S.V., Roy-Chowdhury, A.K.: Frugal following: power thrifty object detection and tracking for mobile augmented reality. In: Proceedings of ACM SenSys (2019)

10. Augmented and Virtual Reality: the First Wave of 5G Killer Apps: Qualcomm - ABI Research. https://gsacom.com/paper/augmented-virtual-reality-first-wave-5g-killer-apps-qualcomm-abi-research/
11. AT&T integrates 5G with Microsoft Azure to enable next-generation solutions on the edge. https://www.business.att.com/learn/top-voices/at-t-integrates-5g-with-microsoft-azure-to-enable-next-generatio.html
12. Chen, K., Li, T., Kim, H.S., Culler, D.E., Katz, R.H.: MARVEL: enabling mobile augmented reality with low energy and low latency. In: Proceedings of ACM SenSys (2018)
13. Chen, X., Ding, N., Jindal, A., Hu, Y.C., Gupta, M., Vannithamby, R.: Smartphone energy drain in the wild: analysis and implications. ACM SIGMETRICS Perform. Eval. Rev. 43(1), 151–164 (2015)
14. Chen, X., et al.: A fine-grained event-based modem power model for enabling in-depth modem energy drain analysis. In: Proceedings of the ACM on Measurement and Analysis of Computing Systems, vol. 1, no. 2, pp. 1–28 (2017)
15. Dash, P., Hu, Y.C.: How much battery does dark mode save? An accurate OLED Display Power Profiler for Modern Smartphones. In: Proceedings of ACM MobiSys (2021)
16. Ding, N., Hu, Y.C.: GfxDoctor: a holistic graphics energy profiler for mobile devices. In: Proceedings of ACM EuroSys (2017)
17. Ding, N., Wagner, D., Chen, X., Pathak, A., Hu, Y.C., Rice, A.: Characterizing and modeling the impact of wireless signal strength on smartphone battery drain. In: Proceedings of ACM SIGMETRICS (2013)
18. Dong, M., Zhong, L.: Self-constructive high-rate system energy modeling for battery-powered mobile systems. In: Proceedings of ACM MobiSys (2011)
19. Huang, J., Qian, F., Gerber, A., Mao, Z.M., Sen, S., Spatscheck, O.: A close examination of performance and power characteristics of 4G LTE networks. In: Proceedings of ACM Mobisys (2012)
20. Li, Y., Peng, C., Yuan, Z., Li, J., Deng, H., Wang, T.: MobileInsight: extracting and analyzing cellular network information on smartphones. In: Proceedings of ACM MobiCom (2016)
21. Linux event trace. https://www.kernel.org/doc/html/v4.18/trace/events.html
22. Liu, L., Li, H., Gruteser, M.: Edge assisted real-time object detection for mobile augmented reality. In: Proceedings of ACM MobiCom (2019)
23. Monsoon power monitor. https://www.msoon.com/online-store
24. Narayanan, A., Ramadan, E., Carpenter, J., Liu, Q., Liu, Y., Qian, F., Zhang, Z.L.: A First look at commercial 5G performance on smartphones. In: Proceedings of ACM WWW (2020)
25. Narayanan, A., et al.: Lumos5G: mapping and predicting commercial MmWave 5G throughput. In: Proceedings of ACM IMC (2020)
26. Narayanan, A., et al.: A variegated look at 5G in the wild: performance, power, and QoE implications. In: Proceedings of ACM SIGCOMM (2021)
27. Pathak, A., Hu, Y.C., Zhang, M., Bahl, P., Wang, Y.M.: Fine-grained power modeling for smartphones using system call tracing. In: Proceedings of ACM EuroSys (2011)
28. Pathak, A., et al.: Measuring and evaluating TCP splitting for cloud services. In: Proceedings of PAM (2010)
29. "Pokémon Go" maker Niantic wants to turn AR into 5G's first killer app. https://www.fastcompany.com/90545662/pokemon-go-maker-niantic-wants-to-jumpstart-5g-augmented-reality

30. Qiu, H., Ahmad, F., Bai, F., Gruteser, M., Govindan, R.: AVR: augmented vehicular reality. In: Proceedings of ACM MobiSys (2018)
31. Ran, X., Chen, H., Zhu, X., Liu, Z., Chen, J.: DeepDecision: a mobile deep learning framework for edge video analytics. In: Proceedings of IEEE INFOCOM (2018)
32. Ran, X., Slocum, C., Gorlatova, M., Chen, J.: ShareAR: communication-efficient multi-user mobile augmented reality. In: Proceedings of ACM HotNets (2019)
33. Ran, X., Slocum, C., Tsai, Y.Z., Apicharttrisorn, K., Gorlatova, M., Chen, J.: Multi-user augmented reality with communication efficient and spatially consistent virtual objects. In: Proceedings of ACM CoNEXT (2020)
34. Ren, P., et al.: Edge AR X5: An edge-assisted multi-user collaborative framework for mobile web augmented reality in 5G and beyond. IEEE Trans. Cloud Comput. (2020)
35. Schulman, A., Schmid, T., Dutta, P., Spring, N.: Phone power monitoring with BattOr. In: Proceedings of ACM MobiCom (2011)
36. Shye, A., Scholbrock, B., Memik, G.: Into the wild: studying real user activity patterns to guide power optimizations for mobile architectures. In: Proceedings of IEEE/ACM MICRO (2009)
37. Sun, L., Sheshadri, R.K., Zheng, W., Koutsonikolas, D.: Modeling WiFi active power/energy consumption in smartphones. In: Proceedings of IEEE ICDCS (2014)
38. Telcos seek killer app to recoup billions spent on 5G. https://www.bloomberg.com/news/articles/2021-08-10/telcos-seek-killer-app-to-recoup-billions-spent-on-5g-networks
39. Verizon teams with NFL, AWS to showcase 5G edge. https://www.fiercewireless.com/operators/verizon-teams-nfl-aws-to-showcase-5g-edgewww.business.att.com/learn/top-voices/at-t-integrates-5g-with-microsoft-azure-to-enable-next-generatio.html
40. Wang, Z., Qian, Z., Xu, Q., Mao, Z.M., Zhang, M.: An untold story of middleboxes in cellular networks. In: Proceedings of ACM SIGCOMM (2011)
41. Xu, F., Liu, Y., Li, Q., Zhang, Y.: V-edge: fast self-constructive power modeling of smartphones based on battery voltage dynamics. In: Proceedings of USENIX NSDI (2013)
42. Yue, C., Sen, S., Wang, B., Qin, Y., Qian, F.: Energy considerations for ABR video streaming to smartphones: measurements, models and insights. In: Proceedings of ACM Multimedia Systems (2020)
43. Zhang, L., et al.: Accurate online power estimation and automatic battery behavior based power model generation for smartphones. In: Proceedings of IEEE/ACM/IFIP CODES+ISSS (2010)
44. Zhang, W., Han, B., Hui, P., Gopalakrishnan, V., Zavesky, E., Qian, F.: CARS: collaborative augmented reality for socialization. In: Proceedings of ACM HotMobile (2018)

Routing

A First Measurement with BGP Egress Peer Engineering

Ryo Nakamura[1]([✉])[iD], Kazuki Shimizu[2], Teppei Kamata[3],
and Cristel Pelsser[4][iD]

[1] The University of Tokyo, Tokyo, Japan
upa@nc.u-tokyo.ac.jp
[2] Juniper Networks K.K., Tokyo, Japan
kshimizu@juniper.net
[3] Cisco Systems G.K., Tokyo, Japan
tkamata@cisco.com
[4] University of Strasbourg, Strasbourg, France
pelsser@unistra.fr

Abstract. This paper reports on measuring the effect of engineering egress traffic to peering ASes using Segment Routing, called BGP-EPE. BGP-EPE can send packets destined to arbitrary prefixes to arbitrary eBGP peers regardless of the BGP path selection. This ability enables us to measure external connectivity from a single AS in various perspectives; for example, does the use of paths other than the BGP best paths improve performance? We conducted an experiment to measure latency to the Internet from an event network, Interop Tokyo ShowNet, where SR-MPLS and BGP-EPE were deployed. Our findings from the experiment show BGP-EPE improves latency for 77% of target prefixes, and peering provides shorter latency than transit. We further show factors on which the degree of improvement depends, e.g., the performance-obliviousness of BGP and the presence of remote peering. Also, we find 91% of peer ASes forwarded packets towards prefixes that the peers did not advertise.

Keywords: BGP egress peer engineering · Segment routing · Internet latency

1 Introduction

Since latency over the Internet impacts the quality of experiences (QoE) of users [13,23], reducing the latency is a fundamental challenge on the Internet. A portion of the challenge is to optimize path selection at inter-AS connections. The BGP path selection algorithm does not care about performance, for example, it sometimes chooses paths based on freshness [11] or IP addresses of neighbors [27]. Thus, many studies have developed alternate routing systems to outperform BGP [5,6,19,28,33]. They steer egress traffic from their own ASes to peer ASes based on performance and link capacity in contrast to BGP.

O. Hohlfeld et al. (Eds.): PAM 2022, LNCS 13210, pp. 199–215, 2022.
https://doi.org/10.1007/978-3-030-98785-5_9

Egress traffic engineering is not an emerging topic. The LOCAL_PREF attribute of BGP is a primitive mechanism to choose specific paths for egress traffic [16, 28], and a Locator/Identifier Separation Protocol-based method has been proposed [14]. Segment Routing (SR) [18] is also one of the techniques to steer egress traffic to specific peers, called BGP Egress Peer Engineering (BGP-EPE) [17]. SR-based BGP-EPE steers specific traffic to given peers using encapsulation; therefore, it is independent of underlying BGP and IGP policies, unlike LOCAL_PREF. Moreover, SR and BGP-EPE are standardized and have been implemented on well-matured commercial routers [32]. These characteristics enable us to measure the potential benefit of egress traffic engineering without impacting other traffic on a real network where SR is deployed.

To the best of our knowledge, this paper reports the first measurement result using SR-based BGP-EPE deployed on a real network. The aim of this measurement is to clarify the potential benefit of egress traffic engineering from a latency perspective and not to propose a methodology to find better egress paths. The effectiveness of egress traffic engineering is still controversial [7], and this paper provides a case study to this argument. We conducted our experiment at an AS where SR-based BGP-EPE was deployed, via 45 unique ASes (3 transit ASes and 43 peer ASes, of which one peer AS is identical to a transit AS). We performed ping and traceroute to addresses spread on the IPv4 address space. The AS where we conducted the measurement is Interop Tokyo ShowNet [3], an event network built for and operated during a technology exhibition in Japan. Therefore, the measurement period was short—from April 12 to 16 in 2021; however, in summary, this paper shows the following findings:

- BGP-EPE reduces latency for 77% of target prefixes, but the gain depends on the BGP best path selection at the measurement point.
- Peering tends to have shorter latency than transit, and this trend increases on inter-continental paths.
- 91% of ASes peering with ShowNet allowed detouring toward prefixes that the ASes did not advertise.

2   Methodology

2.1   Segment Routing and BGP Egress Peer Engineering

Segment Routing (SR) [18] is an emerging source routing architecture implemented in recent commercial routers. The concept of SR is to represent any topological entities as *segments*, and SR-capable routers perform packet forwarding by segments embedded in packets. A segment can indicate, e.g., an IGP node or adjacency between routers. A list of segments in a packet informs routers where the packet needs to flow. SR currently leverages two data planes: MPLS (SR-MPLS) and IPv6 (SRv6). A segment is identified by an MPLS label in SR-MPLS and by an IPv6 address in SRv6. These identifiers are called Segment Identifiers (SIDs). Since we used SR-MPLS for the measurement, we focus on SR-MPLS in the rest of this paper.

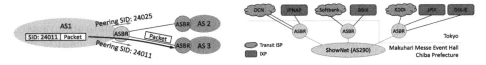

Fig. 1. Overview of BGP-EPE.   **Fig. 2.** External diagram of ShowNet.

SR is one of the techniques to steer egress traffic to specific peers. This capability is called BGP Egress Peer Engineering (BGP-EPE) and has been standardized in RFC9087 [17]. BGP-EPE-capable routers represent eBGP peers as segments called BGP Peering Segments or SIDs. Figure 1 illustrates an overview of SR-based BGP-EPE. The AS border router (ASBR) of AS 1 has two eBGP peers and assigns BGP Peering SIDs for them. When the ASBR receives a packet encapsulated with the SID, the router pops the MPLS header and then transmits the IP packet to the peer corresponding to the SID. Because SR-based BGP-EPE is a mechanism to carry packets toward selected peers, a methodology to choose better peers for given destinations is needed to benefit from egress traffic engineering. However, the methodology is not the focus of this paper. Instead, we measured all possible paths to clarify the potential latency benefit.

2.2 Experimental Environment

Interop Tokyo ShowNet. We conducted the measurement experiment with the SR-based BGP-EPE at Interop Tokyo ShowNet [3]. Interop Tokyo [2] is a large annual exhibition of network technologies in Japan, and ShowNet (AS290) is an event network built at Interop Tokyo. In 2021, Interop Tokyo was held from April 14 to 16, and ShowNet was built in the event hall. The network provided Internet connectivity for exhibitors and visitors at the event, and simultaneously demonstrated new technologies, and conducted several inter-operability tests. The ShowNet backbone in 2021 was composed of SRv6 L3VPN and SR-MPLS, on which we put the measurement experiment.

Figure 2 illustrates a simplified diagram of ShowNet focusing on BGP-EPE. ShowNet had three ASBRs, ASR9902 from Cisco Systems, MX204 from Juniper Networks, and NE8000-X4 from Huawei, connected to one major Japanese Internet Service Provider (ISP) and one or two Internet eXchange Points (IXPs) each. The ASBRs assigned BGP Peering SIDs to transit providers and peer ASes who agreed to join the experiment. ShowNet started peering at the IXPs on the evening of April 12. Eventually, we performed the measurement over 101 eBGP peers of 45 unique ASes listed in Table 1.

Table 1. Number of eBGP peers and ASes involved in the measurement.

	JPNAP	BBIX	JPIX	DIX-IE	Transit	Total
# of eBGP peers	25	32	34	6	4	101
# of ASes	24	26	30	6	3	45 (unique)

Measurement Procedure. The high-level measurement procedure is simple: a Linux server deployed at ShowNet performed ping and traceroute to targeted IPv4 addresses via each eBGP peer by SR-based BGP-EPE. We used scamper [24] for ping and traceroute; ping is performed over UDP with a probe count of five, and traceroute using UDP-paris [8].

We leveraged two techniques in addition to SR-based BGP-EPE: BGP Link State (BGP-LS) [29] to automate detecting new peer ASes and Linux network namespace to measure multiple egress ASes in parallel. Peering with ShowNet was automated and ASBRs dynamically assigned BGP Peering SIDs for the peers. Therefore, the measurement server also dynamically learned the SIDs through BGP-LS using cRPD [22] from Juniper Networks. To accomplish extensive measurements at the ephemeral event network, we ran 8 scamper processes parallel at the server. Each scamper ran on a Linux network namespace, which has a separated routing table, with a hardware-assisted virtual interface by Single Root I/O Virtualization [26]. In this setup, we executed the following procedure in succession: configuring a namespace to encapsulate packets with appropriate SIDs for a peer, and spawning scamper on the namespace.

The target IP addresses of the measurement are 2,638,382 IPv4 addresses. These addresses were extracted from the source IPv4 addresses in ICMP Echo Replies from a packet trace of MAWI [12] on April 8 and 9, 2020[1]. We kept the IPv4 addresses that responded to ping at the end of March 2021. Finally, we extracted one address per /24 prefix. As a result, we obtained 2.6M target addresses. Note that the trace contains reply packets for probes sent from a host of USC's ANT Project [30][2]. Hence, we indirectly used a partial list of theirs.

2.3 Ethical Considerations

As presented in the previous section, our traffic analysis did not consider user traffic. Our experiment involves sending packets destined to the target addresses even when a peer does not advertise their prefixes. It is obviously not an intended behavior on peering links. Therefore, we arranged an agreement with ASes before peering. The agreement states that the purpose of this experiment is measurement and demonstration of SR-based BGP-EPE, the experiment sends UDP or ICMP probe packets having arbitrary destinations to ShowNet peers, the amount of measurement traffic to a peer is up to 15 Mbps (actual throughput was about 3.5 Mbps), and the measurement results are used only for sharing information with network communities and research purposes.

3   Data

Our data was collected at the event network for five days; therefore, the analysis in this paper is a point-in-time, not a longitudinal, analysis. On the other hand,

---

[1] We used an unanonymized version of the trace with a responsible person's consent.
[2] MAWI Traffic Archive FAQ, https://mawi.wide.ad.jp/mawi/faq.html.

the number of samples we obtain is reasonable with respect to the length of the experiment. This section describes the data we collected and its preprocessing.

In our experiments, a single scamper process performs ping or traceroute to 2.6M target addresses via an eBGP peer chosen from the 101 eBGP peers. Eventually, 688 ping iterations and 176 traceroute iterations finished during the period. Thus, we have results of six or seven ping and one or two traceroute iterations for each eBGP peer.

The probe count for ping is five; therefore, at most we obtain 35 RTTs for a destination address via an egress eBGP peer. Because small samples cause statistical errors, we omit ping results with less than 10 RTTs for a pair from further analysis. Figure 3 shows the histogram of numbers of measured RTTs to a destination address via an eBGP peer. About 25% of pings failed, and 28.6% have less than 10 RTTs. After the exclusion of pairs with less that 10 RTTs, the number of remaining target IP addresses is 2,303,253. Through all the ping measurements, we sent 9,062,842,170 probes and received 6,027,615,205 replies. Thus, its success rate is 66.51%. A reason for the low success rate is that it includes ping probes to non-advertised prefixes via peering ASes. The ping success rate via the transit ASes is 77.58%, and via peering ASes is 66.18%. Further analysis on filtering packets to unintended destinations at peering ASes is described in Sect. 4.3.

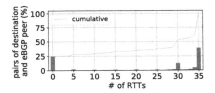

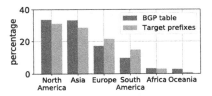

Fig. 3. Histogram of numbers of measured RTTs to a destination address via an egress eBGP peer.

Fig. 4. Percentages of prefixes per region in the BGP table versus in our the target prefixes.

Besides, because the selection process of the target IPv4 addresses does not consider the distribution of the addresses on the IPv4 address space, we summarize the measured RTTs by prefixes in the BGP table. We treat RTTs to a target IP address as RTTs to a prefix that includes the address. The remaining 2.3M target addresses cover 38.06% of prefixes in the BGP table of an ASBR at ShowNet as of April 16, 2021, which is the last day of the measurement. We call these prefixes having measured RTTs target prefixes.

To verify the diversity in the target prefixes and assess a potential bias, we compare these with all prefixes in the BGP table from a regional perspective. Mapping of prefixes and regions is generated from AS number allocation: (1) obtaining prefix-to-ASN mapping from the BGP table, and (2) obtaining ASN-to-region mapping from Geoff Huston's page [20]. Figure 4 shows the percentages of prefixes in each region. As shown, the distribution of target prefixes is similar to the BGP table on a regional allocation basis. The differences are not significant (less than 6% in all regions). Thus, we conclude that the target prefixes properly represent the diversity of prefixes in the BGP table.

4   Analysis

In this section we analyze the data collected during our experiment. Section 4.1 provides a case study of how BGP-EPE improves latency against the BGP best paths. Section 4.2 compares latency through peering and transit. Finally, Sect. 4.3 reveals behaviors of ASes when they receive packets having destinations that the ASes do not advertise. Note that information that can reveal specific ASes, e.g., AS numbers and AS names, is anonymized because of a non-disclosure agreement at ShowNet. ShowNet is sponsored by equipment vendors, transit service providers and connections at IXPs; therefore, we cannot expose matters that are disadvantageous to the contributors.

4.1   How Best are the Best Paths

Reducing latency by steering egress traffic away from the BGP best path is a fundamental ability of BGP-EPE. We first clarify the room for latency improvement by comparing RTTs via the best paths and alternative paths. For this comparison, we extracted the minimum RTTs to each target prefix via the best paths versus all received paths. We call paths that achieved the minimum RTTs among all received paths *alternate paths* in accordance with the previous literature [7,28]. We choose the minimum, not median or average, because of the small number of samples. Appendix A shows the results with the median values.

Figure 5 shows CDF of RTTs to the target prefixes via the best paths (hereafter called $RTT(best)$) and alternate paths (hereafter called $RTT(alternate)$). The graph demonstrates alternate paths achieve better latency than the best paths, as expected. The difference increases when RTT is over about 100 ms.

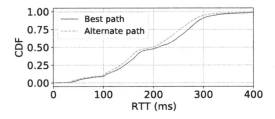

Fig. 5. CDF of RTTs to the target prefixes via the best or alternate paths.

Figure 6 shows the potential latency improvement with the alternate paths. Figure 6a shows improvement calculated from $RTT(best)$ minus $RTT(alternate)$ for each prefix. 23% of the target prefixes have no improvement, which means

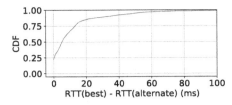 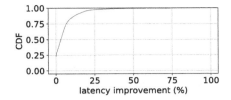

(a) Differences between $RTT(best)$ and $RTT(alternate)$ for each prefix

(b) Rate of latency improvement to $RTT(best)$ for each prefix

Fig. 6. CDF of latency improvement by the alternate paths.

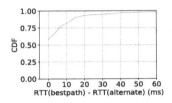 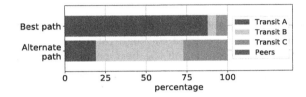

Fig. 7. CDF of improved latency to prefixes accommodating Alexa top sites.

Fig. 8. Percentage of egress ASes on the best paths and alternate paths.

that the best paths are the best. Meanwhile, BGP-EPE improves latency for 77% of the prefixes, e.g., 44% of the prefixes benefit from up to 10 ms latency improvement, and 18% of the prefixes get 10–20 ms latency improvement. Figure 6b shows a relative version of Fig. 6a: rate of latency improvement by $RTT(alternate)$ to $RTT(best)$. The latency improvement for 97% of the target prefixes is within 25%, and the prefixes between 75% and 97% benefit from 6.6% to 25% improvement.

In addition to analyzing all the target prefixes, we pick prefixes of popular services to clarify the benefit derived from BGP-EPE. From the viewpoint of an ISP accommodating end-users, improving latency for such prefixes brings better QoE of the users. As popular services, we used Alexa top 1 million sites [1] obtained on July 21, 2021. We resolved the domains' IP addresses and picked $RTT(best)$ and $RTT(alternate)$ for prefixes that contain the IP addresses. Eventually, we obtained 781,501 IP addresses of 548,680 domains in the Alexa list, corresponding to 25,096 prefixes out of the target prefixes. The result focusing on the Alexa top sites is shown in Fig. 7. As with Fig. 6, latency to the prefixes accommodating Alexa top sites is also improved, e.g., latency for 43% of the prefixes is improved, and 36% of prefixes get up to 20 ms latency improvement.

Even though egress traffic engineering is a promising approach for improving latency, the result where latency for approximately 77% of target prefixes can

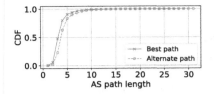

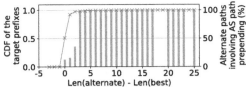

Fig. 9. AS path length of the best and alternate paths.

Fig. 10. CDF of the differences in AS path length of the best and alternate paths for each prefix, and percentages of alternative paths involving AS path prepending.

be improved seems a significantly higher ratio than the previous report [7]. We found that a cause of the high ratio is the imbalance of egress ASes, first hop ASes on the paths, on the best paths. Figure 8 shows the percentage of egress ASes on the best paths and alternate paths. Transit A occupies 88% of egress ASes on the best paths. However, its percentage is 19% in the alternate paths, and the other two transit ASes occupy approximately 54% and 27%, respectively. Paths via the peer ASes also appear in Fig. 8; however, their presence is relatively small (0.06% of the best paths and 0.05% of the alternate paths). Thus, peers are not visible in the figure.

The imbalance of egress ASes on the best paths arose from the order in which ShowNet established eBGP sessions with the transit providers. ShowNet established the eBGP session with transit A before others. As a result, the oldest paths survived in accordance with the BGP path selection algorithm [11]. If ShowNet established eBGP sessions in a different order, the result might change.

We next focus on AS path length of the best paths (hereafter called $Len(best)$) and alternate paths (hereafter called $Len(alternate)$) to the target prefixes. Figure 9 shows that the alternate paths are slightly longer than the best paths, as expected. The solid line in Fig. 10 shows CDF of differences in AS path length calculated from $Len(alternate)$ minus $Len(best)$ for each prefix. We can see several prefixes have longer best paths than their alternate paths, where $x < 0$. This is because ShowNet prefers peers over transit providers by configuration using LOCAL_PREF. The best paths to these 9 prefixes are advertised from peers to ShowNet, and these paths involve AS path prepending by origin ASes. On the other hand, the alternate paths to the prefixes through transit ASes are not prepended. As a result, ShowNet routers choose the longer paths via peers as best by a higher LOCAL_PREF. The shortest paths would be used if ShowNet did not prefer peers over transit.

About half of the prefixes have best and alternate paths of the same length ($x = 0$). We found that both best and alternate paths to 99.9% of those prefixes are advertised from the transit ASes. Further, the egress AS of 88% of the best paths to the prefixes is transit A, and 55% of the prefixes derive the latency improvement from their alternate paths through transit B or C. This result also demonstrates the performance-obliviousness of BGP, which sometimes does not choose better paths when AS path lengths are the same. Moreover, some prefixes have very long alternate paths compared with their best paths, e.g., $Len(alternate)$ is 25 hops longer than $Len(best)$ for two prefixes. These significant differences arise from AS path prepending. The bars in Fig. 10 show percentages of alternate paths involving AS path prepending, and 100% of alternate paths are prepended where $x > 5$. For the length difference above 5, the length is artificially increased and no longer reflects the latency of the path.

This section provides two findings: (1) BGP-EPE can reduce latency as the previous studies reported, even in a leaf of the Internet; (2) however, the degree of the latency improvement highly depends on the situation. 77% of the target prefixes got latency improvement. Furthermore, latency to prefixes of Alexa top sites is also reduced. In addition to large content providers benefiting from egress traffic engineering [28,33], the result demonstrates that a single ISP also can benefit from BGP-EPE to bring better QoE for their end-users. On the other hand, as Fig. 8 shows, the relatively high degree of improvement arises from the imbalance of the BGP best paths, which is due to the deployment process of ShowNet. A similar situation could happen anywhere, and the degree of improvement by BGP-EPE depends on the quality of the main best egress AS.

4.2 Peering Versus Transit

SR-based BGP-EPE can selectively send packets to a destination via peer *or* transit ASes. This characteristic enables us to measure and compare latency to a destination through peers or transit providers. Network operators prefer peering over transit from a cost perspective. However, clarifying the difference in performance is still challenging because it fundamentally requires egress traffic engineering or layer-7 techniques and the help of a large CDN [4]. In this study, we filled the former requirement.

To compare latency via peering and transit, we extracted the minimum RTT for each prefix via the peer ASes advertising the prefix (hereafter called $RTT(peering)$) and, also, the minimum RTT via each transit (hereafter called $RTT(transit)$). Note that SR-based BGP-EPE only influences the egress traffic. Return paths from destinations to ShowNet were the same regardless of egress ASes; hence differences between peering and transit reflect only outbound paths.

Figure 11 shows a first comparison between $RTT(peering)$ and $RTT(transit)$. Figure 11a and 11b present the two types of RTTs to each prefix in scatter plots. The x-axis indicates RTT via peering, and the y-axis indicates that of transit. Therefore, when a dot is above $x = y$, peering is better than the transit for the prefix. Since ShowNet had three transit providers, a prefix is represented by up to three dots in the figures if probes to the prefix succeeded. Both Fig. 11a coloring dots per region of the prefixes and Fig. 11b coloring dots per transit show more dots above the line: 1360 dots above $x = y$ versus 832 dots under $x = y$. Figure 11c shows the CDF of $RTT(transit)$ minus $RTT(peering)$ for each prefix. The figure also demonstrates that peering provides shorter latency than transit. The ratio of prefixes with better latency via peering is 39%, 59%, and 52% for transit A, B, and C, respectively.

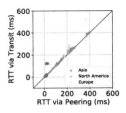
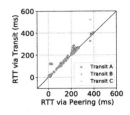
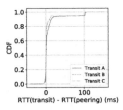

(a) Categorized by regions   (b) Categorized by transits   (c) Latency improvement with peering

Fig. 11. Peering vs. transit. Each dot in a and b indicates a prefix; the x-axis and y-axis values are RTT to the prefix via peering and transit, respectively. (Color figure online)

To clarify the difference in more detail, we analyze the results from a regional perspective in the following sections. To determine regions of prefixes, we used the procedure described in Sect. 3.

Asia. Figure 12 shows results for the subset of prefixes from Fig. 11 allocated in Asia. Almost all ASes peering with ShowNet were Japanese ASes; hence most prefixes in Fig. 12 are located in Japan. In other words, this result compares domestic peering versus transit paths. In Fig. 12a, we observe a group of prefixes with over 100 ms RTTs via the transit providers but less than 50 ms RTTs via peering. We found that these prefixes belong to a Japanese local ISP in a region far from major cities. In Japan, cores of major ISP backbone networks converge on two urban cities: Tokyo and Osaka. A previous experiment reports that regional ISPs outside of Tokyo and Osaka often have long latency via transit ISPs due to economic reasons, so that IXPs extended to regional areas can provide significant improvement in RTT for such regional ISPs [31]. The group that appeared in Fig. 12a implies such a condition in Japan.

Figure 12b zooms on the 0–40 ms range of Fig. 12a to avoid the outliers described in the previous paragraph. The figure shows there is no significant difference in trends between peering and transit in the domestic connection. Moreover, latency improvement with peering is also not significant except for the outlier group as shown in Fig. 12c.

North America. Figure 13a focuses on prefixes allocated in North America. It shows the same trend—no significant difference between peering and transit. However, peering certainly improves latency, as shown in Fig. 13b. This result indicates peering improves latency on inter-continental connections rather than domestic as shown in Fig. 12. Paths from Japan to North America involve long distances over submarine and regional fiber-optic cables; therefore, underlying cable routes of intermediate providers have a relatively larger impact on latency than domestic connections. Besides, we can see that transit B and C achieved

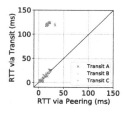
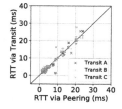
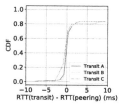

(a) RTTs via peering and transit

(b) Focusing on 0–40 ms in Figure 12a

(c) Latency improvement with peering

Fig. 12. Peering vs. transit for prefixes in Asia.

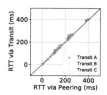
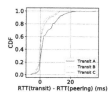
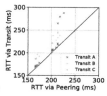
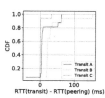

(a) RTTs via peer- ing and transit

(b) Latency improve- ment with peering

(a) RTTs via peer- ing and transit

(b) Latency improve- ment with peering

Fig. 13. Peering vs. transit for prefixes in North America.

Fig. 14. Peering vs. transit for prefixes in Europe.

more comparable latency with peering than transit A. We also attribute the difference to their cable routes.

Europe. Figure 14, which focuses on prefixes in Europe, clearly shows differences between the transit providers. The notable point is that transit C achieves comparable latency to peering. AS paths to the prefixes in Fig. 14 are advertised from a peer AS in Europe via remote peering [10] at an IXP. In addition, we found in the traceroute data that transit C also peers with the AS in Europe at the same IXP. Namely, the paths are, `ShowNet-the IXP-the AS in Europe`, and `ShowNet-Transit C-the IXP-the AS in Europe`. Therefore, ping via the peering and transit C flow through the same inter-continental cable route from the IXP to the remote peer AS in Europe.

The result indicates that although peering improves latency on an inter- continental connection, the improvement depends not only on peering but also on other factors, e.g., underlying cable routes have an impact on latency in long- distance connections. The IXP provides a better path from Japan to Europe than others thanks to remote peering. ShowNet peered with the European AS directly at the IXP; however, it is not necessarily so. BGP's performance obliviousness can lead to long RTTs when shorter delay paths are possible.

4.3   Detouring

So far, previous sections have analyzed paths received from the eBGP peers. Yet, SR-based BGP-EPE can send packets destined to arbitrary destinations to any SID-assigned eBGP peers regardless of received prefixes. Using this ability, we now observe the behavior of ASes when they receive packets having destinations that the ASes do not advertise. Such an experiment can cause unintended or abusive detouring. We however had the consent of the peers, under the agreement mentioned in Sect. 2.3.

First, we determine ASes who did not forward packets to destinations they did not advertise, using the traceroute data. As a result, we found that only four peer ASes blocked packets to non-advertised prefixes. The remaining 39 peers carried packets to the Internet; the rate of ASes not blocking such packets is 91%. Blocking packets to inappropriate destinations requires packet filtering in the data plane, e.g., access control lists, at ASBRs in addition to typical AS path- or prefix-based filtering on the BGP control plane. As a case study in New Zealand reported [21], not every AS spends effort for such filtering. However, commoditization of BGP-EPE might increase the possibility that unintended detouring will happen.

Next, the result raises a question: can BGP-EPE improve latency by detouring to such ASes? Figure 15 gives an answer. Figure 15 shows the CDF of $RTT(best)$, $RTT(alternate)$, and the minimum RTTs to the target prefixes via all possible paths including detouring (hereafter called $RTT(detouring)$). The lines of best paths and alternate paths are identical to Fig. 5. As shown, detouring improves latency, especially in the area of RTTs between 200–300 ms.

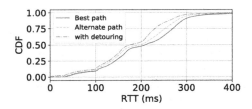

Fig. 15. CDF of the minimum RTTs to the target prefixes with detouring in addition to Fig. 5.

To clarify factors involved in the latency improvement with detouring, we compare the improvement from a regional perspective. Figure 16 shows histograms of latency differences between the best or alternate paths versus detouring for prefixes in each region. The x-axis is $RTT(best)$ or $RTT(alternate)$ minus $RTT(detouring)$ for each prefix, and the y-axis is the number of target prefixes. In contrast to Asia and North America, where reduced latencies are mainly of less than 25 ms, RTTs to prefixes in Europe are significantly improved (25–50 ms). Since RTTs from Japan to Europe are approximately around 200 ms,

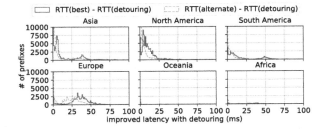

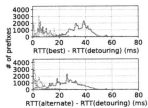

Fig. 16. Histograms of latency improvement with detouring in each region.

Fig. 17. Latency improvement by the top 5 ASes.

the prefixes in Europe considerably contribute to the latency improvement with detouring shown in Fig. 15.

We found that one peer AS mainly contributes to improving latency to Europe. Figure 17 shows the histogram of improved latency for the five most beneficial peer ASes. The gain of a peer AS is calculated by totaling up $RTT(best)$ or $RTT(alternate)$ minus $RTT(detouring)$ for each prefix that the peer AS provides the minimum RTT. The x-axis and the y-axis are identical to Fig. 16. As shown, the peer AS represented as the solid blue line reduces latency by 20 to 50 ms. This AS is a large AS in Europe (ranked within the top 100 in CAIDA AS Rank [9]). Thus, detouring via the AS brings shorter latency to broad networks in Europe.

These results provide two findings: (1) a security issue on peerings and (2) the potential of partial transit [15,25]. Although detouring is fundamentally abusive, current deployments often do not prevent malicious ASes from detouring. A mechanism to filter packets along with the BGP control plane is needed. On the other hand, the significant latency improvement from Japan to Europe indicates that an AS can provide peer ASes with shorter latency by selectively advertising prefixes. It is similar to partial transit, which advertises a partial BGP table to customers. If the European AS advertises the prefixes to customers under an agreement, the customers can derive the latency benefit from the partial transit service of the AS without abusive detouring.

5   Related Work

Performance-aware routing, in contrast to performance-agnostic BGP, is a long-standing issue that many studies have tackled. Early work aimed for multi-homed end networks to effectively choose upstream based on performance and cost [5,19]. Those implementations involving the monitoring aspect have reached programmable switches [6]. On the other hand, [28,33] propose inter-domain performance-aware routing for large content providers. They establish BGP sessions with peers and dynamically shift egress traffic from a peering link to another to achieve better performance and avoid congestion. However, the degree of improvement reachable via performance-aware routing is still controversial;

BGP mostly chooses suitable routes, so that latency gains are small [7]. In addition to the previous studies based on large content providers, this paper provides a new case study at a single AS with a standardized technique.

Measuring the Internet while resisting routing, e.g., longest prefix matching and BGP best paths, is difficult. Measuring transit and peering selectively is a typical example. Ahmed et al. [4] accomplished this feat using client-side JavaScript and with the help of a commercial CDN. They showed peering improves end-to-end latency by at least 5% for 91% ASes. Sect. 4.2 reproduces similar results, but the methodology is different. We demonstrated that SR-based BGP-EPE enables such measurement from a single AS without any help.

6 Conclusion

We provide the first latency measurement with SR-based BGP-EPE that enables engineering egress traffic to peering ASes. We conducted the experiment at an ephemeral event network, Interop Tokyo ShowNet, in which SR-MPLS and BGP-EPE were deployed for five days in April 2021. Despite the short measurement period, the collected data brings three findings: (1) using paths other than the BGP best paths certainly improves latency; however, the gain depends on the performance-obliviousness of the BGP configuration, (2) peering provides shorter latency than transit, especially in inter-continental connections depending on underlying cable routes, and (3) 91% of peer ASes forwards packets to the Internet, although they do not advertise a full BGP table. To conclude, egress traffic engineering is effective in improving latency, but the gain depends on various factors. Meanwhile, the experiment demonstrated the potential of BGP-EPE for measuring external connectivity. A stable network where BGP-EPE is deployed would bring an opportunity for a more comprehensive and accurate measurement of the long-standing issue of performance-agnostic BGP.

Acknowledgments. We would like to thank our shepherd Dr. Marcel Flores and the anonymous reviewers for their insightful feedback. We also thank all the people involved in Interop Tokyo ShowNet 2021.

Appendices

A   Other Metrics for Representative RTTs

We chose the minimum, not median, RTTs for each prefix to avoid statistical errors. Figure 18a shows the median version of Fig. 5. As shown, there is no significant difference between minimum and median in a broad view. However, Fig. 19, which shows the median version of improved latency with peering (Fig. 11c, 12c, 13b, and 14b), includes such errors. Accidentally overestimated RTTs cause inaccurate latency differences between peering and transit.

Throughout the paper, we summarized RTTs by prefixes in the BGP table. Figure 18b shows the not-summarized version, which means per-address RTT, of

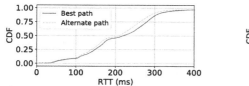
(a) Median RTT on a per-prefix basis

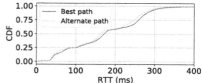
(b) Minimum RTT on a per-address basis

Fig. 18. CDF of RTTs to target prefixes or addresses.

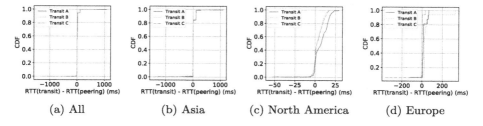

(a) All   (b) Asia   (c) North America   (d) Europe

Fig. 19. Peering vs. transit with median RTTs on a per-prefix basis.

Fig. 5. Differences between the figures, e.g., the per-address version has a higher rate with RTTs under 100 ms, arises from a bias on the distribution of target addresses. In addition, Fig. 20 shows the per-address version of peering versus transit (Fig. 11c, 12c, 13b, and 14b). The figure shows results similar to the per-prefix versions. This is because the number of prefixes advertised from the peers was small (3526 unique prefixes). As a result, there were no especially large prefixes that accommodated many target addresses.

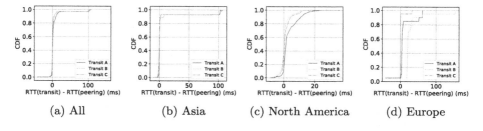

(a) All   (b) Asia   (c) North America   (d) Europe

Fig. 20. Peering vs. transit with minimum RTTs on per-address basis.

References

1. Alexa top 1 million sites. http://s3.amazonaws.com/alexa-static/top-1m.csv.zip
2. Interop Tokyo 2021 (2021). https://interop.jp/en/

3. Interop Tokyo 2021 ShowNet (2021). https://www.interop.jp/shownet/en/
4. Ahmed, A., Shafiq, Z., Bedi, H., Khakpour, A.: Peering vs. transit: performance comparison of peering and transit interconnections. In: 2017 IEEE 25th International Conference on Network Protocols (ICNP), pp. 1–10 (2017). https://doi.org/10.1109/ICNP.2017.8117549
5. Akella, A., Maggs, B., Seshan, S., Shaikh, A.: On the performance benefits of multihoming route control. IEEE/ACM Trans. Netw. **16**(1), 91–104 (2008)
6. Apostolaki, M., Singla, A., Vanbever, L.: Performance-driven internet path selection. In: Proceedings of the Symposium on SDN Research, SOSR '21. Association for Computing Machinery, New York (2021). https://doi.org/10.1145/3482898.3483357
7. Arnold, T., et al.: Beating BGP is harder than we thought. In: Proceedings of the 18th ACM Workshop on Hot Topics in Networks, pp. 9b–16. HotNets '19. Association for Computing Machinery, New York (2019). https://doi.org/10.1145/3365609.3365865
8. Augustin, B., et al.: Avoiding traceroute anomalies with Paris traceroute. In: Proceedings of the 6th ACM SIGCOMM Conference on Internet Measurement, IMC '06, pp. 153–158. Association for Computing Machinery, New York (2006). https://doi.org/10.1145/1177080.1177100
9. CAIDA: As rank: A ranking of the largest autonomous systems (as) in the internet. https://asrank.caida.org/
10. Castro, I., Cardona, J.C., Gorinsky, S., Francois, P.: Remote peering: more peering without internet flattening. In: Proceedings of the 10th ACM International on Conference on Emerging Networking Experiments and Technologies, CoNEXT '14, pp. 185–198. Association for Computing Machinery, New York (2014). https://doi.org/10.1145/2674005.2675013
11. Chen, E., Sangli, R.S.: Avoid BGP best path transitions from one external to another. RFC 5004 (2007). https://doi.org/10.17487/RFC5004. https://rfc-editor.org/rfc/rfc5004.txt
12. Cho, K., Mitsuya, K., Kato, A.: Traffic data repository at the wide project. In: Proceedings of the Annual Conference on USENIX Annual Technical Conference, ATEC '00, p. 51. USENIX Association, USA (2000)
13. Claypool, M., Claypool, K.: Latency can kill: precision and deadline in online games, pp. 215–222. Association for Computing Machinery, New York (2010). https://doi.org/10.1145/1730836.1730863
14. Dac Duy Nguyen, H., Secci, S.: LISP-EC: enhancing lisp with egress control. In: 2016 IEEE Conference on Standards for Communications and Networking (CSCN), pp. 1–7 (2016). https://doi.org/10.1109/CSCN.2016.7785189
15. Faratin, P., Clark, D., Bauer, S., Lehr, W., Gilmore, P., Berger, A.: The growing complexity of internet interconnection. Commun. Strat. **1**, 51–72 (2008)
16. Feamster, N., Borkenhagen, J., Rexford, J.: Guidelines for interdomain traffic engineering. SIGCOMM Comput. Commun. Rev. **33**(5), 19–30 (2003). https://doi.org/10.1145/963985.963988
17. Filsfils, C., Previdi, S., Dawra, G., Aries, E., Afanasiev, D.: Segment routing centralized BGP egress peer engineering. RFC 9087 (2021). https://doi.org/10.17487/RFC9087. https://rfc-editor.org/rfc/rfc9087.txt
18. Filsfils, C., Previdi, S., Ginsberg, L., Decraene, B., Litkowski, S., Shakir, R.: Segment routing architecture. RFC 8402 (2018). https://doi.org/10.17487/RFC8402. https://rfc-editor.org/rfc/rfc8402.txt

19. Goldenberg, D.K., Qiuy, L., Xie, H., Yang, Y.R., Zhang, Y.: Optimizing cost and performance for multihoming. SIGCOMM Comput. Commun. Rev. **34**(4), 79–92 (2004)
20. Huston, G.: AS Names. https://bgp.potaroo.net/cidr/autnums.html
21. Jager, M.: Securing ixp connectivity. APINIC 34 (2012). https://conference.apnic.net/34/pdf/apnic34-mike-jager-securing-ixp-connectivity_1346119861.pdf
22. Juniper Networks: Containerized routing protocol daemon (CRPD) (2021). https://www.juniper.net/us/en/products/routers/containerized-routing-protocol-daemon-crpd.html
23. Khan, F.: The cost of latency—digital realty (2015). https://www.digitalrealty.com/blog/the-cost-of-latency
24. Luckie, M.: Scamper: a scalable and extensible packet prober for active measurement of the internet. In: Proceedings of the 10th ACM SIGCOMM Conference on Internet Measurement, IMC '10, pp. 239–245. Association for Computing Machinery, New York (2010). https://doi.org/10.1145/1879141.1879171
25. Norton, W.: DrPeering white paper - the art of peering: the peering playbook, 7. partial transit (regional) (2010). http://drpeering.net/white-papers/Art-Of-Peering-The-Peering-Playbook.html#7
26. PCI-SIG: Single root i/o virtualization and sharing specification revision 1.1 (2010). https://pcisig.com/single-root-io-virtualization-and-sharing-specification-revision-11
27. Rekhter, Y., Hares, S., Li, T.: A Border Gateway Protocol 4 (BGP-4). RFC 4271 (2006). https://doi.org/10.17487/RFC4271. https://rfc-editor.org/rfc/rfc4271.txt
28. Schlinker, B., et al.: Engineering egress with edge fabric: steering oceans of content to the world. In: Proceedings of the Conference of the ACM Special Interest Group on Data Communication, SIGCOMM '17, pp. 418–431. Association for Computing Machinery, New York (2017). https://doi.org/10.1145/3098822.3098853
29. StefPrevidi, S., Talaulikar, K., Filsfils, Clarence Filand Patel, K., Ray, S., Dong, J.: Border Gateway Protocol - Link State (BGP-LS) Extensions for Segment Routing BGP Egress Peer Engineering. RFC 9086 (2021). https://doi.org/10.17487/RFC9086. https://rfc-editor.org/rfc/rfc9086.txt
30. The ANT Lab: IP Address Space Hitlists. https://ant.isi.edu/datasets/ip_hitlists/format.html
31. Tsurumaki, S.: How do we improve internet connectivity outside major cities? A Japanese approach. APNIC Blog (2021). https://blog.apnic.net/2021/09/02/how-do-we-improve-internet-connectivity-outside-major-cities-a-japanese-approach/
32. Ventre, P.L., et al.: Segment routing: a comprehensive survey of research activities, standardization efforts, and implementation results. IEEE Commun. Surv. Tutor. **23**(1), 182–221 (2021). https://doi.org/10.1109/COMST.2020.3036826
33. Yap, K.K., et al.: Taking the edge off with espresso: scale, reliability and programmability for global internet peering. In: Proceedings of the Conference of the ACM Special Interest Group on Data Communication, SIGCOMM '17, pp. 432–445. Association for Computing Machinery, New York (2017). https://doi.org/10.1145/3098822.3098854

RouteInfer: Inferring Interdomain Paths by Capturing ISP Routing Behavior Diversity and Generality

Tianhao Wu [ID], Jessie Hui Wang[✉) [ID], Jilong Wang, and Shuying Zhuang

Institute for Network Sciences and Cyberspace, BNRist, Tsinghua University,
Beijing, China
{wth20,zhuangsy18}@mails.tsinghua.edu.cn,
{jessiewang,wjl}@tsinghua.edu.cn

Abstract. Accurate inference of interdomain paths between arbitrary source and destination is the foundation for many research areas, especially for the security of the Internet routing system. The widely used method to solve this problem is using standard policies based on the business relationship model, but it is far from satisfactory. We conduct an in-depth analysis on the inherent limitations of the path inference by standard routing policies and show that the routing behaviors of ISPs are diverse and standard import policies are oversimplified. Then we develop RouteInfer, an algorithm for accurately inferring interdomain paths by capturing ISP routing behaviors diversity and generality. RouteInfer uses a 3-layer policy model to extract the fine-grained policies and coarse-grained policies of ASes and can achieve high accuracy as well as good generalization ability. After extracting policies, we find another inherent challenge that there is still a huge number of ASes without inferred policies. To overcome this challenge, RouteInfer formulates the prediction of route decisions as a ranking problem and develops a learning-based approach especially for predicting route decisions. We carefully design node, link, and path features based on the understanding of actual route decisions. Overall, on average, RouteInfer achieves 81.64% accuracy. Compared with state-of-the-art inference algorithms, RouteInfer increases the inference accuracy by about 30.04% to 182.3%. Furthermore, we analyze the inferred policies and the route decision model to understand routing behaviors deeply. We find that many ASes set fine-grained policies for CDN ASes. Besides, most of the violations of the standard preference rule are related to p2p links in European IXPs.

Keywords: Interdomain path inference · BGP routing policy · Network measurement

1 Introduction

The Internet routing infrastructure serves a key role in ensuring the reachability, availability of online services and ensuring that packets can find their

O. Hohlfeld et al. (Eds.): PAM 2022, LNCS 13210, pp. 216–244, 2022.
https://doi.org/10.1007/978-3-030-98785-5_10

destinations. The interdomain routing protocol (i.e., BGP) and a huge number of network operators together determine the selected paths between any source-destination pairs in the Internet. Interdomain path inference is of great importance for a wide range of applications and research areas, such as deploying BGP security mechanisms [1–3], optimizing peer-to-peer applications [4], designing routing-based attacks and countermeasures towards bitcoin [5–8], censorship [9,10], Tor [11], etc.

The widely used method to solve this problem is using standard routing policies in the business relationship model [12]. The business relationship model assumes there are commonly two classes of AS relationships including customer-provider (c2p) and peer-peer (p2p). In terms of standard import policies, each AS sets local preferences as follow (which we also call *the standard preference rule*): prefer paths received from customers over paths received from peers over path received from providers. In terms of standard export policies, ASes would never announce routes received from a provider or a peer towards another provider or peer (also called the valley-free rule).

However, prior works have found path inference based on standard policies performs poorly [13,14]. In this paper, we first use multiple data sources to take an in-depth look at the problem of path inference by standard policies, including BGP routing data, Internet Routing Registry (IRR) data, and BGP community data. The analysis shows that interdomain path inference by standard policies is faced with several fundamental problems. First, routing behaviors of ISPs are diverse, i.e., ISPs not only consider the business relationships with neighbor ASes when setting policies but also set policies for a specific prefix (which are denoted as prefix policies) or a specific destination AS (which are denoted as destination AS policies) or a specific neighbor (which are denoted as neighbor policies) to achieve their performance or economical goals. Three kinds of policies (prefix policies, destination AS policies, and neighbor policies) are all widely used by each AS. Over 40% ASes set multiple kinds of policies. However, to our knowledge, all inference algorithms [4,15–18] use the single-kind policy model to model routing policies, e.g., modeling all policies by prefix policies [15–17], or neighbor policies [4], or standard policies [18]. Second, the inaccuracy of path inference is mainly due to the oversimplified standard import policies. Third, there is still a huge number of ASes whose policies we cannot infer from BGP routing data. Prior works use some naive default policies as the routing policies of those ASes. But we prove that they also perform poorly in path inference. These problems are overlooked by state-of-the-art inference algorithms.

To address the above problems, we design and develop RouteInfer[1], an algorithm that infers interdomain paths between arbitrary sources and destinations in the Internet by capturing ISP routing behavior diversity and generality. First, to capture routing behavior diversity, RouteInfer uses a *3-layer policy model* to model ISP routing policies. The 3-layer policy model uses three kinds of policies to represent an AS's routing behaviors. Each AS has fine-grained policies and

---

[1] The source code of RouteInfer and analysis results can be found at https://github.com/DiceWu/RouteInfer.

coarse-grained policies at the same time. We try to infer the internal details of an AS's policies as much as possible. Second, to predict route decisions of ASes without inferred policies, we explore the intrinsic generality and similarity of route decisions among different ASes. RouteInfer uses a kind of data-driven approach, learning to rank, to train a *route decision model* learned from empirical data. Our model considers various well-designed useful attributes including node, link, and path features. We use the model to predict route decisions of ASes without inferred policies.

Overall, RouteInfer takes into account a full consideration of the diversity and generality of routing behaviors among ISPs. Our evaluations show that, on average, RouteInfer achieves 81.64% accuracy. Compared to the current state-of-the-art algorithms, RouteInfer increases the accuracy by about 30.04% to 182.3%. The two key components (3-layer policy model and route decision model) both benefit the whole algorithm. Compared with single-kind policy models, our 3-layer policy model increases the accuracy by up to 133% and has good generalization ability. The route decision model based on the learning to rank algorithm performs up to 313% better than predicting route decisions by default policies and is an explainable model which gives us opportunities to understand routing behaviors deeply.

Furthermore, we conduct analyses of inferred policies and the explainable route decision model to improve our understanding of ISP routing behaviors. We make the following observations from the analysis:

- ASes in high tiers tend to set fine-grained policies while ASes in low tiers tend to set coarse-grained policies.
- We find that many ASes set prefix policies for the prefixes belonging to CDN ASes.
- We find the tier of next-hop AS is the most important feature in the route decision model. The business relationship is a less important feature in the route decision.
- We find that many ASes prefer the routes received from providers to the routes received from peers, which does not follow the standard preference rule. We also find those violations are related to p2p links in European IXPs.

The paper is organized as follows. Section 2 introduces existing research efforts in interdomain path inference. Section 3 discusses the inherent problems in path inference by standard policies. Section 4 details RouteInfer's design and implementation. Section 5 compares RouteInfer with state-of-the-art algorithms. Analyses of inferred policies and the route decision model are also presented in Sect. 5. Section 6 concludes the paper.

2   Related Work

Inferring interdomain paths have been a long-standing problem in the past two decades and the pioneering and most classic approach is using standard routing policies [12,19] proposed by Lixin Gao and Jennifer Rexford. Several algorithms

[18,20] infer interdomain paths by computing paths that are compliant with standard policies. However, many works [13,21] have proven the accuracy is disappointing.

Thus some researchers try to conduct measurement analysis to understand routing behaviors of ASes in the real world [13–15,21,22]. First, they find that business relationships are too coarse-grained to model routing policies [13,14]. For example, Anwar et al. [14] find about 14–35% of route decisions cannot be explained by the business relationship model and prefix policies can explain 10–20% of unexpected routing decisions. Second, Muhlbauer et al. [13] find that fine-grained policies can be aggregated into coarse-grained policies and actual routing policies are somewhere in-between prefix policies and neighbor policies. Third, they find the main problem of standard policies is the standard preference rule rather than the standard export policy rule [13,21,22]. For example, Deng et al. [21] find that using the standard preference rule causes significant degradation of the overall accuracy, compared with only using standard export policies to infer paths. Giotsas et al. [22] use the BGP community data to infer ground-truth of export policies and found only 1.7% of paths violate the valley-free rule. Fourth, Muhlbauer et al. [15] found the path diversity in Internet routing, i.e., there may exist multiple paths between a source AS to a destination prefix. One router per AS is not sufficient to capture path diversity because one router only contains one route towards a destination prefix.

Inspired by the above measurement and analysis studies, several works proposed the improvement of path inference algorithms [4,15–17]. To overcome the challenge of path diversity, Muhlbauer et al. [15] allow each AS to consist of multiple quasi-routers. A quasi-router is a logical router rather than a physical router. A quasi-router represents part of routers in an AS that all choose the same best path towards a destination. If an AS has multiple paths towards a prefix, then multiple quasi-routers account for each route towards the prefix. To overcome the challenge that business relationship is too coarse-grained, researchers proposed to use fine-grained policy models to infer routing policies. For example, [15–17] model ISP routing policies by a prefix policy model (i.e., each policy is set for a specific destination prefix). Madhyastha et al. [4] model policies by a neighbor policy model (i.e. each policy is set for a specific neighbor). In this paper, we prove modeling routing policies by single-kind models cannot capture ISP routing behaviors diversity and cannot achieve high accuracy. To solve this problem, we propose to use a three-layer policy model to extract and represent the routing policies of ASes.

Many works [16,17] have found that if inferring paths by fine-grained policy model such as prefix policy model, there are some ASes whose policies they cannot infer. To tackle this problem, prior works use default policies for those ASes without inferred policies. For example, Muhlbauer et al. [15] let the ASes without inferred policies select the shortest path when they make route decisions, [16,17] use standard policies as the default policies of the ASes without inferred policies. Tian et al. [23] are the first to introduce a data-driven learning-based approach to model route decisions of ISPs. However, they only use one kind of feature which cannot capture enough information related to route decisions. In this paper, we develop a particular learning-based approach to train a route decision model for predicting the route decisions of the ASes without policies. We take full consideration of node, link, and path features related to route decisions in practice.

3 Limitation of Standard Routing Policy

In this section, we elaborate the inherent problems of using standard policies to infer interdomain paths.

The widely used standard policies for path inference is based on the business relationship model [19]. The model assumes that all ASes set standard routing policies on the basis of neighbor's relationship. Standard routing policies say all ASes prefer routes learned from customers over routes learned from peers over routes learned from providers and they would never announce routes learned from a provider or a peer towards another provider or peer. However, there are at least two problems. First, if multiple neighbors with the same relationship send routes towards a prefix to an AS a, which one AS a prefers? Second, if AS a receives multiple shortest paths with the highest preference, which one to choose? Standard routing policies cannot answer these questions. Besides, the terrible accuracy (only 14% in prior validations [13,21]) also arouses our curiosity. Therefore, we have a strong temptation to answer the questions: "Whether standard routing policies can capture ISP routing behaviors? If not, why?" We conduct three measurement experiments based on three data sources to find the answer. The details of the datasets and the process of data sanitization are presented in Sect. 5.1.

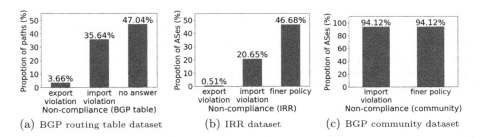

(a) BGP routing table dataset   (b) IRR dataset   (c) BGP community dataset

Fig. 1. Non-compliance of standard routing policies

BGP Routing Table. We first use BGP routing tables to find the answer. We split BGP routing data into a training set (90%) and a test set (10%). The training set is used to infer business relationships between ASes by the state-of-the-art AS relationship inference algorithm AS-Rank [24]. Based on the topology with relationships, we infer AS paths towards the destination ASes in the test set. We simulate the process of route announcement and route decision of the

ASes in the Internet according to standard policies. After routing convergence, we examine whether the inferred paths are consistent with the observed paths in the test set. For example, there is a path $AS1, AS2, AS3, AS4, p1$ in the test set. $p1$ is the destination prefix and $AS4$ is the destination AS. We first examine the inferred path between $AS3$ to $p1$, then between $AS2$ to $p1$, then between $AS1$ to $p1$. Once we find a mismatch (supposing the inferred path between $AS2$ to $p1$ is not equal to $AS2, AS3, AS4$), then we stop the examination and try to find reasons of the mismatch. There are three kinds of reasons. (1) Violation of standard export policy: a neighbor AS should not announce the best route to the AS in standard export policy, while the neighbor AS announces in reality, (2) Violation of standard import policy: an AS chooses a route received from a provider rather than the route received from a customer, or chooses a route received from a provider rather than the route received from a peer, or chooses a route received from a peer rather than the route received from a customer, (3) No answer in standard import policies: *no answer* means that standard import policies do not tell us which one is the best route among several routes with the highest preference and shortest path length. If an AS does not choose the best route among several routes with the highest preference and shortest path length, then we say this path is inferred wrongly due to the no answer problem in standard import policies.

Figure 1(a) shows the result. Only 3.66% of paths are inferred wrongly due to violation of standard export policy. 35.64% of paths are inferred wrongly due to violation of standard import policy and 47.04% of paths are due to no answer in standard import policies. Obviously, violation of standard import policies and the no answer problem are the main culprits of terrible accuracy.

aut-num:	AS4670	aut-num:	AS18060	aut-num:	AS17843
import:	from AS3561	import:	from AS4739	import:	from AS3786
	action pref=100;		action pref=10;		action pref=10;
	accept {204.70.0.0/16}		accept AS473		accept ANY
(a) prefix policy		(b) destination AS policy		(c) neighbor policy	

Fig. 2. Real-world examples of three kinds of routing policies observed from IRR data

Internet Routing Registry. Next, we choose to use IRR data [25] to investigate ISP routing behaviors. IRR records the routing policies of some ASes. First, we can learn that there are commonly three kinds of policies in the wild as shown in Fig. 2, including prefix policy, destination AS policy, and neighbor policy. The prefix policy is set for a specific destination prefix, the destination AS policy (in short, destAS policy) is set for a specific destination AS, and the neighbor policy is set for a specific neighbor AS. We can see that the prefix policy is finer than the destAS policy and the destAS policy is finer than the neighbor policy. 10038 ASes record their routing policies in the IRR database (but maybe not all of their policies). We count the kinds of policies each AS set and show the statistic in Fig. 3. We can see that not all ASes use a single kind of policies, and over 40% ASes set multiple kinds of policies. *Therefore, it is of great importance to capture routing behavior diversity when modeling routing policies.* Second, from IRR data, we can know how the ASes set local preferences for their neighbors. We can find that whether there exist violations of standard import policy, e.g., set higher preference for peers than customers. The dataset of the business relationship is obtained from CAIDA AS relationship database [26]. We can also know whether the policy is finer than the standard import policy, e.g., set different preferences for neighbors with the same relationship. Third, some ASes record their export policies in IRR data, e.g. to $AS1$ announce $AS2$. Thus we can examine whether these export policies obey the valley-free rule to find violations of standard export policy.

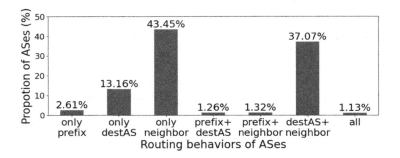

Fig. 3. Routing behavior diversity

Figure 1(b) shows the result of our analysis of IRR data. Only 0.51% of ASes violate standard export policies, while 20.65% of ASes violate standard import policies. This result also indicates standard import policies are more oversimplified than standard export policies. Besides, we find that 46.68% of ASes set finer policies than standard policies. Therefore, standard policies are too coarse-grained to capture ISP routing behaviors.

BGP Community. The third data source we choose is BGP community data. What can BGP community data tell us? First, some ASes will tag the preference set for their neighbors, e.g., $AS1273$ (Vodafone) tags a BGP community value $1273: 70$ to a route, which represents $AS1273$ set preference of the route to 70. We can investigate whether the ASes obey standard import policies when setting preferences. Second, we can find that whether the ASes set different preferences for neighbors with the same relationship. If an AS sets different preferences for neighbors with the same relationship, it means that the AS sets finer policies than standard policies.

Not all ASes tag BGP communities to routing data and we do not know the semantics of all ASes' community values. We get a semantic dictionary of 247 community values of 56 ASes. From BGP routing data, we observe the preference communities of 17 ASes in these 56 ASes and show the statistic in Fig. 1(c). We find that 16 ASes (94.12%) violate standard import policies and set fine-grained policies. Only *AS*11537 obey the standard routing policies.

In conclusion, standard routing policy cannot model ISP routing behaviors because the routing behaviors are diverse among different ASes. Especially the oversimplified standard import policies contribute to most of the errors in path inference. These observations will guide our design in the next section.

4   Design of RouteInfer

4.1   Overview

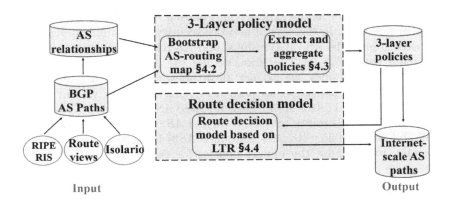

Fig. 4. Overview of RouteInfer

In this section, we present a new path inference algorithm, RouteInfer, that is designed to address the challenges discussed above. Figure 4 shows the overview of RouteInfer, which consists of two key components: a 3-layer policy model for capturing routing behavior diversity and a route decision model based on learning to rank algorithm for predicting route decisions of ASes without inferred policies. RouteInfer works in three steps as follows:

1. We construct an AS-routing map from BGP routing data, initialize policies for each AS, and remove edge ASes with simple policies.
2. We extract prefix policies from BGP routing data and aggregate fine-grained policies into coarse-grained policies.
3. We train the route decision model for predicting route decisions for ASes without inferred policies based on the routing behaviors which are inferred from other ASes.

Next, we explain the design details and the benefits of each step.

4.2   Bootstrap AS-Routing Map

We start from building an AS-routing map based on public BGP data.

Quasi-Router. Muhlbauer et al. [15] have proven that many ASes choose multiple paths towards a given prefix due to hot potato routing, thus we should not model each AS by a single entity. So we allow each AS to consist of multiple quasi-routers which is similar to [15]. We initialize each AS with one quasi-router. In the next step, we will add quasi-routers to capture the path diversity when necessary.

Initial Policies. As mentioned in Sect. 3, compared with standard import policies, standard export policies do not induce too many errors in path inference (this statement is also confirmed with some prior observations [13,21]), thus we use the valley-free rule as the export policy of each AS and leave import policies for further inference. In the area of network security, AS-Rank [24] algorithm is often used to infer the AS relationships, and AS relationships are used to infer interdomain paths [5,7–9]. Therefore, we use the AS-Rank algorithm to infer AS relationships. Besides, we extract all 3-tuples corresponding to three consecutive ASes in AS paths, e.g. for path $AS1, AS2, AS3, AS4$, we can get tuples $(AS1, AS2, AS3)$ and $(AS2, AS3, AS4)$. A tuple $(AS1, AS2, AS3)$ indicates that $AS2$ announces $AS3$'s routes to $AS1$. If we find $AS2$ violates the valley-free rule, we will add export policy (to $AS1$ announce $AS3$) for $AS2$ as a supplement.

Besides, we initialize the import policies for each AS. First, all ASes will set the same preference for all routes received from any neighbor. So ASes will use the shortest path to decide which path to choose and use the smallest AS number for the final tie-break. Please notice that this is just a naïve initial state for ASes to decide the best paths toward a destination. In the next step, we will extract import policies for ASes from BGP routing tables.

Remove Periphery ASes. A huge number of ASes in low tiers only have simple behaviors. Removing these ASes from topology can improve our algorithm efficiency and do not harm the performance. Many edge ASes only have one single neighbor to access the rest of the Internet. We call them *periphery ASes*. It's unnecessary to infer policies of periphery ASes. Considering the AS topology is an undirected graph, we remove all the leaf nodes iteratively until the graph has no leaf node. Suppose AS a is a single-homed ASes with two single-homed customers (AS b and AS c). In the first iteration, AS b and AS c will be removed because they are leaf nodes in AS graph. Then in the second iteration, AS a will be removed because it becomes a leaf node after the first iteration. After removing periphery ASes, the number of ASes is reduced from 60,000 to 45,000.

4.3   Extract and Aggregate Policies

The goal of this step is to get import policies (i.e., preference rules) of ASes and capture routing behavior diversity as much as possible. In the following, we first introduce how we extract prefix policies from observed AS paths. Next, we introduce our approach of aggregating fine-grained policies into coarse-grained policies to get a 3-layer behavior model for capturing routing behavior diversity.

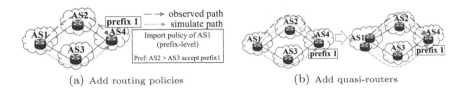

(a) Add routing policies   (b) Add quasi-routers

Fig. 5. Example of prefix policies extraction in one iteration

Extract Prefix Policies. Similar to Muhlbauer et al. [15], we use a heuristic to extract the prefix policies of ASes iteratively. In each iteration of the heuristic, we simulate route announcements and route decisions of ASes in the whole AS-routing map and compare the simulated AS paths with observed paths. If there exists a discrepancy, we will alter the AS-routing map by either adding quasi-routers or adding routing policies. Adding quasi-routers is to capture interdomain path diversity and ensure an AS can choose multiple paths towards a prefix. Adding policies is to ensure simulated paths are consistent with observed paths.

Figure 5(a) shows an example of adding routing policies. The simple topology consists of four ASes and $prefix1$ belongs to $AS4$. The simulated path from $AS1$ to $prefix1$ is $(AS1, AS2, AS4)$, but the actual path observed from BGP data is $(AS1, AS3, AS4)$. So we can add a prefix import policy for $AS1$, i.e., *AS2>AS3 accept prefix1*, trying to make the simulated path match the observed path. Figure 5(b) shows an example of adding quasi-router. In this scenario, we observe two different paths from $AS1$ towards $prefix1$. But $AS1$ only has one quasi-router and the router chooses one path. So we add a quasi-router with no policy for $AS1$, and add policies for this quasi-router to make the router choose the other path towards $prefix1$. After adding routing policies and quasi-routers, we re-simulate route decisions and route announcements in the whole AS-routing map. Similarly, we keep searching for mismatches between simulated and observed paths and add quasi-routers or policies iteratively, until all observed paths match with corresponding simulated paths.

Policy Aggregation. To capture the routing behavior diversity of ASes, we propose a 3-layer policy model. Each AS's routing policies consist of three layers, including prefix policies, destAS policies, and neighbor policies. When we infer an interdomain path, we will apply the finest policies which can be used to infer the path. For example, if an AS a receive a route whose destination prefix is $p1$ from neighbor AS b and prefix $p1$ belongs to destination AS d. We first check whether AS a has the prefix policy set for prefix $p1$. If AS a has the policy, we will apply this prefix policy to infer the path. Otherwise, we will check whether AS a has the destAS policy set for destination AS d. If AS a has the policy, we will apply this destAS policy to infer the path. Otherwise, we will check whether

AS a has the neighbor policy set for neighbor AS b. If AS a has the policy, we will apply this neighbor policy to infer the path. Otherwise, we have no policy to infer paths and we will introduce our solution in Sect. 4.4.

To get destAS policies and neighbor policies, we use policy aggregation from prefix policies that are inferred before. To be specific, *policy aggregation* is aggregating fine-grained policies to coarse-grained policies when there are no conflicts. Conflicts mean preference ranking loops after aggregation. For example, if we have three import policies as follows: AS1 > AS2 accept prefix1, AS2 > AS3 accept prefix2, AS3 > AS1 accept prefix3 (three prefixes belong to the same AS). If we aggregate the three policies, we get a preference ranking loop which is AS1 > AS2 > AS3 > AS1. Therefore, we cannot aggregate these three policies. Prefix policies will first be aggregated into destAS policies. Then, destAS policies will be aggregated into neighbor policies.

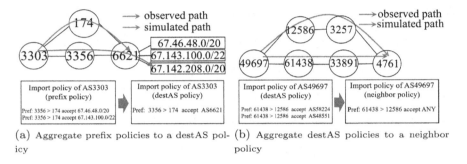

(a) Aggregate prefix policies to a destAS policy

(b) Aggregate destAS policies to a neighbor policy

Fig. 6. Example of policy aggregation

Figure 6 shows two examples of policy aggregation and also shows why we need policy aggregation. Figure 6(a) depicts an example of aggregating prefix policies to a destAS policy. We can infer two prefix policies of $AS3303$ which are for prefix 67.46.48.0/20 and prefix 67.143.100.0/22. But when we want to infer the route from $AS3303$ to prefix 67.142.208.0/20, we do not have routing policies to match and we infer the path wrongly. However, we can aggregate the two prefix policies to a destAS policy as shown in Fig. 6(a), since the two prefix policies are both set for the prefixes belonging to $AS6621$ and there is no conflict between the two prefix policies. Therefore, for any routes whose destination AS is 6621, we know $AS3303$ prefers the routes received from $AS3356$ to the routes received from $AS174$. Figure 6(b) depicts an example of aggregating destAS policies to a neighbor policy. Similarly, we have two destAS policies whose destination ASes are $AS58224$ and $AS48551$, but we cannot use these policies to infer the path from $AS49697$ to $AS4761$. However, we can further aggregate destAS policies to a neighbor policy. The neighbor policy tells us $AS49697$ will prefer the routes received from $AS61438$ to the routes received from $AS12586$ no matter the destination of the routes. Thus we can use this policy to infer the path from $AS49697$ to $AS4761$.

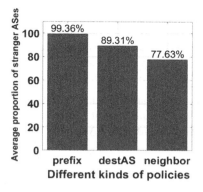

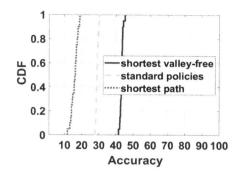

Fig. 7. Average proportion of stranger ASes

Fig. 8. Accuracy of using default policies to predict route decisions

Challenge Caused by Incomplete Routing Data. After policy extraction and aggregation, there is still a huge number of ASes whose policies we cannot extract from public routing data due to incomplete routing data. Those ASes are like strangers, we do not know their routing behaviors. So we call those ASes *stranger ASes*. Figure 7 shows the average proportion of stranger ASes. First, we randomly select 100,000 destination prefixes. For each prefix p, we count the proportion of ASes which do not have any prefix policy towards p. We find 99.36% ASes without the prefix policies towards a given prefix p on average. Then, we randomly select 100,000 destination ASes, and for each destination AS d, we find the proportion of ASes which do not have any destAS policy towards d. We find 89.31% ASes without the destAS policies towards a given destination AS d on average. Besides, we randomly select 100,000 destination prefixes and try to infer the paths towards those prefixes. We find about 77.63% ASes even do not have any neighbor policy to infer the path.

Existing solutions for inferring paths involving stranger ASes are setting default policies to those ASes. When inferring the path, if an AS has inferred policies, then they use the policies to infer the path. If an AS does not have inferred policies, then they use default policies to infer the path. Commonly used default policies include choosing the shortest path [15] as the best path, choosing the shortest valley-free path as the best path, and using standard policies [16,17] to select the best path. However, the accuracy of those solutions is disappointing, which is only 15.8%, 43.23% and 28.86% respectively as shown in Fig. 8.

4.4   Route Decision Model Based on Learning to Rank Algorithm

Millions of routing policies inferred in our 3-layer policy model allow us to use a data-driven machine learning-based approach to train a model for predicting how an AS select the best route among several candidate routes. In this subsection, we propose a route decision model to predict route decisions of stranger ASes.

Crucially, our algorithm integrates various *node, link, and path* attributes that might help infer route decisions of ASes. We first introduce our designed features based on the understanding of actual route decisions. Second, we introduce the design of our route decision model.

Feature Design. The AS which makes route decisions is called decision AS. The first AS in a candidate route is called next-hop AS. The process of route decisions can be characterized by the following three types of features: (A) Properties of the route; (B) Properties of the next-hop AS; (C) Properties between decision AS and next-hop AS.

Path Length (Type A). This feature is based on best practices. Many ASes prefer to choose the paths whose length is the shortest.

Tier of Next-Hop AS (Type B). This feature consists of two parts. One is the degree of the next-hop AS. The other is the AS rank [27] of the next-hop AS. In AS rank, ASes are ranked by their customer cone size, which is the number of their direct and indirect customers. Those two attributes measure an AS's tier in the Internet. This feature folds in the following intuition: ASes may prefer the routes received from high-tier ASes. For example, Anwar et al. [14] find that Cogent prefers the path received from Tier-1 AS. We explain the detail of this intuition in Appendix C.

Business Relationship (Type C). This feature is based on the consensus that route decision depends on economic interests. The business relationship between the decision AS and the next-hop AS is the most related feature to reflect the economic consideration. The data of the business relationship is from the first step of bootstrapping AS-routing map. Since it is a discrete variable, this feature is encoded by one-hot vectors[2].

Co-located IXP and Co-located Private Peering Facility (Type C). Those two features are based on the intuition that if there are many co-located IXPs or facilities between the decision AS and a neighbor AS, the decision AS is likely to choose the route received from the neighbor AS as the best path. We extract the information of co-located IXP and co-located private peering facilities from IXP data.

Model Design. Predicting route decisions is to choose the best route among several candidate routes. This problem can be formulated as a ranking problem, i.e., ranking candidate routes according to the preferences set by decision AS and selecting the most preferred route as the best route. *Learning to rank (in short, LTR)* [28] is a class of machine learning algorithms for solving real-world ranking problems. To achieve this goal, we use a state-of-the-art pairwise LTR algorithm, LambdaMART [29] to learn the route behaviors from observed routing data and predict route decisions of stranger ASes.

---

[2] In machine learning, one hot encoding is a method of converting categorical values into binary vectors.

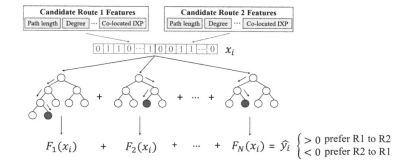

Fig. 9. Framework of the route decision model based on LambdaMART

We begin by reviewing the LambdaMART algorithm. LambdaMART is a pairwise learning to rank algorithm which is approximated by a classification problem, i.e., learning a binary classifier that can tell which route is preferred in a given pair of candidate routes.

The structure of LambdaMART is based on the multiple additive regression tree (MART) which is also called gradient boosting decision tree (GBDT). MART combines many weak learners (which are decision trees here) to come up with one strong learner. All the trees are connected in series and each tree tries to minimize the error of the previous tree. The final model aggregates the result of each tree and thus a strong learner is achieved. Figure 9 shows the framework of our route decision model. Each input instance includes the features of two candidate routes. The sum of each output of trees can be used to predict the preference between two candidate routes.

LambdaMART defines the gradient λ as follows:

$$\lambda_{ij} = \frac{-\sigma}{1 + e^{\sigma(s_i - s_j)}} \mid \Delta_{NDCG} \mid \tag{1}$$

σ is the parameter that determines the shape of the sigmoid. s_i and s_j are the predicted preference of candidate route $r1$ and candidate route $r2$. Normalized discounted cumulative gain (NDCG) is a traditional measure of goodness induced for improving the effectiveness of the model.

LambdaMART uses the Newton-Raphson step to compute the leaf value of the decision tree. For a function $g(\gamma)$, a Newton-Raphson towards the extremum of g is

$$\gamma_{n+1} = \gamma_n - \frac{g'(\gamma_n)}{g''(\gamma_n)} \tag{2}$$

We use the following steps to get our route decision model. After we infer the policies from public routing data, we simulate route announcements and route decisions in our AS-routing map for each prefix. For the ASes which we know its best route towards destination prefix, we query the AS's adj-rib-in database which contains all candidate routes of the AS. Therefore, we can get millions of triplets (decision AS, best route, candidate route) for training our route decision model. We extract features introduced above from those triples as the input of the LambdaMART model. The model is initialized as a constant value. Then the model creates N trees iteratively. In each iteration, we assign leaf values by the newton step and update the model. The pseudocode of our route decision model is shown in Appendix D.

In conclusion, we infer interdomain paths in the following steps. Suppose we want to infer the routes towards prefix p. First, the route is announced from the original AS which hosts the prefix p. Then, we simulate the process of route announcements and route decisions of each AS. When an AS a received a route from a neighbor AS, it will first query its 3-layer policies. AS a will search for the policy which is set for the route. It will first consider prefix policies, then destAS policies, then neighbor policies. If there are even no neighbor policies for it to make the route decision, AS a will use our route decision model to predict the best route. After that, AS a will announce the best route to neighbor ASes according to the export policies we set for AS a. After routing convergence, we can get the best paths between all ASes to the destination prefix p. Those paths are the inference results of our RouteInfer algorithm.

5   Evaluation and Analysis

In this section, we evaluate our inference algorithm RouteInfer. We evaluate the overall accuracy of RouteInfer against state-of-the-art interdomain path inference algorithms. Besides, we evaluate the improvement of two key components (i.e., 3-layer policy model and route decision model) respectively. Furthermore, we analyze inferred routing behaviors of ASes and try to find reasons for the discrepancy between standard policies in theory and routing behaviors in reality. We demonstrate that RouteInfer can achieve high accuracy in path inference and help us better understand routing behaviors in the following five aspects:

Overall Accuracy (Sect. 5.2). RouteInfer achieves higher accuracy compared with five state-of-the-art interdomain path inference algorithms with about 81.64% accuracy on average.

Improvement of 3-Layer Policy Model (Sect. 5.3). Our 3-layer policy model performs up to 133% better than single-kind policy models. Besides, the 3-layer policy model can achieve high accuracy and good generalization ability at the same time.

Improvement of Route Decision Model (Sect. 5.4). Our route decision model based on learning to rank performs up to 313% better than default policies used in prior works. Besides, our model is explainable and can tell us which features are important for route decisions.

Analysis of 3-Layer Policies (Sect. 5.5). We further analyze the 3-layer policies we get. We find that ASes in high-tiers tend to set fine-grained policies and ASes in low-tiers tend to set coarse-grained policies. Besides, we find most of ASes set prefix policies for the prefixes belonging to CDN ASes.

Analysis of Route Decision Model (Sect. 5.6). We investigate feature importance of our explainable model. We find that the tier of next-hop AS is the most important feature. Besides, we find that many ASes prefer the routes received from providers to the routes received from peers, and it does not follow the standard preference rule. We also find those violations are related to p2p links in European IXPs.

5.1   Datasets

BGP Routing Data. We use BGP routing data from RouteViews [30], RIPE RIS [31] and Isolario [32] as the input data of RouteInfer. Snapshots of BGP routing tables are on the first day of January 2020, which are collected from around 747 vantage points (VPs) by 50 route collectors. We preprocess the raw dataset by filtering mistakes or noises that impact the path inference. We remove duplicated ASes that result from path prepending and filter paths with AS loops or reserve AS numbers. IXPs typically have their own AS number and should not add their ASN in the BGP path in best practices [33]. But sometimes it may happen due to debugging. Thus we remove IXP AS numbers from the BGP paths. Please notice that the Internet topology constructed from BGP routing data is incomplete, i.e., there are many invisible links [34]. We do not try to improve the completeness of the topology and it is a limitation of our work.

IRR Data. IRR data is mainly used to investigate the challenge mentioned in Sect. 3. We get IRR data from RADb [25] which provides the largest routing registry mirror site in the Internet on August 1, 2021. IRR data is recorded by Routing Policy Specification Language (RPSL) [35]. Thus we need to parse the IRR data according to the semantic of RPSL.

BGP Community Data. BGP community is a transitive BGP attribute used to attach metadata on BGP paths. This dataset is used to investigate the challenge mentioned in Sect. 3 and to validate the accuracy of inferred policies in Sect. 5.3. BGP community value is extracted from BGP routing data mentioned before (snapshots on January 1, 2020). The semantics of BGP communities is not standardized, many ASes publicly document the meaning of their BGP communities on their websites [36,37], one step [38], and IRR database [25], enabling us to assemble a dictionary that records how the ASes set import policies by BGP communities. Finally, we know the meanings of BGP community values of 56 different ASes.

IXP Data. IXP data is used to identify the co-located IXPs and co-located facilities used in the feature extraction of our route decision model and also used in the analysis in Sect. 5.6. IXP data can be used to identify where p2p links are located. We get IXP data from PeeringDB [39], the Euro-IX IXP Service Matrix [40], and Packet Clearing House [41] on January 1, 2020.

5.2   Overall Accuracy

Evaluation Methodology. To evaluate the accuracy of inferred paths, we split BGP routing data into a training set and a test set. We use the training set as the input of RouteInfer and use the test set to evaluate the accuracy of the inferred paths. This evaluation methodology is widely used in prior path inference works [4, 15–17].

We give a brief introduction of five state-of-the-art path inference algorithms. SIGCOMM06 [15] is the first work to use the prefix policy model to infer policies. It initializes import policies by choosing the shortest path and initializes export policies by announcing all routes to all neighbors. It infers the prefix policies of ASes by iterative simulation. KnownPath [16] also uses prefix policy model to infer AS paths. It infers paths based on known paths observed from the BGP routing table and uses standard policies to infer unknown paths of ASes. iPlane Nano [4] is the

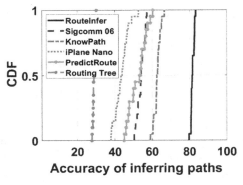

Fig. 10. Overall accuracy against other algorithms

first work to use the neighbor policy model to infer policies. It infers the export policies of ASes by extracting the three consecutive ASes in AS paths and infers import policies by comparing observed paths and alternative routes. Routing Tree [18] algorithm infers paths using standard policies. It uses a three-stage breadth-first search to quickly compute paths from all source ASes to a destination AS. PredictRoute [17] uses prefix policy model to infer policies. It trains Markov chains towards each prefix to predict paths. For the ASes which is not in the Markov chain, PredictRoute will use standard policies to infer paths.

We randomly select 90% (672) VPs and use the routing data observed from those VPs as the training set and the routing data observed from the remaining 10% (75) VPs as the test set. We conduct a classic 10-fold cross-validation, repeated 10 times.

Figure 10 depicts the overall inference accuracy for RouteInfer and the other five state-of-the-art algorithms. We can see that, compared with the five algorithms, RouteInfer is always more accurate and stable, with accuracy between 79.63% and 83.39%. RouteInfer improves the average accuracy 182.3% than that of Routing Tree, 87% than that of iPlane Nano, 55.9% than that of PredictRoute, 50.79% than that of SIGCOMM06, and 30.04% than that of KnownPath.

5.3   Improvement of 3-Layer Policy Model

Next, we evaluate the improvement of the two key components of RouteInfer, the 3-layer policy model and the route decision model respectively. First, we evaluate the improvement of the 3-layer policy model.

Comparison with Single-Kind Policy Model. We compare the accuracy of the 3-layer policy model with single-kind policy models, including prefix policy model, destAS policy model, neighbor policy model, and standard policies. Please notice that, for some single-kind policy models, we cannot infer the policies of all ASes. We first investigate in our test set, how many routes for which we have corresponding policies to infer the path and how many routes with inferred policies can be inferred correctly. For a given route, if we have inferred policies of each AS in the route, we say this route is covered by our inferred policies. We define *coverage* that is the proportion of routes which we have inferred policies. We define *accuracy* which is the proportion of covered routes that are inferred correctly. Figure 11(a) shows the coverage and accuracy of different policy models. We can see that the prefix policy model can achieve 100% accuracy for covered routes but has limited coverage. As the example shown in Fig. 5(a), if we infer a route and we do not have the prefix policy which is set for the destination prefix of that route, then we can only use the default policy to infer the routes. On the contrary, if using standard policies, we can infer any end-to-end route in the Internet. However, it can not achieve high accuracy for those routes. Therefore, single-kind policy models do not have good generalization ability. Our 3-layer policy model consists of three kinds of policies. Coarse-grained policies ensure that our policy model can achieve extensive coverage. Fine-grained policies ensure that our policy model can achieve high accuracy in path inference. Thus, the 3-layer policy model has good generalization ability, with high accuracy and extensive coverage at the same time.

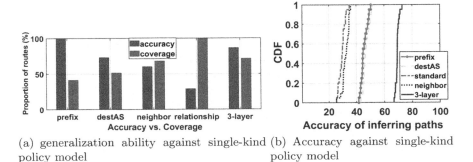

(a) generalization ability against single-kind policy model
(b) Accuracy against single-kind policy model

Fig. 11. Improvement of 3-layer policy model

Then we set default policies for the ASes without policies and investigate the accuracy of each policy model, If there are some ASes we cannot infer their policies, the import policies of those ASes will be set to choosing the shortest valley-free path. Figure 11(b) depicts the accuracy of the 3-layer policy model and single-kind policy model. We can see that the 3-layer policy model achieves higher accuracy than single-kind policy models, with accuracy between 66.82% and 72.98%. 3-layer policy model improves the average accuracy of 52.38% than that of prefix policy model, 47.61% than that of destAS policy model, 133.7% than that of business relationship model (standard policies), and 114.9% than that of neighbor policy model.

Validation of 3-Layer Policies by BGP Communities. We try to use the BGP community data to validate our inferred policies. Please notice that we can not guarantee the quality of BGP community data. But we can use the consistency between our results and the BGP community data to judge whether our results are reliable. As mentioned in Sect. 3, we know the semantics of BGP community values of 56 ASes and only 17 ASes community values can be found in BGP routing data. For example, we find $AS1273$ uses community value $1273\colon 70$ to the route received from neighbor $AS2129$, and it means setting preference 70. $AS1273$ uses community value $1273\colon 90$ to the route received from neighbor $AS12969$, and it means setting preference 90. Thus, we can know the policy that $AS1273$ prefers $AS12969$ to $AS2129$. We extract 13492 policies of those 17 ASes from their BGP community data. 12643 policies can be used to validate our inferred policies (other policies cannot be inferred due to incomplete routing data). In those 12643 policies, about 79.46% policies are consistent with our inferred policies. We can see that our inferred policies are highly consistent with BGP community data.

5.4   Improvement of Route Decision Model

In this subsection, we evaluate the improvement of the route decision model based on learning to rank.

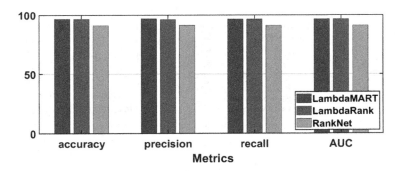

Fig. 12. Performance of three models

Model Selection. Typically, LTR approaches can be categorized into three groups: pointwise, pairwise, and listwise approaches. Pointwise approaches aim to predict the preference of a single route. Pairwise approaches aim to predict the preference between a pair of routes. Listwise approaches aim to predict the preference rank of the entire list of candidate routes. It should be noted that we can only know a decision AS prefers the best route to another candidate route.

We do not know the relative preference between the two routes which are not selected as the best route. Therefore, the pairwise approach is more suitable for solving our problem.

Among the pairwise algorithms, RankNet [42], LambdaRank [43], and LambdaMART [29] have proven to be very successful pairwise LTR algorithms for solving real-world ranking problems [44]. First, we evaluate which model is the best for our problem. We want to know that given two candidate routes, can models predict which one the AS prefer? We use four classic metrics, accuracy, precision, recall, and area under curve (AUC) to evaluate the performance of three models as shown in Fig. 12. All three models perform strongly with over 90% of four metrics (the higher the better). We can see that LambdaRank and LambdaMART perform better than Ranknet. Besides, LambdaRank and LambdaMART are based on the decision tree and the gradient boosting decision tree. They are explainable and can give us an opportunity to conduct further analysis.

Comparison with Default Policies. Next, we try to figure out the accuracy for predicting route decisions using our LTR models. Predicting route decisions represents finding the best route among multiple candidate routes. Figure 13 depicts the accuracy of three LTR models and three default policies. We can see that, compared with using default policies to predict route decisions, three LTR models are more accurate, with accuracy between 60.38% and 67.07%. LambdaMART performs the best among the three LTR models.

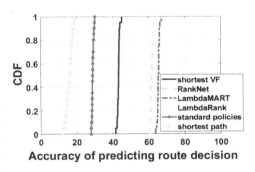

Fig. 13. Accuracy of predicting route decision against default policies

Route decision model based on LambdaMART improves the average accuracy of 51.11% than that of shortest valley-free, 126.4% than that of standard policies, and 313.2% than that of the shortest path.

5.5 Analysis of 3-Layer Policies

In this subsection, we further analyze policies inferred in our 3-layer policy model. Our analysis mainly wants to answer the following two questions: (1) Whether ASes in the different tiers have different routing behaviors? (2) Many ASes set prefix policies for traffic engineering. Which ASes do those prefixes belong to? Whether there are some ASes for which most of ASes set prefix policies?

Tier vs. Routing Behaviors. We first investigate the relationship between tier and routing behaviors. We classify ASes into three classes according to their routing behaviors. If an AS sets at least one prefix policy, we call it *prefix-level AS*. If an AS does not set any prefix policy but set at least one destAS policy, we call it *destAS-level AS*. If an AS does not set any prefix policy or destAS policy and only set neighbor policy, we call it *neighbor-level AS*. We do not consider ASes with fewer inferred policies (less than 100 policies) since we have little information on their routing behaviors. We count the degree and AS rank of the three classes of ASes as shown in Fig. 14. We can see that prefix-level ASes tend to have large degrees and small AS ranks. On the contrary, neighbor-level ASes tend to have small degrees and large AS ranks. Therefore, ASes in high-tiers tend to set fine-grained policies while ASes in low-tiers tend to set coarse-grained policies.

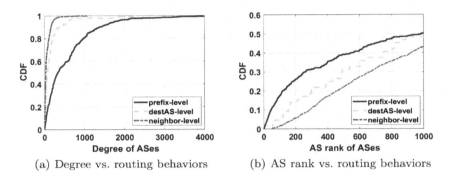

(a) Degree vs. routing behaviors   (b) AS rank vs. routing behaviors

Fig. 14. Tier vs. routing behaviors.

Destination ASes for Which Most of ASes Set Prefix Policies. Next, we investigate most of ASes set prefix policies for the traffic from which ASes. If an AS sets a prefix policy, we map the destination prefix of the policy to the corresponding destination AS. For each destination AS, we count how many ASes set prefix policies for it. We rank the destination ASes according to the number of ASes which set prefix policies for the destination AS shown in Table 1. Interestingly, all top destination ASes are worldwide CDN service providers. Anwar et al. [14] found destination ASes owned by Akamai account for most of the routing decisions which deviate from standard routing policies. Our analysis confirms their findings and shows deep reasons. Not only Akamai but almost all CDN ASes are the destination ASes for which most of ASes set prefix policies. The reason why the paths towards those ASes deviate from standard policies is that most ASes set fine-grained prefix policies for the traffic from those ASes. This result also tells us we should use prefix policies to infer the paths towards CDN ASes.

5.6   Analysis of Route Decision Model

In this subsection, we try to analyze our explainable LTR route decision model and try to answer the questions: What is the importance of the features used in our route decision model? What is the difference between standard routing policies and the model learned from empirical data?

Table 1. Top 10 destination ASes

Rank	Destination AS	Organization	Number of ASes set prefix policy for it
1	AS20940	Akamai International B.V.	349
2	AS16625	Akamai Technologies, Inc.	337
3	AS13335	Cloudflare, Inc.	337
4	AS54994	Quantil Networks Inc.	310
5	AS21433	Accenture UK Limited	306
6	AS21859	Zenlayer Inc	295
7	AS41264	Google Switzerland GmbH	295
8	AS199524	G-Core Labs S.A.	283
9	AS45102	Hangzhou Alibaba Advert-ising Co., Ltd.	278
10	AS15133	MCI Communications Services	277

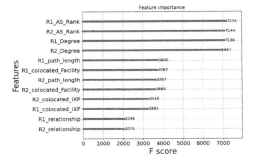

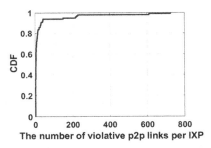

Fig. 15. Feature importance of route decision model. R1 and R2 represents two candidate routes.

Fig. 16. The number of violative p2p links per IXP

Feature Importance Analysis. We rank all features by their F scores which are calculated by the number of times a feature appears in a tree. As shown in Fig. 15, we find the most important feature is the degree and AS rank of next-hop AS. Sometimes, ASes prefer to choose the routes whose next-hop ASes are in high-tiers. We find the feature of path length is as equal importance as the feature of co-located facilities and IXPs between decision AS and next-hop AS. Sometimes, ASes prefer to choose the routes with more co-located IXPs and facilities between the decision AS and the next-hop AS. Perhaps counter-intuitively, the less important feature is the business relationship between the decision AS and the next-hop AS. This result proves standard import policies are oversimplified indeed and confirms our measurement results in Sect. 3. What are the reasons for these discrepancies with the standard preference rules? We investigate this in the following analysis.

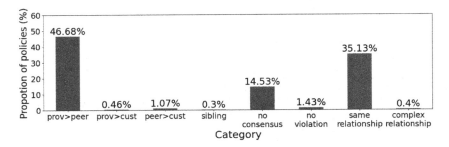

Fig. 17. Analysis of the violations of standard preference rule. No consensus means three algorithms do not reach a consensus on the relationship of links. Same relationship means two neighbor ASes have the same relationship but different preferences. Sibling means the violation is due to a sibling-to-sibling relationship link. Complex relationship means the violation is due to a partial transit relationship or a hybrid relationship link [45].

Violations of Standard Preference Rule. The standard preference rule says the local preference is customer>peer>provider. So there exist three kinds of violations: (1) provider>peer (2) provider>customer (3) peer>customer. We count the proportion of the three violations from our inferred routing policies. To investigate the violations of standard policies, we need to know the business relationship between ASes. A single relationship inference algorithm may have many faults. Therefore, we use three state-of-the-art algorithms, AS-Rank [24], ProbLink [46] and TopoScope [47] to infer AS relationships respectively. We only consider the links for which all three algorithms reach a consensus on their relationship. Figure 17 depicts the statistic of the violations of the standard preference rule. We can see that most of the violations are because the ASes prefer the routes received from a provider to the route received from a peer. We further analyze why they do not prefer the peer. We call these p2p links *violative p2p links*. Then we use IXP data to locate those violative p2p links to corresponding IXPs and count the number of violative p2p links in each IXP. IXP data can tell us a list of interconnection facilities and associated AS. We check the interconnection IXP list of two ASes and find the shared IXP. The result is shown in Fig. 16. We can see that it obeys power-law distribution. Therefore, a small number of IXPs contain most of the violative p2p links. Table 2 shows the top 10 IXPs with most of the violative p2p links. Those ten IXPs contains 81.65% violative p2p links. We can see that all IXPs are located in Europe. But if all large IXPs are located in Europe, our finding is meaningless. Therefore, we collect the largest IXPs [48] and show them in Table 3. Brazil, Russia, USA all have large IXPs. But they do not contain too many violative p2p links. Therefore, we can see that many violations of the standard preference rule are because the ASes prefer a provider to a peer and those violations are related to the IXPs in Europe.

Table 2. Top 10 IXPs with most of violative p2p links

Rank	IXP	Country
1	DE-CIX Frankfurt	Germany
2	AMS-IX	Netherlands
3	France-IX Paris	France
4	Equinix Paris	France
5	Hopus	France
6	LINX LON1	United Kingdom
7	Equinix Stockholm	Sweden
8	Netnod Stockholm BLUE	Sweden
9	Netnod Stockholm GREEN	Sweden
10	VIX	Austria

Table 3. Top 10 IXPs ranked by size

Rank	IXP	Country
1	IX.br	Brazil
2	DE-CIX	Germany
3	AMS-IX	Netherlands
4	LINX	United Kingdom
5	MSK-IX	Russia
6	DATAIX	Russia
7	NL-ix	Netherlands
8	Equinix	USA
9	HKIX	China
10	SIX	USA

6 Conclusion and Future Work

With an in-depth analysis on the limitations of standard routing policies, we propose RouteInfer, an accurate interdomain path inference algorithm by capturing routing behavior diversity and generality. RouteInfer increases the accuracy by about 30.04% to 182.3% compared with existing algorithms. The two key components (3-layer policy model and route decision model) both benefit the whole algorithm. Compared with single-kind policy models, our 3-layer policy model increases the accuracy by up to 133%. Route decision model based on learning to rank performs up to 313% better than predicting route decisions by default policies. Furthermore, we analyze the inferred policies and our route decision model. We find that most of ASes set prefix policies for CDN ASes. Most of the violations of the standard preference rule are related to p2p links in European IXPs.

A bunch of works on the security of Internet routing are based on a complete and accurate Internet routing map. However, almost all existing works use standard policies which perform poorly to get the Internet routing map. Prior works [49] have proven that the success of a system or the analysis in simulation does not guarantee success or the same findings in the real-world. Therefore, in future work, we will focus on analyzing the change and the impact on those security systems after we get a more accurate Internet routing map.

Acknowledgement. We thank the anonymous reviewers and our shepherd, Romain Fontugne, for their comments and suggestions that help significantly improve our paper. This work was supported in part by the National Natural Science Foundation of China under Grant 62072269 and in part by the National Key Research and Development Program of China under Grant 2020YFE0200500.

A   The Influence of Bias

The bias of BGP routing data is a general challenge in Internet-scale measurement studies because BGP routing data is collected from a few vantage points. In this section, we want to investigate the influence of bias on the accuracy of RouteInfer, i.e., how the accuracy of RouteInfer varies with the distance to vantage points. We define the distance of vantage points as the minimum routing hop to vantage points. For example, there are two paths $AS1, AS2, AS3, AS4$ and $AS5, AS6, AS7, AS3, AS8$. In this scenario, $AS1$ and $AS5$ are vantage points. In the first path, $AS3$ is 2 hops from $AS1$. In the second path, $AS3$ is 3 hops from $AS5$. Therefore, the distance between $AS3$ to vantage points is 2 hops. Again, we split the routing data into a training set and a test set. We use the training set as the input of RouteInfer and use the test set to evaluate the accuracy of inferred paths. We classify the paths in the test set by their distance to vantage points. The result is shown in Fig. 18.

We can see that as the distance increases, the accuracy is higher. Thus, bias has little influence on the performance of RouteInfer.

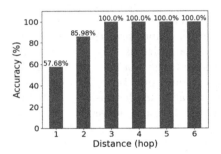

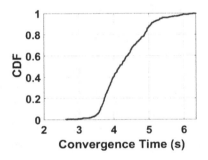

Fig. 18. Distance to vantage points vs. accuracy

Fig. 19. Convergence time

B   Convergence Time

RouteInfer simulates the process of routing decision and routing announcement of the Internet. We need to wait until the simulation gets convergence to get inferred paths. In this section, we analyze the convergence time of one simulation. The result is shown in Fig. 19.

The convergence time is between 2.62 s to 6.35 s. Average convergence time is 4.28 s.

C   The Intuition of Choosing Routes from High Tier ASes

In this section, we will explain the details of the reason why we think route decisions are related to the tier of the next-hop AS. We focus on the Tier-1 ASes and the ASes which connect with Tier-1 ASes. Like the experiments by the BGP routing table in Sect. 3, we split BGP routing data into a training set (90%) and a test set (10%). The training set is used to infer business relationships between ASes. The business relationships are then used to infer the paths. We use the test set to check whether the predictions of route decisions are right. For the Tier-1 ASes, we find that about 50.09% wrong predictions of their route decisions are because the Tier-1 AS chooses the route from a Non-Tier1 AS according to standard policies rather than the route from another Tier-1 AS in reality. For the ASes which connect with Tier-1 ASes, we find that about 58.04% wrong predictions of their route decisions are because the ASes choose the route from a Non-Tier1 AS according to standard policies rather than the route from another Tier-1 AS in reality. Therefore, we find that many Tier1 AS prefer the routes from other Tier1 AS. Besides, if an AS connects to a Tier1 AS, the AS may prefer the routes from the Tier1 AS. Our intuition is based on these findings.

D   The Pseudocode of Route Decision Model

Algorithm 1. Route decision model based on LambdaMART

Input: AS topology; AS relationships; IXP data; Routing policies;

Output: A route decision model which can predict route decisions of stranger ASes;

1: **for all** prefix p **do**
2:    run simulation for p
3:    **for** AS a whose path is known **do**
4:        $br \leftarrow$ best route of a
5:        **for** candidate route cr of a **do**
6:            extract feature vectors from (a, br, cr)
7:        **end for**
8:    **end for**
9: **end for**
10: **set** number of trees N, number of training samples m, number of leaves per tree L, learning rate η
11: **for** $i = 0$ to m **do**
12:    $F_0(x_i) = 0$
13: **end for**
14: **for** $k = 0$ to N **do**
15:    **for** $i = 0$ to m **do**
16:        $y_i = \lambda_i$
17:        $w_i = \frac{\partial y_i}{\partial F_{k-1}(x_i)}$
18:    **end for**
19:    $\{R_{lk}\}_{l=1}^{L}$ // Create L leaf tree on $\{x_i, y_i\}_{i=1}^{m}$
20:    $\gamma_{lk} = \frac{\sum_{x_i \in R_{lk}} y_i}{\sum_{x_i \in R_{lk}} w_i}$ // Assign leaf values based on Newton step
21:    $F_k(x_i) = F_{k-1}(x_i) + \eta \sum_l \gamma_{lk} I(x_i \in R_{lk})$ // Take step with learning rate η
22: **end for**

References

1. Lychev, R., Goldberg, S., Schapira, M.: BGP security in partial deployment: is the juice worth the squeeze? In: Proceedings of the ACM SIGCOMM 2013 Conference on SIGCOMM, pp. 171–182 (2013)
2. Cohen, A., Gilad, Y., Herzberg, A., Schapira, M.: Jumpstarting BGP security with path-end validation. In: Proceedings of the 2016 ACM SIGCOMM Conference, pp. 342–355 (2016)
3. Gilad, Y., Cohen, A., Herzberg, A., Schapira, M., Shulman, H.: Are we there yet? On RPKI's deployment and security. In: NDSS (2017)
4. Madhyastha, H.V., Katz-Bassett, E., Anderson, T.E., Krishnamurthy, A., Venkataramani, A.: iPlane nano: path prediction for peer-to-peer applications. In: NSDI, vol. 9, pp. 137–152 (2009)
5. Apostolaki, M., Marti, G., Müller, J., Vanbever, L.: SABRE: protecting bitcoin against routing attacks. In: 26th Annual Network and Distributed System Security Symposium, NDSS 2019, San Diego, California, USA, 24–27 February 2019 (2019)
6. Tran, M., Shenoi, A., Kang, M.S.: On the routing-aware peering against network-eclipse attacks in bitcoin. In: 30th USENIX Security Symposium (USENIX Security 21) (2021)
7. Apostolaki, M., Zohar, A., Vanbever, L.: Hijacking bitcoin: routing attacks on cryptocurrencies. In: 2017 IEEE Symposium on Security and Privacy (SP), pp. 375–392. IEEE (2017)
8. Tran, M., Choi, I., Moon, G.J., Vu, A.V., Kang, M.S.: A stealthier partitioning attack against bitcoin peer-to-peer network. In: 2020 IEEE Symposium on Security and Privacy (SP), pp. 894–909. IEEE (2020)
9. Nasr, M., Zolfaghari, H., Houmansadr, A.: The waterfall of liberty: decoy routing circumvention that resists routing attacks. In: Proceedings of the 2017 ACM SIGSAC Conference on Computer and Communications Security, pp. 2037–2052 (2017)
10. Houmansadr, A., Wong, E.L., Shmatikov, V.: No direction home: the true cost of routing around decoys. In: 21st Annual Network and Distributed System Security Symposium, NDSS 2014, San Diego, California, USA, 23–26 February 2014 (2014)
11. RisNithyanand, R., Starov, O., Zair, A., Gill, P., Schapira, M.: Measuring and mitigating AS-level adversaries against Tor. In: 23rd Annual Network and Distributed System Security Symposium, NDSS 2016, San Diego, California, USA, 21–24 February 2016. The Internet Society (2016)
12. Gao, L., Rexford, J.: Stable internet routing without global coordination. IEEE/ACM Trans. Netw. **9**(6), 681–692 (2001)
13. Mühlbauer, W., Uhlig, S., Bingjie, F., Meulle, M., Maennel, O.: In search for an appropriate granularity to model routing policies. ACM SIGCOMM Comput. Commun. Rev. **37**(4), 145–156 (2007)
14. Anwar, R., Niaz, H., Choffnes, D., Cunha, Í., Gill, P., Katz-Bassett, E.: Investigating interdomain routing policies in the wild. In: Proceedings of the 2015 Internet Measurement Conference, pp. 71–77 (2015)
15. Mühlbauer, W., Feldmann, A., Maennel, O., Roughan, M., Uhlig, S.: Building an AS-topology model that captures route diversity. ACM SIGCOMM Comput. Commun. Rev. **36**(4), 195–206 (2006)
16. Qiu, J., Gao, L.: AS path inference by exploiting known AS paths. In: Proceedings of IEEE GLOBECOM. Citeseer (2005)

17. Singh, R., Tench, D., Gill, P., McGregor, A.: PredictRoute: a network path prediction toolkit. In: Proceedings of the ACM on Measurement and Analysis of Computing Systems, vol. 5, no. 2, pp. 1–24 (2021)
18. Gill, P., Schapira, M., Goldberg, S.: Modeling on quicksand: dealing with the scarcity of ground truth in interdomain routing data. ACM SIGCOMM Comput. Commun. Rev. **42**(1), 40–46 (2012)
19. Gao, L.: On inferring autonomous system relationships in the internet. IEEE/ACM Trans. Netw, **9**(6), 733–745 (2001)
20. Mao, Z.M., Qiu, L., Wang, J., Zhang, Y.: On AS-level path inference. In: Proceedings of the 2005 ACM SIGMETRICS International Conference on Measurement and Modeling of Computer Systems, pp. 339–349 (2005)
21. Deng, W., Mühlbauer, W., Yang, Y., Zhu, P., Xicheng, L., Plattner, B.: Shedding light on the use of AS relationships for path inference. J. Commun. Netw. **14**(3), 336–345 (2012)
22. Giotsas, V., Zhou, S.: Valley-free violation in internet routing - analysis based on BGP community data. In: 2012 IEEE International Conference on Communications (ICC), pp. 1193–1197. IEEE (2012)
23. Tian, Z., Shen, S., Shi, W., Xiaojiang, D., Guizani, M., Xiang, Yu.: A data-driven method for future internet route decision modeling. Futur. Gener. Comput. Syst. **95**, 212–220 (2019)
24. Luckie, M., Huffaker, B., Dhamdhere, A., Giotsas, V., Claffy, K.C.: AS relationships, customer cones, and validation. In: Proceedings of the 2013 Conference on Internet Measurement Conference, pp. 243–256 (2013)
25. The Internet Routing Registry - RADb. https://www.radb.net/
26. AS Relationships - CAIDA. https://www.caida.org/catalog/datasets/as-relationships/
27. AS Rank: A ranking of the largest Autonomous Systems. https://asrank.caida.org/
28. Liu, T.-Y.: Learning to rank for information retrieval (2011)
29. Burges, C.J.C.: From RankNet to LambdaRank to LambdaMART: an overview. Learning **11**(23–581), 81 (2010)
30. Routeviews - University of Oregon Route Views Project. http://www.routeviews.org/routeviews/
31. Routing Information Service (RIS) - RIPE Network. https://www.ripe.net/analyse/internet-measurements/routing-information-service-ris
32. Isolario project. https://www.isolario.it/
33. Jasinska, E., Hilliard, N., Raszuk, R., Bakker, N.: RFC7947: internet exchange BGP route server (2016)
34. Oliveira, R., Pei, D., Willinger, W., Zhang, B., Zhang, L.: The (in) completeness of the observed Internet AS-level structure. IEEE/ACM Trans. Netw. **18**(1), 109–122 (2009)
35. Alaettinoglu, C.: Routing Policy Specification Language (RPSL). RFC **2622**, 1–69 (1999)
36. AS286. https://as286.net/AS286-communities.html
37. AS9002. https://lg.retn.net/bgp-communities.html
38. One Step. https://onestep.net/
39. PeeringDB. https://www.peeringdb.com/
40. Euro-IX. https://www.euro-ix.net/en/
41. Internet Exchange Point Datasets—PCH. https://www.pch.net/ixp/data
42. Burges, C., et al.: Learning to rank using gradient descent. In: Proceedings of the 22nd International Conference on Machine Learning, pp. 89–96 (2005)

43. Burges, C., Ragno, R., Le, Q.: Learning to rank with nonsmooth cost functions. In: Advances in Neural Information Processing Systems, vol. 19, pp. 193–200 (2006)
44. Chang, Y., Chapelle, O., Liu, T.-Y.: The Yahoo! learning to rank challenge. http:// learningtorankchallenge.yahoo.com
45. Giotsas, V., Luckie, M., Huffaker, B., Claffy, K.C.: Inferring complex as relationships. In: Proceedings of the 2014 Conference on Internet Measurement Conference, pp. 23–30 (2014)
46. Jin, Y., Scott, C., Dhamdhere, A., Giotsas, V., Krishnamurthy, A., Shenker, S.: Stable and practical AS relationship inference with Problink. In: 16th USENIX Symposium on Networked Systems Design and Implementation (NSDI 19), pp. 581–598 (2019)
47. Jin, Z., Shi, X., Yang, Y., Yin, X., Wang, Z., Wu, J.: TopoScope: recover AS relationships from fragmentary observations. In: Proceedings of the ACM Internet Measurement Conference, pp. 266–280 (2020)
48. List of Internet exchange points by size. https://en.wikipedia.org/wiki/List_of_ Internet_exchange_points_by_size
49. Smith, J.M., Birkeland, K., McDaniel, T., Schuchard, M.: Withdrawing the BGP re-routing curtain: understanding the security impact of BGP poisoning through real-world measurements. In: NDSS (2020)

DNS and Routing

Measuring the Practical Effect of DNS Root Server Instances: A China-Wide Case Study

Fenglu Zhang[1], Chaoyi Lu[1], Baojun Liu[1,4(✉)], Haixin Duan[1,2,3], and Ying Liu[1(✉)]

[1] Tsinghua University, Beijing, China
{zfl20,lcy17}@mails.tsinghua.edu.cn, {lbj,duanhx}@tsinghua.edu.cn
liuying@cernet.edu.cn
[2] Qi An Xin Group, Beijing, China
[3] Peng Cheng Laboratory, Shenzhen, China
[4] Beijing National Research Center for Information Science and Technology
(BNRist), Beijing, China

Abstract. DNS root servers are deployed using multiple globally distributed anycast instances, and the scale of instances across the globe has been rapidly growing. This paper presents a measurement study that investigates the practical effect of root server instances deployed in the Chinese mainland. Our analysis of this issue includes two-fold. First, we measure the catchment area of the root server instances and answer the question about which domestic networks are served. Our results show that some of the instances are not accessible from major ISP networks due to limits of BGP routing policies, and a number of root queries still turn to further instances outside the international gateway. Second, we evaluate the impact of deploying new instances on query performance and root server selection in resolvers. We confirm that root instances contribute to lowered query delay from networks within their catchment area. Through reviewing source code of mainstream DNS implementations, we find that less-latent root servers are generally preferred thus deploying root server instances increase their possibilities to absorb DNS root requests from nearby resolvers. We make recommendations to improve the operational status of the DNS root server system.

1 Introduction

The DNS root is the starting point of the domain name space that bootstraps all DNS queries. To resist denial-of-service (DoS) attacks and improve stability of the DNS, all 13 root servers are deployed using *anycast* [18] with multiple *root server instances* that act collectively behind. Through BGP configuration, each DNS root query is routed to one instance, preferably the closest to its origin [34]. Network operators may host an instance, or peer with networks of root server operators to improve access to the DNS Root Server System (RSS) [13].

© The Author(s), under exclusive license to Springer Nature Switzerland AG 2022
O. Hohlfeld et al. (Eds.): PAM 2022, LNCS 13210, pp. 247–263, 2022.
https://doi.org/10.1007/978-3-030-98785-5_11

In recent years, there has been rapid deployment of new instances in the RSS, with an aim of providing faster and more reliable service to *"underserved"* areas (e.g., areas perceiving poor root query performance) [43]. At the time of writing, 1,469 root server instances are operating across the globe, which is 44.7% more compared to the number in 2019 [6]. However, information about their hosting networks and peering ASes is kept private, and the *practical effect* of the instances is still opaque to network operators. A set of research questions that are critical to understanding the deployment process are still not answered, including: *Which networks are within their catchment area? Which networks are still not served by close instances? How are they actually absorbing DNS root queries from nearby resolvers?* A few existing studies and tools focus on measuring delay to root servers [23, 28, 32], root manipulation [27] and the health status of root servers [5, 22, 42], but insights into the practical effect of root server instances is still lacking from the perspective of recursive resolvers.

We believe that seeking answers to the above questions helps examine the operational status of root server instances and can provide guidelines to their future deployment. In this paper, as a first step forward, we perform a case study on the practical effect of the 16 root server instances that have been deployed in the Chinese mainland[1], an understudied region with a large Internet population. Taking advantage of a side channel embedded in the DNS censorship mechanism [35], we propose a novel methodology to measure the catchment area of domestic root server instances (Sect. 3). While the instances do serve nation-wide areas, our results also show that some of them are not accessible from major ISP networks due to limits of BGP routing policies (Sect. 4). One `I-Root` instance even cannot be accessed from all three major ISP networks. As a result, a number of root queries still turn to further instances outside the international gateway, despite that 16 closer domestic instances are operating. Further, we investigate how deploying domestic instances can actually impact root server selection and absorb queries from recursive resolvers within their catchment area (Sect. 5). For this task, we measure the delay to root servers and review the source code of 4 types of common recursive resolver implementations: BIND 9 [25], Unbound [40], Knot Resolver [16] and PowerDNS Recursor [41]. We confirm that deploying domestic instances effectively lowers query delay, and their corresponding root servers will thus be preferred by the selection algorithms (especially in BIND and Knot Resolver).

From our findings, we make recommendations to multiple parties (including network operators and DNS software vendors) to improve the efficacy of the RSS. We believe that this work provides valuable insights into understanding the operational status of root server instances.

---

[1] Due to different network policies, in this paper we exclude Hong Kong SAR, Macao SAR and Taiwan from the scope of our study.

Table 1. Root server instances deployed in the Chinese mainland

Root	Global	Local	Geo-locations
F-Root	0	4	Hangzhou, Beijing, Chongqing, Xining
I-Root	1	0	Beijing
J-Root	2	0	Beijing, Hangzhou
K-Root	1	2	Guangzhou, Guiyang, Beijing
L-Root	6	0	Beijing (2), Shanghai, Zhengzhou, Wuhan, Xining

2   Background and Related Work

DNS Root Server System (RSS). Due to early payload size limits, there are only 13 root servers in the RSS [13], which are named by A-Root through M-Root. The 13 root servers are administered by twelve root server operators, such as Verisign and ICANN. All root servers in the RSS serve one unique copy of the DNS root zone managed by IANA [19]. To resist denial-of-service (DoS) attacks and improve stability of the DNS, all root servers are currently deployed using *anycast* [18] that allows multiple *root server instances* to act collectively using the same address. Over 1,400 instances are now operating in the RSS [6] and at the time of our experiment in this paper (Dec 2020), 16 instances have been deployed in the Chinese mainland. Table 1 shows their details.

Catchment Area of Root Server Instances. To improve their access to the RSS, local networks may *peer* to root server operator networks through exchanging BGP routing information [21,24], or may apply to *host* a root server instance [20,26,39] in their networks or Internet exchange points (IXes). According to their different catchment area, the RSS comprises both *Global* and *Local* root server instances. Local instances only serve a limited network range and their catchment area is limited to the hosting ASes or the boundaries of BGP confederation [7,34]. By contrast, Global instances let BGP alone determine their service scope. As listed in Table 1, the Chinese mainland hosts 6 Local and 10 Global instances.

Unauthorized Root Servers. Unauthorized root servers are those established outside of the RSS. As one type of DNS manipulation, operators of unauthorized root servers take control of the entire DNS name space in their service area. Previous studies have discovered one server potentially masquerading F-Root nodes in 2013 [17] and confirmed an unauthorized root mirror that exclusively serves CERNET (China Education and Research Network) in 2016 [27].

Related Work. To understand the performance and security of the RSS, efforts have been devoted to investigating the impact of uneven distribution of root server instances on end-user query latency [28,32], evaluating effects of anycast through examining DNS traffic and BGP data [12,34,37,49], and detecting DNS root manipulation in the wild [17,27]. However, little has been done to understand the practical effect of anycast instances behind root servers, or how their deployment and operation can be improved in the future.

In addition, a series of works examine how common DNS resolvers select and query authoritative servers (NSes, instead of root servers) [8,38,50]. Almost all of them answer this question by designing simulation experiments or inspecting outgoing DNS queries. They conclude most implementations prefer authoritative servers with the lowest latency, while others choose randomly. However, the reasons behind remain unrevealed, as few of them provide source code analysis.

3   Vantage Points and Methodology

In this section, we elaborate on how we collect vantage points that have broad coverage in the Chinese mainland, as well as our approach to measuring the catchment area of domestic root instances and delay to root servers.

3.1   Vantage point (VP) Selection and Validation

There are three major ISPs in the Chinese mainland, including China Telecom, China Unicom and China Mobile. Typically, the ISP networks are managed at a provincial level (there are 31 provinces in the Chinese mainland, excluding Hong Kong SAR, Macao SAR and Taiwan), and the network policies may differ in each province. However, common global measurement platforms (e.g., RIPE Atlas [44]) do not have good provincial coverage of VPs in China.

For our study, we select a Chinese commercial network looking glass platform that supports DNS queries. The platform operates over 300 VPs in all 3 major ISPs and multiple provinces, as well as in CERNET (China Education and Research Network) that serves universities. Each VP allows us to issue basic IPv4 DNS queries to custom server addresses, but does not offer additional DNS functionalities (e.g., NSID [10] that requests the identity of DNS server instances).

Since the advertised VP locations on commercial platforms cannot be relied on [48], we validate the locations of each VP before our experiment. After establishing a custom DNS server, we launch DNS queries from each VP to the server and check the source addresses of incoming queries against the MaxMind database [36]. If the locations do not match what they advertise, we remove the VPs from consideration. Meanwhile, to avoid DNS hijacking by middleboxes (e.g., NXDOMAIN rewriting [46]), on each VP we send DNS queries to 5 IP addresses that *do not* provide DNS service (i.e., normally, the queries will time out). We remove all VPs that receive DNS responses in the test and put detailed analysis on the filtered VPs in Appendix B. In the end, we select **182 vantage points** that advertise the correct location and are not affected by DNS hijacking. As shown in Table 2, they cover 31 provinces in the Chinese mainland. Due to the consideration of limited vantage points, we have to exclude the regional (province) differences analysis from the scope of our study.

Table 2. Count and coverage of selected vantage points

ISP	# VPs	Provincial coverage
China Telecom	71	26/31
China Unicom	74	28/31
China Mobile	24	21/31
CERNET	13	8/31
Total	**182**	**31/31**

3.2 Methodology

Catchment Area of Domestic Root Instances. The Chinese mainland hosts 16 root server instances (as listed in Table 1) and we seek to measure whether they are able to serve domestic networks. To find the exact instance that responds to a DNS server, one may issue NSID [10] or CHAOS-class queries [14] that return instance-specific strings (e.g., "s1.ash" represents the Ashburn instance of I-Root). A DNS traceroute [47] also reveals the path of root queries and gives clues about the destination instances. However, these DNS functionalities are not supported by most measurement platforms that offer broad ranges of Chinese VPs, including ours.

We try to overcome the challenges by posing another question: *are DNS queries from VPs in the Chinese mainland to root servers resolved domestically or overseas?* If resolved domestically, then the catchment area of domestic instances covers the networks of corresponding VPs. Fortunately, we find that this task is possible by leveraging the DNS censorship mechanisms of China [35], which are deployed at the international gateway to block access to certain websites [15] (we also confirm the location of censorship systems through offline discussions with large ISPs). On detection of DNS queries carrying censored domains (e.g., google.com), forged responses are injected before the authentic ones arrive [9]. As shown in Fig. 1 (top), if a root query carrying a censored domain leaves the international gateway, its response will contain an A record pointing to blocked IP addresses [31]. Note that we have removed VPs that witness DNS hijacking by middleboxes (see Sect. 3.1 and Appendix B) so responses carrying A records can only come from the censorship systems. By contrast, if resolved by domestic instances, root queries do not pass the censorship systems and should receive normal responses that carry delegation data of Top-Level Domains, as shown in Fig. 1 (bottom).

Leveraging this side channel provided by DNS censorship, Fig. 2 overviews our approach to determining whether root queries are responded by domestic instances. From VPs in the Chinese mainland we send DNS queries of censored domains (e.g., [nonce].google.com) to each root server. Domains in the queries are prefixed with a nonce value, such that they must arrive at the root servers instead of being answered from cache (e.g., of middleboxes). If censored responses (Fig. 1 top) are returned, the root queries must have passed the international

```
$ dig @a.root-servers.net. censored-domain.com
;; ANSWER SECTION:
censored-domain.com.    120    IN    A    (CENSORED_ADDRESS)
```
```
$ dig @a.root-servers.net. censored-domain.com
;; ANSWER SECTION:
com.            172800    IN    NS    a.gtld-servers.net.
com.            172800    IN    NS    b.gtld-servers.net.
...
```

Fig. 1. Censored (top) and normal (bottom) responses to root queries

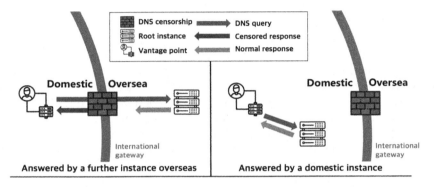

Fig. 2. Using DNS censorship to determine if domestic instances serve root queries

gateway for instances overseas. Otherwise, if normal responses (Fig. 1 bottom) are captured, the root queries are resolved by domestic instances.

Delay to Root Servers. To study the practical impact of domestic instances on root query performance, we also measure the Round-Trip-Time (RTT) of DNS queries from each VP to all 13 root servers. Because root servers are non-recursive (i.e., they never query other servers), the RTT can be acquired by simply sending DNS queries to root servers and recording the arrival time of their responses. Again, to ensure that the queries must arrive at the root servers, we register a (non-censored) domain name exclusively for this task and prefix it with a nonce value in each query (i.e., [nonce].example.com).

4 Catchment Area of Domestic Root Instances

The Chinese mainland hosts 16 root server instances. However, as information about their hosting networks and peering ASes is not made public, it is still unclear which domestic networks can be served by them. In this section, we present our measurement results on the catchment area of domestic root server instances. We believe the results are helpful for future deployment of domestic instances to cover networks that are currently not served.

Table 3. Ratio of root queries that receive normal responses. Root servers with domestic instances (F, I, J, K and L) are marked with lighter backgrounds.

Root	Telecom	Unicom	Mobile	CERNET
A-Root	0.80%	0.50%	2.36%	**100.00%**
B-Root	0.94%	2.79%	2.08%	**100.00%**
C-Root	1.22%	3.29%	1.25%	**100.00%**
D-Root	0.85%	0.95%	5.69%	**100.00%**
E-Root	0.70%	0.00%	1.81%	**100.00%**
F-Root	**99.34%**	3.24%	1.53%	**100.00%**
G-Root	1.78%	0.99%	6.11%	**100.00%**
H-Root	0.85%	2.43%	2.22%	**100.00%**
I-Root	1.69%	0.09%	6.81%	**100.00%**
J-Root	1.27%	**98.24%**	23.47%	**100.00%**
K-Root	**100.00%**	**98.29%**	2.22%	**100.00%**
L-Root	**98.50%**	**98.38%**	**95.83%**	**100.00%**
M-Root	2.02%	0.05%	0.00%	**100.00%**
Total	23.84%	23.79%	11.65%	**100.00%**

4.1 Which Networks Are Served by Domestic Root Instances?

Our experiment that leverages DNS censorship to measure catchment area started on Dec 5, 2020 and lasted for 72 hours. On each VP we send 10 DNS queries of *censored* domains (e.g., [nonce].google.com) to all 13 root servers every 24 hours and inspect whether they yield censored or normal responses. We retry if a query fails and the test issues 130 root queries per day from each VP.

Table 3 shows the nation-wide ratio of root queries that receive normal responses (i.e., served by domestic instances) per ISP network. We first find that *all* root queries from CERNET VPs are answered domestically, which is expected because an unauthorized root server has been confirmed to exclusively serve CERNET [27]. We also find that the domestic instances of F, J, K and L-Root (all of them deploy instances in the Chinese mainland, as listed in Table 1) have *nation-wide catchment area* for VPs in *at least one of the three major ISPs*, as they answer over 95% of root queries from these networks (marked bold in Table 3, e.g., Telecom to F-Root). Zooming into individual VPs, as shown by Fig. 3, we find that the catchment area of most domestic instances in a given ISP network only have minor differences between geo-locations.

For root servers that *do not* deploy domestic instances (e.g., A and B-Root, marked by darker backgrounds in Table 3), we do not expect that root queries trigger normal responses because they should arrive at instances beyond the international gateway and pass the censorship systems. However, in our results their ratio of normal responses does not reach 0%. We suppose that the normal responses are due to occasional failure of DNS censorship and potential unau-

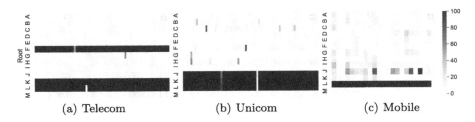

Fig. 3. Ratio of root queries that receive normal responses per VP. Darker cells indicate that more DNS queries from the corresponding VPs are resolved by domestic instances.

thorized root servers deployed in domestic ISP networks, and we will discuss them in Sect. 6.

4.2   Why Are Some Networks Not Served By Domestic Instances?

From Table 3 we also find that from some ISP networks to root servers that *do* deploy domestic instances, their ratio of getting normal responses is still very low, e.g., Mobile to K-Root, Telecom to J-Root and all three major ISPs to I-Root. The above results suggest that, these networks are still not well-served by the domestic instances.

The Domestic I-Root Instance. As shown in Table 1, one Global I-Root instance is deployed in the Chinese mainland, but it does not seem to be serving VPs in all three major ISPs. To locate the hosting network of this instance, we perform ICMP traceroute from 15 other controlled domestic VPs and find the second-last hops (the last hop is the root anycast address) belong to CSTNET (China Science and Technology Network). CSTNET offers Internet services to research institutions and hi-tech enterprises, but has a smaller user base than CERNET.

We then tried to figure out if CSTNET served by I-Root instance. As the looking glass platform does not cover CSTNET, we employ seven volunteer VPs in CSTNET and run the same experiments described in Sect. 3.2. Similarly, 100% queries receive censored responses when they carry sensitive domains, meaning that they pass the international gateway. However, the CSTNET VPs show an average delay of only 3.62 ms to I-Root, which is significantly lower than three major ISPs (over 100ms on average, see results in Fig. 4 of Sect. 5.1). Further, we ask all CSTNET VPs to send NSID queries [10] to I-Root. The responses carry an "s1.bei" string, and we confirm with Netnod (the operator of I-Root) that it represents the Beijing instance.

As a result, we conclude that the domestic I-root instance serve CSTNET only (possibly because three major ISPs do not peer with CSTNET or Netnod), and that it locates physically in the Chinese mainland but out of the international network gateway. In fact, this can be a result of a security incident in 2010 where this instance returned incorrect responses due to DNS censorship [11].

Other Unshared Domestic Instances. Similarly, we locate the hosting networks of other domestic instances through ICMP traceroute. From Table 3, VPs in China Mobile are not served by domestic F, J and K-Root instances, and our traceroute shows that these instances locate in networks of China Telecom and China Unicom. VPs in China Telecom cannot access domestic J-Root instances, which we find in China Unicom.

Combined with discussions with ISPs and DNS root operators, we conclude that root instances in the Chinese mainland are typically advertised from ISP networks instead of IXes, and that root instances hosted in one ISP are typically *unshared* with other networks due to limits of BGP routing policies. For F and K-Root, some are *Local instances* (see Table 1) thus their catchment area does not cover networks of other ISPs. Meanwhile, major ISPs do not directly peer with each other[2], thus *Global instances* deployed in the Chinese mainland are not accessible from some domestic ISPs either (e.g., Mobile to J-Root).

5 Impact of Domestic Instances on Root Server Selection

In Sect. 4, we measure the catchment area of domestic instances by sending DNS queries directly to each root server. However, whether the instances can actually absorb root queries depend on how *recursive resolvers* in their catchment area select from 13 root servers (i.e., the domestic instances are queried only when the corresponding root servers are selected by recursive resolvers). In this section, we first study how deploying domestic instances affects the nation-wide delay to root servers, and then show how it affects root server selection from the perspective of mainstream recursive resolver implementations.

5.1 Do Domestic Instances Serve Root Queries with Lower Delay?

During the same time period and using the same set of VPs, we measure their delay to all 13 root servers. On each VP we perform 10 DNS queries of (custom) *non-censored* domains (e.g., [nonce].example.com) to each root server in every 24 hours and record their RTTs. We retry if a query fails and the test issues 130 root queries per day from each VP.

Figure 4 shows the delay from VPs in each ISP to 13 root servers. All root queries from CERNET are answered within 30 ms because of an unauthorized root server. For the other three major ISPs, we confirm that *root server instances deployed in the Chinese mainland effectively serve networks within their catchment area with lower delay.* Corresponding Fig. 4 with Table 3, we find that for networks with high ratio (>95%, the ISPs are also framed in Fig. 4) of queries that are resolved by domestic instances, their delay to the corresponding root servers is significantly lower (50ms on average). By contrast, VPs spend hundreds of milliseconds to query instances beyond the international gateway when

---

[2] We also tried to validate through inspecting BGP routing information in Route-Views [45]. However, the dataset has little coverage of ASes in China.

their network is not served by the domestic instances (e.g., Mobile to F-Root, Telecom to J-Root and all three major ISPs to I-Root), or when no instances are deployed in the Chinese mainland (e.g., A and B-Root).

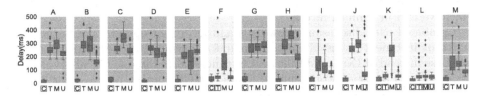

Fig. 4. Root server delay from VPs of different ISPs (C: CERNET, T: Telecom, M: Mobile, U: Unicom). Root servers with domestic instances are marked with lighter backgrounds. Framed networks correspond to high ratio (>95%) of domestically resolved queries in Table 3.

5.2   How Do Domestic Instances Affect Root Server Selection?

Deploying domestic instances improves root query performance within their catchment area, and we further investigate *whether they will actually be selected* (among all 13 root servers) by recursive resolvers because of lowered delay. A series of previous study demonstrated that most resolver prefer authoritative servers with lowest latency. However, the actual reasons behind remain unrevealed. To this end, we take the perspective of mainstream recursive resolver implementations and review their source code of root selection algorithms.

We select the latest versions (as of Oct 2021) of four popular open-source recursive DNS implementations: BIND 9 [25] (9.17.18), Unbound [40] (1.13.2), Knot Resolver [16] (5.4.2) and PowerDNS Recursor [41] (4.5.6). To review and dynamically debug their root selection algorithms, we start a docker container [3] that installs Ubuntu 18.04 and links to a GDB remote debugger [4]. All DNS software is compiled from source code and started in the container. In the GDB debugger, we extract and review the root selection algorithms by following their execution.

Based on the result of source code reviewing and dynamic debugging, we also *quantify* the differences of root selection algorithms in a test network environment. We simulate and inspect 100,000 outgoing root queries from each DNS implementation. Our set of 13 root servers is: RTT=10 ms (1 server), RTT = 50 ms (3 servers), RTT = 100 ms (5 servers), RTT = 250 ms (3 servers) and RTT = 500 ms (1 server). We do not consider response errors or timeouts during simulation.

Root Server Selection Algorithm Overview. We first find that all four recursive DNS implementations *reuse authoritative server (NS) selection algo-*

rithms to select from root servers[3]. For this task, DNS standards [2] vaguely suggest that recursive resolvers should "find the best server to ask". From the comments in their source code, we find that the designers of DNS software reach a consensus that *least-latent servers will be preferred* (e.g., "Find best RTT in the bunch" in the comments of Unbound and "Address with smaller expected timeout is better" in the comments of Knot Resolver). However, as we will show later, the root selection results for Unbound and PowerDNS Recursor do not match this design goal due to untuned timing implementations.

BIND 9 and Knot Resolver. BIND and Knot Resolver significantly prefer root servers with the smallest Round-Trip-Time (RTT) while trying other servers in fewer cases. Through source code debugging, our findings echo with [8,38,50] that use pure traffic analysis to demonstrate that resolvers prefer least-latent NSes. As shown in Figs. 5(a) and (b), during our simulation BIND 9 selects the least-latent root server (RTT = 10 ms) in 98.1% cases, while the ratio for Knot Resolver is 95.3%.

Unbound and PowerDNS Recursor. Despite that they are designed to consider server RTT, Unbound and PowerDNS Recursor tend to select root servers *randomly* due to untuned timing implementations. Unbound selects from a set of servers randomly and disregards one only if its RTT is *400* ms *longer* than the least-latent. However, previous works [23,32] and Fig. 4 already show that only few locations across the globe witness a delay to root servers of over 400 ms, thus Unbound will not remove any root server from consideration. As shown in Fig. 5(c), during our simulation Unbound only disregards one root server (RTT = 500 ms) and evenly distributes root queries among all other servers.

For PowerDNS Recursor, it is designed to select the least-latent server and update its RTT, but *decays* the adjusted RTT for all servers with the same factor. The longer the query interval, the lower the decay factor and adjusted RTTs will be. Since root servers are not frequently queried ([12] shows the root query interval from 97% of addresses is longer than 100 s), the priority for root servers not selected in the current round will be significantly increased in the next round. During our simulation, when we set the query rate to 30s/query, the selection already looks random (Fig. 5(d)) because of significant decay. We believe the implementations of Unbound and PowerDNS do not properly switch to lower latency authoritative servers. And we will contact the developers of these two resolvers, and hope to improve the implementation in the future.

Summary. Through source code debugging and simulation, we confirm that BIND and Knot Resolver significantly prefers least-latent root servers (for over 95% of queries). Considering their large share among recursive resolvers (e.g., BIND is deployed on over 60% of recursive resolvers [1,29]), we conclude that domestic root server instances can effectively absorb queries from networks

---

[3] As part of our contribution, we list pseudo-code and details of all root selection algorithms at https://github.com/anonymous-researcher123/software-analysis/blob/main/software_analysis.pdf.

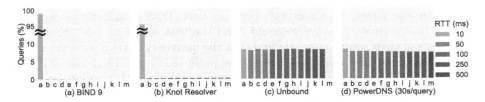

Fig. 5. Simulation results of root server selection algorithms with 100,000 root queries. (From source code we learn that the algorithm of PowerDNS depends on query interval and we show the results under 30 s/query).

within their catchment area because of lowered delay compared to other root servers.

6   Discussion

Ethics. The major ethical concern of this study is sending DNS queries through VPs in the Chinese mainland. To acquire VPs, we leverage a commercial network looking glass platform and pay for their service. On each VP we send plain DNS queries over UDP to root servers, which is within the business scope of the platform. We also strictly limit the DNS query rate on each VP (at around 30 queries per hour) to comply with its service regulations.

To measure the catchment area of domestic root server instances, we leverage the DNS censorship mechanisms of China, which has been thoroughly studied by a series of previous works [9,15,31,35]. In our methodology we use its known characteristics (i.e., injection of DNS responses) and do not study or provide new insights into the censorship systems. All domains carried by our queries are non-existent sub-domains (because of nonce prefixes) under benign Second-Level Domains (e.g., [nonce].google.com and our own domain name). We do not make connections to any censored IP address. Because we only perform DNS lookups, our study poses no harm or potential judicial risks to the VP operators.

Errors Caused By DNS Censorship Failure. In Table 3 we find that for queries to root servers that do not deploy domestic instances (e.g., 3 major ISP networks to A and B-Root), a small portion (1% to 3%) receive uncensored normal responses. We confirm through a separate experiment that for the selected VPs, the DNS censorship has an overall success rate of around 97% (details of the experiment are provided in Appendix A). As a result, the root queries do leave the international gateway and are resolved by instances overseas, but receive normal responses because of censorship failure.

Potential Unauthorized Root Servers. From Table 3 we also find that, from some ISP networks to root servers without domestic instances (e.g., Mobile to D-Root and G-Root), the ratio of normal responses (5% to 6%) is higher than the average failure rate of DNS censorship (around 3%). In Figure 3 we zoom into the ratio of censored responses for each VP. A small number of VPs in China Mobile and China Unicom even receive around 20% to 40% uncensored normal responses from root servers without domestic instances, which is not likely a result of DNS censorship failure. It is also not caused by DNS hijacking or caching by middleboxes because we have removed such VPs (see Sect. 3.1) and use nonce domain prefixes to make every query unique. Finally, we suppose these normal responses are provided domestically by unauthorized root servers.

Recommendations. Our study reveals several major ISP networks that are not served by domestic root server instances and we make the following recommendations. 1) For networks that are not covered by the catchment area of nearby instances, if allowed in terms of political and commercial interests, we recommend BGP peering with the root server networks. Alternative measures that improve access to the RSS (e.g., running a local root copy [30]) can be adopted. 2) Root server operators may take these areas into prior consideration for future deployment of instances. 3) To inform operators about whether their networks can be served, we recommend making BGP peering information between ISPs and root servers more transparent (e.g., disclosing which networks host a root server or peer with them). 4) We do not recommend establishing or using unauthorized root servers which may cause security risks. 5) For developers of recursive DNS software, we recommend they review whether the implementation is consistent with their original design goals. 6) For the DNS community, while the status of root servers has been heavily monitored, systems that measure root servers from resolvers' perspective still need to be developed.

7   Conclusion

In this paper we study the practical effect of root server instances deployed in the Chinese mainland. Through design of novel methodology we measure the catchment area of domestic instances, and find that some of them are not accessible from major ISP networks due to limits of BGP routing policies. We also evaluate the impact of deploying new instances on root server selection in recursive resolvers by measuring root delay and reviewing source code of common recursive resolver implementations. While most software is designed to prefer less-latent servers, some do not meet this goal due to untuned implementations. Our results also show that domestic root instances significantly lower query delay from major ISP networks, which increases their possibility to absorb DNS queries. We believe that multiple parties should take actions to improve the stability and operational status of the DNS Root Server System in China.

Acknowledgement. We thank all the anonymous reviewers for insightful comments and valuable suggestions to improve this paper. This paper benefits from the contributions of a number of people, in particular, Ziqian Liu, provided excellent suggestions that improved the paper. This work was supported by the National Natural Science Foundation of China (grants 62102218, U1836213, U19B2034). Baojun Liu is partially supported by the Shuimu Tsinghua Scholar Program.

A   Success Rate of DNS Censorship

We use the same set of VPs from the looking glass platform to measure the success rate of DNS censorship. On each VP we launch DNS queries of censored domain names (e.g., [nonce].google.com) to a self-built DNS server located in the US. This design ensures that all DNS queries should leave the international gateway and pass the DNS censorship system. As shown in Table 4, the DNS censorship system has an overall success rate of 97%, which explains why 1% to 3% of DNS queries to root servers without domestic instances receive (uncensored) normal responses (see Sect. 4.1).

Table 4. Success rate of DNS censorship

ISP	Ratio of censored responses
China Telecom	96.25%
China Unicom	96.56%
China Mobile	97.82%
CERNET	94.86%
Total	**96.72%**

To further confirm that the queries leave the international gateway, in Fig. 6 we plot the RTTs of normal responses from A-Root (without domestic instances). All normal responses to VPs in China Telecom, Unicom and Mobile have an RTT of around 200 ms, significantly longer than responses from CERNET (a baseline delay for domestic responses). From the results we are confident that the 1% to 3% normal responses come from root instances overseas, rather than domestic servers.

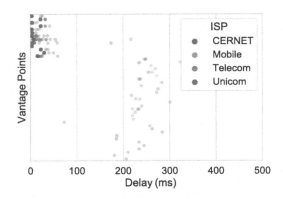

Fig. 6. Delays of normal responses from A-Root to domestic VPs

B Removed VPs that Perceive DNS Hijacking Accidents

During VP validation, we find multiple DNS hijacking accidents in large ISP networks. As shown in Table 5, domains are pointed to rogue addresses or show negative results (NXDOMAIN). Our results echo with [33] reporting that DNS hijacking behaviors are more prevalent for VPs of China Mobile. All VPs are then removed from consideration.

Table 5. Removed VPs that perceive DNS hijacking

Response type	Telecom	Unicom	Mobile	CERNET	Total
Polluted IP	28	13	39	6	**86**
Localhost IP	2	0	8	2	**12**
NXDOMAIN	4	7	16	2	**29**
Empty	0	0	2	0	**2**
Other IP	5	3	3	0	**11**
Total	**39**	**23**	**68**	**10**	

References

1. BIND DNS Holds Lead. https://www.serverwatch.com/server-news/bind-dns-holds-lead/
2. Domain Names - Concepts and Facilities. RFC 1034, November 1987. https://doi.org/10.17487/RFC1034, https://rfc-editor.org/rfc/rfc1034.txt
3. Docker: Empowering App Development for Developers (2021).D https://www.docker.com/
4. GDB: The GNU Project Debugger - GNU.org (2021). https://www.gnu.org/software/gdb/
5. Measuring the Health of the Domain Name System (2021). https://www.icann.org/en/system/files/files/dns-ssr-symposium-report-1-03feb10-en.pdf
6. Root Server Technical Operations Association (2021). https://root-servers.org/
7. Abley, J.: Hierarchical anycast for global service distribution (2003)
8. Ager, B., Mühlbauer, W., Smaragdakis, G., Uhlig, S.: Comparing DNS resolvers in the wild. In: Proceedings of the 10th ACM SIGCOMM Conference on Internet Measurement, pp. 15–21 (2010)
9. Anonymous: Towards a Comprehensive Picture of the Great Firewall's DNS Censorship. In: 4th USENIX Workshop on Free and Open Communications on the Internet (FOCI 14). USENIX Association, San Diego, August 2014. https://www.usenix.org/conference/foci14/workshop-program/presentation/anonymous
10. Austein, R.: DNS name server identifier (NSID) option. RFC 5001, August 2007. https://doi.org/10.17487/RFC5001, https://rfc-editor.org/rfc/rfc5001.txt
11. van Beijnum, I.: Misadventure at root I in China (2010). https://web.archive.org/web/20110622092029/, http://arstechnica.com/tech-policy/news/2010/03/china-censorship-leaks-outside-great-firewall-via-root-server.ars

12. Castro, S., Wessels, D., Fomenkov, M., Claffy, K.: A day at the root of the internet. ACM SIGCOMM Comput. Commun. Rev. **38**(5), 41–46 (2008)
13. Conrad, D.: Brief overview of the root server system (2020). https://www.icann. org/en/system/files/files/octo-010-06may20-en.pdf
14. Conrad, D.R., Woolf, S.: Requirements for a mechanism identifying a name server instance. RFC 4892, June 2007. https://doi.org/10.17487/RFC4892, https://rfc-editor.org/rfc/rfc4892.txt
15. Crandall, J.R., Zinn, D., Byrd, M., Barr, E.T., East, R.: ConceptDoppler: a weather tracker for internet censorship. In: ACM Conference on Computer and Communications Security, pp. 352–365 (2007)
16. CZ.NIC: Knot resolver (2021). https://www.knot-resolver.cz/
17. Fan, X., Heidemann, J., Govindan, R.: Evaluating anycast in the domain name system. In: 2013 Proceedings IEEE INFOCOM, pp. 1681–1689. IEEE (2013)
18. Hardie, T.: Distributing authoritative name servers via shared unicast addresses. RFC 3258, April 2002. https://doi.org/10.17487/RFC3258, https://rfc-editor.org/rfc/rfc3258.txt
19. IANA: Root Zone Management (2021). https://www.iana.org/domains/root
20. ICANN: Hosting IMRS in Your Network (2019). https://www.dns.icann.org/imrs/host/
21. ICANN: IMRS Peering Information (2019). https://www.dns.icann.org/imrs/peering/
22. ICANN: The ITHI (Identifier Technologies Health Indicators) Project (2021). https://ithi.research.icann.org/about.html
23. ISC: Atlas Data Viewer (2021). https://atlas-vis.isc.org/
24. ISC: BGP Peering Network with F-Root (2021). https://www.isc.org/froot-peering/
25. ISC: BIND 9 (2021). https://www.isc.org/bind/
26. ISC: Host an F-Root Node (2021). https://www.isc.org/froot-process/
27. Jones, B., Feamster, N., Paxson, V., Weaver, N., Allman, M.: Detecting DNS root manipulation. In: Karagiannis, T., Dimitropoulos, X. (eds.) PAM 2016. LNCS, vol. 9631, pp. 276–288. Springer, Cham (2016). https://doi.org/10.1007/978-3-319-30505-9_21
28. Koch, T., Katz-Bassett, E., Heidemann, J., Calder, M., Ardi, C., Li, K.: Anycast in context: a tale of two systems. In: Proceedings of the 2021 ACM SIGCOMM 2021 Conference, pp. 398–417 (2021)
29. Kührer, M., Hupperich, T., Bushart, J., Rossow, C., Holz, T.: Going wild: large-scale classification of open DNS resolvers. In: Proceedings of the 2015 Internet Measurement Conference, pp. 355–368 (2015)
30. Kumari, W.A., Hoffman, P.E.: Running a root server local to a resolver. RFC 8806, June 2020. https://doi.org/10.17487/RFC8806, https://rfc-editor.org/rfc/rfc8806.txt
31. Levis, P.: The collateral damage of internet censorship by DNS injection. ACM SIGCOMM CCR **42**(3), 10–1145 (2012)
32. Liang, J., Jiang, J., Duan, H., Li, K., Wu, J.: Measuring query latency of top level DNS servers. In: Roughan, M., Chang, R. (eds.) PAM 2013. LNCS, vol. 7799, pp. 145–154. Springer, Heidelberg (2013). https://doi.org/10.1007/978-3-642-36516-4_15
33. Liu, B., et al.: Who is answering my queries: understanding and characterizing interception of the DNS resolution path. In: 27th USENIX Security Symposium (USENIX Security 18), pp. 1113–1128 (2018)

34. Liu, Z., Huffaker, B., Fomenkov, M., Brownlee, N., Claffy, K.C.: Two days in the life of the DNS anycast root servers. In: Uhlig, S., Papagiannaki, K., Bonaventure, O. (eds.) PAM 2007. LNCS, vol. 4427, pp. 125–134. Springer, Heidelberg (2007). https://doi.org/10.1007/978-3-540-71617-4_13
35. Lowe, G., Winters, P., Marcus, M.L.: The great DNS wall of China. MS New York Univ. **21**, 1 (2007)
36. MaxMind: IP Geolocation and Online Fraud Prevention (2021). https://www.maxmind.com/en/home
37. Moura, G.C.M., et al.: Anycast vs. DDoS: evaluating the november 2015 root DNS event. In: Gill, P., Heidemann, J.S., Byers, J.W., Govindan, R. (eds.) Proceedings of the 2016 ACM on Internet Measurement Conference, IMC 2016, Santa Monica, CA, USA, 14–16 November 2016, pp. 255–270. ACM (2016). http://dl.acm.org/citation.cfm?id=2987446
38. Müller, M., Moura, G.C., de O. Schmidt, R., Heidemann, J.: Recursives in the wild: engineering authoritative DNS servers. In: Proceedings of the 2017 Internet Measurement Conference, pp. 489–495 (2017)
39. Netnod: Host an I-Root (2021). https://www.netnod.se/host-an-i-root
40. NLnet Labs: Unbound (2021). https://www.nlnetlabs.nl/projects/unbound/about/
41. PowerDNS: PowerDNS Recursor (2021). https://www.powerdns.com/recursor.html
42. RSSAC: RSSAC002: RSSAC Advisory on Measurements of the Root Server System (2015)
43. RSSAC: RSSAC057: Requirements for Measurements of the Local Perspective on the Root Server System (2021)
44. RIPE NCC: Ripe Atlas: A Global Internet Measurement Network (2021). https://atlas.ripe.net/
45. University of Oregon: Route Views Project (2021). http://www.routeviews.org/routeviews/
46. Weaver, N., Kreibich, C., Paxson, V.: Redirecting DNS for ads and profit. FOCI **2**, 2–3 (2011)
47. Weber, J.: Detect DNS spoofing: dnstraceroute (2016). https://weberblog.net/detect-dns-spoofing-dnstraceroute/
48. Weinberg, Z., Cho, S., Christin, N., Sekar, V., Gill, P.: How to Catch when proxies lie: verifying the physical locations of network proxies with active geolocation. In: Proceedings of the Internet Measurement Conference 2018, IMC 2018, Boston, MA, USA, 31 October–02 November 2018, pp. 203–217. ACM (2018). https://dl.acm.org/citation.cfm?id=3278551
49. Wicaksana, M.: IPv4 vs IPv6 anycast catchment: a root DNS study, August 2016. http://essay.utwente.nl/70921/
50. Yu, Y., Wessels, D., Larson, M., Zhang, L.: Authority server selection in DNS caching resolvers. ACM SIGCOMM Comput. Commun. Rev. **42**(2), 80–86 (2012)

Old but Gold: Prospecting TCP to Engineer and Live Monitor DNS Anycast

Giovane C. M. Moura[1,2]([✉]), John Heidemann[3], Wes Hardaker[3], Pithayuth Charnsethikul[3], Jeroen Bulten[4], João M. Ceron[1], and Cristian Hesselman[1,5]

[1] SIDN Labs, Arnhem, The Netherlands
giovane.moura@sidn.nl
[2] TU Delft, Delft, The Netherlands
[3] USC/ISI, Marina Del Rey, USA
[4] SIDN, Arnhem, The Netherlands
[5] University of Twente, Enschede, The Netherlands

Abstract. DNS latency is a concern for many service operators: CDNs exist to reduce service latency to end-users but must rely on global DNS for reachability and load-balancing. Today, DNS latency is monitored by active probing from distributed platforms like RIPE Atlas, with Verfploeter, or with commercial services. While Atlas coverage is wide, its 10k sites see only a fraction of the Internet. In this paper we show that passive observation of TCP handshakes can measure *live DNS latency, continuously, providing good coverage of current clients of the service.* Estimating RTT from TCP is an old idea, but its application to DNS has not previously been studied carefully. We show that there is sufficient TCP DNS traffic today to provide good operational coverage (particularly of IPv6), and very good temporal coverage (better than existing approaches), enabling near-real time evaluation of DNS latency from *real clients*. We also show that DNS servers can optionally solicit TCP to broaden coverage. We quantify coverage and show that estimates of DNS latency from TCP is consistent with UDP latency. Our approach finds previously unknown, real problems: *DNS polarization* is a new problem where a hypergiant sends global traffic to one anycast site rather than taking advantage of the global anycast deployment. Correcting polarization in Google DNS cut its latency from 100 ms to 10 ms; and from Microsoft Azure cut latency from 90 ms to 20 ms. We also show other instances of routing problems that add 100–200 ms latency. Finally, *real-time* use of our approach for a European country-level domain has helped detect and correct a BGP routing misconfiguration that detoured European traffic to Australia. We have integrated our approach into several open source tools: **ENTRADA**, our open source data warehouse for DNS, a monitoring tool (**Anteater**), which has been operational for the last 2 years on a country-level top-level domain, and a DNS anonymization tool in use at a root server since March 2021.

© The Author(s), under exclusive license to Springer Nature Switzerland AG 2022
O. Hohlfeld et al. (Eds.): PAM 2022, LNCS 13210, pp. 264–292, 2022.
https://doi.org/10.1007/978-3-030-98785-5_12

1   Introduction

Latency is a key performance indicator for many DNS operators. DNS latency is seen as a bottleneck in web access [65]. Content Delivery Networks (CDNs) are particularly sensitive to DNS latency because, although DNS uses caching extensively to avoid latency, many CDNs use very short DNS cache lifetimes to give frequent opportunities for DNS-based load balancing and replica selection [14]. Latency is less critical at the DNS root [25], but unnecessary delay should be avoided [7]. Because of public attention to DNS latency, low latency is a selling point for many commercial DNS operators, many of whom deploy extensive distributed systems with tens, hundreds, or more than 1000 sites [8].

DNS deployments often use *IP anycast* [33,47] to reduce latency for clients. A *DNS service* is typically provided by two or more *authoritative DNS servers* [22], each defined in DNS on a separate IP address with an NS record [35]. With IP anycast, the IP address assigned to the authoritative DNS server is announced from many physically distributed *sites*, and BGP selects which clients go to which site—the anycast *catchment* of that site. DNS clients often select the lowest-latency authoritative server when they have a choice [40,43]. We show (Sect. 5) that this preference shifts client traffic to sites with the lowest latencies. (Although we focus on anycast, our approach can also be used to evaluate multiple unicast services serving the same zones).

DNS latency has been extensively studied [9,42,59]. Previous studies have looked at both absolute latency [59] and how closely it approaches speed-of-light optimal [28,63]. Several studies measure DNS latency from measurement systems with distributed vantage points such as RIPE Atlas [53], sometimes to optimize latency [7,34]. Recent work has shown how to measure anycast catchments with active probes with Verfploeter [12,13], and there is ongoing work to support RTT measurements. However, approaches to measure latency provide mixed coverage: large hardware-based measurements like RIPE Atlas only have about 11k active vantage points and cover only 8670 /24 IPv4 network prefixes [51] (May 2020), and commercial services have fewer than that. Verfploeter provides much better coverage, reaching millions of networks, but it depends on a response from its targets and so cannot cover networks with commonly-deployed ICMP-blocking firewalls. It is also difficult to apply to IPv6 since it requires a target list, and effective IPv6 target lists are an open research problem [16]. Finally, with the cost of active probing, Verfploeter is typically run daily and is too expensive to detect hourly changes (and RTT measurement support will require twice as much probing).

The main contribution of this paper is to fully evaluate and show operational results from *passive latency observations in DNS*. We show that passive observations of latency in TCP can provide continuous updates of latency with no additional traffic, providing operationally-useful data that can complement active probing methods such as Verfploeter or static observers such as RIPE Atlas. Such observations are not possible with DNS over UDP, and active probing is typically less frequent.

Observing latency from TCP, and in DNS, is not completely new, but prior work has not validated its accuracy and coverage. The TCP handshake has been used to estimate RTT at endpoints since 1996 [20], and it is widely used in passive analysis of HTTP (for example, [57]). Even in DNS, using TCP has been touched upon—the idea was shared with us by Casey Deccio, and .cz operators have used it in their service as described in non-peer-reviewed work that was independent from ours [31,32]. We validate that latency measured from UDP and our estimates from TCP match (Sect. 2.2). We show that DNS servers can choose to solicit TCP from selected clients to increase coverage, if they desire, with an implementation in Knot (Sect. 2.1).

Our second contribution is to show that *TCP-handshakes provide an effective estimate* of DNS latency. Although DNS most often uses UDP, leaving DNS-over-TCP (shortened to DNS/TCP) to be often overlooked, we show that there is enough DNS/TCP traffic to support good coverage of latency estimation. Prospecting through DNS traffic can find the latency "gold". Unlike prior approaches, passive analysis of TCP provides more coverage as busy clients send more queries, some with TCP. It provides good coverage of DNS traffic: for .nl, the top 100 ASes that send DNS/TCP traffic are responsible for more than 75% of *all* queries (Sect. 2.1), and we cover recursive servers sending the majority of queries. By scaling coverage with actual traffic, continuous passive RTT estimation can *increase temporal coverage* beyond current active approaches. For .nl, we cover 20k ASes every hour (Sect. 2.1). Finally, passive analysis is the only approach that provides good coverage for IPv6 networks, overcoming the problem of active probing with stateless IPv6 addresses [46].

Our final contribution is to show that *TCP-based latency estimation matters*—it detects latency problems in operational networks, improving *latency engineering* in anycast (Sect. 4). We identify *DNS polarization* as a problem that occurs when an Internet "hypergiant" [17,27,48] with a global footprint sends traffic over their own backbone to a single anycast location rather than taking advantage of an existing global anycast service. We show the importance of detecting and correcting this problem, reducing latency inflation by 150 ms for many clients of Google and Microsoft as they access .nl ccTLD and two commercial DNS providers. We have instrumented our open-source ENTRADA [61,70] with DNS/TCP RTT analysis. We provide a new tool, Anteater, that analyzes DNS/TCP RTT continuously to detect errors and failures in real-time (we released it freely at [37]), and extend an existing DNS analysis tool (dnsanon). These tools have been operational for more than two years at SIDN, the Netherlands ccTLD (.nl) operator, and were deployed in March 2021 by the B-Root root DNS server. During that deployment, our tools have detected several problems. In one case, some users experienced large increases in RTT due to traffic from Europe going to an anycast site in Australia (Sect. 4.4).

Our tools are freely available, including our changes to Knot [10], dnsanon, Anteater, and ENTRADA. Part of our data is from public TLDs, so privacy concerns prevent making data public. Our analysis follows current ethical guidelines: we never associate data with information about specific individuals, and our analysis is part of improving operations.

2   DNS/TCP for RTT?

While UDP is the preferred transport layer for DNS, TCP support has always been required to handle large replies [6] and all compliant resolvers are required to use TCP when the server sets the TC (truncated) bit [35]. TCP has also always been used for zone transfers between servers, and now increasing numbers of clients are using TCP in response to DNSSEC [2], response-rate limiting [66], and recently DNS privacy [23].

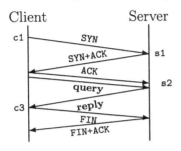

Fig. 1. TCP handshake and RTT measurements

The RTT between a TCP client and server can be measured passively during the TCP session establishment [20,34] or during the connection teardown [57]. In our work, we measure the RTT during the session establishment, as shown in Fig. 1: we derive the RTT between client and server by computing the difference between times $s2$ and $s1$, measured at the server. (In Sect. 2.2 we validate against client measurements of transaction time $c1$ and $c3$, which will be two RTTs (plus usually negligible server processing time)).

When we have multiple observations per target region (AS or prefix), we take the median. We choose median so that frequent retries will change the result, but occassional retries will not.

For passive TCP observations to support evaluation of anycast networks for DNS, (a) enough clients must send DNS over TCP so they can serve as *vantage points* (VPs) to measure RTT, and (b) the RTT for queries sent over TCP and UDP should be the same.

We next verify these two requirements, determining how many clients can serve as VPs with data from three production authoritative servers (Sect. 2.1) – two from the .nl zone, and B-root, one of the Root DNS servers [56]. We then compare the RTT of more than 8k VPs with both TCP and UDP to confirm they are similar (Sect. 2.2), towards two large anycast networks: K and L-Root, two of the 13 anycast services for the Root DNS zone.

2.1   Does TCP Provide Enough Coverage?

To assess whether DNS/TCP has enough coverage in production authoritative servers, we look at production traffic of two DNS zones: .nl and the DNS Root. For each zone we measure: (a) the number of resolvers using the service; (b) the number of ASes sending traffic; (c) the fraction of TCP queries the servers receive; (d) the percentage of resolvers using both UDP and TCP; and (e) the RTT of the TCP packets.

Our goal is to get a good estimate of RTT latency that covers recursive servers accounting for the majority of client traffic. If every query were TCP, we could determine the latency of each query and get 100% coverage. However, most DNS queries are sent over UDP instead of TCP.

Table 1. DNS usage for two authoritative services of .nl (Oct. 15–22, 2019).

	Queries		Resolvers		ASes	
	Anycast A	Anycast B	Any. A	Any. B	Any. A	Any. B
Total	5 237 454 456	5 679 361 857	2 015 915	2 005 855	42 253	42 181
IPv4	4 005 046 701	4 245 504 907	1 815 519	1 806 863	41 957	41 891
UDP	3 813 642 861	4 128 517 823	1 812 741	1 804 405	41 947	41 882
TCP	191 403 840	116 987 084	392 434	364 050	18 784	18 252
ratio TCP	5.02%	2.83%	21.65%	20.18%	44.78%	43.58%
IPv6	1 232 407 755	1 433 856 950	200 396	198 992	7 664	7 479
UDP	1 160 414 491	1 397 068 097	200 069	198 701	7 662	7 478
TCP	71 993 264	36 788 853	47 627	4 6190	3 391	3 354
ratio TCP	6.2%	2.63%	23.81%	23.25%	44.26%	44.85%

We, therefore, look for *recursive representation*—if we have a measured query over TCP, is its RTT the same as the RTTs of other queries that use UDP, or that are from other nearby recursive resolvers? If network conditions are relatively stable, the TCP query's RTT can represent the RTT for earlier or later UDP queries from the same resolver. Since /24 IPv4 prefixes (and /56 IPv6 prefixes) are usually co-located, DNS/TCP measurements from one IP can also represent other resolvers in the same prefix. Our goal is to find latency for DNS recursive resolvers, not all client networks—since recursive resolvers that generate the most traffic are most likely to send TCP queries, we expect good coverage even if TCP use is rare.

.nl Authoritative Servers. .nl currently (Oct. 2019) has four Authoritative DNS services, each configured to use IP anycast. We next examine data from two of these services. Anycast Services A and B employ 6 and 18 sites distributed globally. Each is run by a third-party DNS operator, one headquartered in Europe and the other in North America. They do not share a commercial relationship, nor do they share their service infrastructure.

DNS/TCP Usage: we analyze one week of traffic (2019-10-15 to -22) for each service using ENTRADA. That week from each service handles about 10.9 billion queries from about 2M resolvers spanning 42k Autonomous Systems (ASes), as can be seen in Table 1. The data shows that TCP is used rarely, accounting for less than 7% of queries for each anycast service. However, those queries represent more than a fifth of resolvers and 44% of ASes. (In all cases, TCP queries come from IP addresses that also send UDP queries).

AS Representation: We have TCP data for roughly 44% of all ASes (Table 1). This coverage is lower than we would prefer, but *these are the ASes that account for the majority of traffic*: the top DNS/TCP 10 ASes are responsible for half of all queries, while the top DNS/TCP 100 ASes account for 78% for Service A and 75% for B (Fig. 2). Although we miss many ASes, we next show we cover the prefixes in those ASes with recursive servers and we account for a large fraction of DNS traffic.

Traffic Coverage: We see that 5% of all queries are TCP, and they originate from about 20% of all resolvers (Table 1). While these are incomplete, we next show

Table 2. Traffic coverage for resolvers that use TCP in addition to UDP for DNS queries for `.nl` (Oct. 15–22, 2019).

	Anycast A	Anycast B
IPv4	4 005 046 701	4 245 504 907
TCP resolvers (DNS/UDP + DNS/TCP)	2 306 027 922	1 246 213 577
Ratio (%)	57.7%	29.35%
IPv6	1 232 407 755	1 433 856 950
TCP resolvers (DNS/UDP + DNS/TCP)	533 519 527	518 144 495
Ratio (%)	43.29%	36.13%

Table 3. DNS queries (in millions) for root DNS (E and G missing) – 2019-10-15 – 2019-10-22.

	A	B	C	D	F	H	I	J	K	L	M
Total	70601	40601	59033	88136	144635	31702	66582	115162	76761	105041	42702
IPv4	58552	33925	47675	74565	125020	25706	55874	96727	61378	88046	33687
UDP	56921	32334	45568	70969	118738	25234	51208	87891	60312	84059	31925
TCP	1631	1591	2107	3596	6282	472	4665	8836	1065	3986	1762
Ratio TCP	2.87%	4.92%	4.62%	5.07%	5.29%	1.87%	9.11%	10.05%	1.77%	4.74%	5.52%
IPv6	12049	6675	11357	13571	19614	5995	1070	18435	15383	16994	9014
UDP	11659	6280	10966	13071	18919	5825	936	15511	15108	16576	8268
TCP	389	394	391	499	694	169	1342	2923	274	418	746
Ratio TCP	3.34%	6.29%	3.57%	3.82%	3.67%	2.92%	14.34%	18.84%	1.82%	2.52%	9.03%

that they cover the majority of DNS traffic. In Table 2, we see that 29–58% of the total traffic (depending on IP version and anycast service) is from resolvers that have sent some TCP. As such, we have latency for at least 29% and up to 58% of DNS traffic. In addition, if we want full coverage, we describe below how we can induce coverage when it is necessary.

Root DNS: To confirm that DNS/TCP provides coverage beyond `.nl`, we also look at how many TCP queries are seen at most Root DNS servers [56] over the same period. Table 3 shows RSSAC-002 statistics [24,69] from 11 of the 13 Root DNS services reporting at this time. We see the ratio of TCP traffic varied for each service (known as "letters", from A to M) and IPv4 or IPv6, overall ranging from 2.8 (A Root over IPv4) up 18.9% (J Root over IPv6). This data suggests the root letters see similar DNS/TCP rates as `.nl`.

Inducing Coverage. While TCP coverage is not complete, we can get complete coverage by actively managing traffic to induce occasional TCP queries, as is often done in web systems (for example, [58]). The DNS specification includes the TC ("truncated") bit to indicate a truncated reply that must be retried over TCP. DNS Receiver Rate Limiting [66] (RRL) uses this mechanism to force possible UDP-based address spoofers to resend their queries with TCP. Switching to TCP allows TCP cookies to prevent spoofing [15].

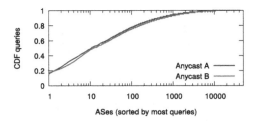

Fig. 2. `.nl`: queries distribution per AS.

A DNS server can use this same mechanism to solicit TCP queries from selected clients, allowing us to determine RTTs. We have implemented this capability in the Knot DNS server [11], building on Knot's RRL implementation. Our implementation tracks each block (/24 IPv4 prefix, or /56 IPv6 prefix). When a UDP request from that block arrives, if there are insufficient TCP queries in the last hour, it returns an answer with the TC bit set with some probability. The probability of not setting the bit and the required number of RTT observations per hour are both configurable. (However, our measurements pre-date and so do not use this mechanism).

The cost of forcing TCP is two additional round trips, and some resolvers fail to convert to TCP [41]. TCP solicitation should therefore be used sparingly, although other deployed systems diverting some traffic to identify service problems (for example, Facebook [58]). To ensure the server's increased TCP load is negligible, RTT induction should be configured to balance better measurements against available computational resources.

Temporal Coverage. Next we investigate how much *temporal coverage* passive analysis of DNS/TCP provides. We require TCP connections to observe latency in each time period with confidence, so traffic rate per AS determines our temporal precision. We hope traffic allows temporal precision of 0.5 to 4 hours so passive analysis can support near-real-time monitoring over the day (Sect. 4.4).

To evaluate the number of TCP queries per AS in a given time interval, we analyze `.nl` traffic from Anycast A and B. We single out one day of traffic (the first day of Table 1, 2019-10-15). On this day, Anycast A and Anycast B received UDP queries from ∼37k ASes over IPv4, and from ∼6.4k ASes over IPv6 (notice that numbers in Table 1 are higher given they cover the whole week).

To evaluate how many ASes report enough data to estimate RTTs each hour, Fig. 3 shows TCP queries per hour for Anycast A. As a baseline, IPv4 (Fig. 3a) sees about 26.3k ASes that send UDP queries per hour (IPv4), and 4.8k for IPv6. Of these, about 8.8k also send TCP queries (1.8k for IPv6), allowing some IPv4 RTT information about 33% of ASes and for IPv6, 38% of ASes. However, these ASes that *also* send TCP queries are responsible for the majority of *all* queries (blue line in Fig. 3): more than 90% of IPv4 queries and more than 60% of all IPv6 queries. If we only consider ASes that send *at least* 10k TCP queries/hour, we still account for most of the traffic (yellow line in Fig. 3).

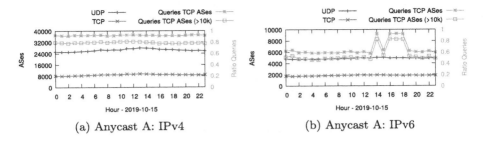

Fig. 3. .nl temporal coverage for Anycast A (Color figure online)

We conclude that a large number of ASes can be measured every hour with DNS/TCP. (We repeated the same analysis Anycast B (Appendix A) and also for another day 2019-10-21, both of them hold the same results [39]).

Summary: We see that TCP data provide good operational coverage and great temporal coverage. More importantly, TCP provides the *only* insight into IPv6 latency, since current active methods do not generalize to IPv6.

2.2 DNS/UDP vs. DNS/TCP RTT

We expect round-trip times measured with DNS/TCP and DNS/UDP to be similar. Next, we investigate that assumption.

We can compare DNS/UDP and DNS/TCP RTTs by comparing *query response times* and accounting for TCP connection setup. DNS/UDP makes a direct request and gets a response, while in DNS/TCP we set up the TCP connection (with a SYN–SYN/ACK handshake), so a TCP DNS request should take two RTTs (assuming no connection reuse, TCP fast-open, or other optimizations). We expect similar RTT estimates after dividing by two to account for TCP's handshake.

To confirm this claim we measure DNS/UDP and DNS/TCP query response times using RIPE Atlas [52]. Atlas provides about 11k devices in different locations around the world, allowing us to test many network conditions. As *targets*, we evaluate two large, globally distributed, production and public DNS anycast networks: L-Root, with 167 anycast sites, and K-Root, with 79 sites, which are two of the thirteen authoritative servers for the Root DNS zone. To measure DNS/UDP latency from probes to these root letters, we leverage existing measurements that run continuously on Ripe Atlas, every 4 min.

We then create DNS/TCP measurements towards L and K-Root ([k,l]root-tcp in [50]), within daily limits on query for RIPE Atlas. We study about 8.6k probes, running every 8 minutes (twice the interval of UDP measurements) for 24 hours, with results in Table 4. In these measurements, each Atlas probe directly queries the IPv4 address of the K and L-Root, without using a recursive resolver. For a fair comparison, we consider only probes that are present in both UDP and TCP measurements (∩ Probes): 8.5k and 8.9k for K

Table 4. DNS/UDP vs. DNS/TCP Atlas measurements. Datasets: [50].

	K-Root		L-Root	
	UDP	TCP	UDP	TCP
Date	Sept 4–5, 2020		Sept 5–6, 2020	
Freq.	4 min	8 min	4 min	8 min
Probes	10608	8680	10595	8999
∩ Probes	8577		8901	
Queries	3759080	1516801	3756572	1600283
∩ Queries	3044067	1499078	3160277	1583243

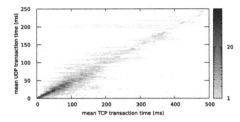

Fig. 4. L-Root: Density plot (log-scale) of number of Atlas observers with mean UDP and TCP DNS transaction times.

and L-Root, respectively. In the same way, we only evaluate queries from these matching probes: ∼3M UDP queries and ∼1.5M for TCP measurements, for each Root Letter (∩ Queries). Both measurements consider retries: UDP in the application and TCP by the kernel. In total, we analyze 9.2M queries for both letters. Then, for each Atlas probe, we compute its latency distribution.

Figure 4 shows a density plot of the number of RIPE Atlas observers with a given combination of mean DNS/UDP and DNS/TCP transaction times. Each combination is the mean of around 360 observations, and we report densities as log scale across the 8.9k Atlas probes available during the measurement. (We omit a handful of outliers with UDP means more than 250 ms.) We see a strong trend on the diagonal with a 1:2 UDP:TCP ratio, corresponding with TCP requiring two round trips. Slight variations from the diagonal represents queueing; considerable variation suggests experiments with retries. We see similar results (not shown due to space) for K-Root, and for median, and for 90%ile RTTs (see [39] for CDFs). The data shows a strong correlation between UDP and TCP, but also some outliers in the lower-left corner due to retransmission.

We can quantify similarity by computing the correlation coefficient of median UDP and half the median: the correlation is 0.913 for K-Root and 0.930 for L-Root. We also did a Student's t-Test, evaluating the hypothesis that the UDP mean and half the TCP mean are statistically identical with a 95% confidence. This test could not be rejected the majority of the time (64% of the time, in 5558 cases for K-Root and 5733 cases for L-Root), suggesting the results were often indistinguishable. Manual examination shows outliers are common in the cases where the hypothesis is rejected, suggesting a TCP-level retransmission. Although retransmission detection is possible, our results show usability even when minimizing computational requirements so as to optimize for low-overhead, real-item deployments. This experiment proves that passively observed TCP RTTs often provide a good representation of the RTTs that DNS/UDP will see.

3   Prioritizing Analysis

We have shown that DNS/TCP can be mined to determine RTTs (Sect. 2). Operational DNS systems must serve the whole world, there are more than 42k active ASes sending DNS queries to authoritative servers. Both detection and resolution of networking problems in anycast systems is labor intensive: detection requires both identifying specific problems and their potential root causes. Problem resolution requires new site deployments or routing changes, both needing human-in-the-loop changes involving trouble tickets, new hardware, and new hosting contracts.

Overview: We use two strategies to *prioritize* the analysis of problems that are most important: per-anycast site analysis and per client AS analysis, and rank each by median latency, interquartile range (IQR) of latency, and query volume.

We focus on anycast sites because that part of the problem is under operator control. If we find sites with high latency, we can examine routing and perhaps correct problems [7,68].

Clients ASes examine the *user* side of the problem (at recursive resolvers), since client latency is a goal in DNS service. While performance in client ASes can be difficult to improve because we do not have a direct relationship with those network operators, we show in Sect. 4 that we can address problems in some cases.

Finally, we consider median latency, interquartile range, and query volume to prioritize investigation. Median latency is a proxy for overall latency at the site. The interquartile range (the difference between 75%ile and 25%ile latencies), captures the *spread* of possible latencies at a given site or AS. Finally, query volume (or rate) identifies locations where improvements will affect more users. We sort by overall rate rather than the number of unique sources to prioritize large ASes that send many users through a few recursive resolvers (high rate, low number of recursive IPs).

Prioritization by Site: Figure 5 shows per-site latency for .nl, broken out by protocol (IPv4 and IPv6) and site, for two anycast services (A and B). For each site, we show two bars: the fraction of total queries and the number of ASes (filled and hatched bar in each cluster). We overlay both with whiskers for latency (with median in the middle and 25%ile and 75%ile at whisker ends). In these graphs some sites (such as CDG for Anycast B in IPv6) stand out with high interquartile ranges, while others with lower interquartile range (for Anycast B, LAX-A and NRT in IPv4 and NRT and GRU in IPv6). We look at these cases in detail in Sect. 4.

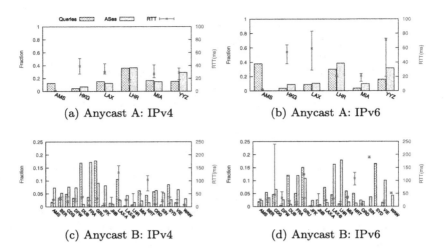

(a) Anycast A: IPv4   (b) Anycast A: IPv6

(c) Anycast B: IPv4   (d) Anycast B: IPv6

Fig. 5. .nl distribution of queries and ASes per site (pink bars) and latency (median, 25%ile, and 75%ile, (green lines), for each anycast site, for two services (Anycast A and B) and two protocols (IPv4 and IPv6). Data from 2020-10-15 to -22. (Color figure online)

Prioritization by Client AS: Figure 6 and Fig. 19 (Appendix B) show the latency distribution for the ten ASes with the largest query volume for Anycast A and B of .nl. (Due to space constraints, we show the complete list of AS names in Appendix C). While many ASes show good latency (low median and small interquartile range), we see the top two busiest ASes for Anycast A in IPv4 (Fig. 6a) show a high median and large interquartile range (Fig. 6b). These ASes experience anycast polarization, a problem we describe in Sect. 4.3.

Figure 7 shows latencies for the top ASes for B-root, with quartile ranges as boxes and the 10%ile and 90%iles as whiskers. Rather than split by protocol, here we show both rankings and by query rate (Appendix B) on the x-axis. While rank gives a strict priority, showing ASes by rate helps evaluate how important it is to look at more ASes (if the next AS to consider is much, much lower rate, addressing problems there will not make as large a difference to users). We identify specific problems from these graphs next.

4 Problems and Solutions

Given new information about IPv4 and IPv6 latency from DNS/TCP (Sect. 2), and priorities (Sect. 3), we next examine anycast performance for two of the four anycast services operating for .nl, and for B-root. For each problem, we describe how we found it, the root causes, and, when possible, solutions and outcomes. We show two problems that have been documented before (Sect. 4.1 and Sect. 4.2) and a new problem (Sect. 4.3). While some of these problems may have been eventually discovered when users encountered them, we have discovered

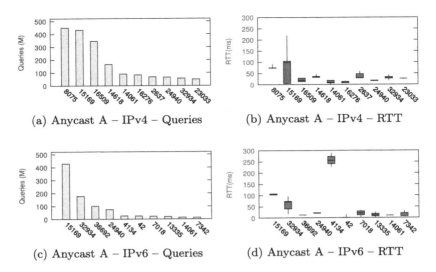

(a) Anycast A – IPv4 – Queries

(b) Anycast A – IPv4 – RTT

(c) Anycast A – IPv6 – Queries

(d) Anycast A – IPv6 – RTT

Fig. 6. `.nl` Anycast A queries and RTT for the top 10 ASes ranked by most queries (bars left axis). Data; 2019-10-15 to -22. ASes list on Appendix C).

each from our prioritized monitoring of DNS/TCP latency (Sect. 3). Our near-real-time monitoring (Sect. 4.4) supported the discovery of these problems before user complaints.

4.1   Distant Lands

The first problem we describe is *distant lands:* when a country has no any-cast server locally and has limited connectivity to the rest of the world. When trans-Pacific traffic was metered, these problems occurred for Australia and New

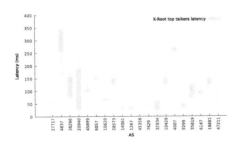

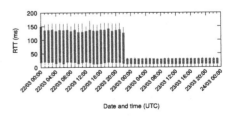

Fig. 7. `B-root`: latency of top talkers by rank

Fig. 8. Anycast B and Comcast: RTT before and after resolving IPv6 miscon-figuration.

Zealand. Today we see this problem with China. China has a huge population of Internet users, but its international network connections can exhibit congestion [73].

Detection: We discovered this problem by observing large interquartile latency for .nl's Anycast B in v4 (Fig. 5c) and v6 (Fig. 5d) at Tokyo (NRT, both v4 and v6), Singapore (SIN, v6), and CDG (v6), all with 75%iles over 100 ms.

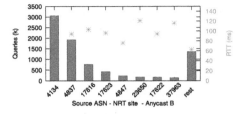
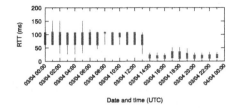

Fig. 9. Anycast B, Japan site (NRT): top 8 querying ASes are Chinese, and responsible for 80% of queries.

Fig. 10. .nl Anycast A and Microsoft (IPv4): RTT before and after depolarization.

These wide ranges of latency prompted us to examine which recursive resolvers visiting these sites and showed high latency. Many queries come from ASes in Asia (Fig. 9). NRT sees many queries (6.1% of total, more than its "fair share" of 5.2%). Of the top 10 ASes sending queries to NRT, 9 are from China (see Fig. 9).

We see many Chinese ISPs that also send IPv6 traffic to Paris (CDG), resulting in a large RTT spread. Not only must their traffic traverse congested, international links, but they also then travel to a geographically distant anycast site, raising the 75%ile RTT at CDG over 100 ms (even though its median is under 22 ms).

Resolution: While we can diagnose this problem, the best resolution would be new anycast servers for Anycast B inside China (or manipulate BGP to attempt to steer traffic to nearby Tokyo or Singapore sites). The operator is considering deployment options, but foreign operation of sites in China has only been recently allowed [73], and anycast operation from China risks service for some non-Chinese clients traversing the Chinese national firewall.

4.2   Prefer-Customer to Another Continent

The second root-cause problem we found is when one AS prefers a distant anycast site, often on another continent, because that site is a customer of the AS. (Recall that a common BGP routing policy is *prefer customer*: if an AS can satisfy a route through one of its customers, it prefers that choice over an alternate route through a peer or transit provider. Presumably, the customer is paying the AS for service, while sending the traffic to a peer or via transit is either cost-neutral or incurs additional cost).

We have seen this problem in two situations: at .nl Anycast B's Brazil site, and B-root for its site in South America. While the ISP should be able to choose where it sends its traffic, anycast service operators would like to know when such policies result in large client latencies, so that can consider exploring peering options that might lower latency.

.nl **Detection:** We detected this problem for .nl Service B by observing high IPv6 median latency (124 ms) for queries is in São Paulo, Brazil (GRU) in Fig. 5d. Examination of the data shows that many of the high-latency queries are from Comcast (AS7922), a large U.S.-based ISP. As with China and CDG, this case is an example of queries traveling out of the way to a distant anycast site, ignoring several anycast sites already in North America. We confirmed that North American clients of this AS were routing to the Brazil site by checking CHAOS TXT queries [1] from RIPE Atlas probes to Anycast B (data: ComcastV6 [50]).

.nl **Resolution:** We contacted .nl Anycast B's operator, who determined that the issue was with one of their upstream providers. This provider had deployed BGP communities to limit the IPv4 route to South America. After our contact, they deployed the same community for IPv6, and the Comcast traffic remained in the US.

We first confirm the problem was resolved by analyzing traces from Anycast B, and by confirming that Comcast IPv6 clients were now answered by other North American sites. The solution reduced 75%ile latency by 100 ms: in Fig. 8 before the change, IPv6 shows IQR of 120 ms for Anycast B. After this change on 2020-03-23t00:00, we see the IQR falls to 20 ms. Second, we also verified with Atlas probes hosted on Comcast's network (data: ComcastV6-afterReport in [50]), and the median RTT from Comcast Atlas was reduced from 139 ms to 28 ms.

B-root **Detection:** B-root has observed high latencies for traffic going to a South-American anycast site of B-root. As with .nl and GRU, we examined traffic and identified a primarily-North American ISP that was sending all of its traffic to the South American site, ignoring all other lower-latency sites. We then confirmed that an AS purchases transit from this ISP.

B-root **Resolution:** We have not yet a completely satisfactory resolution to this problem. Unfortunately, the AS that purchases transit from the North American ISP does not directly peer with B-root, so we cannot control its peering. We currently poison the route to prevent latency problems, which significantly reduces traffic arriving at this site.

4.3 Polarization with Google and Microsoft

We next describe *anycast polarization*, a problem we first described in June 2020 [39]. We are the first to explain and demonstrate the impact of polarization on performance, although subsequent work reported it in a testbed study [64]. Like prefer-customer, it involves high latency that derives from traffic being

Table 5. Anycast A: Polarized ASes and query distribution (Oct 15-22,2019).

	Queries	Queries top site	(% top site)
Google	860 775 677	860 774 158	99.9998
IPv4	433 145 168	433 145 119	99.9999
IPv6	427 630 509	427 629 039	99.9997
Microsoft	449 460 715	449 455 487	99.9988
IPv4	449 439 957	449 434 729	99.9988
IPv6	20 758	20 758	100

needlessly sent to another continent. But it follows from BGP's limited knowledge of latency (AS path length is its only distance metric) and the flattening of the Internet [27].

Detecting the Problem. We discovered this problem by examining DNS/TCP-derived latency from the top two ASes sending queries to .nl Anycast A. As seen in Fig. 6b and Fig. 6d, AS8075 (Microsoft) and AS15169 (Google) show very high IPv4 median latency (74 ms and 99 ms), and Google shows a very high IQR. (99 ms) Google also shows a high IPv6 median latency (104 ms).

Both Google and Microsoft are "hypergiants", with data centers on multiple continents (for .nl, ~85% of Google's traffic is from its Public Resolvers [38,62]). Both also operate their own international backbones and peer with the Internet in dozens of locations. These very high latencies suggest much of their DNS traffic is traveling between continents and not taking advantage of .nl's global anycast infrastructure. This problem occurs in hypergiants with backbones that do not consider multiple exits and anycast—by default they will route all their traffic to one global anycast size, creating polarization. For companies with islands connected by transit providers (without a corporate backbone), each island will compute routing locally, so anycast "just works".

Confirming the Problem: .nl Anycast A has six sites, so we first examine how many queries go to each site. Table 5 shows the results—all or very nearly all (four or five "nines") go to a single anycast site due to routing preferences. For Google, this site is in Amsterdam, and for Microsoft, Miami.

While a preferred site is not a problem for a small ISP in one location, it is the root cause of very high latency for these hypergiants, who often route global traffic internally over their own backbones, egressing to one physical location. Even if it is the best destination for some of their traffic, one location will not minimize latency for multiple, globally distributed, data centers. Such routing defeats latnecy advantages of distributed anycast deployment [43,59].

Depolarizing Google to .nl Anycast A. *Root-cause:* We first investigated Google's preference for AMS. .nl directly operates the AMS site (the other 5 sites are operated by a North American DNS provider). We determined (working with both the AMS and Google operators) that Google has a direct BGP peering with the site at AMS. BGP prefers routes with the shortest AS-PATH, and in addition, ASes often prefer Private Network Interconnect (PNIs) over equal length paths through IXPs, so it is not surprising it prefers this path. (The general problem of BGP policy interfering with the lowest latency is well documented [4,5,7,28,34,59]. We believe we are the first to document this problem with hypergiants and anycast through PNI).

We next describe how we worked with the AMS operators and Google to resolve this problem. We document this case as one typical resolution to show the need for continuous observation of DNS latency through DNS/TCP to find the problem and confirm the fix.

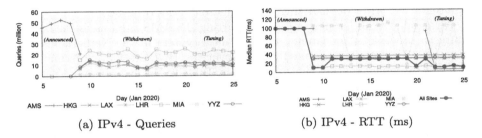

(a) IPv4 - Queries   (b) IPv4 - RTT (ms)

Fig. 11. .nl Anycast A: queries and median RTT per site from Google (AS15169) – January 2020.

Figure 11 show the effects of our traffic engineering on anycast use and query latency for IPv4 (IPv6 figures in Appendix D). Each graph shows traffic or median client latency for each of the 6 .nl Anycast A sites. (Query latency is determined by DNS/TCP traffic over each day.) The graphs show behavior over January 2020, January 5th to 9th (the left, pink area) before any changes, the 9th to the 21st (the middle, green area) when the AMS route was withdrawn, and finally after the 21st (the right, blue region) when AMS was restored, but with different kinds of policy routing.

These graphs confirm that initially, AMS received all traffic from Google, causing Anycast A to appear to be a *unicast* service to Google, precluding locality in a global anycast service. We see that the median latency for Google is about 100 ms (Fig. 6a). Withdrawing the AMS peering with Google corrects the problem, spreading queries across multiple anycast sites, benefiting from geographic locality. Median latency drops to 10 to 40 ms, although still around 100 ms at YYZ in Miami for IPv4. LHR is now the busiest site, located in Europe.

Use of the North American sites considerably lowers median latency. We show in Fig. 12 the depolarization results for all sites combined, for IPv4 and IPv6. For both IPv4 and IPv6, we see median latency for all sites combined reducing 90 ms, from 100 to 10ms. The IQR was reduced from 95 to 10 ms for IPv4. For

Table 6. BGP manipulations on AMS site of Anycast A – IPv4 and IPv6 prefixes to Google (AS15169) on Jan 21, 2020 (Time in UTC). NE: No Export

Op.	Day	Time	Prepend	Community	AMS(%)
1	21	15:00	2x	–	>0
2	22	9:53	2x	NE	>0
3	22	9:59	1x	–	100
4	22	10:21	1x	NE	100
5	22	10:37	1x	NE,15169:13000	100
6	22	11:00	2x	NE	>0

IPv6, we observed few queries over TCP between Jan. 1 and 9, so they are not representative. After depolarizing, we see more queries over TCP.

Although overall latency improves, omitting the AMS site misses the opportunity to provide better latency to their data centers in the Netherlands and Denmark. We therefore resumed peering over the BGP session, experimenting with several policy routing choices shown in Table 6. We experimented with 1x and 2x AS-PATH prepending, no-export, and a Google-specific "try-not-to-use this path" community string [18]. We found that no-export and the community string had no effect, perhaps because of the BGP session, and neither did single prepending. However, double AS-PATH prepending left AMS with about 10% of the total traffic load. Full details of our experiments are in our technical report [39].

Depolarizing Microsoft to .nl Anycast A. Detection: We discovered Microsoft anycast polarization through analysis of DNS/TCP across ASes (Fig. 6b and Fig. 6d) AS8075 (Microsoft) and AS15169 (Google) Microsoft's preferred site for .nl Anycast A is Miami (MIA), a different preference than Google's, but the outcome was the same: large latency (median 80 ms) because global traffic goes to one place.

Resolution: Again, we worked with the operators at .nl Anycast A MIA and Microsoft to diagnose and resolve the problem. We confirm that Anycast had

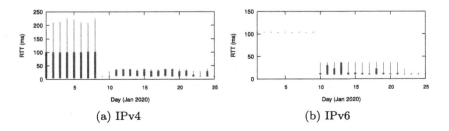

(a) IPv4	(b) IPv6

Fig. 12. Google depolarization results and RTT.

a peering session with Microsoft in MIA, and not at any other sites. Again, the result was a short AS-PATH and a preference for all Microsoft data centers to use the Microsoft WAN to this site rather than other .nl Anycast A anycast sites (having different upstream providers per anycast site may cause such traffic distributions [34]).

Options that could mitigate this polarization include de-peering with Microsoft in MIA, peering with Microsoft at the remaining sites, or possibly BGP-based traffic engineering. Because our ability to experiment with BGP was more limited at this site, and we could not start new peerings at other sites, the operator at MIA de-peered with Microsoft at our recommendation.

Figure 10 shows latency for this AS before and after our solution. Removing the direct peering addressed the problem, and Microsoft traffic is now distributed across all .nl Anycast A sites. As a result, the IQR falls from about 80 ms to 13 ms. The median latency also falls by 70 ms, from 90 ms to 20 ms. Our technique identifies problems with polarization and shows the dramatic improvement that results.

4.4 Detecting BGP Misconfiguration in Near Real-Time

Because it poses no additional cost on the network, passive measurement of anycast latency with DNS/TCP is an ideal method for *continuous, on-the-fly* detection of BGP misconfiguration. To this end, we have developed and deployed Anteater within .nl, which is a *live* monitoring system that retrieves DNS/TCP RTT continuously.

We show the Anteater architecture in Fig. 13. First, traffic is collected at authoritative DNS servers of .nl, which is then exported to ENTRADA [61,70], an open-source DNS traffic streaming warehouse that employs Hadoop [60] and continuously ingests pcap files from these servers. (We also use ENTRADA for other applications as well [36,67]). ENTRADA that extracts RTT for incoming TCP handshakes, making it available for queries using Impala [26], an open-source SQL engine for Hadoop. With Hadoop, ENTRADA supports scalable analysis of large traffic.

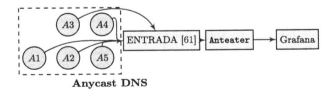

Fig. 13. Anteater monitoring at .nl

Anteater then retrieves DNS/TCP RTT data for each anycast server, anycast site, and various ASes, on an hourly basis (given that .nl authoritative servers have good temporal coverage in 1h frames Sect. 2.1). It stores the information

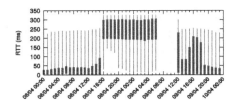
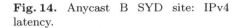

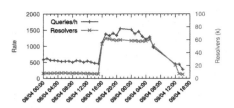

Fig. 14. Anycast B SYD site: IPv4 latency.

Fig. 15. Anycast B SYD: queries rate and resolvers.

on a relational database (PostgreSQL). We then use Grafana [19], a data visualization dashboard and alert system. We then configure RTT thresholds that triggers Grafana to send .nl operators email alerts. Anteater has been used in .nl for the past two years and its proven helpful in detecting BGP misconfigurations. We have released Anteater at [37]. Next we illustrate this use-case with one example from that deployment.

EU Traffic Winding up in Australia: On 2020-04-08, .nl operators received an alert from Anteater that detected a jump in median DNS RTT for Anycast B, from 55 ms to more than 200 ms (see Fig. 14) but only for IPv4 traffic, and not for IPv6.

To investigate this change, we evaluated the number of ASes (Fig. 14), resolvers, and query rates (Fig. 15) using Anteater's Grafana dashboard. We see that the number of resolvers, queries, and latency grow, with many more ASes, and about 3× more queries and resolvers. To rule out DDoS attacks or a sudden burst in popularity for our domain, we confirmed that these ASes and resolvers have migrated from other sites (mostly Germany, site FRA) and went to SYD. Since many of these clients are in Europe, this nearly antipodal detour explains the latency increase.

We reached out to the operator of .nl Anycast B SYD. They confirmed and were already aware of the routing change. They informed us that a set of their SYD prefixes had accidentally to propagated through a large, Tier-1 transit provider. Since this provider peered with many other ASes in many places around the globe, their propagation of the Anycast B anycast prefix provided a shorter AS-Path and sent traffic to SYD. We also confirmed these routing changes on the RIPE RIS database of routing changes [54].

While catchment changes are not bad, route leaks that mis-route Europe to Australia are not an improvement. The lightweight nature of DNS/TCP observations of latency support 24 × 7 monitoring and allowed us to detect this problem, which is why we developed Anteater to monitor the .nl operations.

5   Anycast Latency and Traffic

While DNS/TCP can be used to discover anycast latency, does latency matter? DNS caching means *users* are largely insulated from latency. We next confirm

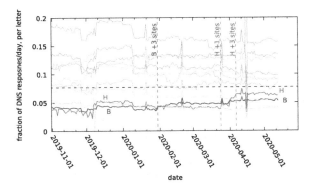

Fig. 16. Fraction of traffic going to each root anycast service, per day, from RSSAC-002 data. B- and H-Root are bold lines.

that latency does influence *traffic* to services when users have the choice of several. A causal relationship between client selection and latency was previously shown experimentally [43] and through code analysis [71], and our operational measurements adds operational measurement confirmation to these results.

Prior work has considered recursive resolver preference for lower latency [44]. Here we turn that analysis around and explore how changing anycast infrastructure shifts a client's preferences towards authoritative name servers. We confirm that lower latency results in increased traffic from recursive resolvers that have a choice between multiple anycast service addresses providing the same zone. (This question differs from studies that examine the optimality of a specific anycast service with multiple sites [28,29].)

To examine this question, we use public RSSAC-002 statistics for the root server system [56]. From this we use the "traffic-volume" statistic, which reports queries per day for each root anycast service. (Recall that the Root DNS is provided by 13 different anycast service addresses per IP version, each using a different anycast infrastructure.) We show 6 months of data here (2019-11-01 to 2020-05-31), but we have noticed similar trends since 2016. This analysis omits G- and I-Root, which did not provide data during this period.

Figure 16 shows the fraction of traffic that goes to each anycast service in the root server system for one year. Two root letters deployed additional sites over this period: B-Root originally had 2 sites but added 3 sites in 2020-02-01, then optimized routing around 2020-04-01. H-Root originally had 2 sites but deployed 4 additional sites on 2020-02-11 and 3 additional sites on 2020-04-06. While other letters also added sites, B and H's changes were the largest improvements relative to their prior size. We see that B and H's share rises from about 4% in 2019-11 to about 6% in 2020-05.

This data confirms that when new sites are created at a root letter, they offer some clients lower latency for that letter. Lower latency causes some clients to shift more of their traffic to this letter (automatically, as described in [43]), so its share of traffic relative to the others grows.

6   Related Work

Passive TCP Evaluation: Janey Hoe was the first to extract RTT from the TCP handshake [20], and several groups have used it since then (*e.g.,*, Facebook HTTP traffic [57]). We use this old idea, but we apply it to DNS RTT estimation and to use to engineer and monitor Anycast DNS services in near real-time. In a non-peer-reviewed work performed previously but independently from our own, .cz operators [31,32] also employed DNS/TCP RTT to evaluate latency from their services. While both use the same idea (derive latencies from the TCP handshake), ours provides a comprehensive validation (Sect. 2). We also act on the results, by carefully manipulating BGP to solve the identified problems, and reduce latency in up to 90% (Sect. 4). Besides, our work includes freely three tools: dnsanon, Anteater, and a modified version of KnotDNS. Linux ss and ip utilities [30] can be also used to retrieve TCP information such as RTT. However, they only provide *averages*. Although TCP congestion control may interact with latency, since DNS/TCP is usually short (a single query and reply), such interactions will be rare.

Anycast DNS Performance: Having a single upstream provider has been previously proposed as a solution to avoid routing unexpected behavior [4]. Later research evaluated the impact of *number of sites* and anycast performance, showing that, counterintuitively, sometimes more sites actually increase latency [59]. The behavior of anycast under DDoS has been examined [42], using data from the 2015 attacks against the Root DNS servers [55]. Our discovery of polarization in Google has been showin in subsequent testbed experiments [64]. We had already shared results of polarization for multiple hypergiants [39], and are the first to quantify the performance and show the benefits of BGP-based fixes.

There is one approach to measure anycast latency today: active measurements. RIPE Atlas [52] measures latency from about 11k physical devices distributed worldwide. Commercial services are known to have fewer vantage points. Our approach instead uses passive analysis of TCP traffic from real clients. It provides far better coverage than RIPE Atlas (Sect. 2.1). We expect that Verfploeter will soon support RTT measurements. Even when it does support RTT measurements, our approach can provide coverage for all networks interacting with the service. In addition, since our analysis is passive, it places no additional strain on other networks and can run 24×7. Last, a previous work proposed using new BGP communities to improve the site catchment, which, in turn, requires protocol level changes [28]. Contrary to their approach, ours relies only on passive TCP traffic and does not involve protocol changes.

Anycast Optimization for Large CDNs with Multiple Providers: Going beyond how many sites and where to place them, McQuistin *et al.* [34] have investigated anycast networks with multiple upstream providers, as is common for large CDNs. When different sites have different peers or transits catchment inconsistencies can result, as we saw with Google and Anycast A (Sect. 4.3). They propose taking active measurements of catchments each day and operator evaluation of catchment changes Our work also detects catchment changes, but only when it affects latency (see Sect. 4.3 and Sect. 4.3), fortunately when changes matte.r Schlinker *et al.* [57] describe how Facebook monitors their CDN for web content, detecting anycast latency problems for their users. Our work instead focuses shows how TCP results can summarize latency for a mostly UDP-based workload, and studies authoritative DNS traffic, from recursive resolvers (not end-users).

Performance-Aware Routing: Todd *et al.* [3] compare data from proposals for performance-aware routing from three content/cloud providers (Google, Facebook, and Microsoft) and show that BGP fares quite well for most cases. Others proposed to perform traffic engineering based on packet loss, latency and jitter [45,49].

DNS over TCP, TLS, and HTTP: There is recent interest in DNS over TCP and TLS [23,72] and HTTP [21] to improve privacy. Most such work emphasizes stub-to-recursives resolvers, while we focus on recursive-to-authoritative, where only now IETF is considering alternatives to UDP. Increased use of DNS over connection-oriented transport protocols will improve coverage we can provide.

7   Conclusions

We have shown that DNS TCP connections are a valuable source of latency information about anycast services for DNS. Although TCP is not (today) the dominant transport protocol for DNS, we showed that there is enough DNS/TCP to provide good coverage for latency estimation. We also showed how we prioritize the use of this information to identify problems in operational anycast networks. We have used this approach to study three operational anycast services: two anycast servers of .nl, and one root DNS server (B-root). We documented one new class of latency problems: anycast polarization, an interaction where hypergiants get pessimal latency (100–200 ms) because of a poor interaction between their corporate backbones and global anycast services. We showed how we addressed this problem for .nl's Anycast A with both Google and Microsoft. We also documented several other problems for anycast latency discovered through our analysis of DNS/TCP and showed that it enables continuous monitoring. Last, we release freely two tools (dnsanon and Anteater) and a modified version of KnotDNS. We believe this approach will be of use to other DNS operators.

Acknowledgments. We thank the operators of .nl Anycast A and B and B-root for their time and collaboration. We also thank Casey Deccio for first proposing using TCP hanshake to measure DNS latency. Finally, we thank Klaus Darilion and our paper's anonymous reviewers for their paper suggestions.

John Heidemann's research in this paper is supported in part by the DHS HSARPA Cyber Security Division via contract number HSHQDC-17-R-B0004-TTA.02-0006-I (PAADDOS) and by NWO. His and Wes Haradaker's research are also supported in part by NSF CNS-1925737 (DIINER), Giovane C. M. Moura, Joao Ceron, Jeroen Bulten, and Cristian Hesselman research in this paper is supported by the Conconrdia Project, an European Union's Horizon 2020 Research and Innovation program under Grant Agreement No 830927.

A   Extra Graphs on Temporal Coverage

Figure 17 show the temporal coverage of Anycast B for .nl. Figure 18 shows temporal coverage for 2019-10-21. Together these graphs show that a core of many ASes are covered by TCP at all times of day.

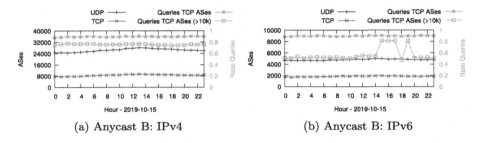

(a) Anycast B: IPv4   (b) Anycast B: IPv6

Fig. 17. .nl temporal coverage for Anycast B

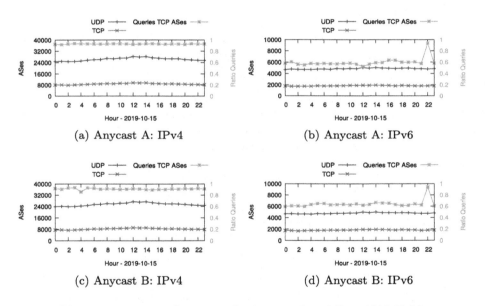

(a) Anycast A: IPv4   (b) Anycast A: IPv6

(c) Anycast B: IPv4   (d) Anycast B: IPv6

Fig. 18. .nl temporal coverage for Anycast A and B on 2019-10-21

B   Anycast Extra Data

Figure 19 shows the the latency for the top 10 ASes of Anycast B.

Figure 20 shows the latency for B-root top talkers by data size (log scale).

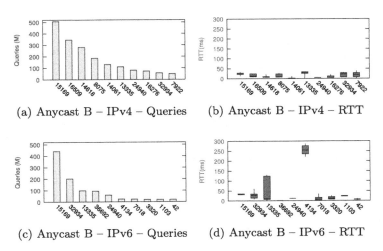

(a) Anycast B – IPv4 – Queries   (b) Anycast B – IPv4 – RTT

(c) Anycast B – IPv6 – Queries   (d) Anycast B – IPv6 – RTT

Fig. 19. `.nl` Anycast B query RTT for the top 10 ASes ranked by most queries (bars left axis). Data: 2019-10-15 to -22.

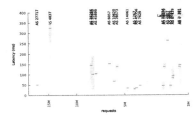

Fig. 20. `B-root` latency of top talkers by data size (log scale)

C   Anycast A and B Top ASes

Table 7 shows ASes names and countries for top ASes observed for Anycast A and Anycast B, as shown in Fig. 6 and discussed in priorization (Sect. 3) (Fig. 21).

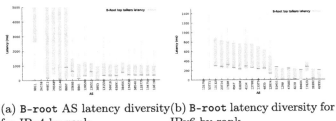

(a) `B-root` AS latency diversity for IPv4 by rank

(b) `B-root` latency diversity for IPv6 by rank

Fig. 21. Latency analysis to `B-root` by AS latency diversity.

Table 7. ASes in the top 10 lists of Anycast A and B

AS number	AS name	Country
42	WoodyNet (PCH)	US
1103	SURFNet BV	NL
2637	Georgia Institute of Technology	US
3320	Deutsche Telekom AG	DE
4134	China Telecom Backbone	CN
7018	AT&T Services, Inc.	US
7342	Verisign infrastructure and Operations	US
7922	Comcast	US
8075	Microsoft Corporation	US
13335	Cloudflare	US
14061	DigitalOcean LLC	US
14618	Amazon.com Inc.	US
15169	Google	US
16276	OVH SAS	FR
16509	Amazon.com Inc.	US
23033	Wowrack.com	US
24940	Hetzner Online GmbH	DE
32934	Facebook, Inc.	US
36692	Cisco OpenDNS, LLC	US

D Depolarizing Google: IPv6 Graphs

Figure 22 shows the IPv6 depolarization graphs for Anycast A and Google.

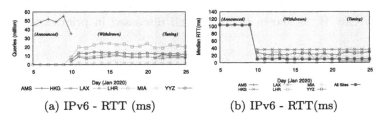

(a) IPv6 - RTT (ms) (b) IPv6 - RTT(ms)

Fig. 22. .nl Anycast A (IPv6): queries and median RTT per site from Google (AS15169) – January 2020.

References

1. Allman, M., Floyd, S., Partridge, C.: Increasing TCP's initial window. RFC 2414, IETF, September 1998
2. Arends, R., Austein, R., Larson, M., Massey, D., Rose, S.: DNS security introduction and requirements. RFC 4033, Internet Request For Comments, March 2005
3. Arnold, T., et al.: Beating BGP is harder than we thought. In: Proceedings of the 18th ACM Workshop on Hot Topics in Networks, HotNets 2019, pp. 9–16. Association for Computing Machinery, New York (2019)
4. Ballani, H., Francis, P.: Towards a global IP anycast service. In: Proceedings of the 2005 Conference on Applications, Technologies, Architectures, and Protocols for Computer Communications, SIGCOMM 2005, pp. 301–312. Association for Computing Machinery, New York (2005)
5. Ballani, H., Francis, P., Ratnasamy, S.: A measurement-based deployment proposal for IP anycast. In: Proceedings of the 2006 ACM Conference on Internet Measurement Conference, IMC, pp. 231–244. ACM, October 2006
6. Bellis, R.: DNS transport over TCP–implementation requirements. RFC 5966, Internet Request For Comments, August 2010. https://www.rfc-editor.org/rfc/rfc5966.txt
7. Bellis, R.: Researching F-root anycast placement using RIPE Atlas. Ripe blog, October 2015
8. Calder, M., Fan, X., Hu, Z., Katz-Bassett, E., Heidemann, J., Govindan, R.: Mapping the expansion of Google's serving infrastructure. In: Proceedings of the ACM Internet Measurement Conference, pp. 313–326. ACM, Barcelona, October 2013
9. Castro, S., Wessels, D., Fomenkov, M., Claffy, K.: A day at the root of the internet. ACM Comput. Commun. Rev. **38**(5), 41–46 (2008)
10. Charnsethikul, P.: Knot extensions to support TCP soliciation, March 2021. https://ant.isi.edu/software/dnsrtt/
11. CZ.NIC: Knot DNS, November 2011. https://www.knot-dns.cz/
12. de Vries, W.B., Aljammaz, S., van Rijswijk-Deij, R.: Global scale anycast network management with verfploeter. In: Proceedings of the IEEE/IFIP Network Operations and Management Symposium. IEEE, Budapest, April 2020
13. de Vries, W.B., de O. Schmidt, R., Haraker, W., Heidemann, J., de Boer, P.T., Pras, A.: Verfploeter: broad and load-aware anycast mapping. In: Proceedings of the ACM Internet Measurement Conference, London, UK (2017)
14. Dilley, J., Maggs, B., Parikh, J., Prokop, H., Sitaraman, R., Weihl, B.: Globally distributed content delivery. IEEE Internet Comput. **6**(5), 50–58 (2002)
15. Eddy, W.: TCP SYN flooding attacks and common mitigations. RFC 4987, IETF, August 2007
16. Gasser, O., et al.: Clusters in the expanse: understanding and unbiasing IPv6 hitlists. In: Proceedings of the Internet Measurement Conference 2018, IMC 2018, pp. 364–378. Association for Computing Machinery, New York (2018)
17. Gigis, P., et al.: Seven years in the life of hypergiants' off-nets. In: Proceedings of ACM SIGCOMM 2021. Virtual Event, August 2021
18. Google: Google BGP communities, January 2020. https://support.google.com/interconnect/answer/9664829?hl=en
19. Grafana Labs: Grafana documentation, July 2020. https://grafana.com/
20. Hoe, J.C.: Improving the start-up behavior of a congestion control scheme for TCP. In: Proceedings of the ACM SIGCOMM Conference, pp. 270–280. ACM, Stanford, August 1996

21. Hoffman, P., McManus, P.: DNS Queries over HTTPS (DoH). RFC 8484, IETF, October 2018
22. Hoffman, P., Sullivan, A., Fujiwara, K.: DNS terminology. RFC 8499, IETF, November 2018
23. Hu, Z., Zhu, L., Heidemann, J., Mankin, A., Wessels, D., Hoffman, P.: Specification for DNS over transport layer security (TLS). RFC 7858, Internet Request For Comments, May 2016
24. ICANN: RSSAC002: RSSAC Advisory on Measurements of the Root Server System, November 2014. https://www.icann.org/en/system/files/files/rssac-002-measurements-root-20nov14-en.pdf
25. Koch, T., Li, K., Ardi, C., Katz-Bassett, E., Calder, M., Heidemann, J.: Anycast in context: a tale of two systems. In: Proceedings of the ACM SIGCOMM Conference. ACM, Virtual, August 2021. https://www.isi.edu/
26. Kornacker, M., et al.: Impala: a modern, open-source SQL engine for Hadoop. In: Cidr. vol. 1, p. 9 (2015)
27. Labovitz, C., Iekel-Johnson, S., McPherson, D., Oberheide, J., Jahanian, F.: Internet inter-domain traffic. In: Proceedings of the ACM SIGCOMM Conference, pp. 75–86. ACM, New Delhi, August 2010
28. Li, Z., Levin, D., Spring, N., Bhattacharjee, B.: Internet anycast: performance, problems, & potential. In: Proceedings of the 2018 Conference of the ACM Special Interest Group on Data Communication, SIGCOMM 2018, pp. 59–73. Association for Computing Machinery, New York (2018)
29. Liang, J., Jiang, J., Duan, H., Li, K., Wu, J.: Measuring query latency of top level DNS servers. In: Proceedings of the International conference on Passive and Active Measurements, pp. 145–154. PAM, March 2013
30. Linux Foundation: networking:iproute2 [Wiki], March 2021. https://wiki.linuxfoundation.org/networking/iproute2
31. Andzinski, M.: Passive analysis of DNS server reachability, June 2019. https://centr.org/library/library/centr-event/rd14-andzinski-passive-analysis-of-dns-server-reachability-20190529.html
32. Andzinski, M.: Passive analysis of DNS server reachability, November 2019. https://www.nic.cz/files/nic/IT_19/prezentace/12_andzinski.pdf
33. McPherson, D., Oran, D., Thaler, D., Osterweil, E.: Architectural Considerations of IP Anycast. RFC 7094, IETF, January 2014
34. McQuistin, S., Uppu, S.P., Flores, M.: Taming anycast in the wild internet. In: Proceedings of the Internet Measurement Conference, IMC 2019, pp. 165–178. Association for Computing Machinery, New York (2019). https://doi.org/10.1145/3355369.3355573
35. Mockapetris, P.: Domain names - implementation and specification. RFC 1035, IETF, November 1987
36. Moura, G.C.M., Müller, M., Wullink, M., Hesselman, C.: nDEWS: a new domains early warning system for TLDs. In: NOMS 2016–2016 IEEE/IFIP Network Operations and Management Symposium, pp. 1061–1066 (2016)
37. Moura, G.C.M.: Anteater, March 2021. https://github.com/SIDN/anteater
38. Moura, G.C.M., Castro, S., Hardaker, W., Hesselman, C.: Clouding up the internet: how centralized is DNS traffic becoming? In: Proceedings of the ACM Internet Measurement Conference, p. to appear. ACM, Virtual Conference, October 2020
39. Moura, G.C.M., Heidemann, J., Hardaker, W., Bulten, J., Ceron, J., Hesselman, C.: Old but gold: prospecting TCP to engineer DNS anycast (extended). Technical report ISI-TR-739, USC/Information Sciences Institute, June 2020. https://www.isi.edu/. Accessed April 2021

40. Moura, G.C.M., Heidemann, J., de O. Schmidt, R., Hardaker, W.: Cache me if you can: effects of DNS time-to-live (extended). In: Proceedings of the ACM Internet Measurement Conference. p. to appear. ACM, Amsterdam, the Netherlands, October 2019

41. Moura, G.C.M., Müller, M., Davids, M., Wullink, M., Hesselman, C.: Fragmentation, truncation, and timeouts: are large DNS messages falling to bits? In: Hohlfeld, O., Lutu, A., Levin, D. (eds.) PAM 2021. LNCS, vol. 12671, pp. 460–477. Springer, Cham (2021). https://doi.org/10.1007/978-3-030-72582-2_27

42. Moura, G.C.M., et al.: Anycast vs. DDoS: evaluating the November 2015 root DNS event. In: Proceedings of the ACM Internet Measurement Conference, pp. 255–270. ACM, Santa Monica, November 2016

43. Müller, M., Moura, G.C.M., de O. Schmidt, R., Heidemann, J.: Recursives in the wild: engineering authoritative DNS servers. In: Proceedings of the ACM Internet Measurement Conference, pp. 489–495. ACM, London (2017)

44. Müller, M., Moura, G.C.M., de O. Schmidt, R., Heidemann, J.: Recursives in the wild: engineering authoritative DNS servers. Technical report ISI-TR-720, USC/Information Sciences Institute, September 2017

45. Nanda, P., Simmonds, A.: A scalable architecture supporting qos guarantees using traffic engineering and policy based routing in the internet. Int. J. Commun. Netw. Syst. Sci. (2009)

46. Narten, T., Draves, R., Krishnan, S.: Privacy extensions for stateless address autoconfiguration in IPv6. RFC 4941, IETF, September 2007

47. Partridge, C., Mendez, T., Milliken, W.: Host anycasting service. RFC 1546, IETF, November 1993

48. Pujol, E., Poese, I., Zerwas, J., Smaragdakis, G., Feldmann, A.: Steering hypergiants' traffic at scale. In: Proceedings of the 15th International Conference on Emerging Networking Experiments and Technologies, pp. 82–95 (2019)

49. Quoitin, B., Pelsser, C., Bonaventure, O., Uhlig, S.: A performance evaluation of BGP-based traffic engineering. Int. J. Netw. Manage. **15**(3), 177–191 (2005)

50. RIPE NCC: RIPE Atlas measurement IDS, December 2019. https://atlas.ripe.net/measurements/ID. Where ID is the experiment ID: kroot-udp: 10311, kroot-tcp: 26995926, lroot-udp: 10308, lroot-tcp:26995949, GoDNS-21: 23859473, GoTrace-21: 23859475 GoDNS-22: 23863904, GoTrace-22: 23863901, Comcast V6: 24269572, ComcastV6-afterReport: 24867517, ChinaNetV6: 24257938, DNS/TCP:22034303, DNS/UDP: 22034324

51. RIPE NCC: RIPE atlas probes, May 2020. https://ftp.ripe.net/ripe/atlas/probes/archive/2020/05/

52. RIPE Ncc Staff: RIPE atlas: a global internet measurement network. Internet Protocol J. (IPJ) **18**(3), 2–26 (2015)

53. RIPE Network Coordination Centre: RIPE Atlas (2015). https://atlas.ripe.net

54. RIPE Network Coordination Centre: RIPE - Routing Information Service (RIS) (2020). https://www.ripe.net/analyse/internet-measurements/routing-information-service-ris

55. Root Server Operators: Events of 2015–11–30, November 2015. http://root-servers.org/news/events-of-20151130.txt

56. Root Server Operators: Root DNS, November 2019. http://root-servers.org/

57. Schlinker, B., Cunha, I., Chiu, Y.C., Sundaresan, S., Katz-Bassett, E.: Internet performance from Facebook's edge. In: Proceedings of the Internet Measurement Conference, IMC 2019, pp. 179–194. ACM, New York (2019)

58. Schlinker, B., et al.: Engineering egress with edge fabric: steering oceans of content to the world. In: Proceedings of the ACM SIGCOMM Conference, pp. 418–431. ACM, Los Angeles, August 2017

59. de Oliveira Schmidt, R., Heidemann, J., Kuipers, J.H.: Anycast latency: how many sites are enough? In: Kaafar, M.A., Uhlig, S., Amann, J. (eds.) PAM 2017. LNCS, vol. 10176, pp. 188–200. Springer, Cham (2017). https://doi.org/10.1007/978-3-319-54328-4_14, https://www.isi.edu/

60. Shvachko, K., Kuang, H., Radia, S., Chansler, R.: The hadoop distributed file system. In: 2010 IEEE 26th Symposium on Mass Storage Systems and Technologies (MSST), pp. 1–10. IEEE (2010)

61. SIDN Labs: ENTRADA - DNS Big Data Analytics, January 2020. https://entrada.sidnlabs.nl/

62. SIDN Labs: .nl stats and data, August 2020. http://stats.sidnlabs.nl

63. Singla, A., Chandrasekaran, B., Godfrey, P.B., Maggs, B.: The internet at the speed of light. In: Proceedings of ACM Hotnets. ACM, Los Angeles, October 2014. http://conferences.sigcomm.org/hotnets/2014/papers/hotnets-XIII-final111.pdf

64. Sommese, R., et al.: Manycast2: using anycast to measure anycast. In: Proceedings of the ACM Internet Measurement Conference, IMC 2020, pp. 456–463. Association for Computing Machinery, New York (2020)

65. Souders, S.: High-performance web sites. Commun. ACM **51**(12), 36–41 (2008)

66. Vixie, P.: Response rate limiting in the domain name system (DNS RRL), June 2012. http://www.redbarn.org/dns/ratelimits, http://www.redbarn.org/dns/ratelimits

67. Wabeke, T., Moura, G.C.M., Franken, N., Hesselman, C.: Counterfighting counterfeit: detecting and taking down fraudulent webshops at a ccTLD. In: Sperotto, A., Dainotti, A., Stiller, B. (eds.) PAM 2020. LNCS, vol. 12048, pp. 158–174. Springer, Cham (2020). https://doi.org/10.1007/978-3-030-44081-7_10

68. Wei, L., Flores, M., Bedi, H., Heidemann, J.: Bidirectional anycast/unicast probing (BAUP): optimizing CDN anycast. In: Proceedings of the IEEE Network Traffic Monitoring and Analysis Conference, IFIP, Berlin, June 2020. https://www.isi.edu/

69. Wessels, D.: RSSAC002-data, May 2020. https://github.com/rssac-caucus/RSSAC002-data/

70. Wullink, M., Moura, G.C., Müller, M., Hesselman, C.: ENTRADA: a high-performance network traffic data streaming warehouse. In: 2016 IEEE/IFIP Network Operations and Management Symposium (NOMS), pp. 913–918. IEEE, April 2016

71. Yu, Y., Wessels, D., Larson, M., Zhang, L.: Authority server selection in DNS caching resolvers. SIGCOMM Comput. Commun. Rev. **42**(2), 80–86 (2012)

72. Zhu, L., Hu, Z., Heidemann, J., Wessels, D., Mankin, A., Somaiya, N.: Connection-oriented DNS to improve privacy and security. In: Proceedings of the 36th IEEE Symposium on Security and Privacy, pp. 171–186. IEEE, San Jose, May 2015. https://www.isi.edu/

73. Zhu, P., et al.: Characterizing transnational internet performance and the great bottleneck of China. Proc. ACM Meas. Anal. Comput. Syst. **4**(1), 1–23 (2020). https://doi.org/10.1145/3379479

A Matter of Degree: Characterizing the Amplification Power of Open DNS Resolvers

Ramin Yazdani[✉], Roland van Rijswijk-Deij, Mattijs Jonker,
and Anna Sperotto

Faculty of Electrical Engineering, Mathematics and Computer Science,
University of Twente, Enschede, The Netherlands
{r.yazdani,r.m.vanrijswijk,m.jonker,a.sperotto}@utwente.nl

Abstract. Open DNS resolvers are widely misused to bring about reflection and amplification DDoS attacks. Indiscriminate efforts to address the issue and take down all resolvers have not fully resolved the problem, and millions of open resolvers still remain available to date, providing attackers with enough options. This brings forward the question if we should not instead focus on eradicating the most problematic resolvers, rather than all open resolvers indiscriminately. Contrary to existing studies, which focus on quantifying the existence of open resolvers, this paper focuses on infrastructure diversity and aims at characterizing open resolvers in terms of their ability to bring about varying attack strengths. Such a characterization brings nuances to the problem of open resolvers and their role in amplification attacks, as it allows for more problematic resolvers to be identified. Our findings show that the population of open resolvers lies above 2.6M range over our one-year measurement period. On the positive side, we observe that the majority of identified open resolvers cut out when dealing with bulky and DNSSEC-related queries, thereby limiting their potential as amplifiers. We show, for example, that 59% of open resolvers lack DNSSEC support. On the downside, we see that a non-negligible number of open resolvers facilitate large responses to `ANY` and `TXT` queries (8.1% and 3.4% on average, respectively), which stands to benefit attackers. Finally we show that by removing around 20% of potent resolvers the global DNS amplification potential can be reduced by up to 80%.

Keywords: DDoS · Reflection and amplification · DNS · Open resolvers

1 Introduction

Distributed Denial of Service (DDoS) attacks are one of the common means for causing disruption on today's Internet. In DDoS attacks, the attacker typically leverages a large number of nodes on the Internet to exhaust the resources of a target network or host. In case of a Reflection & Amplification (R&A)

O. Hohlfeld et al. (Eds.): PAM 2022, LNCS 13210, pp. 293–318, 2022.
https://doi.org/10.1007/978-3-030-98785-5_13

DDoS attack [35], the attacker issues specifically crafted requests with a spoofed source IP address to cause (unaware) servers to send large responses to the victim. R&A attacks are made possible by the existence of connection-less networking protocols such as Domain Name System (DNS) [25], Network Time Protocol (NTP) [36], and Connectionless Lightweight Directory Access Protocol (CLDAP). In September 2017, for example, the largest reported DDoS attack to date targeted thousands of IPs of Google with a traffic rate of 2.5 Tbps [1]. This was a R&A DDoS attack using a combination of DNS, CLDAP and Simple Network Management Protocol (SNMP) servers.

Open DNS resolvers, that is DNS resolvers configured to respond to requests from any address on the Internet, have been widely misused to bring about R&A attacks. Evidently, the potential strength of an attack depends on the number of resolvers misused in the attack. We argue, however, that there are more aspects that contribute to attack potential. Namely, the configuration of a resolver can affect the effective size of responses, i.e., it factors into attack strength. Existing research [19] has revealed that specific DNS query types such as ANY and TXT have been misused more frequently in real world DDoS attacks. However, an Internet-wide and detailed study of the effect of the resolver internal configuration on response amplification has not been investigated and is not yet well understood.

Contrary to existing studies, which focus on quantifying the existence of open resolvers, our paper focuses on infrastructure diversity and aims at characterizing resolvers in terms of their ability to bring about varying attack strengths. The contribution of this paper is twofold. First, we identify the main factors that determine the potential attack strength and link these factors to the internal configuration of a resolver. Second, we perform a measurement-based, Internet-wide characterization of open resolvers to quantify which of the determining factors are prevalent in the wild. This mapping stands to help network operators and the network security community by enabling them focus on more powerful reflectors first.

The remainder of this paper is organized as follows. We discuss related work in Sect. 2. In Sect. 3 we identify and explain the factors that determine attack potential. We introduce our methodology for Internet-wide characterization in Sect. 4. The results of our measurement are then presented in Sect. 5. Finally, we conclude in Sect. 6.

2 Related Work

Several studies have investigated open DNS resolvers. Kührer et al. [24] classify open DNS resolvers based on the authenticity of their responses and the software that these resolvers are running. Similarly, [32] investigates open DNS resolvers that respond with incorrect answers. A classification of amplifiers based on hardware, architecture and operating system is provided in [25]. Our paper differs from these studies. We are not concerned about how legitimate the responses returned by open resolvers are or in purely profiling the software behind them, but rather in characterizing the amplification power that these resolvers stand to provide, when misused, to bring about R&A attacks.

Rijwsijk et al. studied the impact of DNSSEC support on providing higher DDoS amplification power at the authoritative nameserver side [34]. The authors show that DNSSEC support significantly increases the amplification power of a domain name. We extend this research by investigating DNSSEC support at the open DNS resolver side as a key aspect of R&A attacks. Moura et al. [30] conducted a study to measure the problem of large UDP DNS responses. The authors analyze DNS queries and responses at the authoritative name servers of the .nl ccTLD and show that large DNS responses and server-side IP-fragmentation are rare. Our research differs from this work in a couple of aspects. We focus on open DNS resolvers as they provide a misuse potential for DDoS attacks. Besides, we explore query patterns that result in large response sizes rather than generic queries issued by real clients on the Internet.

Moon et al. [29] developed a service called AmpMap to quantify the amplification risk of six UDP-based protocols, using a budget of 1.5 k queries per server in their study. As it is not feasible to apply this method to all existing open resolvers without causing disturbance, the authors limited their measurement to 10 k DNS resolvers. In addition, ten popular domains were used in their queries. Our study differs both in scope as well as in approach. We target the entire open resolver population and in our setup we observe both the DNS query generation point as well as the authoritative nameserver.

Jiang et al. [21] investigated the caching behavior of over 19 k open resolvers when a revoked (ghost) domain is queried. We explore caching pattern of open resolvers from a different angle as our aim is to determine whether or not an open resolver is capable of evading the rate limiting mechanisms when resolving frequent queries for a domain name.

Nawrocki et al. [31] studied the behavior of attackers in terms of which sets of open DNS resolvers they misuse in attacks. Their results show that attackers efficiently detect new resolvers and steadily rotate between them. The authors link the behavior to the fact that resolvers disappear, either because they change away from open status, or because they are subject to IP address churn (e.g., home routers). Our work focuses on configuration aspects of open resolvers that could factor into decision-making processes.

Open DNS resolvers also exist in IPv6 address space. Hendriks et al. [20] explored the potential provided by open resolvers running on IPv6 addresses. Our methodology can be further extended to characterize open resolvers running in IPv6 address space. We leave this as a future work.

Lack of destination side source address validation results in hosts behind a firewall to become partially accessible to externals leveraging source IP address spoofing [16, 22]. DNS resolvers residing in such networks are known to be vulnerable to DNS cache poisoning attacks, but can also be misused in DDoS attacks. Our study focuses on open DNS resolvers and thus we do not cover resolvers accessible through IP address spoofing.

Finally, an important consideration is that the bandwidth of open resolvers plays an important role in determining amplification power. Leverett et al.

studied the impact of bandwith availability in DDoS attacks [27]. Our study focuses specifically on characterizing the internal configuration of resolvers and the associated, thus far not studied effects on amplification potential.

3   Factors that Determine Attack Potential

Our measurement-based characterization in Sect. 5 will show that there are millions of open resolvers on the Internet, corroborating earlier findings in the literature. This is problematic as it gives attackers plenty of choices for performing DNS-based R&A. However, our intuition is that not every open resolver is likely to be equally effective as amplifier. The amplification capabilities of a resolver depend on a number of factors. In this section we analyze typical DNS configurations and highlight how those have an impact on amplification. We focus on support of specific DNS protocol features, handling of ANY queries, caching behavior and TCP support.

3.1   Support for DNS Protocol Features

In the original DNS specification [28], DNS messages over UDP are limited to a maximum of 512 bytes, putting a cap on the amplification potential of 'classic' DNS. This means that open resolvers that only support classic DNS are moderate amplifiers at best. The Extension Mechanisms for DNS (EDNS0) were introduced in 1999 [15]. The goal of EDNS0 was to overcome a number of limitations in the existing DNS protocol that were hampering the development of new functionality. Support for DNS messages over UDP of more than 512 bytes is one of the features of EDNS0. Thus, if an open resolver supports EDNS0 it can be a much more potent amplifier. How potent depends on the specifics of the configuration and implementation of EDNS0. Algorithm 1 shows the possible variants of the DNS and EDNS0 implementation.

In an EDNS0 exchange, the client sending the query can specify the maximum DNS message size it is willing to receive over UDP ($client_{max_{UDP}}$). As the function GETEDNS0RESPONSE (line 11) shows, the server has two implementation options. It can impose its own maximum UDP message size limit and apply that to the response (*variant a*), or it can only use the client's value from the query (*variant b*). If the response size exceeds the maximum response size over UDP, the response will be truncated. Here, there are two implementation options, as the TRUNCATERESPONSE procedure (line 1) shows. In *variant 1*, the server truncates to a small response, that either contains no data or a minimal number of resource records (RRset), such that the response is correct and passes DNSSEC validation. In terms of putting a cap on amplification, this is the most favorable option. In *variant 2*, the truncated response is filled with RRsets from the original response until the maximum UDP response size is about to be exceeded. In terms of amplification, this is the worst option.

The original DNS specification also lacks critical security features, which makes the protocol vulnerable to so-called cache poisoning attacks. The DNS

Algorithm 1. EDNS0 code variants

1: **procedure** TRUNCATERESPONSE($response, max_{UDP}$)
2:   *variant_1*:
3:   ▷ Find minimal RRset TC_{min}
4:     **return** TC_{min}
5:   *variant_2*:
6:     **for all** $RRset \in response$ **do**
7:         **if** $|TC_{resp} \cup answer| > max_{UDP}$ **then**
8:             **return** TC_{resp}
9:         **else**
10:              $TC_{resp} \leftarrow TC_{resp} \cup answer$
11: **function** GETEDNS0RESPONSE(response)
12:   *variant_a*:
13:     $max_{UDP} \leftarrow min(client_{max_{UDP}}, server_{max_{UDP}})$
14:   *variant_b*:
15:     $max_{UDP} \leftarrow client_{max_{UDP}}$
16:
17:     **if** $|response| \leq max_{UDP}$ **then return** $response$
18:   **else**
19:         **return** TruncateResponse($response, max_{UDP}$)

Security Extensions [10–12] address this vulnerability. It is known from the literature [34] that DNSSEC can be abused in amplification attacks. This is because DNSSEC responses are generally larger than unsigned DNS responses, as they include digital signatures and – depending on the message type – public key material. Reports of DDoS attacks in the news suggest that attackers increasingly use DNSSEC-signed domains in amplification attacks [14]. This is supported by observations using DDoS honeypots [23] as well as in a recent work that studies R&A attacks using IXP traces [31]. Whether or not an open resolver supports DNSSEC is thus a factor that influences its usability for amplification from an attacker's point of view. Clients can signal to a nameserver that they wish to receive DNSSEC data by setting the DNSSEC OK flag (DO) in an EDNS0 query. Resolvers can have three levels of DNSSEC support:

   i. *No DNSSEC support* – the resolver does not return DNSSEC-specific record types at all;
  ii. *Pass-through of DNSSEC-specific records* – the resolver returns DNSSEC-specific record types returned by upstream resolvers or authoritative nameservers, but does not set the DO flag in queries to upstream servers;
 iii. *DNSSEC fully supported* – the resolver returns DNSSEC-specific record types and sets the DO flag in queries to upstream servers.

The difference between the latter two forms of DNSSEC support is subtle, yet important. In the pass-through case, responses will typically not include signatures. If an attack uses a DNSSEC-specific record type, such as DNSKEY, this affects amplification. Open resolvers with full DNSSEC support will return a significantly larger response to such a query because they will include the signatures.

The final protocol feature we need to consider is processing of the optional *authority* and *additional* sections in a DNS response. According to the original DNS specification [28], a DNS response contains three sections: answer, authority and additional. The *authority* section contains records that point to an authoritative nameserver for the domain. This optional section – when included in a response – typically contains the NS records listing (part of) the authoritative nameservers for a domain. The *additional* section contains additional information related to the query, such as the A and AAAA records for nameservers listed in the authority section. Whether or not an open resolver includes the two optional sections in a response affects the amplification potential of that resolver, since responses will be larger if either one or both of these sections is included. If a domain is DNSSEC-signed, the authority and additional section may also include signatures. There are three implementation options regarding the optional authority and additional sections:

i *Minimal responses* – the resolver only returns the authority and/or additional section if required by the DNS specification (i.e. in a NO DATA or REFERRAL response);
ii *Pass-through* – the resolver includes authority and additional sections only if these are returned by an upstream nameserver in response to a query from the resolver;
iii *Active synthesis* – the resolver attempts to populate the authority and additional sections based on information it already has in its cache for the domain being queried.

Table 1 summarizes the impact of the DNS protocol features on amplification as just discussed. The right-hand column gives an intuition about the impact of the specific feature on amplification potential. Negative signs indicate that this variant of the feature makes an open resolver less potent as amplifier, positive signs indicate the opposite.

3.2 Handling of ANY Queries

The next factor that affects the amplification potential of a resolver is how it handles the so-called ANY query type. An ANY query signals to a resolver or authoritative nameserver that the sender wishes to receive all records pertaining to the name in the query. As a result, any record that exists in a zone, such as IP address records (A and AAAA) and TXT records (containing, e.g., domain verification tokens) are requested *at once*. Responses to ANY queries are therefore potentially the largest possible DNS response for a name. Because of this, ANY queries are frequently used for amplification attacks [37]. On the side of the DNS resolver, an ANY can be dealt with in three ways:

Table 1. Impact of protocol features on amplification

DNS protocol version

Short ID	Description	Impact
P1-classic-only	The open resolver only supports the classic DNS protocol [28]	−−
P2-EDNS0-server-lim	The open resolver supports EDNS0; it imposes its own maximum size on UDP messages	+
P3-EDNS0-client-lim	The open resolver supports EDNS0; it returns responses up to the maximum size requested by the client	++

Message truncation

Short ID	Description	Impact
TC1-minimal	Truncation is done to a minimal size (e.g. no data at all or a single RRset)	−−
TC2-maxfill	Truncated responses are filled up to the maximum UDP message size (as set for EDNS0 responses), by adding RRsets until adding another RRset would exceed the maximum UDP message size.	++

DNSSEC support

Short ID	Description	Impact
SEC1-DNSSEC-no	DNSSEC is not supported and DNSSEC-specific record types are not returned	−−
SEC2-DNSSEC-passthru	DNSSEC is not supported, but DNSSEC-specific record types are returned if included in a response from an upstream server	+
SEC3-DNSSEC-support	DNSSEC is supported, DNSSEC-specific record types are returned and the DO flag is set in queries to upstream servers	++

Authority and additional section processing

Short ID	Description	Impact
AA1-no	The authority and additional sections are not returned to queries, unless required	−
AA2-passthru	The authority and additional sections are returned if and as present in responses from upstream servers	=
AA3-synthesize	The authority and additional sections are actively synthesized based on data in the resolver's cache	+

i *Refuse or restrict type* ANY *queries* – this is uncommon at present, but we expect the number of DNS resolvers that exhibit this behavior to increase as standardized in RFC 8482 [9].

ii *Return whatever is cached for the query name* – the resolver returns whatever records it has cached for the query name. If it has no cached information, it forwards the query to an upstream resolver or authoritative nameserver and returns whatever response these give to the ANY query;

iii *Return a full* ANY *response* – the resolver returns a full ANY response, either from its cache, or, if not in the cache, from the response to a follow-up query to an upstream resolver or authoritative nameserver (which the resolver then also caches).

The latter two options entail that the open resolver can return potentially large responses to ANY queries. This is not guaranteed, however. Both options have advantages as well as disadvantages for attackers. Option ii may return a smaller response if the open resolver already has cached information for the

Table 2. Impact of implementation choices for handling `ANY` queries

Short ID	Description	Impact
`ANY1-refuse`	The open resolver refuses `ANY` queries or returns a minimal response.	− −
`ANY2-return-cached`	The open resolver returns whatever it has in its cache for the queried name.	+
`ANY3-any-upstream`	The open resolver sends the `ANY` query upstream and returns whatever the authoritative nameserver responds with.	+

queried name. An attacker, however, can also prime such a resolver, by sending it one or more queries for the query name used in an attack to pre-populate the cache. Resolvers that follow implementation option iii will always return the largest possible response to an `ANY` query, provided that the authoritative nameserver also returns a full response to an `ANY` query.

Table 2 summarizes the implementation choices for `ANY` query handling. The columns are similar to Table 1.

3.3 Caching

The third major factor that affects the potential of an open resolver as amplifier is whether or not the resolver has its own cache and how this cache is implemented. If the resolver caches responses, it will typically only interact with the authoritative nameserver for the domain abused in an amplification attack infrequently. This means that any form of mitigation, such as Response Rate Limiting [39] at the authoritative nameserver, is likely to be ineffective. This is an advantage for an attacker seeking to misuse the resolver.

A second aspect to consider if the resolver has a cache is for how long the resolver caches responses from authoritative nameservers to `ANY` queries. One particular option that, e.g., the popular open source resolver Unbound[1] supports, is to use the minimum of the TTLs observed in the records received in the `ANY` response from the authoritative. This is of particular interest in case, for attack purposes, a DNSSEC-signed domain is used that, in turn, uses `NSEC3` [26] for authenticated denial-of-existence. The zone of such a domain will contain a so-called `NSEC3PARAM` metadata record that stores parameters specific to the `NSEC3` mechanism. This metadata record has a TTL of 0 by default. Consequentially, a resolver receiving an `NSEC3PARAM` record as part of an `ANY` responses may decide not to cache at all. This makes such a resolver a much less effective amplifier because of the previously explained effect of resolver caching on the response rate.

Table 3 summarizes the implementation options with respect to caching and indicates their effect on the amplification potential of a resolver.

---

[1] http://unbound.net/.

Table 3. Impact of cache implementation choices

Short ID	Description	Impact
cache1-none	The open resolver does not have a cache.	−−
cache2-ANY-minTTL	The open resolver has a cache but does not cache ANY responses with one or more records with a TTL of 0 seconds.	=
cache3-caches	The open resolver has a cache and also caches ANY responses with one or more records with a TTL of 0 seconds.	++

Table 4. Impact of TCP support

Short ID	Description	Impact
TCP1-no	The open resolver does not support TCP fallback when sending queries to upstream servers.	−−
TCP2-yes	The open resolver supports TCP fallback for queries to upstream servers.	+

3.4 TCP Support

The final characteristic that we consider is whether or not the open resolver supports TCP fallback to upstream resolvers or authoritative nameservers. If an upstream nameserver receives a query from the open resolver that it is unable or unwilling to answer over UDP, it will send back a truncated response (see also Sect. 3.1). This indicates to the initiator of the query (in this case the open resolver) that they should retry the query over TCP. If the open resolver does not support TCP fallback, this has two consequences. First, it limits the maximum size of responses it can return to the maximum size its upstreams are willing to send over UDP. Second, it means that forced truncation of queries such as ANY by upstream servers can be used as a mitigation mechanism to make the open resolver an ineffective amplifier. Table 4 shows the implications of TCP support.

4   Data Collection Methodology

In this section we present our data collection methodology and discuss the ethical considerations that we made towards our measurement design.

4.1 Scanning and Testing Open Resolvers

Our data collection methodology is based on two main steps: *open resolver identification* and *systematic testing of amplification power* (following the characteristics described in Sect. 3).

The *open resolver identification* step consists of scanning the entire IPv4 address space, randomly and on a weekly basis. For each contacted IP, our scan issues a DNS A query for a unique subdomain (by binding the IP address and the timestamp to the query name) of a domain under our own control. If we receive

Table 5. Queries issued in our *systematic testing of amplification power* step

#	Query Type	ENDS0 enabled	EDNS buffer size (B)	DO bit set	Amplification factor ($\times$)	Description
1	A	No	–	No	1.9	0-day churn investigation
2	A	Yes	4096	Yes	8.5	DNSSEC support test
3	ANY	No	–	No	2.4	Classic ANY
4	ANY	Yes	16384	No	32.4	EDNS0 enabled ANY
5	ANY	Yes	16384	Yes	38.0	EDNS0 and DO enabled ANY
6	ANY	Yes	16384	No	153.7	ANY with 12KB response size
7	TXT	No	–	No	2.3	Classic TXT
8	TXT	Yes	16384	No	24.8	EDNS0 enabled TXT
9	TXT	Yes	16384	Yes	31.4	EDNS0 and DO enabled TXT
10	TXT	Yes	16384	No	125.9	TXT with 11KB response size
11–13	2×A & ANY	No	–	No	1.9	A and ANY cache test
14,15	2×ANY	No	–	No	1.9	0–TTL response caching

the correct answer for the query – indicating that a full resolution process has taken place – we infer that IP address is an open resolver. Our scan utilizes the ZIterate [8] tool of the Zmap library [18] to create a random permutation of the IPv4 address space for each week in which we scan. We then rely on the MassDNS tool [4] to issue the unique subdomain queries to each IPv4 address.

The second step aims at checking the internal configuration of an open resolver. To derive logical and consistent results, we note that there is a time-critical dependency between the *open resolver identification* and the *systematic testing of amplification power* steps of our data collection methodology. Previous studies have revealed that there is considerable IP churn among open resolvers [24,25], which entails that any meaningful interaction with the open resolvers that we discover needs to happen as close as possible in time to the identifying scan. We therefore run the *systematic testing of amplification power* step on the same day as the *open resolver identification*.

For the second step we issue 15 queries to each identified open resolver. Note that our goal is not to come up with a complete list of patterns that cause high amplification factors [29]. We rather aim to investigate a limited number of known high amplification patterns and explore the extent to which such patterns are supported among open DNS resolvers. A summary of the queries is provided in Table 5. The corresponding typical amplification factor for each query in this table is derived by dividing the TCP/UDP message size of the response to that of the respective query. Note that these amplification factors are given to provide a sense of typical amplification power that each query causes. This can however differ based on the implementation of a recursive resolver and domain name in question.

We use unique queries, which means that none of the queries cause a cascading interference with the following queries, as the resolver will treat each query independently. To start, we repeat an A query (query #1) to verify that an open resolver identified in the first step of our methodology is still responsive (due to churn). Then we proceed with queries that provide answers to the following aspects. First, we focus on deriving DNSSEC support and EDNS0 buffer sizes. This is done by sending A queries with the EDNS0 flag enabled and an EDNS0 buffer size of 4096 bytes (query #2). Next, we focus on how resolvers handle ANY queries, as we have identified those as a critical factor for amplification. We do this by first testing for ANY query support with classic ANY queries (query #3), then with ANY queries with EDNS0 and DNSSEC enabled (queries #4 and #5). Finally, we test for ANY queries that trigger large responses (query #6). While ANY queries are deprecated and are likely to be increasingly blocked in the future, we argue that R&A attacks might shift towards domains with large TXT records [38] which, due to their variable length, can also result in sizable amplification. Therefore, we decided to also include queries to test how resolvers handle TXT records. Similar to ANY queries, we do this for classic TXT records (query #7), EDNS0 and DNSSEC enabled TXT queries (queries #8 and #9), and TXT queries with very large responses (query #10). For the queries with a large response size (queries #6 and #10) our authoritative nameserver responds with a truncated answer which would trigger the resolvers to retry using a TCP fallback. We then test if a resolver is a caching resolver by sending two consecutive A queries (queries #11 and #12) and checking if the resolver contacts our authoritative nameserver for both queries. This is followed by sending an ANY query (query #13) for the same domain name to investigate whether ANY queries with a cache entry for an A record are resolved using the cache. Finally we test how resolvers treat queries for a record with a zero TTL set on our authoritative nameserver. We do this by sending two identical ANY queries (queries #14 and #15). We use the dnspython library [2] to conduct the scans in this second step. Note that multiple of our queries result in responses which are larger than common path MTU sizes, which can lead to responses getting dropped rather than fragmented [13]. We do not investigate resolvers that fail to respond to us due to such limitations in the middle-boxes on the path because we consider this out-of-scope.

4.2   Ethical Considerations

We designed our methodology with the following aspects in mind. First, we want to minimize the number of queries per host and open resolver. For this reason, we run our scans on a weekly basis, with the exception of a short dedicated measurement to quantify churn (Sect. 5), which was done on a daily basis for open resolvers discovered during the *open resolver identification* phase. Second, we took care of distributing the scan randomly across the input space (by using ZIterate). This diffuses our queries sent towards a specific network over time and reduces bursts. We also offer additional information about our research and an opt-out mechanism. Finally, we use a specific query name in our scans that makes it easy for network operators to discover the purpose behind our scans. We have full control over the authoritative nameserver for the domain name that we use to measure. The PTR record of the IP address of our scanning host also points to a domain name on which we host an information page.

During the study period we received seven opt out requests for our scans. Two requests directly reached us using our contact info on the webpage of our project. The others were forwarded to us through our ISP. Two out of seven complaints did not respond to our request to provide us with the IP address ranges that they wished to be excluded from being scanned. For the remaining five we stopped further scanning.

One could argue that other projects that monitor the existence of open DNS resolvers exist and that they could be used as input for our data collection. While such projects do exists, and we initially did consider them as data providers. Projects such as the OpenResolverProject [5] and The Measurement Factory [6] have already stopped their measurements at the time of our study. There exist other projects which do not share their data set. Thus, we ultimately decided on running our own IPv4 open resolver scans. This is furthermore essential due to considerations such as keeping the amount of time between open resolver identification and systematic testing as short as possible, but also to address the unpredictability and difficulty of quantifying the effects of scanning from different vantage points.

5   Results

5.1   Open Resolvers over Time

Figure 1 shows the number of open DNS resolvers that correctly resolved our queried domain name over time. We observe the population of open resolvers to gradually decrease from roughly 3 millions at the start of our measurement period to roughly 2.6 millions towards the end. As a reference point we also include the numbers reported by the Shadowserver project. For dates with a missing data-point in the Shadowserver dataset we use the nearest data-point.[2] A substantial difference is initially noticed comparing our results to those published by the Shadowserver DNS scanning project: 38% more detected through our scans, on average. The Shadowserver project – as we infer from their webpage – considers a host to be a recursive DNS resolver only if the response is issued by the queried host. However, it has been shown [25] that a large body of DNS forwarders (roughly 800k hosts in our scans), due to potential misconfigurations, fail to correctly change the IP address in forwarded DNS queries. This results in answers being returned from non-contacted hosts and is the main source of difference between our results and the numbers reported by the Shadowserver project. Also the Shadowserver project has been running on a daily basis and for a longer period compared to our scans. This would increase the chance of networks asking to be excluded from their scans as well as more networks blocking the IP addresses of the scanning hosts. The vantage point of a measurement also has an impact on the visibility of hosts to the scanner. These differences have been investigated earlier for scanning other protocols such as HTTP(S) and

---

[2] The discontinuity seen on the plot for our scans on 2021-06-28 was the result of a one-day measurement failure.

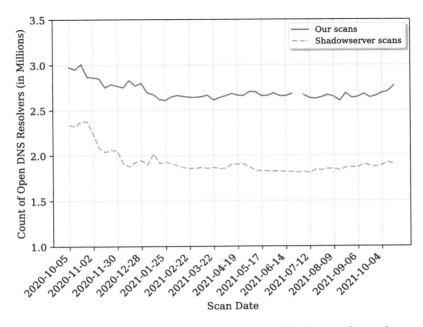

Fig. 1. Number of open resolvers over our study period that correctly resolve queries

SSH [17,40]. Scanner configuration parameters such as scanning rate and time of the day would also cause differences in measurement results. Since we don't have access to the raw data of the Shadowserver project, it is not possible for us to further investigate the potential sources of differences. Overall, a negative growth in the number of open resolvers is visible, which might be due to the efforts of researchers and operators in patching open DNS resolvers. Verifying this is, however, out of the scope of our paper.

Key Takeaway: Despite a decreasing trend, open resolvers still exist in the magnitude of millions.

5.2 IP Address Churn

A share of open resolvers become unresponsive after our initial discovery (i.e., on the same day still). This can be due to the IP address churn caused by DHCP lease of IP addresses as well as honeypot type hosts that apply rate limiting and do not respond to subsequent queries. We do not discern these two cases in this paper. However, we send extra probes at the beginning of our followup scans to quantify the percentage of hosts that are already no longer responsive. Previous studies have explored the churn of open DNS resolvers on a weekly scale [24,25]. In order to investigate this in a more fine-grained way, we sent daily queries to the open resolvers that correctly resolved our main scan query. According to [24], 52.2% of open resolvers disappear in the first week. Our results represent

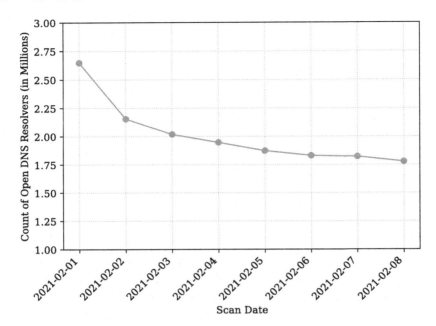

Fig. 2. Count of open resolvers discovered on 2021-02-01 which were still responsive on the consecutive days till 2021-02-08

a lower IP churn (32% of open resolvers are not responsive after a week, as seen in Fig. 2). This difference may be caused by the large reduction in the magnitude of open DNS resolvers in the time period between two studies. We observed a 19% IP churn one day after our main scan.

Key Takeaway: The IP churn rate of resolvers has significantly decreased compared to the previous studies. This could 'benefit' attackers, as their list of open resolvers to misuse needs to be renewed less frequently.

5.3   DNSSEC Support and Supported EDNS0 Buffer Sizes

To determine DNSSEC support by open resolvers, we sent, to the list of open resolvers collected during the main scan, A queries with EDNS0 enabled and DNSSEC OK (DO) bit set to 1. The EDNS0 buffer size of our queries was set to 4096 bytes. Based on the presence of an RRSIG record in the DNS response that we get back, we can infer DNSSEC support for each open resolver. On average 59% of open resolvers during the study period lack DNSSEC support (see Fig. 3). For open resolvers for which we inferred DNSSEC support, we have extracted the advertised EDNS0 buffer sizes that resolvers return to our scanner (see Table 6). 53.24% of resolvers advertise an EDNS0 buffer size of 512 bytes (also the default value for BIND DNS software which is one of the widely deployed DNS implementations). Although these open resolvers support

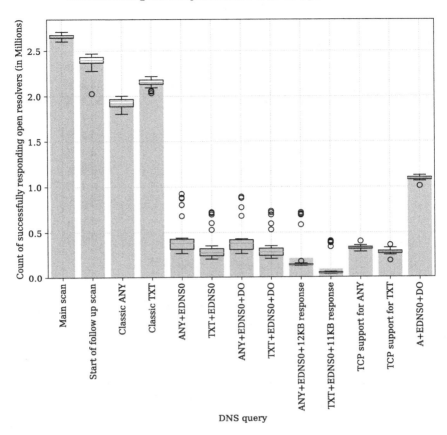

Fig. 3. Distribution of responsive open resolvers for each query category in the period of 2021-01-25 till 2021-10-11

DNSSEC, they only offer a limited amplification power. 30.31% of resolvers advertise a size of 4096 bytes which is the RFC recommended value [15]. This considerably large group of resolvers are potentially dangerous as they advertise to handle pretty large responses. Roughly 16% contribute to the next eight common values which cover a range of EDNS0 buffer sizes with the value of 8192 bytes standing out. Considering the way EDNS0 buffer sizes are negotiated between DNS clients and servers (as we discussed in Sect. 3), an attacker still needs to select authoritative nameservers that do not impose a limit on EDNS0 buffer support to be able to leverage this feature.

Key Takeaway: A large group of open resolvers lack DNSSEC support. This stands to substantially limit attackers when misusing DNSSEC.

Table 6. Average EDNS0 buffer size distribution between 2021-01-25 and 2021-10-04 (Top 10)

EDNS buffer size (B)	#Resolvers	Percentage
512	525.3k	53.24%
4096	299.0k	30.31%
4000	56.3k	5.71%
1232	54.8k	5.55%
1280	33.6k	3.41%
1220	8.7k	0.88%
8192	3.1k	0.31%
1224	2.5k	0.25%
1472	1.6k	0.16%
1460	0.6k	0.07%

5.4 ANY Query Handling

We used multiple variants of ANY queries to explore how open resolvers handle such query types. Our results show that roughly 72.6% of open resolvers successfully return an answer for a classic ANY query, for which the answer fits within a 512-byte packet. Only 16.2% of open resolvers successfully respond to EDNS0 enabled ANY queries (without the DO bit set). Setting the DO bit further decreases the resolution success to 15.9%. Finally, 8.1% of resolvers are capable of responding to an ANY query that has an answer of approximately 12 KB.

Key Takeaway: Only a limited number of open resolvers are capable of handling ANY queries with very large response sizes.

5.5 TXT Query Handling

Multiple TXT queries were sent to each open resolver to explore the consequences of changing various DNS protocol fields in the way open resolvers react to our queries. Our experiments reveal that on average approximately 80.9% of open resolvers during the study period successfully resolve a classic TXT query for which the answer fits a 512-byte packet. This is surprising as classic TXT queries have been part of the DNS standard from its beginning. We further observe that only 12.3% of open resolvers successfully respond to EDNS0 enabled TXT queries. Setting the DO bit doesn't have a noticeable impact in this case. Finally, only 3.4% of resolvers are capable of responding to a TXT query that has an answer of approximately 11 KB. Comparing the behavior of resolvers when dealing with TXT and ANY queries, we observe a higher success rate for classic TXT queries, while when it comes to EDNS0 enabled requests, ANY queries have a higher success rate.

Given the amplification potential of open resolvers supporting large TXT and ANY queries, we also investigate if these resolvers are concentrated in specific

Table 7. Distribution of resolvers at the start of followup scans on 2021-03-29 (Top 10) with the network type field categorized as: ISP (Fixed Line ISP), ISP/MOB (Dual service ISPs with fixed line and mobile), DCH (Data Center/Web Hosting/Transit), COM (Commercial), MOB (Mobile ISP), EDU (University/College/School), CDN (Content Delivery Network), SES (Search Engine Spider), ORG (Organization), GOV (Government)

| Network type | | AS distribution | |
Type	#Resolvers	ASN	#Resolvers
ISP	40.49%	AS4134	7.68%
ISP/MOB	33.97%	AS4837	5.10%
DCH	11.45%	AS4766	2.84%
COM	9.97%	AS45090	2.69%
MOB	1.83%	AS47331	2.40%
EDU	1.21%	AS5617	2.29%
CDN	0.33%	AS12389	1.67%
SES	0.29%	AS3462	1.53%
ORG	0.21%	AS209	1.36%
GOV	0.20%	AS9318	1.18%

Table 8. Distribution of resolvers successfully resolving a TXT query with a response size of 11 KB on 2021-03-29 (Top 10)

| Network type | | AS distribution | |
Type	#Resolvers	ASN	#Resolvers
ISP/MOB	58.51%	AS5617	32.29%
ISP	26.31%	AS4134	6.86%
DCH	8.11%	AS3462	2.17%
COM	4.71%	AS4766	1.33%
MOB	1.49%	AS131090	1.26%
EDU	0.39%	AS5384	1.24%
CDN	0.32%	AS56044	1.23%
GOV	0.07%	AS53006	1.01%
ORG	0.05%	AS3269	0.97%
SES	0.05%	AS37671	0.94%

Table 9. Distribution of resolvers successfully resolving an ANY query with a response size of 12 KB on 2021-03-29 (Top 10)

| Network type | | AS distribution | |
Type	#Resolvers	ASN	#Resolvers
ISP/MOB	41.59%	AS5617	14.51%
ISP	37.56%	AS12389	9.80%
DCH	8.68%	AS4134	7.00%
COM	5.17%	AS4538	2.56%
EDU	3.35%	AS4812	2.29%
MOB	2.87%	AS4837	1.82%
SES	0.28%	AS3462	1.28%
CDN	0.24%	AS6805	1.24%
GOV	0.12%	AS3352	0.85%
ORG	0.11%	AS9269	0.82%

networks/ASes. We use IP2Location data [3] to determine the network type of resolvers. Moreover, we use RouteViews data [7] to map resolver IP addresses to autonomous systems. Table 7 shows the distributions of mappings in the entire open resolvers set. Tables 8 and 9 show the distributions for resolvers that successfully resolve queries with large responses (i.e., the 12 kB ANY and 11 kB TXT cases, respectively). These resolvers appear to be concentrated in a couple of ASes, while type of the networks that they are located does not deviate too much from the distribution for the entire open resolvers set.

Key Takeaway: TXT queries have the potential to take over ANY based amplification. Although not all open resolvers are capable of handling TXT queries, due to the legitimate use cases of TXT records (e.g., to publish domain verification tokens), TXT-based amplifications could be harder to mitigate than ANY-based ones.

5.6   TCP Fallback

In Sect. 3 we discussed the implications of TCP support between open DNS resolvers and authoritative nameservers. To explore this we send TXT and ANY queries, to which our authoritative nameserver is set to respond with a truncated answer. We then investigate queries for which we see (followup) TCP DNS queries on our authoritative nameserver. Our results show that, on average, 10.7% of open resolvers over the study period fallback to TCP for TXT queries when the answer is truncated. For ANY queries, 12.4% of queries result in a TCP fallback, as shown in Fig. 3. These numbers are way lower than those reported by Moura et al. [30] (80% of TCP fallback in IPv4). We suspect the main reason behind this difference to be the resolver set under inspection. While we focus on open resolvers which typically are not well configured, their study investigates DNS queries arriving at the authoritative nameservers which are not necessarily issued by open resolvers.

Key Takeaway: While truncation can be used as a mechanism to avoid returning large DNS responses during attacks, there is a small yet non-negligible number of resolvers that can still be misused to bring about harm as they fall back to TCP.

5.7   Caching

A Query Caching. To test how A queries are cached, we sent two consecutive A queries to open resolvers. We then investigated whether open resolvers contact the authoritative nameserver under our control for these queries. 37.77% of open resolvers on 2021-03-29 contact our authoritative nameserver only once while correctly resolving the two queries. We infer the presence of cache for this group of resolvers. Note that this is a lower bound estimation for caching open resolvers due to the existence of complex caching implementations (e.g., in case of public DNS resolvers) [33].

Table 10. TTL values returned by resolvers for a zero-TTL response on 2021-03-29 (Top 10)

TTL	Count
0	1647.0k
60	74.9k
1	43.7k
30	34.1k
5	27.7k
300	14.8k
3600	8.7k
600	6.0k
59	2.7k
10	1.9k

Key Takeaway: The fact that majority of open resolvers do not respond from cache provides an opportunity to deploy response rate limiting on authoritative nameservers or upstream resolvers as a measure to dampen the impact of amplification attacks.

ANY Query Caching. We examined caching behavior for ANY queries in two different ways. Initially we sent an ANY query for the same domain name sent in the A query cache test of the previous step. We did this to investigate how ANY queries are handled when a potential response exists in the cache. Our analysis reveals that only 6.9% of open resolvers (also on 2021-03-29) rely on their cache to resolve such a query and others contact our authoritative nameserver.

We performed another test to explore how open resolvers deal with a zero TTL response. To this end, we sent two ANY queries for which our authoritative nameserver is configured to return a response with a TTL value of zero. 26.22% of open resolvers contact our authoritative nameserver only once in order to respond to these queries. Thus, we infer that these resolvers use their cache in order to respond such queries, despite the zero TTL value. As discussed in Sect. 3.3, this would make a large group of open resolvers less effective when there is a record with a 0-TTL set for a zone. In Table 10 we show the distribution of TTL values returned by these caching resolvers. 88% of resolvers return the TTL value of zero, as set on our authoritative nameserver for the domain name.

Key Takeaway: While resolvers might respond to ANY queries from their cache, the vast majority of them do recursive resolution to respond to these queries, which makes response rate limiting an effective measure to limit their amplification power when ANY queries are misused.

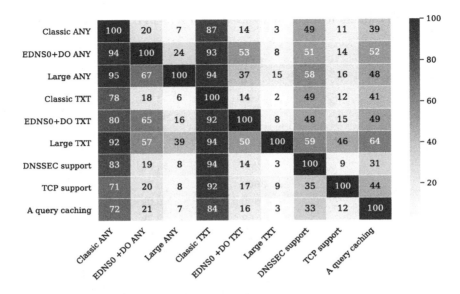

Fig. 4. Correlations between support for various DNS features on 2021-03-29

5.8   Feature Overlaps and Common Resolver Configurations

Now that we have experimented with all DNS features in question, we check which supported features mutually overlap among open resolvers that support them. We do this to get an initial insight into DNS protocol features that might be commonly supported together if we disregard all other features. A heatmap is given in Fig. 4. Each entry of this table represents the percentage of open resolver supporting the feature of the respective row as well as the corresponding column. At first glance, we see that the majority of open resolvers that support one of the features, also support Classic ANY and TXT queries. Note that the asymmetry seen in the table for mutual features is due to the difference in absolute number of open resolvers supporting each feature. For example, while 39% (roughly 21K out of 53K) of open resolvers that support large TXT queries also support large ANY queries, this fraction drops to only 15% (roughly 21K out of 140K) if we consider the reverse order. A similar pattern is seen when looking at EDNS0 enabled ANY and TXT queries with DO bit set. Surprisingly, this behavior is swapped when exploring classic ANY and TXT queries. In this case a larger portion of open resolvers that support classic ANY queries, also support classic TXT queries if we compare it to the reverse situation.

Open resolvers having similar software configurations, would intuitively exhibit similar behavior. To study common behaviors we group open resolvers that react similarly to our set of DNS queries in Table 5. To do so we use the set of features given in Table 11. Using these features, we put open resolvers with a common behavior (feature support) into the same group. We summarize 10

Table 11. Features considered for grouping open resolvers

Feature	Description
1	Resolver being still responsive at the start of the followup scans
2	Resolver responding to classic ANY queries
3	Resolver responding to EDNS0 enabled ANY queries
4	Resolver responding to EDNS0 enabled ANY queries with DO bit set
5	Resolver responding to EDNS0 enabled ANY queries with a large response
6	Resolver responding to classic TXT queries
7	Resolver responding to EDNS0 enabled TXT queries
8	Resolver responding to EDNS0 enabled TXT queries with DO bit set
9	Resolver responding to EDNS0 enabled TXT queries with a large response
10	Resolvers that support DNSSEC
11	Resolver that implement caching for A queries
12	Resolvers that fallback to TCP for TXT queries with a large response
13	Resolver that fallback to TCP for ANY queries with a large response

Table 12. Common groups of open resolvers (Top 10)

Group	Description	Count	Percentage
1	Resolver being still responsive at the start of the followup scans and support classic TXT and ANY queries and support DNSSEC	457.9k	17.3%
2	Resolver being still responsive at the start of the followup scans and support classic TXT and ANY queries	228.5k	8.7%
3	Resolver being still responsive at the start of the followup scans and support classic TXT and ANY queries and implement caching	227.0k	8.6%
4	Resolvers that disappear after our initial scan and are not responsive anymore	166.3k	6.3%
5	Resolver being still responsive at the start of the followup scans and implement caching	142.6k	5.4%
6	Resolver being still responsive at the start of the followup scans but do not support additional features	138.2k	5.2%
7	Resolver being still responsive at the start of the followup scans and support classic TXT and ANY queries, DNSSEC and implement caching	106.0k	4.0%
8	Resolver being still responsive at the start of the followup scans and support DNSSEC	78.7k	3.0%
9	Resolver being still responsive at the start of the followup scans and support classic TXT and ANY queries, implement caching and fallback to TCP for large ANY responses	44.8k	1.7%
10	Resolvers that disappear after our initial scan but are responsive to classic TXT and ANY queries later on	44.2k	1.7%

most common groups of resolvers in Table 12 which covers roughly 62% of open resolvers in our study.

Key Takeaway: The groups of open resolvers with the most common behavior offer a limited amplification factor and thus can be assigned a lower priority to be rooted out by operators.

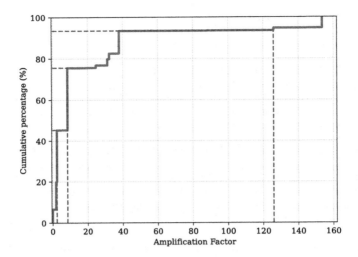

Fig. 5. Amplification factor CDF (considering relevant queries indexed in Fig. 4) for open resolvers on 2021-03-29

5.9 Ranking Open DNS Resolvers

As we have previously shown, each resolver reacts differently to amplification. To study the worst-case scenario, we assign to each open resolver the highest amplification factor that is supported by that specific resolver when responding to our set of queries (indexed in Table 5). This gives us an upper bound to the amplification potential for a given resolver. Figure 5 shows the CDF plot for supported amplification factors. We observe that roughly 6.5% of open resolvers offer an amplification factor of 125× or more. On the other hand, around 75% of open resolvers offer an amplification factor of 8.5× and a bit less than half of all open resolvers (45%) provide an amplification factor of only 2.4×. A non-negligible group of open resolvers (around 6%) do not respond to our followup queries, for which we assign an amplification factor of 0×. We are of course aware that these numbers depend on the configuration of the zone we set up for testing. However, we do not aim to present sharp borderlines on the amplification factor of open resolvers, but rather to differentiate among them.

We then proceed with ranking resolvers based on their highest amplification factor. At the basis of this study is the intuition that not all open resolvers will be equally potent in a DDoS attack. To quantify the usefulness of such a ranking, we group all open resolvers in our dataset based on their maximum amplification factor. We then calculate the maximum possible attack traffic contribution of each group of resolvers by multiplying the maximum amplification factor with the number of resolvers in that group. In Fig. 6 we derive the residual DNS amplification power if resolvers are rooted out, starting with the most powerful ones. Figure 6 shows that removing the top 6.5% of open resolvers halves the cumulative amplification power, while removing the top 25% of resolvers further

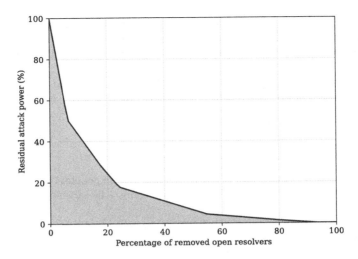

Fig. 6. Residual attack power when rooting out open resolvers based on their amplification rank

reduces the amplification power to only 18%. This confirms our initial intuition that not all resolvers are equally potent. Moreover, it clearly indicates that a priority-based strategy in open resolvers takedown could be very effective in taking the edge off of DNS-based R&A attacks.

Key Takeaway: The majority of open resolvers only offer limited amplification power, while a small group of resolvers is causing very large amplification. This creates an opportunity for operators to prioritize their efforts in discriminately eradicating open resolvers starting with the most-powerful ones.

6 Conclusion

To this day, DNS (R&A) attacks remain one of the most-used forms of DDoS attack. In this type of attack, misconfigured open DNS resolvers are misused to typically send large DNS responses to victims. Despite community efforts, going back well over a decade, to reduce the number of open DNS resolvers on the Internet, millions remain online and open today. This led us to ask: *are all open resolvers equal, in terms of how they can be abused for attacks, or can we identify traits of open DNS resolvers that make them more potent attack vectors?*

By using domain knowledge about how the DNS works, and what features can be misused in R&A attacks, we created a measurement setup that allows us to identify the attack potential of open resolvers. Our results show that – like many phenomena on the Internet – attack potential shows a long-tailed distribution, with a fraction of open resolvers responsible for the vast majority of the attack potential. With this outcome, operators can prioritise takedowns of open resolvers and focus on the most potent ones first. With the scarce time that they have, if they were to focus on just the 20% most potent amplifiers, they could reduce the Internet-wide attack potential by up to 80%, making it much more challenging for attackers to bring about crippling DNS R&A attacks.

Acknowledgments. We would like to thank the anonymous PAM reviewers for their valuable feedback on our paper. This research is funded by the EU H2020 projects CONCORDIA (#830927) and partially funded by SIDNfonds.

References

1. 2.5Tbps DDoS Attack on Google. https://cloud.google.com/blog/products/identity-security/identifying-and-protecting-against-the-largest-ddos-attacks. Accessed 11 Jan 2022
2. dnspython. https://www.dnspython.org/. Accessed 11 Jan 2022
3. IP2Location. https://www.ip2location.com/. Accessed 11 Jan 2022
4. MassDNS, A high-performance DNS stub resolver. https://github.com/blechschmidt/massdns. Accessed 11 Jan 2022
5. Open Resolver Project. https://web.archive.org/web/20200603050044/http://openresolverproject.org/. Accessed 11 Jan 2022
6. The Measurement Factory. http://dns.measurement-factory.com/surveys/openresolvers.html. Accessed 11 Jan 2022
7. University of Oregon Route Views Project. http://www.routeviews.org. Accessed 11 Jan 2022
8. ZIterate, ZMap IP permutation generator. https://github.com/zmap/zmap/blob/main/src/ziterate.1.ronn. Accessed 11 Jan 2022
9. Abley, J., Gumundsson, Ó., Majkowski, M., Hunt, E.: Providing minimal-sized responses to DNS queries that have QTYPE=ANY. RFC 8482, January 2019. https://doi.org/10.17487/RFC8482, https://rfc-editor.org/rfc/rfc8482.txt
10. Arends, R., Austein, R., Larson, M., Massey, D., Rose, S.: RFC 4033 - DNS security introduction and requirements (2005). http://tools.ietf.org/html/rfc4033
11. Arends, R., Austein, R., Larson, M., Massey, D., Rose, S.: RFC 4034 - resource records for the DNS security extensions (2005). http://tools.ietf.org/html/rfc4034
12. Arends, R., Austein, R., Larson, M., Massey, D., Rose, S.: RFC 4035 - protocol modifications for the DNS security extensions (2005). http://tools.ietf.org/html/rfc4035
13. Bonica, R., Baker, F., Huston, G., Hinden, R., Troan, O., Gont, F.: RFC 8900 - IP fragmentation considered fragile (2020). https://www.rfc-editor.org/info/rfc8900
14. Constantin, L.: Attackers use DNSSEC amplification to launch multi-vector DDoS attacks (2016). http://www.computerworld.com/article/3097364/security/attackers-use-dnssec-amplification-to-launch-multi-vector-ddos-attacks.html
15. Damas, J., Graff, M., Vixie, P.: RFC 6891 - extension mechanisms for DNS (EDNS(0)) (2013). http://tools.ietf.org/html/rfc6891
16. Deccio, C., Hilton, A., Briggs, M., Avery, T., Richardson, R.: Behind closed doors: a network tale of spoofing, intrusion, and false DNS security. In: Proceedings of the ACM SIGCOMM Internet Measurement Conference, IMC, pp. 65–77 (2020). https://doi.org/10.1145/3419394.3423649
17. Durumeric, Z., Bailey, M., Halderman, J.A.: An internet-wide view of internet-wide scanning. In: 23rd USENIX Security Symposium (USENIX Security 2014), pp. 65–78 (2014)

18. Durumeric, Z., Wustrow, E., Halderman, J.A.: ZMap: fast internet-wide scanning and its security applications. In: Proceedings of the 22nd USENIX Security Symposium, pp. 605–619 (2013)
19. Fachkha, C., Bou-Harb, E., Debbabi, M.: Fingerprinting internet DNS amplification DDoS activities. In: 2014 6th International Conference on New Technologies, Mobility and Security (NTMS), pp. 1–5. IEEE (2014)
20. Hendriks, L., de Oliveira Schmidt, R., van Rijswijk-Deij, R., Pras, A.: On the potential of IPv6 open resolvers for DDoS attacks. In: Kaafar, M.A., Uhlig, S., Amann, J. (eds.) PAM 2017. LNCS, vol. 10176, pp. 17–29. Springer, Cham (2017). https://doi.org/10.1007/978-3-319-54328-4_2
21. Jiang, J., Liang, J., Li, K., Li, J., Duan, H., Wu, J.: Ghost domain names: revoked yet still resolvable (2012)
22. Korczyński, M., Nosyk, Y., Lone, Q., Skwarek, M., Jonglez, B., Duda, A.: Don't forget to lock the front door! inferring the deployment of source address validation of inbound traffic. In: Sperotto, A., Dainotti, A., Stiller, B. (eds.) PAM 2020. LNCS, vol. 12048, pp. 107–121. Springer, Cham (2020). https://doi.org/10.1007/978-3-030-44081-7_7
23. Krämer, L., et al.: AmpPot: monitoring and defending against amplification DDoS attacks. In: Bos, H., Monrose, F., Blanc, G. (eds.) RAID 2015. LNCS, vol. 9404, pp. 615–636. Springer, Cham (2015). https://doi.org/10.1007/978-3-319-26362-5_28
24. Kührer, M., Hupperich, T., Bushart, J., Rossow, C., Holz, T.: Going wild - large-scale classification of open DNS resolvers. In: Proceedings of the 2015 ACM Internet Measurement Conference - IMC 2015, pp. 355–368. ACM Press, New York (2015). https://doi.org/10.1145/2815675.2815683, http://dl.acm.org/citation.cfm?doid=2815675.2815683
25. Kührer, M., Hupperich, T., Rossow, C., Holz, T.: Exit from hell? Reducing the impact of amplification DDoS attacks. In: 23rd USENIX Security Symposium (USENIX Security 2014), pp. 111–125 (2014)
26. Laurie, B., Sisson, G., Arends, R., Blacka, D.: RFC 5155 - DNS security (DNSSEC) hashed authenticated denial of existence (2008). http://tools.ietf.org/html/rfc5155
27. Leverett, E., Kaplan, A.: Towards estimating the untapped potential: a global malicious DDoS mean capacity estimate. J. Cyber Policy **2**(2), 195–208 (2017)
28. Mockapetris, P.: RFC 1035 - domain names - implementation and specification (1987). http://tools.ietf.org/html/rfc1035
29. Moon, S.J., Yin, Y., Sharma, R.A., Yuan, Y., Spring, J.M., Sekar, V.: Accurately measuring global risk of amplification attacks using AmpMap. Technical report, Technical report CMU-CyLab-19-004 (2020)
30. Moura, G.C.M., Müller, M., Davids, M., Wullink, M., Hesselman, C.: Fragmentation, truncation, and timeouts: are large DNS messages falling to bits? In: Hohlfeld, O., Lutu, A., Levin, D. (eds.) PAM 2021. LNCS, vol. 12671, pp. 460–477. Springer, Cham (2021). https://doi.org/10.1007/978-3-030-72582-2_27
31. Nawrocki, M., Jonker, M., Schmidt, T.C., Waehlisch, M.: The far side of DNS amplification: tracing the DDoS attack ecosystem from the internet core. In: Proceedings of the 2021 ACM Internet Measurement Conference (IMC 2021) (2021). https://doi.org/10.1145/3487552.3487835
32. Park, J., Khormali, A., Mohaisen, M., Mohaisen, A.: Where are you taking me? Behavioral analysis of open DNS resolvers. In: 2019 49th Annual IEEE/IFIP International Conference on Dependable Systems and Networks (DSN), pp. 493–504. IEEE (2019)

33. Randall, A., et al.: Trufflehunter: cache snooping rare domains at large public DNS resolvers. In: Proceedings of the ACM SIGCOMM Internet Measurement Conference, IMC, pp. 50–64 (2020). https://doi.org/10.1145/3419394.3423640

34. van Rijswijk-Deij, R., Sperotto, A., Pras, A.: DNSSEC and its potential for DDoS attacks. In: Proceedings of ACM IMC 2014. ACM Press, Vancouver (2014). https://doi.org/10.1145/2663716.2663731

35. Rossow, C.: Amplification hell: revisiting network protocols for DDoS abuse. In: Proceedings of the 2014 Network and Distributed Systems Security Symposium (NDSS 2014), no. February, pp. 23–26. Internet Society, San Diego (2014). http://www.internetsociety.org/sites/default/files/01_5.pdf

36. Rudman, L., Irwin, B.: Characterization and analysis of NTP amplification based DDoS attacks. In: 2015 Information Security for South Africa (ISSA), pp. 1–5. IEEE (2015)

37. Santanna, J.J., et al.: Booters - an analysis of DDoS-as-a-service attacks. In: 2015 IFIP/IEEE International Symposium on Integrated Network Management (IM), pp. 243–251. IEEE, Ottawa, May 2015. https://doi.org/10.1109/INM.2015.7140298

38. van der Toorn, O., Krupp, J., Jonker, M., van Rijswijk-Deij, R., Rossow, C., Sperotto, A.: ANYway: measuring the amplification DDoS potential of domains. In: 2021 17th International Conference on Network and Service Management (CNSM) (2021)

39. Vixie, P., Schryver, V.: DNS response rate limiting (DNS RRL). Technical report (2012). https://web.archive.org/web/20160307112057/, http://ss.vix.su/~vixie/isc-tn-2012-1.txt. Accessed 11 Jan 2022

40. Wan, G., et al.: On the origin of scanning: the impact of location on internet-wide scans. In: Proceedings of the ACM Internet Measurement Conference, pp. 662–679 (2020)

Routing II

IRR Hygiene in the RPKI Era

Ben Du[1]([✉]), Gautam Akiwate[1], Thomas Krenc[1], Cecilia Testart[2],
Alexander Marder[1], Bradley Huffaker[1], Alex C. Snoeren[1], and KC Claffy[1]

[1] CAIDA/UC San Diego, San Diego, USA
bendu@ucsd.edu, {gakiwate,snoeren}@cs.ucsd.edu,
{tkrenc,amarder,bhuffake,kc}@caida.org
[2] MIT, Cambridge, USA
ctestart@csail.mit.edu

Abstract. The Internet Route Registry (IRR) and Resource Public Key
Infrastructure (RPKI) both emerged as different solutions to improve
routing security in the Border Gateway Protocol (BGP) by allowing
networks to register information and develop route filters based on information other networks have registered. RPKI is a crypto system, with
associated complexity and policy challenges; it has seen substantial but
slowing adoption. IRR databases often contain inaccurate records due to
lack of validation standards. Given the widespread use of IRR for routing security purposes, this inaccuracy merits further study. We study
IRR accuracy by quantifying the consistency between IRR and RPKI
records, analyze the causes of inconsistency, and examine which ASes
are contributing correct IRR information. In October 2021, we found
ROAs for around 20% of RADB IRR records, and a consistency of 38%
and 60% in v4 and v6. For RIPE IRR, we found ROAs for 47% records
and a consistency of 73% and 82% in v4 and v6. For APNIC IRR, we
found ROAs for 76% records and a high consistency of 98% and 99% in
v4 and v6. For AFRINIC IRR, we found ROAs for only 4% records and
a consistency of 93% and 97% in v4 and v6.

1 Introduction

The Border Gateway Protocol (BGP) is the protocol that networks use to
exchange (announce) routing information across the Internet. Unfortunately,
the original BGP protocol lacked mechanisms for route authentication, allowing for unauthorized announcement of network addresses, also known as *prefix
hijacking* [25]. Prior to the adoption of security mechanisms like Resource Public
Key Infrastructure (RPKI), the primary means of protecting against unauthorized origin announcements was to register their routing information in public
databases and use these databases to verify route advertisements (for those networks with resources and incentive to do so). These databases, first deployed
by various organizations in 1990s, now are collectively known as the Internet
Routing Registry (IRR) [7]. However, the IRR depends on voluntary (although
sometimes contractually required) contribution of routing information. Moreover, many Internet Service Providers (ISPs) are reluctant to share their routing

O. Hohlfeld et al. (Eds.): PAM 2022, LNCS 13210, pp. 321–337, 2022.
https://doi.org/10.1007/978-3-030-98785-5_14

policies to avoid leaking sensitive business information [18,26]. Perhaps more critically, the IRR information is not strictly—and sometimefirs not at all—validated. As such, the accuracy of IRR information is not guaranteed [44].

While attempts to create variations of the IRR by adding validation mechanisms have been proposed none have ever gained traction [22,27]. After years of debate, a significant set of stakeholders including many ISPs agreed on an alternative to improving routing security known as the Resource Public Key Infrastructure (RPKI) [31]. RPKI tackles the data integrity problem by allowing networks to register their prefixes with their origin AS and using cryptography to authenticate these records, with each Regional Internet Registry (RIR) operating as a "root" of trust.

Similar to the IRR, operators can use RPKI to discard routing messages that do not pass origin validation checks. Although the RPKI deployment process is standardized and network equipment supports Route Origin Validation (ROV), additional challenges arise because of the configuration and operation of relying parties [28]. Furthermore, there are concerns that RPKI gives too much power to the RIRs [17,23,43], which combined with associated legal risks [43,48] and business concerns [46] hindered its adoption.

As of now, the IRR and RPKI operate in parallel. The routing security initiative known as Mutually Agreed Norms for Routing Security (MANRS) requires its participants to use either IRR or RPKI to facilitate routing security globally but does not enforce the requirement [3]. For example, Telia Carrier (recently rebranded to Arelion), a participant of MANRS, helps its customers keep their IRR records current, and drops all RPKI invalid routes [5]. Google also requires their peers and customers to register in an IRR database [4]. In addition, various large cloud service providers, Internet Service Providers (ISPs), and transit providers such as Cloudflare, Comcast, and Cogent have registered in RPKI and deployed RPKI-based filtering [15].

To reduce cost and complexity, networks may choose not to deploy RPKI filtering and continue using only existing IRR-based route filtering. However, IRR information may be inaccurate due to *improper hygiene*, since there is no penalty to the address space owner for not updating the origin information after changes in routing policy or prefix ownership [30]. Such inaccurate information limits the ability of networks to construct correct BGP route filters and, thus, compromises routing security.

Networks who decide to move to RPKI may not (continue to) keep their IRR records accurate, which means an increase in RPKI adoption can further increase inconsistency between IRR and RPKI, and therefore widen the gap between routing decisions based on IRR and RPKI. In this paper, we study the inconsistency between the data registered in the IRR and RPKI and the underlying causes for those inconsistencies.

2   Background and Related Work

IRR and RPKI studies have focused on deployments, limitations, and impact on routing security. In contrast, we conduct a joint analysis of the IRR and RPKI to shed light on the data consistency across these two infrastructures. In this section, we provide background on both the IRR and RPKI.

2.1   Internet Routing Registry

The IRR, first introduced in 1995 as a combination of the internal routing policy storage system from RIPE and functionality extensions from Merit [8], was designed to facilitate sharing of routing policies across networks to improve routing security. Currently, the IRR consists of 25 distributed databases maintained by RIRs, commercial corporations, and non-profit organizations [33]. Networks can use the Routing Policy Specification Language (RPSL) to register and retrieve routing policy information in a set of distributed IRR databases maintained by different organizations. RPSL formats objects as lists of attribute-value pairs. The following objects are of particular relevance: (1) `mntner` objects contain authentication information required to create, modify, and delete other IRR objects; (2) `aut-num` objects contain the name and routing policies of an Autonomous System (AS). (3) `route` and `route6` objects contain IPv4 and IPv6 prefixes and their origin AS information.

The `route` and `route6` objects are particular significance to routing security. Every route objects has two mandatory attributes: `route` and `origin`. The example route object below shows `AS7377` intends to announce `137.110.0.0/16`.

`route: 137.110.0.0/16   origin: AS7377`

This data allows researchers to better understand the Internet topology and identify anomalies in BGP. Di Battista *et al.* [9] extracted BGP peering information from the IRR and Wang *et al.* [47] infer AS relationships from IRR routing policies. Shi *et al.* [42] and Schlamp *et al.* [41] used IRR information to detect and filter potential BGP hijacking events. This use of IRR data critically depends on its accuracy.

To find out the accuracy of the IRR in practice, in 2013 Khan *et al.* [26] conducted a comparative analysis of prefix origin information in IRR and BGP. They found that 87% of prefix origin pairs in 14 IRR databases matched with those in BGP. 55% of the mismatching prefix origin pairs were outdated in the IRR. They also found that the quality of IRR data depended on the routing registries, RIRs, and ASes. They found that stub ASes were more likely to register in IRR than small transit providers, followed by tier-1 transit ASes. Routing registries maintained by the RIPE NCC, APNIC, and AFRINIC had more consistency with BGP than that of ARIN and LACNIC.

2.2 Resource Public Key Infrastructure

RPKI was introduced in 2012 to help prevent BGP prefix origin hijacking. In contrast to the lack of information validation in the IRR, RPKI binds IP addresses and AS numbers to public keys using certificates. Each of the five Regional Routing Registries (RIRs) operates as the root of trust, a.k.a. *trust anchor*, for its corresponding service region. There are currently two RPKI deployment models: *hosted RPKI* and *delegated RPKI*. In hosted RPKI, The RIRs host Certificate Authority (CA) certificates and sign Route Origin Authorizations (ROAs) for the IP address space and AS numbers of their registered members. In delegated RPKI, the RIR members can host their own CA certificates to sign ROAs for their own or their customers' address space.

The most important RPKI object for BGP origin information validation is the `ROA` object. Inside a `ROA` object, IP `Prefix` specifies the IPv4 or IPv6 address resource owned by the network. `ASN` specifies the AS number used to announce the `IP Prefix` in BGP. `Max Length` specifies the length of the most specific subprefix of the `IP Prefix` allowed in BGP. The example ROA below allows `AS7377` to announce in BGP `137.110.0.0/16` and any subprefix whose length does not exceed 20.

(`IP Prefix, ASN, Max Length`) (`137.110.0.0/16, AS7377, 20`)

Deploying RPKI can bring significant security benefits even with limited deployment [16], but was slow to take off due to early instances of collateral damage from insufficient/erroneous RPKI deployment [19]. Chung *et al.* [14] found that when RPKI was first deployed in 2012, 27.47% of invalid announcements were caused by misconfigurations, and by 2019, the fraction of misconfigurations dropped to 5.39%. Apparently RPKI promotion efforts have had positive effects in RPKI deployment. In 2020, Testart *et al.* [45] found that more transit and content providers had started to enforce RPKI-based filtering and thus fewer illicit BGP announcements were propagating across networks. In 2020, Kristoff *et al.* [28] found that the caching servers of up to 20% of deployed RPKI relying parties did not fetch complete or timely copies of RPKI data.

3 Datasets

The IRR and the RPKI datasets are the main focus of this paper. Additionally, we used CAIDA's Inferred AS to Organization Mappings (as2org) [12], Routeviews Prefix to AS mappings for IPv4 and IPv6 (pfx2as) [13], AS Relationships [11], and AS Rank [10] datasets to facilitate our analysis of the causes of inconsistency between the IRR and RPKI.

IRR Dataset. We collected historical IRR database dumps from the four IRR databases: the Routing Assets Database (RADB) [32], the RIPE IRR [36], the APNIC IRR [6], and the AFRINIC IRR [1]. RADB publicly hosts IRR archives starting in 2016 and we downloaded monthly snapshots from August 2016 to

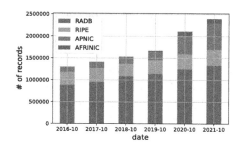

(a) RADB has the most v4 records.

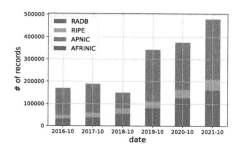

(b) APNIC has the most v6 records.

Fig. 1. Number of v4 and v6 IRR records in RADB, RIPE, APNIC, and AFRINIC IRR databases.

Table 1. RPKI coverage of IPv4 and IPv6 address space expanded almost 10×.

Date	IPv4			IPv6		
	ROAs	Prefixes	ASNs	ROAs	Prefixes	ASNs
2016–10	23k	22k	3,874	3.5k	3.3k	1,911
2017–10	38k	35k	5,067	6.1k	5.3k	2,519
2018–10	50k	46k	6,465	9.0k	8.1k	3,370
2019–10	92k	84k	10,232	15k	14k	5,274
2020–10	160k	143k	16,276	26k	24k	8,651
2021–10	205k	185k	21,265	40k	37k	10,878

October 2021. We downloaded CAIDA's quarterly snapshots from October 2016 to October 2021 of the RIPE, APNIC, and AFRINIC databases and obtained their **authoritative** IRR information (which only include IP address space administrated by the respective RIRs). We extracted the `route` and `route6` objects from the databases above and referred to them as the *RADB IRR dataset*, the *RIPE IRR dataset*, the *APNIC IRR dataset*, and the *AFRINIC IRR dataset* respectively. Figure 1 summarizes these datasets including their growth over time. As of October 2021, RADB had the most v4 records and the APNIC IRR had the most v6 records.

RPKI Dataset. RIPE NCC publishes daily validated ROA objects from all five RPKI trust anchors (APNIC, ARIN, RIPE NCC, AFRINIC, LACNIC) from 2011 to now, even after the retirement of their RPKI Validator [38,40]. These snapshots include both IPv4 and IPv6 RPKI information. We downloaded the monthly validated ROA archive starting August 2016 to October 2021 and refer to it as the *RPKI dataset.*By definition, each ROA can contain a list of prefixes and the MaxLength values for each prefix. But in this paper, we consider each unique (`IP Prefix`, `ASN`, `Maxlength`) a unique ROA, adhering to the data format published by RIPE NCC [39]. Table 1 summarizes the number of IPv4 and IPv6 ROA objects.

MANRS Participants. The Mutually Agreed Norms for Routing Security (MANRS) project [3] publishes its list of participants on its website. We downloaded 787 AS numbers of network operators and CDN-and-cloud providers as of October 25, 2021 and refer to it as the *MANRS dataset*. We compared the IRR hygiene of MANRS ASes and that of other ASes in Sect. 6.

4 Methodology

We present the steps we used to investigate the hygiene of IRR records. We use prefix origin pairs found in the *IRR datasets* and classify them according to their consistency with information found in the *RPKI dataset*. Thereby, we use the cryptographically signed ROAs as baseline for our analyses. Then, based on on the classified IRR records, we classify ASes by their maintenance practices.

4.1 Classification of IRR Records

To classify IRR records by their consistency with ROAs, we define the following four classes: Records that show full consistency in prefix and origin AS fall in **consistent**. When the ASN in an IRR record does not equal that of the ROA, the IRR record is in **inconsistent ASN**. When the ASNs are the same, but the prefix length differs, the IRR record is in **inconsistent length**. Otherwise, if there is no corresponding prefix in the ROA, the record falls into **not in RPKI**. We apply the following algorithm, a modified version of Route Origin Validation [24] and similar to the IRR Explorer [35], for the four IRR datasets *RADB IRR*, *RIPE IRR*, *APNIC IRR*, and *AFRINIC IRR*:

1 We choose snapshots of the same date from the *IRR dataset* and the *RPKI dataset*.
2 We denote each `route` or `route6` object as R_x. We denote the list of ROAs in the RPKI dataset as $ROALIST$.
3 For each record R_x, we denote the prefix as P_x and origin AS as AS_x.
4 We look for exact matching prefixes or covering prefixes of P_x in $ROALIST$. The resulting list of candidate ROAs are denoted L_{ROA}
5 If L_{ROA} is empty, then we put R_x in **not in RPKI**.
6 For each candidate ROA, C_{ROA}, in L_{ROA}, we put C_{ROA} in a list, M_{ROA}, if the origin AS in C_{ROA} equals AS_x.
7 If M_{ROA} is empty, then we classify R_x as **inconsistent ASN**.
8 For each C_{ROA} in M_{ROA}, we put C_{ROA} in a final list, V_{ROA}, if the prefix length of P_x does not exceed maxLength field in C_{ROA}.
9 If V_{ROA} is empty, we classify R_x as **inconsistent length**, otherwise as **consistent**.

Using the example from Sect. 2.2, if the *RPKI dataset* contains ROA (`137.110.0.0/16`, `AS7377`, `20`), a record (`137.110.0.0/24`, `AS195`) from the *RADB IRR dataset* falls into **inconsistent ASN** while (`137.110.0.0/24`, `AS7377`) falls into **inconsistent length**.

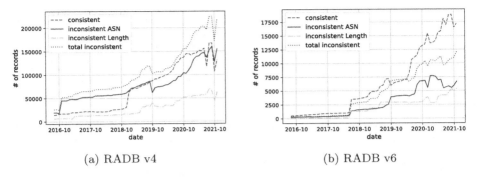

(a) RADB v4   (b) RADB v6

Fig. 2. RADB IPv6 records were more consistent with RPKI than IPv4 records.

4.2 Classification of ASes Registered in IRR

To further study the IRR record maintenance practices of different ASes, we discard all IRR records in the **Not in RPKI** category and group the ASes into three categories based on the classification of the remaining IRR records:

1) An AS is **Entirely consistent (EC)**, if all its IRR records are classified **consistent**.
2) An AS is **Entirely inconsistent (EI)**, if all associated records are classified either **inconsistent ASN** or **inconsistent length**.
3) An AS is **Mixed**, if it is associated with both **consistent** and **inconsistent** IRR records.

5 Prefix Origin Pair Consistency

Thus far, we have introduced our datasets and our methodology to determine inconsistencies in IRR records and characterize the maintaining ASes. In this section, we provide the results of our longitudinal analysis for the two *IRR datasets*, in IPv4 and IPv6, respectively. Specifically, we look at the consistency of all IRR records with a corresponding ROA in the *RPKI dataset*.

5.1 IPv4 vs. IPv6

RADB IRR. We begin by investigating the records in the *RADB IRR dataset*. From a total of 1.33M IRR records in October 2021, we found a corresponding ROA for 279,402 (21%) of the v4 prefix origin pairs. We found that 107,882 (or 38%) pairs are **consistent** with the ROA, while 127,099 (46%) showed an **inconsistent ASN** and the remaining 44,421 pairs (16%) exhibited an **inconsistent length**.

However, the fractions varied across our 5-year observation window (Fig. 2a) We observed an increase in the fraction of prefixes with a corresponding ROA, starting with 882,220 (5%) in 2016, peaking at 30% in August 2021 and dropping to 1,335,602 (20%) in October 2021. We attribute this increase to accelerated adoption of RPKI during that time period (Table 1). The total number of **consistent** records increased by around 1000%, from 14,359 in October 2016 to its peak of 167,370 in August 2021. Also, the number of **inconsistent** records increased by around 850%, from 26,057 in October 2016 to 222,982 in August 2021.

We noticed some outstanding events in Fig. 2a: In October 2016, there was a sudden increase of 26,647 **inconsistent ASN** records. Those records were registered under `AS26415` (Verisign), with a description of `verisign customer route`. Customers of Verisign registered their prefixes under their own AS numbers (27 total) in RPKI, which caused this inconsistency. Later, in September 2019, Verisign deleted 26,682 records from RADB in an effort to clean up their records in RADB. Figure 2a also shows an increase of 34,430 **consistent** records in January 2019. Those records were registered by 10 TWNIC ASes. We speculate that this event was the outcome of TWNIC obtaining an delegated RPKI CA certificate from APNIC in late 2018 [29]. Later, from July 2021 to October 2021, fluctuations in the green line were caused by TWNIC RPKI records disappearing and reappearing from our *RPKI dataset*, possibly due to instability from the retirement of the RIPE NCC RPKI Validator [38].

Next, we look at the consistency of RADB v6 records. Figure 2b shows that for around two years until May 2018, there were few records in any category, constituting fewer than 5% of all prefix origin pairs in the *IRR RADB data set*. After that, the fraction of prefixes with a corresponding ROA increased to more than 10% and peaks 20%, which indicates a steady adoption of RPKI for v6 prefixes. Of 27,540 prefixes with a matching ROA in October 2021, around 16,506 (60%) were **consistent**, 5,977 (22%) **inconsistent ASN**, and 5,057 (18%) **inconsistent length**. Interestingly, the number of inconsistent records stabilized after October 2020, while consistent records continued to increase. This contrasts with our IPv4 observations, where the inconsistency was high. Also, on November 25, 2019 the RIPE NCC announced the complete exhaustion of IPv4 address space [37], after which the growth rate of **consistent** records increased as a potential outcome of the greater incentive to deploy IPv6 operationally.

The sudden increase of records in all three categories in June 2018 can be attributed to 2,411 **consistent** records of 7 APNIC ASes, 827 **inconsistent ASN** records of 2 (a subset of the 7) ASes, and 1,180 **inconsistent length** records of 2 ASes operated by Advanced Wireless Network Company Limited (AWN), which is a large Thai ISP. Later in September 2019, `AS45430` registered 2 prefixes in RPKI, causing 1,313 IRR records that belonged to `133481` to become **Inconsistent**. Using CAIDA's AS Rank Dataset [10], we found that both ASes belonged to AWN, and `AS45430` was the provider of `AS133481`. This is an example of the cause of some **Inconsistent ASN** cases in Sect. 5.3, where the customer AS failed to remove their IRR record after the provider AS reclaimed its address space.

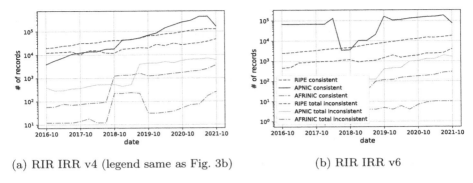

(a) RIR IRR v4 (legend same as Fig. 3b)   (b) RIR IRR v6

Fig. 3. In IRR databases maintained by the RIRs, the number of consistent records was at least 10 times the number of inconsistent records within the same RIR.

RIPE IRR. In October 2021 in the *RIPE IRR dataset*, there were 125,424 **consistent**, 30,764 **inconsistent ASN**, and 16,543 **inconsistent length** v4 records (Fig. 3a). For IPv6, the three categories had 18,154, 3,374, and 721 records, respectively (Fig. 3b). In the RIPE IRR, the prefix origin consistency for v4 and v6 records were similar. The consistent records have grown steadily while there have been minimal increase in the number of records in the inconsistent categories, showing good IRR hygiene over time.

Comparing the RADB and the RIPE IRR, we confirm prevailing knowledge that RIPE IRR has better-maintained records. As of October 2021, 8.3% of total records in *RADB IRR dataset* were **consistent** compared to 34.4% of total records in the *RIPE IRR dataset*. RIPE IRR's better hygiene may be due to RIPE NCC's authorization: To create a `route` object, a validation process first checks if the maintainer (`mntner`) has the authority to announce the IP prefix by either looking for parent maintainer information or referencing IP address space ownership information [36]. Our *RIPE IRR dataset* only included route objects in the authoritative RIPE IRR, which contained only prefixes managed by the RIPE NCC.

In the *RADB IRR dataset*, 28.3% of records had matching ROAs in the *RPKI dataset*, and the corresponding fraction for the *RIPE IRR dataset* was 45.2%. This shows that a larger fractions of networks registered in the RIPE IRR have also registered in the RPKI.

APNIC IRR. In July 2021 in the *APNIC IRR dataset*, there were 438,143 **consistent**, 3,426 **inconsistent ASN**, and 3,702 **inconsistent length** v4 records. For IPv6, the three categories had 182,563, 1,014, and 928 records, respectively. We found that the APNIC IRR had the highest consistency with RPKI compared to all other IRRs. The sudden drop in the solid purple line in Fig. 3b shows the number of **consistent** records decreased by 128,056 in July 2017. This decrease was caused by AS10091 (Starhub, Singapore) and AS45224 (Lanka Bell Limited, Sri Lanka) removing the entirety of their IRR records (65,491 and 62,555 records) from the APNIC IRR. Figure 3b also shows that there were significantly more v6 records in the APNIC IRR than the other RIR IRRs. Dhamdhere et al. [37] found that APNIC made a big push towards IPv6 deployment because it was the first geographical region to experience IPv4 exhaustion. We speculate that the IPv6 push caused such a high presence of IPv6 records in the APNIC IRR.

AFRINIC IRR. In October 2021 in the *AFRINIC IRR dataset*, there were 3,702 **consistent**, 180 **inconsistent ASN**, and 82 **inconsistent length** v4 records. For IPv6, the three categories had 299, 5, and 5 records, respectively. Although the number of consistent records exceeded that of inconsistent records, the AFRINIC IRR overall contained few records compared to other IRRs. Figure 3a shows a increase of both **consistent** and **inconsistent** records in October 2018 (dash-dotted blue and pink lines). We found this event is caused by AS30844 (Liquid Telecom, UK) registering its prefixes in RPKI and caused 1,082 **consistent** and 212 **inconsistent ASN** IRR records. We speculate that AFRINIC has the lowest number of IRR records compared to other RIRs because AFRINIC only launched its IRR in 2013, and had used the RIPE IRR before then [1].

Overall, the IRR databases operated by RIRs showed higher consistency with RPKI compared to RADB, as a result of the RIR's ability to regulate the creation process of `route` objects with address ownership information. In the following sections, we conduct inconsistency analysis only on RADB and RIPE IRR records due to the low inconsistency of APNIC IRR records and scarcity of AFRINIC IRR records.

5.2   Causes of Prefix Length Inconsistency

We further analyze the **inconsistent length** category. Networks that registered such records were one step away from good hygiene. Those networks successfully kept the origin ASes of their prefixes consistent in IRR and RPKI, but registered too-specific prefixes in the IRR. We speculate that this phenomenon could be caused by RPKI misconfiguration instead of bad IRR hygiene. To find out whether the networks registered inaccurate IRR records or incorrectly used the RPKI `Max Length`, we compared the **inconsistent length** records to their BGP announcement and corresponding RPKI ROAs. For each **inconsistent length** IRR record, we looked for its exact or covering prefix in BGP. If the BGP prefix origin pair was the same as that in the IRR record, we labeled it *BGP matches IRR but not RPKI*, and this indicates that the IRR record was correct and the network likely misconfigured RPKI. If the BGP prefix was less specific than the IRR record prefix length and the RPKI ROA `Max Length`, we label it *BGP matches RPKI but not IRR*, and this indicates that the IRR record was indeed inaccurate.

Figure 4a shows that as of October 2021, out of 44,421 **inconsistent length** v4 records in RADB, 713 (1.6%) agreed with BGP (*BGP matches IRR but not*

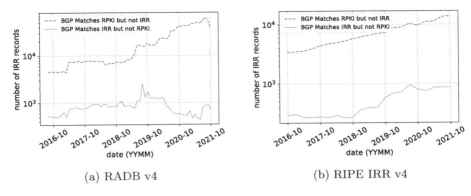

(a) RADB v4   (b) RIPE IRR v4

Fig. 4. BGP sometimes agrees with IRR records but not RPKI, showing that some IRR records in the Inconsistent Length category may actually be correct.

RPKI) and 39,968 (90.0%) disagreed with BGP (*BGP matches RPKI but not IRR*). Most prefix-length inconsistency in the IRR was caused by networks registering too-specific prefixes in the IRR, while in BGP and RPKI, they aggregated the prefixes. In much fewer cases, networks used the correct prefixes in IRR and announced them in BGP, but registered less-specific prefixes in RPKI and failed to set the proper *Max Length* attribute. Figure 4b shows a similar situation for v4 records in the RIPE IRR. Of 16,543 **inconsistent length** records, 866 (5.2%) were *BGP matches IRR but not RPKI* and 13,872 (83.9%) were *BGP matches RPKI but not IRR*. We found similar distributions for v6 records in both RADB and the RIPE IRR (not shown due to space constraints).

To summarize, prefix length inconsistency came from two types of mistakes with different operational impacts. The first type of mistake is having incorrect IRR entries that do not correctly reflect their prefix owners' routing intentions in BGP due to mismatching prefix lengths. If the upstream provider of the prefix owner requires it to register its exact BGP announcements in IRR, the prefix owner's current BGP announcements may be dropped (e.g. the upstream provider sees (`137.110.0.0/24`, `AS7377`) in IRR but sees (`137.110.0.0/16`, `AS7377`) in BGP).

The second type of mistake is misconfiguring the RPKI Max Length field. A too-small Max Length value in RPKI will almost immediately cause disruption to the prefix owner if its upstream provider uses RPKI filtering. The prefix owner's BGP announcement will be marked *RPKI invalid* and the upstream provider will drop the prefix owner's BGP announcement. Some operators reported that the Max Length feature of RPKI can cause confusion especially for RPKI newcomers because no similar feature exist in the IRR [34]. Gilad et al. [21] stated that the use of Max Length brings more harm than good to routing security, and operators have drafted proposals to discourage the use of the RPKI Max Length attribute [20].

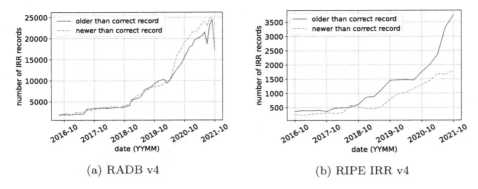

(a) RADB v4   (b) RIPE IRR v4

Fig. 5. Sometimes inconsistent ASN records are registered more recently than their corresponding consistent records.

5.3   Analysis of ASN Inconsistency

We further analyze the causes of **inconsistent ASN** records. Networks may stop maintaining their IRR records after initial registration, inducing outdated information [26]. To study such registration practices, we compared records within the same IRR dataset. First, we defined *conflicting* records to be any two IRR records with the same IP prefix but different origin ASes. Then, we took each **inconsistent ASN** record and looked for *conflicting* records in the same IRR dataset. We called the corresponding *conflicting* record a **correct** record if it was categorized as **consistent** (Sect. 5.1). We compared the registration dates of the **inconsistent ASN** record and the **correct** record.

We found 34,174 (26.9%) [5,524 (18.0%)] **correct** records for 127,099 [30,764] **inconsistent ASN** RADB [RIPE] v4 records in the October 2021 snapshot. Figure 5a shows that in RADB, 17,319 (13.6%) records were older than their **correct** records and 16,855(13.2%) were newer. Figure 5b shows that in RIPE IRR, 3,741 (12.1%) records were older than their **correct** records and 1783 (5.8%) were newer.

This result contradicts the intuition that an **inconsistent ASN** record should be older than its **correct** counterpart, because the inaccurate IRR records are likely stale [26]. To explore this surprising phenomenon, we used the October 2021 snapshots of the *IRR datasets* and use the CAIDA AS Relationship dataset [11] from October 2021 to examine the relationship between the ASes that registered those records. We retrieved the AS relationships for 10,382 (30.4%) out of 34,174 **correct** records for RADB and 3,203 (58.0%) out of 5,524 for RIPE IRR. In RADB, we found that out of 5,468 **inconsistent ASN** records with older **correct** records, 4,464 (81.6%) **correct** records were registered by providers of the networks that registered the **inconsistent ASN** records. Similarly in RIPE IRR, out of 839 **inconsistent ASN** records, 563 (67.1%) fell into the same situation. Such a high percentage of provider-customer relationships suggests that the providers first registered their prefixes in an IRR database, and then assigned address space to their customers. Those customers also registered their assigned prefixes in the same IRR database but failed to delete the IRR records after their providers revoked the address space. We found anecdotal evidence that some large ISPs such as Advanced Wireless Network Company Limited (AWN) in Thailand (Sect. 5.1) had customers who failed to delete outdated IRR records.

To prevent this inconsistency, providers could proactively require their customers to remove their IRR entries upon reclamation of address space to promote good IRR maintenance. Alternatively, if 0providers still intend to allow their customers to use such address space, the providers could register additional ROAs in RPKI under their customers' ASes.

6   ASes Behind IRR Inconsistency

We took the October 2021 snapshots for the *RADB IRR dataset* and the *RIPE IRR dataset* and classified the ASes according to Sect. 4.2. We used the CAIDA Inferred AS to Organization dataset [12] and the MANRS dataset [3] to classify the ASes by their RIR and whether they were MANRS participants. We labeled the ASes in RIPE, ARIN, APNIC, LACNIC, and AFRINIC regions as EU, NA, AP, SA, and SA respectively. Table 2 shows that LACNIC (SA) ASes had the best IRR hygiene among all RIRs as of October 2021. Although there were more **entirely consistent (EC)** ASes than **entirely inconsistent (EI)** ASes, the number of **consistent** records was lower than **inconsistent ASN** and **inconsistent Length** records combined. This discrepancy is because the **entirely consistent (EI)** ASes registered fewer v4 records in RADB. We also used the CAIDA AS Rank [10] dataset to look at the AS *customer cone* size distribution in each category, but found no correlation between AS size and AS registration practice in RADB. Table 3 shows that the authoritative RIPE IRR had few users outside of the RIPE service region, and the ASes had good IRR hygiene as a result of the validation requirement of the RIPE Database.

As of October 2021, of 787 MANRS ASes, 326 appeared in the *RADB IRR dataset* and had corresponding ROAs in the *RPKI dataset*. The MANRS ASes had better IRR hygiene than ASes in RADB, because the fraction of **entirely consistent (EC)** ASes were higher (53.1% vs. 45.2%). However, fewer MANRS ASes registered in the RIPE IRR compared to RADB so the fraction of **entirely consistent (EC)** ASes dropped below that of RIPE ASes (63.6% vs. 71.2%). Note that MANRS **only** requires their participants to register in either IRR or RPKI. MANRS ASes are not required to keep their records consistent between IRR and RPKI, and any MANRS AS that appears in Table 2 and Table 3 registered in both IRR and RPKI, which is more than required by MANRS.

7   Limitations

Incomplete IRR Data Coverage. We do not have historical IRR data for all IRR database providers. Although RADB mirrors all IRR databases, its IRR archives only include information directly registered in RADB itself. The number

Table 2. Classification of ASes that registered v4 records in RADB. MANRS ASes were more consistent than other ASes.

AS Class	Record	General AS count (9,675)						MANRS ASes (326)
		Total	EU	NA	AP	SA	AF	
EC	54,488	4,375 (45.2%)	562	1,084	1,184	1,452	67	173 (53.1%)
EI	367,795	3,513 (36.3%)	415	1,366	1,075	271	50	43 (13.2%)
Mixed	489,172	1,787 (18.5%)	271	428	739	324	16	110 (33.7%)

Table 3. Classification of ASes that registered v4 records in RIPE IRR. Most ASes were in the RIPE region and were highly consistent.

AS class	Record	General AS count (13,109)						MANRS ASes (220)
		Total	EU	NA	AP	SA	AF	
EC	75,589	9,339 (71.2%)	9,039	175	85	31	6	140 (63.6%)
EI	18,613	1,478 (11.3%)	1,309	86	63	7	4	7 (3.2%)
Mixed	144,284	2,292 (17.5)	2,193	70	26	0	3	73 (33.2%)

of consistent and inconsistent IRR records in our analysis is treated as a lower bound of the actual situation.

Sparse IRR Data Granularity. Changes to IRR and RPKI databases happen daily or even hourly as networks change configurations to adapt to routing needs. Our dataset does not have the granularity to monitor such frequent events and provides only a longitudinal analysis.

Aggregated RPKI Data. The RPKI infrastructure has a hosted model and delegated model, which may have different consistency with IRR databases. We cannot distinguish which model our RPKI data is collected from.

8   Summary

The recent growth of RPKI usage gives us the opportunity to study the accuracy of the IRR. In this paper we explored IRR hygiene by comparing the consistency between IRR and RPKI records and analyzing the IRR maintenance practices of ASes. Although RPKI has gained popularity, it still has far fewer participating ASes or database records. Comparing RADB and RPKI, we found 61.4% of v4 and 40.1% of v6 records (that appeared in both databases) were inconsistent. In contrast, the RIPE IRR had only 27.4% v4 and 18.4% v6 inconsistent records. We discovered some causes of inconsistency: complicated customer-provider relationships among ASes in the IRR, and possible misconfiguration in the RPKI. Finally, we found that ASes participating in the routing security intiative MANRS were more likely to keep IRR records consistent with RPKI than ASes in general.

Future Work. Our work helps to broadly identify inaccurate and suspicious IRR records and can serve as the foundation for IRR false registration detection.

On the operational side, the future of IRR can be promising, as new tools such as IRRd Version 4 [2] have been developed to help operators automatically validate IRR information against RPKI. This could further improve the accuracy of the IRR and contribute to better routing security.

Acknowledgment. This material is based on research sponsored by the National Science Foundation (NSF) grants CNS-1901517, OAC-2131987, CNS-2120399, and OAC-1724853. The views and conclusions contained herein are those of the authors and should not be interpreted as necessarily representing the official policies or endorsements, either expressed or implied, of NSF. We appreciate network operators who gave us valuable insight. We also thank our shepherd for the helpful feedback.

References

1. AFRINIC's Internet Routing Registry (2021). https://afrinic.net/internet-routing-registry
2. IRRd Version 4.2.0 (2021). https://irrd.readthedocs.io/en/stable/
3. Mutually Agreed Norms for Routing Security (2021). https://www.manrs.org/
4. Peering with Google (2021). https://peering.google.com/#/options/peering
5. Routing Security (2021). https://www.teliacarrier.com/our-network/bgp-routing/routing-security.html
6. APNIC Internet Routing Registry (2022). https://www.apnic.net/about-apnic/whois_search/about/what-is-in-whois/irr/
7. Alaettinoglu, C., et al.: Routing policy specification language (RPSL). RFC 2622, RFC Editor, June 1999
8. Bates, T., et al.: Representation of IP routing policies in a routing registry (ripe-81++). RFC 1786, RFC Editor, March 1995
9. Battista, G.D., Refice, T., Rimondini, M.: How to extract BGP peering information from the internet routing registry. In: Proceedings of the 2006 SIGCOMM Workshop on Mining Network Data, MineNet 2006, pp. 317–322. Association for Computing Machinery, New York (2006). https://doi.org/10.1145/1162678.1162685
10. CAIDA: AS Rank (2021). https://asrank.caida.org/
11. CAIDA: AS Relationships (2021). https://www.caida.org/catalog/datasets/as-relationships/
12. CAIDA: Inferred AS to Organization Mapping Dataset (2021). https://www.caida.org/catalog/datasets/as-organizations/
13. CAIDA: Routeviews Prefix to AS mappings Dataset (pfx2as) for IPv4 and IPv6 (2021). https://www.caida.org/catalog/datasets/routeviews-prefix2as/
14. Chung, T., et al.: RPKI is coming of age: a longitudinal study of RPKI deployment and invalid route origins. In: Proceedings of the Internet Measurement Conference, IMC 2019, pp. 406–419. Association for Computing Machinery, New York (2019). https://doi.org/10.1145/3355369.3355596
15. Cloudflare: Is BGP Safe Yet? (2022). https://isbgpsafeyet.com/
16. Cohen, A., Gilad, Y., Herzberg, A., Schapira, M.: One hop for RPKI, one giant leap for BGP security. In: Workshop on Hot Topics in Networks, 7 p., November 2015
17. Cooper, D., Heilman, E., Brogle, K., Reyzin, L., Goldberg, S.: On the risk of misbehaving RPKI authorities. In: Proceedings of the Twelfth ACM Workshop on Hot Topics in Networks. HotNets-XII, Association for Computing Machinery, New York (2013). https://doi.org/10.1145/2535771.2535787

18. Durand, J., Pepelnjak, I., Doering, G.: BGP operations and security. BCP 194, RFC Editor, February 2015
19. Gilad, Y., Cohen, A., Herzberg, A., Schapira, M., Shulman, H.: Are we there yet? On RPKI's deployment and security. In: Network and Distributed System Security Symposium (2017)
20. Gilad, Y., Goldberg, S., Sriram, K., Snijders, J., Maddison, B.: The use of maxLength in the RPKI. Internet-Draft draft-ietf-sidrops-rpkimaxlen-09, IETF Secretariat, November 2021. https://www.ietf.org/archive/id/draft-ietf-sidrops-rpkimaxlen-09.txt
21. Gilad, Y., Sagga, O., Goldberg, S.: MaxLength considered harmful to the RPKI. In: Proceedings of the 13th International Conference on Emerging Networking EXperiments and Technologies, CoNEXT 2017, pp. 101–107. Association for Computing Machinery, New York (2017). https://doi.org/10.1145/3143361.3143363
22. Goodell, G., Aiello, W., Griffin, T., Ioannidis, J., McDaniel, P.D., Rubin, A.D.: Working around BGP: an incremental approach to improving security and accuracy in interdomain routing. In: NDSS, vol. 23, p. 156. Citeseer (2003)
23. Heilman, E., Cooper, D., Reyzin, L., Goldberg, S.: From the consent of the routed: improving the transparency of the RPKI, SIGCOMM 2014, pp. 51–62. Association for Computing Machinery, New York (2014). https://doi.org/10.1145/2619239.2626293
24. Huston, G., Michaelson, G.: Validation of route origination using the resource certificate public key infrastructure (PKI) and route origin authorizations (ROAs). RFC 6483, RFC Editor, February 2012
25. Huston, G., Rossi, M., Armitage, G.: Securing BGP - a literature survey. IEEE Commun. Surv. Tutor. **13**(2), 199–222 (2011). https://doi.org/10.1109/SURV.2011.041010.00041
26. Khan, A., Kim, H.C., Kwon, T., Choi, Y.: A comparative study on IP prefixes and their origin ASes in BGP and the IRR. SIGCOMM Comput. Commun. Rev. **43**(3), 16–24 (2013). https://doi.org/10.1145/2500098.2500101
27. Kim, E.Y., Xiao, L., Nahrstedt, K., Park, K.: Secure interdomain routing registry. IEEE Trans. Inf. Forensics Secur. **3**(2), 304–316 (2008). https://doi.org/10.1109/TIFS.2008.922050
28. Kristoff, J., et al.: On measuring RPKI relying parties. In: Proceedings of the ACM Internet Measurement Conference, IMC 2020, pp. 484–491. Association for Computing Machinery, New York (2020). https://doi.org/10.1145/3419394.3423622
29. Ku, C.H.: 98% of Taiwan's IP address holders have signed RPKI ROAs (2020). https://blog.apnic.net/2020/10/16/98-of-taiwans-ip-address-holders-have-signed-rpki-roas/
30. Kuerbis, B., Mueller, M.: Internet routing registries, data governance, and security. J. Cyber Policy **2**(1), 64–81 (2017)
31. Lepinski, M., Kent, S.: An infrastructure to support secure internet routing. RFC 6480, RFC Editor, February 2012. http://www.rfc-editor.org/rfc/rfc6480.txt
32. Merit Network: The Internet Routing Registry - RADb (2021). https://www.radb.net/
33. Merit Network, Inc.: Internet Routing Registry (2018). http://www.irr.net
34. Michaelson, G.: IRR and RPKI: a problem statement (2017). https://conference.apnic.net/44/assets/files/APCS549/Global-IRR-and-RPKI-a-problem-statement.pdf
35. NLNOG: IRR explorer (2021). https://irrexplorer.nlnog.net/
36. RIPE NCC: Managing Route Objects in the IRR (2019). https://www.ripe.net/manage-ips-and-asns/db/support/managing-route-objects-in-the-irr

37. RIPE NCC: The RIPE NCC has run out of IPv4 Addresses (2019). https://www.ripe.net/publications/news/about-ripe-ncc-and-ripe/the-ripe-ncc-has-run-out-of-ipv4-addresses
38. RIPE NCC: Ending Support for the RIPE NCC RPKI Validator (2021). https://www.ripe.net/publications/news/announcements/ending-support-for-the-ripe-ncc-rpki-validator
39. RIPE NCC: RPKI Dataset (2021). https://ftp.ripe.net/ripe/rpki/
40. RIPE NCC: RPKI Validator (2021). https://rpki-validator.ripe.net/
41. Schlamp, J., Holz, R., Jacquemart, Q., Carle, G., Biersack, E.W.: HEAP: reliable assessment of BGP hijacking attacks. IEEE J. Sel. Areas Commun. **34**(6), 1849–1861 (2016). https://doi.org/10.1109/JSAC.2016.2558978
42. Shi, X., Xiang, Y., Wang, Z., Yin, X., Wu, J.: Detecting prefix hijackings in the internet with argus. In: Proceedings of the 2012 Internet Measurement Conference, IMC 2012, pp. 15–28. Association for Computing Machinery, New York (2012). https://doi.org/10.1145/2398776.2398779
43. Shrishak, K., Shulman, H.: Limiting the power of RPKI authorities. In: Proceedings of the Applied Networking Research Workshop, ANRW 2020, pp. 12–18. Association for Computing Machinery, New York (2020). https://doi.org/10.1145/3404868.3406674
44. Testart, C.: Reviewing a historical internet vulnerability: why isn't BGP more secure and what can we do about it? TPRC (2018)
45. Testart, C., Richter, P., King, A., Dainotti, A., Clark, D.: To filter or not to filter: measuring the benefits of registering in the RPKI today. In: Sperotto, A., Dainotti, A., Stiller, B. (eds.) PAM 2020. LNCS, vol. 12048, pp. 71–87. Springer, Cham (2020). https://doi.org/10.1007/978-3-030-44081-7_5
46. Wählisch, M., Schmidt, R., Schmidt, T.C., Maennel, O., Uhlig, S., Tyson, G.: RiPKI: the tragic story of RPKI deployment in the web ecosystem. In: Proceedings of Fourteenth ACM Workshop on Hot Topics in Networks (HotNets). ACM, New York (2015)
47. Wang, F., Gao, L.: On inferring and characterizing internet routing policies. In: IMC 2003, pp. 15–26. Association for Computing Machinery, New York (2003). https://doi.org/10.1145/948205.948208
48. Yoo, C.S., Wishnick, D.A.: Lowering legal barriers to RPKI adoption. U of Penn Law School, Public Law Research Paper (19-02) (2019)

Peering Only? Analyzing the Reachability Benefits of Joining Large IXPs Today

Lars Prehn[1]([✉]), Franziska Lichtblau[1], Christoph Dietzel[1,2],
and Anja Feldmann[1]

[1] MPII, Saarbrücken, Germany
{lprehn,franziska.lichtblau,anja}@mpi-inf.mpg.de
[2] DE-CIX, Cologne, Germany
christoph.dietzel@de-cix.net

Abstract. Internet Exchange Points (IXPs) became a fundamental building block of inter-domain routing throughout the last decade. Today, they offer their members access to hundreds—if not thousands—of possible networks to peer.

In this paper, we pose the question: How far can peering at those large IXPs get us in terms of reachable prefixes and services? To approach this question, we first analyze and compare Route Server snapshots obtained from eight of the world's largest IXPs. Afterwards, we perform an in-depth analysis of bi-lateral and private peering at a single IXP based on its peering LAN traffic and queries to carefully selected, nearby looking glasses. To assess the relevance of the prefixes available via each peering type, we utilize two orthogonal metrics: the number of domains served from the prefix and the traffic volume that a large eyeball network egress towards it.

Our results show that multi-lateral peering can cover ~20% and ~40% of the routed IPv4 and IPv6 address space, respectively. We observe that many of those routes lead to out-of-continent locations reachable only via three or more AS hops. Yet, most IXP members only utilize "local" (i.e., single hop) routes. We further infer that IXP members can reach more than **half of all routed IPv4** and more than one-third of all routed IPv6 address space via bi-lateral peering. These routes contain almost all of the top 10K egress prefixes of our eyeball network, and hence they would satisfy the reachability requirements of most end users. Still, they miss up to 20% of the top 10K prefixes that serve the most domains. We observe that these missing prefixes often belong to large transit and Tier 1 providers.

1 Introduction

Traditionally, the Internet follows a hierarchical structure. At the top of this hierarchy resides a set of large transit providers—also called Tier 1 networks—that exchange traffic with each other at no monetary compensation. The literature commonly refers to this type of interconnection (and business relation) between two ASes as "peering".

© The Author(s), under exclusive license to Springer Nature Switzerland AG 2022
O. Hohlfeld et al. (Eds.): PAM 2022, LNCS 13210, pp. 338–366, 2022.
https://doi.org/10.1007/978-3-030-98785-5_15

When logically descending from the top, higher-tier networks deliver traffic for their lower-tier customers, i.e., they provide transit. Since the early 2000s, the "topology flattening" phenomenon gradually superseded this hierarchical structure. Lower-tier networks started to shift more of their transit traffic to newly established peering connections. The continuous acquisition of new peering partners is often incentivised by cost reduction and potential latency improvements [2].

The fast and widespread deployment of Internet eXchange Points (IXPs) has further accelerated the establishment of new peering connections.

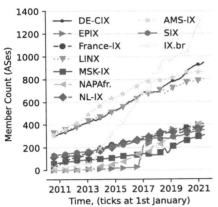

Fig. 1. Number of members over time based on PeeringDB

Traditionally, IXPs allow physically-close networks to exchange traffic via a shared layer-2 switching fabric; thus, they eliminate unnecessary routing detours, which reduces the overall latency and helps to "keep local traffic local". Today, the largest IXPs have grown to multiple hundreds—sometimes even thousands—of members (see Fig. 1) and handle peak traffic volumes of more than 10 Tb/s [4, 27, 38].

As different networks have different negotiation positions, various forms of peering have emerged. The simplest form, bi-lateral peering, refers to a direct connection between two ASes via the IXP's switching fabric.

To ease the life of their customers, most IXPs also offer Route Servers that redistribute all routes they received from one IXP member to all others via a single BGP session per member. As this form of peering involves more than two networks, the community refers to it as multi-lateral peering. As a third option, networks can establish private peering sessions amongst each other. Instead of using the IXP's layer-2 fabric, ASes establish these peering sessions via a dedicated cross-connect in the same colocation facility (or via layer-2 transport for different colocation facilities).

While peering itself is a well-established concept that has been broadly discussed in the research literature (e.g., [1,6,10,11,20,22,45,50]), we still lack fundamental insights into the actual extent and importance of the routes available at large IXPs. In this paper, we take a closer look at how the different forms of peering translate into transit-free prefix reachability. We characterize and compare the multi-lateral peering routes available at the Route Servers of the world's largest IXPs and further estimate the bi-lateral and private peering routes available at one large IXP in Europe that we refer to as L-IXP. We contrast our reachability analysis using two dimensions of importance: the number of top domains that a route serves and the traffic volume that one of the largest European eyeball networks egresses towards it.

In particular, our contributions can be summarized as follows:

- **Characterization of Multilateral Peering:** We analyze and compare
Route Server snapshots from eight of the ten largest IXP peering LANs worldwide (see, Sect. 4). We find that all Route Servers show consistent insights:
(1) only 10% of Route Server peers provide more than 100 routes while 30%
provide less than ten routes, (2) approximately half of the Route Server routes
have a minimum path length of three ASes (announced by close and distance
peers alike) and about two-thirds of all routes lead to out-of-continent destinations, and (3) most large Route Servers have a prefix overlap of ˜50% while
the actually reachable IPs overlap by ˜60–70%.
- **Characterization of Bi-lateral & Private Peering:** For one of Europe's
largest IXPs, we infer routes available via bi-lateral and private peering (see
Sect. 5.1). Similar to Ager et al. [1], we observe that most ASes use the
switching fabric to establish additional transit sessions. As such connections
can drastically influence our inferences of available routes, we developed a
methodology to increase the coverage of relationship inference algorithms at
IXPs, and we use the resulting relationships to isolate transit connections
during the inference process. Similarly, we introduce a methodology to infer
routes available via private peering based on the careful selection and querying
of looking glass utilities.
- **Route Importance:** We compare the IPv4 and IPv6 routes available via
multi-lateral, bi-lateral, and private peering against two top-10K prefix lists:
one based on the number of served domains and one based on the traffic
volume of a large European eyeball network (see Sect. 6). We find that nearly
all top-10k IPv4 prefixes are available via bi-lateral peering. For IPv6, we
observe that prefixes serving many domains are often unavailable (up to 15%)
or can only be obtained via private peering.

2   Background

In this section, we provide an introduction to the different interconnection models
and highlight important observations from related work. We refer to Fig. 2 as a
visualization of the individual components explained throughout this section.

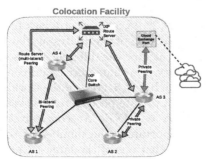

While interconnection agreements
can be rather complex in practice,
the scientific literature abstracts mainly
into two categories: transit and peering.

In a transit agreement, a customer
pays a transit provider for delivering
its traffic from its egress router to
any IP. In a (settlement-free) peering
agreement, two ASes—usually of similar size and with roughly equal traffic volume towards each other—forward
each other's traffic without substantial

Fig. 2. Illustration of different peering
types at an IXP. (Color figure online)

amounts of money flowing in either direction. As neither of the peering partners is a provider for the other, both ASes have to negotiate where to physically interconnect and who is bearing the infrastructure costs. Over time and with the spread of Internet Exchange Points (IXPs) across the globe the peering ecosystem itself became rather complex and different peering practices emerged. In the following, we give an overview of the fundamentals of current peering models.

Internet Exchange Points. As establishing a single BGP peering session for every interconnection partner separately is rather wasteful, operators started building common switching infrastructure that could be shared (w.r.t. usage and cost) among ASes. These switching infrastructures—envisioned to keep local traffic local— belong to so-called Internet eXchange Points (IXPs) located in well-connected colocation facilities. Those colocation facilities provide dedicated infrastructure (e.g., rack space, electricity, and cooling) for the housing of peering equipment. Figure 2 gives an abstract example for a layer-2 peering fabric. While IXPs may attract very diverse sets of members, previous work reported that they observe traffic for 40% or more of all theoretically possible peering connections [13]. As some large IXPs observe traffic originated by or destinated towards tens of thousands of ASes and millions of servers [22] and could theoretically reach 70% of all routed addresses [10], it nowadays is also common that networks pay remote-peering providers to get access to remote IXPs [20]. A recent study by Nomikos et al. [57] revealed that around 90% of 30 tested IXPs had more than 10% of their members connecting via remote peering. They further reported that for certain large IXPs up to 40% of members can be connected via remote-peering.

Bi-lateral Peering. This practice describes a BGP peering session between two member ASes at an IXP via the shared peering fabric as depicted in Fig. 2 (green arrows). While legal processes and concerns of peering policy leakage slow down the acquisition of bi-lateral peering partners [49], Marcos et al. proposed a framework that allows IXP members to quickly provision peering sessions based on an intent abstraction and digitally handled legal contracts [50]. Interestingly, Ager et al. showed in 2012 that also Tier1 providers peer at IXPs and that they use their IXP peerings not only as backup routes. They further showed that these Tier1 providers also abuse the peering LAN for transit connections to their customers [1].

Multi-lateral Peering. As briefly discussed in Sect. 1, IXPs provide a Route Server for their members to establish multi-lateral peerings. In addition to reducing the number of needed interconnections to reach most IXP members[1], Route Servers can also implement additional functionality (e.g., the frequently used per-peer blackholing [28]) to make them more attractive to IXP members. Those services are often realized by attaching a specifically formatted BGP Community onto Route Server announcements. As a route server has to store such information to act properly based on it, some IXP members do not establish a session with the route server as they expect that it might expose their peering

---

[1] A Route Server reduces the number of totally needed BGP sessions for a fully-meshed topology from $n * (n-1)/2$ to n, where n is the number of BGP speakers.

policies [23]. As a notable example of such exposition, Giotsas et al. showed that it is possible to uncover 200k multi-lateral peering agreements by analyzing the BGP community values visible at few Route Servers [34].

Private Peering. When present at the same colocation facility, e.g. because they are members of the same IXP, two networks can establish a private peering session via direct cross-connect avoiding the IXP's peering fabric. Especially large ASes prefer this peering practice as it is provides a very fine-grained control over their peering sessions. Hence, networks that, e.g., need to egress a high traffic volume often require direct peering sessions on dedicated physical infrastructure with guaranteed capacity. This form of interconnection usually comes with monetary compensation for certain Service-Level Agreements (SLAs). Even though private peering keeps the peering policies of an AS hidden and often provides dedicated capacity, even private peering sessions can suffer from outages when, e.g., the entire colocation facility goes down—a not so uncommon scenario as Giotsas et al. reported (160 outages in 5 years) [32].

Cloud and Content Provider Connectivity. Many Cloud and Content providers peer at hundreds of physically distinct locations [11] to thousands of different networks [6]. While they often require private peering connections, they sometimes also rely on bi-lateral peering to ensure that they directly connect with as many eyeball ASes as possible [24] or to gain tens of milliseconds of latency improvements over their transit providers [69]. Hence, it is unsurprising that those providers also dominate the peering LAN traffic (as shown for two medium-sized IXPs by Cardona et al. [19]). Yet, as most networks try to establish private peering connections with them directly in the colocation facilities, those facilities have established so-called cloud exchanges—specific ports which directly provide connectivity (called virtual private interconnection (VPI)) to any number of cloud service providers within the colocation facility [79].

Identifying Peering Partners. Many network operators rely on a network policy database called PeeringDB to identify potential peering partners [62]. In particular, PeeringDB differentiates between four peering policy types: (1) open: A network with an open peering policy that peers with any other network, (2) selective: A network that will peer under certain conditions, e.g., minimum traffic volume or location, (3) restrictive: A network that already has an existing set of peers and needs strong, convincing arguments to establish a peering connection, and (4) no peering: These networks do not peer at all and rely entirely upon transit [58]. Notably, the vast majority of peering policies in PeeringDB are of the 'open' type. Yet, PeeringDB is known to have certain inaccurate entries [45,74]. Further, many small networks—especially in developing regions—do simply not register in PeeringDB [45].

3   Preface: Data Sets

While we introduce each data set separately when using it, this section summarizes the used data sets to provide a better overview of time coherence and caveats.

3.1 Main Data Sets

PeeringDB Snapshots (2010/08/01–2021/06/01, Monthly). PeeringDB is a community-effort database containing information about the infrastructure and policies for IXPs, colocation facilities, peering LANs, and networks [62]. PeeringDB is known to have a small set of inaccurate entries [45,74]. Similarly, Lodhi et al. reported that PeeringDB underrepresents small—especially developing country—networks [45]. The Center for Applied Internet Data Analysis (CAIDA) produces monthly snapshots of this database [17].

Route Server Snapshots (2021/06/06–21, Once). WWe compiled a set of Route Server snapshots for the largest (in terms of members) peering LAN for eight of the world's largest IXPs. We received these snapshots via multiple personal contacts throughout 15 days.

IXP Traffic Data (2021/05/01–2021/06/07). We obtain IPFIX traffic captures from one of the largest European IXPs. The traffic is sampled at a rate of 1 out of 10K (1:10k) flows. The captures encompass all traffic exchanged via the peering LAN; hence, it contains traffic exchanged via multi-lateral and bi-lateral peering sessions but misses private peering traffic. In particular, we utilize the data from May 2021 to analyze how our observation period influences our results and subsequently report most of our results based on the first week in June 2021.

ISP Traffic Data (2021/06/10). We obtain a single workday of egress traffic captured from all border routers from a large European eyeball network. The data was sampled at a rate of 1:1K packets.

Domain-Based Prefix Top List (2021/04/30). We obtain a recently recomputed domain-based prefix top list from Naab et al. [55]. Their methodology relies on a domain top list as input, then resolves those domains to IP addresses from a single physical location, and finally aggregates the number of Fully Qualified Domain Names that is served by every norm-prefix (i.e., a /24 prefix in IPv4 and a /48 prefix in IPv6). We use the prefix top list that relied on Umbrella's domain top list [25] as input, as it was the only one that could provide us with 10K IPv6 prefixes. Notably, this domain-based prefix top list is biased towards the European service region as DNS load-balancing [71] and caching [67] may lead to strongly regionalized address resolutions.

Please note that we handled our traffic data sets in compliance with **measurement ethics** and best practices. We performed all data analyses on servers located at the respective premises of our vantage points using data collected as a part of their routine network analysis. We analyzed flow data summaries based on packet headers that did not reveal any payload information. We further anonymized all flow attributes not explicitly needed for the results presented in this paper. This is in line with Ethical Committee policies. For the remaining data sets, we rely on publicly available sources only.

3.2   Orthogonal Data Sets

Maxmind GeoLite2 Snapshot (2021/06/01). We utilize a snapshot of Maxmind's GeoLite2 database [53] to geolocate Route Server prefixes. While they can have significant inaccuracies on a city or country-level [21], even freely available databases achieve near-perfect continent-level predictions [52].

CAIDA's AS Relationships Snapshot (2021/06/01). CAIDA produces monthly snapshots of the business relationships inferred by ASRank [47] based on routing information collected by RouteViews [61] and RIPE/RIS [56] from the first five days within the month [14]. While it misses many peering links, this data is reasonably complete for transit links [35,59,60]. Further, the inference algorithm is known to near-perfectly infer transit relationships but often misinfers peering relationships as transit [30,39,40], i.e., it overestimates the number of transit relationships.

CAIDA's IP-to-AS Mapping Snapshot (2021/06/10). CAIDA generates daily IP to AS mappings based on routing information from selected Route Views [61] collectors [18].

CAIDA's AS-to-Org Mapping Snapshot (2021/04/01). CAIDA produces quarterly snapshots of AS-to-Organization mappings generated based on the WHOIS databases of all Regional and some National Internet Registries [16]. Notably, WHOIS data is known to contain malformatted and hard-to-parse entries [44], leading to potential inaccuracies in the inferred AS-to-Organization mapping. The April snapshot is the latest available snapshot before our measurement period.

4   Multilateral Peering

We start our analysis with the lowest-hanging fruit: multi-lateral peering. While some IXPs have explicit APIs that could be used to re-build the current routing table of their route servers, we explicitly request Route Server snapshots for the largest peering LAN of different IXPs. Out of the ten IXPs shown in Fig. 1, only Nl-IX and EPIX did not fulfil our request. Our eight Route Server snapshots are from differents days between 6th and 21st June, 2021[2] and contain the entire routing information base for each session, i.e., they contain all paths from all neighbours (rather than just one best path) for a given prefix. Using those snapshots, we look at what routes an AS may expect from the Route Server and how consistent those findings are across different IXP Route Server. In particular, we arrive at the following takeaways:

– Large Route Servers across the world are very similar: They not only have the same distribution of routes per peer but also share the majority of reachable

---

[2] As we obtained similar results for all Route Server related plots for a set of inital snapshots that we obtained throughout January and February, we do not expect any major inconsistencies due to a two week offset.

prefixes and IPs, i.e., joining a second, third, etc. Route Server only negligibly improves reachability.

- Due to the growing trend of remote peering, Route Servers provide only a limited amount of in-continent routes.
- We observe that most routes (at all analyzed Route Servers) contain at least three hops. While both close and distant peers announce those lengthy, unattractive routes, we find that members often only use one-hop Route Server routes.

How Consistent are the Distribution of Routes to Peers Across Route Servers? Our snapshots show that connecting to the Route Server immediately provides routes from up to 650 IXP members. Yet, Richter et al. already reported that not all IXP members announce the same number of prefixes [68]. As a first look at how similar Route Servers are, we analyze whether this distribution is consistent across them. Figure 3 shows the number of prefixes (y-axis, logarithmic) announced by every peer (x-axis) per Route Server. Indeed, we observe strong consistency across different IXP Route Servers regardless of the protocol. For the AMS-IX Route Server (top curve), the top ~1.5, 10, 30, and 70% of Route Server peers announce routes for more than 10K, 1K, 100, and 10 IPv4 (1K, 100, 20, and 5 IPv6) prefixes. While most Route Servers are close to AMS-IX, peers at NAPAfrica (bottom curve) announce around an order of magnitude fewer prefixes.e fewer prefixes, most other IXPs are closer to AMS-IX.

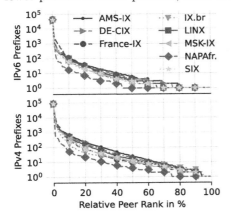

Fig. 3. Number of prefixes announced per peer

Notably, not all prefixes are necessarily exported to all peers by the Route Server. To estimate how many prefixes can only be received conditionally, we inspect the Route Server snapshots for BGP communities that control its redistribution rules. For, e.g., DE-CIX, we inspect routes with the 0:6695 Community that is used to exclude all peers; this community is usually combined with other BGP Communities of the form 6695:X which instruct the Route Server to explicitly redistribute a route to peer X. Overall, we find that 31.3% of IPv4 and 11.2% of IPv6 Route Server prefixes are not globally exported.

Do Route Servers Help to Keep Local Traffic Local? As briefly discussed in Sect. 2, IXPs initially were established as a solution to interconnect geographically close ASes following the idea to "keep local traffic local". Yet, given that many peers announce tens of thousands of prefixes to hundreds of millions of hosts, we now want to take a look at how strictly this idea is followed through by today's Route Servers. We first use a naïve approach to answering this question:

We look at the AS path length (after removing AS Path Prepending). Figure 4 shows the Route Server prefixes of different IXPs separated by the number of ASes in their shortest route. We observe that for around half of all prefixes the shortest path contains three or more ASes. This result goes against the "keep local traffic local" idea, as local routes would likely either directly lead to an access/eyeball network or indirectly via a national service provider. However, given that the AS path length is often not a good proxy for geographic distance, we now switch to a more insightful perspective.

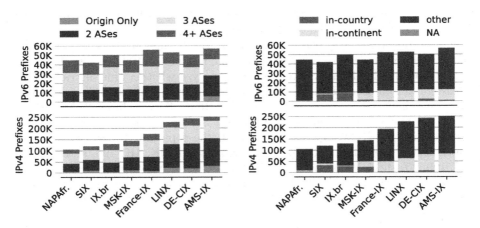

Fig. 4. Length of shortest AS path per prefix

Fig. 5. Geolocation of prefixes relative to Route Server

Rather than looking at the AS path, we now directly map the visible prefixes to countries and continents using a snapshot of Maxmind's GeoLite2 database [53] from 1st June 2021. While perfect IP-to-geolocation mapping is a long-standing research problem, previous work showed that for various public geolocation databases 99% of predictions stay within 600 km of the actual location [21]. Similarly, Maxmind claims that for many countries 0% of predictions are off by more than 250 km [52]. While this large radius might influence the accuracy of country-level predictions, it provides us with near-perfect accuracy for continental predictions as most of our Route Servers have even more distance between their location and the closest continental border. Figure 5 shows the Route Server prefixes of different IXPs separated by whether they lead to in-country, in-continent, or out-of-continent ("other") hosts. Notably, there is a small number of prefixes for which the database did not include a mapping ("NA"). Interestingly, looking at host locations provides an even more drastic result than looking at AS paths: Regardless of the actual Route Server, around two-thirds of all prefixes lead to out-of-continent hosts.

While the growing trend of remote-peering [57] can easily lead to many out-of-continent routes, it is unclear whether it also contributes to the high number of lengthy routes. To better understand whether this correlation exists, we want to compare the path length of each route with the RTT (as a proxy for distance) to its next-hop interface. Hence, we run ping measurements from a server directly connected to the switching fabric of L-IXP towards each member interface.[3] To account for latency inflations due to, e.g., congestion, we repeated those measurements 100 times and collected the minimum RTT towards each interface throughout all runs. Finally, we associate the shortest path of each prefix with the minimum RTT we measured for its respective next-hop interface. Notably, if there was more than one possible shortest path, we picked the one for which the next-hop RTT was the lowest. Figure 7 shows for each prefix of a given minimum path length the minimum latency to its next-hop.[4] We observe that there is no strict correlation between the distance of a peer and the length of the routes it provides (Fig. 6).

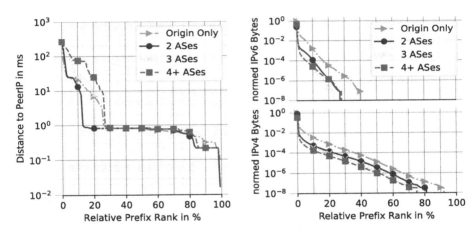

Fig. 6. Distance to next-hop per prefix, separated by length of shortest AS path

Fig. 7. peering LAN bytes per prefix, separated by length of shortest AS path

Now that we know that even local peers forward lengthy routes to the route server, the question becomes whether those routes see any traffic. For one of our observed IXPs, we obtained IPFIX captures sampling 1 out of every 10K packets traversing its peering LAN. While we can observe multilateral and bilateral peering traffic in this data set, we have no insights into traffic exchanged via private peering established via direct interconnects as it does not traverse the public peering infrastructure. Based on the captured flows between the 1st of June and the 7th of June[5], we calculate the aggregated number of Bytes destined

---

[3] We neither had probing devices at other peering LANs, nor was our probing device at L-IXP IPv6-enabled at the time of our study.

[4] We explicitly avoid the classification into remote and local peers based on RTT estimates alone given the caveats presented in [57].

[5] We provide details on how we choose this time window in the next section.

towards each prefix. Figure 7 groups Route Server prefix by their shortest path and shows for each prefix (x-axis) the number of bytes (y-axis, logarithmic) relative to the prefix with the most bytes (i.e., we show bytes normalized by the prefix with the maximum byte count, ρ). We observe that 6% of prefixes reachable via one hop carry at least 1% of ρ's bytes while only less than 0.5% of 2 or more hop prefixes carry that much traffic. Apart from the top 6%, prefixes reachable via two or more hops carry around an order of magnitude less traffic— with only minor differences between two, three, and four or more hops. Finally, we observe that 8, 19, 24, and 25% of IPv4 (60, 72, 73, and 77% of IPv6) prefixes with a shortest path of 1, 2, 3, and 4+ hops carry no traffic at all, respectively.

Those observations are likely tied to how long-established IXP members engage with a Route Server: In contrast to new members, long-established members already acquired many bi-lateral peering sessions. It is common that members attribute higher local preference values to such bi-lateral sessions as they often come with Service Level Agreements (SLAs). Hence, long-established members often peer with the Route Server to get an idea of which routes are available at all but only hand-pick routes they actually use based on, e.g., how consistently they are available or how much performance benefit they may introduce. As local preference values only de-prioritize (rather than filtering them) multilateral peering routes, Route Servers are also used as automatic fall-back in case a bi-lateral peering session suffers from, e.g., an outage [32,68].

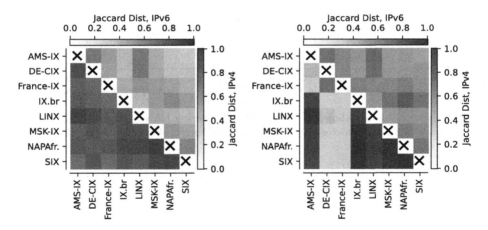

Fig. 8. Similarity of prefixes between Route Servers

Fig. 9. Similarity of addresses between Route Servers

How Route Server Specific are Multi-lateral Peering Routes? Until now, we saw that most Route Servers have very similar characteristics; hence, we now try to understand where the actual difference lies. As a similarity metric, we use the Jaccard distance. The Jaccard distance between two sets of elements,

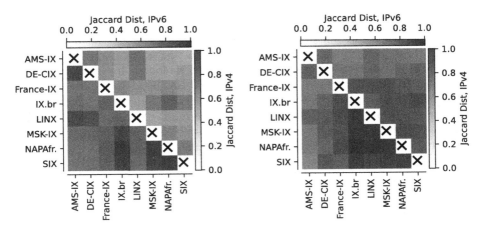

Fig. 10. Similarity of addresses between Route Servers without HE's 2002::/16 route

Fig. 11. Similarity of prefixes between Route Servers for common peers

A and B, is calculated as $JD(A,B) = \frac{|A \cap B|}{|A \cup B|}$. In comparison to other common similarity metrics (e.g., the overlap coefficient $OC(A,B) = \frac{|A \cap B|}{min(|A|,|B|)}$), the Jaccard distance also produces small values when A is entirely contained in a significantly larger B, i.e., it not only considers the similarity of elements but also the cardinalities of the sets. For each pair of Route Servers we now compute the Jaccard Distance between prefixes (see, Fig. 8) and reachable IP addresses (see, Fig. 9). As the Jaccard index is symmetric, we show results for IPv4 in the top-right triangle and results for IPv6 in the bottom-left triangle.

While we observe that certain Route Server combinations show more overlap than others (e.g. AMS-IX and DE-CIX), the average similarity for IPv4 lies at around 50% (77% for IPv6). As certain prefixes can be more-specifics of others, it is also unsurprising that the similarity of reachable IP addresses lies roughly 13% higher for IPv4. While we observe similar behaviour for many IPv6 combinations, we observe that France-IX and DE-CIX are different from the others but similar to each other. We observe that this "clustering" is mainly the result of a single route: 2002::/16 announced by AS6939 (Hurrican Electric). When ignoring this route (see Fig. 10), the takeaways for IPv6 are roughly the same as for IPv4.

Finally, we want to know whether ASes with memberships at multiple IXPs share the same routes with the respective Route Servers. Hence, we rerun the same analysis but, this time, focus only on routes announced by the same member ASes at both IXPs (see Fig. 11). While this comparison shows naturally higher overlap compared to Fig. 8, we observe that certain Route Server combinations still show a Jaccard distance of less than 70%; yet those routes barely make a difference for the number of reachable IPs (Figure not shown).

Summary. We observe that the distribution of prefixes across Route Server peers that was presented by Richter et al. [68] is also present in many other

Route Servers across the world. In general, we show that the characteristics of routes at various Route Servers are very similar. We observe that the majority of routes at Route Servers lead to out-of-continent destinations—likely a side-effect of the growing remote-peering trend. Surprisingly, we found that most routes at Route Servers contain three or more ASes and that the distance of the peer is not a factor for this phenomenon, i.e., even local peers provide many unattractive routes to the Route Server. Nevertheless, the peering LAN traffic from one IXP suggests that its members primarily use the routes to direct destinations, and mostly rely on the Route Server for failover or analysis purposes.

5   Inferring Peering Relationships

After we analyzed the routes that are available to newly joined IXP members via multi-lateral peering, we are now interested in the routes that can be obtained by establishing bi-lateral and private peering sessions.

Similar to the work of Richter et al. [68], we infer bi-lateral peerings (and the prefixes that are announced via them) by observing the traffic that flows through the IXP's peering LAN. As shown by Ager et al., some ASes may "abuse" the peering LAN for additional transit connections to their customers. Given that our reachability analysis might be rather sensitive to the presence of transit relationships[6], we substantially extend the method used by Richter et al. to account for them.

As the inference approach for bi-lateral peerings relies on traffic data, we now limit the scope of our analysis to **one** large European IXP, L-IXP. While the IXP's peering LAN may cover most of the bi-lateral peering agreements, it offers no visibility into the private peerings that happen within the co-located data centers; hence, we rely on carefully selected looking glasses within those data centers to uncover routes that are available via private peering. Notably, this approach does not allow us to accurately distinguish between dedicated private peerings and connections to, e.g., cloud exchanges (as discussed in Sect. 2).

5.1   Bilateral Peering

We bootstrap our analysis in a similar way to Richter et al. [68]: Whenever we observe traffic destined towards IP I flowing from A to B, we deduct that the respective covering /24 (or /48 for IPv6) for I must have been announced from B to A. Notably, this approach relies on the assumption that an ASes will *eventually* send traffic to most, if not all, of the prefixes it received from a neighbor. Hence, we first have to understand for how long we need to observe peering LAN traffic before we arrive at a rather static "snapshot".

Picking a Reasonable Window Size. On the one hand, a small window size (e.g., an hour) may underestimate the available routes as not all of them

---

[6] As customers can potentially send traffic destined for the entire Internet to their transit providers, incorporating such connections would bloat up the set of reachableprefixes.

necessarily continuously see traffic; on the other hand, a large time window (e.g., a year) is more likely to yield an extensive list, yet may provide an overestimate as certain routes are withdrawn in the meantime. To get a better sense of what might be a good window size, we test by how much a certain window size would affect the number of /24s and /48s for which we observe traffic. For various window sizes between 4 hours and 14 days, we calculate the prefix counts and then move the window forward by one hour. Using this method, we generate, e.g., 739, 719, 575, and 407 data points for the window sizes 4 hours, 1 day, 7 days, and 14 days throughout the entire May 2021.

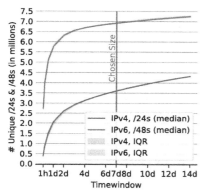

Fig. 12. Influence of window size on visible prefixes

Figure 12 show the median prefixes (y-axis) that we observed for a given window size (x-axis) as well as the Inter Quartile Ranges (IQR) for IPv4 and IPv6. While the knee of the curve (i.e., the point at which further increases of the window size start to yield smaller improvements) lies at around one and a half days, we observe a continuous, almost linear, increase after a window size of six days. We decided to choose a window size of seven days. While this choice might yield a small number of already withdrawn prefixes, it covers workdays as well as weekend days— which are known to exhibit rather different traffic characteristics [29, 41, 43, 72].

Removing Transit Sessions. Now that we have some understanding of the routes that are announced between each member pair, we have to isolate and ignore transit sessions as they might substantially inflate the set of reachable prefixes. Perfectly identifying the business relationships of links has been an academic goal for more than two decades. The current state of the art algorithm, ASRank [47], is well-known for its high accuracy when it comes to identifying transit relationships (even in narrow contexts [64]). CAIDA hosts two versions of monthly-updated business relationship information: serial-1 and serial-2. While serial-1 relies solely on routing information (i.e., AS paths), serial-2 contains serial-1's information but is further extended with topology information inferred via additional sources, e.g., traceroute paths that were mapped to AS Paths. As a result, serial-2 contains more relationships but also inherits inaccuracies from its data extensions (e.g., from IP-to-AS mapping [7,51]). Surprisingly, neither serial-1 nor serial-2 can cover more than 21.2% or 22.3% of the 220k+ IPv4 IXP member pairs that exchanged traffic during that period.

Improving Relationship Coverage via Route Server Paths. Whether the ASRank algorithm produces an inference for a given AS link mostly depends on the set of AS paths that it is executed on. Hence, we can improve our inference coverage by providing additional AS paths that 'cross' (i.e., contain two consecutive IXP members) the IXP's peering fabric. To uncover such paths, we revisit the Route Server of our IXP.

Our main idea is as follows: Our Route Server snapshot contains various routes as well as their respective Route Server redistribution communities, i.e., Route Server specific communities to express the instructions: (1) announce to all neighbor, (2) don't announce to any neighbor, (3) announce to a specific neighbor, and (4) do not announce to a specific neighbor. Notably, instruction (1) and (2) are usually paired with instructions of type (3) and (4) but not with one another. By simulating the redistribution, we can deduce the paths that each IXP member received via its Route Server session(s).

More formally, we construct paths as follows: Let AS A announce some route with AS path (A, p') to the Route Server where p' refers to some (potentially empty) sequence of ASes—we ignore the few routes that contain AS_SETs. A also attaches a set of (potentially large) BGP communities that we translate into the previously explained instructions (1)–(4). To retrieve the set RP of Route Server peers to which the route is redistributed, we first sort the set of instructions in the order we introduced them[7]. While we set RP to all Route Server neighbors for instruction (1), we set RP to the empty set for instruction (2); if both instruction (1) and (2) are present we ignored the route. Notably, if n either instruction (1) nor (2) is present, we defaulted to instruction (1). Afterward, we first added and then discarded specific ASes to/from RP according to the instructions of type (3) and (4). respectively. Finally we constructed paths of the form $(B, A, p'), \forall B \in RP$ which 'cross' the IXP at the link (B, A).

We combine those paths with routes gathered from five days of the rib snapshots from the route collector projects RIPE RIS and RouteViews (i.e., the same data sources that CAIDA uses to produce serial-1 data). For IPv4-related inferences, we use the publicly available ASRank script that is hosted by CAIDA. For IPv6, we apply the necessary changes described by Giotsas et al. [33] to adjust the inference script to IPv6 routig policies. Both scripts require a list of Route Server ASNs for their inference. To generate this list, we extract all ASNs with the type 'Route Server' from PeeringDB. After these steps, our extended relationship data set covers 69.0% and 63.2% of traffic-carrying IPv4 and IPv6 links.

Improving Relationship Coverage via Manual Search. At this point, we still have various ASes with limited coverage. Hence, we decided to manually search for additional relationship information. We invested three days of manual relationship look-ups for ASes that either (i) are in the top 30 contributors of unclassified links, (ii) have only less than 10% of their links covered, or (iii) have more than 10% of their links inferred to be transit connections.

For our manual search, we mostly relied on entries in PeeringDB (e.g., [63]), RADb/Whois (e.g., [66]), and targeted web searches (e.g., [76]) that clearly described (at least some) relationships of a given ASN—please note that the

---

[7] This order represents a conservative approach—if both the instruction to add AS X and to delete X are present, x will ultimately not be included in the set of Route Server peers.

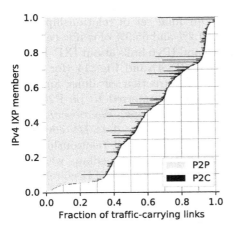

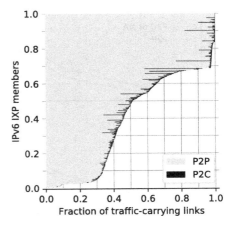

Fig. 13. Coverage of relationships for traffic-carrying links (IPv4).

Fig. 14. Coverage of relationships for traffic-carrying links (IPv6).

three given examples are chosen randomly and may or may not belong to members of our studied IXP. For autnum objects in RADb/Whois, we used an approach similar to that described in [47] to infer transit relationships (even though we did not automate the process). We used as-set objects in RADb/Whois with clearly defined names (most commonly, e.g., `AS<XXX>:AS-CUSTOMER(S)`, `AS<XXX>:AS-TRANSIT(S)`, `AS<XXX>:AS-UPSTREAM(S)` or `AS<XXX>:AS-PEER(S)`) to identify relationships. For PeeringDB and the targeted web searches, we searched for exhaustive enumerations of, e.g., providers as part of, e.g., the network infrastructure description. Whenever possible, we differentiated between IPv4 and IPv6 relationships as well as regional relationships (i.e., if a websites described AS X as peer in Europe but as provider in Asia, we noted it as peer giove that our IXP operates in Europe).

While investigating the relationships for the ASes mentioned above, we observed diminishing coverage improvements; hence, we decided to not extend our manual search beyond them. Notably, whenever an AS explicitly specified its providers and customers but not its peers, we assumed that all remaining links are peering relationships.

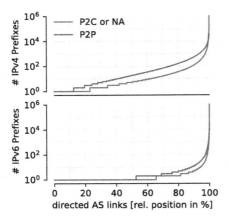

Fig. 15. Norm-prefixes per directed AS link

Our final set of relationships covers 74.2% and 65.9% of traffic-carrying IPv4 and IPv6 links at our IXP. Figure 13 (for IPv4) and Fig. 14 (for IPv6) show the fraction of links for each AS that are inferred to be P2P and P2C relationships. We observe that in both plots our data set covers at least a fourth of all relationships for 93% of ASes. On median, we cover 66% of IPv4 and 51% of IPv6 relationships. While we observe that overall only 1.2% (IPv4) and 1.5% (IPv6) of all inferred links have transit relationships, we also observe that these relationships are distributed across almost all IXP members; hence, it is rather the norm than the exception to establish additional sessions with transit providers via the IXP's peering fabric. Beyond its coverage, we are also interested in the filtering impact of our relationship data set. Figure 15 shows the number of available IPv4 and IPv6 norm-prefixes per traffic-carrying, directed[8] AS link. We observe that certain links carry traffic for more than 10^6 norm-prefixes. Yet, when only considering links that our data set classifies as peering links, we filter out all links that carry traffic for exceptionally many prefixes. Hence, we continue our analysis using only the links explicitly inferred as peering links, i.e., we not only ignore those links explicitly inferred as transit links but also those for which we have no inferred relationship.

5.2 Private Peering

As previously discussed in Sect. 4, our traffic captures do not contain any private peering connections. Therefore, we rely on queries to carefully selected looking glasses (LGs) to infer routes available via private peering. To automatically query looking glass interfaces, we write identification and querying interfaces—similar to those described in [31]—for common looking glass utilities including, e.g., HSDN [73], RESPAWNER [54], and COUGAR [26]. To initially find ASes with looking glasses, we rely on PeeringDB [62] as well as various online lists [8,9,37, 42,46,75]. We first narrow down our selection by removing all LGs from ASes that are not members of our IXP. Afterwards, we removed all LGs that our indentification interface could not map to a LG template. Then, we manually went through the looking glass interfaces of the remaining 63 ASes and validated whether they could look at the routing table of a router that is located within one of the IXPs contiguous colocation facilities—we heavily relied on the naming and

---

[8] If A and B exchange traffic in both directions, we treat the links (A, B) and (B, A) separately.

excluded all entries for which the location was not exactly matching a colocation name. Finally, after removing LGs requiring captchas, exploring rate-limiting, or explicitly stating 'no automation allowed', we are left with LGs from 17 different ASes to trigger.

Triggering Looking Glasses. As looking glasses are usually provided on a voluntary basis from operators to operators, we do not want to abuse them with gazillions of bursty queries. First, we limit the set of norm-prefixes for which we query the LGs to those that are (1) necessary for the analysis in Sect. 6 and (2) not yet covered by multi-lateral or bi-lateral peering. Second, when a looking glass yields a longest-prefix match rather than an exact match and returns a covering prefix that is likely not a default route (i.e., a routes less specific than /8 and /16 for IPv4 and IPv6, respectively), we no longer query for any other norm-prefixes covered by this less-specific. Third, we waited 39.3 seconds[9] on average between two consecutive queries to the same looking glass. With those safeguards in place, we queried looking glasses as follows:

1. **Querying a LG.** We choose a looking glass in round-robin fashion and performed—depending on the LG utility—either an exact match or, preferably, a longest-prefix match query against it.
2. **Ignoring transit routes.** If the LG returned a route for which the first-hop would be a transit provider to the AS the looking glass resides in, we ignore that route. Similarly, if we can't find a relationship and the first hop is a Tier 1 provider, we also ignore the route (given that it likely represents a transit relationship).
3. **Requiring IXP routes.** To ensure that the route is locally available at the IXP, we ensured that the first-hop AS is also an IXP member.

If no route remains after steps 2 and 3, we wait 2 seconds and then query the next looking glass until we have exhausted our LG list. If one LG returned a non-filtered route we marked the norm-prefix as reachable (and queried the next round-robin-order LG for the next norm-prefix), otherwise we mark it as unreachable.

In total, we were able to uncover 2.33M, 6.73M, and 6.77M IPv4 (3.41B, 3.41B, and 3.45B IPv6) norm-prefixes available via multi-lateral, bi-lateral, and private peering covering 19.8, 57.1, and 57.4% (37.3, 37.4, 37.8%) of all routed IPv4 (IPv6) addresses (according to Geoff Houston's Routing Table Analysis Report [36]), respectively. These results provide a real-world calibration for the 70+ % of reachability theoretically calculated by Böttger et al. [10] in 2018.

6 Route Importance

In this section, we present a qualitative analysis of the uncovered peering prefixes with two different measures of importance: (a) How many domains in a top N

---

[9] A result of multiple small waits between queries to different LGs in combination with the answer time of the other LGs.

ranking are served by transit-free reachable prefixes, and (b) how many of the top destination prefixes of a large eyeball network are reachable without transit. The findings of this section can be summarized as follows:

- For both rankings, around half of the top-100 norm-prefixes can be reached via multi-lateral peering.
- For our traffic-based ranking, nearly all prefixes can be reached via bi-lateral peering with few exceptions that can mostly be reached via private peering.
- For our domain-based ranking, the same holds true for IPv4. For IPv6, we observe that bi-lateral peering has a substantially lower impact. While, in general, more prefixes remain unreachable than for IPv4, most of the top norm-prefixes can be obtained via private peering.
- We observe that the prefixes that remain unreachable even via private peering mostly lead to large Transit and Tier 1 providers.

6.1 Prefix Rankings

Traffic-Based Ranking. To provide a traffic-based importance ranking from an independent source, we use traffic statistics from one of the largest European ISPs. In particular, we collect egress traffic from all the ISP's eyeball source addresses at all edge routers over one day (10th June 2021) at a sample rate of 1:1000 packets. For each destination IP, we sum the number of egress bytes throughout the day, aggregate these values to norm-prefixes, and cluster the top 10k norm-prefixes for IPv4 and IPv6.

Domain-Based Ranking. To quantify the importance of IPs with another metric, we obtain a domain-based importance ranking. Thus, we rely on re-computed results from a previous work by Naab et al. [55]. The domain-based norm-prefix top list is generated by picking a common domain top list (e.g., from Alexa [3], Majestic [48], or Umbrella [25]), resolving these domains to as many IPs as possible, and then ranking each norm-prefix by the number of Fully Qualified Domain Names (FQDNs) that can be resolved to an IP. We requested an updated snapshot of the top list from the authors of [55] and promptly received a re-computation from 30th April 2021. We decide to use the Umbrella-based norm-prefix top list because it is the only one from which we can derive 10K IPv4 as well as 10k IPv6 prefixes.

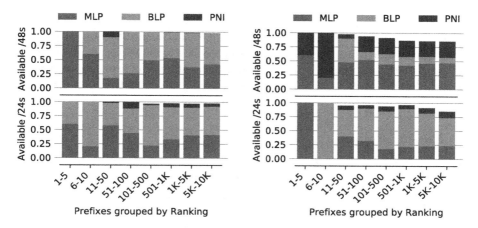

Fig. 16. Coverage of eyeball-based top-10K prefix ranking

Fig. 17. Coverage of domain-based top-10K prefix ranking

6.2   Reachability of the Top-10K

Now that we got the domain- and traffic-based top 10 IPv4 and IPv6 norm-prefixes, we can analyze how many of those prefixes are reachable via different peering types.

Traffic-Based Ranking. Figure 16 separates the top 10k prefixes into different classes based on their respective ranking (x-axis) and shows for each class the fraction of reachable prefixes (y-axis) for IPv4 at the bottom and IPv6 at the top. In addition, each prefix is colored by the lowest-requirement peering type (requirement and economical costs for PNI > BLP > MLP) that it can be reached by (if any). We observe that the top 100 prefixes for both protocols can be fully covered using all peering types. In general, we observe that only very few prefixes can not be reached. Notably, the vast majority of top-10k prefixes can solely be reached via bi-lateral peering agreements. This result benefits aspiring IXP members who, if they carefully select a few private peering partners, can keep their operational costs minimal.

Domain-Based Ranking. Figure 17 shows our results for the domain-based top 10k prefixes in the same style as the previous figure. First, we observe that significantly more—especially lower rank—prefixes are unreachable (e.g., approx. 15% of the lowest 5k IPv4 prefixes are not reachable). Second, we see a drastic shift in patterns for IPv6: The difference between routes available via multi-lateral and bi-lateral peering is almost negligible compared to IPv4. Consequently, IXP members have to rely substantially more on private peering to reach the prefixes with the highest domain counts. Yet, for approx. 15% of 500-or-lower prefix class prefixes IXP members still have to rely on their transit as they are unreachable via peering.

To reduce their operational costs, members of large IXPs may egress most—if not all—of their high-volume destination traffic via (mostly bi-lateral) peering connections while using their transit to egress low-volume yet domain-heavy prefixes. Notably, between 25 and 50% of both top-10k prefix lists can be reached via multi-lateral peering—a finding that further highlights the importance of Route Server connections especially for new IXP members.

6.3   Missing Routes

To get some idea of which routes were not available, we mapped norm-prefixes to ASes via a longest-prefix match on the previously mentioned IP-to-AS data set from CAIDA. We further map each origin AS to a class using CAIDA's AS Classification data set [15].

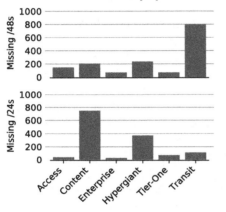

Fig. 18. Unavailable prefixes by origin AS type.

We further refine the classification using lists of Tier 1 Networks [77] and Hypergiants [12]. Figure 18 shows the number of missing norm-prefixes (y-axis) that are originated by the ASes of different classes (x-axis) for IPv4 (bottom) and IPv6 (top). For IPv4, we observe that most of the missing/24 prefixes belong to content providers/hypergiants. In particular, we observe that more than half of the prefixes in both of those classes can be attributed to Amazon's AS14618 and AS16509. Notably, most of the missing prefixes for Amazon do not see any peering LAN traffic (regardless of the business relationship) throughout our measurement period. As most of these prefixes are unique to the traffic-based prefix ranking, we suspect that our eyeball vantage point has access to routes that are only announced via private peering on dedicated connections, and, hence, remain hidden from the peering LAN. Taking Amazon out of the picture, the most prominent class would be the same as for IPv6: Transit ASes. Notably, the individual contributions made by single ASes are much more uniformly distributed; out of the 61 and 231 total ASes contributing to the IPv4 and IPv6 Transit AS class, the top ASes contribute no more than 21 and 29 prefixes respectively. Further, we observe that the vast majority of the prefixes that belong to Transit ASes are only present in the domain-based top list but not in the traffic-based top list. In summary, our observations suggest that ASes can indeed offload high-volume prefixes to peering links by joining an IXP but they still require transit to reach the heavy tail of (potentially low-traffic) domains.

6.4   Limitations

Next, we discuss limitations and specifically elaborate on the generalization of our findings. **Multi-lateral Peering:** We analyzed the Route Servers of different IXPs based on separate snapshots generated throughout seven days. Hence, our observations may be biased by sequences of high-frequency updates (as described by Ariemma et al. [5]). Yet, we discussed our results with some of the IXP operators that provided Route Server snapshots, and they told us that they did not observe unusual behavior during the days from which the snapshot was taken. Yet, as many prefixes can only be seen when aggregating updates over some amount of time, a single snapshot might miss unstable routing information. **Bi-lateral Peering:** Our analysis of bi-lateral peering reachability relied on sampled peering LAN traffic data and inferred business relationships. While we used an entire week of traffic data to partially overcome the problem of missing traffic for existing routes, we likely still missed a few routes as (1) they genuinely did not receive any traffic during our observation period or (2) they small amounts of traffic yet the sampling algorithm did not incorporate any of their packets. While we did our best to improve the coverage of inferred business relationships, we can not guarantee for the correctness of the business inference algorithm. While both algorithms were shown to provide high-quality inferences on public data [33,47], we utilize them in a rather different context which could potentially lead to iimpairments in their performance [64]. **Private Peering:** For the inference of private peering routes, we used a very small set of looking glasses and queried them in a restrictive manner. Especially for our findings regarding the summed reachability, our observations can only be seen as a lower bound. If our number of vantage points would have been significantly higher and we could have triggered queries at a high rate, the amount of private peering prefixes would have certainly increased leading to overall higher estimates for the total achievable reachability. **Regional Importance Bias:** The utilized data sets to infer peering relations and qualify the importance of IPs and prefixes (see Sect. 5 and Sect. 6) are biased towards the European service region. While it is for the conducted analysis required to compare reachability at IXPs and relevance (ISP data set and DNS) in the very same region, it may not necessarily apply to others. As different cultures may have unique eyeball behaviors, a traffic-based ranking for other large eyeball networks around the world may lead to different prefixes especially in the lower part of the top-10k ranking. As address resolution is often location-skewed (e.g., due to DNS load balancing) our domain-based ranking is likely biased towards norm-prefixes primarily used in the European region. While we expect unmatching biases (e.g., comparing American top lists to European IXP) to lower the overall top list coverage based on, e.g., routing policy differences [34], we do not expect that such a comparison would yield considerable differences.

7   Discussion

Our results suggest that networks that peer at one of the larger IXPs can indeed move most traffic to bi-lateral peerings, yet (especially for IPv6) not all prefixes that serve a high number of domains are reachable via peering. While an assessment of the quality of those available peering relationships (i.e., the capacity and latency guarantees they provide) goes beyond the scope of this work, previous works already hinted at certain obtainable benefits [2], e.g., Schlinker et al. [69] showed that the latencies for 10% of Facebook's traffic can be decreased by up to 10ms when switching from transit to peering routes.

That many high-volume prefixes can be served via bi-lateral peering at IXPs is strongly correlated with the observation that Hypergiants—large content providers such as Google, Facebook, or Amazon [12]— interconnect at tens (if not hundreds) of IXPs (see PeeringDB). According to Pujol et al. [65], these relatively few Hypergiants can be responsible for up to 80% of all ingress traffic of large eyeball networks.

Similar to hypergiants, the routes of many lower-tier networks are also available via peering. To them, broadly announcing their routes allows them to reduce the volume of ingress traffic delivered via some of their transit providers. Over time, such an approach may transform an asymmetric traffic ratio into a symmetric one, and allows these networks to re-negotiate their previous transit providers into a peering relationship.

In contrast, we observe that many of the domain-based top prefixes belong to large transit providers and Tier-1s. To reach those prefixes, IXP members often still have to rely on transit.

But how do those findings relate to different types of networks? **Large networks and hypergiants** already established thousands of peering connections [6] and use sophisticated traffic engineering strategies [70,78] among those connections. Their egress traffic mapping is already automated to a degree where adding new peers does not pose a challenge anymore which leads to constant growth of their peering edges and continuous dwindling of dependence on their transit connections.

In contrast, **small (access) networks** may rely on a few border routers operated mostly manually by a small group of network engineers. Adding new bi-lateral peers for these networks often poses a challenge in terms of resources and network complexity (operational costs). Hence, despite our findings, many of such networks may only peer with a Route Server and a few carefully selected bi-lateral peers on purpose. To them, the reduced supplier cost that comes with sophisticated peering is often not worth the increasing added operational complexity.

Medium-Sized Networks. (e.g., smaller national service providers) sit in between those two extremes. While many of them have neither automated their egress traffic mapping nor their peer acquisition yet, they are typically run by competent IT staff capable of anticipating how much their network would benefit from a particular peer. The earlier those networks transition from a few expensive yet feature-rich routers to a distributed fleet of cheaper routers (with potentially partial visibility), the sooner they can quickly scale their peering edge allowing them to take full advantage of the opportunities provided by large IXPs.

8   Conclusion

Throughout this paper, we analyzed the routes available via multi-lateral, bi-lateral, and private peering. For multi-lateral peering, we analyzed Route Server snapshots from eight of the world's largest peering LANs and showed that most of their routes lead to out-of-continent locations via three or more AS hops. While remote peering might be a major contributor to the geographic distance of Route Server destinations, we observe that close and distant IXP members alike provide lengthy, unattractive routes to the Route Server. When comparing those findings to peering LAN traffic, obtained through a collaboration with one large IXP, we saw that mostly one-hop routes saw substantial traffic. In fact, we observed that 25% and 77% of IPv4 and IPv6 Route Server prefixes with at least four hop long paths see no traffic at all. This indicates that even though Route Servers provide many routes, most IXP members only make use of local routes. Afterwards, we used two heuristic-based methodologies to infer bi-lateral and private peering routes from the IXP's peering LAN traffic. During our inferences, we carefully isolated transit connections that were established over the peering LAN—a phenomenon previously reported by Ager et al. [1]. Based on our inference, we observe that at least 19.8, 57.1, and 57.4% (37.3, 37.4, 37.8%) of all routed IPv4 (IPv6) address space can be reached at our IXP via multi-lateral, bi-lateral, and private peering, respectively. Those results provide practical contrast to the 70+ % reachability theoretically calculated by Böttger et al. [10]. Finally, we show that almost all of the top 10k egress prefixes of a large European eyeball network can be reached via bi-lateral peerings. In contrast, we also find that up to 15% of top 10k domain-serving prefixes can not be reached via any type of peering at our IXP. Notably, we observe that most of these prefixes belong to large transit and Tier 1 providers.

References

1. Ager, B., Chatzis, N., Feldmann, A., Sarrar, N., Uhlig, S., Willinger, W.: Anatomy of a large European IXP. In: Proceedings of the ACM SIGCOMM 2012 Conference on Applications, Technologies, Architectures, and Protocols for Computer Communication, pp. 163–174 (2012)
2. Ahmed, A., Shafiq, Z., Bedi, H., Khakpour, A.: Peering vs. transit: performance comparison of peering and transit interconnections. In: 2017 IEEE 25th International Conference on Network Protocols (ICNP), pp. 1–10. IEEE (2017)
3. Alexa: The top 500 sites on the web (2021). https://www.alexa.com/topsites. Accessed 21 June 2021

4. AMS-IX: Total traffic statistics (2021). https://stats.ams-ix.net/index.html. Accessed 27 June 2021. Archived version. https://web.archive.org/web/20210627072325/stats.ams-ix.net/index.html

5. Ariemma, L., Liotta, S., Candela, M., Di Battista, G.: Long-lasting sequences of BGP updates. In: Hohlfeld, O., Lutu, A., Levin, D. (eds.) PAM 2021. LNCS, vol. 12671, pp. 213–229. Springer, Cham (2021). https://doi.org/10.1007/978-3-030-72582-2_13

6. Arnold, T., et al.: Cloud provider connectivity in the flat internet. In: Proceedings of the ACM Internet Measurement Conference, pp. 230–246 (2020)

7. Augustin, B., et al.: Avoiding traceroute anomalies with Paris traceroute. In: Proceedings of the 6th ACM SIGCOMM Conference on Internet Measurement, pp. 153–158 (2006)

8. BGP4.as: BGP looking glasses for IPv4/IPv6, traceroute & BGP route servers (2021). https://www.bgp4.as/looking-glasses. Accessed 21 June 2021

9. bgplookingglass.com: BGP looking glass database (2021). http://www.bgplookingglass.com/. Accessed 21 June 2021

10. Böttger, T., et al.: The elusive internet flattening: 10 years of IXP growth. arXiv e-prints (2018)

11. Böttger, T., Cuadrado, F., Tyson, G., Castro, I., Uhlig, S.: Open connect everywhere: a glimpse at the internet ecosystem through the lens of the Netflix CDN. ACM SIGCOMM Comput. Commun. Rev. **48**(1), 28–34 (2018)

12. Böttger, T., Cuadrado, F., Uhlig, S.: Looking for hypergiants in peeringDB. ACM SIGCOMM Comput. Commun. Rev. **48**(3), 13–19 (2018)

13. Brito, S.H.B., Santos, M.A.S., Fontes, R.R., Perez, D.A.L., Rothenberg, C.E.: Dissecting the largest national ecosystem of public internet eXchange points in Brazil. In: Karagiannis, T., Dimitropoulos, X. (eds.) PAM 2016. LNCS, vol. 9631, pp. 333–345. Springer, Cham (2016). https://doi.org/10.1007/978-3-319-30505-9_25

14. CAIDA: The CAIDA as relationships dataset, 2021/06 (2021). https://publicdata.caida.org/datasets/as-relationships/. Accessed 21 June 2021

15. CAIDA: The CAIDA UCSD as classification dataset, 2021–04-01 (2021). https://www.caida.org/catalog/datasets/as-classification

16. CAIDA: The CAIDA UCSD as to organization mapping dataset, 2021/06 (2021). https://www.caida.org/data/as_organizations. Accessed 21 June 2021

17. CAIDA: The CAIDA UCSD peeringDB dataset, 2010/08-2021/06 (2021). https://www.caida.org/catalog/datasets/peeringdb. Accessed 21 June 2021

18. CAIDA: Routeviews prefix to as mappings dataset for IPv4 and IPv6, 2021/06. https://www.caida.org/datasets/routeviews-prefix2as/. Accessed 21 June. 2021

19. Cardona Restrepo, J.C., Stanojevic, R.: IXP traffic: a macroscopic view. In: Proceedings of the 7th Latin American Networking Conference, pp. 1–8 (2012)

20. Castro, I., Cardona, J.C., Gorinsky, S., Francois, P.: Remote peering: more peering without internet flattening. In: Proceedings of the 10th ACM International on Conference on Emerging Networking Experiments and Technologies, pp. 185–198 (2014)

21. Chandrasekaran, B., et al.: Alidade: IP geolocation without active probing. Department of Computer Science, Duke University, Technical report CS-TR-2015.001 (2015)

22. Chatzis, N., Smaragdakis, G., Böttger, J., Krenc, T., Feldmann, A.: On the benefits of using a large IXP as an internet vantage point. In: Proceedings of the 2013 Conference on Internet Measurement Conference, pp. 333–346 (2013)

23. Chiesa, M., di Lallo, R., Lospoto, G., Mostafaei, H., Rimondini, M., Di Battista, G.: PrIXP: preserving the privacy of routing policies at internet exchange points. In: 2017 IFIP/IEEE Symposium on Integrated Network and Service Management (IM), pp. 435–441. IEEE (2017)

24. Chiu, Y.C., Schlinker, B., Radhakrishnan, A.B., Katz-Bassett, E., Govindan, R.: Are we one hop away from a better internet? In: Proceedings of the 2015 Internet Measurement Conference, pp. 523–529 (2015)

25. CISCO: Cisco umbrella 1 million (2021). https://umbrella.cisco.com/blog/cisco-umbrella-1-million. Accessed 21 June 2021

26. COUGAR: Cougar looking glass utility (2021). https://github.com/Cougar/lg. Accessed 21 June 2021

27. DE-CIX: DE-CIX Frankfurt statistics (2021). https://www.de-cix.net/en/locations/germany/frankfurt/statistics. Accessed 27 June 2021. Archived version. https://web.archive.org/web/20210620110006/www.de-cix.net/en/locations/germany/frankfurt/statistics

28. Dietzel, C., Feldmann, A., King, T.: Blackholing at IXPs: on the effectiveness of DDoS mitigation in the wild. In: Karagiannis, T., Dimitropoulos, X. (eds.) PAM 2016. LNCS, vol. 9631, pp. 319–332. Springer, Cham (2016). https://doi.org/10.1007/978-3-319-30505-9_24

29. Feldmann, A., et al.: The lockdown effect: implications of the COVID-19 pandemic on internet traffic. In: Proceedings of the ACM Internet Measurement Conference, pp. 1–18 (2020)

30. Feng, G., Seshan, S., Steenkiste, P.: UNARI: an uncertainty-aware approach to as relationships inference. In: Proceedings of the 15th International Conference on Emerging Networking Experiments and Technologies, pp. 272–284 (2019)

31. Giotsas, V., Dhamdhere, A., Claffy, K.C.: Periscope: unifying looking glass querying. In: Karagiannis, T., Dimitropoulos, X. (eds.) PAM 2016. LNCS, vol. 9631, pp. 177–189. Springer, Cham (2016). https://doi.org/10.1007/978-3-319-30505-9_14

32. Giotsas, V., Dietzel, C., Smaragdakis, G., Feldmann, A., Berger, A., Aben, E.: Detecting peering infrastructure outages in the wild. In: Proceedings of the Conference of the ACM Special Interest Group on Data Communication, pp. 446–459 (2017)

33. Giotsas, V., Luckie, M., Huffaker, B., Claffy, K.: IPv6 AS relationships, cliques, and congruence. In: Mirkovic, J., Liu, Y. (eds.) PAM 2015. LNCS, vol. 8995, pp. 111–122. Springer, Cham (2015). https://doi.org/10.1007/978-3-319-15509-8_9

34. Giotsas, V., Zhou, S., Luckie, M., Claffy, K.: Inferring multilateral peering. In: Proceedings of the Ninth ACM Conference on Emerging Networking Experiments and Technologies, pp. 247–258 (2013)

35. He, Y., Siganos, G., Faloutsos, M., Krishnamurthy, S.: Lord of the links: a framework for discovering missing links in the internet topology. IEEE/ACM Trans. Netw. 17(2), 391–404 (2008)

36. Houston, G.: Address span metrics (2021). https://bgp.potaroo.net/as6447/. Accessed 27 June 2021

37. ipinsight.io: Looking glass (2021). https://whois.ipinsight.io/looking-glass/. Accessed 21 June 2021

38. IX.br: Total traffic (2021). https://ix.br/agregado/. Accessed 27 June 2021. Archived version. https://web.archive.org/web/20210627071318/ix.br/agregado/

39. Jin, Y., Scott, C., Dhamdhere, A., Giotsas, V., Krishnamurthy, A., Shenker, S.: Stable and practical {AS} relationship inference with problink. In: 16th {USENIX} Symposium on Networked Systems Design and Implementation ({NSDI} 2019), pp. 581–598 (2019)

40. Jin, Z., Shi, X., Yang, Y., Yin, X., Wang, Z., Wu, J.: TopoScope: recover as relationships from fragmentary observations. In: Proceedings of the ACM Internet Measurement Conference, pp. 266–280 (2020)

41. Karagiannis, T., Papagiannaki, K., Faloutsos, M.: BLINC: multilevel traffic classification in the dark. In: Proceedings of the 2005 Conference on Applications, Technologies, Architectures, and Protocols for Computer Communications, pp. 229–240 (2005)

42. Kernen, T.: Looking glass (2021). http://traceroute.org/. Accessed 21 June 2021

43. Lakhina, A., Papagiannaki, K., Crovella, M., Diot, C., Kolaczyk, E.D., Taft, N.: Structural analysis of network traffic flows. In: Proceedings of the Joint International Conference on Measurement and Modeling of Computer Systems, pp. 61–72 (2004)

44. Liu, S., Foster, I., Savage, S., Voelker, G.M., Saul, L.K.: Who is .com? learning to parse WHOIS records. In: Proceedings of the 2015 Internet Measurement Conference, pp. 369–380 (2015)

45. Lodhi, A., Larson, N., Dhamdhere, A., Dovrolis, C., Claffy, K.: Using peeringDB to understand the peering ecosystem. ACM SIGCOMM Comput. Commun. Rev. **44**(2), 20–27 (2014)

46. lookinglass.org: BGP looking glass services (2021). https://lookinglass.org/. Accessed 21 June 2021

47. Luckie, M., Huffaker, B., Dhamdhere, A., Giotsas, V., Claffy, K.: AS relationships, customer cones, and validation. In: Proceedings of the 2013 Conference on Internet Measurement Conference, pp. 243–256 (2013)

48. Majestic: The majestic million (2021). https://majestic.com/reports/majestic-million/. Accessed 21 June 2021

49. Marcos, P., Chiesa, M., Dietzel, C., Canini, M., Barcellos, M.: A survey on the current internet interconnection practices. ACM SIGCOMM Comput. Commun. Rev. **50**(1), 10–17 (2020)

50. Marcos, P., et al.: Dynam-IX: a dynamic interconnection exchange. In: Proceedings of the 14th International Conference on Emerging Networking EXperiments and Technologies, pp. 228–240 (2018)

51. Marder, A., Luckie, M., Dhamdhere, A., Huffaker, B., Claffy, K., Smith, J.M.: Pushing the boundaries with bdrmapIT: mapping router ownership at internet scale. In: Proceedings of the Internet Measurement Conference 2018, pp. 56–69 (2018)

52. MAXMIND: Geoip2 city accuracy (2021). https://www.maxmind.com/en/geoip2-city-accuracy-comparison?country=&resolution=250&cellular=excluding. Accessed 27 June 2021. Archived version. https://web.archive.org/web/20210627075223/www.maxmind.com/en/geoip2-city-accuracy-comparison?country=&resolution=250&cellular=excluding

53. MAXMIND: Geolite2 free geolocation data (2021). https://dev.maxmind.com/geoip/geolite2-free-geolocation-data. Accessed 27 June 2021

54. Mazoyer, G., Schmidt, M., Correa, A.J., et al.: Respawner looking glass utility (2021). https://github.com/gmazoyer/looking-glass. Accessed 21 June 2021

55. Naab, J., Sattler, P., Jelten, J., Gasser, O., Carle, G.: Prefix top lists: gaining insights with prefixes from domain-based top lists on DNS deployment. In: Proceedings of the Internet Measurement Conference, pp. 351–357 (2019)

56. RIPE NCC: Routing information service (RIS) (2021). https://www.ripe.net/analyse/internet-measurements/routing-information-service-ris. Accessed 21 June 2021

57. Nomikos, G., et al.: O peer, where art thou? Uncovering remote peering interconnections at IXPs. In: Proceedings of the Internet Measurement Conference 2018, pp. 265–278 (2018)
58. Norton, W.B.: The Internet Peering Playbook: Connecting to the Core of the Internet. DrPeering Press (2014)
59. Oliveira, R., Pei, D., Willinger, W., Zhang, B., Zhang, L.: The (in) completeness of the observed internet AS-level structure. IEEE/ACM Trans. Netw. **18**(1), 109–122 (2009)
60. Oliveira, R.V., Zhang, B., Zhang, L.: Observing the evolution of internet AS topology. In: Proceedings of the 2007 Conference on Applications, Technologies, Architectures, and Protocols for Computer Communications, pp. 313–324 (2007)
61. University of Oregon: University of Oregon route views project (2021). http://www.routeviews.org/routeviews/. Accessed 21 June 2021
62. PeeringDB: PeeringDB (2021). https://www.peeringdb.com. Accessed 21 June 2021
63. PeeringDB: Hivelocity Inc (2021). https://web.archive.org/web/20220130161818/www.peeringdb.com/net/2159
64. Prehn, L., Feldmann, A.: How biased is our validation (data) for AS relationships? In: Proceedings of the ACM Internet Measurement Conference, p. TBA (2021)
65. Pujol, E., Poese, I., Zerwas, J., Smaragdakis, G., Feldmann, A.: Steering hypergiants' traffic at scale. In: Proceedings of the 15th International Conference on Emerging Networking Experiments and Technologies, pp. 82–95 (2019)
66. RADb: aut-num: As213045 (2021). https://web.archive.org/web/20220130152317/www.radb.net/query?keywords=AS213045
67. Randall, A., et al.: Trufflehunter: cache snooping rare domains at large public DNS resolvers. In: Proceedings of the ACM Internet Measurement Conference, pp. 50–64 (2020)
68. Richter, P., Smaragdakis, G., Feldmann, A., Chatzis, N., Boettger, J., Willinger, W.: Peering at peerings: on the role of IXP route servers. In: Proceedings of the 2014 Conference on Internet Measurement Conference, pp. 31–44 (2014)
69. Schlinker, B., Cunha, Í., Chiu, Y.C., Sundaresan, S., Katz-Bassett, E.: Internet performance from Facebook's edge. In: Proceedings of the Internet Measurement Conference, pp. 179–194 (2019)
70. Schlinker, B., et al.: Engineering egress with edge fabric: steering oceans of content to the world. In: Proceedings of the Conference of the ACM Special Interest Group on Data Communication, pp. 418–431 (2017)
71. Schomp, K., Bhardwaj, O., Kurdoglu, E., Muhaimen, M., Sitaraman, R.K.: Akamai DNS: Providing authoritative answers to the world's queries. In: Proceedings of the Annual Conference of the ACM Special Interest Group on Data Communication on the Applications, Technologies, Architectures, and Protocols for Computer Communication, pp. 465–478 (2020)
72. Shafiq, M.Z., Ji, L., Liu, A.X., Wang, J.: Characterizing and modeling internet traffic dynamics of cellular devices. ACM SIGMETRICS Perform. Eval. Rev. **39**(1), 265–276 (2011)
73. Shin, D., Guaitanele, R.G., Vine, B.: HSDN PHP looking glass (2021). https://github.com/hsdn/lg. Accessed 21 June 2021
74. Snijders, J.: PeeringDB accuracy: is blind faith reasonable? (2013). https://archive.nanog.org/sites/default/files/wed.general.peeringdb.accuracy.snijders.14.pdf. Accessed 24 June 2021
75. subnets.ru: Looking glass list (2021). http://subnets.ru/wrapper.php?p=1. Accessed 21 June 2021

76. Virtua.Cloud: Our network (2022). https://web.archive.org/web/20220130154537/www.virtua.cloud/our-infrastructure/our-network
77. Wikipedia: Tier 1 network, May 2021. https://en.wikipedia.org/wiki/Tier_1_network
78. Yap, K.K., et al.: Taking the edge off with espresso: scale, reliability and programmability for global internet peering. In: Proceedings of the Conference of the ACM Special Interest Group on Data Communication, pp. 432–445 (2017)
79. Yeganeh, B., Durairajan, R., Rejaie, R., Willinger, W.: How cloud traffic goes hiding: a study of Amazon's peering fabric. In: Proceedings of the Internet Measurement Conference, pp. 202–216 (2019)

On the Latency Impact of Remote Peering

Fabricio Mazzola[1]([envelope]), Pedro Marcos[2], Ignacio Castro[3], Matthew Luckie[4], and Marinho Barcellos[4]

[1] UFRGS, Porto Alegre, Brazil
fmmazzola@inf.ufrgs.br
[2] FURG, Rio Grande, Brazil
pbmarcos@furg.br
[3] QMUL, London, UK
i.castro@qmul.ac.uk
[4] University of Waikato, Hamilton, New Zealand
mjl@wand.net.nz, marinho.barcellos@waikato.ac.nz

Abstract. Internet Exchange Points (IXPs) play an essential role in the Internet, providing a fabric for thousands of Autonomous Systems (ASes) to interconnect. Initially designed to keep local traffic local, IXPs now interconnect ASes all over the world, and the premise that IXP routes should be shorter and faster than routes through a transit provider may not be valid anymore. Using BGP views from eight IXPs (three in Brazil, two in the U.S., and one each in London, Amsterdam, and Johannesburg), a transit connection at each of these locations, and latency measurements we collected in May 2021, we compare the latency to reach the same addresses using routes from remote peers, local peers, and transit providers. For four of these IXPs, at least 71.4% of prefixes advertised by remote peers also had a local peering route, BGP generally preferred the remote route due to its shorter AS path, but the local route had lower latency than the remote route in the majority of cases. When a remote route was the only peering route available at an IXP, it had slightly lower latency than a corresponding transit route available outside the IXP for >57.6% of the prefixes for seven of the eight IXPs.

1 Introduction

How to deliver traffic is an increasingly complex aspect of the Internet today as many applications generate large volumes of traffic and have strict service requirements. As a consequence, Autonomous Systems (ASes) are constantly increasing their interconnection capacities and expanding their footprint. Internet Exchange Points (IXPs) are key elements of this process, as they can shorten Internet paths and reduce interconnection cost [4,10,17,31]. As of May 2021, there were more than 800 IXPs deployed worldwide [22,29,46]. The largest IXPs have surpassed 1000 members [32,35,36] and 10 Tbps of peak traffic [7,16,19,36].

An original motivation of IXPs was to keep local traffic local by having ASes physically present at an IXP facility. However, IXPs no longer only interconnect members physically present at IXP facilities. Remote peering – where an AS is not physically present at an IXP facility and reaches the IXP through a layer-2 provider – allows ASes to widen their peering footprint with a quicker setup, no additional hardware, and lower installation costs compared to local peering [9,15,20]. For example, ASes from 85 different countries connect to LINX remotely [36] as of May 2021. To cope with the demand for peering, IXPs and remote peering resellers have expanded their offerings [12,25,48] with some IXPs having up to 55 official partners selling remote peering services [8,32,37]. Network operators prefer to steer traffic through IXPs instead of transit providers because of the reduced transit and operational costs [18,21]. However, the ability to interconnect with remote members at IXPs adds complexity to traffic engineering choices.

Given the public debate about remote peering performance [1,2,5,6,34,41, 43], which is currently data-poor, and to understand the latency properties of BGP routes at IXPs, we analyze latency and latency variability when using different interconnection methods (remote peering, local peering, and transit) to reach addresses in prefixes announced by remotely connected members in eight IXPs identified in Table 1. These eight IXPs include six of the world's ten largest IXPs by membership, and are deployed in five countries (three in Brazil, two in the U.S., and one each in London, Amsterdam, and Johannesburg). Our contributions are as follows.

First, we find that inferring remote ASes using the state-of-the-art methodology [42] based on latency and colocation data is insufficient for some IXPs (Sect. 3). Incomplete and/or inaccurate colocation data in regions, such as Latin America, yields a high number of unknown inferences (more than 68.6% for three IXPs). Because we need to infer which ASes are remotely connected to a given IXP in order to identify prefixes announced by remote ASes, we infer geographically distant remote ASes [15] and complement these inferences with ground-truth data (Sect. 4). We found that at least 26.2% of all ASes connected to major IXPs, such as PTT-SP and AMS-IX, were remotely connected members in May 2021. These remotely connected members announced fewer than ≈15% of the prefixes visible at the IXP, for most IXPs.

Next, we classify prefixes announced by remote ASes in BGP data collected from PCH and IXP looking glass servers. We focus our analysis on prefixes that had routes available through both remote and local ASes (Sect. 5). We found that for 82.5% of these prefixes, on average, the AS path for the route from the remote peer was shorter or had the same length as the route from the local peer in the four IXPs with most of these prefixes (LINX, AMS-IX, Eq-Ash, and Eq-Chi). Using BGP views from RouteViews peers, we confirmed that remote routes tended to preferred by BGP. However, our latency measurements indicate that the local route had a lower latency in most cases.

Finally, we examine the prefixes announced exclusively by remote members at IXPs (Sect. 6). Our findings suggest that remote routes can have lower latency to reach addresses in prefixes announced by remote ASes when compared with a transit route, though not by a considerable margin for six out of eight IXPs: using the remote route or the transit had a latency difference no higher than 5 ms for 78.1% of the measured prefixes. However, for NAPAfrica in South Africa,

Table 1. The eight IXPs analyzed in our study, along with the availability of BGP VPs and ground truth data on remote peering.

IXP	Location	Observed Interfaces	BGP LG	VPs PCH	Reseller Ground Truth
PTT-SP	Sao Paulo, BR	2,169	✓	✗	✓
LINX	London, UK	911	✓	✓	✓
AMS-IX	Amsterdam, NL	907	✓	✓	✗
NAPAfrica	Johannesburg, ZA	542	✗	✓	✗
PTT-RJ	Rio de Janeiro, BR	462	✓	✗	✓
PTT-CE	Fortaleza, BR	395	✓	✗	✓
Eq-Ash	Ashburn, VA, US	365	✗	✓	✗
Eq-Chi	Chicago, IL, US	259	✗	✓	✗

remote peering routes had a lower latency than transit routes, with a latency benefit of more than 40 ms for 81.4% of the measured prefixes.

2 Measurement Architecture

In this section, we discuss the measurement architecture we used. First, we present the IXPs we measured (Sect. 2.1). Next, we describe the datasets we used in our work, including the IXP ground truth and BGP routing data (Sect. 2.2). Finally, we characterize the vantage points (VPs) along with the active measurements we performed (Sect. 2.3).

2.1 Peering Infrastructure Selection

To identify networks connected via remote peering, and prefixes and routes announced via remote peering, we need peering infrastructures that have (1) publicly available BGP routing data, and (2) an active measurement VP attached to the IXP switching fabric. Table 1 presents the eight selected IXPs where we had both BGP routing data and active measurement capability. These IXPs include six of the world's ten largest IXPs by membership [22,29] and are deployed in five different countries. The three Brazilian IXPs (i.e., PTT sites) are part of the largest ecosystem of public IXPs in the world (IX.br) and are the leading Latin American IXPs in terms of average traffic volumes (≈12.9, 9.2, and 1.4 Tbps, respectively) [3,13,14]. The eight IXPs together comprise 3466 unique ASes.

2.2 Datasets

Remote Peering Reseller Ground Truth Data. We obtained ground truth information for the ASes remotely connected via resellers for four of the analyzed IXPs: LINX, PTT-SP, PTT-RJ, and PTT-CE. The data set contains information about the ASN and IP interface of remote ASes reaching the IXPs through shared ports or VLANs associated with resellers. For the PTT IXPs, we obtained the ground truth data from their operators on the 20th April 2021. The set of ASes reaching LINX through resellers or locally connected to the IXP is publicly available at their member portal [37] (collected on 5th May 2021). LINX representatives confirmed that ASes with Port Type labeled as ConneXions correspond to ASes using resellers. The ground truth for the four IXPs comprise a list of 1634 unique ASes using remote peering through resellers.

Membership and Interface Addresses. To identify the peering router's IP and ASN of all members at each IXP, we combine multiple public data sources for all IXPs except for LINX, which publishes this information through their member portal [37]. We collected membership data and subnet information from Euro-IX [22] and the publicly available databases of Hurricane Electric (HE) [29], PeeringDB (PDB) [46], and Packet Clearing House (PCH) IXP Directory [44]. In cases of conflicts, we followed the preference ordering described in [42]: *Euro-IX > HE > PDB > PCH*.

BGP Datasets and Sanitization. We used two sources of routing data: (i) Looking Glass (LG) of the IXP which observes routes from the IXP's Route Server and (ii) routes from the archive collected by PCH [45]. For IXPs with both PCH and LG views, we used data archived by PCH because it has greater visibility of routes advertised by IXP members. For example, when comparing both datasets for AMS-IX and LINX, we observed 3.4–3.9x more routes and 1.9–2.0x more prefixes from PCH than from LG views. As our goal is to understand the latency difference between routes announced at IXPs by different peering types (i.e., remote and local peering), we prefer the dataset from PCH whenever it is available, as it provides us with better visibility of the IXP routes (*PCH > LG*). On IXPs with only LG views (PTT sites), we have observed that LGs are configured to output only the best routes at the time of our BGP routing data collection, lowering the number of cases with multiple routes for the same prefix. Additionally, we collected BGP data from RouteViews collectors at each IXP to understand the types of routes that RouteViews peers actually chose. For each IXP, we obtained a BGP snapshot corresponding to the same period our measurements were performed (5–6 May 2021). We discarded: (i) routes with artifacts, such as reserved/unassigned ASes [30] and loops; (ii) prefixes shorter than /8 or longer than /24.

2.3   Data Plane Measurements

Vantage Points. At each IXP listed in Table 1, we used RouteViews collectors which were directly connected to the IXP LAN to conduct active measurements using scamper [38]. Figure 1 illustrates the measurement architecture of each RouteViews collector and how we used them to conduct active measurements.

Measurement Types. We conducted two types of measurements. In the first, we measured the latency to each IXP member's peering router. These measurements use the IP address that the collector has in the IXP LAN (X.2), so

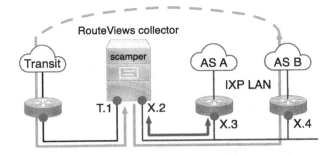

Fig. 1. Architecture of our data plane measurements. We used RouteViews collectors with an interface connected to a transit provider and an interface in the IXP LAN as VPs for data plane measurements. Delay measurements to the peering router of each IXP member (e.g., X.3) used the collector's IP address in the IXP LAN (X.2), so the probes and responses crossed the IXP LAN. Other measurements used the Transit IP address T.1 as the source address, and were delivered to each IXP member using the layer-2 address corresponding to their IXP LAN IP address (e.g., X.4).

that probes and responses cross the IXP LAN, as in when we probe X.3 in Fig. 1. In the second, we measured the path and latency to IP addresses within prefixes announced by each IXP member. Note that these prefixes are peering routes, and not transit routes. These measurements go out via a selected IXP member (e.g. AS B, using the layer-2 address of X.4 in Fig. 1) but used the collector's Transit IP address T.1 as the source address, so that we could receive a response. This strategy allowed us to maintain the same return path from the probed address back to the RouteViews collector, while varying the forward path as we selected different IXP members. We provide further details about the measurement methodology in the sections describing our results (Sect. 4, 5, 6).

3   Challenges in Inferring Remote Peering

Our method needs to know which networks connect via remote connections at IXPs. However, there are two different notions of remote peering.

Notions of Remote Peering. Conversations with IXP and reseller representatives revealed that notions of remote peering varied. Some considered remote peering based on the AS connection type (e.g., using shared ports via resellers), regardless of location (even those in the same city as the IXP). Other representatives viewed remote peering based on the geographical distance to the IXP.

Figure 2 shows different ways that ASes can connect to IXPs. *Local ASes* connect directly to an IXP switch using a router deployed in the same facility as the switch (ASes A, B, C). ASes can also connect via resellers. *Resellers* provide ports and transport to the IXP, usually connecting the routers of the remote ASes to the IXP switches via layer-2 transport. ASes located close to the IXP (ASes D, E) use resellers to lower peering equipment and installation costs. Resellers

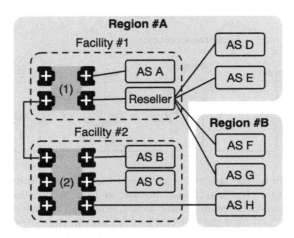

Fig. 2. ASes connect to IXPs via local (ASes A, B, C) and remote connections, either via a reseller (ASes D, E, F, G) or by purchasing transport from the remote location to the IXP switch (AS H). Remote networks can be physically located near the IXP (ASes D, E) or be geographically distant (ASes F, G, H).

can also bridge large geographical distances by connecting members located far from the IXP (ASes F, G). Finally, an AS may also connect remotely without any reseller ports, using its own port at the IXP and purchasing transport to the port from the remote location (AS H).

Available Data Limits Accuracy of Remote Peering Inferences. The current state-of-the-art methodology for inferring remote peering proposed by Giotsas *et al.* [27] infers remote peering (1) through a reseller and/or (2) geographically distant from the IXP. The method combines delay measurements with additional features, such as port capacity and AS presence at colocation facilities; if an AS is not present in one of the feasible IXP facilities, their method infers the AS is remotely connected. We used available ground truth (Sect. 2.2) for four IXPs (LINX, PTT-SP, PTT-RJ, and PTT-CE) and applied their method to all interfaces connected to these IXPs.

We implemented the four steps from the Giotsas *et al.* [27] method. The first step (*ping measurement campaign*) measures the latency to IXP member interfaces from a VP within the IXP. Using the scamper probers on the Route-Views collectors (Sect. 2.3), we performed delay measurements to the peering interfaces of IXP members every two hours for two days, and discarded measurements where the replies might have come from outside the peering infrastructure because they had an IP-TTL value that appeared to have been decremented (i.e., the received IP-TTL was not 64 or 255). The second step (*colocation-informed RTT interpretation*) computes a geographical area where the IXP member router could be located using an AS to colocation facility mapping obtained from PeeringDB and IXP websites. Then, we obtained publicly available RIPE Atlas IPv4 traceroute measurements collected on the same days as our ping campaign and

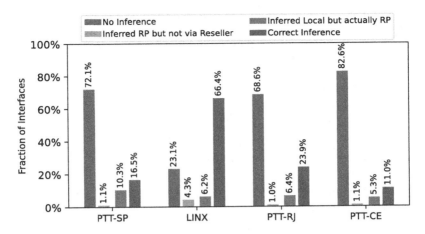

Fig. 3. Classification of interfaces we obtained when we applied our implementation of the current state-of-the-art methodology for inferring remote peering [27]. The high percentage of no inference for the three Brazilian IXPs was a consequence of the method's high reliance on public information (PeeringDB) which was not widely available for members of Brazilian IXPs.

applied step 3 (*multi-IXP router inference*) and step 4 (*finding remote peers via port capacities and lack of private connectivity*) to complete the methodology.

Figure 3 presents the results we obtained. In [27], public information about AS presence at colocation facilities was missing for ≈25% of remote peers and ≈18% of local peers. When we reproduced the study, the number of unknown inferences for LINX was low and the fraction of remote and local interfaces inferred was similar with the published work [27], which we hypothesize was because the PeeringDB coverage for LINX members that had valid information about presence in IXP facilities was high (83.0%). The case for Brazilian IXPs was different. For PTT-SP and PTT-CE, only 27.0% of the members had PeeringDB entries that reported both the IXP and facilities where they were present, leading the current state-of-the-art method to only classify 17.1%, on average, of the interfaces at the Brazilian IXPs. This low classification was because few ASes connected to the Brazilian IXPs shared their information in PeeringDB. Openly publishing peering data has only recently been encouraged by IXP operators in Brazil as best practice [39].

In addition, 5.3–10.3% of the interfaces inferred as local peerings were actually remote, according to ground truth. We believe the misclassification was related to incorrect information about the presence of ASes in colocation facilities. In many cases, an AS using a reseller recorded the facility their reseller connected to in their PeeringDB record, leading the method [27] to infer the AS was locally connected. The other 1.0–4.3% of interfaces inferred as remote were correct, but they did *not* observably connect to the IXP via a reseller. In summary, the methodology of [27] may not be suitable for accurately inferring remote peering for IXPs that have incomplete or inaccurate publicly available data.

Table 2. Number and percentage of routes and prefixes announced by members using a shared port via resellers. Members connecting to an IXP via a reseller announced fewer routes than members connecting locally. LINX had a considerable percentage (78.7%) of the same prefixes being announced by both remote and local peers.

IXP	Reseller Remote Peering			
	Interfaces (I)	Routes (R)	Prefixes (P)	P also Local
PTT-SP	1,265 of 2,169 (58.3%)	28,385 of 154,509 (18.4%)	27,148 of 158,880 (17.1%)	577 of 27,148 (2.1%)
LINX	189 of 911 (20.7%)	107,533 of 1,018,593 (10.6%)	90,633 of 486,171 (18.6%)	71,357 of 90,633 (78.7%)
PTT-RJ	172 of 462 (37.2%)	5,525 of 128,961 (4.3%)	5,502 of 128,478 (4.3%)	25 of 5,502 (0.5%)
PTT-CE	214 of 395 (54.2%)	7,098 of 26,025 (27.3%)	7,095 of 26,012 (27.3%)	10 of 7,095 (0.1%)

4 Remote Peering at IXPs

Inferring remote peering (RP) based solely on reseller connections is imprecise, as it ignores geographically distant ASes not using reseller ports which also incur a latency penalty. However, examining only remote peers that are geographically distant overlooks RP through resellers. This diversity in the notion of RP led us to evaluate RP both by (1) connection type (*Reseller RP*), and (2) geographical distance to the IXP (*Geographical RP*).

To identify members using Reseller RP, we used ground truth that identified members connected to an IXP using a reseller for four IXPs (Sect. 2.2). To infer members using Geographical RP at all eight IXPs, we used the method in [15], which uses latency measurements and empirically obtained thresholds as a proxy of physical distance, with the following approach. For each IXP, we associated IXP member ASes and their assigned IXP IP addresses using the datasets mentioned in Sect. 2.2. We performed latency measurements to these addresses on 5-6 May 2021. From each RouteViews scamper instance, we probed each interface every two hours for two days, and used the minimum latency for each address to account for cases of transient congestion. To ensure that the ping replies returned directly over the peering infrastructure, we discarded measurements where the replies had an IP-TTL value that appeared to have been decremented (i.e., not 64 or 255). If the minimum latency from a given interface was 10 ms or higher, we classified the member's router as remotely connected to the IXP; a latency of 10 ms would roughly correspond to a distance of up to 1000 km from the IXP [33, 49]. We adopted [15]'s method because its latency threshold alone yielded accurate results for single metropolitan area peering infrastructures [27], which is the case of the analyzed IXPs in our work (see Sect. 2.1).

To further assess the correctness of our inferences – and similar to step 2 in [27] (*colocation-informed RTT interpretation*) – we obtained the colocation

Table 3. Number and percentage of routes and prefixes announced by inferred geographically remote members. Members we infer to connect to an IXP from some geographical distance announced fewer routes than members connecting locally. LINX, AMS-IX, Eq-Ash, and Eq-Chi all had a considerable percentage (71.4%) of the same prefixes announced by both remote and local peers.

IXP	Geographical Remote Peering			
	Interfaces (I)	Routes (R)	Prefixes (P)	P also Local
PTT-SP	681 of 2,169	20,289 of 158,932	19,612 of 154,561	1,118 of 19,612
	(31.4%)	(12.8%)	(12.7%)	(5.7%)
LINX	121 of 911	92,975 of 1,015,040	71,452 of 482,643	65,060 of 71,452
	(13.3%)	(9.2%)	(14.8%)	(91.1%)
AMS-IX	238 of 907	67,397 of 978,225	63,323 of 485,933	56,503 of 63,323
	(26.2%)	(6.9%)	(13.0%)	(89.2%)
NAPAfrica	40 of 542	7,256 of 159,100	7,252 of 144,513	88 of 7,252
	(7.4%)	(4.6%)	(5.0%)	(1.2%)
PTT-RJ	61 of 462	3,861 of 129,135	3,850 of 128,652	355 of 3,850
	(13.2%)	(3.0%)	(3.0%)	(9.2%)
PTT-CE	139 of 395	6,870 of 26,610	6,869 of 26,597	8 of 6,869
	(35.2%)	(25.8%)	(25.8%)	(0.1%)
Eq-Ash	35 of 365	49,157 of 967,133	46,752 of 525,688	43,455 of 46,752
	(9.6%)	(5.1%)	(8.9%)	(92.9%)
Eq-Chi	17 of 259	8,382 of 347,788	8,120 of 271,855	5,795 of 8,120
	(6.6%)	(2.4%)	(3.0%)	(71.4%)

facilities of each of the eight analyzed IXPs in public data sources (IXP websites and PeeringDB) and computed the distance between them. We observed that Equinix Ashburn has the largest distance between facilities (i.e., 80 km), which corresponds to a latency of ≈1 ms. Therefore, any IXP peer interface with latency consistently higher than 10 ms is unlikely to be a local peer at the IXPs we examined.

4.1 Remotely Connected Members

Tables 2 and 3 summarize the number and percentage of interfaces connected via remote peering at each IXP.

Reseller RP. We observed a large percentage of Reseller RP at the three Brazilian IXPs, representing more than 37.2% of their member base (Table 2). According to network operators at these IXPs, the IXPs' members are spread across Brazil, which has a large land mass, and members connect to the IXP to reach large content and cloud providers. We encountered a substantially smaller fraction of Reseller RP at LINX (20.7%).

Geographical RP. We inferred that at least a quarter of the ASes connected to PTT-CE, AMS-IX, and PTT-SP were Geographical RP (Table 3). The remaining IXPs had less than 13.3% Geographical RP members inferred. This indicates that even though remote peering is widely used at IXPs (as shown by [27, 42]), a considerable fraction of member ASes are physically connected to the IXPs or closely located to them.

4.2   Remotely Announced Prefixes and Routes

For each IXP, we examined the proportion of BGP routes in the IXP routing data, and the percentage of prefixes that could be reached via both local and remote peers (i.e. local and remote routes). To identify whether routes were local or remote, we compared routes observed in the BGP data with inferred remote networks. We labeled routes as remote when the next-hop IP interface belonged to the IXP subnet and belonged to the list of networks we classified as remote.

We show the percentage of remote interfaces, routes, and prefixes we inferred at each IXP, along with absolute numbers, in Table 2 for Reseller RP and in Table 3 for Geographical RP. In all IXPs, remote peers announced proportionally fewer routes than local peers, both for Reseller RP (Table 2) and Geographical RP (Table 3). For example, in PTT-SP and PTT-RJ, the fraction of peers using Reseller RP was 3.2x and 8.7x higher than the fraction of routes they announced, respectively. For LINX, the 189 remote peers (20.7% of all interfaces) announced just 10.6% of the routes (107 k/1 M). For the Geographical RP inferences, PTT-RJ shows the highest difference between the fraction of remote interfaces and remote routes (4.4x), with 61 (13.2%) remote interfaces announcing just 3.0% of all routes (67 k/981 k). The results suggest that remotely connected ASes tend to announce fewer prefixes than local networks into the IXP. Conversations with IXP network operators revealed that remote peers mainly use their connections to obtain specific content not available at their local IXPs.

Interestingly, we observed a sizeable percentage of prefixes announced by both remote and local peers in some IXPs. At LINX, AMS-IX, Eq-Ash, and Eq-Chi, at least 71.4% of remotely announced prefixes also had a route announced by a local peer in May 2021. These cases can be a problem for traffic engineering since remote peering is invisible to Layer-3 protocols, and there is no guarantee that BGP will choose the lowest latency route.

5   Choosing Between Remote and Local Peering

Sending traffic via an IXP rather than a transit provider can potentially offer lower latency by keeping local traffic local. However, it is currently unknown whether remote peering might hinder that benefit. The geographical distance of an AS or its connection type can introduce undesired latency implications to peering. In this section, we first investigate whether remote routes have shorter AS paths than local routes (Sect. 5.1). Next, we analyze routing data from Route-Views collectors at each IXP and find that remote routes are chosen by BGP

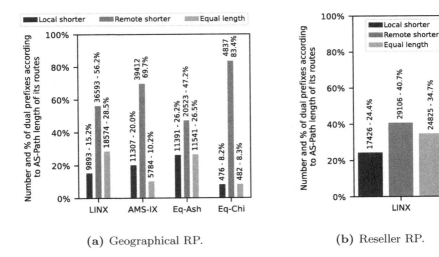

(a) Geographical RP.   (b) Reseller RP.

Fig. 4. AS path lengths of prefixes reachable via both remote and local peers. Regardless of the method to infer RP, the majority of prefixes with both local and remote routes had remote routes with an AS path length shorter or the same length as the local route, and therefore likely chosen by BGP, a hypothesis we have confirmed using data from RouteViews peers (Sect. 5.2).

in the majority of cases (Sect. 5.2). Then, we measure latency, and compare the latency of remote routes with the latency of local routes (Sect. 5.3). Finally, we measure the latency variation of each route and evaluate if remote peering introduces higher latency variability compared to the local route (Sect. 5.4).

5.1 Which Route had the Shortest AS Path?

Prefixes with both local and remote routes can be problematic for traffic engineering because an AS might choose a higher-latency route with a shorter AS path, since AS path length is the BGP second tie-breaker (after local preference) [47]. To examine whether this was the case, we compared the AS path length of routes for every prefix announced via remote and local peerings seen in IXP routing data, reporting the analysis for the IXPs that had a considerable number of these cases, namely LINX, AMS-IX, Eq-Ash, and Eq-Chi (Sect. 4.2). To compare routes, we selected the shortest AS path route of each type, local and remote. In order to observe the path lengths as they appear in the routing data, we do not reduce paths with AS path prepending.

Remote Routes had Shorter AS Paths than Local Routes. Figure 4 shows the percentage of prefixes with a shorter AS path length per peering type. In Fig. 4a, most Geographical RP routes (an average of 82.5%) had shorter (or equal) AS path lengths, with the remaining 17.4% having a shorter AS path for the local route. Thus, BGP may choose a remote route over a local route if

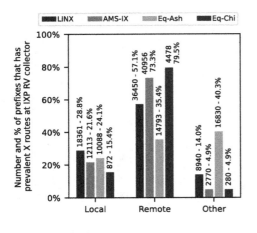
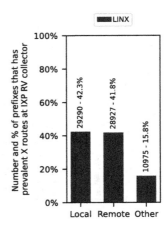

(a) Geographical RP routes.   (b) Reseller RP routes.

Fig. 5. The type of selected route by peers of RouteViews collectors at each IXP for prefixes with both local and remote routes. The remote route was more likely to be selected for Geographical RP. For Reseller RP, preference between remote and local routes was the same – ≈42%.

BGP uses AS path length as a tie breaker. The difference in AS path lengths for most prefixes with different length routes was a single ASN (82.1%, 79.0%, 73.9%, 89.9% for LINX, AMS-IX, Eq-Ash, and Eq-Chi). This happened because the local route was usually announced by large transit providers connected to the IXPs, which include the transit provider's ASN in the path.

Figure 4b, shows the distribution when looking at the Reseller RP inferences for LINX. We only show LINX because the PTT-SP, PTT-RJ, and PTT-CE results are similar but from a much smaller number of prefixes associated with resellers (fewer than 600 prefixes each). Again, we find that the remote routes tend to have shorter AS paths – 40.7% of remote prefixes had the shortest AS path, whereas only 24.4% of local prefixes had the shortest AS path. The difference in path length for most prefixes with different length routes was also a single ASN – 62.5% of the prefixes with different AS path lengths for LINX.

5.2   Are Shorter AS Path Remote Routes Chosen?

Next, we want to understand the extent to which remote routes are preferred over local routes. We analyze how frequently the remote routes appear in routes shared by RouteViews peers in the IXPs (Sect. 2.2). For each prefix with both local and remote routes announced, we find all the routes the RouteViews peers see and compare them with the routes in the dataset used in the previous section. A remote (or local) route is prevalent among RouteViews peers when most peers see the route. It was also possible that most peers reported a different route, neither local nor remote, which we did not observe in the IXP routing data that we used.

Table 4. Number of prefixes that had lower latency via remote or local peers. Generally, a route from a local peer had lower latency than a route from a remote peer to reach addresses in the same prefix.

IXP	Reseller RP		Geographical RP	
	Remote lower	Local lower	Remote lower	Local lower
PTT-SP	131 (51.1%)	125 (48.9%)	112 (20.9%)	423 (79.1%)
LINX	21,001 (45.5%)	25,155 (54.5%)	13,721 (33.0%)	27,903 (67.0%)
AMS-IX	–	–	6,644 (38.8%)	10,477 (61.2%)
NAPAfrica	–	–	14 (28.0%)	36 (72.0%)
PTT-RJ	10 (76.9%)	3 (23.1%)	53 (26.1%)	150(73.9%)
PTT-CE	4 (57.1%)	3 (42.9%)	4 (66.7%)	2 (33.3%)
Eq-Ash	–	–	2,230 (9.4%)	21,561 (90.6%)
Eq-Chi	–	–	830 (25.0%)	2,486 (75.0%)

Figure 5 shows how often each kind of route was preferred according to RouteViews peers: the local, the remote, or a different route which was not in our data set (*other* in Fig. 5). We find that the remote route was more commonly chosen. For Geographical RP routes at LINX, AMS-IX, and Eq-Chi, these remote routes were chosen for at least 57.1% of the prefixes, compared to 28.8% or fewer local routes, and 14.0% or fewer other routes. When a remote route was prevalent among RouteViews peers, the remote route had the shortest AS path among the routes (local, other) for most prefixes (83.5%, 90.0%, 81.3%, and 98.5% of these prefixes, respectively, for LINX, AMS-IX, Eq-Ash, and Eq-Chi). When local routes were prevalent, they were not always the shortest AS path routes available, and the IXP had a remote route with shorter or equal AS path length (64.5%, 39.7%, 76.6%, and 61.0%, respectively, for LINX, AMS-IX, Eq-Ash, and Eq-Chi). This suggests that operators might have been using local policy to prefer local routes so that the remote routes with shorter AS paths were not selected by BGP.

For Reseller RP routes (Fig. 5b) the situation was different: preference between remote and local routes was similar ($\approx 42\%$), with other paths accounting for the remaining 15.8%. For 75.2% of the prefixes with remote routes prevalent, the remote paths had shorter AS paths. When local routes were prevalent, 58.4% of prefixes had a remote alternative with shorter or equal AS path length available at the IXP.

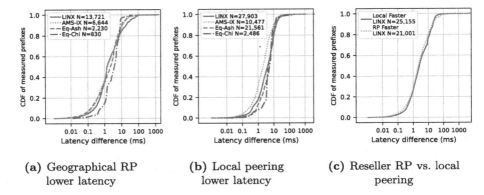

(a) Geographical RP lower latency

(b) Local peering lower latency

(c) Reseller RP vs. local peering

Fig. 6. Latency difference between remote and local routes measured by end-to-end latency to reach an address in a remote prefix. For Geographical RP, when local routes had lower latency, the advantage compared to the remote route was more than 5 ms for at least 44.7% of prefixes in three IXPs

5.3 Is There a Latency Penalty Using a Remote Route?

Considering the current preference for peers to select remote routes, we wanted to understand whether they were also the best route latency-wise. We performed active measurements, using traceroutes toward IP addresses within the prefixes set seen in IXP routing data. Since we did not have a pre-selected list of responding servers, we initially probed the first ten addresses in the IP block of the prefix, followed by thirty IP addresses randomly selected, from a system external to the IXP. Because not every prefix had a responsive address, the set of measured prefixes is smaller than the original set of prefixes. We then ran ICMP-Paris traceroute measurements to these IP addresses from RouteViews VPs in the IXPs over two days and compared the latency of the remote and local routes, provided we had obtained at least five responses from addresses in each type of route. Because a prefix can have multiple remote or local routes, we used the lowest latency measured when comparing each route type – i.e., we compared the lowest latency local and remote routes.

Local Routes had Predominantly Lower Latency than Remote Routes. Table 4 shows the number (percentage) of prefixes where a remote route had lower latency than the local routes. Looking at Geographical RP first, local routes had lower latency than remote routes for nearly all analyzed IXPs. When focusing on the IXPs with a higher prevalence of prefixes with both local and remote routes (e.g., LINX, AMS-IX, Eq-Ash, and Eq-Chi), up to 90.6% of the measured prefixes had lower latency using a local route. Similarly, for the Reseller RP inferences in LINX, the majority of prefixes also had a lower latency local route.

The previous analysis was binary – which route had the lowest latency. We now analyze the differences in latency. Figure 6 shows the latency difference

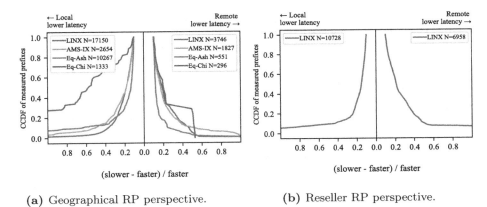

(a) Geographical RP perspective.   (b) Reseller RP perspective.

Fig. 7. Relative comparison of end-to-end latencies. For Geographical RP, when either the local or remote route had lower latency, the route had up to 30.7% lower latency than when compared with the other route type for 75.1% of prefixes in three IXPs. For Reseller RP, when a remote route had lower latency, its advantage over the local route tended to be higher than vice-versa.

between remote and local routes. The figures have a different number of points, as the number of prefixes with lower latency for remote or local routes shown in Table 4 are different. Figure 6a shows that when a Geographical RP provided a route with lower latency than the local route, the advantage was small: for at least 72.9% of the prefixes, the latency benefit of the remote route was restricted to 5 ms or less for three IXPs. In contrast, when the local route was faster, as shown in Fig. 6b, the latency advantage was more pronounced. For at least 44.7% of prefixes in three IXPs, the latency benefit for the local route was more than 5 ms when compared to the corresponding remote route. When looking at Reseller RP for LINX in Fig. 6c, we observe that the distribution of latency differences was similar for both remote and local routes, with nearly 20% of the prefixes having a latency difference above 10 ms.

Figure 7 shows a CCDF of the *relative* latency difference between remote and local routes when the latency differed by more than 5 ms. The left side of the figure shows the prefixes where the local route had lower end-to-end latency than the remote route, while the right side shows when the remote route had a lower latency than the local route. The x-axis represents how much faster one route was when compared with the other. For example, an x equals 0.2 shows that for some fraction of prefixes (in the y-axis), one type of route was 20% faster than the other type of route. We see on the left side of Fig. 7a that local routes are up to 30% faster (better) for 75.1% of prefixes observed in three IXPs. For Eq-Chi, 50% of prefixes are at least 57.8% faster (better) via a local route than using the remote one. On the right side, we see a similar pattern, where remote routes have RTTs less than 30.7% lower (better) for 75.1% of prefixes observed in three IXPs. The situation was different for Reseller RP inferences for LINX.

Table 5. Breakdown per IXP when comparing remote and local routes for each prefix in terms of latency and AS path length – Geographical RP only. A large number of local routes had lower latency but had a longer AS path than the remote route.

IXP	Total prefixes	Remote lower latency, *longer* AS path length	Remote lower latency, *equal* AS path length	Local lower latency, *longer* AS path length	Local lower latency, *equal* AS path length
LINX	41,624	1,177 (2.8%)	2,185 (5.2%)	12,950 (31.1%)	9,636 (23.2%)
AMS-IX	17,121	1,397 (8.2%)	657 (3.8%)	4,798 (28.0%)	1,828 (10.7%)
Eq-Ash	23,791	270 (1.1%)	674 (2.8%)	9,547 (40.1%)	5,579 (23.5%)
Eq-Chi	3,316	57 (1.7%)	161 (4.9%)	2,149 (64.8%)	111 (3.3%)

As shown in Fig. 7b, when the remote routes via reseller had lower latency, they were at least 20% faster for 54.6% of prefixes, while when the local route had lower latency, they were at least 20% faster for only 32.5% of measured prefixes. In summary, the results suggest that with proper configuration and knowledge about these cases, ASes can decide which route to select and steer their traffic, potentially enabling better performance according to their specific goals.

The Path with Lowest Latency was Not Always Preferred by BGP. Table 5 shows the percentage of prefixes where the route with lowest latency would not match the route specified in a BGP tie-breaker. We observed a small percentage of prefixes where the remote route had lower latency but also had a longer AS path when compared to the local route (no more than 8.2%.). In contrast, there were proportionally more cases of prefixes for which the local route had lower latency but a longer AS path than the remote route, varying from 28% (AMS-IX) up to 64.8% (Eq-Ash). When both the remote and local routes had the same path length, the local peering predominantly had a latency advantage over the remote routes despite the latency benefit not being higher than 5 ms for most routes. The results for Reseller RP, obtained from LINX, follow a similar pattern (as in Table 5) and are omitted. In summary, the results indicate that the shortest AS path route may often not match the route with the lowest latency.

5.4 Do Remote Routes Have More Latency Variability than Local Routes?

In discussion with network operators, there was a concern about potential latency variability that could be introduced by a layer-2 connection or the geographic distance separating the AS's router to the IXP. To compare the relative latency variability of remote routes over local routes, we performed active measurements by sending at least 120 ping packets from the scamper prober at the IXP Route-Views node to an address in each of the prefixes with both local and remote routes seen in Table 4 over ≈4 days (depending on the size of the IXP): at least 60 packets via the local route and at least 60 via the remote route. We computed the latency standard deviation for the best remote and local routes for the prefixes we used in the latency comparison in the previous section.

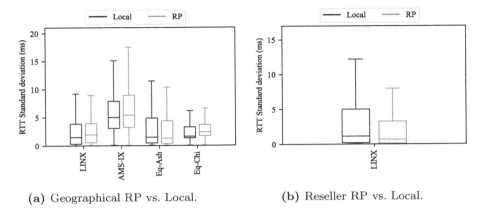

(a) Geographical RP vs. Local.   (b) Reseller RP vs. Local.

Fig. 8. Latency variability to remotely announced prefixes via remote and local routes. The latency variability to reach remote destinations was similar for both local and remote routes, suggesting that reseller connections and geographical distance had limited impact on latency variability.

Remote and Local Routes had Similar Latency Variability. Figures 8a and 8b show the latency variability was similar between remote and local routes. Regardless of peering type or remote peering perspective, 75% of the prefixes had less than 10 ms of latency variability. More specifically, for three of the four analyzed IXPs, the same fraction of prefixes had latency variability below 5 ms. The results indicate that variability was *not* a distinguishing feature at least for the IXPs we considered.

6   Does Remote Peering have Lower Latency than Transit?

When remotely announced prefixes do not also have routes from a local peer at the IXP, ASes must decide between delivering their traffic via the remote peer at the IXP or using a transit provider. Which connection type presents the lower latency to reach these prefixes? Discussions in the network operator community concern whether remote peering is an inferior alternative to transit in both latency and connection stability [34,40].

To assess whether remote peering or transit had lower latency to reach addresses in prefixes exclusively announced at an IXP via remote peers, we performed traceroute measurements through the remote peers at eight IXPs, as well as a transit provider from the same location (§6.1). We compared the latency variability of both RP and transit to reach these remotely announced prefixes (Sect. 6.2).

Table 6. Latency comparison between remote peering or transit, showing the number of prefixes with lower latency. For Reseller RP, in four IXPs, at least 64.9% of the prefixes had lower latency via Reseller RP routes than via transit. For Geographical RP, seven of eight IXPs had at least 57.6% of prefixes with lower latency via remote peering routes than via transit.

IXP	Reseller RP latency		Geographical RP latency	
	Remote lower	Transit lower	Remote lower	Transit lower
PTT-SP	8,886 (74.2%)	3,085 (25.8%)	5,657 (72.0%)	2,205 (28.0%)
LINX	10,342 (77.7%)	2,973 (22.3%)	2,724 (71.0%)	1,108 (29.0%)
AMS-IX	–	–	2,651 (57.6%)	1,950 (42.4%)
NAPAfrica	–	–	1,787 (98.1%)	35 (1.9%)
PTT-RJ	1,929 (64.9%)	1,045 (35.1%)	1,113 (59.6%)	754 (40.4%)
PTT-CE	3,014 (71.7%)	1,190 (28.3%)	2,648 (71.3%)	1,065 (28.7%)
Eq-Ash	–	–	708 (28.9%)	1,740 (71.1%)
Eq-Chi	–	–	1,204 (94.6%)	69 (5.4%)

6.1   Does Transit Offer Lower Latency than Remote Peering?

We collected latency measurements to addresses in prefixes announced by remote peers both using the remote routes and a transit route using a similar approach to Sect. 5.3 – we first identified remote prefixes without a local route and responsive IP addresses in each prefix. We collected at least five latency samples for each remote prefix using a remote peer and the transit provider.

Table 6 shows the number of probed prefixes per IXP, along with the connection type (remote or transit) with lowest latency. Note that the number of prefixes with a measurement is lower than the number of prefixes observed in the routing table (Sect. 5.3), as in some cases we failed to identify a responsive address for the prefix. The remote route had lower latency for most prefixes: 57.6% of the prefixes had lower latency with Geographical RP routes for seven out of eight IXPs, and 64.9% for Reseller RP.

Remote Routes can have a Substantial Latency Advantage. Figure 9a and 9b show the absolute latency difference for Geographical RP. Figure 9a shows that some remote routes had latencies substantially lower than the the transit alternative in some IXPs. In NAPAfrica, 81.4% of remote routes with lower latency than transit had at least 40 ms lower latency. When we discussed our results with resellers, they suggested that high IP transit prices, along with poor ISP interconnectivity and performance in Africa, made remote peering a lower latency and cheaper option, in line with the published literature [23,24,28]. For the remaining IXPs, the latency difference between remote routes and transit was not substantial. Regardless of which route had lower latency, in six IXPs, we observed that the latency difference was below 5 ms for at least 78.1% of the measured prefixes.

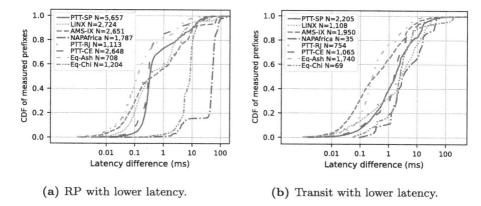

(a) RP with lower latency.   (b) Transit with lower latency.

Fig. 9. Latency difference between Geographical RP and transit provider routes measured by latency to addresses in remote prefixes. Remote peering had a substantial advantage for a few IXPs (NAPAfrica, Eq-Chi), but not as a substantial advantage for others (less than 5 ms for 78.1% of measured prefixes).

Figure 10a and 10b show the results for Reseller RP. Figure 10a suggests that any latency advantage of remote peering was not substantial. For more than 67.2% of remote routes with lower latency, the latency advantage was within 1 ms. In comparison, Fig. 10b suggests that when transit was faster for three out of four IXPs, the latency advantage was a bit higher: in at least 53.1% of transit routes with lower latency, the advantage was more than 1 ms.

6.2   RTT Variability of Remote Prefixes

In Sect. 5.4, the latency variability to reach addresses using either remote or local routes was similar. To understand if using a transit provider introduces more latency variability, we performed ping measurements to exclusively announced prefixes seen at Table 6. Similar to the previous measurements, we sent at least 120 ping probes from to each prefix over up to 4 days (depending on the size of the IXP): 60 (at least) via the transit provider and 60 (at least) via the remote route. We then computed the latency standard deviation among the ping probes for the measurements via remote peering and transit.

Transit and Remote Peering had Similar Latency Variability. Figures 11a and 11b show the latency variability for remote peering. The latency variability to reach prefixes exclusively announced at an IXP via a remote peer was equivalent for both remote and transit. PTT-SP and Eq-Ash were the only IXPs where a fraction of the prefixes had higher latency variability (see Fig. 11a).

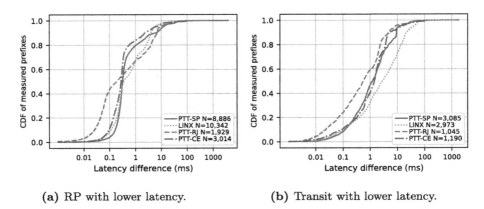

(a) RP with lower latency.   (b) Transit with lower latency.

Fig. 10. Latency difference between Reseller RP and transit measured by the latency to reach remote prefixes. When Reseller RP had lower latency, the latency advantage was not substantial (below 1 ms for over 67.2% of the measured prefixes). When transit routes had lower latency, the latency advantage was a bit higher (more than 1 ms for 53.1% of the measured prefixes in three IXPs).

Still, for all the IXPs, the standard deviation for 75% of the prefixes was below 10 ms. We observed a similar trend for Reseller RP inferences, where resellers and transit had comparable latency variability.

7   Related Work

With the growing deployment of remote peering, there have been several efforts to investigate this interconnection practice. We divide related work into two categories: (1) methods to identify remote peering at IXPs, and (2) studies to explore implications of remote peering on the Internet.

Inferring Remote Peering. Two main related methodologies have been proposed in the literature. In 2014, Castro *et al.* [15] introduced a conservative inference method based on measuring propagation delay to IXP interfaces connected to it via pings. Responses to ping probes sent to IXP interfaces that presented latency more than 10 ms and whose IP-TTL had not been decremented were classified as remote. The authors reported that 91% of the 22 studied IXPs showed networks connecting via remote peering. Further, using ground-truth traffic from a National Research and Education Network, the paper demonstrated that a network could offload up to 25% of its transit-provider traffic via remote peering.

In 2018, Nomikos *et al.* [42] also proposed a methodology to infer remote peering. Using ground-truth data from seven IXPs, the authors showed that latency alone was not sufficient to make accurate inferences in some cases, such as IXPs with switching fabrics distributed across different countries. The paper proposed combining latency measurements with additional remote peering features, such

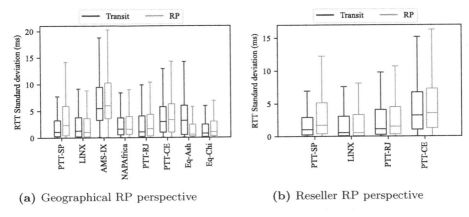

(a) Geographical RP perspective   (b) Reseller RP perspective

Fig. 11. Latency variability to remotely announced prefixes via remote peers and transit providers. The latency variability to reach addresses in remote prefixes was similar between transit and remote peering in all IXPs (latency standard deviation less than 10 ms for 75% of measured prefixes), suggesting that neither transit or the remote peering had a substantial effect on latency variability.

as port capacity and AS presence at colocation facilities, to obtain a more trustworthy inference methodology. Their method computes the geographical area where an IXP member's router could be located and associates the router with the feasible facilities that a local peering could use. They used this method to infer RP in 30 IXPs worldwide, and reported that 90% of the analyzed IXPs had more than 10% of their members using remote peering, with two of the largest IXPs in terms of members (DE-CIX and AMS-IX) having up to 40% of remote members. In 2021, the authors extended the previous work [27], with changes in the methodology and additional analysis on Wide-Area IXPs.

Implications of Remote Peering. In 2017, Giotsas *et al.* [26] proposed a methodology for detecting peering infrastructure outages, such as colocation facilities and IXPs. The authors reported that the rise of remote peering made it easier for localized failures in IXP and colocation facilities to become widespread. For two outages observed in London (2016), they showed that more than 45% of the interfaces related to the affected links were from outside England, with more than 20% of them being located outside Europe.

In 2019, Bian *et al.* [11] proposed a methodology to characterize anycast based on archived BGP routing information collected globally. While trying to infer anycast prefixes, the authors found that remote peering caused a significant element of inaccuracy in their method. They reported that RP can cause unintended consequences on anycast performance and potentially affect 19.2% of the anycast prefixes. Active measurements found that 38% of such prefixes were indeed impacted with an average latency increase of 35.1 ms.

8 Limitations and Future Work

Route Selection. Route selection is a complex problem faced by network operators, as there are many metrics that could affect traffic delivery performance. In this paper we focused on investigating AS-Path length and latency (Sect. 5 and Sect. 6). Analyzing routing by other metrics is challenging, because of the lack of reliable information in publicly available datasets regarding transit costs, economic decisions, and local preference.

Path Relevance. Despite analyzing a considerable number of remote routes, one question that stands is the relevance of such paths, both in terms of destination popularity and traffic carried. Investigating this problem requires data protected by confidentiality terms and not publicly available (e.g., IXP traffic data) for all IXPs. Additionally, many IXPs do not have an implemented and automated way to measure traffic flowing through each announced route, and are able to only share aggregated traffic per AS.

IPv6. We focused on IPv4 IXP interfaces and IPv4 announced prefixes. Six out of eight RouteViews collectors used in our work did not have IPv6 transit that would enable us to study IPv6. We hope to investigate IPv6 routes in the future.

Distributed IXPs. Our analysis considered only IXP facilities within a single metropolitan area, avoiding wide-area peering infrastructures. Our method would not work for distributed IXPs because we used a delay-based methodology and ground truth data to infer remote peering [15]. In distributed IXPs, local members connected at facilities far from the IXP region could present very high latencies and, consequently, be inferred as remote.

Future Work. Our findings help to characterize the latency impact of remote peering. Beyond the analysis we performed, we believe that considering additional IXPs, and analyzing IPv6 prefixes would improve the community's understanding of remote peering in the context of other available route types. Improving current methodologies is also crucial to promote further research on RP implications to performance and security. Our methodology used a 10 ms latency threshold to infer geographical remote peering. While the threshold is conservative, it was adequate to identify networks connected far from IXPs. However, a deeper analysis of the impact of using different latency thresholds (e.g., 2 ms and 5 ms) is needed. We also plan to leverage our ground truth data about networks connected via resellers to investigate better approaches to infer remote peering connections.

9 Final Remarks

IXPs are critical infrastructures that support ever-increasing data volumes and service requirements of modern Internet services. However, the recent growth of remote peering introduces new challenges for traffic engineering because peering may no longer keep local traffic local. Our paper shed light on the latency impact of reaching addresses in remotely announced prefixes at IXPs via remote routes, local peering routes, and regular transit, and had the following key findings.

Inferring Remote Peering is Still Challenging. Using IXP ground truth and delay measurements, we showed that current state-of-the-art methodologies have limitations. We show that relying on public network data can result in a sizable fraction of unknown inferences for some IXPs, caused by public data being unavailable for some classes of networks. Compared to the European, American, and Asian IXPs evaluated in [42], reduced data availability in some regions, such as Latin America, limits the accuracy of remote peering inferences.

The Route Preferred by BGP is not Always the Lowest Latency Route. When investigating the use of remote routes in the BGP routing, we detected a high prevalence of prefixes announced both by remote and local peerings in four IXPs (LINX, AMS-IX, Eq-Ash, and Eq-Chi). We found that most remote routes for these prefixes had a shorter or equal AS path length compared to the available local routes and tended to be preferred by the peers of RouteViews collectors. Despite being shorter and indeed preferred, they were not necessarily the lowest latency route. For at least 61.2% of these prefixes in seven IXPs, the local route had lower latency compared to the geographically distant remote peering routes.

Remote Routes are a Reliable Option to Deliver Traffic at IXPs. Some prefixes have only remote routes at IXPs, and ASes must choose between delivering their traffic via remote peering or a transit provider. Our measurements suggest that relying on remote routes can be an advantageous option for end-to-end latencies. In some scenarios (NAPAfrica and Eq-Chi), remote routes at the IXPs had considerably better latency results when compared to transit, showing latency improvements of at least 40 ms for 81.4% of the measured prefixes, when the remote route was faster than transit. For the other six IXPs, we observed that the latency difference of using the remote route or the transit was no higher than 5 ms for 78.1% of the measured prefixes.

The Connection Type or Geographical Distance does not Directly Impact Latency Variability for Remote Routes. A concern about remote peering growth at IXPs is that networks using a reseller or being geographically distant limits the original performance benefits of peering. Our measurements suggest that remote peering does not introduce additional latency variability to reach addresses in these prefixes. For 75% of the remote prefixes, we observed less than 10 ms of latency variability for remote connections.

Acknowledgment. We thank the anonymous reviewers and our shepherd, Shuai Hao, for their valuable feedback on our paper. We are also very thankful to all network operators and NIC.br for their valuable insights regarding the deployment and different aspects of remote peering. This study was sponsored (in part) by the Coordenacao de Aperfeicoamento de Pessoal de Nivel Superior - Brasil (CAPES) - Finance Code 001, by the EPSRC (EP/W032473/1, EP/S033564/1), and by National Science Foundation (NSF) grant CNS-2120399. The views and conclusions contained herein are those of the authors and should not be interpreted as necessarily representing the official policies or endorsements, either expressed or implied, of the sponsors.

References

1. Panel: Remote peering, with a look at resellers as well, 29th Euro-IX Forum, Krakow, Poland (2016). https://www.euro-ix.net/media/filer_public/ba/61/ba61bc32-f506-4ac7-b037-4dab8549c8a2/e-an-20161108-remote_peering.pdf
2. Panel: What are the challenges of remote peering?, European peering forum 2016, Sofia, Bulgaria (2016). https://www.peering-forum.eu/agenda?year=2016
3. IX.br–Brazilian public IXP project (2020). https://ix.br/intro
4. Ager, B., Chatzis, N., Feldmann, A., Sarrar, N., Uhlig, S., Willinger, W.: Anatomy of a large European IXP. In: SIGCOMM (2012)
5. Ali, Z.: Panel: Remote peering, ripe 65, Amsterdam, Netherlands (2012). https://ripe65.ripe.net/presentations/196-RIPE65_EIXWG_ZA.pdf
6. Almeida, L.: Good practices for ISP connection to international IXPs. In: IX Forum 13 Brazil (2019). https://youtu.be/bIfwuFVm0iI
7. AMS-IX: AMS-IX infrastructure (2018). https://ams-ix.net/technical/ams-ix-infrastructure
8. AMS-IX: The AMS-IX partner program (2018). https://www.ams-ix.net/ams/partners
9. AMS-IX: Pricing (2021). https://www.ams-ix.net/ams/pricing
10. Augustin, B., Krishnamurthy, B., Willinger, W.: IXPs: mapped? In: IMC, pp. 336–349 (2009)
11. Bian, R., Hao, S., Wang, H., Dhamdere, A., Dainotti, A., Cotton, C.: Towards passive analysis of anycast in global routing: unintended impact of remote peering. SIGCOMM CCR **49**(3), 18–25 (2019)
12. BICS: BICS launches remote peering to offer communications providers an affordable solution for network expansion (2014). https://www.prnewswire.com/news-releases/bics-launches-remote-peering-to-offer-communications-providers-an-affordable-solution-for-network-expansion-248317651.html
13. Brito, S.H.B., Santos, M.A.S., Fontes, R.R., Perez, D.A.L., Rothenberg, C.E.: Dissecting the largest national ecosystem of public internet exchange points in Brazil. In: Karagiannis, T., Dimitropoulos, X. (eds.) PAM 2016. LNCS, vol. 9631, pp. 333–345. Springer, Cham (2016). https://doi.org/10.1007/978-3-319-30505-9_25
14. Carisimo, E., Fiore, J.M.D., Dujovne, D., Pelsser, C., Alvarez-Hamelin, J.I.: A first look at the Latin American IXPs. In: SIGCOMM CCR (2020)
15. Castro, I., Cardona, J.C., Gorinsky, S., Francois, P.: Remote peering: more peering without Internet flattening. In: CoNEXT, pp. 185–198 (2014)
16. CGI.br: IX.br reaches mark of 10 tb/s of peak Internet traffic (2021). https://cgi.br/noticia/releases/ix-br-reaches-mark-of-10-tb-s-of-peak-internet-traffic/
17. Chatzis, N., Smaragdakis, G., Feldmann, A., Willinger, W.: There is more to IXPs than meets the eye. In: SIGCOMM CCR (2013)
18. Cloudflare: Bandwidth costs around the world. The Cloudflare Blog (2016). https://blog.cloudflare.com/bandwidth-costs-around-the-world/
19. DE-CIX: DE-CIX Frankfurt statistics (2018). https://www.de-cix.net/en/locations/germany/frankfurt/statistics
20. DE-CIX: Connect to DE-CIX via a reseller (2021). https://www.de-cix.net/en/access/how-to-connect/connect-via-reseller

21. Dr Peering: What are the economics of Internet peering? (2012). https://drpeering. net/FAQ/What-are-the-economics-of-peering.php
22. Euro-IX: Euro-IX. the IXP database (2021). https://ixpdb.euro-ix.net/en/
23. Fanou, R., Valera, F., Dhamdhere, A.: Investigating the causes of congestion on the African IXP substrate. In: IMC, pp. 57–63 (2017)
24. Formoso, A., Chavula, J., Phokeer, A., Sathiaseelan, A., Tyson, G.: Deep diving into Africa's inter-country latencies. In: INFOCOM, pp. 2231–2239 (2018)
25. France-IX: Angola cables launches remote peering service at France-IX Marseille (2017). https://www.franceix.net/en/events-and-news/presse/angola-cables-lance-un-service-de-peering-distance-france-ix-mar/
26. Giotsas, V., Dietzel, C., Smaragdakis, G., Feldmann, A., Berger, A., Aben, E.: Detecting peering infrastructure outages in the wild. In: SIGCOMM, pp. 446–459 (2017)
27. Giotsas, V., et al.: O peer, where art thou? Uncovering remote peering interconnections at IXPs. IEEE/ACM Trans. Netw. **29**(1), 1–16 (2021)
28. Gupta, A., Calder, M., Feamster, N., Chetty, M., Calandro, E., Katz-Bassett, E.: Peering at the Internet's frontier: a first look at ISP interconnectivity in Africa. In: PAM, pp. 204–213 (2014)
29. Hurricane Electric: Internet exchange report (2021). https://bgp.he.net/report/exchanges
30. IANA: IANA autonomous system (AS) numbers (2020). https://www.iana.org/assignments/as-numbers/as-numbers.xml
31. Internet Society: IXPs make the Internet faster and more affordable (2021). https://www.internetsociety.org/issues/ixps/
32. IX.br: IX.br members (2018). http://ix.br/particip/sp
33. Katz-Bassett, E., John, J.P., Krishnamurthy, A., Wetherall, D., Anderson, T., Chawathe, Y.: Towards IP geolocation using delay and topology measurements. In: IMC, pp. 71–84 (2006)
34. Levy, M.J.: Peer locally, with local network on local IXs or not! (alternate title: Remote peering is bad for content) (2019). https://www.globalpeeringforum.org/pastEvents/gpf14/presentations/Wed_2_MartinLevy_remote_peering_is_bad_for.pdf
35. LINX: 100GE member facing port milestone reached (2021). https://www.linx.net/newsletter/linx-newsletter-august-2021/
36. LINX: LINX quick facts (2021). https://quickfacts.linx.net/
37. LINX: Members by IP/ASN (2021). https://portal.linx.net/members/members-ip-asn
38. Luckie, M.: Scamper: a scalable and extensible packet prober for active measurement of the Internet. In: IMC, pp. 239–245 (2010)
39. Mendes, J.L.: IX forum 14: PeeringDB (2020). https://forum.ix.br/files/apresentacao/arquivo/1020/IX_Forum_14_Sao_Paulo-peeringdb-20201204-V3.pdf
40. NANOG: Virtual or remote peering (2017). https://mailman.nanog.org/pipermail/nanog/2017-August/091963.html
41. Nipper, A., Hedges, B., Verhoef, E., Sirota, J.: Remote peering panel–providers. In: IX Forum 12 Brazil (2018). https://www.youtube.com/watch?v=HQZY-DJNlxU&ab_channel=NICbrvideos
42. Nomikos, G., et al.: O peer, where art thou? Uncovering remote peering interconnections at IXPs. In: IMC, pp. 265–278. New York, NY, USA (2018)
43. Norton, W.B.: The great remote peering debate (2012). http://drpeering.net/AskDrPeering/blog/articles/Ask_DrPeering/Entries/2012/9/18_The_Great_Remote_Peering_Debate.html

44. PCH: Packet clearing house, Internet exchange directory (2020). https://www.pch.net/ixp/dir
45. PCH: PCH. daily routing snapshots (2021). https://www.pch.net/resources/
46. PeeringDB: PeeringDB. IXPs and colocation database (2020). https://www.peeringdb.com
47. Rekhter, Y., Hares, S., Li, T.: A Border Gateway Protocol 4 (BGP-4). RFC 4271 (January 2006)
48. Telecomdrive Bureau: Epsilon grows remote peering presence at LINX (2020). https://telecomdrive.com/epsilon-grows-remote-peering-presence-at-linx/
49. Trammell, B., Kühlewind, M.: Revisiting the privacy implications of two-way internet latency data. In: Beverly, R., Smaragdakis, G., Feldmann, A. (eds.) PAM 2018. LNCS, vol. 10771, pp. 73–84. Springer, Cham (2018). https://doi.org/10.1007/978-3-319-76481-8_6

Internet Applications

Know Thy Lag: In-Network Game Detection and Latency Measurement

Sharat Chandra Madanapalli(✉) ⓘ, Hassan Habibi Gharakheili ⓘ, and Vijay Sivaraman ⓘ

The University of New South Wales, Sydney, Australia
{sharat.madanapalli,h.habibi,vijay}@unsw.edu.au

Abstract. Online gaming generated $178 billion globally in 2020, with the popular shooter, action-adventure, role-playing, and sporting titles commanding hundreds of millions of players worldwide. Most online games require only a few hundred kbps of bandwidth, but are very sensitive to latency. Internet Service Providers (ISPs) keen to reduce "lag" by tuning their peering relationships and routing paths to game servers are hamstrung by lack of visibility on: (a) gaming patterns, which can change day-to-day as games rise and fall in popularity; and (b) locations of gaming servers, which can change from hour-to-hour across countries and cloud providers depending on player locations and matchmaking. In this paper, we develop methods that give ISPs visibility into online gaming activity and associated server latency. As our first contribution, we analyze packet traces of ten popular games and develop a method to automatically generate signatures and accurately detect game sessions by extracting key attributes from network traffic. Field deployment in a university campus identifies 31 k game sessions representing 9,000 gaming hours over a month. As our second contribution, we perform BGP route and Geolocation lookups, coupled with active ICMP and TCP latency measurements, to map the AS-path and latency to the 4,500+ game servers identified. We show that the game servers span 31 Autonomous Systems, distributed across 14 countries and 165 routing prefixes, and routing decisions can significantly impact latencies for gamers in the same city. Our study gives ISPs much-needed visibility so they can optimize their peering relationships and routing paths to better serve their gaming customers.

1 Introduction

Online gaming is experiencing explosive growth: 2.9 billion players collectively contributed $178 billion to global revenues in 2020, representing a 23% growth over the year before [2]. Popular online games like Fortnite, Call-of-Duty, League of Legends and Counter-Strike account for hundreds of millions of online players. Interestingly, most of these games are free-to-play, and generate their whopping revenues from in-game purchases (in-game currency, emotes, skins, stickers, weapons, backblings, battle passes, and other such trinkets). Game publishers and platforms are therefore strongly motivated to give gamers the best possible experience to keep them engaged, and thus deploy their game servers on cloud platforms across multiple countries in an effort to minimize network latency for users.

O. Hohlfeld et al. (Eds.): PAM 2022, LNCS 13210, pp. 395–410, 2022.
https://doi.org/10.1007/978-3-030-98785-5_17

Network latency (aka "lag") is indeed one of the largest sources of frustration for online gamers. A typical shooting game requires no more than a few hundred kbps of bandwidth, so a higher speed broadband connection does not by itself have a material impact on gaming experience. By contrast, a 100 ms higher latency can severely handicap the gamer [20], since their gunshots will be slower to take effect, and their movements lag behind others in the game. A whole industry of "game acceleration" is dedicated to address the latency issue, ranging from gaming VPNs/overlays (*e.g.,* WTFast [6] and ExitLag [1]) to gaming CDNs (*e.g.,* SubSpace [5]); indeed, one innovative eSport hosting company (OneQode [4]) has even gone to the extent of locating its servers in the island of Guam to provide equidistant latency to several Asian countries.

Internet Service Providers (ISPs), who have hitherto marketed their broadband offering based purely on speed, are now realizing that they are blind to latency. This is hurting their bottom line, since gamers are vocal in online forums comparing gaming latencies across ISPs, and quick to churn to get any latency advantage. With new game titles and seasons launching every week, and their popularity waxing and waning faster than the phases of the moon, ISPs are struggling to stay ahead to keep gamers happy, and consequently bearing reputational and financial damage.

ISPs have almost no tools today to give them visibility into gaming latencies. Traditional Deep Packet Inspection (DPI) appliances target a wide range of applications spanning streaming, social media, and downloads, and have evolved to largely rely on hostnames found in DNS records and/or the TLS security certificates of a TCP connection. Tracking modern games requires specialized machinery that can track UDP flows with no associated DNS or SNI signaling by matching on multiple flow attributes in a stateful manner. Further, game developers and publishers use different cloud operators in various countries to host their game servers, and use dynamic algorithms for game server selection depending on the availability of players and match making. These factors have made it very challenging for ISPs to get visibility into game play behaviors, limiting their ability to tune their networks to improve gaming latencies.

In this paper we develop a method to detect games, measure gaming latencies, and relate them to routing paths. Our first contribution in Sect. 2 analyzes ten popular games spanning genres, developers, and distributors. We identify key game-specific attributes from network traffic to automatically construct game signatures, and consolidate these into an efficient classification model that can identify gaming sessions with 99% accuracy within first few packets from commencement. Deployment of our classifier in a University network over a month identified 31 k game sessions spanning 9,000 gaming hours, and we highlight interesting patterns of game popularity and engagement in terms of session lengths.

Our second contribution in Sect. 3 uses the servers identified using our classifier from the previous contribution to measure game servers location and latencies. We perform BGP route and Geolocation lookups, coupled with active ICMP and TCP latency measurements, to map the AS-path and latency to the 4,500+ game servers identified. We illustrate the spread of game servers across 31 ASes, 14 countries, and 165 routing prefixes, and the resulting impact on latency for each game title. We further show that different ISPs serving gamers in the same city can offer radically different gaming latency, influenced by their peering relationships and path selection preferences.

Table 1. List of games.

Game	Genre	Developer	Distributor/Publisher
Fortinite	Shooter	Epic Games	Epic Games
Call of Duty: Modern Warfare (CoD:MW)	Shooter	Infinity Ward	Blizzard Entertainment
World of Warcraft (WoW)	RTS	Blizzard Entertainment	Blizzard Entertainment
League of Legends (LoL)	MOBA	Riot Games	Riot Games
Counter Strike: Global Offensive (CS:GO)	Shooter	Valve Corp.	Steam
FIFA 20/21	Sports	Electronic Arts	Origin
Rocket League	Sports	Psyonix	Steam
Hearthstone	Card game	Blizzard Entertainment	Blizzard Entertainment
Escape From Tarkov	Shooter Survival	Battlestate Games	Battlestate Games
Genshin Impact	Action RPG	miHoYo	miHoYo

Our study gives ISPs much-needed visibility into gaming behaviors and game server locations so they better optimize their networks to improve gaming latencies.

2 Game Detection

In this section, we begin by illustrating the network behavior of a representative online game (Sect. 2.1), followed by developing: (i) a method to automatically generate signatures of gaming flows (Sect. 2.2), and (ii) a deterministic classifier that combines the signatures to passively detect games using in-network attributes (Sect. 2.3). The classifier is evaluated (Sect. 2.4) and deployed (Sect. 2.5) to observe the gaming patterns in our university network.

We first collected and analyzed hundreds of *pcap* traces by playing ten popular online games (shown in Table 1) that represent a good mix across genres (*e.g.,* Shooting, Strategy, Sport), multiplayer modes (*e.g.,* Battle-Royale, Co-Operative, Player-vs-Player), and developers/distributors. These traces (labeled lab data[1]) were collected by playing games on a desktop computer in our university research lab. Next, we collected over 1000 hours of game-play packet traces selected from a full mirror (both inbound and outbound) of our university campus Internet traffic (on a 10 Gbps interface) to our data collection system from the campus border router[2]. Selected *pcaps* (labeled field data) were recorded by filtering the IP address of the game servers (to which our lab computer connected while playing). This helped us collect all game-play traffic to those "known" servers when someone on our campus played any game.

2.1 Anatomy of Multiplayer Games

Let us start with an illustrative example from a popular online game: Fortnite. It is a third person shooter (TPS) game developed by Epic Games which has risen in popularity with a game mode called Battle Royale wherein 100 players fight each other to be the last

---

[1] Dataset available on request from the corresponding author.
[2] Ethics clearance (HC16712) obtained from UNSW Human Research Ethics Advisory Panel

one standing. Fortnite is played by over 350 million players around the world [3]. In what follows, we outline the anatomy of a Fortnite game session by manually analyzing a packet capture (*pcap*) trace from our labeled lab data.

Gamer Interaction: A gamer first logs in to the Epic Games launcher and starts the Fortnite game client. The game starts in a lobby where users have access to their social network, collectibles, player stats, and game settings. When the user decides to play, the client contacts Fortnite's matchmaking server that groups players waiting in a queue and assigns a server on which the online game runs. Subsequently, the match starts, and its duration depends on how long the player lasts in the battle royale – the last one/team standing wins among 100 players. After the game, the user returns to the lobby area, where they may choose to start another game.

Network Behavior: From the *pcap* trace, we observe that the client communicates with various service endpoints (which can be identified by their unique domain name) for joining the lobby, matchmaking and social networking (as shown in Table 3 in Appendix A). These communications occur over encrypted TLS connections and constitute "fore-play" before game-play begins. Once the game starts, the actual game-play traffic is exchanged over a UDP stream between the client and a game server (which is usually different from the foreplay endpoints). However, the IP address of the gaming server is not resolved by DNS lookup – we, therefore, believe the server IP address is exchanged over the encrypted connection during the matchmaking process. The lack of the server identity/name (common across other game titles) makes the game-flow detection challenging. We note that the game server and other servers may or may not be co-located – *e.g.,* the game server may be very close to the user, but the matchmaking server could be operating from a different cloud in a different country.

The Fortnite game-play stream (identified using a five-tuple: SrcIP, DstIP, SrcPort, DstPort and Protocol) has a packet rate of 30–40 pkt/sec upstream and about 30 pkt/sec downstream throughout the game – fluctuations depend on player actions. However, this profile of flow rate (as used in some prior works to classify applications [12]) is insufficient to detect the game since we observed a similar pattern in other games. That being said, the UDP stream has some idiosyncratic characteristics: it connects to port 9017 on the server in our example trace; it starts with a few packets of payload size of 29 bytes; the first upstream packet contains 28 trailing 0x00s; etc. These features, albeit simple, seem to be unique to Fortnite. The other competitive games we analyzed displayed similar patterns of user activity and interaction including contacting various services and having idiosyncratic patterns in the first few packets. We next describe methods to analyze multiple gaming flows to extract such signatures automatically.

2.2   Signature Generation

As briefly mentioned above, game-play servers typically lack DNS records, and the flow rate profile is quite similar across games. Therefore, identifying the game-play flows (among a mix of traffic) becomes challenging and requires us to inspect packets of flows for patterns. While signatures can be generated manually by playing the game to collect packet traces, we develop a method to automatically extract signatures from a collection of flows associated with game servers captured in our field dataset.

Dataset: From the lab and field packet traces (described above), we obtained over 20,000 labeled flows, with each game at least having 500 flows. We filtered and cleaned the field traces to remove non-game-play flows using simple heuristics such as flow duration (games typically tend to last for more than a minute at the very least) and protocols (excluding ICMP traffic). A flow record in our dataset contains: (i) game name, (ii) transport-layer protocol (UDP/TCP), (iii) server-side port number – *e.g.,* 9017 for the Fortnite example considered in Sect. 2.1, (iv) packet size (in bytes) arrays of upstream and downstream directions each for five intial packets – *e.g.,* up:[29,29,50,314,78] and down:[29,29,116,114,114], and (v) payload byte (in hex strings) arrays of upstream and downstream directions each for five initial packets – *e.g.,* ["17aabb...","28a004..."]. We note that while client-side port numbers can be useful, they are often obfuscated due to the presence of NAT and hence are not considered in this study. Further, we extract packet-level attributes from just the first five upstream and five downstream packets as they are enough to capture game-specific handshakes.

To extract game signatures from our dataset, we focused on extracting specific patterns, which could be a *static* value (consistent across all flows of a game title) or a range of *dynamic* values. To illustrate, Fortnite[3] comes with the following specific signatures: the server UDP port number is a *dynamic* value between 9000 and 9100; 1st upstream and downstream packets have a *static* size of 29 bytes ($u\_0\_len = d\_0\_len = 29$)[4]; second to tenth byte of 1st upstream packet are 0x00. ($u\_0\_b\_1 = ... = u\_0\_b\_9 = 0x00$)[5]

Static Signatures: We extract static signatures from *protocol, packet size* and *payload byte content* specific to each game title by checking if an attribute has the same value for more than α fraction of the flows. If so, the attribute and its value are added to that specific game's signature (*e.g.,* "$u\_0\_len = 29$" or "$u\_0\_b\_9 = 0x00$"). Note that if α is set to a small value (say, 0.5), the game's signature becomes richer (containing more attributes to match) and more specific to that game. A rich signature demands more stringent requirements from a flow (*i.e.,* higher chance of rejecting a flow with minor deviation from expected attributes – resulting in false-negatives). Setting α to a value close to 1 makes the signature fairly generic, which would imply a chance of overlap with other games – resulting in false positives. We empirically tuned it at 0.90 to strike a balance and detect the games accurately. In addition, we use another parameter k to specify the depth of packet payload (in number of bytes) to be analyzed. We found that most of the static payload byte values can be captured by looking at just the first 10 bytes of each packet, meaning $k = 10$.

Dynamic Signatures: We extract dynamic signatures for *server-side port numbers* as they often do not have a fixed value but lie in a specific range of possible values (configured by their developers). Since we collected a rich set of flows in the field dataset, we use the *min* and *max* of the port numbers to identify an expected range. We further expand the range by rounding the *min* and *max* to the nearest 100 to capture those port

---

[3] A snippet of our signatures for three representative games is shown in Fig. 9 (in Appendix C)

[4] "d_0_len": first letter denotes the direction ("d" for downstream and "u" for upstream), second letter ("0") denotes the packet index, and third letter ("len") denotes the packet size.

[5] "$u\_0\_b\_9$": the letters "u" and "0" are same as above while third letter ("b") denotes byte, and fourth letter ("9") denotes the byte index.

numbers that might have missed out in our traces. Doing so gives us a signature like $port = [9000 - 9100]$ for Fortnite.

Thus, we obtain the static and dynamic signatures of each game title from a set of game flows along with parameters k and α as input. Note that signatures may overlap across games. For example, u_0_len is 29 for both games Fortnite and Call of Duty Modern Warfare (CoD:MW), shown in Fig. 9. Therefore, we need a model that can classify flows based on the attributes of packets as they arrive.

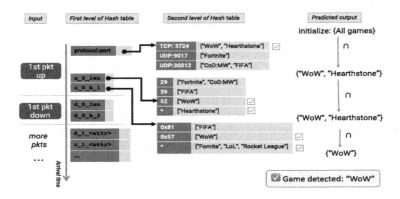

Fig. 1. The structure of our classifier, illustrating a progressive classification of a flow.

2.3   Game Classifier

We employ a *two-level hash table* (Fig. 1) that is constructed by combining all the game signatures extracted above, enabling us to rapidly detect game-play flows (and dismiss undesired traffic). The first level contains the packet attributes (*e.g.,* u_0_len, $u\_0\_b\_0$) as keys. The second level contains the possible values of the attribute as key, and possible game titles that have the same value as the entry of the hash table.

Flow of Events: Given the pre-populated hash table, we demonstrate our classification algorithm for an illustrative example in Fig. 1. We initialize the predicted output by the set of all possible games in our dataset (shown on the right side). For each incoming packet of a given flow (shown on the left side), the attributes are extracted and looked up in the hash table. For each attribute, a set of possible game classes is inferred. For an illustrative WoW (World of Warcraft) flow, upon arrival of the first packet, the protocol and port are identified as TCP:3724. Looking them up in the hash table followed by intersection with {all games} gives us the set {''WoW'', ''Hearthstone''} as output. We then proceed by looking up the packet size of 52 bytes. While 52 only yields WoW in our hash table, keep in mind that Hearthstone corresponds to a wildcard (* : indicating that attribute values were not static) meaning that the size of the first upstream packet in Hearthstone can be anything (including 52) and hence no change in the output game set. Upon extracting the second byte of the first upstream packet ($u\_0\_b\_1$)

we narrow it down to WoW. When the set of games reduces to one game, we declare it as classified. Thus, the classifier rapidly eliminated other possibilities and detected a WoW game-play flow by analyzing the protocol, port, packet size, and the first few bytes of the upload packet. Note that packets' inter-arrival time in a game-play flow is in the order of milliseconds, giving sufficient room for hash table lookups (in the order of microseconds) in between packets.

We intentionally employ an algorithmic model rather than a machine learning model since the latter requires all the input attributes to be collected, stored and processed in memory to make a classification decision, which is more expensive in memory and compute. Our classifier model detects the game or rejects non-gaming flows progressively on a per-packet basis, without necessarily requiring the attributes of all ten initial packets. Whenever the possible games reduce to an empty set, we do not process packets of that flow further by classifying it as a non-gaming flow. This helps us quickly eliminate flows (often on the first packet) that do not form a part of our game set. For example, none of the games use HTTP(S), so a majority of the traffic using TCP:80 or TCP:443 is eliminated straight away and is never detected as a game. This avoids unnecessary per-flow state maintenance (no state is maintained for flows rejected on the first packet) and helps our detection method scale.

2.4   Evaluation

Our model (signatures and classifier algorithm) achieves an overall accuracy of **99.6%** (with a precision of 100% and a false negative rate of 0.36%) when it is applied to our field dataset. We found that flows of nine game titles receive a perfect accuracy 100%, while 4.5% of WoW flows are not detected as a game flow. Note that our game-specific signatures are generated based on traffic patterns found in $\alpha = 0.90$ fraction of labeled game flows; hence a minority of flows that do not conform to those signatures will not be detected as gaming flows. Our model may miss some game flows but indeed detects games correctly and confidently. We observe that the model is able to detect all games in our dataset within the first two packets (first upload and first download) as the signatures across the ten games are fairly unique, resulting in a rapid detection.

2.5   Field Deployment and Insights

The game detection system was deployed in our university campus network (with users from offices and student dormitories) during the month of Sep 2021 to obtain insights into the game playing patterns, as well as to determine corresponding gaming servers that clients connect to and their latency from our campus (discussed in Sect. 3). Our classifier (loaded with the signatures) is implemented as a DPDK [14] application running on a server which receives campus traffic mirror from optical taps (observed total traffic peak: 8Gbps). To reduce the rate of false positives in the wild *i.e.,* not detect non-gaming traffic as games, we made our algorithm more conservative to analyze all attributes of the initial ten packets of each flow before classifying the flow. Also, we monitored the activity of the flow for the first minute of its lifetime, ensuring packet rates match the expected rate of gaming flows (typically less than 100 pkts/sec).

The system detected over 31k game-play sessions, constituting nearly 9000 hours worth of game-play across the ten titles. We found that the top three games by the number of gaming sessions were CoD:MW (9545), Fortnite (7930), and League of Legends (6290). Interestingly, LoL dominated by the total number of gaming hours – LoL was played for 2611 hours, followed by CoD:MW for 1575 hours and Fortnite for 1562 hours. This highlights the games with which gamers generally engage most.

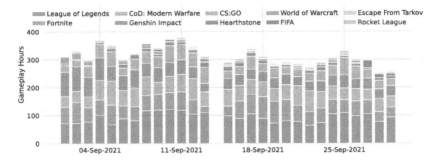

Fig. 2. Dynamics of daily game-play hours across ten titles during field trial.

Figure 2 shows the dynamics of daily game-play hours across the ten titles. Unfortunately there was a power outage in our lab on 14 Sep, causing data to be missed for that day. We make a couple of observations: (a) there is a slight decreasing trend of daily gaming hours during this period (more gaming hours in the first half than the second half) due to academic term starting on 13-Sep following a study break; and (b) gaming hours fluctuate across game titles – as an example, Genshin Impact (shown in brown) was more popular early in September (≈87 h daily), but then trended down to less than half that (≈37 h daily) towards the end of the month; Fortnite (shown in green) was played for 475 hours in the third week when Chapter 2 Season 8 was released, but this dropped to 325 hours in the fourth week once the excitement wore off – such ebb and flow is the norm in gaming [17], requiring ISPs to have constant visibility so they can tune their networks accordingly.

Table 2. Summary of detected game-play sessions in our field trial.

# Game Session	# Game Hour	# Game Server	# IP Prefix	# AS	# Country
31673	8956	4523	165	31	14

Figure 3 shows the distribution of game-play session duration across the ten titles. We observe a few patterns of user engagement with various games: Several CS:GO, Genshin Impact, and WoW gamers spend more than an hour in each gaming session, with CS:GO being the most engaging game with median duration of 32 minutes. Rocket

Fig. 3. Distribution of game-play session duration across the ten titles.

League is played for a relatively fixed duration of 10 minutes. Further, the impact of game modes is pronounced in games like CoD:MW with three bumps on its corresponding curve, highlighting three clusters of game modes, namely 5v5, GroundWar, and BattleRoyale offered by this game title.

Lastly, we analyzed short game flows (with duration less than 2 min), which can indicate game abandonment. While only 3.5% of the flows with local servers (within Australia) were short, it quadruples to more than 12% when the game is played on remote servers. Though correlation should not be interpreted as causation, it does indicate that gamers tend to abandon games more often when the latency to the server is high. The next section draws insights into game server locations and latencies.

3 Mapping Game Server Locations and Latencies

Having measured gaming behaviors in the University campus over a one-month period, we now shift focus to the game servers, including their location and latency. This covers over 31 k gaming sessions played against 4,500 unique game servers, spread across 14 countries and 165 routing prefixes and 31 ASes, as shown in Table 2.

3.1 Methods and Tools

We employed an IP Geolocation service [11] to tag the location of every server IP address. We also used the online Looking Glass tool exposed by the University's ISP, that offers `ping`, `traceroute`, and BGP queries to obtain routing prefix (*i.e.,* the subnet of the server IP address) and its AS path. Furthermore, we estimated the latency (we will use latency interchangeably with round-trip-time or RTT) by actively pinging the game servers ourselves. Since only 26% of the servers responded to ICMP pings, we used two additional tools – `HPing3` [18] was used to perform TCP ping using SYN packets to servers of TCP-based games (WoW and Hearthstone), and `fping` [19] to ping the entire subnet of the game server (since the entire prefix is housed in the same AS), yielding min, average, and max RTT to all servers in the subnet that respond. To corroborate the validity of (subnet) fping, we compared its average value to (endpoint) ping where available, and found the mean absolute percentage error (MAPE) to be less than 3%.

3.2   Mapping Game Servers from the University

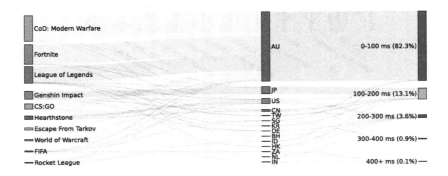

Fig. 4. Sankey diagram depicting game sessions, countries, and latency bands.

A high level view of sessions of each of the ten game titles as they map to servers in various countries and at different latency bands is shown in Fig. 4. Most countries map to a single latency band (needless to say Australia (AU) is the home country), though some countries (like US) map to multiple latency bands, due to disparities in routing paths to multiple ASes in the same country, or to different subnets within the same AS. Specifically, 82.3% of the game-play sessions connected to servers within Australia with fairly low latency of 2–20 ms, 13.1% of the sessions experienced 100–200 ms, 3.6% had 200–300 ms, and 1% had latency of 300+ ms.

Our measurements clearly reveal that game providers often use multiple CDNs (each identified by a unique AS number) to host their game servers – for example, while Fortnite largely connects to Amazon cloud locally, some sessions connected to Google cloud in another country. There are several reasons why a gamer's session may be hosted at a server with high latency: (a) no nearer server availability; (b) there may not be enough local players available, and the player is therefore matched with players in other geographies; or (c) the player deciding to team with friends in another country, and the server is chosen in proximity to the majority of players.

To get a better understanding of gaming latency per title, we plot in Fig. 5 the latency distribution across the ten games. Fortnite and Escape from Tarkov predominantly use local servers (50 ms or lower); League of Legends and CoD:MW use only a small number of local servers; while Hearthstone and Genshin Impact do not have any servers operational in the local country (the closest ones being 100+ ms away). It is also interesting to see that servers are clustered for some games (*e.g.,* Hearthstone, Genshin Impact, WoW), highlighting servers co-located in the same CDN. Curiously, though WoW and Hearthstone are from the same publisher (and share the AS owned by Blizzard), only WoW uses local in-country servers.

To highlight the deeper dynamics of latency, we focus on League of Legends (LoL) and show in Fig. 6 the distribution of latency across various server prefixes, color-coded by their country of residence. The game connected to 293 servers located in 8 countries

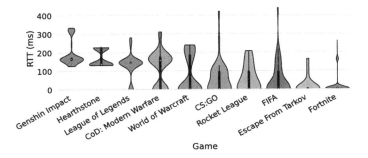

Fig. 5. Latency distribution of game servers from the campus field trial.

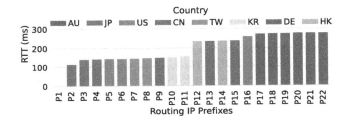

Fig. 6. Latency per IP prefix of the League of Legends servers.

spanning 22 routing prefixes. We observe that it has only one routing prefix locally (P1) that offers a very low latency of under 5 ms. Across other prefixes, we make a couple of observations. First, prefixes (P3, P4, P9) and (P13, P15), while located in China, belong to two different ASes and hence give very different latencies. In fact, P13 is geographically closer to P3 but the latter is one AS hop away while P13 is 3 AS hops away, leading to a latency differential of about 100 ms. Second, prefixes (P5, P6, P16) belong to the same AS and are located in USA. They are all one AS away from the source but P16 has a 120 ms higher latency, illustrating that routing paths can vary for different subnets even within the same AS (in this case owned by Riot Games, the publisher of LoL). Further, counter-intuitively, prefix P16 is geographically closer (to game client) than P5 and P6. This analysis can help ISPs identify game server locations and routing prefixes so they can tune their peering relationships and path selections to improve latency for their gamers.

3.3 Comparing Gaming Latencies from Multiple ISPs

To better illustrate the impact of peering relationships and routing paths on latency, we performed active latency measurements (using an automated script) from several volunteers' home broadband connections in our local city to the game servers discovered in Sect. 2. The volunteers were spread across four residential ISPs (numbered *II-V*, with ISP-*I* representing the University), and we found that the average latency to game

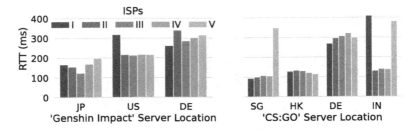

Fig. 7. Measured latency across ISPs to popular external (outside country) game server subnets of Genshin Impact (left) and CS:GO (right).

servers outside the country varied significantly across these ISPs, as illustrated in Fig. 7 for two representative games namely Genshin Impact and CS:GO.

Genshin Impact has no local servers, and a majority of its servers are in Japan (JP). It can be seen that ISP-*III* offers the lowest latency of 119 ms while the latency is much higher (at around 198 ms) with ISP-*V*. The USA serves the next higher number of sessions of Genshin Impact, and in this case ISPs *II-V* provide a latency of around 200 ms, while the University's ISP-*I* has 300+ ms latency. For Denmark (DE), ISP *II* provides the highest latency at 322 ms. Overall, a Genshin Impact gamer would get a better experience if they were with ISP-*III*. However, any ISP with this visibility into game server locations can optimise their routing paths to improve the gamer experience.

The difference across ISPs for CS:GO is even more stark, as shown in the right side of Fig. 7. In this case ISP-*V* offers a significantly worse latency to CS:GO servers in Singapore (SG) and India (IN). Given that CS:GO is a tournament-grade first-person shooting game, the latency handicap induced by ISP-*V* will be unacceptable to gamers, and likely to lead to complaints and churn. The situation is very avoidable – indeed we have reached out to this ISP, urging them to look into their peering relationships and routing path selections to address this issue.

4   Related Work

Signature Generation & Classification: Automatic signature extraction methods were first proposed a decade ago in the context of malware detection [16]. Work in [22] generates regular expressions from the payloads of un-encrypted protocols to detect application types. Bitcoding [13] proposes generating bit-level signatures for network applications by identifying bit positions that do not change in value. In a recent work [21], authors identify smart home devices and their events using signatures based on packet sizes and directions. Our methods build upon the prior work to generate signatures specific to online games. Our signature extraction is similar to [13]. However, it is faster since it looks for constant bytes in the payload instead of bits. Further, our algorithm incorporates port values in addition to byte patterns.

Gaming Applications: Several aspects of gaming applications have been studied in the past, including the impact of device-level attributes such as frame rates, and network-level parameters such as latency and loss across different games. The authors of [7] were among the first to analyze the effect of network parameters like delay, jitters, and packet loss on the game Unreal Tournament using real players. Subsequently, work in [10] analyzed multiple games using real players and [8] used bots to remove the skill bias of players. A common approach taken in these studies was to artificially induce delay/jitters/packet losses and observe the change in experience using MOS, win rates, game scores, etc. The authors in [9] studied the impact of latency on different player actions in games that have varying precision and deadline requirements. Their recent work [15] surveys the impact of different latencies on different game genres and users, concluding that gamers indeed feel the impact of high latency, especially in competitive multiplayer games. Work in [20] shows that latency is a more contributing factor than screen refresh rates in gamer performance. All prior works collectively highlight that reducing latency to gaming servers improves gaming performance and experience.

5   Conclusion and Future Work

The gaming industry is experiencing explosive growth, and ISPs are keen to offer a better gaming experience to their subscribers. However, they are hamstrung by the lack of visibility into gaming patterns, servers, and latencies. We collected and analyzed packet traces from ten popular games across various genres, extracted packet attributes, and developed a deterministic model to identify games based on automatically generated game-specific signatures. We deployed our system on live traffic of a university network, and over a 1-month period detected 31 k game sessions to gain insights into game popularity and gaming engagement. We then related game latencies to routing paths by performing BGP/Geo lookups and active latency measurements to the 4,500+ game servers identified. We illustrated how the spread of games servers across ASes and countries impacts latency. Finally, we showed that ISPs serving gamers in the same city have varying latencies to these game servers, influenced by their peering relationships. While this paper studied ten popular games, we plan to evaluate the efficacy of the proposed method on a wider set of games. If conflicts arise amongst games, the classifier may require richer signatures extracted from more packets and/or deeper payload contents of individual packets. Another avenue for future work is analysis of public peering datasets to offer low-latency peering recommendations within cost budgets to ISPs.

Acknowledgements. We thank our reviewers and specifically our shephard, Anubhavnidhi Abhashkumar, for providing valuable feedback to improve our paper.

A   Fortnite Services

Table 3. Fortnite Services, their name prefixes (suffix=`ol.epicgames.com`) and purpose.

Service	Domain Name Prefix	Purpose
Launcher	`launcher-public-service-prod06`	Epic games launcher for login
Waiting Room	`fortnitewaitingroom-public-service-prod`	The user decides the game mode
Party	`party-service-prod`	Lobby area to invite friends to play
Social Network	`friends-public-service-prod`	In-game social network
Matchmaking	`fortnite-matchmaking-public-service`	Creates matches among waiting players
Anti-cheat	`hydra.anticheat.com`	Third-party anti-cheat service
Data reporting	`data-router`	Anonymous stats reporting

B   Fortnite Game Signature Generation

Game	Protocol	Server Port	Up Pkt sizes	Down Pkt sizes	Up Payloads	Down Payloads
Fortnite	17	9017	[29, 29, 45, 62, 80]	[29,29, 45, 62, 80]	[0x170000, ...]	[0xd7bf45e8, ...]
Fortnite	17	9002	[29, 29, 35, 43, 51]	[29,29, 45, 62, 80]	[0x170000, ...]	[0x570000c0, ...]
Fortnite	17	9035	[29, 29, 37, 89, 74]	[29,29, 45, 62, 80]	[0x170000, ...]	[0x07e86474, ...]
Fortnite	17	9067	[29, 29, 41, 39, 72]	[29,29, 45, 62, 80]	[0x160000, ...]	[0xf0c476e6, ...]

Fig. 8. An illustrative example of signature generation using Fortnite traffic traces.

As shown in Fig. 8 above, each row corresponds to attributes extracted from the first few packets of Fortnite gaming flows from our dataset. The attributes include protocol, transport layer port numbers, packet sizes and payload bytes. In one flow (identified by the standard five-tuple), protocol and server port remain the same but the packet sizes and content vary as more packets arrive. For this illustration, the table shows 5 packet sizes in each direction and (stripped) payload content of the first packet.

Some attribute values (shown in red) are fixed/constant across all the flows (called *static signatures*) and other (shown in green) fall within a close range of values (called *dynamic signatures*). These signatures are same across the flows implying that they can detect a Fortnite game session. Using the static and dynamic signatures, a signature JSON is built as shown in the next section which is then used as an input to the game classifier algorithmic model.

C   Example Game Signatures

Figure 9 shows example signatures generated from our dataset. We can see that while all attributes have a key and a value, only *ports* has a range since it is a dynamic signature. We note that the complexity of signatures varies: some are primarily based on packet size (Rocket League) while others require payload bytes too (Fortnite and Call

```
"Fortnite": {
    "protocol": 17,
    "ports": [9000,9100],
    "u_0_len": 29,
    "d_0_len": 29,
    "u_0_b_0": 0x00,
    "u_0_b_1": 0x00,
    "u_0_b_2": 0x00,
    ...
},
```

```
"Call of Duty MW": {
    "protocol": 17,
    "ports": [30000,45000],
    "u_0_len": 29,
    "u_0_b_0": "0x0d",
    "d_0_len": 29,
    "d_1_len": 29,
    "d_2_len": 116,
    "d_3_len", 114,
    ...
}
```

```
"Rocket League": {
    "protocol": 17,
    "ports": [7700,8800],
    "u_0_len": 80,
    "d_0_len": 48,
    "u_1_len": 48,
}
```

Fig. 9. Signature of three representative game titles.

of Duty MW); some are based on attributes of first two packets (Fortnite and Rocket League) while others require more data (Call of Duty MW). These signatures need to be combined to predict the actual game being played as they may have some common attributes for *e.g.*, both Fortnite and Call of Duty MW have the first upload packet length as 29 and thus require further inspection to classify the game. The classifier model takes into account all attributes and looks at the minimum number of packets to rapidly detect the game.

References

1. Exitlag (October 2021). https://www.exitlag.com/en/
2. Global Games Market to Generate $175.8 Billion in 2021 (2021). https://newzoo.com/insights/articles/global-games-market-to-generate-175-8-billion-in-2021-despite-a-slight-decline-the-market-is-on-track-to-surpass-200-billion-in-2023/
3. Here's how many people play Fortnite (2021). https://www.gamesradar.com/au/how-many-people-play-fortnite/
4. Oneqode: The gaming infrastructure company (October 2021). https://www.oneqode.com/
5. Subspace: Dedicated network for real-time applications (October 2021). https://subspace.com/
6. Wtfast (October 2021). https://www.wtfast.com/en/
7. Beigbeder, T., Coughlan, R., Lusher, C., Plunkett, J., Agu, E., Claypool, M.: The effects of loss and latency on user performance in unreal tournament 2003. In: Proceedings of the ACM SIGCOMM NetGames, pp. 144–151. Portland, Oregon, US (2004)
8. Bredel, M., Fidler, M.: A measurement study regarding quality of service and its impact on multiplayer online games. In: Proceedings of the IEEE NETGAMES Workshop, pp. 1–6. IEEE, Taipei, Taiwan (2010)
9. Claypool, M., Claypool, K.: Latency can kill: precision and deadline in online games. In: Proceedings of the ACM MMSys, pp. 215–222. Phoenix, Arizona, USA (February 2010)
10. Dick, M., Wellnitz, O., Wolf, L.: Analysis of factors affecting players' performance and perception in multiplayer games. In: Proceedings of the ACM SIGCOMM NetGames, pp. 1–7. Hawthorne, NY, USA (2005)
11. Dowling, B.: The trusted source for ip address data (2021). https://ipinfo.io/
12. Habibi Gharakheili, H., Lyu, M., Wang, Y., Kumar, H., Sivaraman, V.: iTeleScope: softwarized network middle-box for real-time video telemetry and classification. IEEE Trans. Netw. Serv. Manag. **16**(3), 1071–1085 (2019)

13. Hubballi, N., Swarnkar, M.: BitCoding: network traffic classification through encoded bit level signatures. IEEE/ACM Trans. Netw. **26**(5), 2334–2346 (2018)
14. Intel: Data plane development kit (dpdk) (2021). https://www.dpdk.org/
15. Jiang, C., Kundu, A., Liu, S., Salay, R., Xu, X., Claypool, M.: A survey of player opinions of network latency in online games (2020). https://ftp.cs.wpi.edu/pub/techreports/pdf/20-02.pdf
16. Kaur, S., Singh, M.: Automatic attack signature generation systems: a review. IEEE Secur. Priv. **11**(6), 54–61 (2013)
17. Quwaider, M., Alabed, A., Duwairi, R.: The impact of video games on the players behaviors: a survey. In: Proceedings of the 10th International Conference ANT, vol. 151, pp. 575–582 (2019)
18. Sanfilippo, S.: Active network security tool (2021). http://www.hping.org/
19. Schweikert, D.: fping homepage. https://fping.org/
20. Spjut, J., et al.: Latency of 30 Ms benefits first person targeting tasks more than refresh rate above 60 Hz. In: Proceedings of the ACM SIGGRAPH Asia 2019 Technical Briefs, pp. 110–113. Brisbane, QLD, Australia (2019)
21. Trimananda, R., Varmarken, J., Markopoulou, A., Demsky, B.: Packet-level signatures for smart home devices. In: Proceedings of the NDSS. San Diego, California (2020)
22. Wang, Y., Xiang, Y., Zhou, W., Yu, S.: Generating regular expression signatures for network traffic classification in trusted network management. J. Netw. Comput. Appl. **35**(3), 992–1000 (2012)

Differences in Social Media Usage Exist Between Western and Middle-East Countries

Jens Helge Reelfs[1]([📧])[iD], Oliver Hohlfeld[1][iD], and Niklas Henckell[2]

[1] Brandenburg University of Technology, Cottbus, Germany
{reelfs,hohlfeld}@b-tu.de
[2] The Jodel Venture GmbH, Berlin, Germany
niklas@jodel.com

Abstract. In this paper, we empirically analyze two examples of a Western (DE) versus Middle-East (SA) Online Social Messaging App. By focusing on the system interactions over time in comparison, we identify inherent differences in user engagement. We take a deep dive and shed light onto differences in user attention shifts and showcase their structural implications to the user experience. Our main findings show that in comparison to the German counterparts, the Saudi communities prefer creating content in longer conversations, while voting more conservative.

1 Introduction

Every social networking platform depends on an active user-base. The recent pandemic disruption has even accelerated the shift of our everyday's life into digital spaces, may it be at work or socially. What constitutes an active user-base and if cultural differences exist in this usage behavior, however, is unclear.

Social network analysis is an active field of research for more than a decade. Research provided a general understanding through the empirical and qualitative analyses of a number of different networks. Examples include structural measurements of classic online social networks [11,23,24,29] as well as more specialized variants such as microblogging [4], picture sharing [6,33], or knowledge sharing [35]. Works in this field analyzed the networks' *structure*, mostly using graph-theory approaches. This way, they showed that social networks usually creates small-world networks [8,20]. The influence of cultural or geographic backgrounds on usage largely remain unknown.

Most studies either focus on analyzing social-media usage *worldwide* or by focusing on specific parts of the world, mostly English speaking. These works have enriched our understanding of social media. Yet it is unclear if or to what extent the obtained measures differ between different geographic regions. Cultural differences are known to exist that drive human behavior in social networks, e.g., the degree of connectivity [15] or how marketers use social media to impact purchase decisions [9]. Yet, little is known on how geographic or cultural backgrounds may impact the way users interact with a social media platform in terms of the generated traffic; that is, content creation and content voting.

O. Hohlfeld et al. (Eds.): PAM 2022, LNCS 13210, pp. 411–425, 2022.
https://doi.org/10.1007/978-3-030-98785-5_18

In this work, we take the rare chance to analyze ground truth information provided by a social network operator to compare interactions with a social media platform of a Western (Germany) and a Middle-Eastern (Saudi Arabia) country. We selected both countries since they represent the largest user-bases of the Jodel platform, while simultaneously representing a largely different (cultural) background. Our data sets capture the entirety of all social media interactions in both countries since the very first post. This way, we can, for the first time, shed light on whether geographic or culture specific differences exist between both countries w.r.t. how the user-bases generate and vote content.

The studied social media platform Jodel is location-based and anonymous. Most importantly, the feature of Jodel to form independent local communities enables us to compare in-country and between country effects and thereby to clearly identify country specific usage differences. Further, it does not display any form of user profiles or other user-related information that would introduce visible social credit; users solely interact framed into their physical proximity and based on their topic preferences. This results in a *pure* form of communication that is reduced to content, since any form of influence by user profiles such as social status is absent. This makes Jodel an ideal platform to study differences in content creation and voting, i.e., the entirety of active interactions with this social network. We shed light on fundamentally different user behavior and engagement patterns within such anonymous spaces having received less attention as of today, across the Kingdom of Saudi Arabia and Germany; and showcase structural implications. Our contributions are as follows.

– While not a primary focus of our work, we empirically show the very different adoption processes of a new social media platform in both countries.
– We show that, invariant to time and community size, users in Saudi-Arabia (Middle-East) behave fundamentally different to the German counterparts (Western country). They prefer creating content, but vote slightly less than the German users. This highlights, for the first time, that country-level differences in the usage culture in social media exist that create drastic differences in user behavior of the very same social media platform.
– We exemplify the implications of shown user engagement to the social media platform. E.g., we show that the availability of more content in Saudi Arabia naturally decreases the available votes per post, which can have serious impact on, e.g., distributed community moderation techniques.

2   The Jodel App

Jodel is a mobile-only messaging application which we show in Fig. 1. It is location-based and establishes local communities relative to the users' location ❶. Within these communities, users can *anonymously* post both images and textual content of up to 250 characters length ❸ (i.e., microblogging) and reply to posts forming discussion threads ❹. Posted content is referred to as "Jodels", colored randomly ❺. Posts are only displayed to other users within close (up to ≈20 km) geographic proximity ❷. Further, all communication is *anonymous* to other users since no user handles or other user-related information are displayed. Only *within* a single discussion thread, users are enumerated to enable referencing to other users. Threads are displayed to the users in three different feeds ❶: i) *recent* showing the most recent threads, ii) *most discussed* showing the most discussed threads, and iii) *loudest* showing threads with the highest voting score.

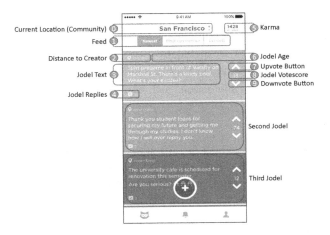

Fig. 1. Jodel iOS mobile application.

Jodel employs a community-driven filtering and moderation scheme to avoid adverse content. For an anonymous messaging app, community moderation is a key success parameter to prevent harmful or abusive content. In Jodel, content filtering relies on a distributed voting scheme in which every user can increase or decrease a post's vote score by up- ($+1$) ❼ or downvoting (-1) ❾ (similar to StackOverflow). Posts reaching a cumulative vote score ❽ below a negative threshold (e.g., -5) are no longer displayed. Depending on the number of vote-contributions, this scheme filters out adverse content while also potentially preferring mainstream content. To increase user engagement w.r.t. posting and voting, Jodesl uses lightweight gamification by awarding *Karma* points ❺.

3   Dataset Description and Ethics

The Jodel network operators provided us with *anonymized* ground truth data of their network, cf. Table 1. The obtained data contains post and interaction *metadata* created within Germany and the KSA only, and spans over multiple years from the beginning of the network in 2014 up to August 2017. It is limited to metadata only without textual content and user records stripped and anonymized. The data enables us to cluster users by their anonymous ID. Further, it contains no personal information and cannot be used to personally

identify users. While users consent to research via the Jodel ToS, we also inform
and synchronize with the Jodel operator about evaluations we perform on their
data. The structure of our available dataset includes 3 categories: interactions,
content, and users.

Table 1. Dataset Statistics. The data ranges from the application start in late
2014 up to the beginning of August 2017. We find the first observation in the KSA in
December 2014.

Type	#SA	#DE	Description
User	1.2 M	3.6 M	User metadata
Content	469 M	285 M	Content (posts, replies)
Interaction	961 M	3.0 G	Interactions incl. user, community and type (post, reply, up-/downvoted)

Dataset Limitations. Our dataset only includes the users' *active* interactions
with the system, where they contribute like registering, creating posts, replying, or voting. Thus, we cannot infer when or how much a user only *passively*
participates—lurkers—who only consume content. Further, the vote interactions
are always mapped to the date and community of the respective content creation.
This prevents us from making detailed analyses depending on the voting time or
place. However, due to the vivid usage of the application (multiple posts/replies
per minute), we generally consider votes to be executed on the same day as
their respective content. Especially since posts are only accessible via the three
different feeds, where they will only stay for a very limited time, casting votes
long after the content creation is usually not possible.

4   The Birth of the Jodel Networks in DE and the KSA

The growth patterns of social networks are less understood given that data captures from the very beginning of a social media platform are typically unavailable. We take the rare chance to begin showcasing the rate in which the Jodel
platform established itself in both countries. Our first peek is relevant to better understand network activity and to define a meaningful aggregate layer for
comparison, e.g., time slices, for studying cultural shifts in social media usage
in the next section. We thus remark that a detailed study of the shown adoption
pattern is beyond the scope of this paper.

4.1   Different Adoption Pattern in Germany and the KSA

We show the adoption of the Jodel network in both networks by the number of
interactions over time in Fig. 2. The figure shows the number of weekly interactions for Germany (solid line) and the KSA (dotted) since the very first interaction till the end of our data set in August 2017. With interaction, we refer to
any interaction with the Jodel system, i.e., either posting, replying, or voting.

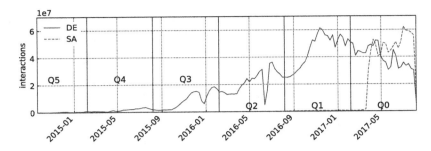

Fig. 2. Jodel activity in Germany (DE) and the Kingdom of Saudi Arabia (SA) over our observation time. While the DE network enjoys a steady growth over time, the usage in the KSA has suddenly surged and remains stable.

The adoption of Jodel in Germany is characterized by a slow but rather steady growth of network activity over time, peaking in 2016/2017. This captures the birth of the Jodel network that originated in Germany and then constantly increased in popularity. In contrast to the steady increasing activity in Germany, the adoption of Jodel in the KSA is characterized by a substantial influx of users and an increase in activity at a short time in March 2017. To our best knowledge, the reason for this behavior is that Jodel went viral via social media in Saudi Arabia—in absence of any marketing campaigns of the operator itself.

While studying the reasons that were driving these adoption processes is beyond the scope of this paper, their adoption processes differ substantially. That is, referring to Table 1, in only 4 months, Jodel KSA has roughly gathered 1.2 million users, while Jodel Germany over six times longer time period accumulates to 3.6 million. Likewise, the amount of interactions equally scales between the KSA with 1 billion and Germany with 3 billion interactions. This observation and differences in adoption allow for putting aggregates, e.g., comparable time slices, for our study into perspective.

Findings. *Adoption pattern and thus associated traffic can differ substantially.*

4.2   Different Adoption Pattern Require Comparable Time Slices

To compare the social media usage in both countries, we need to derive comparable datasets. That is, we need to enable comparisons between two different populations of posts, interactions, and users across a multitude of communities. We thus identify two main dynamics within the lifecycle of communities defining the aggregation dimension: *i)* time and *ii)* per community interaction volume.

Slicing by i) Time. As we are limited in the length of observations, especially for Saudi Arabia, we selected half-year long timeframes backwards from the end of observation. We show these timeframes with vertical bars in Fig. 2 named by country *DE0, DE1, ..., DE5, SA0, SA1*, where the index indicates the partition's age. This simple batching approach creates half-year slices that represent various stages within the community development. In our study, we compare these slices independently in each evaluation to account for the different adoption processes. We have experimented with higher resolutions to enrich our results with more data points (not shown), but our conclusions remain the same for our presented period length. We handle these partitions independently of each other, i.e., early-day users from DE5 may drop out of the statistics in subsequent partitions due to a lack of interactions.

Slicing by ii) Community Interaction Volume. Defining "a" community is not possible on Jodel given that content is displayed relative to the users location and thus differs from user to user. That is, every user might experience a slightly different community to interact with, which cannot be reconstructed from the data. To solve this, we assign each interaction to a nearby major city or district, which generates clusters of interactions that we refer to as communities. This discretization generates an approximation of the individually experienced communities. The resulting approximation is of sufficient accuracy to study and compare the Jodel usage in different parts of the respective countries. Further, the discretization does not normalize for covered area, nor covered population.

We mitigate these inherently hard problems in normalization by simplifying our partitioning approach. By slicing all interactions into quantiles ordered by their corresponding community size, we enable a relative comparison; named is_q0_25, ... representing the corresponding quantile of all interactions, discretized into communities (leading to an approximation). We provide details of this partitioning in Table 2 describing the amount of discretized communities per country. That is, e.g., the single largest SA community is the capital Riyadh at about 30% total interaction volume—hence, it is the only community within the set of $q75\_100$. Due to dividing the interaction volume into equal parts, we encounter a heavy-tailed interaction distribution across communities resulting in only few entries within the upper quantiles; the German community size distribution qualitatively matches the SA counterpart, while the latter is largely shifted in volume within magnitudes of fewer communities (not shown).

We will compare the social media usage based on the resulting data sets.

Table 2. Interaction volume aggregation layer & amount of corresponding communities. Due to the heavy tailed distribution across the community discretization, the upper quantiles consist of fewer communities.

Interactions quantile	#communities SA	#communities DE
≈75..100	1	14
≈50..75	4	29
≈25..50	12	114
≈0..25	78	6,678

5 Geographic Differences in Jodel Usage: DE vs. KSA

Is there a systematic difference between Jodel users in Germany and in the KSA in the way they use the social media platform? In other words, do culture or country specific usage behaviors exist that uniquely define traffic profiles of the very same platform in each country? While social media usage has widely been studied, the question of in-platform variation and behavioral differences is still open. In this section, we set out shedding light on this aspect by comparing the Jodel usage in two countries with a different social and cultural background.

We study the question of (cultural) differences w.r.t. user behavior in Jodel usage by investigating differences in active user *interactions* with Jodel, i.e., posting and voting, accounting for all possible active system interactions. We base this evaluation on two factors introduced in Sect. 4.2: partitioning by *i)* time and *ii)* interaction type, which we discuss next.

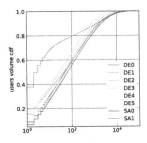
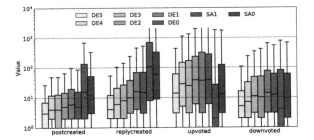

(a) Total per user interactions per time period. Per user interaction volume is very similar over time.

(b) Per user interactions by time period (DE0, ...) and interaction type. Over time, we observe increasing engagement. There is a substantial difference in content creation and upvote activities between SA and DE.

Fig. 3. Differences in per-user interactions by time and country. *a)* While the individual users behave similar across the board w.r.t. interaction volume, *b)* attention shifts towards content creation for the SA user groups, whereas downvoting is less popular in comparison to DE.

Overall Per-user Activity is Country-Independent. First, we subdivide all interactions into independent half-year periods as described in Sect. 4.2 (DE0, ..., DE5, SA0, SA1). These independent periods enable to compare the behevior of the networks at different times to account for differences in the adoption of Jodel in DE and SA. We then aggregate the interactions to each user and present the resulting interactions per user CDF in Fig. 3a. We show each half-year period as separate CDF (series) for each of the two countries. Invariant to time, we observe quite similar heavy tailed distributions; that is, most users are not very active, such that e.g., 60% of all users each have up to only 100 interactions. The distribution for SA1 deviates from the pattern since it captures a timeframe before being popular (considerably fewer data points). In general,

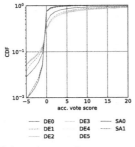 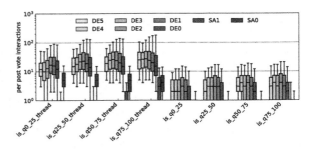

(a)   Accumulate   vote
scores CDF over time.

(b) Vote interaction distributions by time period (DE0, ...) split by community size (q0_25,...) and being a thread start (thread) or is a reply buried within a thread.

Fig. 4. Platform accumulate vote scores and vote interactions per post. *a)* Larger communities experience a stronger heavy tail in vote scores. *b)* Due to their exposure, threads usually collect more votes than replies buried within them.

we observe that irrespective of time and country, users follow a similar usage behavior—also in absolute terms (not shown).

Difference: Posting vs. Voting. Next, we further partition the data by the type of interaction in addition to the time slices used before. That is, we show distributions of interactions per user subdivided into the voting interactions (upvoted, downvoted) and content creation interactions (postcreated, replycreated) as a box plot in Fig. 3b. Note the logarithmic y-axis. Further, the whiskers denote the 5%/95% percentile.

German users tend to increase their engagement over time at increasing platform activity regardless of the interaction type. While upvoting is the most prominent type of interaction for the German users, voting content down and replying to content are roughly equally less prominent. The SA users prefer content creation, especially replying, whereas upvoting happens less frequently.

Remarkably, all time periods within a country are determined by similar behavior. In other words, posting content is the dominant type of interaction in the KSA, while it is voting in Germany. This represents a clear difference in platform usage that can be observed between these two countries (also regardless of community size, not shown).

The ratio of up to overall votes remains positive at a happyratio (upvotes to total votes) of 83% for DE and 71% for SA. The figures for the SA1 partition need to be taken with a grain of salt due to only few users; however, the engagement spread is higher compared to the latest timeframe SA0.

Findings. *Invariant to time and community size, the SA users (Middle-East) behave fundamentally different to the DE counterparts (Western country). They heavily prefer creating content, but vote slightly less than the German users. This highlights, for the first time, that cultural patterns in social media user behavior exist that create drastic shifts in how a very same social media platform is used in* *each country. This finding may be considered even more interesting, given Jodel being an anonymous platform that enables a very pure form of communication; it entirely focuses on posted content in absence of any user profile.*

6   Structural Implications

With the identified fundamental attention shift in user behavior between SA and DE users in content creation and voting, we now aim at studying resulting implications on the platform. According to the operator, the communities in both countries are considered to be well-functioning. That is, regardless of implications arising from different usage profiles, participants are enjoying spending time on the platform to the most part; e.g., by creating content, voting, or just lurking.

6.1   Content Voting

Accumulated Votes Overview. Votes on posted content have two roles in Jodel: *i)* they show content appreciation to others (e.g., enable users to sort by popularity) and *ii)* enable distributed user based content moderation that removes content with negative vote scores (see Sect. 2). Factors influencing vote distributions can thus have structural implications on the platform. To study differences in voting behavior, we first take a look into accumulate vote score (#upvotes - #downvotes) distributions. There are two given bounds for posts gathering votes: *1)* Posts beyond a negative threshold are no more displayed on the platform. *2)* There is no conscious upper bound given by the system, yet posts are only temporarily displayed within the various app feeds (see Sect. 2)

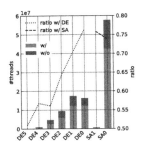

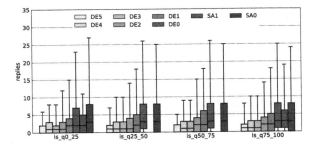

(a) Thread w/o replies over time and response ratio. Most threads can attract replies.

(b) Thread length over time by community size. With increasing engagement (*left*, Fig. 5a), communities experience longer threads on average invariant to community size.

Fig. 5. Thread engagement with responses - how many & how much. *a)* At an increasing ratio over time, within recent time periods, most threads attract replies. *b)* With growing amounts of interactions over time, the average thread length increases to a similar level in DE and SA.

and therefore, the time for interacting with them is inherently limited. Given these constraints, all communities naturally enjoy a rather positive mood. To put an emphasis on the temporal dimension, we show the CDF of vote scores to posts over time (DE0, ...) in Fig. 4a. In the earlier times of DE with less activity, more posts were able to gather more votes as illustrated by the DE3..5 series resembling a broader distribution. There is a slight decrease of accumulated vote scores throughout time, hence interactions per post, for the DE communities— also observed within the KSA. The distributions become more and more long-tailed over time and appear scale-shifted. Noteworthy, a split into community sizes confirms this finding: larger communities may reach far higher absolute scores, but the distributions become more skewed correlated to the observed interaction volume (not shown).

Due to SA users producing much more content, the feeds displayed in the app also get renewed completely at a very high pace. Thus, SA posts compete harder for time to collect possible votes in comparison to their DE cousins; the feeds also promote observed long-tails. What implications does this shift have on experienced vote distributions?

Votes per Post. To better understand the voting interactions and the observed skew in accumulated vote scores, we next normalize observed figures to a per-post basis. The box plots in Fig. 4b show various per post vote interaction distributions across time (DE0, ...), and community size (q0_25, ...), while further distinguishing between threads (thread) and replies (replies).

We find the long tail of high vote scores in the rather long 95% percentile whiskers on the log scaled y-axis. Invariant to time and community size, the median German user enjoys voting on threads with median levels around 10 to 30 votes gathered by each post throughout time. Naturally given by the communication structure and app design, content buried within threads is much less appreciated; they accumulate only two to three votes in DE. As discussed before, the SA posts stand in stark contrast at three to four votes within the main Q0 timeframe. I.e., opposed to German users, the average participant within the Kingdom of Saudi Arabia cannot expect to receive any vote on her content—especially and naturally not on replies.

Findings. *We show that the availability of more posted content in Saudi Arabia decreases the available votes per post, which can influence community moderation techniques that depend on voting.*

6.2   Spinning Faster: Response Time and Volume

While voting or liking is a vital part of a social network, it can only exist because of posted content and replies. We thus next study geographic properties that influence the response time and volume.

In Fig. 5a, we show the amounts of posts with and without replies (bars) and the ratio (lines) across time for both countries. The German communities increase their response cover over time, while it instantly is equally high for the

SA communities at about 90%. I.e., 9 out of 10 users in both countries can expect getting at least a single reply on a thread.

Response Volume. As most users receive a reply, does the total achieved thread length correlate with community size, and how does this interplay with the distribution shift in content creation? We answer this question with distributions given in Fig. 5b as a box plot, which depicts the thread length gathered per post across time (DE0, ...) and community sizes (is_q0_25, ...).

First, the 95% percentile whiskers indicate a long-tailed distribution in the length of threads, which we confirm (now shown). Second, the amount of replies is invariant to community size as the distributions are very similar; however, there still exists a huge spread from the 75% to the 95% percentile (whiskers) due to the long-tailed distribution. Second, we observe an increasing trend over time. This increasing engagement is also apparent when looking deeper into the interactions (cf. Sect. 4.2 and alike split by community size—not shown).

Findings. *Most posts in both countries get a reply; even at larger volumes for SA, the thread lengths are similar to DE.*

Conversations. Having established an understanding of the amount of replies most users experience, we get into more structural detail. We define *conservationness* as the ratio between replies per replier as a proxy for conversations—where lower ratios naturally depict a heterogeneous set of repliers, while higher ratios indicate fewer participants forming a back and forth conversation.

We present the distributions of this ratio over time for both countries in Fig. 6a as box plots; the 95% whisker indicates long-tailed distributions, which we can confirm (not shown). Over time and with increasing network activity,

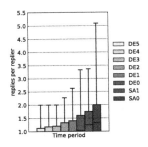
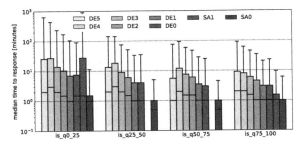

(a) Conversationness - Replies per thread participant are long-tailed and substantially larger within SA.

(b) Thread engagement speed. The median timeframe between consecutive answers within a thread decreases over time in the meanwhile growing DE environment. Likewise, larger communities experience faster responses—in SA widely immediately.

Fig. 6. Thread engagement with responses - who & when. *a)* The observed overall activity increase in DE results in longer conversations over time, the SA users talk substantially longer. *b)* The average time until receiving a response reduces to only few minutes in both countries, SA still takes the lead.

all German communities increase up to about 1.6 replies per thread participant within the 75% quantile in DE0. This indicates a shift from rather random single comments becoming less popular in favor of interacting with each other. Given the high preference on creating content and vividly replying, this trend is particularly apparent and reinforced in the SA communities at rates of up to two replies for the 75% quantile of SA0.

Findings. *Employing a conservationness metric, we identify SA users to be more conversational compared to DE.*

Response Time. We have seen that most threads receive at least some replies. While the counts in responses may matter quantitatively, we also want to shed light on the time-dependent dynamics of the reply interactions. Figure 6b shows a box plot of the distributions of the time between consecutive responses within a thread split by time (DE0, ...) and community size (q0_25, ...); note the log y-scale. Unfortunately, our dataset does not allow for this evaluation on vote interactions (see Sect. 3).

From this evaluation, we gain two major insights: *1)* throughout time with increasing activity and engagement, the German communities establish shorter response times down to only minutes. Having reached a sustainable community size, the response times no longer drop. *2)* The SA communities instantly drop response times substantially below the German counterpart to only a single minute within most threads. Note: High response times within small communities in SA1 are due to small amounts of data; Missing series indicate no present data.

Findings. *In comparison to DE, the SA communities are more vividly responsive as the average response times are considerably lower.*

7   Related Work

The research community established a rich field of understanding human interaction within social media, yet not studying geographic differences in social media usage. Empirical studies on social media focused on the birth and growth [22,27,29], social media usage in specific regions such as the Arab Gulf states [27] specifically focused to global usage [17], information propagation [6], specific platforms such as Facebook [18,24], YouTube [5], SnapChat [33], or Twitter [13]. Such research tries to understand and identify social structures and influence [11,31]. Mathematical modelling [32] and graph methods are common techniques to analyze social ties [14,19]. Platforms may also have rather adverse effects like cyberbullying [10,12,36], or may raise privacy concerns [30].

A recent body of research aims at understanding anonymous social networks. The desire for anonymity can result in throwaway accounts [16] and can also manifest in anonymous self disclosures [2]. Anonymous content platforms have been detailed w.r.t. content [25] and user behavior [1,7,26]. Other empirical work focuses specifically on location based anonymous platforms, e.g., Whisper [34] or Yik Yak [21,28], or analyzes its local content [3].

We complement these works providing a new unique view on the lifecycle of various Jodel communities in Germany and Saudi Arabia with a special focus on happening interactions, differences and resulting platform implications.

8   Conclusions

In this paper, we show that the usage behavior of users in Germany (DE) fundamentally differs from users in Saudi Arabia (KSA) in the anonymous and location based Jodel network. This study is enabled by the feature of Jodel to form independent local communities enables us to compare in-country and between country effects and thereby to clearly identify country specific usage differences. We empirically characterizes usage behavior based on ground truth user interaction data provided by the operator. While we can rule out marketing effects by the operator, our findings motivate future work that study root causes. We find that, independent of time and community size, KSA users prefer content creation (posting & responding), while German users tend to interact slightly more passively (voting). Other than this shift towards content, due to the users in both regions else behaving identical on a per-user measure; we find rather identical community engagement. However, due to much more content being available within SA per user, posts compete harder in gathering votes than the German counterparts, which can have implications for vote-based content moderation schemes. Further, the average number of replies also does not increase in comparison; Still, reply times are much smaller due to higher activity. The average Saudi user tends towards having longer conversations. Overall, we identify time- and geographic-invariant differences between DE and SA user engagement as the latter substantially focus on creating content, giving a slight lead in voting to the Germans. This provides a new interaction-based perspective on geographic difference of social media usage that have not yet been studied.

References

1. Bernstein, M.S., Monroy-Hernández, A., Harry, D., André, P., Panovich, K., Vargas, G.G.: 4chan and/b: an analysis of anonymity and ephemerality in a large online community. In: ICWSM (2011)
2. Birnholtz, J., Merola, N.A.R., Paul, A.: Is it weird to still be a virgin: anonymous, locally targeted questions on Facebook confession boards. In: SIGCHI (2015)
3. Black, E.W., Mezzina, K., Thompson, L.A.: Anonymous social media-understanding the content and context of Yik Yak. SIGCHI (2016)
4. Bollen, J., Mao, H., Pepe, A.: Modeling public mood and emotion: twitter sentiment and socio-economic phenomena. In: ICWSM (2011)
5. Brodersen, A., Scellato, S., Wattenhofer, M.: Youtube around the world: geographic popularity of videos. In: WWW, pp. 241–250 (2012)
6. Cha, M., Mislove, A., Gummadi, K.P.: A measurement-driven analysis of information propagation in the flickr social network. In: WWW (2009)
7. Correa, D., Silva, L.A., Mondal, M., Benevenuto, F., Gummadi, K.P.: The many shades of anonymity: characterizing anonymous social media content. In: ICWSM (2015)

8. Freeman, L.: The Development of Social Network Analysis. Empirical Press, Vancouver (2004). ISBN 1-59457-714-5
9. Goodrich, K., de Mooij, M.: How 'social' are social media? A cross-cultural comparison of online and offline purchase decision influences. J. Mark. Commun. **20**(1–2), 103–116 (2014). https://doi.org/10.1080/13527266.2013.797773
10. Hosseinmardi, H., Ghasemianlangroodi, A., Han, R., Lv, Q., Mishra, S.: Towards understanding cyberbullying behavior in a semi-anonymous social network. In: ASONAM (2014)
11. Kairam, S., Brzozowski, M., Huffaker, D., Chi, E.: Talking in circles: selective sharing in google+. In: SIGCHI (2012)
12. Kayes, I., Kourtellis, N., Quercia, D., Iamnitchi, A., Bonchi, F.: The social world of content abusers in community question answering. In: WWW (2015)
13. Kouloumpis, E., Wilson, T., Moore, J.D.: Twitter sentiment analysis: the good the bad and the omg! In: ICWSM (2011)
14. Kumar, R., Novak, J., Tomkins, A.: Structure and evolution of online social networks. In: Yu, P., Han, J., Faloutsos, C. (eds.) Link Mining: Models, Algorithms, and Applications. Springer, New York, NY (2010). https://doi.org/10.1007/978-1-4419-6515-8_13
15. LaRose, R., Connolly, R., Lee, H., Li, K., Hales, K.D.: Connection overload? A cross cultural study of the consequences of social media connection. Inf. Syst. Manag. **31**(1), 59–73 (2014). https://doi.org/10.1080/10580530.2014.854097
16. Leavitt, A.: This is a throwaway account: temporary technical identities and perceptions of anonymity in a massive online community. In: CSCW (2015)
17. Leskovec, J., Horvitz, E.: Planetary-scale views on a large instant-messaging network. In: WWW (2008)
18. Lewis, K., Kaufman, J., Gonzalez, M., Wimmer, A., Christakis, N.: Tastes, ties, and time: a new social network dataset using Facebook.com. Soc. Netw. **30**(4), 330–342 (2008)
19. Magno, G., Comarela, G., Saez-Trumper, D., Cha, M., Almeida, V.: New kid on the block: exploring the google+ social graph. In: IMC (2012)
20. Manku, G.S., Naor, M., Wieder, U.: Know thy neighbor's neighbor: the power of lookahead in randomized p2p networks. In: STOC (2004)
21. McKenzie, G., Adams, B., Janowicz, K.: Of oxen and birds: is yik yak a useful new data source in the geosocial zoo or just another twitter? In: SIGSPATIAL (2015)
22. Mislove, A., Koppula, H.S., Gummadi, K.P., Druschel, P., Bhattacharjee, B.: Growth of the flickr social network. In: WOSN (2008)
23. Mislove, A., et al.: Measurement and analysis of online social networks. In: IMC (2007)
24. Nazir, A., Raza, S., Chuah, C.N.: Unveiling facebook: a measurement study of social network based applications. In: IMC (2008)
25. Papasavva, A., Zannettou, S., De Cristofaro, E., Stringhini, G., Blackburn, J.: Raiders of the lost kek: 3.5 years of augmented 4chan posts from the politically incorrect board. In: Proceedings of the International AAAI Conference on Web and Social Media, vol. 14, pp. 885–894 (2020)
26. Reelfs, J.H., Bergmann, M., Hohlfeld, O., Henckell, N.: Understanding & predicting user lifetime with machine learning in an anonymous location-based social network. In: WWW LocWeb Workshop (2021). https://doi.org/10.1145/3442442.3451887
27. Reyaee, S., Ahmed, A.: Growth pattern of social media usage in Arab Gulf states: an analytical study. Soc. Networking **4**(02), 23 (2015). Scientific research publishing
28. Saveski, M., Chou, S., Roy, D.: Tracking the yak: an empirical study of yik yak. In: ICWSM (2016)

29. Schiöberg, D., Schneider, F., Schiöberg, H., Schmid, S., Uhlig, S., Feldmann, A.: Tracing the birth of an osn: social graph and profile analysis in google+. In: WebSci (2012)
30. Stutzman, F.D., Gross, R., Acquisti, A.: Silent listeners: the evolution of privacy and disclosure on Facebook. J. Priv. Confidentiality **4**(2), 2 (2013)
31. Tang, J., Sun, J., Wang, C., Yang, Z.: Social influence analysis in large-scale networks. In: SIGKDD (2009)
32. Van Mieghem, P., Blenn, N., Doerr, C.: Lognormal distribution in the digg online social network. Eur. Phys. J. B **83**(2), 251 (2011)
33. Vaterlaus, J.M., Barnett, K., Roche, C., Young, J.A.: "Snapchat is more personal": an exploratory study on Snapchat behaviors and young adult interpersonal relationships. Comput. Hum. Behav. **62**, 594–601 (2016). Elsevier
34. Wang, G., Wang, B., Wang, T., Nika, A., Zheng, H., Zhao, B.Y.: Whispers in the dark: analysis of an anonymous social network. In: IMC (2014)
35. Wang, S., Lo, D., Jiang, L.: An empirical study on developer interactions in stackoverflow. In: SAC (2013)
36. Whittaker, E., Kowalski, R.M.: Cyberbullying via social media. J. Sch. Violence **14**(1), 11–29 (2015). Taylor & Francis

Measuring the (Over)use of Service Workers for In-Page Push Advertising Purposes

George Pantelakis[1], Panagiotis Papadopoulos[2($\boxtimes$)], Nicolas Kourtellis[2], and Evangelos P. Markatos[1]

[1] FORTH/University of Crete, Heraklion, Greece
[2] Telefonica Research, Barcelona, Spain
panpap@ics.forth.gr

Abstract. Rich offline experience, periodic background sync, push notification functionality, network requests control, improved performance via requests caching are only a few of the functionalities provided by the Service Worker (SW) API. This new technology, supported by all major browsers, can significantly improve users' experience by providing the publisher with the technical foundations that would normally require a native application. Albeit the capabilities of this new technique and its important role in the ecosystem of Progressive Web Apps (PWAs), it is still unclear what is their actual purpose on the web, and how publishers leverage the provided functionality in their web applications.

In this study, we shed light in the real world deployment of SWs, by conducting the first large scale analysis of the prevalence of SWs in the wild. We see that SWs are becoming more and more popular, with the adoption increased by 26% only within the last 5 months. Surprisingly, besides their fruitful capabilities, we see that SWs are being mostly used for In-Page Push Advertising, in 65.08% of the SWs that connect with 3rd parties. We highlight that this is a relatively new way for advertisers to bypass ad-blockers and render ads on the user's displays natively.

Keywords: Service workers · Push ads · Push notification advertising

1 Introduction

The proliferation of, and our ever-increasing reliance on, the Web have boosted the development of more complex and user-friendly Web applications that can operate cross-platform (on both desktop and mobile Web). Recent advancements in the contemporary browsers and in the availability of technologies like the SW API have 1) enabled users to receive timely updates via push notifications, 2) their content synced on the background, 3) improved performance (via request caching) and 4) even allowed to work offline.

These rich capabilities of SWs played an important role in the birth and growth of a whole separate type of application software called Progressive Web

© The Author(s), under exclusive license to Springer Nature Switzerland AG 2022
O. Hohlfeld et al. (Eds.): PAM 2022, LNCS 13210, pp. 426–438, 2022.
https://doi.org/10.1007/978-3-030-98785-5_19

Apps (PWAs) [1]. PWAs are built on top of three requirements: HTTPS, *SWs* and a web app manifest. By combining functionalities of different web APIs (e.g., WebRTC, Cache API, Push API), PWAs are capable of providing the benefits of both native apps and websites worlds: reliability, rich user experience, and multi-platform support via a single codebase [2].

The somewhat revolutionary functionality of *SWs* could not avoid drawing the attention of the academic community with regards to its security aspects. Specifically, research studies have shown that this technology provides rich capabilities not only to users and web developers, but to potential attackers as well. In [3], authors present a framework that exploits *SWs* functionality to launch attacks like DDoS, cryptojacking and distributed password cracking. In [4], authors investigate the potential privacy leaks that malicious *SWs* can cause on a victim's browser.

Notwithstanding the important research on the *SW* API, yet it is still unknown what is the prevalence and the growth of the *SW* deployment across the Web and how publishers leverage the provided functionality of *SWs* in their Web applications. In this study, we aim to address these exact questions, by conducting a full-scale analysis of *SWs* (the core component of PWAs) in the wild. Specifically, we crawl a large number of websites to detect the deployment of *SWs*, monitor and characterize their communications across the Internet, and investigate their purpose of existence and operation on the websites found.

In summary, the contributions of our present work are:

1. By crawling the top 150 K sites of the Tranco list, we detect a dataset of 7,444 *SWs*-registering websites. The same crawl after 5 months reveals a high increase (26%) in the adoption of *SWs*.
2. We use Wayback Machine to go back in time and find that, from 2015 till today, there were 1.62× more publishers per year, on average, utilizing *SWs* in their web applications.
3. By analysing our collected dataset, we conduct the first full-scale study of the *SWs* deployment on the Web. Specifically, we investigate with whom the deployed *SWs* communicate over the Internet, what are the websites that use such technology the most, as well as what is the purpose of the deployed *SWs*. Surprisingly, we see that despite the important functionality of *SWs* (e.g., timely notifications, background sync, etc.), yet a stunning 65.08% of the *SWs* that connect with 3rd parties use *SWs* for pushing ads to the users, under the radar of possibly deployed ad-blockers.

2   Service Workers

A Service Worker is a JavaScript script that runs separately from the main browser thread, and can intercept network requests, perform caching or retrieving resources from the cache, and deliver push messages. *SWs* are independent from the Web application they are associated with, so they cannot access the DOM directly. *SWs* are non-blocking and fully asynchronous. Therefore, synchronous XHR and localStorage cannot be used inside a *SW*. Also, a *SW* can

Fig. 1. The Web Push API enables developers to deliver asynchronous notifications and updates to users who opted-in.

Fig. 2. An in-page push advertisement as it appears on the user's screen on top of other windows.

import and execute 3rd party scripts within its context, and receive push messages from a remote server, thus letting the associated website push notifications to the user (even when the website is not open in a browser tab). Finally, a *SW* can be registered to the browser via the `serviceWorkerContainer.register()` or `navigator.serviceWorker.register()` function, which take as argument the (HTTPS only) URL of the remote JavaScript file that contains the worker's script. This URL is passed to the internal browser's engine and is fetched from there. For security purposes, this JavaScript file can be fetched only from the first-party domain, i.e., cannot be hosted by a CDN or a 3rd party server.

2.1 Web Push Notifications

The Web Push API gives web applications the ability to receive messages pushed from a remote server, whether or not the Web app is in the foreground, or even loaded in a browser tab. As shown in Fig. 1, the Web Push API enables developers to deliver asynchronous notifications and updates to (desktop or mobile) users that opt-in, resulting in better engagement with timely new content. For an app to receive push messages, it has to have an active *SW* and subscribe to push notifications (each subscription is unique to a *SW*). The endpoint for the subscription is a unique *capability URL*, and the knowledge of the endpoint is all that is necessary to send a message to the application's users. Therefore, the endpoint URL needs to be kept secret or anyone might be able to send push messages to the app's users.

2.2 In-Page Push Advertising

Web push notification technology itself is nothing new, but it has started to be used for advertising purposes very recently. In fact, push marketing skyrocketed at the end of 2018 [5]. Push ads are a type of native ad format in the form of a notification message from a website, which appears on the user's screen on top of other windows as shown in Fig. 2. Users who click on those messages get redirected to the advertiser's landing page, thus, generating ad-conversion.

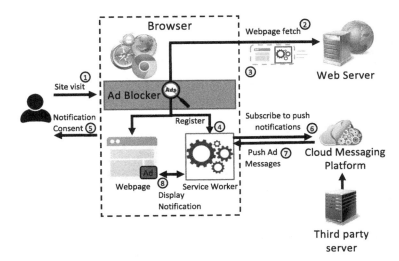

Fig. 3. High level overview of how *SWs* deliver push ads on the user display even with ad blocker deployed.

The in-page push ad delivery is cross-platform and aims to offer an *opt-in based*, highly engaging way for advertisers to reconnect and expand their audiences, while at the same time it achieves higher click-through and conversion rates than other ad formats [6]. A push notification usually consists of: (i) the main image which conveys the sense of the ad impression, (ii) the small icon which explains the main image, (iii) the headline which is the main element to engage users and (iv) the message text that shows the main details of the offer. Contrary to traditional programmatic advertising [7–9], in push ads, advertisers pay for clicks (i.e., Cost-Per-Click) and not for impressions (i.e., Cost-per-Impression). The minimum cost per click starts from $0.0104 [10], but in Real-Time Bidding the median cost per impression has been measured to be as low as $0.0025 [11].

3   Use Case

In Fig. 3, we present a high level overview of how *SWs* and push notifications work. As we can see, first (step 1), the user visits a website they are interested in, thus, instructing a browser to connect with a web server (step 2) that responds back with the web page's HTML/CSS/JavaScript resources, along with a *SW* script, which gets registered (step 3). This snippet will deploy a *SW* inside the user's browser (step 4) which operates independently from the rendered website. Then, the *SW* will ask the user's permission to push notification massages on their display (step 5) and if granted, it will establish a communication channel with a remote messaging platform to subscribe to their push notifications (step 6). Whenever the message publishing entity (e.g., news update feed server,

Table 1. Summary of our dataset

Data	Volume
Websites parsed	150 K
(1st crawl, 12.20) Websites registering a *SW* (SW)	7,444 (4.96%)
SWs that do not communicate with any remote server	336 (4.51%)
SWs communicating only with the first party	2,054 (27.59%)
SWs communicating with at least one 3rd party	5,054 (67.89%)
SWs communicating with at least one ad server	3,289 (44.18%)
SWs communicating with at least one analytics server	164 (3.24%)
(2nd crawl, 05.21) Websites registering a SW	9,383 (6.25%)

article recommendation server, ad server) behind the messaging platform has updates to push to the website's users, it uploads them to the platform which will push them to all subscribed users (step 7). On the user's end, upon message arrival, the deployed *SW* creates a push notification with the received message on the user's display (step 8). As shown, a *SW* may establish a separate communication channel with a remote messaging platform that cannot be monitored or filtered by any potentially deployed ad-blocking browser extension. This means that whenever a user opts-in to receive updates from a website, they may start receiving ad notifications instead, even if they have an ad-blocker deployed.

4   Data Collection

Crawling Infrastructure. After manual inspection, we see that there are websites checking first if the site has push notification permissions, before registering *SWs*. This means that in order to perform a large scale crawl of websites and detect the deployment of *SWs*, and the use of push notifications, some sort of automation for the notification consent is required. To address this, we leverage the crawler presented in [12]. This crawler creates docker containers with fresh instrumented Chromium browser instances and browser automation scripts. The browser has the *RequestPermission* and *PermissionDecided* methods of the class *Permission-ContextBase*, modified to automatically grant permissions on every site. Then, a custom Puppeteer [13] script listening to *serviceworkercreated* event is used to log when a *SW* is registered by a website, the page that registered this *SW* and the URI of the source code. As soon as a *SW* is registered, it can subscribe for push notifications via a Cloud Messaging Platform (e.g., Firebase Cloud Messaging [14]) with an API key passed from the server to the browser, which is also logged by listening for *PushManager.subscribe* events. Then, the custom Puppeteer script logs the communication between the *SW* and the Web.

Creating the Dataset. We create a dataset of websites that utilize *SWs*, by crawling the landing pages of the 150 K top sites of a (deduplicated, pay-level only domains) Tranco list [15] in December 2020. Each site is visited for three

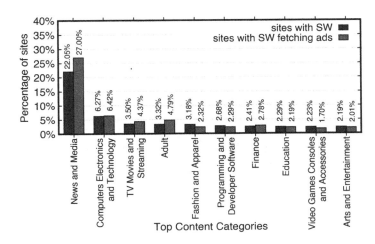

Fig. 4. Top 10 content categories of sites using (i) *SWs* (blue) and (ii) *SWs* that communicate with advertisers (red). As we can see, *SWs* is a technique widely used in sites delivering content related to 'News and Media' and 'Computers Electronics and Technology'. (Color figure online)

minutes, during which, and according to our experiments, is sufficient for a *SW* to be register and make the first touch with the corresponding server(s) (*1st crawl*). After 5 months (April 2021), we revisit the websites of our initial Tranco list to inspect how the ecosystem evolved, i.e., sites dropping *SWs*, new sites adopting *SWs* (*2nd crawl*). Table 1 summarizes the data collected.

Data Analysis. To classify the network traffic of the registered *SWs* in our data, we use the 1Host filterlist [16] and flag the ad-related domains in our weblogs. Additionally, we used SimilarWeb [17] to categorize the sites registering *SW* based on the content they deliver.

Historical Analysis and Static Detection. To explore the evolution of *SWs* across time, we use our set of *SW*-registering sites to extract heuristics and keywords that indicate the registration or use of *SWs*. This way, we develop a crawler that can statically detect the registration of *SWs* in this set of sites. Next, we use Wayback Machine [18], and specifically `waybackpy` Python package [19] to go back in time and find the day that these websites started deploying *SWs* in their visitors' browsers.

Ethical Considerations. It is important to note that during the conduct of this study, we neither gathered or used any user data, nor impeded or tampered with the proper operation of the sites we crawled, in any way. Our research was purely limited in passively monitoring the behavior of *SWs*.

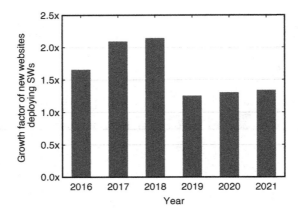

Fig. 5. Growth factor of the *SWs* deployment in our dataset. From 2015 till mid 2021, there are 1.62× more publishers per year, on average, utilizing *SWs* in their Web apps.

5   Measurements

What are the Kind of Sites Deploying *SWs*? By crawling the top 150 K websites of the Tranco list, we find that 7,444 (4.96%) of these sites register one or more *SWs* in the users' browser (Table 1). To understand what kind of sites deploy such a technique, we query Similarweb [17] for the content category of each of our sites and we get a response for 86.7% of them. In Fig. 4, we plot the top-10 categories. We see that *the sites that mostly use* SWs *(in blue) are related to 'News and Media' (22.05%)*, with the categories of 'Computers Electronics and Technology' and 'Arts and Entertainment' following (6.27% and 3.5%, respectively).

What is the Prevalence of *SW* Deployment? By revisiting the sites of the same Tranco list after 5 months (as described in Sect. 4) via the same crawler, we find a total of 9,383 websites registering a *SW* (6.25% of the total sites crawled), which indicates a 26% increase. More specifically, we find (i) 6,173 websites using *SWs* in both crawls, (ii) 1,271 websites that stopped using them at some time after our 1st crawl, and (ii) 3,210 new websites deploying them in their visitors' browsers.

This rapid growth in the prevalence of *SWs* within just 5 months, motivated us to go back in time and observe their evolution across the years. Specifically, by using Wayback Machine web archive [18] and our initial set of *SW*-registering websites, we crawled previous versions of their landing pages to spot when they started using *SWs*. As a result, we crawled all the way back to 2015, when the first websites in our dataset started using *SWs*. As seen in Fig. 5, after 2015, every year we observe an average growth factor of 1.62. In 2017 and 2018 we see this growth increasing, with 2.09× and 2.14× more websites deploying *SWs* than the previous year, respectively.

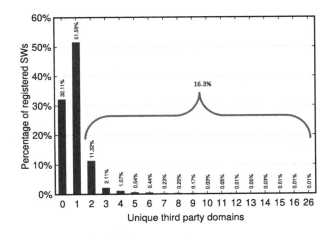

Fig. 6. The number of distinct 3rd parties each SW communicates with. 32.1% of the SWs do not communicate with a 3rd party. The majority (51.6%) communicates with exactly one 3rd party. 16.3% communicate with 2 or more (even 26!) distinct 3rd parties.

What is the Communications between SWs and Web? Next, by analyzing the traffic that the registered SWs generate, we see that 27.59% communicate only with the first party. However, 67.89% of them communicate with at least one 3rd party, and 4.51% of them do not communicate with the web at all (Table 1). In Fig. 6, we plot the number of distinct 3rd parties each registered SW in our dataset communicates with. As we can see, 32.1% of the SWs communicate with no 3rd party (as mentioned: 27.59% connects with the first party only, and 4.51% with no one), when the majority (51.6%) communicates with exactly one 3rd party, proving that there are specific agreements between publishers and 3rd party advertisers, analytics, content or library providers. It is important to note that *there is a significant 16.3% communicating with 2 or more (even 26!) distinct 3rd parties.*

How much do SWs Support Push Advertising? By using the popular filter-list of *1Hosts*, we classify the type of domains the SWs connect with in our dataset. Surprisingly, as we see in Fig. 7, in essence *3rd party communications of SWs are used for advertising*, since the majority (65.08%) of the SWs that connect with 3rd parties, establish these connections to receive content from at least one push advertiser (9.51% receive content from 2 advertisers or more). On the contrary, only 34.92% of the SWs perform at least one request to 3rd parties, but communicate with zero ad servers.

What is the Popularity of Sites Leveraging Push Advertising? In Fig. 8, we plot the popularity rank of the websites that deploy SWs on the users' side. As we see, the sites that tend to deploy ad pushing SWs are of lower popularity ranks in comparison to the ones that use SW only locally, without connecting to any remote server. Specifically, the median site that registers SW that does not

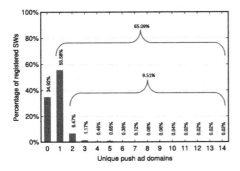
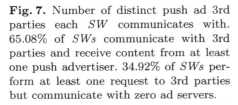
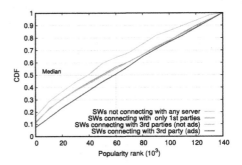

Fig. 7. Number of distinct push ad 3rd parties each *SW* communicates with. 65.08% of *SWs* communicate with 3rd parties and receive content from at least one push advertiser. 34.92% of *SWs* perform at least one request to 3rd parties but communicate with zero ad servers.

Fig. 8. Cumulative distribution function of the popularity rank of the websites with *SWs*. As we see, the sites that tend to deploy ad pushing *SWs* are less popular than the ones that use *SW* only locally, and do not connect to any remote 3rd party server.

connect with any remote server has a popularity rank of around 40000 in Tranco (grey). On the other hand, the median site with *SW* that connects (i) only with first party domains, or with 3rd parties that do not include ads is around 50000 rank (green or orange) (ii) with push ad domains around 60000 rank (red).

Also, as we see in Fig. 4 (in red) where we consider only sites with *SWs* that communicate with ad servers, the content categories are topped by 'News and Media' (27%), 'Computers, Electronics and Technology'(6.42%) and 'Adult' (4.79%). This is somewhat expected, since 'News and Media' sites have higher chances to convince a user to give their consent to receive timely news updates via push notifications, that can also include ads.

In Fig. 9, we further analyze these content categories by selecting their sites in our dataset that communicate with 3rd parties via their deployed *SWs*. Then, we measure what portion of them does that for advertising purposes. We see that **Soccer** sites lead this effort, with a percentage close to 85%. This means that from all Soccer sites using *SWs* to communicate with 3rd parties, 85% use them to communicate specifically with at least one ad server. The 'Animation and Comics' follow closely with 84% and 'File Sharing and Hosting' are next, with 83.78%. The 'News and Media' are in fifth place with a bit more than 77%. These high portions suggest that 75–80% of these websites use *SWs* for ads.

One can not help but wonder why were *SWs* invented in the first place. It is true that several people may argue that *SWs* were invented to provide offline operation, synchronize data in the background, and retrieve updates. However, we see a different picture here: *SWs* that communicate with 3rd parties are primarily used for advertisements, thus opening a new way to reach users' desktop: a way invented for a different purpose. Even if these push notifications require user to give consent, the website is free to abuse this consent at any time by

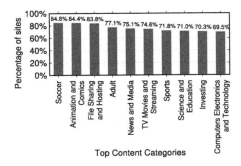

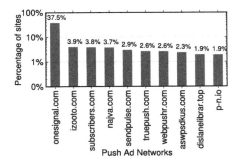

Fig. 9. Breakdown the top-10 categories for sites using *SWs* to serve ads. 'Soccer' sites are the most aggressive in using *SWs* for advertising (84.62%), with 'Animation and Comics' and 'File Sharing and Hosting' following. 'News and Media' sites are next (75%).

Fig. 10. Portion of unique sites collaborating with each of the top ad servers in our dataset. *onesignal.com* dominates the market (37.49%) with the majority of the rest of the ad servers owning less than 4% each (note: y-axis in log-scale).

delivering ad messages instead of the news updates the user was interested in receiving. These ad messages appear via the *SWs* as native ads and cannot be controlled (or filtered out) by ad-blockers. One can only smile in melancholy at the Google Developers guide advising: *"Whatever you do, do not use notifications for advertising of any kind."* [1]

Which are the Dominant Push Ad Networks? In Fig. 10, we plot the top 10 most popular Push Ad Networks in our data, and the portion of the registered *SWs* they communicate with. We see that *onesignal.com* dominates push advertising by owning more than 37.49% of the market, with the majority of the rest Push Ad Networks owning less than 4% each. In Fig. 11, we plot the distribution of all push ad networks in our dataset along with the sites they deliver push ads to. We can see that the distribution can be modeled by two straight lines for large numbers in the x-axis, indicating that the distribution has a piece-wise power-law tail. We can also see the head representing the major player *onesignal.com*.

6 Related Work

The powerful technology of Service Workers provides rich functionality to developers and has triggered an important body of research around its security and privacy aspects. Papadopoulos et al. in [3] are the first to study *SWs* in an attempt to raise awareness regarding a new class of attacks that exploit this exact HTML 5 functionality. Specifically, the authors investigated the potential

---

[1] https://developers.google.com/web/ilt/pwa/introduction-to-push-notifications

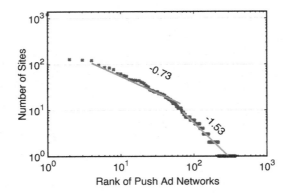

Fig. 11. Distribution of the number of sites that each Push Advertiser in our dataset delivers ad notifications to. The points in the plot tend to converge to two straight lines for large numbers in the x axis, following a piece-wise power-law distribution.

security vulnerabilities of SWs and they demonstrated multiple attack scenarios from cryptojacking to malicious computations (e.g., distributed password cracking), as well as Distributed Denial of Service attacks.

Karami et al. in [4] studied attacks that aim to exploit SWs vulnerabilities to ex-filtrate important privacy information from the user. Specifically, they demonstrated two history-sniffing attacks that exploit the lack of appropriate isolation in these browsers including a non-destructive cache-based version. Finally, the authors proposed a countermeasure and developed a tool that streamlines its deployment, thus facilitating adoption at a large scale.

Chinprutthiwong et al. in [20] described a novel Service Worker-based Cross-Site Scripting (SW-XSS) attack inside a SW, that allows an attacker to obtain and leverage SW privileges. Additionally, they developed a SW Scanner to analyze top websites in the wild, and they found 40 websites vulnerable to this attack including several popular and high ranking websites. Squarcina et al. in [21] demonstrated how a traditional XSS attack can abuse the Cache API of a SW to escalate into a person-in-the-middle attack against cached content, thus, compromising its confidentiality and integrity.

Subramani et al. in [12] proposed PushAdMiner: a new tool to detect Web Push Notifications (WPNs) on the Web. Contrary to our work, the authors focus only on ad related WPNs messages by collecting and analyzing 21,541 WPN messages and 572 ad campaigns, for a total of 5,143 WPN-based ads reporting 51% of them as malicious. Finally, Lee et al. in [22] conducted a systematic study of the security and privacy aspects of PWAs. They demonstrated a cryptojacking and a browser history exfiltration attack. They also suggested possible mitigation measures against the vulnerabilities of PWAs and corresponding SWs.

7   Summary and Conclusion

In this paper, we set out to explore the ecosystem of Service Workers and how websites overuse them to deliver ads (even when user has deployed ad-blockers). We analyzed the top 150 K websites of the Tranco list and our findings can be summarized as follows:

1. A non-trivial percentage (4.96%) of sites deploy a *SW* on the user side.
2. Within a period of 5 months (12.20–05.21), there has been a 26% increase in the adoption of *SWs*.
3. Overall, by using Wayback Machine, we found that from 2015 till today, there were 1.62× more publishers per year, on average, utilizing *SWs* in their web applications.
4. 32.1% of the *SWs* communicate with no 3rd party (27.59% connects with its first party only and 4.51% connects with nobody). The majority (51.6%) communicates with exactly one 3rd party with a significant 16.3% communicating with 2 or more (and up to 26) distinct 3rd parties.
5. Third-party communications are mostly for pushing ads: **A stunning 65.08% of the registered *SWs* that communicates with 3rd party servers, communicate with at least one advertiser**.
6. Most of the ads-pushing *SWs* are deployed on 'News and Media' related sites (27%), with the 'Computers, Electronics and Technology' (6.42%), and 'Adult' (4.79%) related sites following.
7. For some website categories such as 'Soccer' and 'File Sharing', the percentage of ads-pushing *SWs* reaches as high as 85%.

Our study on Service Workers has revealed several surprising results with respect to the use of *SWs* on Web applications and websites. Future research could look into leakage of user personal information and tracking from *SWs*, as well as how ad-blockers can be revamped to still provide effective ad-filtering to their end-users.

Acknowledgements. This project received funding from the EU H2020 Research and Innovation programme under grant agreements No 830927 (Concordia), No 830929 (CyberSec4Europe), No 871370 (Pimcity) and No 871793 (Accordion). These results reflect only the authors' view and the Commission is not responsible for any use that may be made of the information it contains.

References

1. Google Developers: Progressive web apps (2017). https://web.dev/progressive-web-apps/#introduction
2. Pete LePage Sam Richard: What are progressive web apps? (2020). https://web.dev/what-are-pwas/
3. Panagiotis, P., Panagiotis, I., Michalis, P., Evangelos, P.M., Ioannidis, S., Vasiliadis, G.: Master of web puppets: abusing web browsers for persistent and stealthy computation. In: Network and Distributed System Security Symposium (NDSS) (2019)

4. Karami, S., Ilia, P., Polakis, J.: Awakening the web's sleeper agents: misusing service workers for privacy leakage. In: Network and Distributed System Security Symposium (NDSS) (2021)
5. Ann, M.: Are push notifications high engagement marketing tool in 2018? (2021). https://themarketingfolks.com/are-push-notifications-high-engagement-marketing-tool-in-2018/
6. New brave ads use cases show up to 15.8% click-through rate, unmatched engagement (2020). https://brave.com/brave-ads-use-cases/
7. Papadopoulos, P., Kourtellis, N., Markatos, E.P.: The cost of digital advertisement: comparing user and advertiser views. In: Proceedings of the World Wide Web Conference (WWW) (2018)
8. Castelluccia, C., Olejnik, L., Minh-Dung, T.: Selling off privacy at auction. In: Network and Distributed System Security Symposium (NDSS) (2014)
9. Pachilakis, M., Papadopoulos, P., Markatos, E.P., Kourtellis, N.: No more chasing waterfalls: a measurement study of the header bidding ad-ecosystem. In: Proceedings of the Internet Measurement Conference (IMC) (2019)
10. Aksana Shakal. Push ads in 2021: Complete advertiser's guide (2020). https://richads.com/blog/push-notification-advertising/
11. Papadopoulos, P., Kourtellis, N., Rodriguez, P.R., Laoutaris, N.: If you are not paying for it, you are the product: how much do advertisers pay to reach you? In: Proceedings of the Internet Measurement Conference (IMC) (2017)
12. Subramani, K., Yuan, X., Setayeshfar, O., Vadrevu, P., Lee, K.H., Perdisci, R.: When push comes to ads: measuring the rise of (malicious) push advertising. In: Proceedings of the ACM Internet Measurement Conference (IMC) (2020)
13. Google. Puppeteer: Chormium browser automation tool (2020). https://developers.google.com/web/tools/puppeteer
14. Google Developers: Firebase cloud messaging (2021). https://firebase.google.com/docs/cloud-messaging
15. Tranco: The tranco list we used for our crawls. https://tranco-list.eu/list/L564/1000000. Accessed 24 Sep 2020
16. badmojr: 1hosts (pro) (2021). https://hosts.netlify.app/Pro/hosts.txt
17. Similarweb LTD.: Website traffic–check and analyze any website (2021). https://www.similarweb.com/
18. Wayback Machine: Internet archive (2021). https://archive.org/web/
19. Mahanty, A.: Python package & cli tool that interfaces with the Wayback machine API (2021). https://pypi.org/project/waybackpy/
20. Chinprutthiwong, P., Vardhan, R., Yang, G., Gu, G.: Security study of service worker cross-site scripting. In: Annual Computer Security Applications Conference (ACSAC) (2020)
21. Squarcina, M., Calzavara, S., Maffei, M.: The remote on the local: exacerbating web attacks via service workers caches. In: 15th Workshop On Offensive Technologies (WOOT) (2021)
22. Lee, J., Kim, H., Park, J., Shin, I., Son, S.: Pride and prejudice in progressive web apps: abusing native app-like features in web applications. In: Proceedings of the ACM SIGSAC Conference on Computer and Communications Security (CCS) (2018)

Network Properties

ISP Probing Reduction with Anaximander

Emeline Marechal[1]([✉])[iD], Pascal Mérindol[2][iD], and Benoit Donnet[1][iD]

[1] Université de Liège, Montefiore Institute, Liège, Belgium
{emeline.marechal,benoit.donnet}@uliege.be
[2] Université de Strasbourg, iCube, Strasbourg, France
merindol@unistra.fr

Abstract. Since the early 2000's, Internet topology discovery has been an active research topic, providing data for various studies such as Internet modeling, network management, or to assist and support network protocol design. Within this research area, ISP mapping at the router level has attracted little interest despite its utility to perform intra-domain routing evaluation. Since Rocketfuel (and, to a smaller extent, `mrinfo`), no new tool or method has emerged for systematically mapping intra-domain topologies.

In this paper, we introduce Anaximander, a new efficient approach for probing and discovering a targeted ISP in particular. Considering a given set of vantage points, we implement and combine several predictive strategies to mitigate the number of probes to be sent without sacrificing the ISP coverage. To assess the ability of our method to efficiently retrieve an ISP map, we rely on a large dataset of ISPs having distinct nature and demonstrate how Anaximander can be tuned with a simple parameter to control the trade-off between coverage and probing budget.

Keywords: Anaximander · `traceroute` · ISP mapping · Internet topology discovery · Probing reduction

1 Introduction

For the last 20 years, Internet topology discovery has attracted a lot of attention from the research community [9,17]. Those researches have focused on efficient data collection (e.g., Doubletree [10]), on alias resolution [21], on ISP mapping (e.g., Rocketfuel [40] and `mrinfo` [31]), or on Internet modeling [35].

Despite being man-made, much of the Internet is hidden and unknown, for the reason that it is a large and complex system that does not consist in a single authoritative entity. Rather, it is made up of more than 72,000 independent Autonomous Systems (ASes), each having its own commercial practices, physical infrastructure, and logical design (in particular its routing and Traffic Engineering – TE – strategies). More precisely, to deploy a specific routing strategy (from best-effort traffic to more complex strategies, such as fast re-routing),

O. Hohlfeld et al. (Eds.): PAM 2022, LNCS 13210, pp. 441–469, 2022.
https://doi.org/10.1007/978-3-030-98785-5_20

ISPs generally assign an IGP weight to each link and then elaborate more or less complex strategies to control packet forwarding according to a given set of network metrics, related constraints, and technology [36].

Consequently, blindly sampling (a subset of) the Internet is not enough to reveal and discriminate such specific topological and routing patterns, or generic ones if they are any. Instead, in order to conduct relevant TE and IGP performance evaluations [13] and showcase the performance of a given routing proposal (with simulations or analytical models), it is more suitable to rely on distinct ISP maps offering various realistic situations, rather than using an arbitrary chunk of the Internet.

To answer this requirement and offer a framework for reproducible realistic experimentation, one needs to collect intra-domain networks of distinct natures (e.g., Tier-1, Transit, and Stub ASes of diverse sizes). We thus argue it is essential to develop modern, accurate, and advanced topology discovery tools able to skillfully capture the reality of the Internet, in particular considering its atomistic technical nature. The goal is therefore to search for efficient probing designs able to reveal the specifics of any given intra-domain router level map.

While Rocketfuel [40] topologies have been the de facto dataset in use for nearly two decades, we argue that both the resulting topologies and the underlying probing methods are now outdated. Indeed, the Internet structure and practices have evolved over time, and new refined measurements tools have become available as well [2,25]. In this paper, we pursue the same objective as Rocketfuel formerly, i.e., to map specific ISPs at the router level. More specifically, we tackle the following challenge: *Can we infer ISP router level maps with a reduced probing budget without hampering the resulting topological coverage?* Designing efficient probing campaigns is indeed essential to speed up the measurement period and so mitigate forwarding anomalies (e.g., routing changes [48,50]), and the effects of adaptative filtering (e.g., rate limiters [16,37]). Otherwise, the data collected may not be consistent or suffer from poor coverage.

We first point out Rocketfuel limits for capturing nowadays Internet maps but also revisit its successful components when their efficiency is still valuable. Then, we develop our own strategies and evaluate them relying on a large and recent dataset to conduct realistic simulations and support our assumptions. More precisely, we replay measurements offline using different approaches than the initial brute-force approach in order to understand what are the corresponding gains and losses. The reduction strategies we evaluate are diverse and span from the design of the initial hitlist and its scheduling to specific reduction techniques looking at prefix de-aggregation and neighbor marginal utility. To answer our research question, this paper introduces ANAXIMANDER, our new probing method able to recover the same ISP maps as obtained with a brute force approach, but with a network-friendly and efficient probing methodology. For a given set of vantage points, ANAXIMANDER is able to adapt itself to the characteristics of the ISP being mapped. It constructs and manages a target list in order to efficiently cover most of the visible part of the targeted ISP topology. Additionally, our tool offers the opportunity to easily explore the trade-off between AS coverage and probing budget, with a single parameter.

The remainder of the paper is organized as follows: Sect. 2 positions this paper with respect to the state of the art; Sect. 3 describes how we collected and processed the data used throughout the paper; Sect. 4 discusses nowadays Rocketfuel limits; Sect. 5 introduces ANAXIMANDER, our new tool for efficiently probing ISPs; finally, Sect. 7 concludes this paper by summarizing its main achievements.

2   Related Work

Most active probing tools based on `traceroute` embed some heuristics to limit the probing overhead. Such heuristics generally rely on caching previously seen IP addresses to avoid redundancy. For example, for a given prefix P, *Mercator* [14] identifies the furthest router R that was already in the map at the time the probe completed. Then, each subsequent probes to P can start at the TLL of R: if the reply comes from R, Mercator continues to probe the path, otherwise it backtracks and restarts probing with a regular TTL of one. *Atlas* [47] probes IPv6 networks using source routed IPv6 `traceroute`. For each trace, Atlas caches the hop distance to the via-router, i.e., the intermediate router used for source routing. If the same via-router is used in a subsequent trace, then the cache distance provides the initial hop distance and alleviates the need to re-probe from the vantage point to that via-router. *Scriptroute* [41] avoids retracing paths by embedding a list of previously observed IP addresses. A given vantage point stops probing when it reaches an IP address belonging to the list. More generally, Doubletree [10] keeps track of the tree-like structure of routes, either emanating from a single source towards multiple destinations or converging from multiple sources towards a single destination, to avoid probing duplication. Rocketfuel [40], probably the most well-known intra-domain topology discovery tool, relies on two reduction techniques, namely ingress and egress reductions, to reduce its probing budget. While the first considers that probes to a given destination should converge if they enter the targeted ISP at the same ingress node, the second advocates that traces from the same ingress to any prefix beyond the same egress should traverse the same path. Generally speaking, Rocketfuel relies on BGP to guide the probing and builds a router-level map of the targeted domain using Ally. However, it has been shown that Rocketfuel tends to overestimate the path diversity of the targeted domain [42]. Section 4 will investigate more deeply the (other) limits of Rocketfuel. Finally, it is worth noticing heuristics have also been proposed to increase the number of nodes discovered, e.g., POPsicle [11].

With respect to ISP mapping, few other tools than `traceroute` and Rocketfuel exist. There is notably [51], that focuses on the exploration of an essential component of an ISP's infrastructure: its regional access network. By combining several Internet cartography methods (such as public WiFi hotspots and public transit of mobile devices), they are able to get some insight on this specific ISP portion, although it is often remarkably opaque and difficult to measure. There is also `mrinfo` [20], that relies on the Internet Group Management Protocol (IGMP) to enable native router level query. The IGMP reply consists in a list of local multicast interfaces and their link with adjacent interfaces. Recursively querying adjacent interfaces can thus lead to the collection of connected topological information [31]. Pansiot et al. [34] have also provided algorithms for efficiently delimiting AS boundaries to extract ISP maps from such data. Merlin [26] extends `mrinfo` by increasing its efficiency but also mixes IGMP probing with ICMP probing (Paris Traceroute [2] and Ally [40] are used to overcome `mrinfo` limitations). However, IGMP queries are now deprecated and operators filter them at their borders [27], making those techniques unusable. The Internet topology zoo [23] and similar projects like SNDlib[1] expose real intradomain maps manually collected from operators providing their own network maps. However, although useful for TE related reproducible experiments, such datasets are often insufficient as they do not expose large and up to date maps of the Internet. Many are outdated and correspond to small, sometimes partial, IP networks not revealing all relevant information (e.g., IGP weights, node positions, or propagation delays). Eventually, Sybil [6] is a system that can serve a rich set of queries about Internet routes, including what routes go through an ISP of interest. However, in the background, Sybil needs to continuously run measurements in order to maintain its knowledge of routing. This paradigm, which requires a database of (relatively fresh) previously-issued `traceroutes`, is a great departure from the one-shot campaign that can be run more quickly and easily.

Our goal is to provide a light probing framework enabling the deployment of repeated probing campaigns enriched with all available information brought by forwarding traces.

3   Dataset

The `traceroute` data used throughout this paper has been collected by CAIDA with `TNT` [25,44]. `TNT` is a Paris-traceroute [2] extension that is able to reveal the content of MPLS tunnels hidden to `traceroute` exploration [46].

`TNT` has been deployed on the Archipelageo infrastructure [5] between April 17th and 23rd, 2021 over 14 vantage points (VPs), scattered all around the world: Europe (6), North America (1), South America (3), Asia (2), and Australia (2). The overall set of destinations, over 11 million IP addresses, is spread over the 14 vantage points to speed up the probing process.

A total of 936,944 distinct unique IP addresses (excluding `traceroute` targets) have been collected, without counting non-publicly routable addresses, which have been excluded from our dataset. As we are interested in mapping ISPs[2] (as opposed to the whole Internet), we applied `bdrmapIT` [29], a tool for annotating routers and IP addresses with AS ownership. The objective here is to delimit as accurately as possible the ASes maps from the rest of the Internet.

`bdrmapIT`'s inferences are more meaningful when the tool is provided with information about routers, and not only IP addresses found in the traceroutes.

---

[1] http://sndlib.zib.de.

[2] In the remainder of this paper, "ISP" and "AS" are used interchangeably.

Table 1. Various statistics on ASes of interest. Within each type category, ASes are ordered by the number of directed prefixes found in the RIBs (Routing Information Bases), which is a coarse indicator of the AS's importance in the Internet. More precisely, a `traceroute` towards a directed prefix is expected to transit through the AS of interest.

AS		Topology			Directed prefixes	
ASN	Type	Links	Interfaces	Routers	Dependent	Raw number
3491	Tier1	4,399	601	107	0.49%	832,968
6830		6,215	2,985	40	0.22%	832,808
6762		5,338	530	95	0.69%	831,530
174		23,115	4,931	861	1.83%	830,610
3257		8,913	1,477	310	0.83%	829,468
1299		11,999	1,064	204	0.86%	829,309
6453		5,207	831	156	1.70%	829,002
286		1,46	56	11	0.01%	828,926
6461		5,944	1,122	209	0.56%	771,902
12956		8,650	981	91	0.74%	752,128
11537		631	124	33	0.00%	21,823
6939	Transit	11,345	743	132	1.84%	850,999
50673		306	52	5	0.08%	845,664
4637		1,374	402	68	0.18%	814,703
1273		2,800	760	93	0.69%	474,677
7922		33,473	23,356	1,054	0.77%	163,000
2856	Stub	6,959	2,381	37	12.46%	4,423
8764		293	93	7	22.93%	3,149
9198		881	353	44	85.13%	1,748
5400		2,000	395	39	16.46%	1,628
13789		235	60	7	65.26%	685
5432		394	172	4	80.25%	157
1241		472	224	16	91.03%	145
2611		176	124	5	77.97%	59
224		506	417	8	91.30%	23

Therefore, we used MIDAR [22], a tool based on similarities in the IP-ID field, to perform alias resolution (i.e., the process of identifying IP addresses that belong to the same router [21], leading so to a router-level topology) on our set of addresses. We ran MIDAR between April 29th, 2021 and May 1st, 2021. Out of the 900k addresses discovered by TNT, MIDAR found 45,977 routers involving 147,633 addresses.

Additionally, we used APPLE [28] (between May 10th, 2021 and May 12th, 2021), a technique for resolving router IP aliases that complements existing techniques, such as MIDAR. We deployed APPLE on EdgeNet [39], a Kubernetes cluster dedicated to network and distributed systems research, and were able to find 26,729 routers involving 87,532 addresses. In combination with MIDAR, we were thus able to further refine our alias resolution with a total of 57,355 routers involving 192,320 addresses, which represents an increase in coverage of 25% compared to the initial results with MIDAR.

Besides, we used BGPStream [33], an open-source software framework to easily acquire live and historical BGP data. The tool provides access to BGP views from all around the world, coming from the RouteViews [38] and RIPE RIS [43] projects. We collected 44 BGP tables (from as many collectors) in the middle of the TNT campaign, on April 20th, 2021.

Table 1 provides global statistics about the sample of 25 ASes selected for this study and discussed in the paper. We chose ASes with varying sizes and roles in the Internet (11 Tiers 1, 5 Transits, and 9 Stubs) in order to be as representative as possible.

4   Rocketfuel Limits

The main contribution of Rocketfuel was to propose and deploy the pioneer measurement techniques to infer ISP router-level maps. The second challenge was to use as few measurements as possible to speed up the campaign, not only because of the limited capacity of legacy forwarding devices, but also because ISPs (continue to) filter probes using default rate limiters (e.g., only small bursts of ICMP replies are allowed) for both performance and security reasons. Additionally, ISPs are continuously subject to routing changes [30]. In this regard, their approach was to first exploit available routing information to select traces likely to transit the ISP of interest, and second, to apply reduction techniques based on IP routing properties to eliminate traces likely to follow redundant paths in the ISP.

At the time, Rocketfuel was admittedly the best attempt at mapping an ISP, even though it already suffered from some limits [42]. These issues had to do with the inference of numerous false links, due, on the one hand, to the naive use of the basic `traceroute` implementation (later replaced by Paris `traceroute` [2]), and on the second hand, to using alias resolution techniques that are now obsolete.

Nowadays, Rocketfuel suffers from additional problems due to the massive growth of the Internet during the last 20 years, along with all the changes that came with it. More and more edge networks joined the Internet, the interconnections between core networks became denser (flattening the Internet), and networks operational practices (such as the usage of TE, multi-homing, or provider independent addresses [1]) have significantly evolved and rely now on new technologies (e.g., MPLS or Segment Routing). Following this shift in paradigm, while the core principles guiding Rocketfuel's probing remains valuable conceptually, the set of tools and strategies applied on top of them became outdated.

In the next sections, we will review how Rocketfuel's reduction techniques (namely, Egress Reduction – Sect. 4.1 –, Next-hop AS Reduction – Sect. 4.2 –, and Ingress Reduction – Sect. 4.3) are no more suited for today's Internet.

4.1   Egress Reduction

Without going into all the details, Rocketfuel's initial pool of targets is built from BGP tables (i.e., Routing Information Bases – RIBs), that allow one to select measurements expected to transit the ISP of interest. They call this technique *directed probing*, and the number of *directed prefixes* for each AS can be found in Table 1. Egress Reduction advocates that traces from the same ingress to any prefix beyond the same egress should traverse the same path. Such traces are thus redundant, and only one needs to be collected. But in order to find said egresses, Rocketfuel must conduct a pre-probing phase to discover the ISP's egress routers common to several prefixes.

This pre-probing stage is only launched on a subset of their initial pool of targets, that they call the *dependent prefixes*. Dependent prefixes are prefixes originated by the ISP of interest or one of its singly-home customers. Therefore, by definition, all `traceroutes` to these prefixes (from anywhere in the network) should transit the ISP. This allows them to launch their pre-probing phase from a single monitor, with the guarantee that the probes will indeed go through the ISP of interest.

Even though Egress Reduction is admittedly sound in principle, being able to apply it and actually find the egresses shared by several prefixes may prove to be too costly for a marginal reduction not balancing the effort. To demonstrate this, we build the initial target pool from the RIBs (following Rocketfuel's approach) and compute the corresponding portion of dependent prefixes. The raw number of targets in the pool, as well as the corresponding percentage of dependent prefixes can be found in Table 1, in the "Raw number" and "Dependent" columns respectively.

We can observe that the percentage of dependent prefixes greatly varies from one AS to the other. For large Tiers 1, less than 1% of the targets could *potentially* be reduced with Egress Reduction. This is not surprising given that Tiers 1 are involved in almost all Internet traffic (in particular with thousands of customers) and have numerous peering relationships. Additionally, the practice of multi-homing has become more and more prominent, which further explains this very small portion of dependent prefixes. For smaller Transit ASes, the potential reduction can sometimes be slightly better, but is not a panacea either. And for Stubs (or near-Stubs), the potential reduction is indeed greater (from 10% to 90%). However, given the already small number of targets in the pool, there is no use in trying to reduce them further at the cost of additional probes during the pre-probing phase.

All in all, Egress Reduction is not actually helpful. On the one hand, the reduction potential it shows for small ASes does not actually lead to a great saving in terms of absolute number of probes. And on the other hand, the gain for large ASes looks negligible (less than 1%) with respect to the already large number of probes required, as well as for the pre-probing stage.

4.2   Next-hop AS Reduction

The principle behind Next-hop AS Reduction is that the path through an ISP usually depends only on the next-hop AS, not on the specific destination prefix. According to this idea, only one trace from ingress router to next-hop AS is likely to be valuable, which means that all prefixes sharing the same next-hop AS could be reduced to a single probe.

To determine the veracity of this assumption, we evaluated whether we often see multiple different egresses for a given next-hop AS and for a given ingress. We performed the evaluation on our 25 ASes (see Table 1) containing altogether 90,009 (ingress, next-hop AS) pairs, and found that for 30% of the cases, an ingress does see more than one egress when crossing over the same AS. Note that the initial evaluation made by Rocketfuel was conducted on a smaller dataset, i.e., only one AS and 2,500 (ingress, next-hop AS) pairs, and found that the early-exit assumption was violated in only 7% of the cases [40].

To go further, we also simulated the Next-hop AS Reduction on our dataset and found that, in the worst case, this reduction can lead up to a decrease in the discovery of 32% for links, 18% for IP addresses, and 29% for routers. These results confirm that Next-hop AS Reduction now leads to too much false negatives. This can be explained by an increase in peering relationships between ASes [7], notably with IXPs, leading therefore to a flatter but more diverse Internet [8, 49].

4.3   Ingress Reduction

The idea of Ingress Reduction is that routes taken through a network are usually destination-specific. As such, when `traceroutes` from different VPs to the same destination enter the ISP at the same ingress, the path through the ISP is likely to be the same. Therefore, only one `traceroute` from one of the VP would be required.

The first consideration to have is that purely destination-oriented routing is not necessarily the only default rule in use when it comes to forwarding packets, given the rise of TE in the last few years [45]. TE strategies take into account other parameters (such as the type of traffic, its origin, or its flow-id with multipath routing[3]) to optimize the network traffic delivery performance.

Secondly, Ingress Reduction was applicable for Rocketfuel because of its probing design, that initially assigns the complete target list to each VP (meaning that all targets are probed from each VP if no reduction applies). In our case however, our reference dataset subdivides the target list among VPs in order to speed up the probing process (by design, the same destination is not probed from two VPs or more), as it has little impact on the overall quality of discovered data [15].

---

[3] In theory, the transit traffic flows can be load balanced among multiple (possibly inter-domains) routes according to congestion control algorithms.

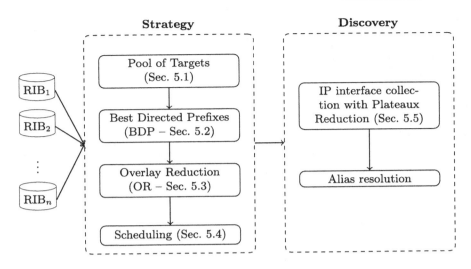

Fig. 1. ANAXIMANDER two steps process.

For those two reasons, we will not consider Ingress Reduction for our study, or any other optimization that could be done on VP placement or targets specific balancing among VPs.

5   Anaximander

This section introduces ANAXIMANDER[4], our new ISP mapping framework. In a nutshell, given a set of vantage points and a targeted ISP $\mathcal{X}$, ANAXIMANDER aims at discovering the most complete map of $\mathcal{X}$ using the minimum amount of probes to enable a quick and efficient measurement campaign.

Figure 1 illustrates the overall behavior of ANAXIMANDER. As Rocketfuel, ANAXIMANDER starts by collecting RIBs. Afterwards comes the *Strategy* phase, which is run completely off-line and has no probing cost. In this step, ANAXIMANDER relies on three core principles: (*i*) finding an initial pool of targets expected to transit the ISP of interest (Sect. 5.1); (*ii*) applying pruning techniques to this initial pool to reduce the number of probes before probing (Sect. 5.2 and 5.3); (*iii*) sorting and scheduling the targets in preparation for the discovery phase (Sect. 5.4). Those three steps are run in sequence (the output of one is used as input for the subsequent). At the end, the Strategy phase produces an ordered list of targets for probing the ISP of interest.

Secondly comes the *Discovery* phase (Sect. 5.5), in which ANAXIMANDER will send probes based on the target list, taking advantage of the scheduling of the targets to speed up the discovery progression and possibly stop the probing

---

[4] Anaximander (610–546 BC) is known to be the first to have published a map of the world. See https://en.wikipedia.org/wiki/Anaximander.

in some portions when the discovery becomes marginal in said portions. Once IP interfaces have been collected, ANAXIMANDER can run alias resolution for generating a router-level map of the ISP, using for instance the combination of MIDAR [22] and APPLE [28].

5.1 Initial Pool of Targets

Rocketfuel's Initial Pool of Targets. We start our investigation with the same initial pool of targets as Rocketfuel, but without applying any of their reduction techniques, as we have shown they do not offer a good trade-off between coverage and efficiency for the current shape of the Internet.

The core principle for selecting targets likely to transit the ISP of interest (i.e., directed probing) is to take advantage of the routing information contained in BGP routing tables. A BGP entry is composed of a prefix (of any length) associated to several attributes, in particular the AS_PATH attribute. If the AS of interest appears in the AS_PATH attribute, sending a probe to this prefix is likely to traverse the ISP (in particular if there exists a vantage point co-located to one of the BGP collectors). The number of targets in the initial pool for each AS can be found in Table 1, in the "Raw number" column.

/24 Internal Prefixes. Anticipating on the results presented in Sect. 6.2, we actually need to expand Rocketfuel's initial pool with additional targets in order to complete our exploration, given the rather low coverage resulting from it (especially for Stubs and small Transit).

A natural lead to discover most of a given intra-domain AS map is to simply add the AS's internal prefixes to the pool of targets. This time however, we consider a finer granularity and divide the raw prefixes into /24 prefixes (e.g., with prefix 109.75.120.0/22, we split it into four /24 prefixes within the range 109.75.120.0/24-109.75.123.0/24). Basically, our initial pool of target is thus composed, on the one hand, of the AS's internal prefixes (broken down into /24 prefixes); and on the other hand, of the raw[5] directed prefixes found in the RIBs.

Limitations. The public BGP information we rely on is already known to be incomplete [32]. As a result, some valid targets may be skipped (i.e., *false negatives*) because of this limitation of the data, although they would have traversed the ISP.

Another important principle in BGP is that there is no single authoritative view of the Internet's inter-domain routing table – all views are in fact relative to the perspective of each BGP speaker [19]. Obviously, the ideal scenario would be to have a VP co-located to each BGP collector, in order to get the exact BGP view from the VP. But since this option is not conveniently available at

---

[5] Understand: not broken down into /24 prefixes.

large scale, we rather combine together multiple RIBs and use this merging as an approximation.

The result of this merging can entail *false positives*, i.e., `traceroutes` that do not traverse the ISP and waste the probing budget. Indeed, the BGP collector that provided the target can be located in a very distant part of the network from the VP that will actually launch the `traceroute`. As their network views potentially do not match (for first AS hops in particular), the probe may not traverse the ISP – even though it would have, had it been launched from the BGP collector instead. These false positives sacrifice the probing budget but not the accuracy, and can be reduced later thanks to our reduction techniques (see Sects. 5.2, 5.3, and 5.4).

5.2   Best Directed Prefixes

This section introduces our first reduction technique, which is based on a simple observation of the workings of BGP routing tables. The BGP information we have access to from the RouteViews [38] and RIPE RIS [43] projects comes in the form of *routing* tables (RIBs), and not *forwarding* tables (Forwarding Information Bases – FIBs). In normal BGP operation, BGP routers typically receive multiple paths to the same prefix. All local routing information learned by a BGP speaker is maintained in the RIB. As such, a prefix can appear multiple times (and with different `AS_PATH`) in the RIB if it has been advertised by multiple BGP neighbors (see Table 2 for an example of this).

For each prefix in the RIB, the route that will actually be used to forward packets and installed into the FIB is determined by the BGP route selection process. BGP has multiple criteria for selecting the *best* route among a set of routes towards a prefix. The first selection criteria is based on local policies defined by network operators, which reflect selfish objectives. Second usually comes the shortest `AS_PATH` criteria, a globally safe criteria, which will select the route with the shortest `AS_PATH`, in order not to burden the network uselessly. If necessary, other more or less arbitrary rules are applied until a tie break is reached. Therefore, when looking at a given RIB to build our initial pool of targets, we are wasting probes on prefixes that *could* be reached through the AS of interest, but that never will, as the route inserted into the FIB can be one that potentially does not go through the AS of interest.

This situation presents the opportunity to perform a first reduction on the initial pool of targets, by building refined FIBs from the collected RIBs. Having no access to the operators' local policy, we approximate it with the *no-valley and prefer customer routing policy* [12], which is a current practice in today's Internet. This policy specifies to prefer a route through a customer AS, over a route through a peer AS, over a route through a provider AS, for economical reasons. In case the routing policy cannot be applied, or if we need a tie-break between two RIB entries, we use the second criteria and select prefixes only if the AS of interest is present in the *shortest* `AS_PATH`. More precisely, we apply this process individually for each prefix in each RIB, before merging the results together. For example, based on the use-case presented in Table 2 (and considering that the

Table 2. Routing Table – Example of multiple paths towards the same prefix. AS 3223 is a pivot AS where traffic can either go towards AS 8262 or AS 3356. If AS 8262 is a customer of AS 3223, and if AS 3356 is a peer of AS 3223 (for example), entry n°3 will be discarded, according to our BGP decision heuristic. Next, entry n°1 will be discarded in profit of the entry with the shortest AS_PATH, i.e., entry n°2. AS 3356 being ANAXI-MANDER's target, this prefix will not be selected for ANAXIMANDER's target list.

#	Prefix	AS_PATH					BGP heuristic
1	72.249.184.0/21	9050	6762	3223	8262	36024	
2	72.249.184.0/21		1230	3223	8262	36024	X
3	72.249.184.0/21		39737	3223	*3356*	36024	

AS of interest is the AS3356), we would not select the prefix 72.249.184.0/21 for ANAXIMANDER's target list, as it is not present in the prefered path. We call this strategy *Best Directed Prefix* (BDP).

5.3   Overlay Reduction

In this section, we present ANAXIMANDER's second reduction technique, relying on a more in-depth analysis of the routing tables.

Forwarding in the Internet is usually done on a longest prefix match basis.[6] As such, a router will always prefer to forward a packet towards the most specific entry to its intended destination. For instance, a router may contain entries for prefix 10.0.0.0/8 as well as a more specific prefix 10.0.5.0/24. Packets towards 10.0.5.12 (or any other address drawn from the more specific prefix) will always be forwarded towards 10.0.5.0/24.

It is thus possible, through BGP, to announce *more specific* prefixes. Given that not all more specific advertisements serve the same purpose, Huston has proposed a classification of these more specific prefixes into three categories, based on the relationship between the more specific and its immediately enclosing aggregate advertisement [18].

The first category is that of the *Hole Punching* more specifics. These more specifics are used traditionally to advertise reachability information, in the case where a block of the aggregate prefix has been attributed to a customer AS. In the routing table, this corresponds to the case where the origin AS of the more specific route is different from the origin AS of the covering aggregate.

The second category covers *Traffic Engineering* use cases. Network operators take advantage of the longest prefix match rule to control the route choices made by other BGP speakers to direct traffic on more specific constrained paths (e.g., towards links with greater capacity, lower latency, or lower cost). In the routing table, this corresponds to the case where the origin AS of the more specific route and its covering aggregate are the same, but where the AS paths differ.

---

[6] If we do not take into account MPLS forwarding [45], for instance.

Table 3. Routing Table – Example of Overlay category with more specific prefixes. AS 3356 is ANAXIMANDER's target.

Prefix	AS_PATH
1.0.4.0/22	4608 4826 *3356* 56203
1.0.4.0/24	4608 4826 *3356* 56203
1.0.5.0/24	4608 4826 *3356* 56203
1.0.6.0/24	4608 4826 *3356* 56203
1.0.7.0/24	4608 4826 *3356* 56203

Finally, the third category is called the *Overlays*. In this category, the more specific and its aggregate share the exact same AS_PATH (see Table 3 for an example of this). These more specific advertisements actually serve no purpose at all, as the handling of packets in the aggregate or in the more specific will be the same.[7] For this reason, the Overlays category is of particular interest for ANAXIMANDER: because there is no variation in the path towards the ISP of interest, it naturally allows us to reduce the number of probes by selecting a single prefix within a group of overlays.

We thus apply *Overlay Reduction* (OR) to BDP obtained earlier (see Sect. 5.2). To do so, we first compute the overlays groups for all the RIBs we have and combine them together to get the most complete view of the Internet. After this, we cycle through the targets in the pool and randomly select only a single prefix per group of overlays and per VP[8]. For example, based on the use-case presented in Table 3 (and considering that the AS of interest is the AS3356), we would only select one of the prefixes present in the table – prefix 1.0.6.0/24 for instance.

5.4   Targets Scheduling

After having exploited all that we can regarding routing information (with BDP and OR), we now start investigating scheduling of our targets, instead of randomly launching probes. The purpose here is twofold: the first objective is to start by probing the targets that will lead to the greatest discovery, and to put the less successful targets (i.e., those that discover only a few elements, or no elements at all) at the end of the queue. This can be useful in the context of a low probing budget, where it is necessary to stop probing as soon as possible. The second more general objective is to find an ordering or a grouping of the probes that exhibits some patterns to be exploited in order to reduce the probing budget when some explored portions becomes marginal in term of discovery.

---

[7] It is believed network operators do this as a messy attempt to mitigate, to some extent, the risks of a more specific routing attack [18].

[8] More precisely, the OR can only be applied on a per-VP basis. Indeed, let us imagine we have two overlays. If those two overlays are taken by two different VPs, we are susceptible to find different addresses and links because of the entry point that will be different for the two VPs.

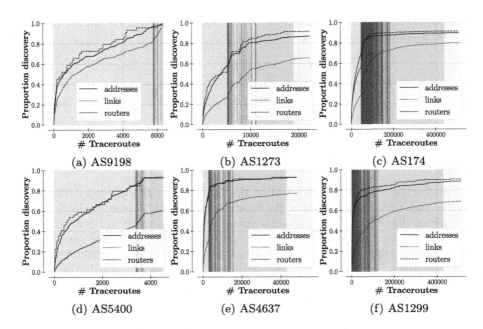

Fig. 2. ANAXIMANDER simulation with targets scheduling. (*i*) /24 internal prefixes in green, (*ii*) direct neighbors in red, (*iii*) one-hop neighbors in violet, and (*iv*) others in yellow. Separation between the ASes is shown with vertical red lines in the direct neighbors group. In the one-hop neighbors and others groups, probes are also grouped by AS, but the separation is not shown for readability purpose. (Color figure online)

To reach these goals, we organize the target list into four main groups: (*i*) first the targets belonging to the /24 internal prefixes of the AS, (*ii*) those belonging to the direct neighbors, (*iii*) those belonging to the one-hop neighbors, and finally, (*iv*) the targets belonging to other ASes. Within each of the main groups, probes are gathered together by AS, with no particular order between the probes of an AS. The direct neighbors group is further sub-divided into three categories: the AS's customers, the peers, and the providers, probed in this particular order.[9] Finally, ASes within a group or category are ordered by increasing size of their customer cone, as defined by CAIDA [3,24]. We will review in the next sections the benefits and reasons for this scheduling.

Results are depicted in Fig. 2, with the X-axis representing the number of `traceroutes` that were launched, and the Y-axis depicting the corresponding levels of discovery during the time progression. Each of the four main groups is represented by a color: green for the internal prefixes, red for the direct neighbors, violet for the one-hop neighbors, and yellow for the others. In the direct neighbors section, the separation between the ASes is shown with vertical red lines. In the

---

[9] To be able to establish such a classification of ASes, we use the CAIDA AS Relationships Dataset [4].

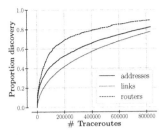

Fig. 3. Simulation with no scheduling of the probes (AS174).

violet and yellow group, probes are also grouped by AS, although the separation is not shown with vertical lines for readability purpose. A router is considered as discovered if we managed to discover at least two of its addresses.[10] Due to space constraints, we present the detailed results only for six ASes (2 Stubs, 2 Transits, and 2 Tier 1) among the 25 we studied, as they are representative of the typical behaviors for their type.

This representation eases the visualization of the probing evolution: one can analyze which group of prefixes is the most important for the discovery of an AS map as `traceroutes` are launched. In the next sections, we will review the contributions of each group successively. For the interested reader, the contributions of each group individually from each others are given in Appendix B.

/24 Internal Prefixes (Green Group). Targets in this group are launched in no particular order. As can be seen in Fig. 2a (AS9198) and Fig. 2d (AS5400), this group represents almost all discovery for Stub ASes. This is expected given the leaf nature of Stubs, which is not to provide transit and carry traffic for others. As such, only probes directed towards the internal prefixes will hit the AS of interest. For larger ASes, internal prefixes also play a major role in the discovery (especially for addresses), with values ranging from 35% (Fig. 2f – AS1299) to 80% (Fig. 2e – AS4637). The effect for links follows the same lead, although it is less impressive. It is not surprising either that internal prefixes lead to high discovery levels for large ASes. Indeed, probes launched directly into the core of the AS naturally discover a lot of internal elements. However, probing only the internal prefixes is not sufficient in this case to discover the complete AS map.

We also notice that starting to probe with the /24 internal prefixes is beneficial, as it allows us to shift the discovery curve to the left, meaning that most of the discovery of an AS happens at the beginning of the probing campaign. To convince ourselves of this effect, let us have a look at Fig. 3, which presents a probing campaign with no scheduling for AS174. With this campaign, we can observe that the discovery curve is, in fact, already shifted to the left, with a steep increase in discovery at the beginning, followed by a slower rise. This has

---

[10] Two addresses are enough to perform alias resolution with MIDAR and APPLE.

to do with the properties of `traceroute` exploration, which is naturally very redundant [10]. Indeed, the first `traceroutes` that are launched arrive in unchartered territory, meaning that all addresses and links discovered are new to the observer. The discovery rate at that time is thus very high. However, as time passes, new elements are discovered for sure, but the probes nevertheless go through the same routers again and again. At this time, only a few elements per `traceroute` are thus valuable, instead of the whole `traceroute`, as previously.

Even though it is naturally shaped to the left, we managed to increase the trend by starting to probe the /24 prefixes. Indeed, we see that for AS174 for example (Fig. 2c), we have already managed to discover 70% of the addresses after having spent only 10% of the probing budget. Compared to the campaign with no scheduling (Fig. 3), we had only discovered 40% of the addresses with 10% of the probing budget. Starting to probe with the /24 prefixes is thus an obvious first step in the right direction to get the most discovery the soonest.

Direct Neighbors (Red Group). The first thing we can notice is that the direct neighbors also represent a substantial part of the AS discovery (for larger ASes), with values ranging from 15% to 40% for addresses, from 25% to 40% for links, and from 10% to 35% for routers (see Fig. 2c, 2b, 2e, and 2f).

With the direct neighbors, we work on both our objectives, i.e., to group targets in some way as to find a discovery pattern that could be further exploited for reduction, and to shift the discovery curve to the left.

We meet our first objective thanks to the grouping of probes by AS. At first, when ANAXIMANDER starts to probe the prefixes of a neighbor, new IP interfaces and links are discovered. After some time though, all routes carrying traffic to the neighbor have been discovered, and it becomes useless to continue probing the neighbor's address space, because paths taken will be redundant with paths already explored. This is reflected in the simulation plots (see Fig. 2e and Fig. 2b for example) by the apparition of *plateaux* in the discovery curve. Indeed, we see that the curve presents small bursts of discovery followed by flat sections, which correspond each time with the beginning of a new neighbor probing. These flat sections correspond to `traceroutes` that were launched but that did not yield any discovery, and present thus the opportunity to be pruned from the list of targets. Some neighbors also do not present any discovery at all. The pattern is exactly the same for other ASes, but is less visible due to the scale of the plots, and the successive reductions applied to the pool of targets, which have already pruned a large number of useless `traceroutes`. In the next section (Sect. 5.5), we will see how this pattern can be exploited for probing reduction.

We meet our second objective by grouping the neighbor ASes into three categories: first the AS's customers, then the peers, then the providers, probed in this particular order. ASes within each category are ordered by increasing size of their customer cone [3,24]. An AS's customer cone is defined as the ASes and IPv4 prefixes that can be reached through this AS by following only customer links. In other words, an AS's customer cone contains its direct customers, plus its customers' customers, and so on. The size of an AS's customer cone actually

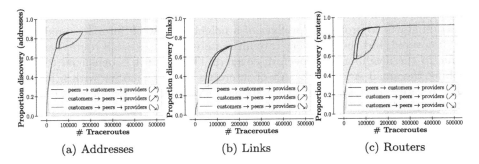

(a) Addresses   (b) Links   (c) Routers

Fig. 4. Alternative scheduling for direct neighbors (AS 174). ↗ stands for ASes ordered by increasing order of their customer cone size, while ↘ stands for the decreasing order. (*i*) /24 internal prefixes in green, (*ii*) direct neighbors in red, (*iii*) one-hop neighbors in violet, and (*iv*) others in yellow. (Color figure online)

reflects the size or the influence of an AS in the routing system. After testing several combinations for the categories and ordering in both the increasing and the decreasing customer cone size, we found the optimal scheduling is indeed the one presented above. The various attempted scheduling for the direct neighbors are presented in Fig. 4 for the particular case of AS 174 (results are similar for all other ASes, but are not presented due to space constraints).

The first thing we notice is that it is more advantageous to start probing the customers rather than the peers (note that the position of the providers does not have much of an impact and has been left at the end of the scheduling). We explain this phenomenon with the *no-valley and prefer customer* routing policy [12], which is a current practice in today's Internet. BGP routing decisions are mostly based on business relationships and guidelines between ASes. For economical reasons, peer ASes should exchange traffic only between each other and each other's customers, as this traffic generates money for them (either the cost is null or they are paid by their customers). However, an AS should avoid forwarding traffic coming from a peer to a provider (creating so a "valley"), as it can only generate costs for the AS (no gain). For this reason, `traceroute` exploration tends to discover customer-provider links more easily than peer-to-peer links, which are subject to more constraints for the traffic they are allowed to carry. As such, launching `traceroutes` towards a peer of the AS of interest will most likely follow a route without passing through said AS of interest, because the `AS_PATH` containing the peering link is also likely to be longer (compared to a direct customer-to-provider one, if any). Links between the AS of interest and its peer will thus be harder to spot, explaining the lower discovery it brings during ANAXIMANDER's probing campaign (as can be seen in Fig. 4).

Furthermore, the increasing customer cone size order presents the advantageous burst we are looking for, followed by a decrease in the discovery rate). On the contrary, we see the decreasing order yielded the opposite trend of a slow increase followed by a speed up in the discovery. This phenomenon is due to the traceroute exploration process of the neighbors. More precisely, when ANAXI-MANDER starts to probe the prefixes of a neighbor, new IP interfaces and links are discovered, but the discovery rate ultimately decreases as all routes carrying traffic to the neighbor have been discovered. Therefore, it is beneficial to start probing the small ASes in the AS of interest's cone (i.e., ASes with a low AS rank) because their address space is smaller; it will thus be explored faster, and the next neighbor (with its associated discovery burst) will be tackled sooner.

One-Hop Neighbors and Others (Violet and Yellow Group). Following the direct neighbors come the one-hop neighbors (violet group) and other ASes even further away (yellow group). Within each group, ASes are also ordered by increasing order of their customer cone [3,24]. Separating the two groups has no effect whatsoever on the efficiency of the probing, but we present it this way to realize what is the contribution of each group to the AS discovery. The global contribution of next-hop neighbors and other ASes is much lower than the two previous groups, with values ranging from a few percents to a small 5%. Although not very visible in the plots, plateaux are also present in those two groups.

Alternative Scheduling. The existence of plateaux may suggest that our scheduling is suboptimal. We have tried several alternative probing scheduling to understand to which extent we can improve the current scheduling. However, our results showed that none of those alternatives have positive effects on the results (see Appendix A). As it happens, grouping together redundant probes to create those plateaux will prove to be a useful characteristic in order to take decisions on marginal benefit while probing. We thus choose to keep the current scheduling, and to work on exploiting this pattern by reducing as much as possible the plateaux, in which no new discovery is made (see Sect. 5.5).

5.5   Discovery Phase with Plateau Reduction

The Strategy phase ends with an ordered list of target, for each ISP of interest. This list, obtained without any probing effort, serves as input for ANAXIMANDER second phase, the *Discovery step*.

In the Discovery step, ANAXIMANDER may rely on any probing mechanism. In our implementation, we use TNT [25], so that we can also reveal the MPLS usage [46] in the targeted AS. Then, from TNT IP level data, we run alias resolution (such as MIDAR [22] and APPLE [28]) for providing a router level map.

For its probing, ANAXIMANDER will take advantage of the plateaux that appeared in the discovery curve due to the grouping of the probes by AS (see Sect. 5.4). When we reach a plateau during the probing of a particular AS, ANAXIMANDER will simply jump to the next AS and continue probing, as the AS marginal utility has become null. Of course, during the actual probing, it is impossible to know whether we are truly encountering the final plateau indicating the end of the discovery, or if additional elements will still be discovered afterwards. On the one hand, if we jump too soon to the next AS, we risk to

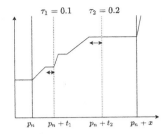

Fig. 5. Plateau Reduction (PR): Effect of parameter τ on probing.

skip some `traceroutes` that would have discovered new elements. But on the other hand, if we jump too late, we waste the probing budget for nothing.

We therefore introduce a simple *threshold parameter*, τ, that allows ANAXI-MANDER to control the trade-off between maximizing the discovery and reducing the probing budget. The threshold parameter τ belongs to the interval $[0, 1]$ and represents the length of the plateau (expressed as the proportion of the probed AS address space) after which we jump to the next AS. In other terms, the lower the parameter, the soonest we jump to the next AS. On one hand, when $\tau = 1$, it means ANAXIMANDER does not take into account the plateau and continues probing even if nothing new is discovered for a group (e.g., prefixes belonging to a neighbor AS). On the other hand, when $\tau = 0$, ANAXIMANDER stops probing the plateau as soon as a single probe is useless. We call the effects of τ on probing the *Plateau Reduction* (PR).

An example of the effect of τ is given in Fig. 5. This figure presents a portion of a (fictitious and simplified) discovery curve during a probing campaign. The two vertical red lines delimit the current AS being probed (for example, a direct neighbor of the AS of interest, let us call it AS $\mathcal{N}$). The first probe belonging to AS $\mathcal{N}$ is p_n and the last probe is $p_n + x - 1$. The address space of AS $\mathcal{N}$ thus contains x probes. If we select $\tau_1 = 0.1$ as the threshold parameter, it means we will stop probing AS $\mathcal{N}$ after having encountered a plateau whose length is greater than 10% of the AS's address space. In this case, we thus stop at the first vertical blue line, i.e., at probe $p_n + t_1$. However, if we select $\tau_2 = 0.2$, we stop probing after having encountered a plateau whose length is greater than 20% of the AS's address space. This corresponds to the second vertical blue line, at probe $p_n + t_2$. In this scenario, we see that a threshold value of $\tau_2 = 0.2$ is more appropriate because it allows us to discover all there is to discover, and to prune the remaining of the plateau, thus reducing the probing budget. On the other hand, if we select $\tau_1 = 0.1$, we will jump too soon to the next AS and possibly lose some information.

6   Evaluation

6.1   Methodology

To assess ANAXIMANDER efficiency, we simulate it on the TNT dataset (see Sect. 3). More precisely, we replay measurements offline in order to understand what are the respective gains and losses of our probing reduction techniques. Our comparison is thus relative and we consider the brute-force approach (probing of the entire Internet at a /24 granularity) as a baseline offering an upper bound on the probing coverage one cannot outperform by construction. While this baseline provides the coverage upper-bound, it is not able to cover the whole topology (for example, backup links are not visible if no failure occurs during the campaign): our goal is to offer the same coverage but with a reduced probing budget.

In practice, we do not assume that the TNT dataset provides a complete picture of the router-level topology of a given ISP. As a matter of fact, different VPs placements can lead to discovering different portions of the AS. There could even be some unlucky sets of VPs that provide very poor visibility for a specific AS of interest (for example, if all VPs have a certain Tier 1 as their primary provider while the goal of the study is to map another Tier 1).

However, such considerations are outside the scope of this work. It is not our goal here to study VPs placement strategies. Rather, we designed ANAXIMANDER to remain a flexible tool that can be launched on any set of VPs, and that will yield the best possible results given that set. This appears to us as the most sensible approach for designing a probing tool, given the difficulty of obtaining VPs to launch a campaign (and the even greater difficulty of placing VPs in strategic locations that would suit the specific purpose of said campaign).

In short, if the initial set of VPs provides very poor visibility into the AS of interest, the resulting maps will obviously not offer high quality absolute coverage. But this is independent of the probing strategies employed (and of ANAXIMANDER, *de facto*), and the maps would not have been any more complete with a brute force approach (or with any other probing strategy). This evaluation argues that ANAXIMANDER is able to recover (almost) the same ISP maps as obtained with a brute force approach, but with a much more efficient probing methodology.

For our evaluations to be relevant nonetheless, we selected 25 ASes (see Table 1) for which we attained good coverage in terms of IP interfaces, links, and routers, given the set of VPs of the TNT dataset. We chose ASes with varying sizes and roles in the Internet (11 Tiers 1, 5 Transits, and 9 Stubs) in order to be the most representative. We evaluate our strategies based on two metrics: the percentage of discovery (i.e., completeness) compared to the complete AS map in the TNT dataset[11]; and the number of `traceroutes` sent (i.e., probing reduction) compared to the initial pool where no reduction is applied.

6.2   Results

We present in Fig. 6 the simulation results for all ASes and all reduction strategies applied successively (first BDP, then OR, then PR, as shown in Fig. 1). A comparsion with Rocketfuel is also available. Fig. 6a, 6b, and 6c present the final ASes coverage (Y-axis) for addresses, routers, and links, respectively. A router is

---

[11] As a reminder, AS maps have been isolated with the tool `bdrmapIT`.

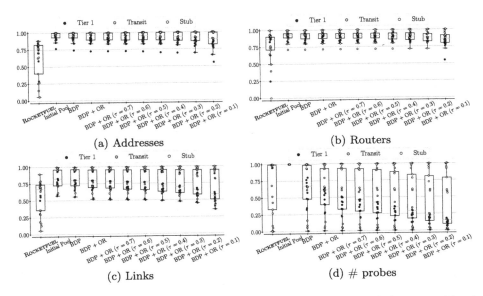

Fig. 6. Efficiency of reduction techniques compared to the initial pool of targets without any reduction, and compared to Rocketfuel. "BDP" stands for "Best Directed Prefixes" (Sect. 5.2) and "OR" for "Overlay Reduction" (Sect. 5.3). The various percentages correspond to the threshold τ for PR (Sect. 5.5). (Color figure online)

considered as discovered if we managed to discover at least two of its addresses.[12] As for Fig. 6d, it displays the corresponding reduction on the number of probes sent, relative to initial pool where no reduction is applied (see "Initial Pool" label on the X-axis).

Results are presented in the form of box plots in order to study the global distribution of ASes' coverage with each strategy. Additionally, each AS is represented by a colored dot (black for Tiers1, blue for Transits, and white for Stubs) to visualize the difference in behaviors depending on the AS type.

Comparison with Rocketfuel. As a reminder, Rocketfuel's initial pool of targets is composed of the directed prefixes found in the RIBs, while ANAXIMANDER's initial pool is composed, on the one hand, of the AS's internal prefixes (broken down into /24 prefixes); and on the other hand, of the raw directed prefixes. The first observation we can make for Rocketfuel in Fig. 6a, 6b, and 6c is that the final discovery levels can vary quite dramatically depending on the AS type, with values ranging from a few percents to a perfect 100%.

For Stub ASes, the global trend is to be situated in the lower part of the box plots. We see the final coverage can very often be quite low, with values that can drop around 5% for both addresses and routers, and even to 0% for links. This is

---

[12] As two addresses are necessary and sufficient to perform alias resolution with MIDAR and APPLE.

actually not surprising given the edge position of the AS in the global network. Such ASes generally appear only at the end of the AS_PATH attribute associated to a unique prefix (internal to the AS) resulting so in very few probes launched towards the AS of interest. For large Tiers 1 however, the final coverage can reach much higher values on average, that is 80% for addresses, 70% for links, and around 87% for routers. For Transit ASes, we observe intermediate and diverse discovery levels, with behaviors similar to Stub ASes for some but that can also span the ones of a Tier 1, depending on the size and role of the Transit AS in the global interconnection.

From these results, we can clearly see that Rocketfuel's initial pool provides quite unreliable coverage and is lacking a lot of targets in order to reconstruct the complete ISP topology. This justifies the need to expand Rocketfuel's initial pool with the /24 internal prefixes in order to complete our exploration. The final levels of discovery for ANAXIMANDER's initial pool (enhanced with /24 internal prefixes) can be found under the label "Initial Pool" on the X-axis. For addresses, routers, and links, we see the positive impact on ASes coverage brought by the addition of the /24 internal prefixes. Indeed, the box plots are much denser and higher than in the case of Rocketfuel, meaning that results are consistently better. More precisely, Stubs now almost always present a perfect coverage for addresses, routers, and links. For Tiers 1, the increase in coverage is less impressive, although still present, with a smaller 10% absolute gain. Transit ASes present once again an intermediate behavior between Stubs and Tiers 1.

These results are also coherent with those presented in Sect. 5.4, where we showed that internal prefixes represent a great part of the AS discovery (or even all discovery for Stubs). Adding the /24 internal prefixes naturally brought the box plots up for all types of ASes.

Best Directed Prefixes (BDP) Reduction. Looking at Fig. 6a, 6b, and 6c for addresses, link, and routers; we notice that the BDP Reduction had little to zero impact on AS coverage. Indeed, the three box plots have been slightly elongated downwards, but this is almost imperceptible (especially for routers that are quite resistant to any reduction strategies).

If we now take a look at the reduction of probes allowed by BDP Reduction (Fig. 6d), we see it already presents a great potential in reduction depending on the type of the AS. The first result is that, for Stub ASes, there is practically no difference between the initial pool and the BDP Reduction, both in terms of probe reduction and discovery, meaning that the reduction was ineffective. Indeed, we can see across the four figures that all Stub ASes globally remain at their position in the box plots. In fact, this is not surprising given that BDP Reduction is applied to the *directed prefixes* in the pool and that their initial pool is composed mostly of the AS's internals prefixes (see Sect. 5.4 for a visualization of this). For this reason, and anticipating on the next sections, none of the reduction techniques of ANAXIMANDER will be effective for Stub ASes. Given the already low number of probes in the initial pool for Stubs, we do not consider it an issue and focus our efforts on reducing the probing budget for larger (transit) ASes.

On the other hand, for Transit and Tier 1 ASes, the effect of the reduction appears clearly with a substantial decrease of 30% on average in the probing budget, without any loss in coverage. Moreover, for some Transits and Tiers 1, BDP Reduction managed to decrease the probing budget by impressive values of up to 90%. The diversity of BGP paths does seem to introduce significant redundancy, and targeting shortest sub-paths looks to be a good option across multiple vantage points.

Overlay Reduction (OR). As already explained for the BDP Reduction, the effects of the strategy are invisible for Stub networks (we can see all Stub ASes remain in their position in all of the box plots).

However, if we take a look at the impact of OR on Tier 1 and Transit networks, we observe, as expected, a probing reduction (more than 10%) without any significant loss in topology discovery (see Fig. 6a, 6b, and 6c).

Plateau Reduction (PR). Results for PR are presented for different threshold values (τ varying from 0.7 down to 0.1 by step of 0.1). Once again, and not surprisingly, the effects of the strategy are invisible for Stub ASes. For larger ASes however, the impact is much more significant. PR allows for an important reduction of the number of probes with more or less decrease in coverage, depending on the AS, the type of element (IP interface, router, or link), and the threshold value.

Let us look in more details at the threshold impact on the levels of discovery. For addresses and routers (Fig. 6a, 6b), we observe virtually no reduction in AS coverage up until a threshold value of $\tau = 0.4$, where the levels of discovery start to very slowly decrease. The effect of PR is a bit more detrimental for links though, where we see a slightly more important decrease in coverage compared to addresses and routers. Regarding the reduction on the number of probes (Fig. 6d), we discern a very clear and steady reduction with each passing value of τ. For $\tau = 0.4$, we managed to reduce the probing budget by an average of 65% with no reduction whatsoever on coverage.

With these results, we can clearly observe the effect of the different values of parameter τ on PR. Smaller values are able to greatly reduce the probing budget, but naturally come at the cost of a decrease in AS coverage. It is up to the users to select a particular threshold value τ that best suits their needs and contraints. Intermediate threshold values might be a better option than the quite radical $\tau = 0.1$ value, as they present a reduction on the probing budget more than acceptable (between 50% and 65%) while maintaining high topology discovery levels. They can also pick a very conservative value ($\tau = 0.7$, for example) that does not decrease the topology discovery at all while still reducing the probing budget of another 10–12%.

6.3   Global Comment

Globally, the general shapes of the box plots are very promising. For addresses and routers in particular, the ASes' coverage distribution remains very high and dense across the various reduction strategies. For links, the coverage distribution remains also rather constant, although it was more spread to start with. And while the coverage remains high, the probing budget is greatly and steadily reduced with each reduction strategy.

All in all, the various reduction strategies we designed are quite effective in reducing the probing budget while still maintaining high coverage. They are also able to adapt themselves to the type of AS being mapped and thus provide flexible but consistent and reliable results across all types of AS.

7   Conclusion

Internet is a complex system made of numerous independent entities called ASes. To understand its structure and characteristics, many attempts have been proposed, developed, and deployed according to the scale and the purpose of the study. In this work, we are interested in the extraction of specific AS router level maps, with a reduced probing budget, and without hampering the resulting topological coverage. Given the difficulty of directing `traceroutes` towards an AS of interest, as well as the fact that many traces lead to redundant paths, the problem is challenging and predictions are not obvious.

To achieve this goal, we proposed ANAXIMANDER, a new efficient approach able to recover the same ISP maps as obtained with a brute force approach, but with a network-friendly and efficient probing methodology. For a given ISP and a given set of vantage points, ANAXIMANDER will design the best list of targets before actively probing the ISP. In addition, our tool also comes with a simple parameter to control the trade-off between maximizing the ISP coverage and reducing the probing budget. Overall, ANAXIMANDER is a generic tool that can adapt to the nature of the AS being mapped (e.g., Tier-1, Transit, or Stubs) thanks to its self-adaptative probing strategies and scheduling. The probing reduction we manage to achieve with our pruning techniques is significant and comes with almost no losses in term of coverage, whatever the kind of AS.

Software Artifacts

The `TNT` data we used throughout the paper is freely available on CAIDA website: https://www.caida.org/data/active/ipv4_tnt_dataset.xml. Reproducibility is therefore quite easy.

Our ANAXIMANDER implementation is tunable with a single parameter (the threshold τ for PR), making it easy to use and flexible. The simulator is developed in Go, and is available at

https://github.com/Emeline-1/anaximander_simulator.

A   Alternative Schedulings

As explained in Sect. 5.4, our grouping of targets by AS has made plateaux appear during the probing, which can be exploited to prune useless probes from the list of targets in real time. However, even if we do manage to reduce the plateaux as much as possible while still maintaining a high coverage, a certain portion of the plateau (shorter or longer depending on the τ parameter) will still be explored. Indeed, ANAXIMANDER is no oracle and cannot know in advance if the final plateau has been reached or if there will still be some discovery afterwards. Therefore, it needs to explore the plateau before deciding whether it is safe to skip this portion and jump to the next AS or not. In short, plateaux are reduced, certainly, but some probes are still wasted on a regular basis in the middle of the probing.

An alternative scheduling would be to launch the exploration of ASes in parallel, rather than explore them sequentially. The Plateau Reduction would still be applied on a per-AS basis, allowing to prune useless probes as usual. At first glance, this new scheduling could have the effect of shifting all bursts of discovery sooner into the probing campaign, and to relegate all remaining plateaux towards the end. We have explored two parallel scheduling.

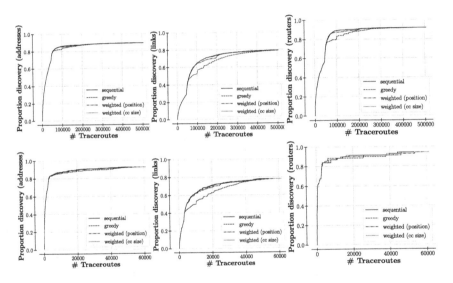

Fig. 7. Comparison of the discovery curves between the different scheduling strategies (AS174 on top, AS4637 bottom). The left column present the results on addresses, the middle column on links, and the left column on routers.

The first one, called *greedy scheduling*, will halt its probing of an AS as soon as it encounters a useless probe, and get back to it at a later time in the probing campaign. This could have, on paper, a beneficial effect on the discovery curve, by shifting it to the left and limiting the useless probes early on the campaign. Let us be careful not to confuse this concept with Plateaux Reduction. In this greedy scheme, ANAXIMANDER does not stop exploring an AS entirely at the first useless probe. It will just get back to it later, to try to relegate a potential plateau towards the end of the probing campaign. The remaining length of the plateaux are still explored at the end of the discovery curve (and they will still be reduced by Plateau Reduction).

The second one, called *weighted scheduling*, attributes a weight to each AS (based on various criteria), and explores this AS's address space in successive batches according to that weight. More precisely, based on the weight of an AS, ANAXIMANDER will explore only a given portion of that AS's address space before jumping to the next one. Once ANAXIMANDER has browsed over all ASes in such a way, it will get back to the first AS in the list and resume its probing with yet another batch. The probing of an AS will thus continue in successive batches, up until all of the AS has been probed, or until the probing is stopped because of a plateau. For our experiments, we have tested two different weighting functions, one based on the AS's relative position in the list of ASes, and the other based on its customer cone size [24]. Each function has been tested with varying parameters and results are presented for the parameters that yielded the best results.

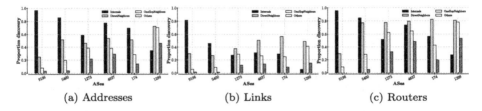

(a) Addresses   (b) Links   (c) Routers

Fig. 8. Individual contribution of each of the four main groups (internal prefixes, direct neighbors, one-hop neighbors, and others).

We present our results (Fig. 7) for two ASes of Interest (one Transit and one Tier 1). Results are not presented for Stub ASes, whose pool of targets is mainly composed of /24 internal prefixes, as the scheduling of probes remains the same in this particular group. Results for the other ASes in our sample of 25 ASes lead to the same conclusions but were not presented due to space constraints.

Across all ASes and all types of elements (addresses, links, or routers), the results are unequivocal: ANAXIMANDER's sequential scheduling always outperforms (or is at least equivalent to) the other scheduling strategies. Looking in more details, we see that the greedy scheduling consistently performs worse than the other three strategies and can thus be discarded. On the other hand, with carefully crafted weight functions, we were able to get as close as possible to the same performance as ANAXIMANDER's current scheduling. More precisely, the weight function based on the customer cone size generally performs better than the one on the position of the AS. This is not surprising, as the customer cone size retains more information than simply the ordering of the AS in the global AS list.

B   Individual Group Contribution

Figure 8a, 8b, and 8c show the contribution of each group of prefixes (internals, direct neighbors, one-hop neighbors, and others) for addresses, links, and routers respectively, so that the reader can really appreciate what is the cost/coverage ratio for each group. The same general trend remains: for any type of AS, internal prefixes are the most likely to enable a good ISP coverage for addresses (this group can even be seen as almost sufficient for stub ASes). For Tier-1 however, probing neighbor ASes becomes necessary to complete the exploration. This is particularly true for links and routers, that really benefit from probing the neighbors, and where internal prefixes are insufficient to cover the whole topology.

References

1. Abley, J., Lindqvist, K., Davies, E., Black, B., Gill, V.: IPv4 multihoming practices and limitations. RFC 4116, Internet Engineering Task Force (July 2005)
2. Augustin, B., et al.: Avoiding traceroute anomalies with Paris traceroute. In: Proceedings of the ACM Internet Measurement Conference (IMC) (October 2006)
3. CAIDA: AS rank v2.1 (March 2020). https://api.asrank.caida.org/v2/docs
4. CAIDA: The caida as relationships dataset (April 2021). https://www.caida.org/catalog/datasets/as-relationships/
5. Claffy, K., Hyun, Y., Keys, K., Fomenkov, M., Krioukov, D.: Internet mapping: from art to science. In: Proceedings of the IEEE Cybersecurity Application and Technologies Conference for Homeland Security (CATCH) (March 2009)
6. Cunha, I., et al.: Sibyl: a practical Internet route oracle. In: Proceedings of the USENIX Symposium on Networked Systems Design and Implementation (NSDI) (March 2016)
7. Dhamdhere, A., Cherukuru, H., Dovrolis, C., Claffy, K.: Measuring the evolution of internet peering agreements. In: Bestak, R., Kencl, L., Li, L.E., Widmer, J., Yin, H. (eds.) NETWORKING 2012. LNCS, vol. 7290, pp. 136–148. Springer, Heidelberg (2012). https://doi.org/10.1007/978-3-642-30054-7_11
8. Dhamdhere, A., Dovrolis, C.: The internet is flat: modeling the transition from a transit hierarchy to a peering mesh. In: Proceedings of the ACM CoNEXT (November 2010)
9. Donnet, B., Friedman, T.: Internet topology discovery: a survey. IEEE Commun. Surv. Tutor. **9**(4), 2–15 (2007)
10. Donnet, B., Raoult, P., Friedman, T., Crovella, M.: Efficient algorithms for large-scale topology discovery. In: Proceedings of the ACM SIGMETRICS (June 2005)
11. Durairajan, R., Sommers, J., Barford, P.: Layer-1 informed Internet topology measurement. In: Proceedings of the ACM Internet Measurement Conference (IMC) (November 2014)
12. Gao, L.: On inferring autonomous system relationships in the internet. IEEE/ACM Trans. Netw. (ToN) **9**(6), 733–745 (2001)
13. Gay, S., Schaus, P., Vissichio, S.: REPETITA: repeatable experiments for performance evaluation of traffic-engineering algorithms. cs.NI 1710.08665, arXiv (October 2017)
14. Govindan, R., Tangmunarunkit, H.: Heuristics for internet map discovery. In: Proceedings of the IEEE INFOCOM (March 2000)

15. Grailet, J.F., Donnet, B.: Virtual insanity: linear subnet discovery. IEEE Trans. Netw. Serv. Manag. (TNSM) **17**(2), 1268–1281 (2020)
16. Guo, H., Heidemann, J.: Detecting ICMP rate limiting in the Internet. In: Proceedings of the Passive and Active Measurement Conference (PAM) (March 2018)
17. Haddadi, H., Rio, M., Iannacone, G., Moore, A.W.: Network topologies: inference, modeling, and generation. IEEE Commun. Surv. Tutor. **10**(2), 48–69 (2008)
18. Huston, G.: BGP more specifics: routing vandalism or useful? (June 2017). https://blog.apnic.net/2017/06/26/bgp-specifics-routing-vandalism-useful/. Accessed 17 May 2021
19. Huston, G.: BGP in 2020–the BGP table (January 2021). https://blog.apnic.net/2021/01/05/bgp-in-2020-the-bgp-table/
20. Jacobson, V.: Mrinfo (1995). http://cvsweb.netbsd.org/bsdweb.cgi/src/usr.sbin/mrinfo/?only_with_tag=MAIN
21. Keys, K.: Internet-scale IP alias resolution techniques. ACM SIGCOMM Comput. Commun. Rev. **40**(1), 50–55 (2010)
22. Keys, K., Hyun, Y., Luckie, M., Claffy, K.: Internet-scale IPv4 alias resolution with MIDAR. IEEE/ACM Trans. Netw. **21**(2), 383–399 (2013)
23. Knight, S., Hung, X.N., Falkner, N., Bowden, R., Roughan, M.: The Internet topology zoo. IEEE J. Sel. Areas Commun. **29**(9), 1765–1775 (2011)
24. Luckie, M., Huffaker, B., Claffy, K., Dhamdhere, A., Giotsas, V.: AS relationships, customer cones, and validation. In: Proceedings of the ACM Internet Measurement Conference (IMC) (October 2013)
25. Luttringer, J.R., Vanaubel, Y., Mérindol, P., Pansiot, J.J., Donnet, B.: Let there be light: revealing hidden MPLS tunnels with TNT. IEEE Trans. Netw. Serv. Manag. (TNSM) **17**(2), 1239–1253 (2020)
26. Marchetta, P., Mérindol, P., Donnet, B., Pescapé, A., Pansiot, J.J.: Topology discovery at the router level: a new hybrid tool targeting ISP networks. IEEE J. Sel. Areas Commun. Spec. Issue Meas. Internet Topol. **29**(6), 1776–1787 (2011)
27. Marchetta, P., Mérindol, P., Donnet, B., Pescapé, A., Pansiot, J.J.: Quantifying and mitigating IGMP filtering in topology discovery. In: Proceedings of the IEEE Global Communications Conference (GLOBECOM) (December 2012)
28. Marder, A.: APPLE: alias pruning by path length estimation. In: Proceedings of the Passive and Active Measurement Conference (PAM) (March 2020)
29. Marder, A., Luckie, M., Dhamdhere, A., Huffaker, B., Smith, J., Claffy, K.: Pushing the boundaries with bdrmapIT: mapping router ownership at internet scale. In: Proceedings of the ACM Internet Measurement Conference (IMC) (November 2018)
30. Mérindol, P., David, P., Pansiot, J.J., Clad, F., Vissicchio, S.: A fine-grained multi-source measurement platform correlating routing transitions with packet losses. Comput. Commun. (COMCOM) **129**, 166–183 (2018)
31. Mérindol, P., Van den Schriek, V., Donnet, B., Bonaventure, O., Pansiot, J.J.: Quantifying ASes multiconnectivity using multicast information. In: Proceedings of the ACM Internet Measurement Conference (IMC) (November 2009)
32. Oliveira, R., Pei, D., Willinger, W., Zhang, B., Zhang, L.: The (in)completeness of the observed Internet AS-level structure. IEEE/ACM Trans. Netw. (ToN) **18**(1), 109–122 (2010)
33. Orsini, C., King, A., Giordano, D., Giotsas, V., Dainotti, A.: BGPStream: a software framework for live and historical BGP data analysis. In: Proceedings of the ACM Internet Measurement Conference (IMC) (November 2016)

34. Pansiot, J.J., Mérindol, P., Donnet, B., Bonaventure, O.: Extracting intra-domain topology from mrinfo probing. In: Proceedings of the Passive and Active Measurement Conference (PAM) (April 2010)
35. Pastor-Satorras, R., Vespignani, A.: Evolution and Structure of the Internet: A Statistical Physics Approach. Cambridge University Press, Cambridge (2004)
36. Psenak, P., Hegde, S., Filsfils, C., Gulko, A.: ISIS segment routing flexible algorithm. Internet Draft (Work in Progress) draft-hegdeppsenak-isis-sr-flex-algo-02, Internet Engineering Task Force (February 2018)
37. Ravaioli, R., Urvoy-Keller, G., Barakat, C.: Characterizing ICMP rate limitation on routers. In: Proceedings of the IEEE International Conference on Communications (ICC) (June 2015)
38. RIPE: Ripe ris, routing information service, see. https://www.ripe.net/analyse/internet-measurements/routing-information-service-ris
39. Senel, B.C., Mouchet, M., Cappos, J., Fourmaux, O., Friedman, T., McGeer, R.: EdgeNet: a multi-tenant and multi-provider edge cloud. In: Proceedings of the International Workshop on Edge Systems, Analytics and Networking (April 2021)
40. Spring, N., Mahajan, R., Wetherall, D.: Measuring ISP topologies with Rocketfuel. In: Proceedings of the ACM SIGCOMM (August 2002)
41. Spring, N., Wetherall, D., Anderson, T.: Scriptroute: a public Internet measurement facility. In: Proceedings of the USENIX Symposium on Internet Technologies and Systems (USITS) (March 2002)
42. Teixeira, R., Marzullo, K., Savage, S., Voelker, G.: In search of path diversity in ISP networks. In: Proceedings of the ACM SIGCOMM Internet Measurement Conference (IMC) (October 2003)
43. University of Oregon: Route views, University of Oregon Route Views project, see. http://www.routeviews.org/routeviews/
44. Vanaubel, Y., Luttringer, J.R., Mérindol, P., Pansiot, J.J., Donnet, B.: TNT, watch me explode: A light in the dark for revealing MPLS tunnels. In: Proceedings of the IFIP Network Traffic Measurement and Analysis Conference (TMA) (June 2019)
45. Vanaubel, Y., Mérindol, P., Pansiot, J.J., Donnet, B.: MPLS under the microscope: revealing actual transit path diversity. In: Proceedings of the ACM Internet Measurement Conference (IMC) (October 2015)
46. Vanaubel, Y., Mérindol, P., Pansiot, J.J., Donnet, B.: Through the wormhole: tracking invisible MPLS tunnels. In: Proceedings of the ACM Internet Measurement Conference (IMC) (November 2017)
47. Waddington, D.G., Chang, F., Viswanathan, R., Yao, B.: Topology discovery for public IPv6 networks. ACM SIGCOMM Comput. Commun. Rev. **33**(3), 59–68 (2003)
48. Wang, F., Mao, Z.M., Wang, J., Gao, L., Bush, R.: A measurement study on the impact of routing events on end-to-end Internet path performance. In: Proceedings of the ACM SIGCOMM (August 2006)
49. Wang, Y., Zhang, K.: Quantifying the flattening of Internet topology. In: Proceedings of the International Conference on Future Internet Technologies (June 2016)
50. Zhang, Y., Mao, Z.M., Wang, J.: A framework for measuring and predicting the impact of routing changes. In: Proceedings of the IEEE INFOCOM (May 2007)
51. Zhang, Z., Marder, A., Mok, R., Huffaker, B., Luckie, M., Claffy, K., Schulman, A.: Inferring regional access network topologies: methods and applications. In: Proceedings of the ACM Internet Measurement Conference (IMC) (November 2011)

Lights on Power Plant Control Networks

Stefan Mehner[✉], Franka Schuster, and Oliver Hohlfeld

Brandenburg University of Technology
Cottbus – Senftenberg, Cottbus, Germany
{stefan.mehner,franka.schuster,oliver.hohlfeld}@b-tu.de

Abstract. Industrial Control Systems (ICS) are critical systems to our society. Yet they are less studied given their closed nature and often the unavailability of data. While few studies focus on wide-area SCADA systems, e.g., power or gas distribution networks, mission critical networks that control power generation are not yet studied. To address this gap, we perform the first measurement study of Distributed Control System (DCS) by analyzing traces from all network levels from several operational power plants. We show that DCS networks feature a rather rich application mix compared to wide-area SCADA networks and that applications and sites can be fingerprinted with statistical means. While traces from operational power plants are hard to obtain, we analyze to which extent easier to access training facilities can be used as vantage points. Our study aims to shed light on traffic properties of critical industries that were not yet analyzed given the lack of data.

1 Introduction

Insights gained from two decades of Internet measurement research enabled the evolution and optimization of Internet technology—including Internet performance and security. This research has provided many fundamental results on network operation or network traffic that form the basis for network planning or optimization (e.g., the finding of the self-similar character of Internet traffic [9] or the evolving application mix [11]). These efforts focus on the Internet as the largest and general-purpose communication network. In contrast, important application-specific networks that increasingly rely on Internet technologies received less attention from a measurements' perspective yet, e.g. power plants.

The Hidden Networks. Critical industrial systems such as power plants rely on industrial control systems (ICS) for their operation. These systems are based on proprietary protocols and typically closed. Especially the access to critical infrastructures in the energy and water sector is highly restricted, which limits the potential for conducting measurement studies. As a result, little is publicly known about networks, which limits research potential for enhancements, e.g., to improve their security. While these networks experience an attack vector of increasing relevance [8], the little public knowledge about their properties and functions limits the design of mitigation strategies. By studying traffic-level properties of operational power plants, we make step towards closing this gap.

O. Hohlfeld et al. (Eds.): PAM 2022, LNCS 13210, pp. 470–484, 2022.
https://doi.org/10.1007/978-3-030-98785-5_21

Related Work. Prior work on measurement of *real* infrastructure traffic focused on SCADA networks. While SCADA networks control the interactions of dispersed assets to enable power and water distribution, Distributed Control Systems (DCS) are dedicated to the control of the local core processes in power plants and water treatment sites [15]. The most recent SCADA work shows that IEC 60870-5-104 is used as the only protocol in the studied infrastructure [10]. In contrast, our work will show that DCS systems feature a much richer application mix. Other studies investigated in water treatment and distribution facilities, a gas utility as well as an electricity and gas utility. They show that SCADA traffic largely differs from Internet traffic given the absence of human users (and thus diurnal patterns) and self-similarity [3]. In later works, the same authors prove that traffic in SCADA networks is periodic and provides a stable connection matrix [2,5]. Since these prior measurements focussed on SCADA infrastructures, we will complete the picture (for the energy sector) by focussing on the DCS part of the energy supply by investigating four operational real power plants.

Our Contribution. In this first of its kind study, we shed light on traffic properties of critical yet unstudied type of infrastructure networks: internal (i.e., not intentionally Internet facing) control networks of three power plants and one power plant simulation facility. Our study is enabled by the rare opportunity to capture traffic traces during maintenance slots at three operational power plant sites. Our main objective is to provide a first empirical perspective on these otherwise hidden networks since traffic properties pave the way for controlled simulation and evaluation studies. Our contributions are as follows.

- We show that DCS networks in power plants feature a rich protocol mix that differs by automation layer. This is in contrast to typical SCADA networks that are often realized using a single protocol only. That is, while a recent survey [6] found in every ICS testbed one dominant protocol, we show that in power plant DCS features 'zoo' of protocols on different network levels.
- We show that the proprietary and publicly undocumented ICS protocols used can be identified by applying statistical clustering approaches. These clusterings even work in the absence of payload by analyzing inter-arrival times and header information.
- We finally applied our methods to a dataset from a plant simulator that serves as training facility. Given that measurements in operational power plants can only be conducted in rare maintenance windows, we study if easier to access simulation facilities are an option for measurements.

2   ICS 101

ICS aim at controlling and supervising machines or processes (e.g., coal firing).

SCADA vs. DCS. There is not one type of ICS, but many [7]. Most prominently, both SCADA and DCS systems enable the supervision and control of industrial processes. Studied types of SCADA networks are wide-area networks that are scattered over hundreds of kilometers, e.g., bulk power grids for power distribution [10] or water treatment and distribution facilities [2,5]. In contrast to the widely studied SCADA network, DCS offer integrated solutions provided by a single vendor and are thus often designed for local use—like the power plant networks studied in this paper. Consequently, the used protocols and traffic patterns in both network types differ and, as a consequence, it is not possible to infer the characteristics of one network type from the characteristics of the other. For example, IEC 60870-5-104 (one of the most widely used SCADA protocols, e.g., studied in [10]) is a telecontrol protocol that does not play any role in DCS. Also, SCADA networks are dominated by a single or few protocols, while—as we will show—the integrated nature of DCS systems yields a much richer protocol mix. The unstudied nature of DCS traffic thus motivates our work.

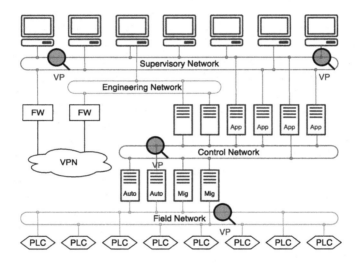

Fig. 1. Network architecture levels of plant DCS with vantage point locations.

ICS Architecture. While ICS differ in their physical extension and associated network characteristics, they are quite similar in terms of network organization. Typically they follow a layered, hierarchical design. The lowest network part, the *Field Network*, consists of the physical level, including sensors and actuators measuring and adjusting basic physical parameters (e.g., temperature, pressure, speeds, feeds). They are connected to programmable logic controllers (PLC). Each PLC controls actuators and/or monitors sensors and hence realizes a low-level control according to an implemented application-specific control loop. In the *Control Network*, inputs from various PLC are collected and evaluated by subsystem-specific servers in order to aggregate all activities corresponding to a subprocess. For power plants, these sub-processes include, for example, temperature monitoring of the boiler. There are also servers that prepare the process data for visualization on the Human Machine Interfaces (HMI) and others that connect legacy systems to the control system. Monitoring and manual adjustment of the physical process is realized in the *Supervisory Network*. Here the operator interacts with the subsystems via HMI that incorporate the data from the Control Network.

Power Plants. ICS in plants use DCS architectures, often realized as large proprietary networks provided by a single vendor. As such, the concrete network design including its configuration (e.g., addressing schemes) is vendor dependent and differs. We observe three typical server types in plants, which are also depicted in Fig. 1. Automation servers (*Auto*) provide so-called automation objects that enable clients to automate well-defined procedures by directly accessing reusable functionality made available by the server. Migration servers (*Mig*) aggregate data from Field-Network communication to representations appropriate for the application servers (*App*) connected to the Control Network. These application servers in turn realize further data preparation for graphical applications, such as the control center's screens, attached to the Supervisory Network. Another characteristic is that these networks are rarely upgraded. In the case of power plants, operators only plan for one network upgrade during the entire lifetime of a power plant, i.e., once installed, the networks run for decades without major changes. This is in stark contrast to classical Internet-networks that are upgraded much more frequently.

3   Power Plant Datasets

Our study is based on packet traces captured at three operational power plants (see Table 1). The traces contain traffic from all physical subprocesses including coal firing, fluid flow, and turbine operation. As our datasets account for two of the leading vendors of control systems that are of widespread use world-wide, they enable us to provide a representative picture of traffic characteristics.

Table 1. Dataset overview

	Vendor	Level	Duration	# packets	# devices
Plant 1	A	Supervisory	3.3 h	38 M	39
		Control	18.6 h	96 M	44
		Field	1.4 h	6 M	52
Plant 2	B	Control	54.9 h	17 M	89
Plant 3	B	Control	2.7 h	61 M	65

Plant 1. The first dataset was captured in the main process control network of a unit of capacity class of 800/900 MW as part of a two-unit coal-fired power plant. We were allowed to monitor vantage points at all three network levels shown in Fig. 1. In this network, process control technology of type A (we omit vendor names due to a non-disclosure agreement) from one of the few major vendors in this field is installed, which is of widespread use in power plants worldwide.

Plant 2. This trace was taken at the control level network of one unit of a multi-unit coal-fired power plant of capacity class (in total) of 1000 MW. The control system is from a different vendor also being a dominant supplier in that field. The main activity of the system is realized by virtualized components encapsulating machine-to-machine communication. Since communication within virtual environments does not leave the hosting machines, virtual machine-to-machine communication is not seen on the wire and a significant proportion of process communication could not be captured by listening at the chosen network switch. That is why the captured process traffic is incomplete. Since virtualization is a new trend in ICS, this trace represents network traffic visible in newer systems.

Plant 3. The third dataset was taken at a third black coal power plant, also at the control level network of the process control system. In contrast, here the control system was shared among both units representing in total 700 MW installed capacity. Here, the applied process control system is of the same type as the one in Plant 2. In contrast, no system components are virtualized and thus more process control traffic is visible.

Some Plant Network Details. We observed that the interaction between the identified network levels is defined by separated networks, each having its own IP subnet. The communication among multiple levels is realized by a certain set of clients and servers that are connected to one or two network levels. In our case, the supervisory network in the studied plants is not intentionally connected to the Internet for remote access. Remote access is a procedure that has also to be manually initiated from inside the power plants and is only performed when necessary. Except for one system that, due to legal regulations, has to regularly report pollution measurements to authorities, no data is made available to outside. In all considered plant networks the IP address assignment is static and the only security devices installed are border firewalls to higher-level networks of the owner company or dedicated networks for remote access. The network link speeds are 1 GBit/s. The average packet rates can be derived from Table 1.

Measurement Setup. The data was captured during the downtime of the physical generation process during a regular maintenance. In this time, the physical processes were stopped (i.e., no power was produced). However, the operators and the system vendors confirmed that the DCS is running in normal operation, only links to physical actuators are deactivated. For this reason, we assume the application mix studied in this work to be the same as in normal operation. Yet the content of control messages and network load might differ to normal operation (not studied). We captured all traces using `tcpdump` [1] and port mirroring at one or several switches placed in the network part/s stated to the datasets. Vantage points were chosen to capture traffic from servers relevant to plant operation. Not all vantage points shown in Fig. 1 were available at all power plants.

Ethics. The operators granted permission to capture traffic during maintenance intervals in which it was ensured that our setup cannot impair physical processes. All traces contain only machine-to-machine traffic. We do not reveal ICS protocol details or network configurations that could help in attacking these power plants.

4 The Rich Application Mix of Power Plant ICS Networks

A common assumption is that ICS networks are dominated by a single protocol only, e.g., which controls the automation process. Prior work showed that this is indeed the case in a number of industrial settings and identified Modbus TCP/MMS [3–5] and IEC 104 [10] as typical protocols used. This originates from the dedicated design of many SCADA networks and is in contrast to the typical Internet application mix that is dominated by different protocols (see e.g., as observed at an IXP [14]). The existence of only a single control protocol can ease network management and dimensioning. In this section, we show that this common assumption of a single dominant protocol is not the case for all industrial settings. We show that the integrated DCS architecture of the studied power plants yields a more complex traffic composition than commonly believed by actually representing a mix of different application protocols.

4.1 Application Mix of Power Plant 1

Approach. We refer to an "application protocol" as a protocol used to transmit *application* payload—regardless of the underlying transport protocol. We thus omit network control protocols such as ARP and LLC, but consider COTP that also is a MAC-layer protocol. Frequently used dissectors (e.g., by tshark or Zeek) can identify common Internet protocols. ICS networks, however, often use proprietary protocols which are not recognized by such tools. We thus manually inspected all traffic traces and created payload based identifiers for each proprietary protocol. We further identify known Internet protocols (e.g., HTTP/NTP) by the destination port in Zeek logs. All well known protocols are mapped by their name, while the remaining ones are shown by their port number.

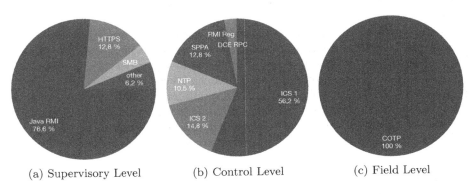

(a) Supervisory Level   (b) Control Level   (c) Field Level

Fig. 2. Application mix of Plant 1 divided into the hierarchical layers.

Protocol Shares Differ Substantially by Level. Figure 2 shows the protocol mix of Power Plant 1 by hierarchical layer. While only COTP is visible at the lowest layer (field), above layers show more protocol variety, as we discuss next.

Field Level. We observe one dominant protocol (COTP as identified by Wiresharks dissector) that is served via Ethernet with 100% traffic share. The reason is that on field level point-to-point communication with sensors and actuators (e.g., using Profinet IO to meet real-time guarantees) is used. The sensor data is then directly encapsulated on top of Ethernet as payload using proprietary protocols. At the control and supervisory level, all communication is IP-based and thus UDP and TCP are the dominant transport protocols. However, both layers differ substantially in transport protocol share. While the supervisory level shows 99.0% TCP communication, the control level shows 40.9% UDP traffic.

Control Level. The application mix at the control level features multiple protocols, see the protocol share by packets in Fig. 2b. This is rooted in multiple functions that are performed at the control level. First, sensor data is obtained from field level devices and then aggregated and processed by migration and automation servers (see Fig. 1). Aggregated data is then prepared for graphical representation (at the supervisory level) by application servers. The communication between the migration and the application servers is based on two protocols. The first is a proprietary TCP-based protocol that we observe on multiple ports, referred to as ICS 1. With a share of 56,2% of the exchanged packets it is the dominant protocol at the control level. The second, referred to as ICS 2, is a UDP-based protocol used to share information between multiple servers via IP multicast. Automation servers, that are responsible for the time-critical automation process, further communicate with application servers by using a proprietary protocol—we call SPPA—on ports 10002 and 10003. In Sect. 5, we describe in detail our approach of identifying the protocols on the different port numbers. Beyond these proprietary ICS protocols, we also see RPC communication with the supervisory layer using Java RMI (for graphical representation) and further classical Internet protocols such as NTP.

Supervisory Level. The communication at the supervisory level is dominated by Java RMI based RPC communication, see Fig. 2a again showing the packet share per protocol. Proprietary or classical ICS protocols known in the SCADA domain are absent. Java RMI based RPC communication is used for graphical representation by browser-based thin clients at the supervisory level, which interact with application servers. As in the control level, there is an RMI registry, here on port 1099, with a share of 5.3%. The app mix is dominated by two RMI RPC-based applications each running on a different port with a share of 44.2% respectively 21.4% of the whole trace. In Fig. 2a we aggregated all such traffic to 'Java RMI'. Beyond, we see also known Internet protocols such as HTTPS between two servers and SMB for file servers.

Takeaway. *Unlike findings in related works that suggest the presence of only a single protocol in ICS networks, depending on the level, ICS networks can feature richer application mixes comprised of multiple protocols. In terms of protocol complexity, ICS networks at higher layers are thus comparable to typical LANs rather than single protocol networks.*

Bugs Can Skew the Traffic Mix. We further observe an unexpected high amount of 68–75% of UDP-based traffic at all levels in this trace. So what is the reason of this? To answer this question we evaluated the application mix and find SNMP to create the high share of UDP traffic. We have consulted the power plant operator and figured out that this is a bug in the control system that unnecessarily pulls status information from network devices. It does not affect the operation of the plant, but disturbs the monitoring of the network components. While similar skews in traffic are normal in Internet-type applications that get updated often, infrastructure in power plants is typically static, remains in operation for years, and can only be updated during few maintenance windows. Thus changes in the traffic composition can alter network dimensioning and thus might night to be incorporated when simulating networks for planning.

Encryption is Uncommon. We observed very little encrypted traffic. The encrypted traffic on port 443 with a share of 12.8% (shown as HTTPS in the plot) was seen only between two pairs of servers in the supervisory level of Power Plant 1. Hence, we observed that encrypted traffic is uncommon, which is in line with similar observations made in other industrial settings [4, 13].

4.2   The Application Mix Differs by Power Plant/Vendor

Is the application mix comparable between the different power plants? That is, given that it is challenging to obtain traffic traces from operational power plants, would it suffice to measure one plant and then generalize? We next answer this question by comparing the application mix for the different power plants.

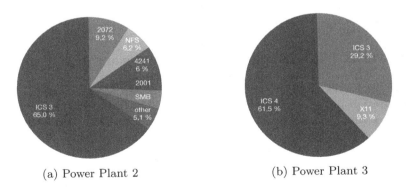

(a) Power Plant 2   (b) Power Plant 3

Fig. 3. Application mix of Power Plant 2 and Power Plant 3

Power Plants with Different Vendor Control Systems. We begin by comparing the application mix for power plants with different control systems. In our case, the control system of power Plant 1 is by a different vendor than power Plant 2 and 3. In this power plants we have a slightly other network architecture, where supervisory and control level networks are merged. We remark that the operators of that power plants only enabled traffic captures at one vantage point. In direct comparison of the port-based application mix (see Fig. 3), we observe different port ranges and number of ports used. At the supervisory level at Plant 1, there is essentially Java RMI traffic running over ports 50000, 50001, etc. At the control level, there are three proprietary ICS protocols that communicate over many ports and represent the largest share of the communication. In contrast, in power plants 2 and 3 we see fewer actively used ports. The (ICS) application protocols also always use the same port number. Further, we see remote procedure call realizations in traffic of both power plant types. Other application-level characteristics differ. That means, that the port-based application mix differs between power plants that run different control systems. This can be explained by the vendor-driven different design of control systems which usually incorporates at least one vendor-specific protocol whose associated port number(s) individualize the app mix.

Power Plants with the Same Vendor Control System. Does running a control system by the same vendor yield comparable application mixes? To answer this question, we compare the application mix of Power Plant 2 and 3—both running a control system from the same vendor. Both plants show a significant share of proprietary TCP-based traffic on port 2010 with 65% respectively 29%. We call this protocol ICS 3 in Fig. 3. The largest share at Plant 3, however, is on port 2000 (named ICS 4 in the plot). After consultation with the operator of Plant 2, the ICS 4 protocol is also in use, but we were unable to see it at this VP. In contrast to Plant 2 we also see 9% X11 traffic in the Plant 3 trace. Probably an engineer performed a remote session to servers due to maintenance reasons. Beyond these dominant application ports, other port-level statistics differ. We thus conclude that the two power plants using a control system by the same vendor offer partially comparable application mixes.

5   Towards Understanding the Proprietary ICS Protocols

The ICS protocols used by the studied power plants are proprietary with no documentation provided, not even to the operator. Our study in Sect. 4 thus relied on a time-consuming manual payload inspection. We therefore now ask if the protocols and their characteristics can be identified purely by statistical means without any a-prior knowledge. We exemplify this study on the control level of Plant 1.

5.1   Clustering Communication by Packet Payload Differences

The payload of a typical ICS protocol mainly consists of few message types and physical (actuator or sensor) values within a well-defined range. Additionally, the nature of automated control loops tendentially lead to recurring physical values transmitted in the payload, generally as well as for each respective protocol. Consequently, it should be possible to identify packets encapsulating the same protocol by comparatively high similarity in the respective payloads.

Approach. We measure differences in packet-level payload by the Levenshtein ratio, which computes the similarity of two binary strings between 0 and 1. To showcase our approach, we extract the payload from the first 10,000 packets for every destination port of interest. Then, using the Levenshtein distance, we compute the similarity for each pair of all packets for every two ports. Finally, we derive the minimum, average, and maximum similarity for every port pair, which is visualized in a heat map as shown in Fig. 4.

Payload Clustering Can Trace Protocols Well. Our analysis reveals that the TCP port ranges 1487 to 3137 and 42239 to 44061 are addressed by communications with highly similar payload (average Levenshtein ratio between 40% and 87%). We call it ICS 1. Concerning the UDP ports 10002 and 10003, which we already know from our prior analysis using the dissector, we identified a average similarity of 74%. We call this SPPA. The port ranges 20202 to 20205 and 20301 to 20304 resulted in an average similarity of 76% and 55%, respectively. On the contrary, e.g., the ports 20202 and 20301 only showed an average similarity of 8%. A look into the trace revealed multicast communication, where both of the ports are either source or destination. Hence, they are considered as related and associated to protocol ICS 2.

Takeaway. *Our payload based classification scheme could—without any a-priori knowledge—identify all used protocols as compared to our manual payload inspection in the previous section.*

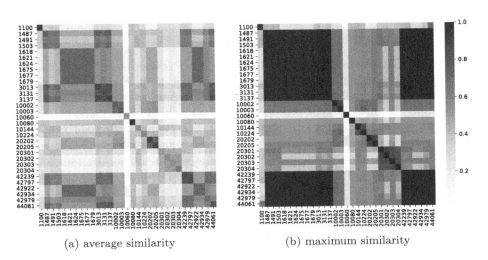

(a) average similarity   (b) maximum similarity

Fig. 4. Payload similarity of all ports (TCP and UDP) in the control level trace. The darker the blue color, the higher the similarity of two protocols payload. (Color figure online)

5.2   What if We Don't Have Payload?

In public traces usually there is no payload available [12]. Hence, a relevant question is, whether it is possible to achieve similar results by only using available metadata like packet inter-arrival times or packet header information, such as the payload size, the transport protocol used, or unicast/multicast communication? This approach assumes that the same protocols behave similarly with regard to this metadata. If this is the case, no knowledge about the protocol and no time-consuming deep packet inspection would be necessary for a traffic characteristic. As before, we compare the resulting protocol clusters to our previous study.

Approach. We employ the implicit application-level traffic classification approach using the packet size and the packet inter-arrival time distribution by Trivedi et al. [16]. For both metrics, the entire range of values is divided into 50 unequal-sized bins each and normalized. We have adopted this approach and modified it as follows: In contrast to protocols like HTTP, or FTP, industrial protocols have rather small payloads as often only sensor measurements are transmitted. For this reason, we have chosen other bin sizes as shown in Table 3. The packet inter-arrival times within a flow also differ for industrial protocols, since these have periodic communication with defined cycles. In Table 4 we show the bin sizes we used for our analysis. We normalized the values to the relative share of each bin for both metrics. We consider three cases, payload length and inter-arrival time individually and combined. Furthermore, we added two more metrics: the transport protocol (TCP/UDP) and the communication type (unicast/multicast). To find similar protocol properties, we used two clustering approaches: DBSCAN (with $\epsilon = 0.3$ and $min\_samples = 3$) and k-means (with $k \in \{3..10\}$ cluster).

Metadata Clustering Does not Identify All Protocols. Both approaches, the payload clustering and the metadata clustering, look at the same question from two different perspectives. Both clustering approaches find clusters that successfully distinct different protocols, but the results differ slightly. In Table 5 we provide a comparison of the results. Here, the column *Payload similarity* contains the results derived from the payload-based protocol clustering using the Levenshtein ratio, which is used as ground truth, here. The port ranges of ICS 1 protocol were clustered to two respectively three clusters. ICS 2 was correctly clustered by DBSCAN for both metrics. In k-means, ICS 2 was in same cluster as SPPA and DCERPC in most cases. By design DBSCAN was not able to cluster protocols that are using only one or two port numbers, because we set $min\_samples = 3$.

Takeaway. *When payload is unavailable, metadata clustering can identify most protocols. Compared to the payload-based identification, yet at a lower accuracy.*

6   Measuring at a Power Plant Training Facility

Traffic can only be captured in rare maintenance windows of operational power plants. Consequently, we study next to what extent a training facility of a real plant does reflect the traffic observed in the real infrastructure. We consider such

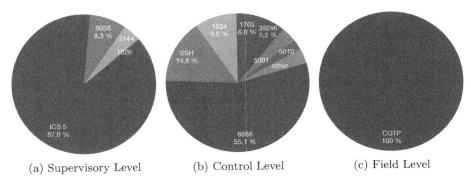

(a) Supervisory Level   (b) Control Level   (c) Field Level

Fig. 5. Application mix of power plant training facility

a facility as ideal environment for generating representative normal as well as attack traffic. Since this training network is not a productive network, interruptions of the normal network functions do not have any consequences.

Dataset. We capture at a training facility for power plant operators that rebuilds the automation network installed in Power Plant 1. The process control system is of the same vendor as Plant 1, but is an older system version. It only lacks the physical production layer which is completely simulated by software. Further details are shown in Table 2.

Application Mix Differs Substantially. Contrary to our expectations the application mix is completely different in both systems. At the supervisory level there is no RPC based communication, but other TCP-based traffic at 10 different ports with a share of about 10% each. Using our payload based classification approach from Sect. 5.1 we were able to identify most of this ports to the same protocol, which we will call ICS 5 in Fig. 5a. The major part of the control level traffic consists of one flow on port 8888. Apart from this we see some other proprietary traffic and SSH communication. Obviously the current system version as used in Plant 1 is in most parts a new development. Another reason is that the simulator acts as training facility for Plant 1 and thus tries to completely mimic the control functionality, but it doesn't implement all the power plant functionality. Just as on the field level in Power Plant 1, we also see exclusively COTP in this trace.

Takeaway. *The training facility shows a completely different protocol mix differs and it might not be sufficient to only capture traffic at simulation facilities to understand real-world ICS networks.*

7   Conclusion

Access to networks that control critical infrastructures, especially DCS, is highly restricted and thus little is publicly know about its properties. We took the rare opportunity to capture traffic traces during maintenance slots at three operational power plant sites and one training facility. Our main objective is to provide a first empirical perspective on these otherwise hidden networks. Unlike prior work that studied SCADA networks, we show that DCS networks in power plants feature a rich protocol mix that differs by automation layer. Any evaluation (e.g., simulation) of plant network traffic must account for these traffic mixes. We further show that the proprietary and publicly undocumented ICS protocols used can be identified by applying statistical clustering approaches— with and without payload. These clusterings even work in the absence of payload by analyzing inter-arrival times and header information. We finally applied our methods to a dataset from training facility that replicates power plant 1. Given that measurements in operational power plants can only be conducted in rare maintenance windows, we study if easier to access simulation facilities are an option for measurements. We observe that the resulting application mixes differ substantially. With this paper we thus aim to shed light on a relevant but not yet studied type of network.

Declarations

Acknowledgement. Franka Schuster acknowledges funding by the German Federal Ministry of Education and Research (BMBF) grant WAIKIKI (funding reference number: 16KIS1198K).

Author contributions. This study has been solely conducted by Stefan Mehner (main author) on a previously captured dataset as part of his PhD thesis. The study design was developed by Stefan Mehner and Oliver Hohlfeld. All authors contributed to the discussion and writing of the paper.

A   Appendix

A.1   Power Plant Training Facility Dataset

Table 2. Dataset overview of power plant training facility

Vendor	Level	Duration	# packets	# devices
A	Supervisory	1.1 h	4 M	25
	Control	19 h	20 M	28
	Field	2.3 h	1.6 M	11

A.2   Bin Sizes Used for Protocol Clustering

Table 3. Bin sizes used for the study to divide the TCP/UDP payload

0	5	10	15	20	25	30	35	40
45	50	55	60	65	70	75	80	85
90	95	100	115	130	145	160	175	190
205	220	235	250	300	350	400	450	500
600	700	800	900	1000	1500	>1500		

Table 4. Bin sizes in milliseconds used for the study to divide the packet inter-arrival times within a flow

0.1	0.2	0.3	0.4	0.5	0.6	0.7	0.8	0.9	1.0
1.1	1.2	1.3	1.4	1.5	1.6	1.7	1.8	1.9	2.0
2.5	3.0	3.5	4.0	4.5	10.0	25.0	50.0	>50	

A.3   Payload Similarity and Clustering Results

Table 5. Comparison of results from payload similarity analysis as well as the clusterings using payload-length (p), inter-arrival times (i) or both metrics (pi) for DBSCAN and Kmeans (n = 5 cluster) clustering approaches

Port	Payload similarity	DBSCAN p	Kmeans p	DBSCAN i	Kmeans i	DBSCAN pi	Kmeans pi
1100	Java RMI	-	A	-	A	-	A
1487	ICS 1	A	A	A	B	A	B
1491	ICS 1	A	A	A	B	A	C
1503	ICS 1	A	A	A	B	A	B
1618	ICS 1	B	B	A	B	B	B
1621	ICS 1	B	B	A	B	B	B
1624	ICS 1	B	B	A	B	B	B
1675	ICS 1	B	B	A	B	B	B
1677	ICS 1	B	B	A	B	B	B
1679	ICS 1	B	B	A	B	B	B
3013	ICS 1	C	A	B	C	C	C
3131	ICS 1	C	A	B	C	C	C
3137	ICS 1	C	A	B	C	C	C
10002	SPPA	D	C	C	D	D	D
10003	SPPA	-	C	-	D	-	D
10060	DCERPC	-	D	-	D	-	D
10080	Java RMI	-	E	-	E	-	E
20202	ICS 2	E	D	D	D	-	D
20205	ICS 2	E	D	D	D	-	D
20301	ICS 2	E	D	D	D	-	D
20302	ICS 2	E	D	D	D	-	D
20303	ICS 2	E	D	D	D	-	D
20304	ICS 2	E	D	D	D	-	D
42239	ICS 1	B	B	A	B	B	B
42797	ICS 1	B	B	A	B	B	B
42922	ICS 1	B	B	A	B	B	B
42934	ICS 1	B	B	A	B	B	B
42979	ICS 1	B	B	A	B	B	B
44061	ICS 1	B	B	A	B	B	B

References

1. Tcpdump and Libpcap: https://www.tcpdump.org
2. Barbosa, R.R.R., Sadre, R., Pras, A.: A first look into scada network traffic. In: 2012 IEEE Network Operations and Management Symposium. pp. 518–521 (April 2012). https://doi.org/10.1109/NOMS.2012.6211945
3. Barbosa, R.R.R., Sadre, R., Pras, A.: Difficulties in modeling SCADA traffic: a comparative analysis. In: Taft, N., Ricciato, F. (eds.) PAM 2012. LNCS, vol. 7192, pp. 126–135. Springer, Heidelberg (2012). https://doi.org/10.1007/978-3-642-28537-0_13
4. Barbosa, R.: Anomaly detection in SCADA systems: a network based approach. Ph.D. thesis. University of Twente (2014). https://doi.org/10.3990/1.9789036536455
5. Barbosa, R.R.R., Sadre, R., Pras, A.: Exploiting traffic periodicity in industrial control networks. Int. J. Crit. Infrastruct. Prot. **13**, 52–62 (2016). https://doi.org/10.1016/j.ijcip.2016.02.004
6. Conti, M., Donadel, D., Turrin, F.: A survey on industrial control system testbeds and datasets for security research. IEEE Commun. Surv. Tutorials **23**(4), 2248–2294 (2021). https://doi.org/10.1109/COMST.2021.3094360
7. Galloway, B., Hancke, G.P.: Introduction to industrial control networks. IEEE Commun. Surv. Tutor. **15**(2), 860–880 (2013)
8. Hemsley, K.E., Fisher, D.R.E.: History of industrial control system cyber incidents. Idaho National Laboratory (2018)
9. Leland, W.E., Taqqu, M.S., Willinger, W., Wilson, D.V.: On the self-similar nature of ethernet traffic. SIGCOMM Comput. Commun. Rev. **23**(4), 183–193 (1993). https://doi.org/10.1145/167954.166255
10. Mai, K., Qin, X., Ortiz, N., Molina, J., Cardenas, A.A.: Uncharted networks: a first measurement study of the bulk power system. In: Proceedings of the ACM Internet Measurement Conference. IMC 2020, pp. 201–213. Association for Computing Machinery, New York, NY, USA (2020). https://doi.org/10.1145/3419394.3423630
11. Maier, G., Feldmann, A., Paxson, V., Allman, M.: On dominant characteristics of residential broadband internet traffic. In: ACM IMC (2009)
12. Mathur, A., Tippenhauer, N.O.: SWaT: a water treatment testbed for research and training on ICS security. In: 2016 International Workshop on Cyber-Physical Systems for Smart Water Networks (CySWater), pp. 31–36 (2016)
13. Ndonda, G.K., Sadre, R.: A two-level intrusion detection system for industrial control system networks using P4. In: 5th International Symposium for ICS & SCADA Cyber Security Research, pp. 31–40 (2018)
14. Richter, P., Chatzis, N., Smaragdakis, G., Feldmann, A., Willinger, W.: Distilling the internet's application mix from packet-sampled traffic. In: Mirkovic, J., Liu, Y. (eds.) PAM 2015. LNCS, vol. 8995, pp. 179–192. Springer, Cham (2015). https://doi.org/10.1007/978-3-319-15509-8_14
15. Stouffer, K., Pillitteri, V., Lightman, S., Abrams, M., Hahn, A.: Guide to Industrial Control Systems (ICS) security. NIST Special Publication 800–82 (2015)
16. Trivedi, C., Trussell, H.J., Nilsson, A.A., Chow, M.Y.: Implicit traffic classification for service differentiation. Technical report. North Carolina State University. Center for Advanced Computing and Communication (2002)

DNS

Assessing Support for DNS-over-TCP in the Wild

Jiarun Mao[1]([✉]), Michael Rabinovich[1], and Kyle Schomp[2]

[1] Case Western Reserve University, Cleveland, OH 44106, USA
{jxm959,michael.rabinovich}@case.edu
[2] Akamai Technologies, Cambridge, MA 02142, USA
kschomp@akamai.com

Abstract. While the DNS protocol encompasses both UDP and TCP as its underlying transport, UDP is commonly used in practice. At the same time, increasingly large DNS responses and concerns over amplification denial of service attacks have heightened interest in conducting DNS interactions over TCP. This paper surveys the support for DNS-over-TCP in the deployed DNS infrastructure from several angles. First, we assess resolvers responsible for over 66.2% of the external DNS queries that arrive at a major content delivery network (CDN). We find that 2.7% to 4.8% of the resolvers, contributing around 1.1% to 4.4% of all queries arriving at the CDN from the resolvers we study, do not properly fallback to TCP when instructed by authoritative DNS servers. Should a content provider decide to employ TCP-fallback as the means of switching to DNS-over-TCP, it faces the corresponding loss of its customers. Second, we assess authoritative DNS servers (ADNS) for over 10M domains and many CDNs and find some ADNS, serving some popular websites and a number of CDNs, that do not support DNS-over-TCP. These ADNS would deny service to (RFC-compliant) resolvers that choose to switch to TCP-only interactions. Third, we study the TCP connection reuse behavior of DNS actors and describe a race condition in TCP connection reuse by DNS actors that may become a significant issue should DNS-over-TCP and other TCP-based DNS protocols, such as DNS-over-TLS, become widely used.

1 Introduction

The DNS protocol, along with the massive infrastructure that runs it, is one of the key components of the Internet, providing mapping services from names to various data records, most notably from human-readable hostnames to IP addresses [28]. Over its decades of development, numerous use cases for DNS have emerged, such as distributing tokens used as proof of website ownership [4], providing access to cryptographic signatures for verifying both the integrity of the DNS records themselves [10] and the follow-up application traffic [13], and facilitating mechanisms for enhancing email security [11,17]. Diverse usage scenarios have led to a wide range of DNS message sizes, including some very large messages.

© The Author(s), under exclusive license to Springer Nature Switzerland AG 2022
O. Hohlfeld et al. (Eds.): PAM 2022, LNCS 13210, pp. 487–517, 2022.
https://doi.org/10.1007/978-3-030-98785-5_22

DNS can use either UDP or TCP as transport, but UDP is overwhelmingly used in practice: only 0.02% of DNS queries in our log of DNS queries at a major content delivery network (CDN) arrive over TCP. Using UDP is attractive because it is light-weight, and most DNS messages fit within a datagram and even within the 512-byte limit stipulated for DNS-over-UDP, per RFC 883 [27]. Moreover, the optional EDNS0 payload size allows larger UDP messages [36].

However, there are still messages that may be too large even for EDNS0 payload size. Further, large UDP responses make DNS an easy vector for amplification denial of service attacks [25,31], since an attacker can (i) elicit a large response from a legitimate server using a comparatively small query and (ii) spoof the source IP address of the victim, causing the server to send its (large) response to the victim. Thus, there is an increased interest in expanding the use of TCP for DNS interactions. Support for TCP allows much larger DNS messages (up to 65535 bytes) and effectively limits amplification attacks as large messages are not transferred until after the TCP handshake verifies the authenticity of the client's IP address; note that packets exchanged during the handshake are all equal size, precluding amplification in packet size – if not number of packets due to server-side retries [22] – during the handshake itself.

According to the protocol, a DNS interaction can occur over TCP at the discretion of either the client or the server. The client can simply send its query over TCP. The server can force a "TCP fallback" by responding to a UDP query with a partial UDP response and the truncated flag (TC) to indicate the truncation. The client should then retry the query over TCP.

The heightened interest in DNS-over-TCP brings an important question: if one party chooses to use TCP for DNS interactions, is there a risk that the other party may not support it properly, given that the current practice is to use UDP virtually exclusively? In fact, a past study of DNSSEC deployment provided an indication that some resolvers may not be TCP-capable [23], adding impetus to a more comprehensive look into this issue.

In this paper, we investigate the support for DNS-over-TCP in the deployed DNS infrastructure from several angles. First, we assess the support for TCP-fallback by recursive resolvers, using various measurement techniques to explore different classes of resolvers, that in the aggregate are responsible for a large portion of Internet DNS activity. Second, we assess DNS-over-TCP support by authoritative DNS servers (ADNS) serving many domains – including popular ones – and a large number of content delivery networks. Third, we study the behavior of these DNS actors with regard to an important aspect of DNS-over-TCP behavior, namely, reuse of TCP connections for multiple queries. Our key findings are:

- We show that the egress resolvers follow complex patterns in interacting with authoritative servers that force TCP-fallback, with only half of resolutions exhibiting a "canonical" pattern of one UDP query followed by one TCP query. Consequently, we design and validate an algorithm for characterizing egress resolvers' TCP-fallback capability from complex patterns.

- Among the egress resolvers we study, we find 2.7% to 4.8% to be incapable of TCP-fallback. Moreover, by analyzing the DNS logs of the major CDN, we show that these TCP-fallback incapable resolvers tend to be generally as active as their TCP-fallback capable counterparts, as they account for 1.1% to 4.4% of DNS queries received by the major CDN from the resolvers we study. We believe content providers are unlikely to move to a technology that leads to failure of such a fraction of DNS queries and potentially cuts off a non-negligible amount of their consumers.
- We find that around 3% of popular websites, and 5% of domains at large, with at least some ADNS failing to answer DNS-over-TCP queries. Moreover, a surprisingly large fraction of CDNs, 11 out of 47 CDNs we consider, have at least one authoritative DNS server with no DNS-over-TCP support. Again, we believe, with these results, resolver operators would be hesitant to unilaterally switch to DNS-over-TCP and potentially block their users from a non-negligible portion of Internet content.
- We identify an edge case in the DNS-over-TCP protocol that can cause unnecessary query retries and uncover some DNS-over-TCP implementation bugs in two major CDNs. We propose simple changes to the protocol that would remove this vulnerability.
- We demonstrate that, despite the steady decrease in the number of open resolvers, active scanning can still discover egress resolvers[1] responsible for a substantial portion of the Internet DNS activity. In all, the egress resolvers discovered via our active scanning techniques contributed 66.2% of the DNS queries in the major CDN's DNS logs. Because this CDN handles a large portion of the global Internet traffic, we believe the discovered egress resolvers are responsible for a generally commensurate fraction of the overall DNS activity.

The datasets collected through active measurements and analyzed in this study that are not related to the major CDN are publicly available at [1].

2   Terminology

DNS literature uses the terms "resolver", "recursive resolver (RDNS)", and "local DNS server (LDNS)" to refer to the servers that provide DNS recursive resolution service to end-user devices. We will use the term resolver. "Open resolver" refers to a resolver that accepts DNS queries from the public Internet, as opposed to being restricted to specific clients. The term "authoritative DNS server (ADNS)" refers to servers that maintain DNS records for a section of the DNS namespace (a "zone") and are able to provide authoritative DNS responses to queries for names within the zone.

Some DNS deployments exhibit complex resolution paths (Fig. 1) involving multiple resolvers as discussed in [33]. Following [33], we refer to the resolver that receives DNS queries directly from end clients as "ingress resolver", while

---

[1] The resolvers that directly interact with authoritative DNS servers – see Sect. 2.

Fig. 1. An example of a complex resolution path which involves ingress and egress resolvers.

an "egress resolver" communicates directly with authoritative DNS servers. The ingress resolver may also act as an egress resolver or may forward queries from the end clients, potentially through several intermediaries, to an egress resolver that obtains the response from the authoritative servers and forwards the response back to the ingress resolver, which finally sends the response back to the client. In the latter case, the ingress resolver is often referred to as a "forwarder".

A DNS query includes multiple fields. Of particular relevance to this paper are the query string, denoted "QNAME", which is a name within the DNS namespace and the query type, denoted "QTYPE", which indicates what type of resource is desired (e.g., "A" for an IPv4 address, "MX" for a mail server, and "TXT" for arbitrary text).

DNS TCP fallback refers to a scenario in which the ADNS sets the TC flag in its response to a UDP query, indicating a truncated response (we also use "TC response" for brevity), and the querying resolver repeats its query through TCP to retrieve the full response. Modern DNS platforms often employ collaborative resolution, where a resolver may forward the follow-up querying tasks to one of its resolver peers [3,30,33], complicating the analysis of TCP-fallback capability. In our characterization of resolvers' TCP behavior, we identify TCP-fallback capable resolvers by the initial UDP query, whether the subsequent TCP fallback arrives from the same resolver or from a peer. Because we find negligible number of DNS interactions to be originally conducted over TCP, we equate DNS-over-TCP capability of resolvers with their TCP-fallback capability in this paper.

3   Related Work

Geoff Huston measured DNS TCP-fallback support among resolvers in 2013 [16]. He found that 83% of 80,505 measured resolvers are capable of TCP-fallback. In our study 8 years later, we find much greater support, with 95.2%–97.3% of 116,851 measured resolvers being TCP-fallback capable. A further explanation for the difference besides time is that Huston did not consider collaborative resolution, where the original UDP and the followup TCP queries come from different resolvers (see Sect. 4.3).

TCP fallback was also considered by Moura et al. as part of a broader study on the implications of large DNS responses [29]. By using a passively collected dataset at .nl TLD, this study observed many more recursive resolvers than we could with active measurements (over 3M vs. over 100K in our study) but at the expense of less accurate analysis due to inability to craft special queries with unique names[2]. In particular, this study could only indirectly bound the effect of collaborative resolution, while we are able to associate queries that belong to the same resolution, via names that are used only once, whether or not they come from the same resolver. Moura et al. also assesses the TCP fallback failure to be more prevalent than we observed: after correcting for the specifics of Google's resolution platform, they found roughly 7–10% of truncated responses to lack a TCP query follow-up[3]. In contrast, we estimate that, out of all queries to a major CDN from the resolvers we study, around 1.1–4.4% of queries are from the resolvers incapable of TCP fallback.

In 2016, Shulman and Waidner [34] studied the support for DNS-over-TCP in ADNS and found nearly 20% of the 170K ADNS serving the top 50K domains in the Alexa list could not return a DNS response over TCP. In contrast, we find 423K (95%) out of 445K tested ADNS in our All Domain List (described in Sect. 5) to be *always* TCP-capable[4]. Clearly, we observe substantially lower levels of incapability. Further, Shulman and Waidner found that the majority of failures (13% of all ADNS) occurred *after* the TCP handshake, while the experimental client was waiting for the DNS response. In our study, we found the opposite: 3.8% of the total tested ADNS failed exclusively during the TCP handshake and only 1.2% ever failed after the TCP handshake.

Vixie and Schryver [37] propose opportunistically setting the TC flag in DNS responses as a mitigation technique for reflection and amplification attacks, rather than dropping queries outright. A legitimate resolver can then retry over TCP, while the attacker gains no amplification from the responses. However, this technique is only effective if the legitimate resolvers support DNS-over-TCP.

Several works [5,7,24,39] study the impact of encrypting DNS (i.e., DNS-over-TLS, or DoT, [14] and DNS-over-HTTPS, or DoH, [12]). In particular, Zhu et al. [39] argue that DNS-over-TLS has acceptable performance costs, in large part due to connection and TLS negotiation reuse. While both DOT and DOH use TCP for transport, these are new protocols that require an explicit adoption by the parties. In contrast, DNS-over-TCP and TCP fallback are part of the existing DNS standard that must be supported by every party. Thus, in principle, an ADNS should be able to switch to TCP unilaterally. Our study examines the extent to which this holds in practice. At the same time, the race condition we uncover (Sect. 6) applies to both DoT, which explicitly adopts the connection management from DNS-over-TCP (see Sect. 3.4 in [14]), and DoH as judged from our personal communication with one of the leading CDNs. Thus, in this aspect, our study informs potential support for encrypted DNS.

---

[2] Other available passive datasets, such as DITL [9] entail a similar limitation.

[3] Indeed, 47% of 15–21% of TC responses initially found without a TCP query follow-up were to Google resolvers, virtually all of which the authors later assessed to be successful fallback to TCP, leaving 7–10% of TC responses still without a TCP followup.

[4] While in Sect. 5 we categorize TCP support by domain to demonstrate the impact to clients using TCP as their transport medium, here we categorize by ADNS for easy comparison to Shulman and Waidner.

4   TCP Fallback Support by Recursive Resolvers

4.1   Methodology

To investigate DNS-over-TCP support in resolvers, we collect datasets from four sources. Three of the datasets are actively collected; each offers a view into a specific population of resolvers and we collect all three to provide a larger view of resolvers on the Internet. The fourth dataset is aggregated logs from the ADNS servers of a major CDN, which we use to assess the coverage of our study and evaluate the activity level of the resolvers collected in the active datasets.

A limitation of our study is that it focuses on DNS interactions over IPv4 and does not consider IPv6. While we are currently expanding our experiments to cover IPv6, we note that IPv4 still dominates DNS traffic: in the major CDN dataset, queries conducted over IPv4 outnumber IPv6 by 11:1. Further, there is no reason to believe that the choice of the network-layer protocol version would affect the application-level behavior of DNS resolvers[5].

Next, we describe the details of the experiments run to produce each dataset.

Open Resolvers Scan. We scan the entire IPv4 public address space (barring reserved addresses and our exclusion list, see Sect. 7) between February 10 and 11, 2021, with DNS queries for names from our experimental zone, in search of open resolvers. If the scanned IP address returns a DNS response with a NOERROR response code and a resource record, the scanner will send follow-up queries to the discovered ingress resolver to assess support for DNS-over-TCP. Because some ingress resolvers dynamically change IP addresses – a previous study shows that 52.2% of the ingress resolvers change their IP addresses within a week [21] – we launch the DNS-over-TCP capability testing right after the discovery of an ingress resolver, to minimize interference caused by address churn. All queries encode the IP address of the ingress resolver and a nonce so that they cannot be answered from cache.

In probing the discovered ingress resolvers, our goal is to test the TCP-fallback capability of the egress resolvers the open resolvers use by forcing the egress resolver to switch to TCP after a UDP query. The scanner sends two follow-up queries, one A-type and one MX-type (for ease of comparison with our other datasets below which use the same type). Our experimental zone has a single ADNS server that is configured to respond to both queries with the TC flag set and 0 resource records, so that the egress resolvers must re-query over TCP to obtain the records.

Enterprise Resolvers Scan. In an effort to assess recursive resolvers used by major enterprises, which are often protected by firewalls that forbid any DNS queries from the outside, we leverage a technique introduced by Klein et al. [18] to induce MX queries from the resolvers used by enterprises to our ADNS. The experiment was conducted on February 15, 2021, and used the Majestic Top

---

[5] Indeed, a study [29] concerning large DNS responses did include both IPv4 and IPv6 traffic and did not note significant variations in behavior between the two.

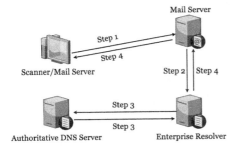

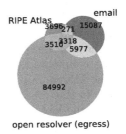

Fig. 2. Inducing a DNS resolution from a private enterprise resolver.

Fig. 3. Egress resolvers discovered in our experiments.

Million "Root Domains List" [26] – which includes many major enterprises – fetched on February 14, 2021.

We measure TCP fallback support of enterprise resolvers using the following process, illustrated in Fig. 2:

1. For each mail server used by the enterprise domain (obtained from the MX records of the domain), in the decreasing preference order, we send an email through SMTP and, if failed, through SMTPS, using Python's *smtplib* library. We stop iterating through the mail servers in this enterprise domain if *smtplib* reports no error. We use random strings as recipients of our emails (i.e., "[random]@majestic.domain"), which are highly unlikely to collide with existing recipients, and we embed the enterprise domain in the sender's email address (i.e., "research@majestic-domain.our.zone").

2. When the destination mail server receives the email for the non-existent recipient, the mail server should generate a delivery-status-notification (DSN) and send it back to the original sender, as required by RFC 5321 [20]. To return the DSN, the mail server must lookup via DNS the MX record of the original sender's domain (i.e., "majestic-domain.our.zone"), although some resolvers send our ADNS an A-type query for the same name, instead. We interpret the latter as a misunderstanding of implicit MX records stated in RFC 2821 [19], which allows mail servers to use the A record of the sender's domain if no MX records are found. For the purposes of our study, either an MX-type or A-type query from the resolver is sufficient, so we use both.

3. The enterprise resolver interacts with our ADNS to resolve either an MX or A query over UDP. Since our ADNS responds to either query with an empty answer section and the TC flag, the resolver must support TCP-fallback in order to successfully obtain the MX and A records.

4. If the mail server receives a successful response from its resolver, the mail server then sends the DSN back to our scanner (which we set up to double as the MX server for our zone). Regardless, we can assess the TCP-fallback capability of the resolver by observing a TCP query from it (or lack thereof).

Note that for the above technique to work, several prerequisites must be met. First, the mail servers must be willing to receive mail from our SMTP client.

Second, the mail server must attempt to send the DSN back to the original sender. Often in our measurement the mail servers indicate an error within the SMTP interaction instead of resolving our MX record and delivering the DSN. Further, some mail servers have catch-all inboxes and provide no feedback about non-existing recipients at all. Another frequent occurrence is that the resolver performs the MX lookup, but the mail server does not send a DSN message to our scanner. In this case, we can still ascertain that the resolver is TCP-fallback capable since the lookup completed.

Another assumption behind this experiment is that enterprise mail servers use the enterprise's general resolution path rather than resolve queries themselves (in which case we would be measuring the TCP-fallback capability of the mail servers rather than the enterprise resolvers). A supporting evidence for this assumption is that there is a large overlap between the resolvers discovered in our enterprise and open resolver scans (see below).

RIPE Atlas Probes Experiment. We use the RIPE Atlas platform to gain an insight into another slice of resolvers. RIPE Atlas [32] is a volunteer-based Internet measurement platform managed by RIPE NCC, where each volunteer deploys a measurement probe in their home or institutional network, and experimenters can conduct various measurements from the probes, including DNS resolutions. RIPE Atlas has probes deployed worldwide, but particularly dense deployment in Europe and North America. We used 11,522 probes in our experiments – all available probes that were suitable for our purpose, i.e., those having an IPv4 prefix and not tagged as having problems in resolving DNS queries.

Similar to the technique in the open resolver scan, we embed the probe ID in the DNS query, which makes each probe's query unique and ensures that no resolvers reuse cached responses to answer queries from multiple probes. Further, we direct the probes to use their configured DNS resolvers – whether they happen to be open or closed – to process our queries. Thus, the RIPE Atlas dataset explores a potentially distinct set of resolvers from our open resolver and enterprise email scans. Like the open resolver scan, a RIPE Atlas probe sends a type-A and a type-MX query to its configured resolver, and our ADNS replies to both of these queries with zero resource records and the TC flag.

DNS Logs of a Major CDN. Lastly, we collect one week in February 2021 of aggregated logs from the authoritative DNS servers of a major CDN. The dataset includes source IP addresses (i.e., egress resolver) and the counts of queries from each address fielded by the CDN during that week. Due to the high aggregation level, we are not able to identify whether the resolvers in the logs are TCP-fallback capable by observing TCP follow-up queries to TC flag responses. Instead, we use the CDN dataset to assess the coverage of our study and use the relative counts of queries to evaluate the popularity of the resolvers we measure.

Measurement Instrumentation Losses. Our measurements are susceptible to packet losses due to unreliable UDP messages, the ADNS potentially not responding to some queries due to overload, and the scanner not exploring discovered ingress resolvers. We can't formally assess the number of UDP datagrams lost in-network before they reach our hosts, but we have no reason to suspect an unusually high packet losses during our experiments. On the ADNS side, we find that 16 out of 13,836,165 total UDP queries were left without response across all three datasets, which is negligible. Among the TCP queries, 13,793 out of 11,692,210 TCP queries were not responded to, a high response rate of 99.9%. Moreover, our classification strategy (see Sect. 4.3) is based on the TCP queries that arrive; thus, the unresponsive TCP queries do not affect the accuracy of our egress resolver classification.

As time is a factor in our algorithm (see Sect. 4.3), we investigate how quickly our ADNS responds to UDP queries. The average response time for UDP queries is 38 μs, with 3.0 ms standard deviation, so the response is usually very quick. Indeed, the ADNS response took greater than 1 s for only 302 (0.002%) of UDP queries, still substantially below the 2 s threshold used in our algorithm. We conclude that delays in our ADNS do not materially affect our analysis.

Another source of measurement loss is on the scanner during the open resolver scan. Our scanner uses an LRU cache to keep track of the most recent 200K {QNAME, QTYPE} pairs that produced answers from scanned ingress resolvers. This is to ensure that our scanner does not send follow-up queries to superfluous repeated responses to our scanning queries that some ingress resolvers keep sending. The entries in the cache are identified using a 64-bit xxHash value for performance, and the check if an arriving response is already present in the LRU cache may return false positives on collisions, in which case our scanner will not measure the responding ingress resolver. Our scanner explored 3,051,701 out of 3,052,913 (99.96%) responding ingress resolvers. The small number of unexplored ingress resolvers slightly reduces the number of assessed egress resolvers but does not materially affect our results.

4.2 Datasets

In the open resolver scan, we discovered 97,797 egress resolvers, and 3,052,913 open ingress resolvers.[6] It is important to note that, while the open resolver scan only engages with DNS resolution systems through open ingresses, the measured egress resolvers include both open and closed ones. In particular, we found a sizable number of egress resolvers discovered through the open resolver scan to also serve enterprise networks.

In the email scan, we discovered 24,653 egress resolvers, serving enterprises responsible for 192,164 websites from the Majestic 1M list. In the rest of the paper, we refer to these resolvers as "serving a domain" or "used by a domain" for brevity, meaning that these resolvers provide resolution services for clients

---

[6] We discover substantially more open ingress resolvers than other recent scans [2,35]. The likely cause of this discrepancy is that those scans do not include ingress resolvers that respond from a different port (not 53) than the port used in probing, a behavior first observed in [33]. Indeed, our results include 2010584 (65.9%) ingress resolvers that do respond from port 53, closely matching the number of resolvers reported by the previous scans.

from the enterprises that operate or are responsible for those domains. We stress that in this experiment, we assess resolvers that the enterprises use, regardless of whether they are operated by themselves or an external DNS service provider.

Finally, in the RIPE Atlas measurement, we discovered 10,795 egress resolvers.

While each of the above datasets aims to capture a distinct class of egress resolvers – the open resolver scan finds public resolvers or those used by open forwarders, the email scan finds resolvers used by enterprises, and the RIPE Atlas scan finds closed resolvers in use by home networks or institutions – unsurprisingly, there is some overlap. Figure 3 is a Venn diagram of the egress resolvers in each dataset. While the overlap is significant, each datasets contributes a significant number of net new egress resolvers. Thus, all three datasets contribute to a more comprehensive picture of DNS-over-TCP support in the wild. In the aggregate, we discover and investigate 116,851 egress resolvers across all three datasets. These resolvers contribute 66.2% of the external queries in the CDN logs. Note that the CDN uses DNS internally as part of the platform operation, and DNS queries originating from the CDN do not represent end-user resolutions. Since this CDN delivers large amounts of popular content accessed by most Internet users, this finding shows that, despite drastic reduction in the number of open resolvers, active measurements can still assess a significant portion of the DNS activity on the Internet. For the rest of the paper, we focus on the aggregate set of egress resolvers, unless otherwise stated.

4.3 Resolver Categorization Algorithm

Our open resolver scan finds a large fraction of failed DNS interactions when the ADNS forces TCP fallback: almost a quarter (24.35%) of the overall type-A resolutions involving TCP fallback ultimately fail, i.e., the ingress resolver returns a response with an error flag, or response with no TC flag and no resource records, or no response at all (despite having been discovered through a successful UDP-based DNS probe) or the response carrying a wrong transaction ID. However, it is unclear if these failures are not due to a potential bias in the set of the ingress resolvers we are able to interact with, since they are selected based on a specific trait (being open to external queries) that distinguishes them from all other ingress resolvers. Thus, our assessment of the resolvers' TCP fallback capability focuses on characterizing egress resolvers rather than on whether or not the ingress resolvers ultimately returns the answer to our scanning host. As noted in Sect. 4.1, we are able to assess the egress resolvers responsible for two-thirds of the overall DNS activity observed by ADNS of the major CDN.

Identifying TCP-fallback capability of an egress resolver in our datasets requires associating the UDP query it sends with the subsequent TCP query. Several factors significantly complicate this seemingly easy task. First, we find that a single query emitted by our scanner often elicits multiple queries at our ADNS (see Sect. 4.4). This complicates matching a UDP query with the followup TCP query because multiple UDP queries may be candidates for being associated with the same TCP query. Second, these queries may come from different egress

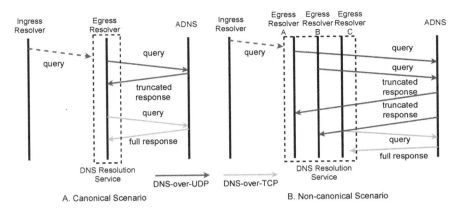

Fig. 4. Examples of a "canonical scenario" where it is trivial to match the UDP and TCP queries and a "non-canonical scenario" where it is hard to tell whether resolver A or B triggers the TCP-fallback.

resolvers, and in fact TCP queries may come from *different* egress resolvers than the UDP queries they succeed, a behavior indicative of collaborative resolution previously reported (e.g., [3, 30, 33]).

To illustrate, in the "canonical" TCP fallback scenario shown in Fig. 4A, matching the UDP and TCP queries, and identifying the resolver involved as TCP fallback capable, is trivial – there is only one query of each type. However, Fig. 4B shows an example of a scenario, where it is unclear, from the ADNS vantage point, which of the two UDP queries triggered TCP-fallback, and which of the two resolvers, A or B is TCP fallback capable.

This section presents our algorithm to determine TCP-fallback capability, as well as the rationale for selecting key parameters of the algorithm.

At the beginning of our data processing pipeline, packet traces captured at our ADNS during the three active measurements are fed to a preprocessing stage. A converter extracts all the DNS messages from the trace, including messages in UDP datagrams as well as reassembling TCP streams to find DNS messages across segments. Next, the few UDP queries that our ADNS did not respond to (see Sect. 4.1) are discarded. In these cases, the egress resolver did not receive a response, let alone one with the TC flag, so we cannot measure TCP-fallback. Conversely, the TCP queries to which our ADNS did not respond are retained because the TCP query even without a response is sufficient to identify TCP-fallback. If the egress resolver repeats the TCP query after the query to which it received no response, the repetitions are discarded to prevent potential incorrect association with other UDP queries.

Next, the algorithm attempts to associate the UDP and TCP queries and mark matched UDP queries as "TCP-fallback success", unmatched UDP queries as "TCP-fallback failure", and the queries that it could not unambiguously match to a single TCP query as "indeterminate". Finally, the algorithm classifies

egress resolvers as TCP-fallback capable or not based on the prevalence of their
UDP query markings.

Associating UDP and TCP-Fallback Queries. The heart of the algorithm
in UDP-to-TCP query matching. It does this by first separating the DNS queries
by QNAME and QTYPE, since the UDP and TCP-fallback query must match
on these fields. The queries are then clustered such that all the UDP queries in a
cluster can plausibly be associated only with the TCP queries in the same cluster, and no cluster can be split without removing some plausible UDP-to-TCP
query association. By "plausible association" we mean a UDP query followed
by a TCP query within a certain time threshold $t_{threshold}$, a parameter in the
algorithm. UDP queries outside any clusters have no plausible associations with
TCP queries and are marked as "TCP-fallback failures". Our matching algorithm proceeds to act upon individual clusters.

Appendix A has the full algorithm for constructing query clusters. Briefly, a
cluster has the following attributes:

1. For any UDP query within a cluster, there must be at least one TCP query
   that is within $t_{threshold}$ seconds after it. Otherwise, the cluster can be split
   after the UDP query in question.
2. For each pair of consecutive TCP queries in a cluster, T_i and T_{i+1}, there is a
   UDP query U that precedes T_i and also precedes T_{i+1} by less than $t_{threshold}$
   seconds. This ensures that U can be plausibly associated with both T_i and
   T_{i+1} – otherwise, the cluster could be split after T_i.
3. A cluster can include no UDP queries (e.g., if there is a spurious isolated
   TCP query or a TCP query that is removed from a preceding UDP query by
   more than $t_{threshold}$), but always includes at least one TCP query.
4. As a corollary of (1), a cluster always ends with a TCP query in chronological
   order.

Figure 5 shows an example of a series of queries that arrive at ADNS in
the aftermath of a single probe to an ingress resolver. UDP query #13 doesn't
precede any TCP query, and therefore is labeled as TCP-fallback failed by our
algorithm. The rest of the queries are split into four clusters The first cluster
consists of queries #1 through #4 because UDP query #1 is within $t_{threshold}$
seconds before TCP query #4. TCP query #5 is in a cluster alone because there
are no UDP queries within the time threshold preceding it. UDP query #6 and
TCP query #7 make up the third cluster, and the remaining queries #8 through
#12 form the last cluster.

Within a cluster, the algorithm scans queries in chronological order and
attempts to greedily assign each UDP query to the next unclaimed TCP query
within the $t_{threshold}$ window. If all UDP queries are successfully assigned to their
own exclusive TCP query, they are marked as TCP-fallback success. Otherwise,
all UDP queries that could plausibly match to the same TCP query are marked
as indeterminate since we cannot determine conclusively which triggered TCP
fallback and which did not.

Returning to the clusters in Fig. 5, while both UDP queries #1 and #3 can
be associated with TCP query #4, this would leave TCP query #2 unmatched

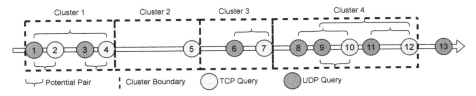

Fig. 5. Splitting queries into clusters based on plausible TCP-fallback association.

– an unlikely scenario. The algorithm instead greedily matches UDP query #1 with TCP query #2, and UDP query #3 with TCP query #4. Thus, both UDP queries are marked as TCP-fallback success. UDP query #6 is trivially associated with TCP query #7 because there are no other UDP queries that can plausibly associate with TCP query #7. In the fourth cluster, the algorithm will attempt to greedily match UDP query #8 with TCP query #10, then UDP query #9 with TCP query #12, and then is left with UDP query #11 that could not match to a dedicated TCP query. At this point the algorithm will mark all three UDP queries as indeterminate because it cannot tell if UDP queries #8 and #9 should share TCP query #10 (and thus be marked indeterminate) leaving UDP query #11 to be exclusively matched to TCP query #12 (and thus marked TCP-fallback success), or UDP query #8 should be exclusively matched to TCP query #10 (thus marked TCP-fallback success) while UDP queries #9 and #11 should share TCP query #12 (and thus be marked indeterminate).

Selecting Time Threshold. The algorithm uses one parameter which must be tuned, $t_{threshold}$ – the time for matching UDP queries to potential TCP-fallback queries. Logically, this time comprises the propagation time of the UDP response with TC flag from the ADNS to the egress resolver, processing time at the egress resolver, and the TCP handshake followed by the initial data segment carrying the TCP query. Clearly, this time can vary substantially among resolvers.

To estimate $t_{threshold}$, we look at scenarios where we can unambiguously associate UDP and TCP queries, i.e., those resolutions that contain exactly one UDP query followed by exactly one TCP query. We call these scenarios "canonical". Because in the canonical scenarios we can be confident that the TCP query is a result of TCP-fallback from the UDP query, we measure the time between the queries and use the times to inform our choice of $t_{threshold}$.

Figure 6 shows the cumulative distribution function (CDF) of the measured time between UDP and TCP queries in the canonical scenarios in our three datasets. In all three datasets, nearly 100% of TCP-fallback happens within 2 s. Thus, we choose 2 s for $t_{threshold}$ as a conservative estimate of the maximum time TCP-fallback should take. The CDFs do show that this threshold will miss a small number of cases where TCP-fallback takes longer than 2 s. However, a resolver that requires more than 2 s to fallback can be treated as TCP-fallback incapable (or at least "impaired") since it will negatively impact the end-user experience.

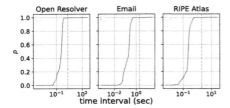
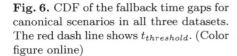

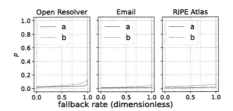

Fig. 6. CDF of the fallback time gaps for canonical scenarios in all three datasets. The red dash line shows $t_{threshold}$. (Color figure online)

Fig. 7. CDF of the (a) optimistic and (b) pessimistic fallback rates of the resolvers across all three datasets. The red dash line shows $t_{threshold}$. (Color figure online)

Categorizing Egress Resolvers. The above algorithm labels individual UDP queries as leading to TCP-fallback success, failure, or indeterminate. However, moving from the characterization of individual queries to the overall characterization of the egress resolvers involves several complicating issues.

One issue is that many egress resolvers in our datasets handle multiple queries, and we find that the labeling of those queries sent by the same resolver may not be consistent. There are many possible causes of this inconsistency. First, UDP queries in complex resolution patterns may be marked indeterminate rather than TCP-fallback success or failure due to coinciding with UDP queries from other egress resolvers, with different TCP fallback capability. Second, UDP queries that arrive from the same IP address may in fact come from different resolvers in a server farm behind a common NAT box, again with different TCP-fallback capability. Finally, egress resolvers may selectively perform TCP-fallback due to rate limits, policy, or other factors. Thus, we characterize the overall TCP-fallback capability of an egress resolver by the predominance of their individual UDP query markings.

Another complication is that indeterminate UDP queries introduce uncertainty into the characterization. To address this issue, we bracket its effect by treating indeterminate queries as TCP fallback-success or failure and considering, respectively, the optimistic and pessimistic successful fallback rates of resolvers. We refer to the resolvers characterized under these assumptions as, respectively, optimistically and pessimistically TCP-fallback (in)capable.

Figure 7 shows the CDFs of the successful fallback rate for egress resolvers in each of our three datasets. A majority of resolvers exhibit successful fallback rate of 1.0, removing the first complication in characterizing their TCP fallback capability. In the aggregated dataset, the successful fallback rate is 1.0 for 102,802 to 110,394 (88.0%–94.5% of all) of the egress resolvers depending on pessimistic or optimistic treatment of indeterminate queries, making these resolvers optimistically or pessimistically TCP-fallback capable. To classify the minority of egress resolvers with the successful fallback rate between 0.0 and 1.0, we opt to take a threshold approach. At around 0.7 on the X-axis (the dotted red line), we note that the lines appear to be fairly flat, meaning that large steps in the threshold would produce small changes in the classification. Thus, we classify the egress resolvers with the successful fallback rate of 0.7 or higher as TCP-fallback capable. In addition to being insensitive to variations in value, this threshold requires the resolver to exhibit fallback success – at least under the optimistic assumptions – in a sizable majority of UDP queries in order to be considered TCP-fallback capable.

In the rest of the paper, we will use a range to represent the number of TCP-fallback capable and incapable resolvers according to the optimistic and pessimistic calculations.

Validating the Algorithm. We validate our algorithm by looking at the end-to-end resolution outcomes for A-type queries in our open resolvers scan, with the following three assumptions:

1. If a DNS query is resolved exclusively by TCP-fallback *incapable* egress resolvers, the ingress resolver should reply to our scanner with a failed DNS response or no response at all.
2. If a DNS query is resolved exclusively by TCP-fallback *capable* egress resolvers, the ingress resolver should reply to our scanner with a successful DNS response.
3. Should our matching algorithm fail to match a UDP query with the fallback due to the latter being delayed by longer than $t_{threshold}$, the end-to-end response would also be delayed. As mentioned earlier, characterizing the resolver involved as incapable is not unjustified because of the excessive response time.

Note that we expect these assumptions to only hold as general trends because – as discussed earlier – the same egress resolver (as represented by its IP address) may exhibit inconsistent TCP-fallback capability in different resolutions but in the end is categorized by the algorithm as either TCP-fallback capable or not.

We consider the end-to-end resolution successful if our scanner receives a response with the matching transaction ID and the NOERROR response code, and which either carries the TC flag (71.8% of successful responses) or, if the TC flag is not set, includes some resource records in the answer section (28.2% of successful responses); otherwise the resolution is considered to have failed. A response that carries the TC flag – which may have zero answer records – we consider successful because, after such a response, a real client would retrieve the answer records through TCP. This assumption is conservative because one cannot preclude the possibility that the upstream resolvers blindly copy back the ADNS response with TC flag, and without the ability to perform TCP-fallback. We could not further assess the TCP-fallback capability of the resolution path by sending a TCP query to the ingress resolver, because most ingress resolvers that we found to be open to UDP queries are not open to TCP queries. However, 65.7% of all transactions considered successful – including 37.5% with the TC flag – contain at least one resource record returned by our ADNS over TCP, precluding the possibility of the success misjudgment.

Of all the resolutions that were handled by optimistically TCP-fallback capable egress resolvers only, 88.9% returned a successful response to our scanner;

in contrast, for the resolutions handled by optimistically TCP-fallback incapable egress resolvers only, 79.9% returned failed responses. Furthermore, for
the 20.1% of queries that were proxied by optimistically TCP-fallback incapable
resolvers only but came back to our scanner as successful responses, we found
that their end-to-end response time is significantly higher than the queries that
were proxied by TCP-fallback capable egress resolvers. Comparing the cumulative distribution functions of the two sets of response times above, shown in
Fig. 8, 75% of resolutions involving all incapable egress resolvers had end-to-end
response time over 1 s, while only 25% of resolutions involving all capable egress
resolvers were as slow.

These results show high correspondence between our algorithm's characterization of TCP-fallback capability of egress resolvers and positive end-to-end
resolution outcomes when fallback is required. We conclude that our algorithm
can successfully characterize resolvers from this perspective.

Table 1. Pattern prevalence of query
clusters. Many rare patterns are aggregated together in "Other".

Cluster pattern	% of clusters
U	0.7%
UU	0.4%
>2 UDP queries	2.0%
T	2.9%
UT	50.4%
UUT	1.7%
UTUT	19.2%
UUTT	13.6%
Other	9.0%

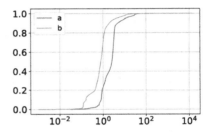

Fig. 8. CDF of the end-to-end response time
for successful TCP-fallback responses with
(a) optimistically TCP-fallback incapable and
(b) optimistically TCP-fallback capable egress
resolvers

4.4   DNS Resolution Patterns

Query clusters represent scenarios unfolding in individual DNS resolutions of
a domain name. We now examine the patterns of UDP and TCP queries in
these clusters. This analysis sheds light on the sequence of DNS transactions
comprising a single resolution when the authoritative DNS server forces a TCP
fallback. Given that each cluster includes a sequence of UDP and TCP queries
for the same QNAME/QTYPE pair, we represent query patterns in clusters as
sequences of symbols "U" and "T" to denote, respectively, the UDP and TCP
queries in a cluster, in chronological order.

Table 1 breaks down the query clusters by pattern. Note that the table
includes patterns composed exclusively of UDP queries even though the algorithm does not consider them as "clusters" for the matching purpose. These

patterns include all UDP queries for a given QNAME/QTYPE pair that cannot be plausibly associated with any TCP queries, i.e., are TCP-fallback failures.

First, we note that 2.9% of clusters contain a singleton TCP query that could not be matched with any UDP query according to our algorithm. This does not match our expectation that unsolicited TCP queries are very rare, and therefore we investigate them further. The singletons account for 0.8% of all DNS queries in our dataset and arrive from 1549 different egress resolvers. One possible explanation for the singletons is TCP-fallback that took longer than $t_{threshold}$ (2) s. Indeed, our ADNS did receive UDP queries from all but 15 of these resolvers at some point during our scans, and 79% of the singletons are preceded by at least one other cluster that does contain a UDP query. Still, since our algorithm could not associate the singletons with any UDP query, they are excluded from our analysis, potentially leading to UDP queries being marked as TCP-fallback failure. In an effort to determine whether the singletons affect our results, we bound their potential impact by marking each as TCP-fallback success, since the egress resolvers involved are clearly capable of DNS-over-TCP. We find that the results of our analysis in Sect. 4.5 do not change discernibly since most of the egress resolvers sending the singletons are determined to be TCP-fallback capable anyway from their other interactions: the number of TCP-fallback capable resolvers increases by just 26 to 33 for optimistic and pessimistic cases, respectively, from over 100K TCP-fallback capable resolvers found without the singletons. Thus, we exclude the singleton TCP queries for simplicity.

Surprisingly, the "canonical" expected scenario, where a single UDP query is followed by a single TCP-fallback query, represents barely a majority of interactions, only 50.4%. Others involve multiple redundant queries, with a sizable number, 83,987 (9.0%), of interactions following complex patterns beyond those listed in the table. While DNS scans typically leave a low-rate residual trickle of queries arriving long after the scan, the fact that so many resolvers, including well-known and well-administered ones, routinely send redundant queries, is unlikely due to obscure bugs. These behaviors more likely represent complicated resolution processes and require a separate study. In the meantime, the complexity and diversity of the cluster patterns highlight the need for a commensurately sophisticated matching algorithm, of the kind we use in this paper, to identify the TCP-fallback capabilities of the resolvers involved.

4.5   Results

In this section, we share the results of our analysis. As shown in Table 2, of the 116,851 egress resolvers discovered across all three datasets, between 111,284 to 113,673 (95.2%–97.3%) are TCP-fallback capable according to the pessimistic and optimistic classification, respectively. This leaves a sizeable number, under either classification approach, of incapable egress resolvers in the wild, suggesting that the Internet is not ready for DNS-over-TCP, as content providers are unlikely to move to a protocol that cuts off a non-negligible amount of their consumers.

Table 2. TCP-fallback capabilities of egress resolvers.

Resolver category	Num.	% resolvers	% queries to CDN
Optimistically capable	113,673	97.3%	98.9%
Pessimistically capable	111,284	95.2%	95.6%
All egress resolvers	116,851	100%	100%

We also note that many resolvers support EDNS0 extended payload [6], which allows handling of oversized messages over UDP and thus reduces the need for TCP. Interestingly, we find that TCP-fallback incapable resolvers are *more* likely to support EDNS0 than their TCP-fallback capable counterparts. From our ADNS logs, 65,501 (56.0%) of all the egress resolvers support EDNS0, while 2037 (64.1%) of optimistically classified, and 3633 (65.3%) of pessimistically classified TCP-fallback incapable resolvers support EDNS0. We note, however, that EDNS0 and DNS-over-TCP are not interchangeable because in EDNS0 the server must agree to the payload size the client advertises and very large messages may still exceed it, and because DNS-over-TCP mitigates amplification attacks while EDNS0 exacerbates them. In any case, TCP support is mandatory per RFC 7766 [8], so egress resolvers that support EDNS0 but not TCP are still in violation of the specification.

We consider the significance of the TCP-fallback incapable egress resolvers, that is, how actively they are used in practice. To this end, we turn to the DNS Logs of a Major CDN dataset to assess how many DNS queries the egress resolvers drive. 2.7%–4.8% of egress resolvers that are TCP-fallback incapable contribute 1.1% to 4.4% of all queries arriving at the CDN from the resolvers we study. Thus, TCP-incapable egress resolvers are roughly as active as their TCP-fallback capable counterparts.

Enterprise-Centric View. Out of the 999,546[7] domains in the Majestic Top Million "Root Domains List" used in our Enterprise Resolvers Scan, we were able to receive DNS queries from resolvers serving 192164 domains, or 19.2%. The rest either refused our SMTP connection or responded with an error within the SMTP interaction, without ever sending our ADNS a DNS query. In this section, we classify the domains based upon the TCP-fallback capability of the DNS resolvers used by the enterprises that own those domains – which we again stress could be operated or administered by the enterprises themselves or third-party DNS service providers. Note that the relationship of domains to resolvers may be many-to-many: we observe both (*i*) domains served by several resolvers, with or without TCP-fallback capability (see below for the techniques we use to detect these cases), and (*ii*) cases where a resolver serves multiple domains. Moreover, the same resolver may successfully fallback to TCP when conducting a resolution on behalf of one domain, yet fail to fallback for another domain.

---

[7] We missed 454 domains due to an issue with retrieving the full list from Majestic's website.

One way we detect that a domain uses multiple resolvers is when the domain's ADNS contains multiple MX records, and our scanner tries several of the listed mail servers searching for one that would accept our email. Some mail servers trigger DNS queries even if they don't accept our email, and we observe these queries coming from different egress resolvers. However, as reported in Sect. 4.3, some DNS interactions involve complex resolution patterns, and we also find that a single attempt at an email to a domain may trigger repeated DNS queries from this domain, sometimes from different egress resolvers. This provides us with another, incidental, way to observe a domain that uses multiple resolvers. Of all the measurable domains, we detected 103,549 (53.9%) domains use multiple recursive resolvers.

We break down the measurable 192,164 domains into the following categories according to the resolvers that serve them, again using our pessimistic and optimistic classification, respectively:

- 190,045–191,371 (98.9%–99.6%) domains use only resolvers classified as TCP-fallback capable in the enterprise dataset, and we observe at least one successful TCP fallback in the email scan of each of these domains. This means that the clients of the enterprises responsible for these domains are unlikely to be negatively impacted by an ADNS-triggered TCP fallback.
- 1028–479 (0.5%–0.3%) domains are served by both TCP-fallback capable and incapable resolvers, and we still observe at least one successful TCP fallback when scanning these domains.
- 937–937 (0.5%–0.1%) domains were not observed to use any TCP-fallback capable resolvers, yet we observe at least one successful TCP fallback when scanning each of these domains. Note that this is possible, since a resolver classified as TCP-fallback incapable may still fallback for some queries (<70%).
- 152 (0.1%) domains do not use any TCP-fallback capable resolvers, and we observed no TCP queries from our email scans of the corresponding domains.
- 2 (0.00%) domains are served by at least one TCP-fallback capable resolver (i.e., the resolver performed fallback for *some* websites), yet no TCP queries were observed when scanning the corresponding domains.

Overall, compared to our resolver-centric results, enterprises are more prepared for unilateral TCP fallback enforced by ADNS, with 98.9%–99.6% of the domains using exclusively TCP-fallback capable resolvers and only 154 domains served by resolvers that did not send any TCP queries during our scan.

5 DNS-over-TCP Support by Authoritative DNS Servers

We now turn to the other side of DNS interactions and consider DNS-over-TCP support by ADNS. Failure to support DNS-over-TCP is a violation of RFC 7766 [8], so in this section we examine whether ADNS in the wild accept unsolicited TCP connections and respond to the DNS queries sent over those connections. To this end, we consider three sets of domain names: (*i*) 10.6 million domains queried in a week through a resolution service operated by the major CDN ("All

Domains"), measured on January 3 and 4, 2022, and (*ii*) popular websites as represented by the Majestic top-1K "root domains" ("Popular Websites"), measured on January 5, 2022 and (*iii*) 47 content delivery networks, measured on January 5, 2022. whose domains we identified in a separate project ("CDNs"). For the All Domains set, we extract second-level domains (e.g., "example.com") from the QNAME in queries the resolution service receives. If the domain includes two-character labels (e.g., "co.uk") we also extract the third label (e.g., "example.co.uk") to cover country-code domains[8]. Next, and for all three sets, we discover the NS records of the ADNS serving the domain names in the sets, using publicly available recursive resolvers. Finally, we resolve – using public recursive resolvers again – the name in each NS record to A records, resulting in one or more IP addresses of the ADNS serving each domain name. We note that, in the case of large-scale ADNS operators, such as CDNs, very high-volume content providers, or third-party DNS service providers, this technique is likely to obtain only a small subset of the potentially large number of ADNS operated by the ADNS platform, since some providers use anycast to distribute queries among their ADNS or return different NS records to different resolvers. Still, even with this incomplete measurement, we find – as discussed below – a number of ADNS with problematic DNS-over-TCP support.

To assess the TCP support of a domain name, we send a TCP query to each ADNS serving the domain name. An ADNS supports TCP if it both accepts the TCP connection and responds to the DNS query, both within a 2 s timeout. We note that a TCP query may fail either because the ADNS does not support DNS-over-TCP or because the ADNS is offline. While accepting a TCP connection is sufficient to determine that the ADNS is online, a time out at this step may simply indicate the ADNS is offline. In this case, we send 5 UDP queries with a 0.5 s interval between each, to check the ADNS status. If the ADNS successfully responds to any one of them, the ADNS is online and TCP-incapable, otherwise it is offline and we discard the ADNS from our experiment. Note that our experiments are measuring either the behavior of the ADNS or the middleboxes fronting the ADNS, and cannot distinguish between the two. However, that is a distinction without meaning: If an ADNS is only accessible through a middlebox that blocks DNS-over-TCP, then our analysis reflects the experience of an actual DNS client attempting, per RFC, to use TCP to communicate with this ADNS. In all, we measure DNS-over-TCP support for 445,293 ADNS servers in the All Domains, 2835 ADNS in the Popular Websites, and 224 ADNS in the CDNs sets, respectively. In addition, 22,980 ADNS servers were found to be offline in the All Domains set and thus excluded; no ADNS were offline in the Popular Websites or CDN sets.

---

[8] While this technique is not exhaustive in discovering all domains from the available QNAMEs, it serves to provide a reasonably broad list for our subsequent measurements. In hindsight, using Mozilla's public DNS suffix list at https://publicsuffix. org/wouldhavebeenbetter.

Table 3. Domains using ADNS with a given DNS-over-TCP capability.

Domain category	All domains		Popular websites		CDNs	
	Num.	%	Num.	%	Num.	%
TCP queries succeed with all ADNS	10,067,248	95.1%	954	96.5%	36	76.6%
TCP queries fail with all ADNS	280,981	2.7%	6	0.6%	10	21.3%
Mixed outcome of TCP queries	242,571	2.3%	29	2.9%	1	2.1%
All domains tested	10,590,800	100%	989	100%	47	100%

Table 3 summarizes the results of this experiment[9]. Over 5% of All Domains fail to resolve a TCP query through some of their ADNS. Among popular websites, which one would hope to be administered well, still around 3% exhibit failures to resolve the website over TCP from at least some of their ADNS. Surprisingly, CDNs are even more likely to fail: 10 of the 47 CDNs studied do not support DNS-over-TCP at all, at least by the ADNS probed. See Appendix B for the tested CDN list and individual CDN results. We conclude that egress resolvers choosing to switch to TCP as their transport medium will encounter a non-negligible amount of resolution failures as a result.

6   Race Condition in DNS-over-TCP Connection Reuse

The RFC standards [8,28] recommend that a client and server keep TCP connections open to amortize the cost of the TCP handshake over multiple DNS resolutions. These standards further recommend letting clients initialize the closing process, but both parties are free to close the connection at will, after either a timeout or the completion of a DNS resolution.

Our ADNS supports TCP connection reuse, using the following policy: (1) A new TCP connection times out if no query arrives on this connection for two seconds, and (2) A TCP connection used by some queries times out after being idle for five seconds. The timeout values are shorter than the defaults of some mainstream DNS server implementations such as BIND9 due to the high traffic in our experiments but still in compliance with the recommended settings of RFC 7766 ("it is RECOMMENDED that the default server application-level idle period be on the order of seconds") [8].

A number of egress resolvers observed across our scans in Sect. 4.1 are shared among multiple ingress resolvers or different enterprise domains. When we happen to scan these resolvers in close time proximity, we observe them reusing their TCP connections to our ADNS. Of the 114909 resolvers that used TCP for some of their queries to our ADNS, we observed 3653 to reuse a TCP connection, with the longest connection lasting over 24 h. Furthermore, these connection-reusing resolvers are very active, accounting for 37.5% of all the queries from the resolvers we discovered in the major CDN's DNS logs. In fact, by deliberately grouping email probes close in time for the enterprises that share egress

---

[9] The table includes only 989 of the 1K popular websites because eleven of these domains either provide no NS records, the name servers listed fail to resolve to IP addresses, or none of the IP addresses responded to TCP or UDP queries.

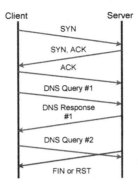

Fig. 9. An example of a race condition, where the client is attempting to reuse an established connection that the server is closing.

resolvers, we were able to induce more connection reuse and observe 13.5% of enterprise resolvers (3135 out of 23197 that established TCP connections to our ADNS) reuse their connections. Clearly, TCP connection reuse is deployed in production on resolvers that are responsible for a significant part of the Internet DNS activity.

As a worrisome observation, we found incidents of a race between a connection reuse attempt from the egress resolver and a connection closing by our ADNS. Significantly, this race condition is not an artifact of a bug in an implementation but is a behavior allowed by the protocol specification. Consider the scenario in Fig. 9, where the client would like to reuse the connection, and the server decides to close the connection while the second query from the client is in flight. In this scenario, the second query arrives at the closing server, in which case the server is either unable to receive the query from the socket, or unable to send the response back, depending upon implementation. In either case, the second query will be unanswered, and the client must retry, adding delay.

While this edge case can occur both when the server times out on an idle connection and when the server does not support connection reuse at all and closes the connection immediately after returning a DNS response, the latter is especially problematic as it makes the race condition more likely. Indeed, with connections closed after idling, a busy resolver interacting with a popular website may never experience long enough idle time for the connection to close, and the race described here would not arise. At the same time, the immediate unilateral closing of the connection by ADNS will have a high chance to coincide with the next client query, triggering the race.

Furthermore, one incident of this edge case may impact more than one query, particularly since TCP, as a streaming protocol, can transmit multiple DNS queries back-to-back, even within a single segment. Also, in the extreme case, a query retried after encountering the race condition might be sent over another active TCP connection to the ADNS – in fact, this may not be uncommon for busy public resolvers and ADNSs serving large or multiple zones (such as those for CDNs). When the ADNS does not support connection reuse, this would lead to repeated failed resolution attempts.

Table 4. TCP connection reuse by popular websites.

Category	Number	%
All established TCP connections can be reused	662	67.3%
None of the established TCP connections can be reused	258	26.2%
Mixed outcome of connection reuse	63	6.4%
All websites that established some TCP connections	983	100%

In order to investigate the prevalence of immediate closing by ADNS, we consider handling of TCP connections by ADNS of (*i*) popular websites and (*ii*) a number of CDNs, since their behavior affects all content providers that subscribe to their service. We focus on ADNS that are likely to be busy in this experiment because, as discussed above, they are more prone to trigger the race.

To assess this behavior, our Popular Websites and CDNs scans described in Sect. 5 actually include two TCP queries over each connection, with the second query sent one second after receiving the response to the first. In accordance with the recommendation of RFC 7766, we expect connection reuse without explicitly including the EDNS0 edns-tcp-keepalive option (see Sect. 6.1).

Popular Websites. Among the 2835 name servers serving the popular websites, 53 servers do not accept TCP connections or fail to respond to the first DNS query in a TCP connection – violating the DNS protocol. Of the remaining servers, only 1861 (66.9%) were observed to respond to the second query at least once. Table 4 breaks down the websites according to their connection reuse behavior. The take-away point is that a third of ADNS servers close their TCP connections immediately after sending a response, and a third of top-1K websites are affected by this behavior as at least some of their ADNS are in this category.

This result shows that roughly a third of popular websites use name servers that leave them highly exposed to the race condition, as some of their name servers do not support connection reuse. Thus, DNS-over-TCP performance for these websites may suffer.

Content Delivery Networks. Turning to the ADNS serving content delivery networks, the results are quite different. Out of 37 CDNs that support DNS-over-TCP by at least some of their ADNS, 33 always support TCP connection reuse, while only two-thirds of the popular websites do. However, two out of four CDN providers that do not support TCP connection reuse are two major CDNs, which we label CDN1 and CDN2. In fact, based on their name servers we probed, these two CDNs behaved abnormally – albeit differently – in response to the resolver's attempt to reuse a connection. Neither explicitly closed the connection between servicing the first query and the second. CDN1 did ACK the second query, but then immediately initiated TCP connection closing. CDN2 ACK'ed the second query as well, but did not send a DNS response before our scanner timed out and initiated closing of the connection[10].

---

[10] We contacted both CDN1 and CDN2 about our findings. CDN1 acknowledged the bug, and CDN2 did not respond.

Overall, we observe that resolvers often follow RFC recommendations and attempt to reuse a TCP connection for DNS-over-TCP queries. At the same time, popular websites commonly close the connections immediately, and some major CDNs, serving large portions of Web traffic, mishandle connection reuse. Either case is problematic: immediate close can lead to a race condition and possible performance degradation, and mishandling leads to a deterministic failure of queries that reuse existing connections and a potentially significant disruption in the DNS resolution process.

6.1 Deployment of edns-tcp-keepalive

RFC 7828 [38] allows clients and servers to negotiate the idle timeout of the current TCP connection through an EDNS0 edns-tcp-keepalive option. The client signals its desired TCP connection keepalive time to the server. Upon receipt, the server can determine the value it wishes to use – either accepting the client's value, modifying it, or rejecting the persistent connection – and return its decision to the client. Support for this EDNS0 option can mitigate the TCP race condition discussed above, especially if the server maintains the connection slightly longer than as negotiated.

RFC 7828 is already supported by some widely deployed DNS software, including BIND9. We assess the adoption of this mechanism by popular websites. To this end, we rescan the authoritative servers of Majestic top-1K websites and the 47 CDNs, including the edns-tcp-keepalive option in the first query to each ADNS. The second query is still sent 1 s after receiving the response to the first, and we set the keepalive to 2 s to be significantly larger than our actual interval.

Unfortunately, we find support for the edns-tcp-keepalive option to be sparse. Only 263 ADNS, serving 140 top-1K websites, negotiate the edns-tcp-keepalive option with our scanner by appending their corresponding options in DNS responses. 244 (92.8%) out of 263 of these ADNS set this value to 30 s, which is the default option value in BIND9, as well as the default waiting time before it timeouts an idle TCP connection. Further, none of the CDN we study support edns-tcp-keepalive, at least judged by the ADNS we probed. In addition, we find that 36 ADNS servers in Popular Websites set the edns-tcp-keepalive option in their responses but close the connection before the specified keepalive value, resulting in a failed second query. This is obviously a non-compliant behavior.

We note that RFC 7828 does not address the situation where a resolver explicitly requests a keepalive in its first query, the ADNS refuses, but before the resolver receives the response with the refusal, another query arrives at the resolver. An opportunistic resolver may pipeline the second query through the current connection, and it will be left unanswered.

6.2 Addressing the Connection Reuse/Closing Race

We showed a high potential for the race between TCP connection reuse and closing: many resolvers attempt to reuse a connection when it is available and many ADNSs close their connections right after sending a response. As long as DNS interactions over TCP are rare, the few TCP queries that do occur are unlikely to encounter another connection for reuse, and the above race will be rarer still. Indeed, on a 5-min packet trace of TCP queries at one of the ADNS servers at the major CDN, resolvers reused only 19 of the 15436 observed TCP connections. Still, we believe this issue needs to be addressed at the protocol level, before it can inflict practical harm, in the case the current activities within the DNS community do lead to a shift towards connection-oriented DNS communication. We stress that this issue extends beyond DNS-over-TCP, as DNS-over-TLS [14] and DNS-over-QUIC [15] explicitly inherit connection reuse policies from DNS-over-TCP. We believe the following simple modifications to these policies would remove a possibility for the race.

- A resolver *must* not reuse a TCP connection unless an explicit ends-tcp-keepalive negotiation has been completed, so that resolver would know for how long the ADNS will maintain the connection.
- Similar to timed wait in TCP, An ADNS *must* retain an active connection for 2MSL (maximum segment lifetimes) beyond the negotiated keepalive duration. At the same time, the resolver *must not* reuse a connection beyond the negotiated keepalive duration.
- As an optional optimization (a further study would be needed to decide if this is worth the complications), a resolver may indicate its support for TCP connection reuse in an EDNS0 option with its initial UDP query. An ADNS that supports persistent connections may then indicate a default keepalive value with its UDP TC response to such a query, allowing the client to immediately learn the possibility of reusing the fallback connection. The client, in the TCP fallback, can choose any keepalive value that does not exceed the indicated default. The ADNS *must* accept this value during the TCP interaction.

7   Ethical Considerations

We realize our scans may be confused for malicious activity by some scanned networks, or be otherwise unwanted. We employ the following measures (representing to the best of our knowledge the best practices developed by the measurement community) to minimize the affect to the Internet.

- We randomly shuffle the targets of our open resolver scan to avoid high probing rates for a given network and triggering alerts for address scanning.
- We encode our contact information in the query strings used in our open resolver measurement. The strings are formatted according to the following pattern: "[keyword]-[target-IP]-email-[email-addr].our.zone".
- All the scanner machines we used in this paper have publicly accessible reverse DNS records, and the organizations of these machines can be looked up in WHOIS database by their IP addresses.
- We embed the same message in the email sent in our enterprise resolver measurements as well.

– We maintain an exclusion list, which includes the IP addresses and the hostnames of the organizations who previously expressed their unwillingness to join experiments. We exclude these IP addresses and hostnames from subsequent measurements.

We received 14 complaints and inquiries (including one notification from a public shared spam reporting service) from our enterprise email scans. We responded to all of them quickly and excluded from our future experiments those who expressed their unwillingness to participate. We did not receive any complaints from our open resolver and RIPE Atlas scan.

8   Conclusion

In this paper, we assess the support of DNS-over-TCP, which has generated significant interest due to its more secure nature. On the one hand, while we find significantly higher support for TCP fallback by recursive resolvers than prior studies, there is still a number of resolvers that are not capable of TCP fallback. In particular, we assess 116,851 egress resolvers, responsible for 66.2% of all queries to a major CDN's ADNS platform, and find that 2.7%–4.8% of them, contributing 1.1% to 4.4% of all queries from the resolvers we measured, were unable to perform a TCP fallback when instructed by an ADNS. Thus, ADNS operators deciding to force DNS-over-TCP usage via TCP fallback face the risk of cutting off a non-negligible amount of their potential users.

On the other hand, we find a number of authoritative name servers, including those serving some popular websites and several content delivery networks, to not accept DNS queries over TCP. Indeed, around 3% of popular websites, and over 5% of domains at large, are served by at least some ADNS failing to answer queries over TCP, while 9 out of 47 CDNs we consider also exhibit this behavior. Thus, a resolver operator choosing to switch to DNS-over-TCP today would essentially make its users unable to reliably access these domains as well as all content delivered by these CDNs.

Further, we uncover a race condition that may occur in DNS-over-TCP and find that 32.4% of authoritative DNS servers serving Majestic top-1K popular websites are vulnerable to this condition. Finally, we observe abnormal behavior by two major CDNs in their DNS-over-TCP support.

We hope our findings will inform DNS operators who consider possible adoption of DNS-over-TCP and help improve DNS-over-TCP support of the platforms that have already adopted it.

Acknowledgement. We thank the anonymous reviewers, and especially our shepherd, Alessio Botta, for useful comments and guidance. We are indebted to CWRU IT organization ("UTech") for its continued support, without which this research would not be possible. The work of Jiarun Mao and Michael Rabinovich was supported in part by NSF through grant CNS-1647145.

A   Matching Algorithm

Algorithm 1. Split an array of DNS queries with a given (QNAME,QTYPE) pair into an array of clusters (as defined in Sect. 4.3). Queries that cannot be assigned to any cluster are added to a pseudo cluster.

Input: array *queries* ← all UDP and TCP queries with the given QNAME and QTYPE pair in chronological order.

Input: float max_time ← maximum delay between a UDP query and a TCP query in TCP-fallback.

Output: array of arrays *clusters* ← each inner array is a cluster of UDP/TCP queries. The last inner array is the pseudo cluster of UDP queries that cannot be assigned to any cluster. The *clusters* appear in the outer array in chronological order, i.e., the first query in a later cluster comes after the last query in an earlier cluster. The queries within a cluster are also in chronological order.

1: **procedure** SPLITINTOCLUSTERS(*queries*, *max_time*)
2:     *clusters* ← empty array
3:     *pseudo_cluster* ← empty array
4:     *cluster* ← empty array
5:     **for** each TCP query q_{tcp} in *queries* in chronological order **do**
6:         qs_{udp} ← UDP queries in *queries* within max_time before q_{tcp}
7:         **if** $(qs_{udp} \cap cluster) = \emptyset$ and $cluster \neq \emptyset$ **then**   ▷ cluster boundary
8:             append *cluster* to *clusters*
9:             *cluster* ← empty array
10:         append each query q in qs_{udp} to *cluster* unless q is already in *cluster*
11:         append q_{tcp} to *cluster*
12:     **if** *cluster* is not empty **then**
13:         append *cluster* to *clusters*
14:     remove all queries in *clusters* from *queries*
15:     **for** each q_{udp} in *queries* **do**   ▷ All remaining queries in *queries* are UDP
16:         add q_{udp} to *pseudo_cluster*
17:     append *pseudo_cluster* to *clusters*
18:     return *clusters*

Algorithm 2. Label DNS queries according to whether they represent TCP-fallback successes, failures, or indeterminate cases.

Input: map m ← QNAME and QTYPE pair ("*qpair*") as **keys** and arrays of chronologically ordered queries with the corresponding *qpair* as **values**.

Input: float max_time ← maximum delay between a UDP query and a TCP query in TCP-fallback.

Output: map *labels* ← queries as **keys** and labels of success, failure, or indeterminate as **values**.

1: $labels$ ← empty map
2: **for** $qpair$, $queries$ in m **do**
3:     $clusters$ ← SPLITINTOCLUSTERS($queries$, max_time)
4:     **for** each $cluster$ in $clusters$ excluding pseudo cluster **do**
5:         $used\_qSet_{tcp}$ ← empty set
6:         $indeterminate\_qSet_{udp}$ ← empty set
7:         $pending\_qSet_{udp}$ ← empty set
8:         $pending\_count\_qs_{udp}$ ← 0
9:         $owners$ ← empty map (from UDP queries to tentatively matching TCP queries)
10:         **for** each $query$ in $cluster$ **do**
11:             **if** $query$ is a UDP query **then**   ▷ **else** statement in line 36
12:                 $first\_q_{tcp}$ ← the first TCP query in $cluster$ following $query$ and not in $used\_qSet_{tcp}$
13:                 **if** $first\_q_{tcp}$ is null **then**
14:                     add $query$ to $indeterminate\_qSet_{udp}$
15:                     add queries in $pending\_qSet_{udp}$ to $indeterminate\_qSet_{udp}$
16:                     $pending\_count\_qs_{udp}$ ← 0
17:                 **else**
18:                     add $first\_q_{tcp}$ to $used\_qSet_{tcp}$
19:                     $owners[query]$ ← $first\_q_{tcp}$
20:                     **if** $indeterminate\_qSet_{udp}$ is empty **then**
21:                         add $query$ to $pending\_qSet_{udp}$
22:                         $pending\_count\_qs_{udp}$ + +
23:                     **else**
24:                         $last\_q_{udp}$ ← last query in $indeterminate\_qSet_{udp}$
25:                         **if** time($first\_q_{tcp}$) − time($last\_q_{udp}$) > max_time **then**
26:                             **for** each q in $indeterminate\_qSet_{udp}$ **do**
27:                                 $labels[q]$ ← indeterminate
28:                                 remove $owners[q]$ from $cluster$
29:                                 remove q from $cluster$
30:                             clear $indeterminate\_qSet_{udp}$
31:                             $used\_qSet_{tcp}$ ← {$first\_q_{tcp}$}
32:                             $pending\_qSet_{udp}$ ← {$query$}
33:                             $pending\_count\_qs_{udp}$ ← 1
34:                         **else**
35:                             add $query$ to $indeterminate\_qSet_{udp}$
36:             **else**   ▷ **if** statement in line 11
37:                 **if** $pending\_count\_qs_{udp}$ > 0 **then**   ▷ Can be 0 if $cluster$ only has a TCP query
38:                     $pending\_count\_qs_{udp}$ − −
39:                     **if** $pending\_count\_qs_{udp}$ = 0 **then**
40:                         **for** each q in $pending\_qSet_{udp}$ **do**
41:                             $labels[q]$ ← success
42:                         clear $pending\_qSet_{udp}$
43:         **for** each q in $indeterminate\_qSet_{udp}$ **do**
44:             $labels[q]$ ← indeterminate
45:     **for** each q in pseudo Q_t cluster **do**
46:         $labels[q]$ ← failure
47: **return** $labels$

B   CDN Targets Tested

Below we list the 47 CDNs we tested in this study, which includes 17 (shown in bold font) out of 25 CDNs listed at CDN Planet (https://www.cdnplanet.com/, accessed on Jan 2, 2022). The parenthetical information lists the domain name employed and whether all, some, or none of the ADNS tested are TCP capable.

advancedhosterscdn(11799613.pix-cdn.org, all),

akamai(www.a1776.g1.akamai.net, all),

amazoncloudfront(www.d2qjncoblxi5md.cloudfront.net, all),

aryaka(hd.itrip.com.top.aads1.net, none), azion(18697b.ha.azioncdn.net, all),

belugacdn(www.cdn.famefocus.com.i.belugacdn.com, none),

bitgravity(www.pc-ap.bitgravity.com, all),

bunnycdn(www.planetedomo.b-cdn.net, some),

cachefly(www.vip1.g5.cachefly.net, none), **cdn77**(www.1650447009.rsc.cdn77.org, all),

cdnetworks(www.kisa.or.kr.cdngc.net, none),

cdnify(karnataka.a.cdnify.io, all), cdnsun(www.239827766.r.cdnsun.net, all),

cdnvideo(bfm.cdnvideo.ru, all),

cedexis(mobile.interflora.fr.fasterize.it.2-01-295f-000e.cdx.cedexis.net, all),

chinacache(hpcc-page.cncssr.chinacache.net, all),

chinanetcenter(www.v4q3iig12pcnka.wscloudcdn.com, none),

cloudflare(www.upra.org.cdn.cloudflare.net, all), cubecdn(mr.sp.cubecdn.net, all),

edgecast(www.cs109.adn.edgecastcdn.net, all),

facebook(scontent.xx.fbcdn.net, all), **fastly**(www.prod.seamless.map.fastlylb.net, all),

google(www.g0e1hw.feedproxy.ghs.google.com, all),

highwinds(www.cds.v2f8x7x9.hwcdn.net, all),

incapsula(www.hs2rptk.x.incapdns.net, all),

internap(www.6a2809e8d5.site.internapcdn.net, none),

keycdn(p-frpa00-v4.kxcdn.com, all),

leasewebcdn(www.5ad9c8cb35308834bf7d93d4e09de97e.lswcdn.net, all),

level3(www.vc.sporttube.com.c.footprint.net, none),

limelight(ualsharp.vo.llnwd.net, none),

maxcdn(www.creative-watch-new-pull.4ncfzftyhcv4rwo.netdna-cdn.com, all),

medianova(img-cimri.mncdn.com, none),

netlify(www.campusmanagement.netlify.com, all),

ngenix(www.cntraveller-st.cdn.ngenix.net, all),

nyiftw(www.nyi.nyiftw.net, all), onapp(316150366.r.worldcdn.net, all),

optimalcdn(www.cdn.optimalcdn.com, all),

quantil(www.oversea.dtwscache.speedcdns.com, none),

reflectednetworks(www.e-static.pornmd.com.sds.rncdn7.com, all),

rocketcdn(www.mediacdn.karnaval.com.streamprovider.net, all),

singularcdn(h2.singularcdn.net.br, all),

stackpath(www.adoramapix-8u9vvrwnlphhiqnu.stackpathdns.com, all),

swiftcdn(secure.aims.jns.swiftserve.com, all),

unicorncdn(xc3uk5s3rf.unicorncdn.net, all), wordpress(www.2.gravatar.com, all),

yottaa(www.a19af6306e7c013695900a3ba3fac80a.yottaa.net, all),

zenedge(104-225-137-39-tls12.zenedge.net, all)

References

1. https://osf.io/6ysxv/
2. Al-Dalky, R., Rabinovich, M., Schomp, K.: A look at the ECS behavior of DNS resolvers. In: Proceedings of the ACM Internet Measurement Conference, pp. 116–129 (2019)
3. Al-Dalky, R., Schomp, K.: Characterization of collaborative resolution in recursive DNS resolvers. In: Beverly, R., Smaragdakis, G., Feldmann, A. (eds.) PAM 2018. LNCS, vol. 10771, pp. 146–157. Springer, Cham (2018). https://doi.org/10.1007/978-3-319-76481-8_11
4. Barnes, R., Hoffman-Andrews, J., Kasten, J.: RFC 8555: automatic certificate management environment (ACME) (2019)
5. Böttger, T., et al.: An empirical study of the cost of DNS-over-HTTPS. In: Proceedings of the ACM Internet Measurement Conference, pp. 15–21 (2019)
6. Damas, J., Graff, M., Vixie, P.A.: RFC6891: extension mechanisms for DNS (EDNS0) (2013)
7. Deccio, C., Davis, J.: DNS privacy in practice and preparation. In: Proceedings of the 15th International Conference on Emerging Networking Experiments And Technologies (CoNEXT), pp. 138–143 (2019)
8. Dickinson, J., Dickinson, S., Bellis, R., Mankin, A., Wessels, D.: RFC 7766: DNS transport over TCP-implementation requirements (2016)
9. DNS-OARC. https://www.dns-oarc.net/oarc/data/ditl (2018)
10. Eastlake, D.: RFC 2535: domain name system security extensions (1999)
11. Hansen, T., Crocker, D., Hallam-Baker, P.: RFC 5585: DomainKeys identified mail (DKIM) service overview (2009)
12. Hoffman, P., McManus, P.: RFC 8484: DNS queries over HTTPS (DoH) (2018)
13. Hoffman, P., Schlyter, J.: RFC6698: The DNS-based authentication of named entities. (DANE) transport layer security (TLS) protocol: TLSA (2012)
14. Hu, Z., Zhu, L., Heidemann, J., Mankin, A., Wessels, D., Hoffman, P.: RFC 7858: specification for DNS over transport layer security (TLS) (2016)
15. Huitema, C., Shore, M., Mankin, A., Dickinson, S., Iyengar, J.: Specification of DNS over dedicated QUIC connections. Internet-draft draft-huitema-quicdnsoquic-07. Work in Progress
16. Huston, G.: https://labs.ripe.net/Members/gih/a-question-of-dns-protocols, August 2013 (2013)
17. Kitterman, S.: RFC 7208: Sender policy framework (SPF) for authorizing use of domains in email (2014)
18. Klein, A., Shulman, H., Waidner, M.: Internet-wide study of DNS cache injections. In: IEEE INFOCOM, pp. 1–9. IEEE (2017)
19. Klensin, J.: RFC 2821: simple mail transfer protocol (2001)
20. Klensin, J.: RFC 5321: simple mail transfer protocol (2008)
21. Kührer, M., Hupperich, T., Bushart, J., Rossow, C., Holz, T.: Going wild: large-scale classification of open DNS resolvers. In: Proceedings of the ACM Internet Measurement Conference (2015)
22. Kührer, M., Hupperich, T., Rossow, C., Holz, T.: Exit from hell? Reducing the impact of amplification DDoS attacks. In: 23rd {USENIX} Security Symposium ({USENIX} Security 14), pp. 111–125 (2014)
23. Lian, W., Rescorla, E., Shacham, H., Savage, S.: Measuring the practical impact of DNSSEC deployment. In: 22nd USENIX Security Symposium, pp. 573–588 (2013)

24. Lu, C., et al.: An end-to-end, large-scale measurement of DNS-over-encryption: how far have we come? In: Proceedings of the ACM Internet Measurement Conference, pp. 22–35 (2019)
25. MacFarland, D.C., Shue, C.A., Kalafut, A.J.: Characterizing optimal DNS amplification attacks and effective mitigation. In: Mirkovic, J., Liu, Y. (eds.) PAM 2015. LNCS, vol. 8995, pp. 15–27. Springer, Cham (2015). https://doi.org/10.1007/978-3-319-15509-8_2
26. Majestic Top Million Root Domains List. https://majestic.com/reports/majestic-million (2021)
27. Mockapetris, P.: RFC 883: domain names - implementation and specification (1983)
28. Mockapetris, P.V.: RFC 1035: domain names-implementation and specification (1987)
29. Moura, G.C.M., Müller, M., Davids, M., Wullink, M., Hesselman, C.: Fragmentation, truncation, and timeouts: are large DNS messages falling to bits? In: Hohlfeld, O., Lutu, A., Levin, D. (eds.) PAM 2021. LNCS, vol. 12671, pp. 460–477. Springer, Cham (2021). https://doi.org/10.1007/978-3-030-72582-2_27
30. Randall, A., et al.: Trufflehunter: cache snooping rare domains at large public DNS resolvers. In: Proceedings of the ACM Internet Measurement Conference, pp. 50–64 (2020)
31. van Rijswijk-Deij, R., Sperotto, A., Pras, A.: DNSSEC and its potential for DDoS attacks: a comprehensive measurement study. In: Proceedings of the ACM Internet Measurement Conference, pp. 449–460 (2014)
32. RIPE: Atlas. https://atlas.ripe.net/ (2021)
33. Schomp, K., Callahan, T., Rabinovich, M., Allman, M.: On measuring the client-side DNS infrastructure. In: Proceedings of the ACM Internet Measurement Conference, pp. 77–90. ACM (2013)
34. Shulman, H., Waidner, M.: Is the internet ready for DNSSEC: evaluating pitfalls in the naming infrastructure. In: International Workshop on Traffic Monitoring and Analysis (TMA) (2016)
35. The Shadowserver Foundation. https://scan.shadowserver.org/dns/ (2020)
36. Vixie, P.: RFC 2671: extension mechanisms for DNS (EDNS0) (1999)
37. Vixie, P., Schryver, V.: DNS response rate limiting (DNS RRL). http://ss.vix.su/~vixie/isc-tn-2012-1.txt (2012)
38. Wouters, P., Abley, J., Dickinson, S., Bellis, R.: RFC 7828: The edns-tcp-keepalive EDNS0 option (2016)
39. Zhu, L., Hu, Z., Heidemann, J., Wessels, D., Mankin, A., Somaiya, N.: Connection-oriented DNS to improve privacy and security. In: 2015 IEEE Symposium on Security and Privacy, pp. 171–186. IEEE (2015)

Measuring the Accessibility of Domain Name Encryption and Its Impact on Internet Filtering

Nguyen Phong Hoang[1]([✉]), Michalis Polychronakis[2], and Phillipa Gill[3]

[1] University of Chicago, Chicago, USA
nguyenphong@uchicago.edu
[2] Stony Brook University, Stony Brook, USA
mikepo@cs.stonybrook.edu
[3] Google Inc., Amherst, USA

Abstract. Most online communications rely on DNS to map domain names to their hosting IP address(es). Previous work has shown that DNS-based network interference is widespread due to the unencrypted and unauthenticated nature of the original DNS protocol. In addition to DNS, accessed domain names can also be monitored by on-path observers during the TLS handshake when the SNI extension is used. These lingering issues with exposed plaintext domain names have led to the development of a new generation of protocols that keep accessed domain names hidden. DNS-over-TLS (DoT) and DNS-over-HTTPS (DoH) hide the domain names of DNS queries, while Encrypted Server Name Indication (ESNI) encrypts the domain name in the SNI extension.

We present *DNEye*, a measurement system built on top of a network of distributed vantage points, which we used to study the accessibility of DoT/DoH and ESNI, and to investigate whether these protocols are tampered with by network providers (e.g., for censorship). Moreover, we evaluate the efficacy of these protocols in circumventing network interference when accessing content blocked by traditional DNS manipulation. We find evidence of blocking efforts against domain name encryption technologies in several countries, including China, Russia, and Saudi Arabia. At the same time, we discover that domain name encryption can help with unblocking more than 55% and 95% of censored domains in China and other countries where DNS-based filtering is heavily employed.

Keywords: DNS · DoTH · ESNI · Domain-based network interference

1 Introduction

Despite its importance, the domain name system (DNS) [41] was not designed with encryption or authentication. Traditional DNS resolutions are transmitted in plaintext, allowing network-level adversaries to easily eavesdrop or tamper with the resolution process [29,43,48], jeopardizing user privacy and security.

Additionally, the domain name information is also visible in the Transport Layer Security (TLS) protocol [47]. During the TLS handshake, the client specifies the domain name in the Server Name Indication (SNI) in plaintext [17], signaling a server that hosts multiple domain names (name-based virtual hosting) to present the correct TLS certificate to the client. However, network observers can also use this information to surveil or interfere with a user's connection.

With the proliferation of network interference and Internet surveillance [25], users have become more aware of their online security and privacy. This has led to DNS and TLS improvements for enhancing user privacy. DNS-over-TLS (DoT) [32], DNS-over-HTTPS (DoH) [31], and Encrypted Server Name Indication (ESNI) [23] are recently proposed privacy-enhancing protocols, to which we refer collectively as domain name encryption technologies.

However, advances in domain name encryption technologies have not gone unnoticed to censors. For instance, China has been blocking ESNI since July 2020 [36]. Russia has also drafted laws to ban the adoption of domain name encryption [12]. Despite these reports, there has yet to be a comprehensive study to shed light on how common blocking of domain name encryption is; and whether domain name encryption approaches can help with evading network interference.

In this paper, we present *DNEye*, a measurement system built on top of a network of vantage points, allowing us to study the accessibility of domain name encryption technologies and whether censors are interfering with them, and to evaluate their efficacy in bypassing network interference. Over a period of six months, *DNEye* conducted 315K measurements to examine the accessibility of 1.6K domains and DoT/DoH (hereafter: DoTH) resolvers around the globe.

While our data shows that DNS manipulation is widespread, we found no major DNS-based filtering of DoTH resolvers' domain names at the autonomous system (AS) level, except for *ordns.he.net*, which is blocked by the Great Firewall via DNS poisoning, and two Cloudflare servers (*cloudflare-dns.com* and *mozilla.cloudflare-dns.com*) blocked in Thailand's AS23969. We then examine whether connections destined for DoTH resolvers suffer from any interference (Sect. 4.2). We detect several ASes in China interfere with connections destined for different DoTH resolvers. We also found only 1.5–2.25% of the domains in the top-level domain (TLD) zone files with ESNI supported. Despite this small number of ESNI-supported domains, we find evidence that China and numerous network operators in Russia have started blocking connections to ESNI-enabled websites (Sect. 4.2).

Finally, we investigated whether domain name encryption can help with bypassing Internet filtering (Sect. 4.3), and found that it can help with unblocking many censored domains. Specifically, except from Iran, we could successfully fetch more than 55% and 95% of the blocked domains in China and other countries where DNS-based network filtering is widely employed.

2   Background

2.1   Common Internet Filtering Techniques

There are several Internet filtering techniques often employed by authoritarian governments to control the free flow of information.

DNS Manipulation. Due to the unencrypted design of the original DNS protocol [41], any on-path network observer can monitor the domain name being queried by a user. The visibility into the plaintext domain name allows any on-path filtering system to trivially conduct DNS-based filtering. Specifically, an on-path observer can forge DNS responses containing non-routable IPs, an IP under its control, or a DNS error code. China's Great Firewall (GFW) is one of the most prominent filtering systems that injects such forged DNS packets in response to "sensitive" DNS queries [8,29,43].

IP Blocking. Once a user obtains the correct IP(s) of the intended website, a TCP connection is established with the web server for data transmission. Upon observing a connection attempt to a forbidden IP, filtering systems often inject RST (reset) packets to interfere with the TCP stream [11,46,54]. In other cases, null routing [53] can also be used to discard traffic destined for certain IPs.

Application-Level Interference. After establishing the TCP connection, the user proceeds with sending an HTTP request with the HTTP Host field specifying the intended domain name. Similarly, for HTTPS-supported websites, clients specify the intended domain name in the SNI field of the TLS handshake [17]. Filtering systems can also monitor these fields to determine the domain name being visited to interfere with the connection, either by injecting RST packets or modifying the HTTP traffic to redirect the user to a blockpage [35,42,46,52].

2.2   Domain Name Encryption Protocols

As discussed in Sect. 2.1, the exposure of the domain information in both DNS and TLS protocols has been widely exploited for network interference [13,29,46, 48].

Encrypted DNS. DoT [32] and DoH [31] were proposed to provide integrity and confidentiality for DNS resolutions by encrypting DNS packets between clients and DoTH resolvers. These protocols have been standardized and supported by many major Internet companies. Google [26] and Cloudflare [5] have provided public DoTH resolvers, while popular web browsers (e.g., Firefox [39], Chrome [9], Safari [14], and Edge [15]) have also supported DoH.

Encrypted SNI. The SNI extension [47] was introduced to enable name-based virtual hosting. Up until TLS 1.2 [17], clients indicate their intended domain name in the SNI field during the TLS handshake in plaintext so that the server can present the appropriate certificate. Encrypted SNI is one of the optional extensions of TLS 1.3 designed to conceal the domain name information [21]. ESNI has been reworked to Encrypted Client Hello (ECH) [22] since June 2020.

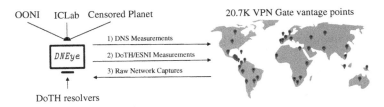

Fig. 1. *DNEye* architecture.

3   *DNEye* Design

Given that the visibility into plaintext domain information is lost due to the introduction of domain name encryption, we are interested in investigating how these new protocols impact Internet filtering systems. We developed *DNEye* to (1) assess the current situation of DNS-based network filtering, (2) examine the accessibility of domain name encryption protocols and whether they are interfered with across different network locations, and (3) evaluate whether these protocols can help with evading network interference. In this section, we first describe how we obtain testing vantage points, their limitations, and ethical considerations. We then explain the process by which we curate our test list of domains and how we use *DNEye* to perform various connectivity measurements. Figure 1 provides an overall view of *DNEye*'s architecture.

3.1   Vantage Points

Vantage Points. The core component of *DNEye* is a network of vantage points (VPs) provided by VPN Gate [45]. VPN Gate is a public VPN relay service where any volunteer can register to be a VPN endpoint by running the SoftEther package [44]. Since these VPs are operated by volunteers around the globe, they often reside in residential networks, allowing us to observe filtering policies which would be usually unobservable via commercial VPNs in data centers [46]. However, since the infrastructure is volunteer-based, these VPs are often short-lived and unsuitable for testing a long list of websites. We describe how we account for this shortcoming by conducting a sliding-window analysis in Sect. 4.1.

Table 1 summarizes the geographical distribution of our VPs by continent and Internet freedom scores assessed by the Freedom House [1]. During six months of our study, VPN Gate VPs provide us with access to 34K unique IPs. We however exclude 13.3K short-lived VPs that were online for less than one day to eliminate unstable data points. In total, *DNEye* has access to about 20.7K VPs in 85 countries, with an average of 10 ASes per country. More importantly, we have access to more than twice the number of countries classified as "not free" than ICLab [42], which is a platform that also relies on VPN services for measuring network interference. Of these "not free" countries, there are 11 countries where we have access to VPs located in at least two different ASes, allowing us to observe centralized country-level filtering policies (if any).

Table 1. Geographical distribution of *DNEye*'s VPN vantage points indicated by the number of countries and ASes across continents. NF, PF, and F columns denote the number of *politically not free, partially free,* and *free* countries.

Continent	Vantages	Countries	ASes	NF	PF	F
Asia	14K	32/48	367	17	8	6
Africa	13	4/54	9	2	0	2
N. America	2.7K	6/23	157	0	1	3
S. America	811	9/14	58	1	4	4
Europe	2.8K	32/50	271	2	3	27
Oceania	282	2/6	16	0	0	2
Total	20.7K	85/195	878	22	16	44

Ethical Considerations. Measuring Internet interference using volunteer-based VPs must be carried out in a thoughtful way that takes into consideration various ethical aspects [34]. There are commercial services (e.g., Luminati [3]) that provide residential VPs, meeting the measurement needs of our study. Nonetheless, studies have reported illicit activities of these services, e.g., malware hosting [40]. We, thus, opt to use VPN Gate for two primary reasons. First, to become a VPN server, the SoftEther VPN package [44] requires all volunteers to manually go through a process that reminds them about the associated risks of joining the VPN Gate research network [6]. Therefore, it is reasonable to expect volunteers, who are willing to be VPN endpoints, to fully understand the potential risks before agreeing to share their network connection. Moreover, the University of Tsukuba and the VPN Gate software also record access logs which serve as an anti-abuse policy used by the project and to assist its volunteers in case of disputes [49]. Since the launch of *DNEye* we have not received any complaints.

3.2   Test List

While it is desirable to test many domains, due to the short-lived nature of VPs, we cannot test a large number of domains. OONI [24], ICLab [42], and Censored Planet [52] are measurement platforms actively monitoring Internet interference around the globe. Since these platforms have implemented testing modules to monitor DNS filtering, we opt to use their collected data as an input for *DNEye*.

We first look for domains reported as censored by these platforms within the past 30 days and visit them to confirm their online status. We consider domains that are censored in at least two ASes per country and reported by at least two platforms. This helps eliminate unreliable data points that could have been caused by generic network errors. To that end, we obtain 1.5K domains that are commonly reported as censored by these prior platforms in 77 countries where we have VPs. Since one of our main goals is to examine the accessibility of domain name encryption protocols, we also add domains for 71 DoTH resolvers publicly available at the time of our study [19]. These resolvers are indexed in Table 4.

3.3   Measurements

Once connected to a VP, we instruct *DNEye* to capture all network traffic during each measurement. Monitoring traffic transmitted over the VPN tunnel enables us to observe network interference (if any) across all layers of the network stack.

Measuring DNS Manipulation. After each VPN tunnel is established, *DNEye* first issues DNS queries for the domains in our test list. This allows us to not only obtain an updated view of DNS filtering across network locations, but also determine whether there are any filtering systems that block these DoTH resolvers via DNS tampering. *DNEye* sends DNS queries to both public DNS resolvers (e.g., Google and Cloudflare) and the local DNS resolver configured by each VP's network provider. Querying both types of resolvers helps us discern whether DNS tampering (if any) is conducted solely by the local resolver or by an on-path system between our clients and the selected public resolvers.

Measuring DoTH and ESNI Connectivity. *DNEye* then uses `kdig` [18] to send encrypted DNS queries to 71 DoTH resolvers to resolve a control domain for which we know the correct answer. This test checks whether each DoTH server returns the control domain's correct IP. The ability to capture network packets allows us to detect at which stage of a connection (i.e., TCP or TLS handshakes) a filtering system tampered with the connection destined for the selected DoTH servers. In addition, to determine whether ESNI is blocked, *DNEye* also attempts to connect to an ESNI-supported website under our control.

Measuring Filtering Circumvention. Finally, to evaluate whether domain name encryption can help evade Internet filtering, *DNEye* instruments a customized web browser with DoH and ESNI enabled to crawl filtered domains from VPs where DNS filtering of these domains was observed in the first step.

However, as later shown in Sect. 4.2, many DoTH resolvers are being blocked in several countries. To prevent any filtering system from interfering with our DoH resolutions, we configure the crawler to use our private DoH resolver, which runs on a non-standard port (i.e., different from 443) and is hosted in an uncensored network. For an ESNI-supported website, the crawler will also obtain its ESNI key and establish an ESNI-enabled TLS connection. Simultaneously, we crawl the same website from an uncensored control environment for later comparison.

Between November 12, 2020, and May 12, 2021, *DNEye* has conducted 315K connectivity measurements for 1.6K domains and DoTH resolvers in 878 ASes across 85 countries. The aggregated dataset will be made available to the public to stimulate future studies in this domain at https://homepage.np-tokumei.net/publication/publication_2022_pam/.

4   Results

4.1   DNS-Based Network Interference

To identify DNS tampering, we apply well-established heuristics in the literature on the data collected by *DNEye* (Appendix B). For each DNS query sent via a VP, we extract all DNS responses captured from that VP's network traffic. In case of a poisoned DNS response, the ability to analyze raw network packets allows us to discern whether it was injected by an on-path filtering system or directly served from the local DNS resolver. Specifically, if the tampering is conducted by an on-path filtering system when querying a public DNS resolver, we will be able to observe more than one DNS response, of which the one arrives the VP first is usually forged by the filtering system [20,29]. In case of a forged response served directly from a local resolver, we will only observe that one response.

Sliding-Window Analysis. Due to the short-lived nature of our VPs, we do not have access to all VPs on the same day. To reduce the impact of unreliable data points, we analyze the data by considering a sliding window of seven days for each measurement. In other words, for each domain tested in a measurement, we aggregate the data we have from the same VP within a window of ± 3 days. Meanwhile, we also compute the average filtering rate (i.e., the number of measurements we mark as "tampering" divided by the total measurements for each VP and domain pair). If the filtering rate of a domain at a VP is higher than 80%, we consider that domain as "blocked" at that VP in that particular measurement. We conservatively choose the 80% threshold to avoid false positives caused by generic network errors instead of network interference.

Table 2. Top five countries where most DNS resolutions are tampered with.

(a) When querying local resolvers		(b) When querying public resolvers	
Country	Domains	Country	Domains
China	305	China	300
Russia	251	Russia	205
Japan	181	Iran	147
Iran	159	Indonesia	134
Indonesia	135	India	98

Regardless of the introduction of DNS encryption protocols, our results confirm that DNS manipulation is still widely employed, aligning with prior reports [29,33,42,48,52]. Table 2 presents the top five countries where most DNS resolutions are tampered with. Japan is not a censorship country, as is evident by its *"free"* classification by the Freedom House [1]. The reason for the high number of DNS resolutions interfered by local DNS resolvers is that VPN Gate is a Japan-based project, thus providing us with a large number of VPs from many residential networks across Japan. Our collected data indicates that many of these VPs are configured with filtering services provided by local DNS resolvers. Hence, queries sent to these resolvers are often interfered with. More specifically, many DNS responses returned by these local DNS resolvers contain IPs redirecting to destinations within the same AS of the VPs where

DNS queries were issued. On the other hand, we could still obtain the correct DNS records for our DNS resolutions when querying public resolvers from these same VPs. As a result, this is not a case of country-level DNS censorship.

DNS Manipulation of DoTH Domains. As laid out in Sect. 3.3, *DNEye* also performs DNS resolutions for domain names of 71 DoTH resolvers to determine whether there is any DNS tampering against these resolvers. Except for China, we did not observe any DNS-based filtering of DoTH domain names at country level. Specifically, `ordns.he.net` is blocked in China by the GFW via DNS tampering. In addition, *DNEye* detected DNS tampering against two Cloudflare servers (*cloudflare-dns.com*, *mozilla.cloudflare-dns.com*) by AS23969 TOT Public Company Ltd, Thailand. DNS resolutions for these two domains are poisoned with a forged IP (i.e., 180.180.255.130), pointing to a blockpage.

4.2 DoTH and ESNI Accessibility

DoTH Accessibility. Since DoTH is still in its early stage of adoption while not all DoTH servers are well-provisioned, any of them may become unavailable during our measurement, e.g., due to maintenance. To determine if a resolver is unavailable due to a generic reason rather than network interference, we aggregate all daily resolutions from all VPs for that particular resolver. If more than 70% of the queries were successfully resolved, we consider that resolver as available on that day. We choose 70% as a conservative threshold to prevent intermittently available resolvers from causing false positives in our analysis.

Figure 2a and b show the percentages of correct resolutions performed daily using DoT and DoH resolvers, respectively. We consider a resolution as correct when the correct IP of our control domain is successfully returned. The result is clustered by country type defined by the Freedom House [1]. The percentages of correct resolutions obtained via VPs in *"not free"* countries are lower than those in *"partially free"* and *"free"* countries. To better highlight this finding, we add to both plots another dash-dot (purple) line, computed from data of the top five *"not free"* countries that have the most number of failed resolutions, namely China, Russia, Iran, Saudi Arabia, and Venezuela. It is visible on the plots that the number of successful resolutions for these five countries has decreased significantly since March. This decrease is driven by the blocking effort of China, where our system detected an increase in network interference with our DoTH resolutions issued from China VPs. In an earlier study, Lu et al. [38] reported successful rates of more than 84% and 99% for resolutions using Cloudflare and Quad9 DoT resolvers, respectively. However, since early March, *DNEye* has detected increasing network interference efforts by the GFW against DoT resolutions destined for several major resolvers, including Cloudflare, Quad9, AdGuard, and CleanBrowsing. Our findings corroborate several anecdotal reports from users in China about DoTH blocking around that same time [4].

DoTH Filtering. To examine how filtering systems interfere with connections destined for DoTH resolvers, we analyze packets captured by *DNEye* for measurements in which failed resolutions were observed. The ability to process raw

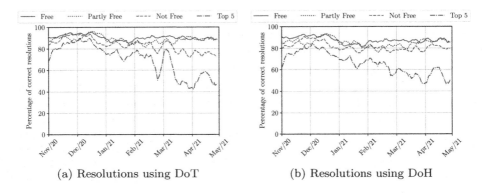

(a) Resolutions using DoT   (b) Resolutions using DoH

Fig. 2. Percentage of correct DoTH resolutions over time.

network packets allows us to pinpoint the stage at which a connection was interfered with, thus being able to identify the employed filtering technique (i.e., TCP packet injection, SNI-based filtering, or packet dropping).

We employ the same sliding-window technique defined in Sect. 4.1 to determine blocking cases of DoTH resolvers. Given a VP, an average failure rate of a DoTH resolver is calculated by dividing the number of failed resolutions by the total number of resolutions performed at that VP within a seven-day window. If the failure rate exceeds 80%, we label the DoTH resolver as "probably blocked" at that VP. To determine whether a DoTH resolver is actually blocked at a VP, we then compute the 90th percentile value of all failure rates for that DoTH resolver at that particular VP. If the value is greater than 80%, we can be confident that there is network interference with connections destined for that resolver at that VP. We employ this 90th percentile threshold in combination with the sliding-window analysis to account for failed resolutions caused by sporadically available VPs and unstable DoTH resolvers rather than actual network interference.

Next, we consider a DoTH resolver to be blocked by an AS if *DNEye* detects network interference from at least two VPs from different subnets of that AS on two separate days. Table 5 in Appendix C depicts the top countries where most AS-level DoTH filtering was detected. China has the most number of ASes that interfere with DoTH connections. The filtering of different DoTH resolvers detected at different ASes indicates that DoTH filtering is implemented by individual Internet service providers rather than a centralized policy (e.g., centralized DNS-based filtering by the GFW [29]).

Another advantage provided by the VPN Gate VPs is that having access to multiple ASes per country allows *DNEye* to identify cases of country-level filtering where multiple ASes interfere with the same domains. For instance, *DNEye* detects SNI-based network interference against the same set of DoH resolvers across different ASes in Saudi Arabia, indicating a centralized filtering policy.

In Iran, we also observe filtering of multiple DoTH resolvers. Notably, SNI-based filtering of TLS connections, destined for both DoT and DoH servers of `dns.google`, were detected from several subnets of AS58224. This same filtering was also detected at AS39501 and AS56402, which are not considered in Table 5 since we did not have VPs from more than one subnet in these two ASes.

Filtering of some DoTH resolvers was also detected in the US, South Korea, and Singapore (Table 5). However, upon verifying the organization information of the filtering ASes, we find that these are filtering cases implemented by corporate and institutional firewalls instead of a country-wide filtering policy.

ESNI Adoption. For ESNI to provide any meaningful privacy and filtering resistance benefits, it needs to be supported by many websites, since if there are only a few ESNI-supported websites, connections to their servers are trivially distinguishable [27,28]. Therefore, we first measure the adoption of ESNI on the web by looking up the ESNI TXT record for more than 350M domains from TLD zone files [2].

Over the course of our measurement period, we find that only about 1.5–2.25% of domains from TLD zone files have a valid ESNI key format (see Appendix D). Of these ESNI-supported domains, 15.4K and 143.3K domains are within the top 100K and 1M popular domains ranked by the Tranco list [37], respectively. We have also measured the deployment of Encrypted Client Hello (ECH) by probing for HTTPS resource records [22] but did not find any evidence of ECH deployment in the wild.

ESNI Filtering. As described in Sect. 3.3, *DNEye* also measures the filtering of ESNI by visiting our control website that has ESNI enabled. This website will reflect the visiting client's IP if the client can successfully connect to our server. Employing the same sliding-window technique defined in Sect. 4.1 in combination with the 90th percentile threshold described above, we detect ESNI filtering in China, Russia, and Iran.

Following a TLS client hello whose SNI field is encrypted, we observe RST packets being injected by China's GFW to tear down connections destined for our ESNI-supported web server. This observation aligns with previous anecdotal reports that China has started filtering all ESNI traffic since July 2020 [36].

Unlike the centralized ESNI filtering policy of China, Internet service providers in Russia are known to implement blocking mechanisms independently in a decentralized manner [50]. Among the networks where we have VPs in Russia, we detect ESNI filtering in AS28890, AS52207, and AS41754, where RST packets are injected to disrupt ESNI connections to our website.

DNEye has also detected ESNI filtering from VPs in Iran's AS56402, AS31549, and AS16322. However, since we did not have measurements from more than one subnet in each of these ASes, we cannot conclude these cases as AS-level filtering with high confidence.

4.3   Network Filtering Circumvention

For the top five countries where most on-path DNS tampering was detected, Table 3 summarizes the number of domains that we (1) could fetch by employing

Table 3. Number of domains that could evade filtering as a result of domain name encryption employment. The filtering technique column indicates the number of domains that fail to evade filtering due to other filtering techniques (i.e., TCP packet injection), HTTP-only site, SNI-based filtering of domains without ESNI support, and server-side blocking.

Country	Circumvented/Total crawled	Filtering technique			
		TCP	HTTP	TLS	SS
China	130/230	11	2	84	3
Russia	53/56	1	1	1	0
Iran	0/49	1	1	47	0
Indonesia	93/98	2	2	0	1
India	20/20	0	0	0	0

domain name encryption, thus evading network filtering, and (2) could not fetch due to other filtering mechanisms at multiple layers of the network stack.

Note that we focus our analysis on those domains tampered with by on-path filtering systems (i.e., Table 2b), rather than those blocked by local resolvers. This is because, instead of using domain name encryption, simply changing to a public resolver is already sufficient to evade filtering employed by a local resolver for some domains. This is the reason why *DNEye* observes fewer filtered domains when querying public resolvers (Table 2b) compared to local resolvers (Table 2a).

Except for Iran, we could successfully unblock more than 50% and 95% of filtered domains in China and other countries, respectively, where on-path DNS filtering is heavily employed.

There are three reasons why some domains fail to evade filtering. First, filtering systems can have several mechanisms deployed at different network layers, as discussed in Sect. 2.1. Thus, domain name encryption alone is not enough to cope with other filtering mechanisms. Second, a few domains are still serving HTTP sites only, allowing straightforward network interference. The third reason, which is also the main one, is because many domains do not support ESNI (see Appendix D). Domain name information of websites without ESNI support is still visible via the TLS handshake and thus susceptible to SNI-based filtering.

Note that DNS-based and SNI-based filtering modules of China's GFW have been shown to maintain different blocklists. Some domains, therefore, are filtered via DNS tampering but not SNI-based interference [46]. There are three domains that we could evade filtering in China but experience server-side blocking.

5   Related Work

The adoption trend of domain name encryption technologies by major Internet companies in the last couple of years has prompted several measurement studies to examine how these new technologies are treated by Internet filtering systems.

Basso [10] created a testing module to detect the blocking of DoTH services for the OONI probe [24]. The author analyzed one-month data of measurements for 123 DoTH resolvers conducted by OONI volunteers at three separate ASes in Kazakhstan, Iran, and China, finding that the most frequently blocked DoTH resolvers belong to Cloudflare and Google. While this study presents some preliminary insight into DoTH filtering, *DNEye* conducts comprehensive measurements from more VPs at many network locations over an extended period of time, providing a more complete view of how filtering systems are treating domain name encryption technologies around the globe. Specifically, the extensive and continuous measurements conducted by *DNEye* have enabled us to discover exactly when a major filtering system like the Great Firewall started blocking a domain name encryption protocol (Sect. 4.2).

Jin et al. [33] conducted a one-off measurement to examine whether DoTH resolvers perform any DNS tampering themselves. Our system, *DNEye*, is designed to also detect on-path filtering systems that interfere with connections destined to DoTH servers. The authors also examined whether encrypted DNS can help with bypassing Internet filtering by using commercial VPNs running in data centers for testing. However, this has several drawbacks, including VPN locations being falsified [55] and limited visibility into residential networks that often have different filtering policies [46]. The paper concludes that the effectiveness of encrypted DNS in evading network interference varies by country.

Chai et al. [13] study the adoption of ESNI and whether it can help bypass Internet filtering in China. They found that 10.9% of the Alexa top 1M domains supported ESNI in 2018. By enabling ESNI in their web crawler, the authors could unblock 66 websites filtered by the GFW based on SNI [13]. Unfortunately, that has not gone unnoticed to China's filtering systems. From July 2020, the GFW has been reported to block all ESNI traffic [36]. Our work complements this earlier work by verifying the support of ESNI for all domains from TLD zone files, finding an increase to almost 15% of top 1M popular domains supporting ESNI (Sect. 4.2).

6 Discussion

From a technical perspective, it is obvious that domain name encryption technologies can help to improve security and privacy for Internet users. Our measurements, however, show mixed results when it comes to the resilience of these technologies to Internet filtering. Specifically, while we found that encrypting DNS resolutions could help evade DNS-based filtering for many domains, almost half of the domains filtered in China and all domains filtered in Iran could not evade filtering despite the use of DoH (Sect. 4.3). This is primarily because the vast majority of domains on the Internet do not have ESNI supported.

As a result, unless ESNI is universally deployed, DNS encryption alone is not enough to resist Internet filtering. Moreover, filtering systems in China and Russia have been blocking ESNI traffic because the collateral damage of this blocking is not substantial enough, since only a small fraction of domains on the Internet have ESNI supported. Even when more websites support ESNI, they should be co-hosted instead of being hosted on separate IPs to increase the potential collateral damage (if being blocked) [30] and to avoid IP-based blocking [27,28].

Another issue with DoTH is the chicken-and-egg problem of resolving the domains of DoTH resolvers. Specifically, the domain of a DoTH resolver would still need to be first resolved via an unencrypted DNS resolution. Although we did not observe any major DNS-based filtering against the domains of DoTH resolvers, the blocking cases of ordns.he.net and two Cloudflare DoH resolvers in Sect. 4.1 show that this is a critical problem in the current implementation of most DoTH resolvers. Although a client can instead use a fixed IP of a DoTH resolver (e.g., 8.8.8.8 or 1.1.1.1), this setting is then susceptible to IP-based blocking unless the DoTH resolver's identity is obfuscated similarly to our own DoH resolver in Sect. 3.3. There have been studies demonstrating the possibility of using machine learning models to detect and filter encrypted DNS resolutions based on network traffic signatures [7,16], we however did not experience such blocking efforts. This is evident by the fact that we could still use our private DoH resolver in all countries where we have measurement vantage points.

7   Limitations

Prior work has shown that an advanced Internet filtering system such as the GFW could block hundreds of thousands of domains [29]. Although it is desirable to test as many domains as possible to obtain a more general view about the filtering mechanisms used against various types of domains, we could not test a large number of domains due to the short-lived nature of VPN Gate vantage points (Sect. 3.2). Another limitation of using VPN Gate is that VPN endpoints often rewrite the packet header, taking away the capability of using incremental IP time-to-live values to pinpoint the location of filtering devices.

8   Conclusion

We present *DNEye*, a measurement system built on top of a distributed network of vantage points, to examine the accessibility of domain name encryption technologies and whether they are interfered with by filtering systems across different network locations. Over a six-month period, *DNEye* conducted 315K measurements from more than 20K vantage points in 85 countries, detecting blocking efforts against domain name encryption technologies in several countries, including China, Russia, and Saudi Arabia.

Measuring the prevalence of ESNI adoption, we find that only 1.5–2.25% of the domains from TLD zone files have a valid ESNI key, indicating that ESNI has not been widely adopted yet. Finally, to evaluate the efficacy of domain name encryption in evading Internet filtering, we instrument a customized browser with DoH and ESNI enabled to crawl a list of filtered domains detected by *DNEye*. Except for network locations where SNI-based filtering is also employed, we could unblock more than 55% and 95% of the blocked domains in China and other countries where DNS-based filtering is employed.

Acknowledgments. We would like to thank our shepherd, Gareth Tyson, and the anonymous reviewers for their thorough feedback on earlier drafts of this paper. This research was supported in part by the Open Technology Fund under an Information Controls Fellowship. The opinions in this paper are those of the authors and do not necessarily reflect the opinions of the sponsor.

A   DoTH Resolvers

Table 4 indexes 71 DoTH resolvers publicly available at the time of our study.

B   DNS Tampering Detection

To identify cases of DNS-based network interference, we employ the following well-established consistency heuristics in the literature [24, 42, 48, 51].

Multiple Responses with Different ASes. We receive multiple responses for a DNS query that belong to different ASes. Previous studies have identified cases where on-path filtering systems inject packets carrying false IP addresses that often are publicly routable [8, 29, 43].

NXDomain or Non-routable Address. We receive an NXDomain or non-routable IP in response to a DNS query from a vantage point while receiving a routable address from the majority of vantage points and our control node.

Different Responses from Control and Aggregate. When a vantage point receives a globally routable IP but different from the IP observed at the control node. We first check whether they belong to the same AS. If both IPs are under the same AS, this is due to the use of CDN and/or DNS-based load balancing but not censorship. If the IP observed by the vantage point belongs to an AS which is different from the response AS we observe at the control node and the majority of other vantage points, this behavior indicates DNS interference by a filtering system that aims to redirect the client to a different server (e.g., for displaying blockpages). However, there are also cases in which different ASes are managed by large CDN providers (e.g., Akamai). We look up organization information of those ASes to exclude cases where different response ASes belong to the same organization to avoid false positives.

Table 4. The list of DoTH resolvers that is used in our measurement.

Index	DoTH Servers	Index	DoTH Servers	Index	DoTH Servers
1	1dot1dot1dot1.cloudflare-dns.com	25	dns.switch.ch	49	doh.xfinity.com
2	cloudflare-dns.com	26	dns.twnic.tw	50	family.cloudflare-dns.com
3	dns10.quad9.net	27	dns-unfiltered.adguard.com	51	fi.doh.dns.snopyta.org
4	dns11.quad9.net	28	doh-2.seby.io	52	free.bravedns.com
5	dns9.quad9.net	29	doh.applied-privacy.net	53	jp.tiarap.org
6	dns.aa.net.uk	30	doh.centraleu.pi-dns.com	54	jp.tiar.app
7	dns.adguard.com	31	doh.cleanbrowsing.org	55	mozilla.cloudflare-dns.com
8	dns.alidns.com	32	doh-de.blahdns.com	56	odvr.nic.cz
9	dns.containerpi.com	33	doh.dnslify.com	57	ordns.he.net
10	dns.digitale-gesellschaft.ch	34	doh.dns.sb	58	resolver-eu.lelux.fi
11	dns.dnshome.de	35	doh.eastas.pi-dns.com	59	security.cloudflare-dns.com
12	dns.dns-over-https.com	36	doh.eastau.pi-dns.com	60	1dot1dot1dot1.cloudflare-dns.com (DoT)
13	dns.dnsoverhttps.net	37	doh.eastus.pi-dns.com	61	adult-filter-dns.cleanbrowsing.org (DoT)
14	dnses.alekberg.net	38	doh.familyshield.opendns.com	62	dns.adguard.com (DoT)
15	dns-family.adguard.com	39	doh.ffmuc.net	63	dns-family.adguard.com (DoT)
16	dns.flatuslifir.is	40	doh-fi.blahdns.com	64	dns.google (DoT)
17	dnsforge.de	41	doh-jp.blahdns.com	65	dns-nosec.quad9.net (DoT)
18	dns.google	42	doh.libredns.gr	66	dns.quad9.net (DoT)
19	dns.hostux.net	43	doh.northeu.pi-dns.com	67	dns-unfiltered.adguard.com (DoT)
20	dnsnl.alekberg.net	44	doh.opendns.com	68	dot.xfinity.com (DoT)
21	dns-nosec.quad9.net	45	doh.pi-dns.com	69	family-filter-dns.cleanbrowsing.org (DoT)
22	dns-nyc.aaflalo.me	46	doh.tiarap.org	70	one.one.one.one (DoT)
23	dns.quad9.net	47	doh.tiar.app	71	security-filter-dns.cleanbrowsing.org (DoT)
24	dns.rubyfish.cn	48	doh.westus.pi-dns.com		

C   AS-Level DoTH Filtering

Table 5 shows the top five countries where most connections to DoTH resolvers were interfered with. The DoTH server names are indexed in Table 4.

D   ESNI Prevalence

Over the course of our measurement period, we frequently query for ESNI TXT records of more than 350M domains from TLD zone files [2]. Only 3%–4.5% of domains respond to our ESNI TXT queries. And, only 48–51% of these TXT records have a valid ESNI key format defined in the Internet drafts [21,23]. Analyzing the key lengths of all ESNI TXT records obtained, we find that the majority of them have 92 characters. These ESNI-supported domains are hosted by Cloudflare, which is the only Internet company supporting ESNI to the best of our knowledge. For domains whose ESNI TXT records that do not have a correct ESNI key format, we find that their authoritative nameservers are configured with a wildcard setup (i.e., *.example.com), thus responding to our ESNI TXT query for _esni.example.com despite not having an actual ESNI key. To that end, only around 1.5%–2.25% of domains on the Internet have ESNI supported.

Table 5. Top five countries where most AS-level DoTH filtering was detected. * indicate cases where both TCP and TLS handshakes were completed but we could not obtain the correct IP of our control domain being resolved.

Country		China						United States				S. Korea			Singapore			Saudi Arabia			Iran
ASN		4134	4837	9808	37963	45090	140314	7155	20473	31898	36352	17870	20473	38121	14061	20473	55430	25019	35819	35753	58224
Index of blocked DoH resolvers	1			X								X						X	X	X	X
	2			X			X											X	X	X	
	4																				X
	5						X														
	6			X			X														
	9			X			X														
	10			X			X														
	11						X														
	13			X																	
	14			X			X														
	16			X			X														
	18	X	X	X	X	X	X														X
	19			X			X														
	20			X			X														
	22			X																	
	23			X																	X
	25			X																	
	26				X		X														
	27						X														
	28			X			X														
	32			X																	
	33			X	X	X															
	34			X			X														
	37			X			X														
	38			X	X	X	X	X				X	X		X	X	X				X
	39			X			X														
	40			X	X	X	X														
	41			X	X	X															
	42			X			X														
	44			X	X	X	X	X		X		X	X		X	X	X				
	45	X	X		X	X															
	47			X			X			X						X					
	48			X			X														
	50														X			X	X	X	X
	51			X			X														
	54						X			X						X					
	55			X	X	X	X											X	X	X	X
	59														X			X	X	X	X
Index of blocked DoT resolvers	60			X			X								X						
	61			X			X														
	62			X			X														
	63			X			X														
	64																				X
	65			X			X														
	66			X			X														
	67			X			X														
	68			X			X														
	69			X			X														
	70			X			X								X						
	71			X			X														
Block (%)	TCP	98.3	97.8	44.8	4.8	95.3	96.2	0*	100	0*	0*	100	0*	100	0*	50	0*	0	0	0	10
	TLS	1.7	2.2	55.2	95.2	4.7	3.8	0*	0	0*	0*	0	0*	0	0*	50	0*	100	100	100	90

References

1. Freedom on the Net (2020). https://freedomhouse.org/countries/freedom-net/scores
2. ICANN Centralized Zone Data Service. https://czds.icann.org
3. Luminati proxy service. https://luminati.io
4. Anecdote: DNS over TLS has stopped working (2021). https://web.archive.org/web/20210329194856/forum.manjaro.org/t/dns-over-tls-has-stopped-working/56422
5. Cloudflare DoT. https://developers.cloudflare.com/1.1.1.1/encrypted-dns/dns-over-tls (2021)
6. How to enable or disable the VPN relay function on VPN gate client? (2021). https://www.vpngate.net/en/join_client.aspx

7. Alenezi, R., Ludwig, S.A.: Classifying DNS tunneling tools for malicious DoH traffic (2021)
8. Anonymous: towards a comprehensive picture of the great firewall's DNS censorship. In: Free and Open Communications on the Internet. USENIX (2014)
9. Baheux, K.: A safer and more private browsing experience with secure DNS. https://blog.chromium.org/2020/05/a-safer-and-more-private-browsing-DoH.html (2020)
10. Basso, S.: Measuring DoT/DoH blocking using OONI probe: a preliminary study. In: NDSS DNS Privacy Workshop (2021)
11. Bock, K., Hughey, G., Qiang, X., Levin, D.: Geneva: evolving censorship evasion strategies. In: ACM Conference on Computer and Communications Security (2019)
12. Chen, C.: Russia wants to outlaw ESNI, DoT, and DoH. https://www.privateinternetaccess.com/blog/russia-wants-to-outlaw-tls-1-3-esni-dns-over-https-and-dns-over-tls
13. Chai, Z., Ghafari, A., Houmansadr, A.: On the importance of Encrypted-SNI (ESNI) to censorship circumvention. In: USENIX FOCI (2019)
14. Cimpanu, C.: Apple adds support for encrypted DNS (DoH and DoT). https://www.zdnet.com/article/apple-adds-support-for-encrypted-dns-doh-and-dot/ (2020)
15. Cornell, J.: How to enable DNS Over HTTPS in microsoft edge. https://www.howtogeek.com/660157/how-to-enable-dns-over-https-in-microsoft-edge/ (2020)
16. Csikor, L., Singh, H., Kang, M.S., Divakaran, D.M.: Privacy of DNS-over-HTTPS: requiem for a dream? In: IEEE EuroS&P (2021)
17. Dierks, T., Rescorla, E.: Transport layer security protocol V1.2. RFC 5246, IETF (2008)
18. DNS, K.: kdig - Advanced DNS lookup utility (2020). https://www.knot-dns.cz
19. DNS over HTTPS: DOH (2020). https://github.com/curl/curl/wiki/DNS-over-HTTPS
20. Duan, H., et al.: Hold-on: protecting against on-path DNS poisoning. In: SATIN 2012 (2012)
21. Rescorla, E., Oku, K., Sullivan, N., Wood, C.: Encrypted server name indication for TLS 1.3 draft-ietf-tls-esni-02 (2019). https://datatracker.ietf.org/doc/html/draft-ietf-tls-esni-02
22. Rescorla, E., Oku, K., Sullivan, N., Wood, C.: TLS encrypted client hello draft-ietf-tls-esni-07 (2020). https://datatracker.ietf.org/doc/html/draft-ietf-tls-esni-07
23. Rescorla, E., Oku, K., Sullivan, N., Wood, C.: Encrypted server name indication for TLS 1.3 draft-ietf-tls-esni-05 (2020). https://datatracker.ietf.org/doc/html/draft-ietf-tls-esni-05
24. Filasto, A., Appelbaum, J.: OONI: open observatory of network interference. In: FOCI 2012 (2012)
25. Fuchs, C., Boersma, K., Albrechtslund, A., Sandoval, M.: Internet and Surveillance: The Challenges of Web 2.0 and Social Media (2011)
26. Google: JSON API for DNS over HTTPS (DoH). https://developers.google.com/speed/public-dns/docs/dns-over-https (2019)
27. Hoang, N.P., Niaki, A.A., Borisov, N., Gill, P., Polychronakis, M.: Assessing the privacy benefits of domain name encryption. In: ACM AsiaCCS (2020)
28. Hoang, N.P., Niaki, A.A., Gill, P., Polychronakis, M.: Domain name encryption is not enough: privacy leakage via IP-based website fingerprinting. In: PoPETs (2021)

29. Hoang, N., et al.: How great is the great firewall? Measuring China's DNS Censorship. In: USENIX Security Symposium (2021)
30. Hoang, N., Niaki, A., Polychronakis, M., Gill, P.: The web is still small after more than a decade. ACM SIGCOMM Comput. Commun. Rev. (2020)
31. Hoffman, P., McManus, P.: DNS queries over HTTPS (DoH). RFC 8484, IETF (2018)
32. Hu, Z., Zhu, L., Heidemann, J., Mankin, A., Wessels, D., Hoffman, P.: Specification for DNS over Transport Layer Security (TLS). RFC 7858, IETF (2016)
33. Jin, L., Hao, S., Wang, H., Cotton, C.: Understanding the impact of encrypted DNS on internet censorship. In: Proceedings of the Web Conference 2021, pp. 484–495 (2021)
34. Jones, B., Ensafi, R., Feamster, N., Paxson, V., Weaver, N.: Ethical concerns for censorship measurement. In: ACM SIGCOMM Workshop on Ethics in Networked Systems Research (2015)
35. Jones, B., Lee, T.W., Feamster, N., Gill, P.: Automated detection and fingerprinting of censorship block pages. In: ACM Internet Measurement Conference (2014)
36. Bock, K., Anonymous, I., Merino, L., Fifield, D., Houmansadr, A., Levin, D.: Exposing and circumventing China's censorship of ESNI (2020). https://geneva.cs.umd.edu/posts/china-censors-esni/esni/
37. Le Pochat, V., Van Goethem, T., Tajalizadehkhoob, S., Korczyński, M., Joosen, W.: Tranco: a research-oriented top sites ranking hardened against manipulation. In: NDSS (2019)
38. Lu, C., et al.: An end-to-end, large-scale measurement of DNS-over-encryption: how far have we come? In: ACM Internet Measurement Conference (2019)
39. McManus, P.: Improving DNS privacy in firefox. https://blog.nightly.mozilla.org/2018/06/01/improving-dns-privacy-in-firefox/ (2018)
40. Mi, X., et al.: Resident evil: Understanding residential IP proxy as a dark service. In: IEEE S&P (2019)
41. Mockapetris, P.: Domain names - concepts and facilities. RFC 1034, IETF (1987)
42. Niaki, A.A., et al.: ICLab: A global, longitudinal internet censorship measurement platform. In: 2020 IEEE SP 2020 (2020)
43. Niaki, A.A., Hoang, N.P., Gill, P., Houmansadr, A., et al.: Triplet censors: demystifying great firewall's DNS censorship behavior. In: USENIX FOCI (2020)
44. Nobori, D.: Virtual ethernet system and tunneling communication with SoftEther. In: The 45th Programming Symposium of Information Processing Society of Japan, pp. 147–158 (2004)
45. Nobori, D., Shinjo, Y.: VPN gate: a volunteer-organized public vpn relay system with blocking resistance for bypassing government censorship firewalls. In: USENIX NSDI '14 (2014)
46. Hoang, N.P., Doreen, S., Polychronakis, M.: Measuring I2P censorship at a global scale. In: USENIX Workshop on Free and Open Communications on the Internet (2019)
47. Nystrom, M., Hopwood, D., Mikkelsen, J., Wright, T.: Transport Layer Security (TLS) Extensions. RFC 3546, IETF (2003). https://datatracker.ietf.org/doc/html/rfc3546
48. Pearce, P., et al.: Global measurement of DNS manipulation. In: USENIX Security Symposium (2017)
49. Procedure to request for logs from the VPN Gate project: Available in Japanese at. https://www.vpngate.net/ja/about_abuse.aspx
50. Ramesh, R., et al.: Decentralized control: a case study of Russia. In: Network and Distributed System Security Symposium (2020)

51. Scott, W., Anderson, T., Kohno, T., Krishnamurthy, A.: Satellite: Joint analysis of CDNs and network-level interference. In: USENIX Annual Technical Conference (2016)
52. Sundara Raman, R., Shenoy, P., Kohls, K., Ensafi, R.: Censored planet: an internet-wide, longitudinal censorship observatory. In: ACM CCS (2020)
53. Turk, D.: Configuring BGP to block denial-of-service attacks. RFC 3882, IETF (2004)
54. Wang, Z., Cao, Y., Qian, Z., Song, C., Krishnamurthy, S.: Your state is not mine: a closer look at evading stateful internet censorship. In: ACM Internet Measurement Conference (2017)
55. Weinberg, Z., Cho, S., Christin, N., Sekar, V., Gill, P.: How to catch when proxies lie: verifying the physical locations of network proxies with active geolocation. ACM IMC (2018)

One to Rule Them All?
A First Look at DNS over QUIC

Mike Kosek[1(✉)] [ID], Trinh Viet Doan[1] [ID], Malte Granderath[1],
and Vaibhav Bajpai[1,2] [ID]

[1] Technical University of Munich, Munich, Germany
{kosek,doan,grandera}@in.tum.de
[2] CISPA Helmholtz Center for Information Security, Saarbrücken, Germany
bajpai@cispa.de

Abstract. The DNS is one of the most crucial parts of the Internet. Since the original DNS specifications defined UDP and TCP as the underlying transport protocols, DNS queries are inherently unencrypted, making them vulnerable to eavesdropping and on-path manipulations. Consequently, concerns about DNS privacy have gained attention in recent years, which resulted in the introduction of the encrypted protocols DNS over TLS (DoT) and DNS over HTTPS (DoH). Although these protocols address the key issues of adding privacy to the DNS, they are inherently restrained by their underlying transport protocols, which are at strife with, e.g., IP fragmentation or multi-RTT handshakes—challenges which are addressed by QUIC. As such, the recent addition of DNS over QUIC (DoQ) promises to improve upon the established DNS protocols. However, no studies focusing on DoQ, its adoption, or its response times exist to this date—a gap we close with our study. Our active measurements show a slowly but steadily increasing adoption of DoQ and reveal a high week-over-week fluctuation, which reflects the ongoing development process: As DoQ is still in standardization, implementations and services undergo rapid changes. Analyzing the response times of DoQ, we find that roughly 40% of measurements show considerably higher handshake times than expected, which traces back to the enforcement of the traffic amplification limit despite successful validation of the client's address. However, DoQ already outperforms DoT as well as DoH, which makes it the best choice for encrypted DNS to date.

1 Introduction

The Domain Name System (DNS) is used for almost all communications across the Internet. As the original DNS specifications [25,26] define UDP and TCP as the underlying transport protocols, DNS requests and responses using DNS over UDP (DoUDP) and DNS over TCP (DoTCP) are inherently unencrypted, which makes them vulnerable to eavesdropping and on-path manipulations [56]. This enables an observer to not only reveal the browsing or application usage behavior [57], but also the identification of device types which are in use [35];

O. Hohlfeld et al. (Eds.): PAM 2022, LNCS 13210, pp. 537–551, 2022.
https://doi.org/10.1007/978-3-030-98785-5_24

hence, a user profile can be created and tracked with only having access to the user's DNS traffic [44,45,48]. Consequently, concerns on DNS privacy have gained attention in recent years.

With the standardization of DNS over TLS (DoT) [38] in 2016 and DNS over HTTPS (DoH) [37] in 2018, encrypted DNS protocols leveraging Transport Layer Security (TLS) on top of TCP have been introduced. Moreover, DNS over DTLS (DoDTLS) [52] has also been standardized as an experimental protocol in 2017, offering encrypted DNS by leveraging TLS on top of UDP.

However, while these protocols address the key issues of adding privacy to DNS [29,33,49,55], they are inherently restrained by their underlying transport protocols. Using UDP as a connectionless protocol, DoDTLS is vulnerable to *IP fragmentation* [28,31,36,50]—a problem which has gained awareness in recent years due to the trend of increasing DNS response sizes [40,46]. Although both DoT and DoH are not affected by *IP fragmentation*, as they leverage the connection-oriented TCP, the underlying TCP connections are still constrained by head-of-line-blocking and missing multiplexing support on the transport layer, as well as an additional connection establishment in comparison to UDP.

These challenges are addressed by QUIC [42,43,54], a connection-oriented encrypted transport protocol using UDP as a substrate. Standardized in early 2021, QUIC features mandatory encryption, solves head-of-line blocking, provides multiplexing, and improves on connection establishment time by combining the transport and encryption handshakes into a single round trip. Consequently, offering DNS using the QUIC transport protocol is the natural evolution for not only the traditional performance-oriented DNS protocols DoUDP and DoTCP, but also the privacy-preserving DNS protocols DoT and DoH (as well as the experimental DoDTLS).

DNS over QUIC (DoQ) is currently being standardized within the *DNS PRIVate Exchange* IETF working group [41] with the design goal to provide DNS privacy with minimum latency. With this objective, DoQ aims to obsolete all other currently used DNS protocols, which lack privacy and/or require more round-trips for handshakes—therefore, promising to make DoQ the *"One to Rule them All"*. Despite its development status, multiple experimental implementations already exist that offer DoQ support for clients [7,10,16,19,21], servers [5,7,8,19], proxies [4,16,21], as well as multipurpose libraries [1,7,12,19]. Moreover, *AdGuard* [3] and *nextDNS* [17] already use DoQ in production systems for their DNS-based ad as well as tracker blocking services, offering publicly reachable DoQ servers and client implementations [10,16]. However, while DoQ was submitted to the Internet Engineering Steering Group (IESG) for publication in December 2021, only one study [33] has explicitly included DoQ as part of an experiment on encrypted DNS based on traffic flow analyses as of January 2022. Hence, no studies focusing on DoQ, its adoption, or its response times exist to this date—a gap we close with our study.

We begin by investigating the adoption of DoQ (see Sect. 3) and identify a maximum of 1,217 resolvers in a single week. Over the course of 29 weeks, we find 1,851 unique X.509 certificates used by the resolvers. However, only 51.6%

of the resolvers in the first week are still reachable in the last week, reflecting the ongoing development and standardization process, during which DoQ implementations and services undergo rapid changes. Analyzing the response times of DoQ in comparison to DoUDP, DoTCP, DoT, as well as DoH (see Sect. 4), we find that QUIC's full potential is only utilized in around 20% of measurements. On the other hand, roughly 40% of measurements show considerably higher handshake times than expected, which traces back to the enforcement of the traffic amplification limit despite successful validation of the client's address, ultimately causing an additional, unnecessary round-trip.

The remainder of this paper is structured as follows: We first present our methodology in Sect. 2. Afterwards, we detail our adoption measurements in Sect. 3 before analyzing the response times of DoQ in Sect. 4. Limitations and future work are discussed in Sect. 5, after which we conclude the paper with Sect. 6.

2 Methodology

To study the adoption and response times of DNS over QUIC (DoQ), we issue measurements from a single vantage point located in the research network of the Technical University of Munich, Germany. Distributed measurement platforms such as RIPE Atlas do currently not support DoQ; nevertheless, we plan to distribute our measurements to multiple vantage points in the future (see Sect. 5).

Adoption. To assess the adoption of DoQ on resolvers worldwide, we issue weekly scans of the IPv4 address space over the course of 29 weeks, starting in 2021-W27 (July 05–11). For this, we leverage the *ZMap* network scanner [22] and target all DoQ ports proposed by the different DoQ Internet-Drafts (I-Ds), i.e., UDP/784, UDP/853, and UDP/8853 [39]. For comparison, we additionally target DoUDP port UDP/53, which we identify by leveraging the *ZMap*'s built-in DNS probing packet that queries an A record for www.google.com [58]. Since *ZMap* does not provide means for the identification of QUIC or DoQ, we issue a custom packet [24] that carries the Initial QUIC handshake frame with an invalid version number of 0 [53]: In this way, if the target operates a QUIC stack on the probed port, a Version Negotiation packet is triggered. As such a packet does not produce state, it allows us to identify the target as *QUIC-capable* without consuming resources on the target itself [43]. However, note that other QUIC services, which are not necessarily DoQ, could be offered on the probed ports. Hence, we further validate targets identified as *QUIC-capable* by the *ZMap* scans, checking if they actually support DNS over QUIC [23]. To do so, we offer the doq Application-Layer Protocol Negotiation (ALPN) identifiers (as required by the DoQ I-Ds [39]), which results in a list of *DoQ-capable* targets. As a final step, a connection to every *DoQ-capable* target on all proposed DoQ ports UDP/784, UDP/853, as well as UDP/8853, is established [15]: For these connections, we offered the QUIC version draft-34 in our Initial frame until 2021-W42, while support for version 1 was added in 2021-W43. Overall, our client supports the QUIC versions draft-34, -32 and -29 since the start of our study, as well as version 1 later on; hence, the client can respond to `Version Negotiation` packets if issued by the resolvers. For DoQ, we offer versions in the order of `draft-06` to `draft-00` [39], for which we added support for new versions within 2 weeks of the `draft` release. By issuing the highest QUIC and DoQ protocol versions supported by our client first, we ensure that we negotiate the highest shared protocol versions between our client and the target resolver. With this, we record the negotiated QUIC and DoQ versions, as well as the X.509 certificate offered by each *DoQ-capable* target, creating the final list of *DoQ-verified* resolvers.

Response Time. To study the response times of DoQ compared to DoUDP, DoTCP, DoT, and DoH, we develop *DNSPerf*, an open-source DNS measurement tool which supports all stated protocols [11]. Using *DNSPerf* to target all *DoQ-verified* resolvers identified in 2022-W02, we issue response time measurements every hour over the course of 2022-W03 (January 17–23). As we specifically scan for DoQ in our adoption measurement, we measure DoUDP, DoTCP, DoT, as well as DoH *optimistically*, i.e., without prior knowledge whether the target resolvers offer the respective DNS protocols in addition to DoQ. In detail, we measure DoUDP and DoTCP according to RFC 1034 [25] on target port `UDP/53` and, respectively, `TCP/53`, DoT according to RFC 7858 [38] preferring TLS version `1.3` on target port `TCP/853`, and DoH according to RFC 8484 [37], also preferring TLS version `1.3` on target port `TCP/443`. Similar to the verification step of the adoption measurement, we again target all proposed DoQ ports.

Our DNS requests query an `A` record for `test.com`. We further explicitly set the `Recursion Desired` flag in all requests to ensure that the resolvers return a valid and recursively queried or cached `A` record, which circumvents resolvers simply returning the corresponding name server or refusing to answer our queries to prevent *Cache Snooping* [20,51] when the flag is not set. As populating the caches can affect the measured response times, every DNS request on every protocol is preceded by an identical cache warming query, which ensures that the actual DNS response time measurement query is directly answered by the resolver from a cached record. For DoQ, we additionally use the negotiated QUIC `Version` along with the token received in a `New_Token` frame of the cache warming query for the handshake of the subsequent DNS response time measurement query, which ensures that the response time measurements are not affected by QUIC's `Version Negotiation` and `Address Validation` features. Overall, these decisions enable comparable DNS response time measurements of all stated protocols.

Round-Trip Time (RTT). If the response time measurement of a protocol:resolver pair is successful, we measure the *round-trip time* to the targets to analyze the path and protocol-specific *RTT* [9]. Since the resolvers can be deployed behind proxies, or the path can have protocol-dependent queuing characteristics, we send probing packets to the same port using the same protocol as the respective response time measurement. Therefore, our implementation enables *RTT* measurements for UDP (DoUDP), TCP (DoTCP, DoT, DoH), as well as QUIC (DoQ) by leveraging protocol-specific probing payloads: For UDP, a randomized payload is sent from a random `Source Port`, while the payload for TCP is a `SYN` packet containing a randomized `Sequence Number`. Finally, QUIC leverages the custom packet that carries the `Initial` QUIC handshake with an invalid version number of `0` (see Adoption above).

Ethical Considerations. To minimize the impact of our active scans, we follow best practices of the Internet measurement community [30,47]. Thus, we display the intent of our scans on a website reachable via the IP address of each scanning machine, also allowing targets to opt-out from our study. Moreover, we honor opt-out requests from previous studies and maintain a University-wide shared blocklist with the excluded targets.

Reproducibility. In order to enable the reproduction of our findings [27], we make the developed tools, the raw data of our measurements, as well as the analysis scripts and supplementary files publicly available [18].

3 Adoption

To study the adoption of DoQ on resolvers worldwide, we issue weekly scans of the IPv4 address space over the course of 29 weeks, as described in Sect. 2. Thus, we record the negotiated QUIC and DoQ versions, as well as the X.509 certificates offered by the target resolvers that support DoQ, for which we also determine the announcing Autonomous Systems (ASes) and geolocations. Overall, we find 1,851 unique X.509 certificates over the course of 29 weeks.

Adoption of QUIC and DoQ Versions. In our scans and in the verification process, we target all proposed DoQ ports `UDP/784`, `UDP/853`, and `UDP/8853`. The DoQ drafts `-00` and `-01` state that port `UDP/784` *MAY* be used for experimentation. `draft-02` defined `UDP/8853` for usage as experimentation as well as for reservation at the Internet Assigned Numbers Authority (IANA). This was changed in `draft-03`, where port `UDP/784` was again stated for experimentation usage; ultimately, `UDP/853` has been established as the final port for reservation at IANA. Over the course of the 29 weeks, we observe a dominance of the usage of port `UDP/784`, with roughly 75–82% of all *DoQ-verified* resolvers offering all observed DoQ `drafts-00`, `-02`, and `-03` on `UDP/784`. Port `UDP/8853` is only observed in combination with `draft-02` at roughly 17–24% of all *DoQ-verified* resolvers, with the remainder (<1%) serving DoQ `draft-02` on port `UDP/853`.

Figure 1 presents the *DoQ-verified* resolvers per week, grouped by negotiated DoQ and QUIC version. Overall, we observe that the number of *DoQ-verified* resolvers rises steadily: Starting with 833 resolvers in 2021-W27 (July 05–11), we see an increase by 46.1% to 1,217 verified resolvers in 2022-W03 (January 17–23). After we added support for QUIC version 1 [43] in 2021-W43, we observe a steady usage of `DoQ Draft 02/QUIC 1` (dark blue bars) until 2021-W50, followed by a steep increase until 2022-W01. Analyzing this observation, we find that the open source DNS server implementation *AdGuard Home (AGH)* [5] changed the default DoQ/QUIC pair from `DoQ Draft 02/QUIC Draft 34` (orange bars) to

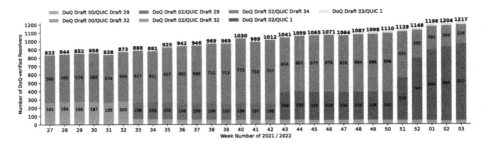

Fig. 1. Number of *DoQ-verified* resolvers per week number of 2021 and 2022 grouped by negotiated DoQ and QUIC version. Support for QUIC version 1 was added in 2021-W43. (Color figure online)

`DoQ Draft 02/QUIC 1` (dark blue bars) starting 2021-W51 [6], matching the pattern we observe. In addition, we find indications of the usage of *AGH* by the updated resolvers within the *Common Names* of their X.509 certificates, and also identify multiple of the updated resolvers to be running *AGH* through random sampling. Hence, we attribute the observed increase in usage of `DoQ Draft 02/QUIC 1` between 2021-W51 and 2022-W01 to this implementation.

Although we offer a total combination of 28 DoQ/QUIC version pairs as of 2022-W03 (see Sect. 2), we observe only 7 pairs across all measurements, with the majority being `DoQ Draft 02/QUIC 1` (dark blue bars, 917 (75.3%)) in 2022-W03. Additionally, we find that only 430 (51.6%) of the initial 833 resolvers are still verified in 2022-W03. As a comparison, 96.5% of the verified DoUDP resolvers from 2021-W27 are still verified in 2022-W03. This fluctuation of DoQ reflects the development process: While DoQ is still in standardization, implementations and services change frequently and are expected to be used in experimental rather than in production environments.

However, both *AdGuard* [3] and *nextDNS* [17] actually do use DoQ in production systems for their DNS-based ad and tracker blocking services, offering publicly reachable DoQ servers as well as client implementations [10, 16]. This is reflected in the *Common Names* of the X.509 certificates offered by the verified DoQ resolvers: In 2022-W03, 199 resolvers (16.5%) state `dns.nextdns.io` as their common name. Analyzing the change over time, we observe that *nextDNS* operates the highest share of resolvers in each week, with a mean of roughly 180 resolvers in 2021-W27 to 2021-W31, increasing to a mean of 199 resolvers in 2021-W32 to 2022-W03. While the increase was observed between 2021-W31 and 2021-W32, *nextDNS* offered `DoQ Draft 02/QUIC Draft 32` (purple bars) until 2021-W32 and downgraded all resolvers to `DoQ Draft 02/QUIC Draft 29` (green bars) in 2021-W33, where this DoQ/QUIC pair is exclusively offered by *nextDNS*. After adding support for QUIC version 1 in 2021-W43, we also observe that all *nextDNS* resolvers offer `DoQ Draft 02/QUIC 1` (dark blue bars) since that week; hence, we attribute the previously observed downgrade to the missing support of QUIC version 1 in our tooling during that timeframe. Considering the publicly reachable DoQ servers of *AdGuard* (identified by the common names

Fig. 2. Geographical locations of the 1,217 *DoQ-verified* resolvers as of 2022-W03, with counts by continent. The blue marker represents our vantage point. (Color figure online)

`dns.adguard.com` and `adguard.ch`), we identify 25 resolvers offering `DoQ Draft 03/QUIC 1` (yellow bars) in 2022-W03 (2.1%). Note that this DoQ/QUIC pair is exclusively offered by the *AdGuard* services, as it differs from the *AdGuard Home (AGH)* open source DNS server implementation detailed above. We find 12–17 resolvers with the common name `dns.adguard.com` and `DoQ Draft 02/QUIC Draft 34` (orange bars) until 2021-W47, after which these resolvers switch to `DoQ Draft 03/QUIC 1` (yellow bars) starting 2021-W48. Moreover, `DoQ Draft 03/QUIC 1` is also offered by 6–8 resolvers using `adguard.ch` starting 2021-W49.

Adoption in Continents and by ASes. Figure 2 presents the geographical locations of the 1,217 *DoQ-verified* resolvers of 2022-W03 with counts per continent based on an IPv4 geolocation lookup service [14]. We observe a strong focus of resolvers operated in Asia (45.19%) and Europe (EU) (32.37%), whereas only 17.83% are operated in North America (NA). However, note that geolocation lookups of IP addresses are known to have inaccuracies, possibly resulting in the incorrect attribution of locations.

The publicly available information of *AdGuard* [2] states that they operate resolvers in 10 countries in the four continents Asia, EU, NA, as well as Oceania (OC). However, this is not reflected in our measurements: We find that 16 resolvers are operated in Russia (EU, MNGTNET (AS199274)), 8 in Cyprus (Asia, ADGUARD (AS212772)), and 1 in Italy (EU, TISCALI-IT (AS8612)) for 2022-W03, resulting in an overall distribution over 2 continents, 3 countries, as well as 3 ASes. Due to the strong divergence, we attribute this observation to the incorrect attribution of the IP geolocation lookups.

On the other hand, *nextDNS* operates globally distributed DoQ resolvers: The 199 *DoQ-verified* resolvers of 2022-W03 are distributed across 66 countries on all 6 continents, with most resolvers located in EU (78, 39.20%), NA (54, 27.14%), and Asia (35, 17.59%). Looking at the distribution over ASes, we find that 55 (27.64%) are attributed to ANEXIA (AS42473), whose *DoQ resolvers* are all operated by *nextDNS*. The remaining 144 resolvers (72.36%) are distributed over 72 ASes, with most ASes hosting 1–2 resolvers.

While our measurements show a slowly but steadily increasing adoption of DoQ on resolvers worldwide, the observed week-over-week fluctuations reflect the ongoing development and standardization process with rapidly changing implementations and services. Considering that these experimental deployments of the resolvers, along with their geographical locations, can substantially affect the overall response times, in particular when multiple RTTs are required, we investigate the measured response times in the following section.

4 Response Times

To study the response times of DoQ in comparison to DoUDP, DoTCP, DoT, and DoH, we issue response time measurements every hour over the course of 2022-W03 (January 17–23), targeting all *DoQ-verified* resolvers identified in 2022-W02 (see Sect. 2). From these 1,204 resolvers, 1,148 answer our requests via DoQ, 663 via DoH, 1,028 via DoT, 630 via DoTCP, and 455 via DoUDP in 2022-W03. A total of 264 resolvers, i.e., *DoX-verified*, offer all stated DNS protocols simultaneously. While the adoption measurements (Sect. 3) are independent of the selected vantage point, we acknowledge that the vantage point introduces a location bias for our response time measurements (see Sect. 5). To counteract these limitations, we restrict our response time analysis to the 264 *DoX-verified* resolvers, enabling a comparative study of all stated DNS protocols. The geographical distribution of these resolvers follows the distribution observed in the adoption scan: Asia dominates with 123 (46.59%) of the *DoX-verified* resolvers, followed by EU with 83 (31.44%), and NA with 51 (19.32%). The remainder are attributed to OC (5 resolvers, 1.89%) and AF (2 resolvers, 0.76%).

To account for the different transport protocol mechanisms leveraged by the measured protocols, we differentiate between the *round-trip time (RTT)*, the *resolve time*, and the *handshake time*. We define the *resolve time* as the time between the moment the first packet of the DNS query is sent until the moment a valid DNS response is received. Considering we ensure that our requested DNS record is cached by the targeted resolver through cache warming (see Sect. 2), the *resolve time* is, therefore, expected to resemble roughly 1 *RTT* for every measured protocol. In addition to the *resolve time*, we define the *handshake time* as the time between the moment the first packet of the session establishment is sent until the moment the (encrypted) session to the resolver is established. Note that since DoUDP uses a connectionless protocol and, therefore, has no connection establishment, it is omitted from the *handshake time* discussion below. The DoTCP *handshake time* resembles the TCP 3-way handshake, i.e., 1 *RTT*. For DoT and DoH, the TLS handshake is added to the TCP handshake: Using TLS 1.2, the *handshake time* is 3 *RTTs* for DoT and DoH, which is decreased down to 2 *RTTs* with the usage of TLS 1.3. Since QUIC combines the handshakes of the connection as well as the encryption in the `Initial` frame, and we ensure that QUIC's `Version Negotiation` and `Address Validation` features do not affect the actual DNS response time measurement query (see Sect. 2), the *handshake time* of DoQ should resemble 1 *RTT*.

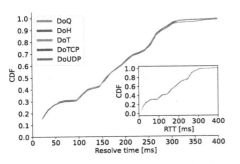
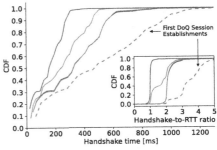

(a) *Resolve time* and *RTT* distribution.   (b) *Handshake time* and *handshake-to-RTT ratio* distribution.

Fig. 3. Distributions of response time metrics, targeting 264 *DoX-verified* resolvers. Please note the different x-axis scales. (Color figure online)

Note that we send every request with a new session for every protocol as a single query; we acknowledge that using a previously established session would reduce the overhead introduced by the *handshake time* for subsequent queries, e.g., by using `edns-tcp-keepalive` on TCP-based sessions. In addition, the stated *handshake times* can further be optimized *between* sessions by the usage of protocol mechanisms such as `TCP Fast Open (TFO)` using TCP, or `0-RTT` for TLS 1.3 ("early data") using TCP as well as QUIC (see Sect. 5). Hence, we investigate the 1,204 *DoQ-verified* resolvers for the support of `edns-tcp-keepalive` and `TFO`, as well as TLS 1.3 0-RTT for QUIC. We do not explicitly investigate the support of TLS 1.3 0-RTT for TCP, which we instead leave open for future work. For `edns-tcp-keepalive`, we find support only on the *AdGuard* resolvers, although they respond with a `timeout` value of 0 which instructs the client to directly close the session after having received the response. As for `TFO`, we find 208 resolvers supporting the TCP extension, of which no resolver is included in our *DoX-verified* set. Finally, none of the *DoQ-verified* resolvers offer support for QUIC 0-RTT. However, the lack of 0-RTT support might be a deliberate choice, as the use of 0-RTT exposes clients to privacy risks [39].

Figure 3 presents the distribution of the *resolve time* and the *RTT* (a, left), as well as the *handshake time* and *handshake-to-RTT ratio* (b, right) of the response time measurements toward the 264 targeted *DoX-verified* resolvers; please note the different x-axis scales. The steps in the CDF lines can be explained by two consecutive hops that have a high difference in their latencies, e.g., when crossing continental borders. For our response time analysis, we only consider measurements which successfully return a valid DNS response containing a `Response Code` within a timeout of 5 s. Further, we limit the analysis of DoQ, DoH, DoT, and DoTCP to measurements for which the corresponding *RTT* measurement is successfully answered by the resolvers. For DoUDP, we exclude the *RTT* measurements, as they were not replied to by any resolver, but include the *resolve* time for comparison. Analyzing the *resolve* time in Fig. 3(a, left), we observe that the distributions of all protocols are almost identical, and match the distributions of the respective RTT as shown in the subplot. Hence, we confirm that the *resolve* time indeed resembles 1 RTT, regardless of the protocol.

In contrast to *resolve time* and RTT, the *handshake time* presented in Fig. 3(b, right) shows a vastly different picture. DoTCP (green line) offers the fastest *handshake* times over all protocols with a median of 156 ms (mean 153 ms), which is expected due to DoTCP only requiring the TCP handshake (1 RTT) for the establishment of the session. On the other hand, DoT (gray line) and DoH (magenta line) show almost identical *handshake* times, with medians of around 322 ms and means of around 315 ms. As both protocols require the TCP handshake plus the TLS handshake for session establishment, the *handshake* times should resemble 3 times the measured *handshake* times of DoTCP when TLS 1.2 is used (3 $RTTs$ in total), and 2 times when TLS 1.3 is used (2 $RTTs$ in total): Analyzing the negotiated TLS versions, we observe that 99.6% of DoT and 96.7% of DoH measurements use TLS 1.3, whereas the remaining ones use TLS 1.2. Analyzing DoQ, we find an unexpected result (solid cyan line): Since QUIC combines the connection and encryption handshakes into 1 RTT, DoQ is expected to have the same distribution as DoTCP. However, with a median of 235 ms and a mean of 233 ms, the DoQ *handshake* times observed are higher than expected, having its distribution in between the distributions of DoTCP, and DoT and DoH.

To investigate this, we analyze the distribution of the relative number of $RTTs$ which are required by the *handshakes* as shown in Fig. 3(b, right, subplot). We divide each successful *DoX handshake time* measurement by its consecutive RTT measurement, thus, showing the distribution of the *handshake-to-RTT ratio* of each measurement pair. For DoTCP (green line), we observe that the *handshake* resembles 1 RTT as expected. Moreover, DoT (gray line) and DoH (magenta line) again overlap and converge into a long tail, roughly resembling the expected 2 $RTTs$ for TLS 1.3 up until the median. On the other hand, DoQ (solid cyan line) differs drastically from the expected *handshake* of 1 RTT: With around 20% of measurements showing an RTT of 1, DoQ converges to 2 RTTs at the 60th percentile; hence, roughly 40% of DoQ measurements require more than 2 $RTTs$, which is twice as much as expected in comparison. To investigate this, we analyze the qlog [32] outputs recorded during our response time measurements, which enable us to analyze the packet exchanges in detail. Using the qlogs, we confirm that the response time measurements are not affected by QUIC's Version Negotiation feature, as we use the previously negotiated QUIC Version of the cache warming session for the handshake of the subsequent DNS response time measurement session (see Sect. 2). However, we attribute the additional 1 RTT to the Address Validation feature of QUIC, which is a requirement for every session to prevent traffic amplification attacks by validating that the client is able to receive packets. To perform Address Validation, the QUIC standard [43] defines 1 *implicit* and 2 *explicit* mechanisms, with the *implicit* mechanism validating the address by receiving a packet protected with a handshake key (i.e., 1 additional RTT). The first *explicit* mechanism uses a Retry token sent by a server as a response to the clients `Initial` frame, instructing the client to re-issue the `Initial` frame with the server-constructed token (i.e., 1 additional RTT). The second *explicit* mechanism also leverages a server-constructed token: If a server issued a token using a `New_Token` frame in a previous session, it can be used in the `Initial` frame of a subsequent session (i.e., no additional $RTTs$).

Analyzing the `qlogs`, we find that in every cache warming session a `Retry` token is sent, and the client is validated using the first *explicit* mechanism. Moreover, we observe that a `New_Token` frame is also issued in every cache warming session, which we use in the subsequent DNS response time measurement session in order to validate the address within the clients first `Initial` frame. For those subsequent measurements, we confirm that every DNS response time measurement session is not affected by an additional `Retry` frame and, thus, no additional RTT, as the `Address Validation` is fulfilled. However, we find that resolvers still enforce the traffic amplification limit of 3 times the amount of data they received despite successful validation of the client's address: Depending on the X.509 certificate issued by a server, its size might exceed the traffic amplification limit, which requires the client to `ACK` data before the server sends the remaining bytes. Hence, an additional RTT is required, resulting in 2 $RTTs$ in total as observed in roughly 40% of DoQ measurements (see Fig. 3, b, right, cyan lines) – 2 times as much as expected.

We further analyze the *handshake times* of cache warming queries: This allows us to investigate the effect of `Address Validation` mechanisms on the DoQ *handshake time* required for the first session establishment between a client and a resolver (see Fig. 3, b, right, dashed cyan lines). With a median of 468 ms and a mean of 487 ms, the *handshake* times for the first session establishment are roughly doubled in comparison to subsequent sessions. Analyzing the `qlogs`, we find that the traffic amplification limit is also enforced in the cache warming sessions following successful `Address Validation`, which can therefore require up to 4 $RTTs$ (i.e., `Initial`, `Version Negotiation`, `Retry`, and `Amplification Limit`) – 4 times as much as expected.

Both our DoQ *handshake time* analyses of cache warming and subsequent queries show that an already validated address is still constrained by the traffic amplification limit until the client sends another frame, which adds 1 RTT to the handshake. However, while the QUIC standard states that the traffic amplification limit is to be enforced *until* a client is successfully validated, we argue that our observations are most likely an unintentional effect of the QUIC implementations used by the DoQ resolvers. Hence, we suggest resolvers to not enforce the traffic amplification limit on already validated client addresses to optimize the performance, which results in a reduction by 1 RTT during the *handshake*.

5   Limitations and Future Work

We acknowledge that the selected vantage point introduces a location bias for our measurements, in particular for the measured latencies in the response time analysis (Sect. 4). The highly varying geographical distances to the resolvers (whose distribution exhibits further biases, see Sect. 3) inherently affect the delays, especially if multiple round-trips are required. Hence, we plan to address this limitation by performing measurements from distributed vantage points worldwide to obtain a more representative view on DoQ response times around the globe.

Moreover, we acknowledge that public DNS resolvers often leverage IP anycast, about which we could not find any publicly available information for DoQ resolvers of *AdGuard* and *nextDNS*. In addition, by cross-referencing anycast IP addresses of public DNS providers used in related work measuring DoT and DoH [33,49,55], we were not able to identify these public DNS providers within our set of *DoQ-verified* resolvers.

Further, we miss resolvers that do not accept DoQ requests without Server Name Indication (SNI) information. For instance, Google requires queries over TLS 1.3 (which, thus, also affects QUIC) to use the SNI extension [13]. As a result, DoQ queries to 8.8.8.8 are not responded to by Google, whereas queries with the `HostName` set to `dns.google.com` in the SNI extension do trigger a DNS response. Since we do not include SNI in our requests due to not knowing the corresponding `HostName` for every identified resolver, we cannot identify and measure resolvers with such requirements. Therefore, the list of DoQ resolvers measured in our study is not exhaustive, as we only consider open resolvers that do not require SNI. Moreover, we only consider IPv4 resolvers in our study; future work should also consider scanning the IPv6 address space as a complement, e.g., based on IPv6 hitlists [34].

Finally, we plan to further evaluate DoQ by using previously established sessions for subsequent queries, as well as TLS 1.3 `0-RTT` between sessions in a future study: Both mechanisms reduce the overhead introduced by the *handshake time*, which affects application layer protocols that typically require multiple DNS queries in rapid succession.

6   Conclusion

DNS over QUIC promises to improve on the established encrypted DNS protocols by leveraging the QUIC transport protocol. In our study, we detailed a slowly but steadily increasing adoption of DoQ on resolvers worldwide, where the observed week-over-week fluctuations reflect the ongoing development and standardization process with rapidly changing implementations and services. Analyzing the response times of DoQ, we showed that the DoQ *handshake* times fully utilize QUIC's potential in around 20% of measurements. However, roughly 40% of measurements show considerably higher *handshake* times than expected, which traces back to the enforcement of the traffic amplification limit despite successful validation of the client's address. While this shows still unused optimization potential, DoQ already outperforms DoT as well as DoH, making it the best choice for encrypted DNS to date.

In conclusion, our study provided a first look at DNS over QUIC. However, we presented only a glimpse of the potential of DoQ: With the expectation that the upcoming standardization of DoQ will cause a surge in adoption along with optimizations of existing implementations, future studies will reveal whether DoQ will truly become the *"One to Rule them All"*.

Acknowledgements. We thank Luca Schumann and Simon Zelenski for their valuable support, as well as Jan Rüth and the anonymous reviewers for their insightful feedback.

References

1. AdGuard C++ DNS libraries. https://github.com/AdguardTeam/DnsLibs. (Accessed 31 Jan 2022)
2. AdGuard DNS. https://web.archive.org/web/20211011184753/adguard.com/en/adguard-dns/overview.html. (Accessed 31 Jan 2022)
3. AdGuard DNS-over-QUIC. https://adguard.com/en/blog/dns-over-quic.html. (Accessed 31 Jan 2022)
4. AdGuard DNS Proxy. https://github.com/AdguardTeam/dnsproxy. (Accessed 31 Jan 2022)
5. AdGuard Home. https://github.com/AdguardTeam/AdguardHome. (Accessed 31 Jan 2022)
6. AdGuard Home Release 0.107.0. https://github.com/AdguardTeam/AdGuardHome/releases/tag/v0.107.0. (Accessed 31 Jan 2022)
7. aioquic. https://github.com/aiortc/aioquic. (Accessed 31 Jan 2022)
8. CoreDNS fork for AdGuard DNS. https://github.com/AdguardTeam/coredns. (Accessed 31 Jan 2022)
9. DNS Measurements. https://github.com/mgranderath/dns-measurements. (Accessed 31 Jan 2022)
10. dnslookup. https://github.com/ameshkov/dnslookup. (Accessed 31 Jan 2022)
11. DNSPerf. https://github.com/mgranderath/dnsperf. (Accessed 31 Jan 2022)
12. Flamethrower. https://github.com/DNS-OARC/flamethrower/tree/dns-over-quic. (Accessed 31 Jan 2022)
13. Google Public DNS: TLS 1.3 and SNI for IP address URLs. https://developers.google.com/speed/public-dns/docs/secure-transports#tls-sni. (Accessed 31 Jan 2022)
14. IP Geolocation API. https://ip-api.com/. (Accessed 31 Jan 2022)
15. Misc DNS Measurements. https://github.com/mgranderath/misc-dns-measurements. (Accessed 31 Jan 2022)
16. NextDNS CLI Client. https://github.com/nextdns/nextdns. (Accessed 31 Jan 2022)
17. NextDNS Knowledge Base. https://help.nextdns.io/t/x2hmvas/what-is-dns-over-tls-dot-dns-over-quic-doq-and-dns-over-https-doh-doh3. (Accessed 31 Jan 2022)
18. One to Rule them All? A First Look at DNS over QUIC. https://github.com/kosekmi/2022-pam-dns-over-quic. (Accessed 31 Jan 2022)
19. quicdog. https://github.com/private-octopus/quicdoq. (Accessed 31 Jan 2022)
20. Refuse queries without RD bit. https://knot-resolver.readthedocs.io/en/stable/modules-refuse_nord.html. (Accessed 31 Jan 2022)
21. RouteDNS. https://github.com/folbricht/routedns. (Accessed 31 Jan 2022)
22. The ZMap project. https://zmap.io/. (Accessed 31 Jan 2022)
23. Verify DoQ. https://github.com/mgranderath/verify-doq. (Accessed 31 Jan 2022)
24. ZMap DoQ. https://github.com/mgranderath/zmap-doq. (Accessed 31 Jan 2022)
25. Domain names - concepts and facilities. RFC 1034 (1987). https://doi.org/10.17487/RFC1034
26. Domain names - implementation and specification. RFC 1035 (1987). https://doi.org/10.17487/RFC1035

27. Bajpai, V., et al.: The dagstuhl beginners guide to reproducibility for experimental networking research. SIGCOMM Comput. Commun. Rev. **49**(1), 24–30 (2019). https://doi.org/10.1145/3314212.3314217

28. Brandt, M., Dai, T., Klein, A., Shulman, H., Waidner, M.: Domain validation++ for MitM-resilient PKI. In: ACM SIGSAC Conference on Computer and Communications Security. CCS '18, pp. 2060–2076. Association for Computing Machinery, New York, NY, USA (2018). https://doi.org/10.1145/3243734.3243790

29. Deccio, C., Davis, J.: DNS privacy in practice and preparation. In: Conference on Emerging Networking Experiments And Technologies. CoNEXT '19, pp. 138–143. Association for Computing Machinery, New York, NY, USA (2019). https://doi.org/10.1145/3359989.3365435

30. Durumeric, Z., Wustrow, E., Halderman, J.A.: ZMap: fast internet-wide scanning and its security applications. In: 22nd USENIX Security Symposium (USENIX Security 13), pp. 605–620. USENIX Association, Washington, D.C. (2013). https://www.usenix.org/conference/usenixsecurity13/technical-sessions/paper/durumeric

31. Fujiwara, K., Vixie, P.A.: Fragmentation avoidance in DNS. Internet-Draft draft-ietf-dnsop-avoid-fragmentation-06, Internet Engineering Task Force (2021). https://datatracker.ietf.org/doc/draft-ietf-dnsop-avoid-fragmentation/. Work in Progress

32. Fujiwara, K., Vixie, P.A.: Main logging schema for qlog. Internet-Draft draft-ietf-quic-qlog-main-schema-01, Internet Engineering Task Force (2021). https://datatracker.ietf.org/doc/draft-ietf-quic-qlog-main-schema/. Work in Progress

33. García, S., Hynek, K., Vekshin, D., Čejka, T., Wasicek, A.: Large scale measurement on the adoption of encrypted DNS (2021). https://arxiv.org/abs/2107.04436

34. Gasser, O., et al.: Clusters in the expanse: understanding and unbiasing IPv6 hitlists. In: Proceedings of the Internet Measurement Conference 2018, IMC 2018, Boston, MA, USA, 31 October–02 November 2018, pp. 364–378. ACM (2018). https://dl.acm.org/citation.cfm?id=3278564

35. Hardaker, W.: Analyzing and mitigating privacy with the DNS root service. In: NDSS: DNS Privacy Workshop (2018)

36. Herzberg, A., Shulman, H.: Fragmentation considered poisonous, or: one-domain-to-rule-them-all.org. In: Conference on Communications and Network Security (CNS), pp. 224–232. IEEE (2013). https://doi.org/10.1109/CNS.2013.6682711

37. Hoffman, P.E., McManus, P.: DNS queries over HTTPS (DoH). RFC 8484 (2018). https://doi.org/10.17487/RFC8484

38. Hu, Z., Zhu, L., Heidemann, J., Mankin, A., Wessels, D., Hoffman, P.E.: Specification for DNS over Transport Layer Security (TLS). RFC 7858 (2016). https://doi.org/10.17487/RFC7858

39. Huitema, C., Dickinson, S., Mankin, A.: DNS over dedicated QUIC connections. Internet-Draft draft-ietf-dprive-dnsoquic-08, Internet Engineering Task Force (2022). https://datatracker.ietf.org/doc/draft-ietf-dprive-dnsoquic/. Work in Progress

40. ICANN: RSSAC002 Data. https://www.dns.icann.org/rssac/rssac002/. (Accessed 31 Jan 2022)

41. IETF: DNS PRIVate Exchange WG. https://datatracker.ietf.org/wg/dprive/about/. (Accessed 31 Jan 2022)

42. Iyengar, J., Swett, I.: QUIC loss detection and congestion control. RFC 9002 (2021). https://doi.org/10.17487/RFC9002

43. Iyengar, J., Thomson, M.: QUIC: A UDP-based multiplexed and secure transport. RFC 9000 (2021). https://doi.org/10.17487/RFC9000

44. Kim, D.W., Zhang, J.: You are how you query: deriving behavioral fingerprints from DNS traffic. In: Thuraisingham, B., Wang, X.F., Yegneswaran, V. (eds.) SecureComm 2015. LNICST, vol. 164, pp. 348–366. Springer, Cham (2015). https://doi.org/10.1007/978-3-319-28865-9_19

45. Kirchler, M., Herrmann, D., Lindemann, J., Kloft, M.: Tracked without a trace: linking sessions of users by unsupervised learning of patterns in their DNS traffic. In: Freeman, D.M., Mitrokotsa, A., Sinha, A. (eds.) Proceedings of the 2016 ACM Workshop on Artificial Intelligence and Security, AISec@CCS 2016, Vienna, Austria, 28 October 2016, pp. 23–34. ACM (2016). https://doi.org/10.1145/2996758.2996770

46. Labs, N.: Measuring the effects of DNSSEC deployment on query load (2006). http://www.nlnetlabs.nl/downloads/publications/dnssec/dnssec-effects.pdf. (Accessed 31 Jan 2022)

47. Learmonth, I.R., Grover, G., Knodel, M.: Guidelines for performing safe measurement on the internet. Internet-Draft draft-irtf-pearg-safe-internet-measurement-05, Internet Engineering Task Force (2021). https://datatracker.ietf.org/doc/draft-irtf-pearg-safe-internet-measurement/. Work in Progress

48. Li, J., Ma, X., Li, G., Luo, X., Zhang, J., Li, W., Guan, X.: Can we learn what people are doing from raw DNS queries? In: IEEE Conference on Computer Communications, INFOCOM 2018, Honolulu, HI, USA, 16–19 April 2018, pp. 2240–2248. IEEE (2018). https://doi.org/10.1109/INFOCOM.2018.8486210

49. Lu, C., et al.: An End-to-End, large-scale measurement of DNS-over-encryption: how far have we come? In: Internet Measurement Conference. IMC '19, pp. 22–35. Association for Computing Machinery, New York, NY, USA (2019). https://doi.org/10.1145/3355369.3355580

50. Moura, G.C.M., Müller, M., Davids, M., Wullink, M., Hesselman, C.: Fragmentation, truncation, and timeouts: are large DNS messages falling to bits? In: Hohlfeld, O., Lutu, A., Levin, D. (eds.) PAM 2021. LNCS, vol. 12671, pp. 460–477. Springer, Cham (2021). https://doi.org/10.1007/978-3-030-72582-2_27

51. Randall, A., et al.: Trufflehunter: cache snooping rare domains at large public DNS resolvers. In: Internet Measurement Conference. IMC '20. Association for Computing Machinery (2020). https://doi.org/10.1145/3419394.3423640

52. Reddy, K.T., Wing, D., Patil, P.: DNS over Datagram Transport Layer Security (DTLS). RFC 8094 (2017). https://rfc-editor.org/rfc/rfc8094.txt

53. Rüth, J., Poese, I., Dietzel, C., Hohlfeld, O.: A first look at QUIC in the wild. In: Beverly, R., Smaragdakis, G., Feldmann, A. (eds.) PAM 2018. LNCS, vol. 10771, pp. 255–268. Springer, Cham (2018). https://doi.org/10.1007/978-3-319-76481-8_19

54. Thomson, M., Turner, S.: Using TLS to secure QUIC. RFC 9001 (2021). https://doi.org/10.17487/RFC9001

55. Doan, T.V., Tsareva, I., Bajpai, V.: Measuring DNS over TLS from the edge: adoption, reliability, and response times. In: Hohlfeld, O., Lutu, A., Levin, D. (eds.) PAM 2021. LNCS, vol. 12671, pp. 192–209. Springer, Cham (2021). https://doi.org/10.1007/978-3-030-72582-2_12

56. Wicinski, T.: DNS privacy considerations. RFC 9076 (2021). https://doi.org/10.17487/RFC9076

57. Zhu, L., Hu, Z., Heidemann, J., Wessels, D., Mankin, A., Somaiya, N.: Connection-oriented DNS to improve privacy and security. In: Symposium on Security and Privacy, pp. 171–186. IEEE (2015). https://doi.org/10.1109/SP.2015.18

58. ZMap: UDP Data Probes. https://github.com/zmap/zmap/blob/master/examples/udp-probes/README. (Accessed 31 Jan 2022)

Application Performance

Zoom Session Quality:
A Network-Level View

Albert Choi, Mehdi Karamollahi, Carey Williamson$^{(\boxtimes)}$, and Martin Arlitt

University of Calgary, Calgary, AB, Canada
{albert.choi1,mehdi.karamollahi,cwill,marlitt}@ucalgary.ca

Abstract. Zoom is a popular videoconferencing application for remote work and learning. In 2020, our university adopted Zoom for delivering online lectures during work-from-home restrictions. Starting in September 2021, however, our university offered both in-person and online classes, leading to increased Zoom usage on our campus network. In this paper, we study this Zoom network traffic in two different ways. First, we perform small-scale active measurements on individual Zoom test sessions to understand communication patterns and traffic structure. Second, we use large-scale passive measurement of campus-level Zoom traffic to understand usage patterns and performance problems. Our results identify 4x growth in Zoom traffic on our campus network since 2020, as well as network-related issues that affect Zoom session quality.

Keywords: Network measurement · Zoom video conferencing · QoE

1 Introduction

Since the onset of the COVID-19 pandemic in early 2020, Zoom has become the primary platform for online learning at many universities worldwide, including the University of Calgary. Zoom grew significantly as a video conferencing platform during the pandemic, due to its ease of use, and the ability to host meetings with a large number of participants [2,17].

In September 2021, our university began to transition back to in-person learning for 50% of its courses. Many students who enrolled for in-person classes also had Zoom-based online lectures for other courses. Due to course scheduling, this situation often required students to be on campus for their online classes, which significantly increased Zoom traffic on our campus network, and led to several anecdotal reports of Zoom performance problems.

In this paper, we describe our approach for studying Zoom network traffic on campus, and our results from analyzing this network traffic. Our work is motivated by fairly broad questions such as how large the Zoom user community is on campus and the number of classes being joined by students while on campus. The data that we collect and analyze also gives insights into the behaviours of students when joining Zoom sessions from on campus, such as when and for how long they join Zoom sessions, and whether they use their camera or microphone. We are also interested in the user-level Quality of Experience (QoE) for Zoom

© The Author(s), under exclusive license to Springer Nature Switzerland AG 2022
O. Hohlfeld et al. (Eds.): PAM 2022, LNCS 13210, pp. 555–572, 2022.
https://doi.org/10.1007/978-3-030-98785-5_25

sessions. Our results provide a better understanding of how Zoom is used on our campus network, and identify several network performance issues.

Our main contributions include tools for analyzing empirical Zoom network traffic data, as well as insights regarding Zoom session quality from a network-level perspective. Our results quantify the performance of Zoom with respect to bandwidth usage and QoE. Table 1 summarizes our main observations, which are discussed more fully in the rest of the paper.

Table 1. Empirical observations about Zoom network traffic

Name	Observation	Section
Control	Zoom uses a TCP connection to manage each session, including chat	4.1
Channels	Zoom uses separate UDP ports for audio, video, and screen sharing	4.1
Adaptivity	Zoom uses bandwidth probing to dynamically adapt video bit rates	4.1
Disruptions	Many Zoom sessions experience disruptions on TCP or UDP connections	4.3
Usage	Zoom has diurnal usage patterns that are driven by class schedules	5.1
Growth	Zoom traffic on our campus network has grown 4x over the past year	5.1
Patterns	Session structure and camera usage are discernible from traffic analysis	5.2
Robustness	Zoom sessions are resilient, and can re-establish connections as needed	5.3

The remainder of this paper is organized as follows. Section 2 provides a brief overview of prior related work. Section 3 describes our active and passive approaches for collecting and analyzing Zoom network traffic. Section 4 presents results from our small-scale experiments with Zoom, while Sect. 5 discusses results from our campus-wide look at Zoom traffic. Section 6 discusses the performance implications of our results. Finally, Sect. 7 concludes the paper.

2 Related Work

Several prior works have studied pandemic effects on Internet traffic, including enterprise networks [1,5], ISP networks [7], mobile networks [9], and academic environments [4,15]. Here we highlight selected papers from the literature.

Feldmann et al. [5] studied pandemic effects on Internet traffic, as viewed by ISPs, IXPs, and mobile network operators. They identified 15–20% growth in Internet traffic volumes within a week of the lockdowns taking place in Europe. Their paper identified new network applications being used in work-from-home environments, including Zoom and Teams, that contributed to the traffic growth. Our study focuses specifically on Zoom in a campus setting, with an emphasis on network-level and application-level performance.

Favale et al. [4] studied changes to network traffic induced by the COVID-19 pandemic in an academic setting. The traffic patterns were observed from Politecnico di Torino, a medium-sized university located in Italy. Their study differs from ours in that the online e-learning platform studied was not Zoom, but rather a custom in-house solution developed based on the BigBlueButton framework. The authors found that incoming traffic was greatly reduced across three university campuses that were studied, since few students were on campus to generate inbound traffic. For the campus that hosted the e-learning platform, however, the outbound network traffic more than doubled. While their university did not adopt Zoom at all, many universities did. Thus our results should be broadly applicable for many Zoom users in academic environments.

Two recent papers [3,10] studied videoconferencing applications, including Zoom. Chang *et al.* [3] developed a cloud-based framework for testing and comparing the QoE for Meet, WebEx, and Zoom. Their work used emulated clients in the cloud to identify QoE differences for these three applications, based on architecture, infrastructure, geographic location, lag, video bit rate, and network bandwidth constraints. They used free-tier versions of these applications, and real mobile devices, in meetings with up to 11 emulated participants. MacMillan *et al.* [10] compared Meet, Teams, and Zoom in an experimental testbed. Their work focused on network utilization, robustness, and fairness [14] between and among these videoconferencing applications under different emulated network conditions. They also studied the scaling properties of these applications with up to 8 participants. Our work differs from both of these papers in that we focus on developing tools to analyze empirically-observed Zoom sessions generated by thousands of users on our campus network. Our companion paper [6] provides a longitudinal (macroscopic) view of Zoom, Teams, Meet, VPN, and other applications on our campus network during the pandemic; here, we provide a detailed (microscopic) look at Zoom.

There are also several Zoom-specific papers that focus on privacy and security issues [11,12], rather than network performance or QoE. Marczak and Scott-Railton [12] studied Zoom network traffic to investigate potential security vulnerabilities with the platform. Mahr et al. [11] analyzed the types of data that Zoom sends in either encrypted or unencrypted form. In our paper, we focus on the network traffic patterns and application-level performance of Zoom.

3   Methodology

Our work uses a combination of active and passive approaches to network traffic measurement. We use the resulting data to study on-campus Zoom sessions from both network-level and application-level perspectives.

We first analyze Zoom traffic at a small-scale to extract insights regarding communication patterns. We do so using Wireshark [16] for a packet-level view of Zoom test sessions under our control. Although all Zoom traffic is encrypted, we can still obtain useful information regarding the Zoom application, such as IP addresses and port numbers, session structure, and bandwidth consumption.

Data collection is done using Windows and Linux laptops. Wireshark is used to capture packets locally during Zoom test sessions. Data collection is done in a controlled environment where we are the only users in a Zoom session. Our active measurements only involve users who opted in for data collection.

Using knowledge from the small-scale experiments, we subsequently analyze campus-wide Zoom traffic at our university, which has approximately 35,000 students, faculty, and staff, and a 10 Gbps external connection to the Internet. The campus-level traffic data consists of summarized traffic logs from our campus network monitor (Endace DAG; Dell PowerEdge running Zeek). The connection logs provide detailed information about each observed connection, such as start time, protocol endpoints, bytes/packets transferred, and connection duration (see Appendix A for an example). These logs are collected in cooperation with our campus IT staff, and with permission obtained via our campus research ethics review process. We conduct TCP/IP traffic analysis using packet headers only (no payloads), focusing on aggregate traffic characteristics from thousands of users, most of whom use transient IP addresses from DHCP/NAT.

We collect our passive measurement data from a mirrored stream of all traffic that passes through the campus edge router. This means that we can observe all traffic that has at least one endpoint on the campus network and at least one endpoint on the Internet. In particular, Zoom traffic is observable when students or instructors on campus connect to a Zoom server. We identify Zoom traffic based on the 118 IPv4 network prefixes[1] indicated on the Zoom Web site. We also use information about the Zoom connection process[2] and local DNS logs to distinguish Zoom MultiMedia Routers (MMR) from other Zoom server types (e.g., API, CDN, logging, Web, XMPP, Zone Controller).

4   Small-Scale Measurements

This section presents results from our small-scale measurements of Zoom test sessions using Wireshark. The purpose is to understand the structure of Zoom traffic, and enable Zoom analysis using our campus-level connection logs.

4.1   Zoom Session Structure

Our first experiment[3] focused on the structure of a Zoom test session that lasted about 45 min. The meeting host was on campus, using the university-licensed version of Zoom on a wireless laptop. The second participant was on their own laptop at home. A third participant joined the meeting late, and then left early.

Figure 1(a) shows a time-series plot of the packet traffic during this Zoom test session, based on the Wireshark trace. After launching the meeting, the host waited for others to join. During this time, communication took place between the host's laptop and the Zoom MMR server, using one TCP control connection (port 443), and three separate UDP connections[4] for audio, video, and screen-sharing (data), respectively. All media traffic was sent to the MMR server on UDP port 8801, with periodic keep-alive packets when idle. TCP is used to manage the session, and handle any chat messages[5] sent during the meeting.

---

[1] https://support.zoom.us/hc/en-us/articles/201362683-Network-firewall-or-proxy-server-settings-for-Zoom.

[2] https://zoom.us/docs/doc/ZoomConnectionProcessWhitepaper.pdf.

[3] Other experiments tested different features (e.g., camera, microphone, chat, screen-sharing, waiting room) to learn more about Zoom, similar to the approach in [8]. See Appendix B for two additional examples of such sessions.

[4] Though UDP is connectionless, we refer to these as UDP connections or *channels*.

[5] Documents sent via chat use a separate TCP connection to an XMPP server.

When the second participant joined 6 min later, Zoom switched into peer-to-peer (P2P) mode (shown in purple). In this mode (P), all media traffic is delivered directly between the two participants using a single UDP connection with ephemeral ports at each end [3]. However, the TCP control (C) connection to the MMR server remained in place. The total bit rate in P2P mode fluctuated between 3 Mbps and 6 Mbps, with an average of 5 Mbps.

When the third participant joined 11 min later, Zoom switched back into server mode, with all traffic from each laptop being sent to the MMR server on UDP port 8801. In this mode, Zoom uses three UDP channels (with ephemeral ports at each client) to send audio, video, and screen-sharing data to each participant. The packet rates and sizes on each channel are quite distinctive (see the CDF plots in Fig. 1(b) and (c)), enabling simple heuristics[6] to identify the channels. These channels are colour-coded in the graph with blue for video (V), orange for audio (A), green for screen-sharing data (D), and black for total UDP traffic volume (T). The total bit rate in this mode was about 3.5 Mbps, substantially higher than the 1.0–1.5 Mbps rate reported for free-tier Zoom [3,10]. As is evident from the graph, video accounts for most of the UDP traffic observed.

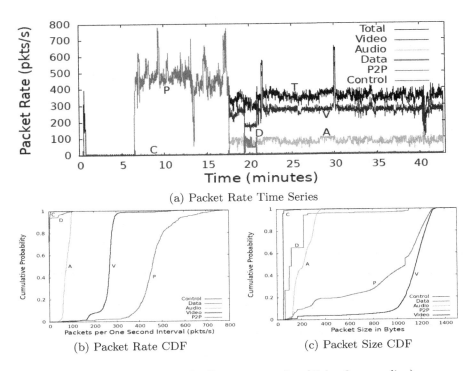

(a) Packet Rate Time Series

(b) Packet Rate CDF   (c) Packet Size CDF

Fig. 1. An example of a Zoom test session (Color figure online)

---

[6] We use threshold-based strategies, with average packet size as the primary feature, and average packet rate as a secondary feature. Directionality is also important.

Several other observations are evident from Fig. 1(a). First, the overall packet rate decreased when switching from P2P mode to Zoom server mode, likely reflecting bandwidth management techniques used by the server. Second, when the third participant leaves, Zoom does *not* switch back into P2P mode; rather, it stays in central server mode for the remainder of the session. Third, when screen-sharing happens (at 20-min mark), the video bit rate is dynamically reduced until screen-sharing is complete. Fourth, the two upward spikes suggest that Zoom uses dynamic bandwidth probing to adapt the video bit rate during the session. Each spike represents a higher packet rate from the MMR server for 10 s. Finally, the TCP control connection (red) lasts throughout the Zoom session, regardless of the number of participants.

4.2   Zoom Session Profiles

In addition to time-series plots of packet traffic, we construct *session profiles* to visualize Zoom session structure and identify performance anomalies.

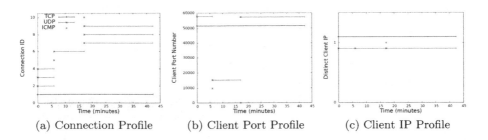

(a) Connection Profile   (b) Client Port Profile   (c) Client IP Profile

Fig. 2. Session profile for a single client in the Zoom test session

Figure 2 shows the session profile for the Zoom test session from Fig. 1. Figure 2(a) shows the *connection profile*, which illustrates the TCP and UDP connections used during a Zoom session. The vertical axis shows a monotonically increasing ID number for each connection (TCP, UDP, or ICMP) in the order of their creation, and the horizontal axis shows the elapsed time duration for each connection. A normal Zoom session has four horizontal lines for each participant, representing one TCP connection and three UDP connections launched almost simultaneously, and with very similar durations. An exception is when switching between P2P mode (with a single UDP connection) and Zoom server mode, since three new UDP connections are created then, while the TCP connection remains the same. Figure 2(b) is a *port profile*, which shows the port numbers used by each client connection, which sometimes reveals OS-specific behaviours. Notably, the UDP port numbers here are consecutive (suggestive of Microsoft Windows), and the P2P session occurred on a distinctly different port than the others. Because of the vertical scale of the graph, some of the concurrent UDP connections blend together, though they are separate connections as seen in Fig. 2(a). Figure 2(c) shows the *IP profile*, which stitches together disrupted connections (if any), and groups them based on the client's IP address. We vertically offset TCP from UDP so that they do not obfuscate each other, and bundle the UDP connections together to reduce visual clutter (e.g., this helps a lot when many clients are being shown).

4.3   Anomalous Zoom Sessions

The session profile plot provides a useful visualization tool for assessing Zoom session quality, and identifying anomalous Zoom sessions.

Figure 3 shows the session profile from a Zoom meeting that had very poor quality (i.e., two Zoom restarts, and two additional audio outages for the user). Figure 3(a) shows that this particular session had numerous disruptions to the TCP control channel, which had trouble reconnecting, and finally stabilized[7] after about 10 min. There were about 40 TCP connection attempts, though only four Zoom impairments were perceptible at the user level. The two Zoom restarts resulted in new UDP connections for all three channels (labelled 'AVD' in Fig. 3(c)). There were also two other disruptions to the audio channel (labeled 'A'), which resulted in the creation of a new UDP connection. The dynamic port selection for the disrupted audio channel is evident in Fig. 3(b), while that for the TCP control channel is less evident, since these port numbers are often contiguous. Figure 3(c) shows the IP profile for this session. The overall structure of the Zoom session is clearer on this plot. In particular, the TCP channel had many disruptions, which affected the control channel and Zoom connectivity. The UDP channels had fewer disruptions, but still degraded session quality.

Surprisingly, even small Zoom meetings in P2P mode can experience disruptions. As an example, the second row of Fig. 3 shows the session profile for a two-person meeting, with one on campus, and the other at home. The on-campus laptop for which we have a Wireshark trace has TCP (red) and UDP (orange) connections that start near time 50 on the graph. The UDP connection was normal, but the TCP connection was disrupted repeatedly for over half an hour. Analysis of the Wireshark trace and the campus-level data shows numerous connection resets, often in alternating fashion with another campus host (green for TCP) that was trying to set up a different meeting with the same Zoom server. The graph also shows a third host (blue for TCP, and magenta for UDP) that had started another meeting with the same Zoom server about an hour earlier. Its session was fine until near the end, when the other sessions started.

Figure 3 leads to several insights. First, it is quite common for multiple meetings on our campus network to share the same Zoom server at the same time. This behaviour differs from that reported in prior work, where every new meeting used a different Zoom server [3]. We attribute this difference to the large number of Zoom meetings on campus, and the limited set of Zoom servers available in our region. Second, things can go wrong when too many Zoom

---

[7] The client contacted a Zone Controller (ZC), and then switched the TCP control channel (but not the UDP channels) to a different Zoom MMR server.

meetings concurrently use the same busy Zoom server. Our Wireshark traces show lots of TCP duplicate ACKs, spurious retransmissions, and the Zoom server sending an "Encrypted Alert" to terminate the TLS session with the client, which then has trouble reconnecting to the server. Third, the network-level effects are most evident on TCP connections. Detailed analysis shows a mix of unsuccessful connection attempts, resets by the server, and resets by the client. Several exhibit sluggish Server Hello messages in the TLS handshake (e.g., taking 2–8 s instead of 25–30 ms), causing the client to timeout and reset the connection.

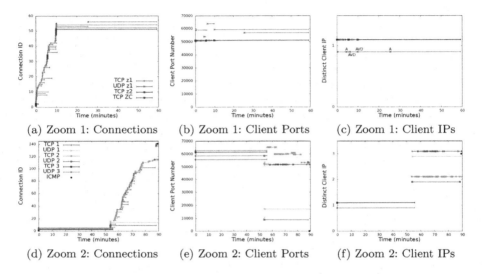

(a) Zoom 1: Connections   (b) Zoom 1: Client Ports   (c) Zoom 1: Client IPs

(d) Zoom 2: Connections   (e) Zoom 2: Client Ports   (f) Zoom 2: Client IPs

Fig. 3. Session profile examples for two anomalous Zoom meetings (Color figure online)

5   Large-Scale Measurements

Our next set of measurements focus on larger examples of Zoom sessions extracted from our campus network traffic logs. For these sessions, we have no packet-level Wireshark traces, since we do not have permission to collect such traces during live classes or meetings. Nonetheless, we use the empirically-observed traffic data from connection logs to infer information about the Zoom sessions.

5.1   Zoom Usage Patterns

Figure 4(a) shows a time series plot of the aggregate Zoom traffic observed on our campus network for a representative day (Wed Sept 22, 2021) from our Fall 2021 semester. The lines on the graph represent the total number of concurrent UDP 8801 connections (purple) to Zoom MMR servers, as well as the corresponding number of Zoom sessions (green) and Zoom meetings (blue) determined using our traffic analysis tools. On this day, the peak load reached about 3,500 concurrent UDP connections, representing about 1,100 Zoom sessions (i.e., users) in about 250 different concurrent Zoom meetings. There were a total of 3,679 different Zoom meetings on this day. Each meeting had about 4 on-campus users, on average, and each user session had about 3 UDP connections.

Figure 4(a) shows that Zoom usage exhibits a diurnal pattern that corresponds to when people are on campus. The busy period starts in the morning with usage peaking mid-day[8] and declining towards the evening. Class schedules are also evident in the overall Zoom traffic, with classes starting every hour between 8:00 am and 5:00 pm on this specific day.

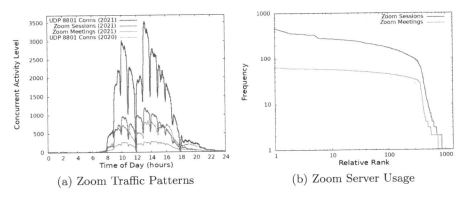

(a) Zoom Traffic Patterns   (b) Zoom Server Usage

Fig. 4. Aggregate Zoom traffic characteristics: demand vs. supply (Color figure online)

Figure 4(a) also illustrates the growth in Zoom traffic on our campus network between Fall 2021 and the corresponding day (Wed Sept 23, 2020) from the Fall 2020 semester, when only 20% of courses were offered in person. We use the count of concurrent UDP 8801 connections for this comparison (i.e., purple line versus thin magenta line). The results show that Zoom traffic has increased 4x from Fall 2020 to Fall 2021; in fact, it now exceeds 1 TB per day [6]. This growth in demand is substantial, and reflects the impacts of mixed modalities for learning, with 30–50% of students back on campus.

Figure 4(b) takes a different perspective, by looking at the supply of Zoom servers. This graph is an IP frequency-rank plot (on a log-log scale), showing the relative frequency with which different Zoom MMR server IPs are used for meetings. The data is from a one-week period in September 2021, during which

---

[8] The dip at 12 noon is an artifact of our campus network monitor, which is restarted every 6 h to avoid possible crashes during high-volume scans [6]. This restart unfortunately loses information about connections in progress at 6:00 am, noon, 6:00 pm, and midnight. This artifact is most evident at 12 noon, when load is higher.

there were 17,120 Zoom meetings, involving a total of 1,374 Zoom MMR servers. However, Fig. 4(b) shows that the usage of Zoom servers is highly non-uniform. In our dataset, the top three/24 Zoom network prefixes accounted for 42%, 35%, and 13% of the meetings, using 183, 150, and 76 MMR servers, respectively. Each of these MMR servers was used, on average, about 40 times during the week, or about 6 times each day.

These results show that the number of Zoom servers available to our campus users is limited, with about 400 servers handling 90% of the meetings. The reason for this is our campus Zoom configuration, which directs work-related meetings to regionally-hosted Zoom servers within Canada (primarily Vancouver and Toronto, as well as Etobicoke, Ontario). The other Zoom server IPs in our dataset appear only a few times, possibly from personal (free-tier) Zoom usage, or on-campus people attending meetings hosted by colleagues elsewhere.

We believe that this mismatch between supply and demand is the root cause of the Zoom performance anomalies that we have observed on our campus network. At peak times of the day, some MMR servers are managing multiple large meetings, and are unable to cope with the corresponding load. This phenomenon might be specific to our university's Zoom configuration, but could occur elsewhere if the supply of regional Zoom servers is quite limited.

5.2 Session Characteristics

By focusing on a single Zoom server IP address at a time, we can identify specific Zoom sessions for classes or meetings. As a sanity check for these sessions, we also check the consistency of the end time, and the data volumes exchanged on each connection. For such an event, we can then determine the number of participants, and assess the arrival patterns for the attendees.

Based on the relative data volumes sent in each direction on the UDP channels, we can also estimate the proportion of participants that are using their camera, microphone, or screen-sharing during a Zoom call. Anecdotally, it has been observed that most students turn their cameras off when attending a Zoom lecture. Our measurements suggest that about 10% of participants are using their camera, and the others have the camera off for most or all of the session.

Figure 5(a) shows an example from a one-hour Zoom session with about 40 on-campus participants. The horizontal axis shows the average packet size sent by each connection, and the vertical axis shows the average packet size received. The points are colour-coded based on our (heuristic) classification of the channels. The points cluster quite tightly into logical groupings, with the video category varying the most. The graph shows that one of the Zoom participants was using screen-sharing, with an average packet size of 600 bytes, while the others were not. Similarly, one participant sent more audio/video than the others, and received more control information. These observations imply that there was a single presenter during the session, with several questions asked via audio or chat. These patterns are consistent with a lecture-based class.

Figure 5(b) shows an example of a large meeting with 120 Zoom participants, about 30 of whom were on campus (including one of the co-authors). The pat-

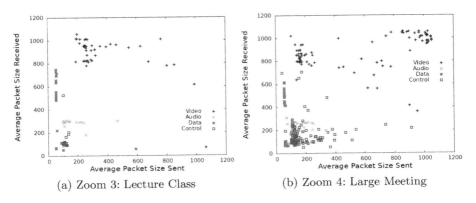

(a) Zoom 3: Lecture Class　　　　　(b) Zoom 4: Large Meeting

Fig. 5. Scatterplot view of Zoom channel usage

terns for the UDP channels resemble those in Fig. 5(a), though more cameras (about 40%) were on during the meeting. In addition, the TCP control channel indicates lots of interaction via the chat interface for questions and answers.

5.3 Session Quality

Figure 6 shows the session profile[9] for the large Zoom meeting. There was a steep arrival pattern for the connections, because of the Zoom waiting room used to admit attendees. The consistency in the end times for the connections suggests that all participants were (likely) in the same meeting.

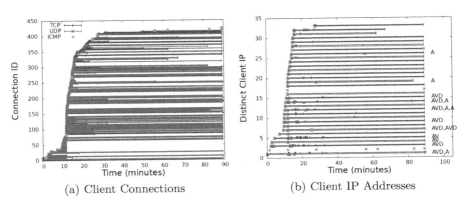

(a) Client Connections　　　　　(b) Client IP Addresses

Fig. 6. Zoom 4: session profile for participants in large Zoom meeting

Figure 6 shows that about a dozen (40%) of the 30 participants had disruptions to their TCP connections during the Zoom session. We have also annotated

---

[9] We exclude the port profile, which is too cluttered to be useful.

the graph with A, V, or D to indicate disruptions to the UDP-based audio, video, or data channels, respectively, that occurred during the meeting. About 10 of the participants (30%) had disruptions, with many of these participants on NAT addresses. Even users on static IP addresses (e.g., IPs on rows 7, 25, and 27) had some disruptions on their UDP channels.

5.4   Anomalous Zoom Behaviour

Figure 7 shows one of the most interesting Zoom sessions that we found in our data. This graph shows the IP profile for a session with about 20 on-campus participants. This session seems to be a lecture-oriented class that lasted about an hour. Several disruptions occurred during this session, at almost periodic intervals that are about 11 min apart. Based on the session profile, it appears that the session host had their network connectivity disrupted (note the ICMP messages), which affected every other meeting participant.

The timing gaps between UDP connections are about 2–10 s each, consistent with Zoom restarts. Even more interesting, Zoom seems to enter a "failover" mode with *four* concurrent UDP connections: three[10] new ones on a randomly chosen[11] Zoom server, and one on the original server. On the graph, this mode manifests in alternating fashion upon each new disruption. This might reflect Forward Error Correction (FEC) to preserve audio quality [10], since the extra UDP channel has packet rates and sizes consistent with audio.

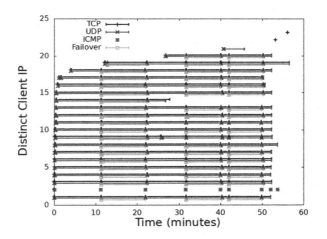

Fig. 7. Zoom 5: example of Zoom failover mode

We have not yet identified the root cause of this anomaly, but have found several other examples like it in our data. Using scatterplot analysis on this

---

[10] There is also a TCP control connection to this new server (not shown on graph).

[11] Curiously, two clients (IPs 9 and 11) choose the *original* Zoom server to handle failover as well, inducing extra connection overhead at an inopportune time.

example, we have determined that all participants have their cameras on, and screen-sharing is in use, though the presenter does not seem to be on campus. This might suggest that the problem is a home networking issue for the presenter, such as buffer overflow at a WiFi router, leading to repeated Zoom failures that affect all participants in a synchronized fashion. We are trying to recreate this phenomenon experimentally in our ongoing work.

6   Discussion

In this section, we highlight the main performance implications from our study, and offer several suggestions for network administrators and Zoom software engineers to improve Zoom performance in the future. We also discuss the technical limitations of our work.

6.1   Performance Implications and Recommendations

The main problem identified in our study is one of supply versus demand. The use of mixed learning modalities on our campus during the Fall 2021 semester quadrupled Zoom traffic demand compared to Fall 2020, while directing this traffic to regional Zoom servers in Canada has inadvertently constrained the supply of MMR servers available. As a result, these servers often host multiple Zoom meetings at the same time, some of which are large and long duration meetings. At busy times of the day, some MMR servers seem to become sluggish (e.g., TLS), compromising session quality and the user-level Zoom experience.

For campus network administrators, our main recommendation is to ensure that a sufficiently large pool of regional servers is available. If this is not possible, then a second option is to reduce the default video bit rate on Zoom sessions, so that traffic loads are lower. A third option is to host a Zoom Meeting Zone within the campus network, though this might be expensive, and would no longer be needed when the pandemic is over. Finally, it is important to consider the load that Zoom places on the campus WiFi network and the NAT infrastructure, to ensure that these are not performance bottlenecks for Zoom.

For Zoom network engineers, one recommendation is to ensure that their regional data centers are adequately resourced to handle peak traffic loads. Better monitoring of these facilities could also identify performance anomalies sooner. Another recommendation is to improve Zoom's load balancing, which currently seems to be random, rather than load-based. These policies lead to non-uniform loads on MMR servers (Fig. 5(b)), and poor selections of failover servers when needed (Fig. 8). A third recommendation is to consider the use of QUIC, rather than UDP, for media streaming, if they are not already doing so. QUIC could provide a simpler solution for robust media streaming, without the need for elaborate FEC and failover strategies. In the longer term, a final recommendation is to consider the use of network-layer or application-layer *multicast*, which seems like a potential solution to reduce network traffic and server load.

6.2 Limitations

There are several limitations to our study. First, our monitoring infrastructure only sees traffic that traverses the edge of the campus network, so we inherently underestimate Zoom traffic when some meeting participants are off-campus. Second, our heuristics for UDP channel classification (i.e., audio, video, data) are simple threshold-based policies, and may not be robust to the many variations possible in empirical Zoom traffic. Third, a similar caveat applies to our heuristics for Zoom meeting classification: overlapping meetings on the same Zoom server make meeting identification quite a challenge, and campus-level NAT means that the same client IP can be in multiple Zoom meetings (same or different) at the same time. Fourth, the restarts of our monitor, plus any packet losses there, result in underestimation of Zoom traffic volume. Finally, our traffic analysis approach currently misses Zoom traffic exchanged in P2P mode, since neither endpoint is a Zoom address. Identifying this traffic (at least when it crosses the campus edge network) is part of our ongoing work.

7 Conclusion

This paper has presented a detailed analysis of Zoom network traffic on a university campus network. Through small-scale experiments, we identified the structural properties of Zoom sessions. We then used the knowledge and insights from the small-scale study to analyze large-scale Zoom traffic at the campus level.

The main take-home messages from our paper are as follows. First, Zoom usage on our campus has increased 4x with the transition to a mix of in-person and online course delivery. Second, this traffic can stress campus network infrastructure, including WiFi and NAT, due to many concurrent meetings, temporally-correlated arrivals, high video bit rates, and long-lasting sessions. Third, many Zoom sessions experience disruptions, seemingly triggered by high demand on a limited supply of regional Zoom servers. These disruptions can degrade the QoE for Zoom users. Finally, our simple analysis and visualization tools provide an effective way to identify and quantify such problems.

Our ongoing work seeks to corroborate the results from our network-level view with the application-level view provided by the Zoom console (dashboard) used by our campus network administrators.

Acknowledgements. The authors thank the PAM 2022 reviewers and shepherd Matteo Varvello for their constructive suggestions that helped to improve our paper. Summer student Kiana Gardner helped with our active measurements, including the collection of Wireshark traces from Zoom test sessions. The authors are grateful to University of Calgary Information Technologies (UCIT) and the Conjoint Faculties Research Ethics Board (CFREB) for enabling the collection of our passive network traffic measurement data. Financial support for this work was provided by Canada's Natural Sciences and Engineering Research Council (NSERC).

Appendix A: Data Format and Analysis Tools

Figure 8 shows an example of the connection log data from the Zoom test session in Fig. 1. This format uses selected columns from the Zeek connection log [13]. Each line summarizes the network traffic on one connection (TCP, UDP, or ICMP). In this example, A.B.C.D is a laptop on the campus WiFi network, K.L.M.N is a laptop on a home network, and W.X.Y.Z is a Zoom MMR server. The number of users varied between 1 and 3, but the third user was off campus, and thus does not appear in the log. In this example, there were two UDP connection attempts before P2P mode was fully established. Also, an ICMP "port unreachable" message was sent when switching back to server mode.

```
Timestamp  Src_IP  SPort Dest_IP DPort Prot Duration    State PSent BytesSent  PRecd BytesRecd
3371.758208 A.B.C.D 51525 W.X.Y.Z   443 tcp  2539.271654 RSTR  12214    1692606  21103   1646631
3372.166462 A.B.C.D 57643 W.X.Y.Z  8801 udp   361.544867 SF     3209    3096498   3008   2793039
3372.391270 A.B.C.D 57644 W.X.Y.Z  8801 udp   361.320242 SF      760      73731    194     20933
3372.515465 A.B.C.D 57645 W.X.Y.Z  8801 udp   361.196108 SF      311      33321    396     41924
3733.570248 K.L.M.N 38099 A.B.C.D  9756 udp     0.157993 SF       23       2622     21      2373
3733.592228 K.L.M.N 45276 A.B.C.D 15326 udp   666.015837 SF   211955  179935922 283443 252424232
4399.609065 A.B.C.D 57193 W.X.Y.Z  8801 udp  1511.283689 SF     7054    1394954   4778    344920
4399.609081 A.B.C.D 57192 W.X.Y.Z  8801 udp  1511.408204 SF   114638   25945097  95585  17170572
4399.609405 A.B.C.D 57194 W.X.Y.Z  8801 udp  1511.407976 SF   354039  388913210 289850 318527540
4399.612464 K.L.M.N     3 A.B.C.D     3 icmp    0.002069 OTH       8       4086      0         0
```

Fig. 8. Zeek connection log entries for Zoom test session (anonymized)

We have written C and Python programs to parse such log entries and produce graphical visualizations of Zoom sessions using gnuplot. Our C programs (called `zoomparse.c`, `zoomplot.c`, and `zoomcount.c`) produce a textual summary, intermediate data for graph plotting, and a statistical summary of Zoom sessions, respectively. We also have a Python program that parses full Zeek connection log entries, and produces a summary of Zoom sessions and Zoom meetings. The latter program relies on a database of Zoom server IP addresses and server types. Our software tools and graph plotting scripts are available from http://www.cpsc.ucalgary.ca/~carey/software.htm.

Appendix B: Additional Zoom Test Sessions

We collected Wireshark traces of several other Zoom sessions in order to identify typical and atypical behaviours. Figure 9 shows two unusual examples.

Figure 9(a) shows the packet traffic for a small meeting with three participants (all on their home networks), during which the presenter used the screen-sharing function to scroll through a large PDF document. In this example, the screen-sharing data volume (green) fluctuated dramatically, and actually exceeded the video traffic volume for most of the session.

Figure 9(b) shows the video and audio packet traffic for an on-campus participant during a seven-person Zoom meeting. (We exclude the data and control

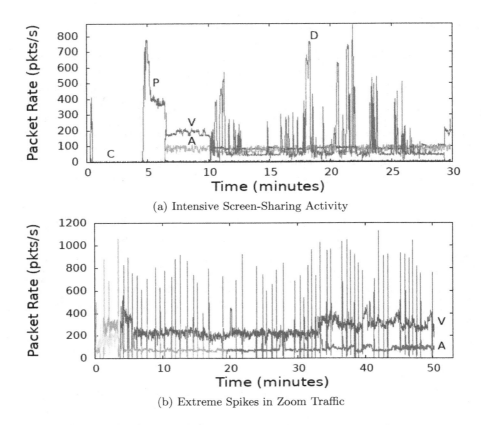

(a) Intensive Screen-Sharing Activity

(b) Extreme Spikes in Zoom Traffic

Fig. 9. Additional examples of Zoom test sessions in Wireshark

traffic from the graph, since it is negligible.) There are extreme spikes in the traffic during this Zoom session, which had very poor QoE (the different colors in the graph show the audio and video disruptions). One of the spikes, near the 20-min mark, reflects Zoom's bandwidth probing, which lasts for 10 s. The other spikes, however, are more extreme, and seem almost periodic. Each spike in the Wireshark trace lasts for only a second or two, and is preceded by a 2–3 s interval with no packets at all. Furthermore, the same pattern occurs in both the audio and video traffic (as well as non-Zoom traffic in the trace).

We do not believe that the traffic spikes in Fig. 9(b) are attributable to Zoom servers. Rather, this phenomenon could reflect congestion on the campus WiFi network (e.g., a large backlog at an AP), or could be a measurement artifact from running Wireshark on the same laptop as the Zoom session. We have observed this pattern in at least three different Wireshark traces, but have not yet been able to recreate it experimentally.

These examples help illustrate the variety of traffic patterns observed during our Zoom test sessions.

References

1. Böttger, T., Ibrahim, G., Vallis, B.: How the internet reacted to Covid-19: a perspective from Facebook's edge network. In: Proceedings of the ACM Internet Measurement Conference (IMC), Pittsburgh, PA, October 2020, pp. 34–41 (2020). https://doi.org/10.1145/3419394.3423621
2. Carman, A.: Why Zoom became so popular. The Verge. https://www.theverge.com/2020/4/3/21207053/zoom-video-conferencing-security-privacy-risk-popularity. (Accessed 19 Sept 2021)
3. Chang, H., Varvello, M., Hao, F., Mukherjee, S.: Can you see me now? A measurement study of Zoom, Webex, and Meet. In: Proceedings of ACM IMC, November 2021, pp. 216–228 (2021). https://doi.org/10.1145/3487552.3487847
4. Favale, T., Soro, F., Trevisan, M., Drago, I., Mellia, M.: Campus traffic and e-Learning during COVID-19 pandemic. Comput. Netw. **176**, Article 107290, 1–9 (2020). https://doi.org/10.1016/j.comnet.2020.107290
5. Feldmann, A., Gasser, O., Lichtblau, F., Pujol, E., Poese, I., Dietzel, C., et al.: The lockdown effect: implications of the COVID-19 pandemic on internet traffic. In: Proceedings of ACM IMC, Pittsburgh, PA, October 2020, pp. 1–18 (202). https://doi.org/10.1145/3419394.3423658
6. Karamollahi, M., Williamson, C., Arlitt, M.: Zoomiversity: a case study of pandemic effects on post-secondary teaching and learning. In: Proceedings of Passive and Active Measurement (PAM) Conference, March 2022 (2022, to appear)
7. Liu, S., Schmitt, P., Bronzino, F., Feamster, N.: Characterizing service provider response to the COVID-19 pandemic in the United States. In: Hohlfeld, O., Lutu, A., Levin, D. (eds.) PAM 2021. LNCS, vol. 12671, pp. 20–38. Springer, Cham (2021). https://doi.org/10.1007/978-3-030-72582-2_2
8. Lu, Y., Zhao, Y., Kuipers, F., Van Mieghem, P.: Measurement study of multi-party video conferencing. In: Crovella, M., Feeney, L.M., Rubenstein, D., Raghavan, S.V. (eds.) NETWORKING 2010. LNCS, vol. 6091, pp. 96–108. Springer, Heidelberg (2010). https://doi.org/10.1007/978-3-642-12963-6_8
9. Lutu, A., Perino, D., Bagnulo, M., Frias-Martinez, E., Khangosstar, J.: A characterization of the COVID-19 pandemic impact on a mobile network operator traffic. In: Proceedings of ACM IMC, Pittsburgh, PA, October 2020, pp. 19–33 (2020). https://doi.org/10.1145/3419394.3423655
10. MacMillan, K., Mangla, T., Saxon, J., Feamster, N.: Measuring the performance and network utilization of popular video conferencing applications. In: Proceedings of ACM IMC, November 2021, pp. 229–244 (2021). https://doi.org/10.1145/3487552.3487842
11. Mahr, A., Cichon, M., Mateo, S., Grajeda, C., Baggili, I.: Zooming into the Pandemic! A forensic analysis of the Zoom application. Forensic Sci. Inte.: Dig. Invest. **36**, Article 301107, 7 (2021). https://doi.org/10.1016/j.fsidi.2021.301107
12. Marczak, B., Scott-Railton, J.: Move fast and roll your own crypto: a quick look at the confidentiality of Zoom meetings. Citizen Lab Research Report No. 126. University of Toronto, April 2020 (2020). (Accessed 23 Sept 2021)
13. Paxson, V.: Bro: a system for detecting network intruders in real-time. Comput. Netw. **31**(23), 2435–2463 (1999). https://doi.org/10.1016/S1389-1286(99)00112-7
14. Sander, C., Kunze, I., Wehrle, K., Rüth, J.: Video conferencing and flow-rate fairness: a first look at Zoom and the impact of flow-queuing AQM. In: Proceedings of PAM Conference, Germany, March 2021, pp. 3–19 (2021). https://doi.org/10.1007/978-3-030-72582-2_1

15. Ukani, A., Mirian, A., Snoeren, A.: Locked-in during lock-down: undergraduate life on the internet in a pandemic. In: Proceedings of ACM IMC, November 2021, pp. 480–486 (2021). https://doi.org/10.1145/3487552.3487828
16. Wireshark.org, Wireshark frequently asked questions. https://www.wireshark.org/faq.html. (Accessed 22 Sept 2021)
17. Zoom, Zoom video conferencing plans and pricing. https://zoom.us/pricing. (Accessed 19 Sept 2021)

Zoomiversity: A Case Study of Pandemic Effects on Post-secondary Teaching and Learning

Mehdi Karamollahi$^{(\boxtimes)}$, Carey Williamson, and Martin Arlitt

University of Calgary, Calgary, AB, Canada
{mehdi.karamollahi,cwill,marlitt}@ucalgary.ca

Abstract. The first wave of the COVID-19 pandemic hit North America in March 2020, disrupting personal and professional lives, and leading to work-from-home mandates in many jurisdictions. In this paper, we examine two years of empirical network traffic measurement data from the University of Calgary's campus network to study the effects of the pandemic on a post-secondary education environment. Our study focuses on the online meeting applications and services used, as well as traffic volumes, directionality, and diurnal patterns, as observed from our campus edge network. The main highlights from our study include: changes to inbound and outbound traffic volumes; reduced traffic asymmetry; significant growth in Zoom, Microsoft Teams, and VPN traffic; structural changes in workday traffic patterns; and a more global distribution of campus network users.

Keywords: Network traffic measurement · Workload characterization

1 Introduction

The COVID-19 pandemic affected everyone's daily life, both personally and professionally. Lockdowns, travel restrictions, and stay-at-home orders were in effect in most parts of the world in 2020, and they had many consequences on people individually and socially. The way that people work and study changed quite drastically, with many people relying much more extensively upon the Internet and online tools for their daily tasks [11].

In a broader sense, the pandemic has provided a glimpse into the possible Future of Work (FoW) [4,23,29], a term used to describe a flexible work-from-home society enabled by digital connectivity, telepresence, and computer networks. With the continuous move to the cloud infrastructures within the organizations and universities around the world [12], most people were aware of the possibility of working remotely before the pandemic occurred, but relatively few have done it. At the very least, the pandemic accelerated the transition to FoW and made it real for many more people, changing some mindsets and possibly influencing remote work and online learning technologies for the future.

© The Author(s), under exclusive license to Springer Nature Switzerland AG 2022
O. Hohlfeld et al. (Eds.): PAM 2022, LNCS 13210, pp. 573–599, 2022.
https://doi.org/10.1007/978-3-030-98785-5_26

In this paper, we study the effects of the pandemic within the context of a post-secondary education environment. We do so from a network-level viewpoint, by studying the changes in the Internet traffic patterns into and out of our campus network. Specifically, we examine two years of empirical connection-level network traffic data to identify changes in the volume, timing, and directionality of traffic, as well as the application mix. Doing so offers insights into how the pandemic affected the work and study habits of our campus community.

A main focus in our study is on the use of Zoom video-conferencing software, which was adopted by University of Calgary (UCalgary) as the preferred solution for remote teaching and learning. Zoom has been adopted by many universities, companies, and other organizations for remote communication purposes.

Zoom is a popular and easy-to-use video-conferencing solution. Zoom offers a free account with some limitations, such as a maximum meeting duration of 40 minutes. However, many organizations (including UCalgary) purchased the corporate license for Zoom so that their members could use it for teaching and learning, as well as meetings and conferences, without the duration limit.

Zoom, of course, is not the only video-conferencing solution on the market. Microsoft Teams and Google Meet are two other online conferencing applications used by our campus community for meeting purposes. Some features are free for the public to use, and the rest are accessible only to licensed organizations. Other popular solutions include FaceTime, Skype, Vidyo, and Webex.

In our work, we study the network traffic of three online meeting applications on our university campus network. We focus on characterizing the network traffic from these applications, as seen on our campus. As a baseline, we provide pre-pandemic traffic measurements from 2019 and the early months of 2020, and compare 2020 traffic with this baseline.

Our main objectives are to answer the following questions:

- How has the campus network traffic changed during the pandemic, and why?
- What are the usage patterns for Zoom as the most prominent online video conferencing application on our campus?
- What other network applications and services are used to support remote work and learning?
- What are the potential implications of these changes on the future usage of our campus network?

The main contributions of this paper are as follows:

- We compare empirical network traffic data from 2019 (pre-pandemic) and 2020 (pandemic) to identify structural changes in traffic patterns.
- We identify the emergence of Zoom and Teams as popular applications for teaching and for meetings, respectively, and characterize Zoom usage.
- We identify temporal and geo-spatial changes in how our research and education community accesses and uses campus network resources.

The results from our work should be of value not only to networking researchers, but also to educators, academic administrators, and IT professionals. Using longitudinal data analysis, we provide several key insights on the growth and evolution of network traffic for online learning, and the performance implications of such traffic on a campus edge network.

The rest of this paper is organized as follows. Section 2 discusses prior related work on network traffic characterization and the effects of the COVID-19 pandemic. Section 3 describes the methodology for our study, focusing on our network environment, our network traffic measurement infrastructure, and our data analysis tools. Section 4 presents the main high-level results from our study, while Sect. 5 provides detailed results regarding Zoom traffic. Finally, Sect. 6 concludes the paper.

2   Related Work

Researchers in academia and in industry rely on network traffic measurement as an increasingly important methodology to obtain data, analyze Internet traffic, assess network performance, identify network security issues, and investigate different features of new protocols and applications. The book by Crovella and Krishnamurthy [9] provides the technical underpinnings of this discipline.

The usage of network traffic measurement and workload characterization techniques is broad and extensive. Classic examples include the characterization of wide-area TCP connections [25], Web traffic [3,6], and email traffic [28]. More recent works have studied video streaming services [1,13], as well as the growth and evolution of online social networks [15,22,30]. Such studies offer insights into the changing nature of Internet traffic, and its potential effects on network performance. We follow a similar approach in our work.

The COVID-19 pandemic has affected Internet usage dramatically. Since the onset of the pandemic, several research works have noted changes in the timing, volume, and directionality of traffic, as many people switched to work-from-home scenarios. One of the first was the weekly blog by Labovitz [16], analyzing data from several networks in Western Europe. As of March 9, 2020, this report noted 20-40% increases in traffic during the evening peak hours, 3x growth in teleconferencing apps (e.g., Skype, Zoom), and 4x growth in gaming traffic [16]. A later report [17] indicated that aggregate traffic was up by over 25%, and that the normalized peak traffic was 25-30% above pre-pandemic levels. Also, DDoS attacks increased by 40-50% after the pandemic [17]. Similar observations arise in our work, along with insights that are specific to Zoom traffic.

The Broadband Internet Technical Advisory Group (BITAG) produced a detailed report on how Internet traffic changed, and how network operators and providers managed the unprecedented circumstances [5]. Though focused on the US, this report provides valuable insights into network operations from many different vantage points, including core, edge, and ISP locations. The report states that the Internet, in general, was robust during the pandemic, and continued to perform well. Several performance issues experienced by some users were attributed to end-user system configurations and outdated wireless equipment. Dramatic growth in VPN usage by campus networks is also reported in this document, along with the notable asymmetry in traffic growth between upstream and downstream. The busy hours for the downstream were in the evening with 12-25% growth, while the upstream peak hours start in the morning and run most of the day until about midnight. Our results also confirm VPN traffic growth, and noticable shifts in network usage patterns.

Feldmann *et al.* [11] provided a multi-perspective look at pandemic effects on Internet traffic, using datasets from ISPs, IXPs, and mobile network operators. The main highlights were shifts of 15-20% in Internet traffic within a week of lockdown. Their paper noted the emergence of non-hypergiants among the contributors to traffic growth, and identified a plethora of network applications being used in work-from-home environments. Our work confirms Zoom as a new potential hypergiant.

Lutu *et al.* [20] presented an analysis of the changes in user mobility patterns and how this affected the cellular traffic of a UK mobile network operator. They observed an overall decrease in mobility (i.e., roaming) by 50%, with non-uniform geographical changes. They reported a 150% increase in voice traffic, a 20% overall decrease in download traffic, and a 10% increase in uplink traffic. Nonetheless, the network operator was able to maintain service quality standards. Our work does not address cellular traffic at all, but we do see reduced WiFi usage from having fewer people on campus.

Liu *et al.* [19] studied how several US providers responded to changes in Internet traffic demands during the pandemic. They also identified some differences between rural versus urban users, which can affect QoS/QoE for online learning applications. The shift to using online meeting applications and platforms for learning and collaboration is also well documented in the literature [26,27]. Our work indicates potential performance problems when Zoom is used for teaching and learning on a large campus edge network.

The closest study to our own so far is by Favale *et al.* [10], who studied traffic on the campus network of the Politecnico di Torino (PoliTO). They analyzed the changes in traffic patterns due to the restrictions in place in Turin, Italy, and the switch to online learning solutions. They observed that the campus inbound traffic drastically decreased, since fewer students were on campus, while outbound traffic more than doubled, due to the remote learning platform installed at the campus to support all online classroom instruction. Furthermore, they provided insight into the growth of online collaboration platforms, VPN, and remote desktop services. Compared to their work, our research spans an entire calendar year of pandemic-related network traffic data (2020), rather than just a few months, with the previous calendar year (2019) as a baseline. Furthermore, our campus uses the widely-adopted Zoom platform for remote teaching and learning, rather than a custom in-house solution. We provide observations on how the usage of online learning and meeting applications has changed in terms of connection counts and traffic volume, and offer insights into these changes.

A recent paper [7] studied three major videoconferencing systems: Zoom, Webex, and Google Meet. They used a cloud-based emulated framework to generate videoconferencing sessions on these applications and then measure, study, and compare them. They measured streaming delay (lag), as well as a range of well-known objective QoE metrics, including PSNR (Peak Signal-to-Noise Ratio), SSIM (Structural Similarity Index Measure), and VIFp (Pixel Visual Information Fidelity). They found that these systems vary in terms of geographic location, resulting in different QoE. For example, Webex sessions created in US-west are subject to artificial detours via relays in US-east, inflating their lags. They saw that high-motion video feeds experience non-negligible QoE degradation on all three systems compared to low-motion video streaming. Finally, systems react differently under bandwidth constraints.

Another recent study [21] compared Zoom, Microsoft Teams, and Google Meet in an experimental testbed. They tried to find the baseline level of Internet performance needed to support common videoconferencing applications for remote learning. Under simulated conditions, they measured the bandwidth utilization, time to recovery from interruptions, and fairness under competitive circumstances.

Our work differs from these papers too, as we study empirically-captured network traffic data from thousands of users on our campus network. Our companion paper [8] developed tools to analyze Zoom sessions and meetings from these captured data and provides a microscopic view of Zoom traffic. This paper, on the other hand, provides a longitudinal (macroscopic) view of Zoom, Teams, Meet, VPN, and other applications involved in remote working and learning during the pandemic.

3   Data Collection and Methodology

This section discusses the methods and technologies used for our network traffic characterization study, as well as some of the limitations of our approach. We start with some brief contextual information about the university environment that we studied.

3.1   University Environment

UCalgary is a medium-sized university with about 30,000 students. The academic schedule is semester-based, with the Fall (September to December) and Winter (January to April) semesters each having a full set of course offerings. There are also Spring (May to June) and Summer (July to August) semesters, each with reduced course offerings.

During the COVID-19 pandemic, the switch from in-person learning to remote online learning took place quite abruptly on March 13th, 2020, during the Winter semester. Online learning remained the norm throughout the rest of the calendar year, though a small number of students (20%) were allowed back on campus in Fall 2020, mainly in capstone and/or lab-based experiential learning courses with limited enrollments.

Videoconferencing. With the shift to remote learning, the students, staff, and faculty members started to use online meetings and screen-sharing applications to continue with the courses, academic tasks, and regular or occasional meetings. The University officially advised its community to use Zoom for teaching and learning, and it has been the dominant way of teaching classes since the lockdown. Microsoft Teams is offered for internal or external meetings. An organizational license was purchased for Zoom, and Microsoft Teams is an integrated application within the Office365 suite available via a campus-wide licence.

Remote Access. Being physically away from campus raised access issues for almost everyone. For example, many faculty, staff, and graduate students needed to access computers in their offices or labs to proceed with their work or research. Even undergraduate students using systems in different labs before the lockdown needed to connect remotely to those systems. Furthermore, certain services require access from a university IP address, augmenting the demand to connect to the campus network. Three different remote access solutions were offered to resolve these issues: Secure Shell (SSH), Virtual Private Network (VPN), and Remote Desktop Protocol (RDP).

Authentication. Our campus network uses an authentication service that checks user credentials before accessing enterprise resources, such as the wireless network, learning management system, email, and Office365 applications.

3.2 Passive Measurement

Passive measurement involves capturing ambient network traffic and analyzing it either online or offline. With this technique, no additional traffic is produced, and the ordinary network traffic is not altered in any way. We collected two years of empirical network traffic data using this approach.

Our monitor uses an Endace DAG (Data Acquisition and Generation) packet capture card. The monitor is installed in the main data center on campus, and receives from the edge routers a mirrored copy of every packet entering or leaving the campus network. Those packets are then sent to a Zeek (formerly known as Bro) worker node [24]. For privacy purposes and to reduce storage requirements, Zeek aggregates all the packets of the same connection and stores a summarized entry for that connection. This summary consists of many fields, including a unique identifier of the connection, the connection's 4-tuple of endpoint addresses/ports, the time of the first packet, duration of the connection, and the number of packets and bytes sent by both the originator and responder.

We use ARC (Advanced Research Computing), an existing HPC (High Performance Computing) cluster at UCalgary, for storage, management, and script-based processing of our traffic data. We also use Vertica, an SQL-based big data analytics platform, to analyze the captured data. Using Vertica is fast and convenient for network traffic analyses, since it supports parallel execution of SQL queries on structured data [18].

3.3   Active Measurement

Active measurement refers to establishing connections and sending data packets to identify entities in the network, characterize traffic, or measure different metrics. In this study, we used active measurement techniques judiciously to identify hosts and servers associated with organizations and autonomous systems under study, and their traffic attributes, such as port numbers. This information is most often essential in network traffic measurement and workload characterization studies. For this purpose, we mainly conducted simple experiments using basic network tools like `nslookup` and `traceroute` and used Wireshark to capture packet-level traffic. We then analyzed the captured logs and extracted the required fields, such as IP addresses associated with the target organizations and the port numbers used by applications. This information may also be utilized in the passive measurement when required.

3.4   Challenges and Limitations

As with any network traffic measurement study, there are challenges and limitations that affect the completeness of our data, and hence the interpretation of results. We discuss these issues here.

First and foremost, it is important to note that our monitoring infrastructure is set up to observe packet traffic that is strictly *between* the university and the Internet. Specifically, the monitor does not see traffic that stays completely within the campus network (e.g., a student in residence connecting to an internal server), nor traffic that is completely external (e.g., a home residential user directly accessing Netflix). The pandemic has thus changed the visibility into Internet usage by our campus community. Some traffic that was not visible previously (e.g., accessing a university Web server while at work) is now visible when people work and learn from home. Conversely, some traffic that was visible previously (e.g., YouTube accessed from the campus WiFi network) is no longer visible when these users directly access the Internet from home. For VPN, however, remote users actually obtain a campus IP address from the BYOD subnet, which is then used to connect to the Internet. Therefore, a connection to the campus VPN contributes to both incoming and outgoing connection counts as seen by the monitor.

A second challenge, as in any longitudinal traffic study, arises from unexpected events that disrupt data collection. Several such incidents occurred during the 2020 year under study. The most pernicious of these were aggressive scanning attacks (horizontal and vertical) that exhausted the memory resources on our monitor, and crashed the system. These outages in data collection are visible in several of the time-series graphs presented in the paper.

To mitigate the foregoing problem, we disabled the scanning module in Zeek, and reconfigured our monitor to do a software restart every 3 h. While this strategy avoids crashes that lose substantial amounts of data, it does limit visibility into long-duration connections. We subsequently experimented with shorter (1 h) and longer (6 h) restart intervals as well, prior to settling on 6-h intervals since

July 2020 (see Appendix for more details). The effects of these configuration changes are also apparent in several of our traffic plots.

Another challenge regarding the videoconferencing applications is that (unlike the on-site proprietary solutions such as the case for Favale *et al.* [10]) we have limited information available about their infrastructure and how the applications behave. In many cases, we had to reverse engineer their behavior based on a few documents. Furthermore, their deployments may have been changed during the pandemic. However, due to the wide adoption and availability of these applications across the globe, our analysis and results should be generalizable to other environments with similar contexts.

Despite these issues, we still believe that our empirical dataset offers great research value. Where appropriate, we exercise caution in our interpretations of results, and contextualize them accordingly.

3.5 Ethical Considerations

Permission to capture network traffic data was authorized via the ethics review process at UCalgary and was carried out with the cooperation of the IT center. Our network monitor is mounted in a secure data center with restricted physical access. A limited amount of traffic data is stored on the monitor at a time, with data summarization and transfer to a secure storage server happening on a daily basis. All data is stored in logs as per-connection summaries. Data analysis is done at an aggregate level, and not individually. Furthermore, most users get transient IP addresses from DHCP and/or NAT when connected to the campus network. Any identification process in the active or passive measurement is limited to the hosts and servers associated with organizations and applications under study, not individual users. Access to the log data is restricted to those specifically authorized to conduct networking and security research. Any security-related vulnerabilities (e.g., compromised machines, amplification attacks) detected in these summarized data are reported to the campus IT team for subsequent follow-up.

4   Measurement Results

This section presents the results from our empirical network traffic study. We start with an overview of the traffic on a year-to-year basis, and then focus on specific applications and services, including authentication, learning management system, and VPN.

4.1 Traffic Overview

Figure 1[1] provides a high-level overview of our campus network traffic volume, in Terabytes (TB) of data per day for calendar years 2019 and 2020. The horizontal

---

[1] This figure uses the direct information from DAGstats and not the logs captured by Zeek. Therefore, it is not affected by the monitor restarts and the reconfiguration in mid-July. However, it is affected by the monitor crash in late March.

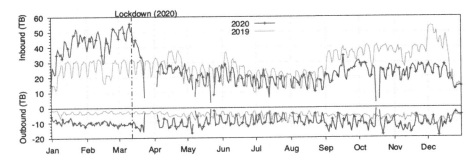

Fig. 1. Daily network traffic data volume in TB for 2019 (green) and 2020 (red). Upper axis is inbound traffic; lower axis is outbound traffic. (Color figure online)

axis shows the time in months, while the vertical axis shows inbound data on the upper part of the plot, and outbound data on the lower (negative y axis) part of the plot. The green lines are for the baseline pre-pandemic year 2019, while the red lines are for the pandemic-affected year 2020.

There are several structural patterns evident in Fig. 1. First, there is generally higher network activity during the main semesters (Jan-Apr and Sept-Dec) than during the Spring/Summer period (May-Aug). Second, there are distinctive weekly cycles. Third, our campus is a net consumer of data, with inbound traffic far exceeding outbound traffic. Fourth, there is a general decline in network traffic in late December when the university is closed for the holiday season, and few people are on campus.

There are also several pandemic-related effects evident in Fig. 1. The most prominent of these is the sharp decline in traffic volumes in mid-March 2020, when classes were cancelled, people were asked to stay home, and remote learning began. Also notable is how the inbound traffic for Fall 2020 (Sept-Dec) is about 25% below that observed for Fall 2019. In over a decade of monitoring our campus network, this is the first time that we have observed a reduction in network traffic volume from one academic year to the next. Furthermore, this decline differs starkly from the Winter semester (Jan-Apr), in which the 2020 traffic prior to the lockdown exceeds that of 2019, for both inbound and outbound (with about 84% growth in overall traffic).

These dynamics in Fall 2020 reflect the fact that most people were still away from campus, working and learning from home. This observation is further supported by the increases in outbound traffic volume in Fall 2020 (almost 50% increase with respect to the prior year). As explained earlier, a connection to the campus VPN generates an incoming connection to the VPN server, as well as outgoing connections to the user's target hosts on the Internet. It results in the symmetry between outbound and inbound traffic volume due to a VPN connection. Therefore, VPN connections have no net effect on the overall asymmetry of the campus traffic observed.

Table 1. Top 10 external organizations by traffic volume on Day2019 (2019-09-24)

Rank	Organization	Flows	% Flows	Bytes (GB)	% Bytes	Outbound	Inbound
1	Apple	11,172,676	6.15	5,417	12.91	791	4,627
2	Netflix	519,633	0.29	5,094	12.14	82	5,012
3	Akamai	16,907,100	9.30	4,815	11.48	131	4,683
4	Google	33,788,336	18.59	3,536	8.43	470	3,066
5	CANARIE	500,082	0.28	3,238	7.72	38	3,200
6	Facebook	7,505,585	4.13	2,891	6.89	130	2,761
7	Microsoft	37,201,566	20.46	2,034	4.85	935	1,098
8	Amazon	25,083,071	13.80	1,941	4.63	210	1,731
9	Fastly	2,934,594	1.61	1,386	3.30	45	1,341
10	UChicago	3,400	0.00	1,185	2.82	16	1,169

Table 2. Top 10 external organizations by traffic volume on Day2020 (2020-09-23)

Rank	Organization	Flows	% Flows	Bytes (GB)	% Bytes	Outbound	Inbound
1	Amazon	12,936,245	14.82	3,259	11.70	928	2,331
2	Akamai	6,225,932	7.13	3,140	11.27	79	3,061
3	Apple	3,950,781	4.53	2,545	9.14	392	2,154
4	Netflix	421,738	0.48	2,393	8.59	89	2,304
5	Microsoft	20,200,909	23.15	2,286	8.20	1,027	1,259
6	Google	15,818,810	18.13	2,268	8.14	744	1,524
7	CANARIE	328,570	0.38	1,551	5.57	21	1,531
8	Facebook	1,548,066	1.77	1,094	3.93	56	1,038
9	Shaw	145,454	0.17	924	3.32	585	339
10	Oracle	37,193	0.04	853	3.06	241	612

The campus is still a net consumer of Internet traffic, and there are two main explanations for it. First, a large subset of campus services is being hosted in the cloud, such as Microsoft Office365 and Learning Management System (LMS). Second, our findings show that video streaming and entertainment services are significant contributors to campus traffic, even in 2020. However, the increase in outbound traffic volume after the lockdown has reduced the degree of asymmetry.

Figure 1 also shows several distinct outages in monitor data collection (e.g., a week in late March, plus a few days in May, late July, and mid-October). These outages were due to intensive scanning attacks on the university network that crashed our monitor. These attacks were more frequent and more extreme during the pandemic than in the previous year. The main takeaway here is that *campus network traffic has changed in both expected (e.g., decline in inbound, increase in outbound) and unexpected ways (e.g., intensive scanning attacks)*.

4.2 Structural Analysis

To better understand the changes in network traffic, we first examined the traffic volumes for hypergiants, such as Google and Microsoft. Table 1 shows the Top 10 external organizations based on total byte traffic volume (in Gigabytes) on a weekday in Fall 2019 (**Day2019**: 2019-09-24). As a representative day, this table

Table 3. Top 10 internal subnets by traffic volume on Day2019 (2019-09-24)

Rank	Subnet	Flows	% Flows	Bytes (GB)	% Bytes	Outbound	Inbound
1	NAT 1	96,802,932	53.25	26,547	63.27	2,434	24,113
2	NAT 2	30,148,603	16.58	4,780	11.39	884	3,896
3	Guest WiFi	7,292,797	4.01	2,050	4.89	170	1,880
4	Other (4)	104,936	0.06	1,210	2.88	36	1,174
5	WLAN	388,178	0.21	399	0.95	28	371
6	Other (6)	4,107,762	2.26	381	0.91	62	320
7	RezNet 1	385,428	0.21	326	0.78	15	311
8	RezNet 2	417,543	0.23	319	0.76	18	300
9	RezNet 3	417,322	0.23	315	0.75	32	283
10	Other (10)	380,008	0.21	312	0.74	17	295

Table 4. Top 10 internal subnets by traffic volume on Day2020 (2020-09-23)

Rank	Subnet	Flows	% Flows	Bytes (GB)	% bytes	Outbound	Inbound
1	NAT 1	23,247,481	24.38	12,824	46.03	2,105	10,719
2	NAT 2	27,246,242	28.58	6,285	22.56	1,280	5,005
3	Guest WiFi	2,627,619	2.76	1,208	4.34	97	1,111
4	VPN (217)	18,315	0.02	900	3.23	698	202
5	Other (6)	5,244,110	5.50	705	2.53	181	523
6	Admin (83)	133,204	0.14	366	1.31	8	357
7	Other (84)	392,222	0.41	297	1.07	273	24
8	Other (33)	178,259	0.19	284	1.02	15	269
9	Other (19)	218,287	0.23	264	0.95	15	249
10	Other (14)	250,297	0.26	232	0.83	8	224

illustrates the pre-pandemic traffic pattern for hypergiants. Apple tops the list at 5.4 TB/day, due to the multiple services it offers, such as iCloud and Apple TV. Netflix (5.1 TB/day) is second with a large number of subscribers and high popularity. The other organizations are popular hypergiants, with some primarily offering their own services, such as Facebook, Google, and Microsoft, and others providing network infrastructure and CDNs (Content Delivery Networks), such as Akamai, Amazon, and Fastly. CANARIE is Canada's national research and education backbone network, connecting Canadian universities, educational institutions, and research organizations to each other and to the Internet.

Table 2 shows the results for the corresponding day in 2020 (**Day2020**: 2020-09-23) to illustrate hypergiant traffic during the lockdown. Significant changes in usage patterns are evident in this table, with Amazon and Akamai now at the top, and significant declines for Apple and Netflix. The latter declines are attributable to fewer users on campus. Table 2 also shows Shaw (a major ISP in western Canada) that was not even in the top 20 on Day2019.

One interesting observation when comparing Tables 1 and 2 is that while traffic for most organizations declined significantly from Day2019 to Day2020, Amazon's traffic increased substantially from 1.9 TB/day to 3.3 TB/day. One contribution to this growth is Zoom, since its services are mainly deployed on AWS, and expanded during the pandemic [2]. In particular, Zoom's traffic on our

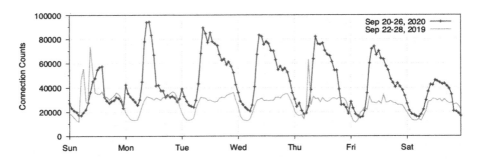

Fig. 2. Hourly connections initiated to authentication servers.

campus rose from 34 GB on Day2019 to 1,358 GB on Day2020, and represents about 4% of total campus traffic. The key takeaway is that *Zoom traffic, at over 1.3 TB/day, is now comparable to the traffic of other hypergiants.*

Insights can also be gleaned by looking at the internal breakdown of campus network traffic. Table 3 shows pre-pandemic traffic on Day2019, broken down by subnets within our campus network. The top subnets on this list include a BYOD subnet for unmanaged devices, campus WiFi subnets, student residences, and some popular locations with NAT access to the Internet.

Table 4 shows the corresponding traffic breakdown for Day2020 to represent internal subnet traffic patterns during the pandemic. While the top three subnets remain the same, their traffic volumes are much lower, since fewer users are on campus. Several new subnets appear in Table 4, including a subnet for VPN traffic, and a subnet used by UCalgary's administration to update the campus community about the pandemic situation. The labels (numbers in parentheses) for these subnets show their relative pre-pandemic rankings on Day2019. Also of note, the traffic volumes from several student residences[2] decreased, since occupancy was limited; these subnets no longer appear in the Top 10. The main insight from our analysis is that *there were significant structural changes in network usage, both internally and externally. For example, VPN and Admin usage rose, while RezNet and WiFi decreased. The latter contribute to the concomitant decreases in Apple and Netflix traffic.*

4.3 Authentication

Our next analysis focuses on the authentication-related traffic, as we study the network usage patterns of our campus community during the pandemic. All faculty, staff, and students must authenticate themselves with their credentials when using enterprise services, such as email, LMS, VPN, and so on.

Figure 2 shows the authentication-related traffic for two selected weeks from our empirical dataset: one in September 2019, and the corresponding one in

---

[2] We have not analyzed the residence traffic in detail, since the number of users seems low. Ulkani *et al.* [31] studied pandemic effects on student residence traffic at UCSD, finding changes (for example) in Zoom and OSN usage.

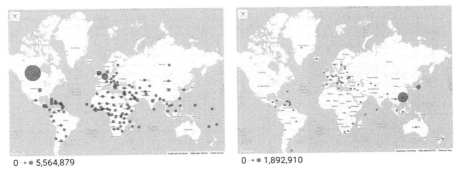

0 · ● 5,564,879   0 · ● 1,892,910

(a) Countries with increase in connections (b) Countries with decrease in connections

Fig. 3. Changes in authentication connections from Sept 2019 to Sept 2020 based on the countries of origin. The maximum numbers in the legends (under the maps) demonstrate the maximum change that a country experienced, i.e., increase (in Canada) for (a) and decrease (in Hong Kong) for (b).

September 2020. The graph shows the number of connections initiated to the authentication servers in each one-hour interval during the week.

There are two main observations evident from Fig. 2. First, prior to the pandemic (September 2019), authentication traffic tended to have two peaks per day on weekdays, with one peak in the morning, and one in the evening. This pattern reflects users logging in from home (e.g., checking email, accessing course Web pages) as part of their daily routine both before and after their time on campus[3] for the workday. Second, there is a substantial increase in authentication traffic in September 2020, as a new cohort of students joins the campus community, and many people are working and learning from home. There is a single peak to the traffic each day, with most authentications happening in the morning, and some sessions lasting several hours[4], if not all day, since there was no need to logout and commute to/from campus anymore. Weekend traffic is substantially lower than weekday traffic, as expected. The weekend peaks are also time-shifted to slightly later in the morning. The main insight is that *working from home shifts the usage patterns and leads to prolonged sessions with campus servers.*

Figure 3 demonstrates the changes to the number of connections to the authentication servers, comparing data from September 2019 to September 2020. Each bubble represents a country and shows the absolute amount of change in the authentication connection counts. The size of the bubbles is relative to the maximum change observed (i.e., increase in connections from Canada). Figure 3(a) shows the countries whose number of authentication connections increased, while

---

[3] Recall that any additional authentication sessions initiated while on campus would not be observable from our monitor.

[4] The mid-July configuration change to the monitor restart interval (now 6 h) contributes to the observed increase in connections as well.

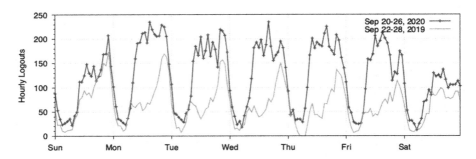

Fig. 4. Hourly LMS Connections during two weeks in Sept 2019 and Sept 2020. (Color figure online)

Fig. 3(b) shows the countries with a decrease in their counts. These maps show that connection count increases were most prominent from locations in Canada, followed by the Netherlands, UK, and the US. For connection count decreases, Hong Kong had the largest change, with Japan, Ukraine, and Indonesia next.

4.4   Learning Management System (LMS)

Figure 4 shows hourly connection counts to our LMS during a week in September 2020 and the corresponding week in September 2019. UCalgary uses D2L (Desire2Learn) for LMS, and it is hosted in Quebec, Canada. Despite being in the cloud (AWS), users are redirected to the campus authentication servers at both the start and the end of LMS sessions, enabling counting of this traffic.

Figure 4 shows significant changes in LMS traffic patterns, similar to those observed for the authentication traffic. In September 2019 (before the pandemic), students were regularly on campus, so their LMS authentication traffic was not always visible from our monitor. A peak in the evening when most people were back home is most evident on the green line. When working from home, however, this traffic is more observable throughout the day, as reflected in the higher activity levels in September 2020, with significant changes in its pattern. Diurnal patterns are still evident, with a decline on weekends.

4.5   Remote Access

This subsection discusses the usage of three popular remote access protocols, namely SSH, VPN, and RDP.

Figure 5(a) illustrates the daily connection counts for these protocols for the entire calendar year of 2020, while Fig. 5(b) shows the daily byte traffic volume associated with these connections. Note that the vertical axes are logscale (base 10) for better visibility of the entire data. Overall, these results show the dominance of SSH (purple line) in terms of the number of connections (some of which may be generated by scripts or automated processes), while VPN connections (orange line) account for the most data bytes. RDP (gold line) has the lowest

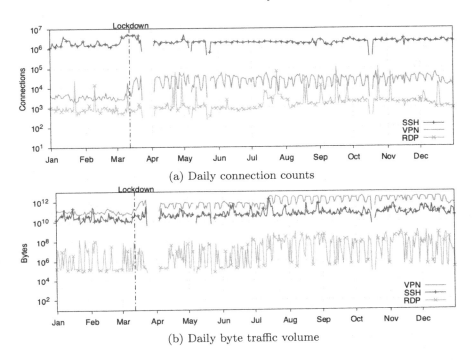

(a) Daily connection counts

(b) Daily byte traffic volume

Fig. 5. Comparison of SSH, VPN, and RDP usage in 2020. (Color figure online)

activity for both connections and data volumes since it is only applicable for Windows users, and requires a registered system on campus in order to establish an RDP connection. Therefore, lower usage for RDP is unsurprising.

Our further investigation revealed that the increase in the number of SSH connections right before the lockdown is attributable to the increase in inbound scanning activity. Interestingly, the SSH connection count remains pretty steady throughout the year and does not exhibit the typical human-driven weekly patterns evident in the VPN traffic. However, the SSH data volume did increase 2–5x compared to the pre-pandemic baseline in February, reflecting changes to the monitor's visibility of this traffic after the July configuration change. The 6-h restart interval improves visibility into long-duration TCP connections (refer to Appendix). This is important for applications like VPN and SSH, which often last several hours, if not all day, and it explains the larger proportionate increase in byte traffic volume than in connection count. On our network, SSH usage seems more research-driven rather than education-driven.

Daily VPN connections and data volume both increased after the lockdown by a factor of about 10x. This increase occurred almost immediately following the work-at-home mandate in mid-March 2020. A later increase is also evident in mid-July 2020, when the change in the monitor configuration enhanced observability of longer-duration connections. Although there are fewer VPN connec-

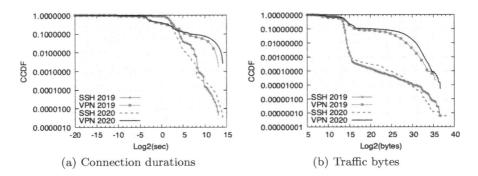

(a) Connection durations   (b) Traffic bytes

Fig. 6. LLCD of connection durations and traffic bytes for SSH and VPN connections during two separate weeks (September 22–28, 2019 and September 20–26, 2020).

tions than SSH, VPN connections tend to have longer durations and transfer more data bytes than SSH connections. Figure 6 illustrates these effects.

The growth in VPN traffic is consistent with observations made by others [5]. For our campus network, the VPN has a broader set of users than the other remote access protocols, since it is available to the entire community. The VPN has greater flexibility as well, since traffic from multiple network applications can be transferred via its connection. Therefore, such an increase in VPN usage is not surprising. In fact, after the lockdown, the primary option to access the campus network was to use the VPN. Many students returned to their home cities or countries, and a lot of newly admitted international students had to commence their programs from abroad. Using the VPN has been the primary means to facilitate this access.

A separate analysis (not shown here) of the origin cities of VPN connections confirms that the increased connection count comes from a larger set of external IPs accessing the network from all over the world. The main insight is that *VPN usage increased dramatically, in terms of connections, data volumes, session duration, IP addresses, and geographical distribution.* Our further investigations did not find any evidence of VPN-related performance degradation on the campus network or repercussions for the nearby clients.

5   Zoom Measurement Results

This section provides an in-depth look at Zoom network traffic, motivated by the growth and volume of this traffic as identified in the previous section. We begin with a look at videoconferencing applications to provide a comparison point for the Zoom traffic.

5.1   Videoconferencing Apps

This subsection discusses the network traffic measurement results for three online meeting applications (i.e., Zoom, Microsoft Teams, and Google Meet). Google

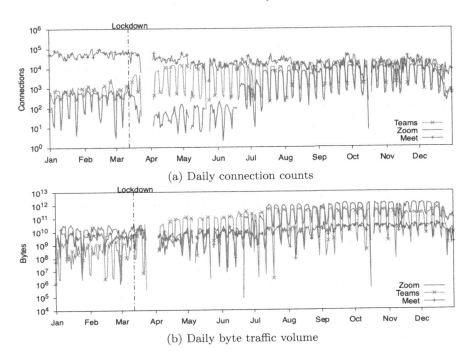

(a) Daily connection counts

(b) Daily byte traffic volume

Fig. 7. Comparison of Zoom, Teams, and Meet usage in 2020. (Color figure online)

Meet is a relatively new video conferencing app launched by Google in 2017. Prior work indicates that Meet usage increased during the COVID-19 pandemic, especially after Google relaxed its meeting size constraints for unpaid users [14]. We identify Zoom traffic based on the ports and IP ranges[5] provided in their Web site documentation. Similar principles apply to our identification of traffic for Teams and Meet. We show graphs of daily connection counts and traffic volume for each of these applications and compare them accordingly.

Figure 7(a) illustrates the daily connection counts for the three applications, while Fig. 7(b) shows the corresponding daily byte traffic volumes for each. Both plots show the entirety of calendar year 2020, illustrating the traffic generated by on-campus users when accessing these externally-supported applications. The gaps in the plots are due to the monitor outages mentioned earlier.

Figure 7 shows the emergence of Zoom in our post-secondary learning environment in 2020. Prior to the work-at-home order in March 2020, Google Meet (red line) was the most popular conferencing app, with almost 100K connections per day. At this time, Zoom (blue line) had only 1K connections per day. By September 2020, however, Zoom had reached a level of connection activity comparable to Meet, while far exceeding Meet in data traffic volume. Similarly,

---

[5] https://support.zoom.us/hc/en-us/articles/201362683-Network-firewall-or-proxy-server-settings-for-Zoom.

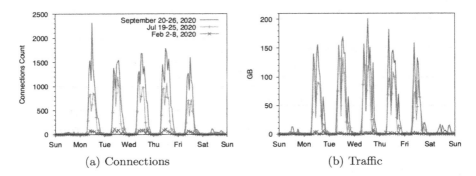

(a) Connections   (b) Traffic

Fig. 8. Hourly connections and byte traffic volume for Zoom on three selected weeks in February, July, and September, 2020.

Microsoft Teams traffic (green line) grew significantly for remote work and learning after March 2020, and has usage patterns very similar to Zoom.

The number of connections to Google Meet has actually decreased after the lockdown. One reason is fewer people on campus, and another is that Teams and Zoom were adopted as the official online meeting and conferencing app for our university. In particular, the total number of Meet connections from July onwards has decreased by 60–70% with respect to that number in February. However, the byte traffic volume for Google Meet did not decline much at all, suggesting more prolonged usage. These observations also suggest that a significant portion of connections to Meet are system-generated probes by the Meet app on the phones or when users access Gmail.

The daily connections to Teams, and its data traffic volume, increased tenfold right after the lockdown. This surge reflects the shift of administrative meetings (for faculty and staff still present on campus) to the remote format. On the other hand, daily Zoom connections and traffic declined after March 2020 since few students remained on-campus. It was not until the Summer 2020 semester that Zoom usage grew, since more classes were offered then.

In mid-July 2020, we made a configuration change in the monitor (as described earlier), which enabled better tracking of long-duration connections. Consequently, there are increases observed in connections and data volumes for both Zoom and Teams since then. With this change, we have a more complete view to compare with the baseline before the lockdown. For example, comparing the measurements in July, August, and September with February (baseline) shows that the total number of connections to Zoom in July is about 9.5x that in February, and this ratio for August and September is 11x and 20x, respectively. The corresponding ratios for the aggregated byte traffic volume are 27x, 36x, and 48x. These numbers illustrate the pronounced effects of Zoom following the lockdown.

The growth in traffic for Teams is even more dramatic. The total number of connections in July, August, and September are (respectively) 9x, 11x, and

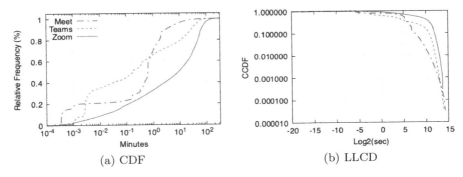

(a) CDF   (b) LLCD

Fig. 9. Distribution of connections durations for three applications (Sept 21–25, 2020).

14x that for February, while total byte traffic volumes are 424x, 447x, and 448x that in February. This increase in Teams traffic after the lockdown shows the prevalence of the application among staff and faculty who are still on campus after the lockdown. In February, Zoom traffic volume was 27x larger than the Teams traffic. However, this dominance decreases to 1.6x, 2x, and 2.6x in July, August, and September, respectively. These trends may reflect different bit rate, video resolution, or compression settings in the two applications [21]. Even with fewer people on campus, there has been *a significant increase in Zoom and Teams traffic on our campus network*.

Figure 7 shows a strong weekly usage pattern for Zoom and Teams, both in the connection counts and the data traffic volume. Every hump represents five consecutive working days of network activity, while the valleys show the weekends where those activities are reduced. However, this weekly pattern is less prominent in the Google Meet traffic, especially for connection counts, which implies the system-generated nature of many of these connections.

Figure 8 takes a closer look at diurnal usage patterns in Zoom traffic at a finer-grain time scale. Figure 8(a) illustrates the hourly counts for Zoom connections in three separate weeks from February, July, and September. Figure 8(b) shows the hourly byte traffic volume (in GB) for the same weeks, with inbound and outbound traffic combined. In both plots, there is a clear diurnal pattern, with increases in connections and byte traffic volume during normal working hours, and a decline overnight. Recall that the week in February was pre-pandemic, and the Zoom traffic was negligible. Nonetheless, the connections were established during working hours. The week in July represents the lockdown period. Although many restrictions were lifted by that time, it was after the monitor's configuration change, and the data is more complete. The week in September is after Fall 2020 classes began, and we see increased traffic, as expected.

Figure 8 shows two notable peaks per weekday in the selected weeks from July and September. The first one is in the morning and the second is in the afternoon, both during working hours. On some days, there is a third peak in

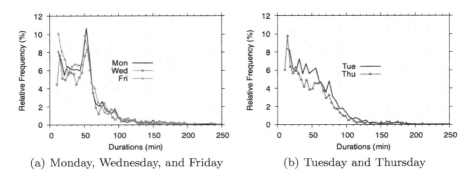

(a) Monday, Wednesday, and Friday   (b) Tuesday and Thursday

Fig. 10. Distribution of Zoom connections durations (Sept 21–25, 2020).

the late evening, especially in the traffic volume graph. All these peaks in the network traffic represent diurnal patterns from human-driven behavior.

Figure 9(a) illustrates the Cumulative Distribution Function (CDF) of the connection durations for each of the three meeting applications under study during five working days of September 2020. For Zoom, 80% of the connections are less than 50 min. For Teams, 90% of the connections last less than one hour. For Google Meet, the vast majority of connections have very short durations, often less than a minute, once again suggesting the machine-generated[6] nature of them rather than human-generated. However, the tail of the distribution for all three applications extends well to the right, with some connections lasting up to 5.5 h, as can be seen in Fig. 9(b). The main takeaway from Fig. 9 is that *Zoom connections tend to have longer durations than Teams and Meet*, reflecting usage of Zoom for classes and workshops with prolonged durations.

We next analyze connection durations for Zoom traffic in particular. At UCalgary, most courses are offered on either the Monday/Wednesday/Friday (MWF) schedule with 50-min lectures, or the Tuesday/Thursday (TuTh) schedule with 75-min lectures. Since most classes were delivered via Zoom after the lockdown, we expect to see some evidence of that in the distribution of Zoom connection durations.

Figure 10 shows the empirical distribution of Zoom connection durations for five consecutive working days from Fall 2020. Figure 10(a) for MWF confirms the expected peak around 50 min. Figure 10(b) for TuTh shows a small peak near 75 min duration, with a wide range of other values observed. Note that for courses with labs or tutorials, the timings may be different. For example, tutorial slots are usually 50 min, regardless of which day of the week they occur. These observations are congruent with our expectations, and *confirm the widespread usage of Zoom for class delivery at UCalgary*.

---

[6] A more detailed analysis shows that some of these are for STUN (Session Traversal Utilities for NAT) protocol traffic on UDP port 19302.

Table 5. Breakdown of transport protocols of Zoom connections on 2020-09-23.

Protocol	Connections	Outbound	Inbound
TCP	308,688	6.16 GB	9.18 GB
UDP	20,461	361 GB	981 GB

5.2 Detailed Traffic Analysis

Via active measurement experiments, we have gained further insights [8] into the structure of Zoom sessions. Note that there are several different ways to set up Zoom, depending on the client application, server deployment, or cloud solution in use. Our university uses the default approach with remote Zoom servers, and no Zoom Meeting Zones located inside the campus.

The connection process to initiate or join a meeting depends on the client's application (e.g., desktop app, mobile app, or Web browser). When using Zoom apps for one-on-one meetings between two parties, direct peer-to-peer connections are often used to carry the media packets. For meetings with more than two participants, a client-server architecture is used, with a cloud-hosted media server as the central point for collecting and distributing media packets for all participants in the Zoom session. Furthermore, such a typical Zoom session involves four logical connections: one TCP connection for control and management of the session (including chat interactions), and three UDP connections, one for audio, one for video, and one for screen sharing (if used). If the Zoom client is unable to connect via the usual procedure, they are directed to use the Web client, which uses TCP only.

To measure Zoom connections and client application usage on our campus, we picked a representative day (Day2020) and examined transport protocol usage based on the number of connections, as well as inbound and outbound data traffic volumes. Table 5 shows this information. TCP accounts for only 1.67% of outbound traffic, and 0.93% of inbound traffic, indicating that few people use Web access to join meetings. Rather, they use the standard procedure of a Zoom meeting connection using client applications.

For a typical Zoom meeting, a client should have three UDP connections for every TCP connection. However, the results in Table 5 show that the number of TCP connections is 15x larger than the number of UDP connections. There are two possible explanations for this discrepancy. First, there might be network connectivity or performance issues when users connect to Zoom from certain subnets (e.g., WiFi), causing TCP problems. Second, there might be many short-lived TCP connections for administrative management of Zoom sessions. We explore both of these possibilities next.

Figure 11 provides evidence to support these hypotheses. The plot illustrates the Log-Log Complementary Distribution (LLCD) function for Zoom connection durations. Considering the logarithmic scale of the y-axis, we can see a rather significant portion of TCP connections have small durations (under 30 s) that cannot be attributed to typical meetings. UDP sessions tend to have longer

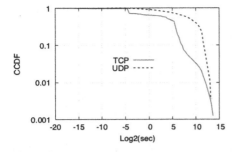

Fig. 11. LLCD of connections durations to Zoom on 2020-09-23.

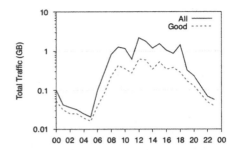

Fig. 12. Hourly TCP traffic of Zoom connections on 2020-09-23.

durations that reflect actual meetings, although the non-negligible portion of relatively short-lived UDP sessions partly indicates the performance issues resulting in Zoom connection interruptions. Waiting rooms, a feature utilized in some Zoom meetings, can also be another cause for the short-lived UDP sessions.

Figure 12 provides another perspective on Zoom session issues on our campus network. It shows the hourly TCP traffic of Zoom connections on Day2020. Connections with typical SYN-FIN handshakes as seen by our monitor are deemed "Good". During the peak hours of the day, only about half of the byte traffic (note the log scale) is exchanged on Good TCP connections, implying that *many connections suffer when too many users on the same network connect to busy Zoom servers*. Note that the administrative machine-generated TCP connections are short-lived with only a few kilobytes of traffic, which do not contribute significantly to overall traffic volume. Although this issue gives us insight into some implications of online learning on our campus network, identifying its root cause requires further investigation, which we leave as future work.

5.3 Zoom Session Management

To better understand Zoom sessions on our campus network, we have analyzed Zoom server usage, as well as the administrative traffic generated between our campus VPN server and the Zoom servers. These results are described next.

Figure 13 is a profile-rank plot to show how connections and byte traffic volumes are distributed across clients and Zoom servers. Figure 13(a) shows the IP frequency-rank profile for servers and clients on Day2020, as well as a year later (**Day2021**: 2021-09-22). Figure 13(b) plots the corresponding IP volume-rank profile for those two days.

Several key insights emerge from these two graphs. First, in 2020, four client IPs dominated the Zoom traffic, while connections are more widely distributed among a larger set of IPs in 2021. This change reflects the presence of more people on campus, with many using BYOD wireless devices. Second, the load increase on Zoom's servers is also evident in these graphs, both in connection counts (2–3x) and traffic volume (1.5x). Third, although about 2,000 server IPs

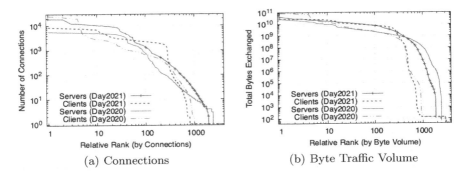

(a) Connections   (b) Byte Traffic Volume

Fig. 13. IP profile-rank plots for Zoom traffic on Day2020 and Day2021.

are seen on a daily basis, most of the traffic is handled by only a couple hundred servers. Furthermore, two stand out in the frequency-rank, reflecting roles in Zoom session management for the campus network. Last but not least, the top 20 server IPs in frequency-rank do not contribute much traffic volume, implying the role of zone controllers, directing clients to selected Zoom Multimedia Routers (MMRs). The main takeway here is that *most of our campus Zoom traffic is handled by a relatively small set of Zoom servers*, leading to possible load issues on those servers. Zoom and other vendors need to provide more detailed information in their client-side dashboard to assist with customer support[7].

Within our own campus network, we have identified one specific server that is directly involved in Zoom session management. This server has at least two different roles. First, it communicates with Zoom servers at the start of each new hosted Zoom meeting to exchange a fixed-size payload, which might be a certificate or authentication credential for licensed users. Second, it generates ICMP "port unreachable" messages to Zoom servers when a Zoom session is aborted, or when an authenticated participant departs prematurely from a meeting. The takeway message from these observations is that *Zoom sessions are complex from the network point of view, and induce extra administrative overhead.*

6   Conclusion

The COVID-19 pandemic has had a profound impact on many aspects of people's lives over the past year. In this paper, we provide a detailed look at the network-level effects on inbound and outbound Internet usage on a large campus edge network with over 30,000 users.

The main highlights from our study include the changes in the volume, timing, and directionality of traffic. With fewer users on campus, we observed

---

[7] For example, a light (green, yellow, or red) on the client's view to indicate the performance of the Zoom server from the server's perspective, and possibly tracking over time to summarize the percentage of total meeting time where server performance was green, yellow, or red.

dramatic changes in the inbound and outbound traffic volumes, as well as a reduction in the degree of asymmetry in the traffic. That is, inbound traffic still dominates outbound, but not by as much as it did prior to the pandemic. There are some perceptible differences in the daily timing of network usage, since commuting to campus is no longer the norm. Furthermore, a geographic analysis of the authenticated users for our campus network shows an increasingly international spread.

Pronounced shifts are also evident in network application usage. The increased traffic volume for Zoom and Teams is dramatic (e.g., 20x–450x), and VPN usage is also much higher (20x) than ever before. Most applications show strong daily and weekly patterns, consistent with the normal workday schedule, even when working from home. Research traffic seems less affected by the pandemic than teaching and learning traffic.

Finally, the results of our analysis reveal that there are issues with Zoom TCP connections and session management on our campus network when many people on campus connect to a limited set of regional Zoom servers during peak hours [8]. These problems manifest themselves with a plethora of short-lived TCP connections, and compromise the user-perceived quality of Zoom sessions. Furthermore, these problems are likely to grow as UCalgary adopts a blended learning model (i.e., a mix of in-person and online learning) in the upcoming academic year.

Acknowledgements. The authors thank the PAM 2022 reviewers and shepherd Tobias Fiebig for their constructive suggestions that helped to improve our paper. The authors are also grateful to UCIT for facilitating our collection of campus-level network traffic data, and to the team at ARC for technical support in the storage and management of our data. Financial support for this research was provided by Canada's Natural Sciences and Engineering Research Council (NSERC).

Appendix

The monitor reconfiguration mentioned earlier happened in the course of a week. On July 6, 2020, we changed the reset interval from one hour to every three hours to test the robustness of the monitor against the large volume of scanning activity and how disabling the scanning module is effective. The experiment was successful, and on July 13, 2020, we again changed the reset interval to every six hours. We then settled with that interval as our subsequent resource monitoring suggested that a longer interval may cause problems.

Figure 14 shows the distribution of connection durations for five working days from June 29 to July 3, 2020 (representing before reconfiguration) and another five working days from July 13 to July 17, 2020 (representing after reconfiguration). Both distributions follow a very similar pattern, with the post-reconfiguration graph stretching slightly to the right and longer tail on the LLCD plot, showing a heavier tail for the distribution that attributes to the connections lasting between 1 to 6 h (note the log2-based x-axis). However, the most significant difference between these distributions (not evident in this figure)

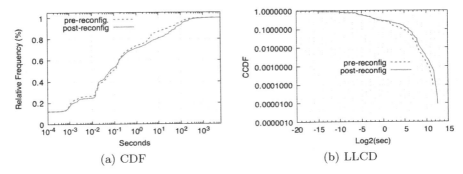

(a) CDF   (b) LLCD

Fig. 14. Distributions of connection durations during five working days of June 29, 2020 to July 3, 2020 (before monitor reconfiguration) and five working days of July 13, 2020 to July 17, 2020 (after monitor reconfiguration).

is that more than 615 million connections were captured during these post-reconfiguration days, while this number for the pre-reconfiguration days was more than 570 million. There is about 45 million difference between the number of connections in these distributions, out of which only about 574 thousand lasted between 1 to 6 h. It shows that the reconfiguration not only helped in capturing longer connections (which is very impactful for some applications, such as Zoom and VPN) but also more connections in general, due to fewer restarts per day.

References

1. Adhikari, V., Guo, Y., Hao, F., Hilt, V., Zhang, Z., Varvello, M., et al.: Measurement study of Netflix, Hulu, and a tale of three CDNs. IEEE/ACM Trans. Networking **23**(6), 1984–1997 (2015). https://doi.org/10.1109/TNET.2014.2354262
2. Amazon Inc., Press Room: AWS and Zoom Extend Strategic Relationship. https://press.aboutamazon.com/news-releases/news-release-details/aws-and-zoom-extend-strategic-relationship. Nov 2020
3. Arlitt, M., Williamson, C.: Internet web servers: workload characterization and performance implications. IEEE/ACM Trans. Networking **5**(5), 631–645 (1997). https://doi.org/10.1109/90.649565
4. Balliester, T., Elsheikhi, A.: The future of work: a literature review, ILO research department working paper, vol. 29, March 2018
5. BITAG Technical Working Group: 2020 Pandemic Network Performance (2021). https://www.bitag.org/documents/bitag_report.pdf. Apr 2021
6. Breslau, L., Cao, P., Fan, L., Phillips, G., Shenker, S.: Web caching and Zipf-like distributions: evidence and implications. In: IEEE INFOCOM 1999. Conference on Computer Communications. Proceedings. Eighteenth Annual Joint Conference of the IEEE Computer and Communications Societies. The Future is Now (Cat. No. 99CH36320), vol. 1, pp. 126–134, March 1999. https://doi.org/10.1109/INFCOM.1999.749260

7. Chang, H., Varvello, M., Hao, F., Mukherjee, S.: Can you see me now? a measurement study of zoom, Webex, and Meet. In: Proceedings of ACM IMC, pp. 216–228, November 2021. https://doi.org/10.1145/3487552.3487847

8. Choi, A., Karamollahi, M., Williamson, C., Arlitt, M.: Zoom session quality: a network-level view, to appear. In: Proceedings of Passive and Active Measurement (PAM) Conference, March 2022

9. Crovella, M., Krishnamurthy, B.: Internet Measurement: Infrastructure, Traffic, and Applications. Wiley & Sons (2006)

10. Favale, T., Soro, F., Trevisan, M., Drago, I., Mellia, M.: Campus traffic and e-learning during COVID-19 pandemic. Comput. Networks **176**, 107290 (2020). https://doi.org/10.1016/j.comnet.2020.107290

11. Feldmann, A., Gasser, O., Lichtblau, F., Pujol, E., Poese, I., Dietzel, C., et al.: The lockdown effect: implications of the COVID-19 pandemic on internet traffic. In: Proceedings of ACM IMC, pp. 1–18, Pittsburgh, October 2020. https://doi.org/10.1145/3419394.3423658

12. Fiebig, T., Gürses, S., Gañán, C., Kotkamp, E., Kuipers, F., Lindorfer, M., et al.: Heads in the clouds: measuring the implications of universities migrating to public clouds. arXiv preprint arXiv:2104.09462 (2021)

13. Gill, P., Arlitt, M., Li, Z., Mahanti, A.: YouTube traffic characterization: a view from the edge. In: Proceedings of ACM IMC, pp. 15–28, San Diego, CA, USA, October 2007. https://doi.org/10.1145/1298306.1298310

14. Google: COVID-19 community mobility reports (2021). https://www.google.com/covid19/mobility/

15. Klenow, S., Williamson, C., Arlitt, M., Keshvadi, S.: Campus-level instagram traffic: a case study. In: Proceedings of IEEE MASCOTS, pp. 228–234, Rennes, France, October 2021. https://doi.org/10.1109/MASCOTS.2019.00032

16. Labovitz, C.: Early effects of COVID-19 lockdowns on service provider networks: the network soldiers on!. https://www.nokia.com/blog/early-effects-covid-19-lockdowns-service-provider-networks-networks-soldier/. Mar 2020

17. Labovitz, C.: Network traffic insights in the time of COVID-19. https://www.nokia.com/blog/network-traffic-insights-time-covid-19-april-9-update/. 9 Apr 2020

18. Lamb, A., Fuller, M., Varadarajan, R., Tran, N., Vandier, B., Doshi, L., et al.: The Vertica analytic database: C-Store 7 years later. In: Proceedings of VLDB Endowment, vol. 5, no. 12, pp. 1790–1801, August 2012. https://doi.org/10.14778/2367502.2367518

19. Liu, S., Schmitt, P., Bronzino, F., Feamster, N.: Characterizing service provider response to the COVID-19 pandemic in the United States. In: Hohlfeld, O., Lutu, A., Levin, D. (eds.) PAM 2021. LNCS, vol. 12671, pp. 20–38. Springer, Cham (2021). https://doi.org/10.1007/978-3-030-72582-2_2

20. Lutu, A., Perino, D., Bagnulo, M., Frias-Martinez, E., Khangosstar, J.: A characterization of the COVID-19 pandemic impact on a mobile network operator traffic. In: Proceedings of ACM IMC, pp. 19–33, Pittsburg, CA, USA, October 2020

21. MacMillan, K., Mangla, T., Saxon, J., Feamster, N.: Measuring the performance and network utilization of popular video conferencing applications. In: Proceedings of ACM IMC, pp. 229–244, USA, May 2021. https://doi.org/10.1145/3487552.3487842

22. Mislove, A., Marcon, M., Gummadi, K., Druschel, P., Bhattacharjee, B.: Measurement and analysis of online social networks. In: Proceedings of ACM IMC, pp. 29–42, New York, NY, USA, October 2007. https://doi.org/10.1145/1298306.1298311

23. Nagel, L.: The influence of the COVID-19 pandemic on the digital transformation of work. Int. J. Soc. Soc. Policy (2020). https://doi.org/10.1108/IJSSP-07-2020-0323

24. Paxson, V.: Bro: a system for detecting network intruders in real-time. Comput. Netw. **31**(23), 2435–2463 (1999). https://doi.org/10.1016/S1389-1286(99)00112-7

25. Paxson, V.: Empirically derived analytic models of wide-area TCP connections. IEEE/ACM Trans. Networking **2**(4), 316–336 (1994). https://doi.org/10.1109/90.330413

26. Porpiglia, F., Checcucci, E., Autorino, R.: Traditional and virtual congress meetings during the COVID-19 pandemic and the post-COVID-19 Era: is it time to change the paradigm? Eur. Urol. **78**(3), 301–303 (2020). https://doi.org/10.1016/j.eururo.2020.04.018

27. Pratama, H., Azman, M., Kassymova, G., Duisenbayeva, S.: The trend in using online meeting applications for learning during the period of pandemic COVID-19: a literature review. J. Innovation Educ. Cult. Res. **1**(2), 58–68 (2020). https://doi.org/10.1007/978-3-030-40716-2_2

28. Ramachandran, A., Feamster, N.: The trend in using online meeting applications for learning during the period of pandemic COVID-19: a literature review. In: Proceedings of ACM SIGCOMM, New York, NY, USA, pp. 291–302, August 2006. https://doi.org/10.1145/1159913.1159947

29. Santana, M., Cobo, M.: What is the future of work? Sci. Mapp. Anal. Eur. Manage. J. **38**(6), 846–862 (2020). https://doi.org/10.1016/j.emj.2020.04.010

30. Schneider, F., Feldmann, A., Krishnamurthy, B., Willinger, W.: Understanding online social network usage from a network perspective. In: Proceedings of ACM IMC, pp. 35–48, Chicago, IL, USA, November 2009. https://doi.org/10.1145/1644893.1644899

31. Ukani, A., Mirian, A., Snoeren, A.: Locked-in during lock-down: undergraduate life on the internet in a pandemic. In: Proceedings of ACM IMC, pp. 480–486, November 2021. https://doi.org/10.1145/3487552.3487828

SSQoE: Measuring Video QoE from the Server-Side at a Global Multi-tenant CDN

Anant Shah[(✉)], Juan Bran, Kyriakos Zarifis, and Harkeerat Bedi

CDN Engineering, Edgecast, 13031 W Jefferson Blvd., Los Angeles, CA 90094, USA
{anant.shah,juan.bran,kyriakos.zarifis,harkeerat.bedi}@edgecast.com

Abstract. Over the past decade, video streaming on the Internet has become the primary source of our media consumption. Billions of users stream online video on multiple devices with an increasing expectation that video will be delivered at high quality without any rebuffering or other events that affect their Quality of Experience (QoE). Video streaming platforms leverage Content Delivery Networks (CDNs) to achieve this at scale. However, there is a gap in how the quality of video streams is monitored. Current solutions rely on client-side beacons that are issued actively by video players. While such approaches may be feasible for streaming platforms that deploy their own CDN, they are less applicable for third-party CDNs with multiple tenants and diverse video players.

In this paper, we present a characterization of video workload from a global multi-tenant CDN and develop SSQoE: a methodology deployed on the server side which estimates rebuffering experienced by video clients using passive measurements. Using this approach, we calculate a QoE score which represents the health of a video stream across multiple consumers. We present our findings using this QoE score for various scenarios and compare it to traditional server and network monitoring metrics. We also demonstrate the QoE score's efficacy during large streaming events such as the 2020 Superbowl LIV. We show that this server-side QoE estimation methodology is able to track video performance at an AS or user agent level and can easily pinpoint regional issues at the CDN, making it an attractive solution to be explored by researchers and other CDNs.

1 Introduction

Streaming video constitutes a large portion of traffic on the Internet. Content Delivery Networks (CDNs) deliver tens of Terabits per second of video for large video streaming platforms that users rely on for news, entertainment, and communication. Live streaming services have further gained popularity with the rise of over-the-top (OTT) services.

The increasing volume of video traffic and the user expectations for high quality necessitate visibility into client-perceived performance of video streaming. A key performance metric for video Quality of Experience (QoE) is the

O. Hohlfeld et al. (Eds.): PAM 2022, LNCS 13210, pp. 600–625, 2022.
https://doi.org/10.1007/978-3-030-98785-5_27

rebuffering experienced by video players. Rebuffering can be caused by a variety of reasons including problems at the client, at the ISP, or at the CDN layer. Content providers that employ their own video players usually extend the players to generate reports about performance metrics directly from the client. Alternatively, third-party services can be utilized to report such data from a set of clients. However, in many cases where commercial third-party CDNs are used for video delivery, the CDN operators may not have visibility into such client reports. Therefore, CDN operators typically use more indirect server and network performance metrics to identify performance degradation of video streams that they deliver. Such metrics may not provide a clear picture of client-perceived performance, and make it harder to evaluate if a problem is impacting clients enough to warrant traffic engineering actions like choosing alternative peering links or sending a client request to a different location.

To address the gap in visibility and the challenges of client-side beacon based monitoring, we characterize the video workload at a multi-tenant CDN that spans over 160 Points of Presence (PoPs) distributed globally, making it one of the largest egress networks in the world [10], and we design and deploy a server-side QoE monitoring tool called SSQoE on the CDN in order to estimate client video QoE based on server logs. In particular, our work makes the following contributions:

- We identify and characterize QoE metrics that can be tracked using only server-side logs and analyze their implications on video performance. These include the timestamp when a video request is received at the CDN, gaps in requests, changes in bitrate, and time taken to serve a request.
- We propose a simple, scalable, and intuitive methodology called SSQoE, which uses these metrics that are available from CDN access logs to estimate rebuffering on the client side. We use other relevant QoE indicators to calculate a QoE score that can be used to track video performance agnostic to the type of video player, device, and type of video traffic.
- We show the value of our methodology by comparing it with commonly used client beacon based reporting. We demonstrate use cases from our deployment, like tracking regional per-PoP anomalies from the 2020 Superbowl event where the CDN served the live video stream to millions of clients.
- We demonstrate the shortcomings of the server and network based monitoring metrics by comparing their efficiency in representing client-perceived performance to our methodology during incidents like transit provider connectivity failures or cache fill errors.

This paper is structured as follows. We describe the current video distribution pipelines commonly used by video providers and motivate our work by elaborating on the challenges faced by multi-tenant CDNs to monitor video performance in Sect. 2. In Sect. 3, we present insights on the video workload delivered by the CDN, and we describe relevant performance indicators. In Sect. 4 we present our QoE score calculation methodology. We validate our methodology using a testbed and production traffic in Sect. 5 and show its value using several examples in Sect. 6. We discuss the limitations, related work, and conclude in Sects. 7, 8, 9 respectively.

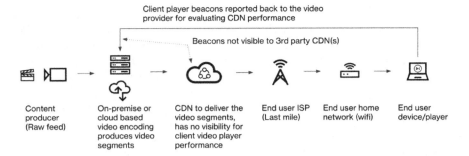

Fig. 1. Live video streaming pipeline. Each step can be a cause of increased latency. Client player reports performance metrics back to content provider or a 3rd party beaconing service using their SDKs. These reports are analyzed to evaluate CDN performance from client's perspective.

2   Background

Video streaming workflows are complex, especially while delivering a live stream. As with any complex system, each involved component can fail and lead to degradation in end-to-end performance. In the case of video streaming, such degradations translate to reduced QoE for the video consumer. In this section, we describe various pieces of a video pipeline starting from data capture to distribution, point out gaps in visibility, and motivate the need for server-side video monitoring.

To deliver scale and achieve robustness, many video streaming providers use multiple CDNs to deliver content to the clients. Third-party beaconing platforms [2] have become a popular mechanism by which content providers monitor CDN performance to get insights on client experience and use beacon data to steer traffic across multiple CDNs.

Components in Video Streaming

Figure 1 illustrates the components of a live video streaming pipeline. An on-premise camera captures the video and the raw feed is sent to the video encoder. Video encoders can be on-premise installations or cloud based services. The video encoder gathers a sufficient video chunk (usually less than 2 to 5 s) before it can generate an encoded video segment that will be distributed. Next, the system generates a manifest file, which describes the set of segments that a video player will need to request for the given video stream. The video encoder encodes the segments into multiple bitrates denoting different quality levels. Each unique time range of video may exist as multiple segments in different bitrates. The video encoder then pushes the segments to a CDN origin server or the CDN can pull them periodically. The client starts the video streaming on their device and requests the video asset. Each client is identified as a unique *session*. First, the manifest is delivered to the client. Based on current network conditions, the player chooses an appropriate bitrate from the manifest and requests the corresponding video segment. These segments, which are available from the CDN origin server, are cached at the CDN edge when a client requests them. The client request traverses through the client ISP link to its backbone and then to the CDN peering point where it finally gets served by the CDN.

Each component in the pipeline adds to the latency and is a potential source of video performance degradation. It is possible that the video ingest at the video encoder is delayed. In such cases most clients will start lagging in their live stream. Next, there can be delay when ingesting the video segments from the encoder to the origin server or at the CDN cache due to degradation in backbone or transit provider connectivity. Delays can also occur at the CDN PoP due to overloaded servers or congestion at the peering link. Congestion is also common at the client ISP, in the middle or the last mile. Finally, the load on the client device, e.g. available RAM, CPU, can also play a role in how the video player performs. Given all these potential sources of delay and performance degradation, the process of pinpointing an exact the root cause for QoE impairments becomes challenging.

QoE Metrics in the Wild

Existing video performance monitoring techniques have been focused on analyzing client-side metrics. The video player instruments a beacon that periodically reports how the player is performing. Those beacons are collected and analyzed to extract QoE insights. Some video providers own the application or video player and therefore can implement their own data collection strategy, which the CDN may not have the visibility into. There are also third-party vendors such as [2] that are commonly used for such beaconing. Key metrics that are monitored by the video providers are:

Startup-delays: This measures delays experienced when starting a stream.

Rebuffering ratio: This is the most commonly monitored metric [2,7,18,21]. It represents the ratio of the amount of time a video player was stalled waiting for new segments to be downloaded over the total video duration. For example, if a client played a 60-second video but in the middle of the playback it ran out of buffered segments and it had to wait for 2 s before resuming, then the rebuffering ratio is $2/60 \doteq 3.3\%$.

Bitrate: This denotes the number of bits used to encode a given segment of video. Higher bitrate represents better video quality. Video providers who use the CDN service to distribute the content expect the bitrate to be high.

Video playback failure: This represents cases where video player had trouble playing the content it received. This can be a result of expired token, digital rights management (DRM) issues, etc. which are used to secure the video segment so that only approved clients, such as paying subscribers, can view the content.

Motivation for Server-side Video QoE Monitoring

Commercial CDNs deliver a mixed workload of video traffic for many live streams. Each video provider (CDN customer) can have a completely different set of configurations for encoding and caching the video segments. Their performance goals could also be different, e.g. some might value lower latency over higher bitrate/quality. Furthermore, popular live streams can have millions of concurrent users requesting the same video asset from the CDN.

Client-side metrics captured via beacons provide a clear view per-session of how the client experiences the video. However, these methods rely on some control over the client. They are by design made for the video provider to consume and not for the CDN provider. Content providers that use their own CDN and video client player (i.e. both ends of the connection) can easily implement this beaconing and use it for CDN performance monitoring. In contrast, commercial CDN operators face the challenge of analyzing the performance of video streams without complete visibility. The root cause of a performance issue can very well be outside of the CDN stack, such as at the encoder or at the client ISP. This large disparity in type of workloads for different CDN customers and type of content, dependency on video player metrics, and lack of complete visibility makes the previously studied client-side approaches less viable for a commercial CDN.

3   Characterizing the CDN Video Workload

In this section we analyze a large CDN video workload and extract insights that serve as guiding principles for designing a server-side QoE monitoring strategy. For this analysis, we use 24 hours (one weekday) of CDN access logs for a large live video streaming provider that powers multiple live sports, news, and entertainment services. The dataset spans more than 10 million HTTP requests.

Unique Session Tracking
In order to extract aggregate performance information for a stream that is delivered through the CDN, we first need to understand performance of each session separately. For that purpose, there needs to be a unique identifier that characterizes a particular client stream. Some video streaming providers maintain a unique session ID per client session, which can make session tracking easier. However, SSQoE does not rely on such a session ID. In particular, we notice that in the majority of cases a unique client ID can be inferred by using the client IP and the device User Agent. In our dataset, 99% of the session IDs map to a unique {client_ip, user_agent} tuple. In the reverse direction, the same {client_ip, user_agent} tuple maps to the same session ID for about 80% of the cases. This may be due to the presence of large carrier-grade NATs [24] which can lead to aggregation of multiple clients into one session. However, based on our analysis of the CDN access logs, this noise is minimal and it is still possible to infer per-session characteristics using the hash of client IP and User Agent tuple.
Takeaway: A session or client ID is important for measuring per-session QoE from the server side. In the absence of such an identifier in the CDN logs, a hash of the client IP and User Agent is an adequate alternative.

Total Duration of Video Sessions
Video streams delivered by multi CDNs can vary significantly in terms of duration. Additionally, the complexity of user viewing patterns is high, especially for

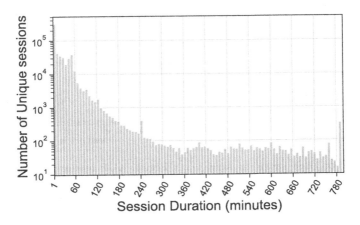

Fig. 2. Session durations. Most sessions are short lived.

live streams where clients can join or leave a stream at anytime. This can add noise when trying to measuring the QoE at scale for millions of users. In Fig. 2 we show the number of sessions ordered by playback duration over the course of one day. As shown in the figure, most sessions are short-lived (note the log scale on the Y-axis). This highlights the variety and scale of our dataset, but also reveals a key observation that needs to be taken into consideration while designing server-side QoE measurements: QoE decisions need to be made near-real time over a short time duration, because most sessions are short lived (in the order of minutes).

Takeaway: Due to the short playback duration and high churn of clients in live streams, tracking the performance of a few sessions over a long period of time will provide little value; instead, tracking a large number of session over a shorter time window is more feasible.

Time Taken to Serve a Request

Next we try to understand which metrics can provide insights on the performance of a session. A metric that impacts video delivery is the amount of time it takes the server to deliver a response. For a given video stream, the time it takes to deliver the same video segment remains fairly constant, and fluctuations in the flow completion time are a good indicator of performance change.

Tracking the time taken to serve a request when grouping the streams by different dimensions or characteristics also reveals insights about misbehaving sections of the traffic. For example, in Fig. 3 we show the distribution of time taken to serve a request grouped by top User Agents of a video provider. For this distribution we look at requests for video segments betweeen 8-10MB to keep the comparison fair across all requests and user agents. The User Agent names are anonymized. Here, we observed the CDN taking several seconds longer to serve the request to one particular User Agent (UA-1). This User Agent belonged to the application of the video provider on an older generation of a large Smart TV

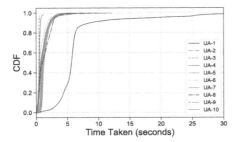
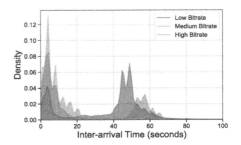

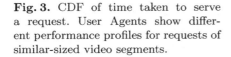

Fig. 3. CDF of time taken to serve a request. User Agents show different performance profiles for requests of similar-sized video segments.

Fig. 4. KDE interarrival times for sessions. During normal operation, the inter-arrival time between requests is short.

manufacturer. When we compared the performance of this User Agent in the client-side QoE monitoring systems, it also accounted for top rebufferring events for that provider on the CDN.

The time taken to download a video segment is not only a function of client player behavior but also of server performance (high CPU utilization times can lead to higher response time), network congestion, and size of the video segment. When the bitrate of a video stream changes, the size of the video segment also changes. For example, ads can be inserted into a video stream, and tracking this change is an important indicator of the behavior of the video stream since the ads can be encoded in different bitrate.

Takeaway: Understanding the time taken to serve subsets of requests of the same stream that share similar characteristics can reveal anomalous behavior in different dimensions, which is important for server-side QoE monitoring.

Request Arrival Times and Bitrate Changes

The behavior of the video player at the client plays an important role in how the user experiences the video stream. Most common players employ Adaptive Bit Rate (ABR) [1]. During playback, players try to estimate the achievable bandwidth, i.e. which corresponding bitrate/quality can be achieved using the current network conditions. When the available bandwidth drops, the ABR algorithm drops the bitrate i.e., requests a subsequent video segment of a lower quality.

It is possible to understand how the client-side player perceives the connection by tracking when the request arrived and what bitrate the client requested. We capture the request timing information in comparison to previous requests on the same session by tracking the inter-arrival time of requests. In Fig. 4 we show the Kernel Density Estimation (KDE) distribution of requests for a live streaming provider over one day. We bucket each request into three bitrate types: Low, Medium, and High. In most cases the request inter-arrival times are in the order of few seconds, indicating normal player behavior where the player maintains sufficient video segments in the buffer to play next. However, we also notice that in some cases, and more commonly when the used bitrate quality is low, the inter-arrival times can be high (greater than 30 s). To evaluate if the high inter-arrival times correlate with change in bitrate, for each case where inter-arrival times are higher than 12 s, we check if the current bitrate matches that of the previous request of the same session. We chose the threshold of 12 s since the particular provider examined here starts playback as soon as the player receives a minimum of 12 s of video. We categorize the bitrate change into Same, Up, or Down based on the direction of the quality change. We see that in more than 70% of the cases where inter-arrival times are high, the subsequent request is for a lower quality segment (direction: Down). This shows that the player suffered some delays and ABR reduced the quality of the video. ABR only switches quality to higher if it is sure the client will not see a negative impact. In about 20% of the cases the direction of change in quality was Up, meaning even though the inter-arrival times increased, the client may not have experienced a rebuffering event.

Takeaway: *The change in bitrate is a good metric to capture client player behavior and to use as indication for client-perceived quality, but it is not enough by itself to accurately estimate if the client experienced rebuffering.*

4   Server-side Video QoE Measurement Methodology

Based on the takeaways from Sect. 3, in this section we present SSQoE: a server-side QoE score calculation method that relies solely on CDN access logs, and requires no other input from the client-side. The goal of this methodology is to be content agnostic (it should work for any video customer at the CDN), player agnostic (it should not make any assumptions about client video player behavior), and to account for noise that is caused by millions of users connecting to the platform as well as from video artifacts like quality change, ad breaks, etc.

Information Needed from the CDN Access Logs
As our approach relies solely on the CDN access logs, we first describe the necessary fields that are extracted from the logs to perform this analysis. We use three key pieces of information, a *timestamp* of when a client requested a video asset, the *segment ID* (file/segment name) of the video asset, and a *session ID*. We know the video length of the segments before hand, either via a configuration file or via estimations done using `ffmpeg` [3]. These fields are easily available in most web server logs. In case of absence of explicit session ID, a hash of the {client_ip, user_agent} tuple can be used. Hashing the tuple obviates the need for IP-level tracking. Note the video asset segment ID usually encodes the information of the bitrate. A full video such as a movie comprises of many segments. Each segment is numbered incrementally, for example, A1.ts, A2.ts, ... , etc. In this example let us say the first letter is the quality type: A is lowest, B is higher than A, C is higher than B, and so on. With this knowledge, we look at requests from each client and check them in sequence. If their quality changes, for example, A1.ts, B2.ts, A3.ts, we then add it to the rate of fluctuation metric.

Player Buffer Estimation

To estimate if the client side video player ran out of video to play (i.e. suffered rebuffering), we estimate the amount of video the player has in its buffer at a given time. For every request received from a player, we add the respective duration of video (in seconds) to the estimated buffer size. We note that the segment length can change across segment types. For example, ad segments used for server-side ad insertion can be shorter than main content video segments. Therefore, for each session we have in memory the amount of video in the player's buffer. Every time we see a request for a segment of a session, we compare the time difference between the previous request and current timestamp. Using this information we can estimate how much video has been consumed. For example, if at a given time the estimated buffer length for a client is 12 s, i.e. we estimate that the player has 12 s of video available in its buffer, and the next request is seen 15 s after the previous request, then we know that for at least for 3 s the player must not have had any video to play. We refer to this as *rebuffer duration*. With this approachs, without the need for any client-side beacons, we can measure a key element that influences user's QoE.

Calculating QoE Score

Estimating video rebuffer duration from the server-side provides the missing piece needed to measure QoE without client-side participation. However, as shown in the previous section, there are other metrics that prove to be useful.

First, video quality is a function of the bitrate. A higher average bitrate means better video quality, and a better viewing experience. It has been shown before that viewers tend to respond negatively to fluctuations in bitrate and prefer a constant bitrate [8]. Thus a constant lower bitrate impacts user engagement less than many quality switches. A session can have low bitrate due its network subscription package limits, device capabilities, etc. It is not accurate to count every low bitrate session as lack or drop in QoE. Therefore, we keep track of jitter in the bitrate i.e., the *number of times the video stream changes its quality*.

Second, we observed that in most cases the time taken to serve the requests for a client remains fairly constant. We use this information to extract an average time taken to serve a client in a time bin. We analyze this at per ASN or per User Agent granularity to be able to compare similar clients. *Any large fluctuations in average time taken metric is also a good indicator of anomalies.*

Finally, we saw that for a stable video stream the player requests video segments at a fairly constant rate from the server, when performance changes or the player falls behind in a live stream it might request more segments to change quality or catch up in a live stream. *Any large fluctuations in average requests rate is also a good indicator of anomalies.*

We define R_b, T_b, B_b, A_b to describe each metric, as described in Table 1. These metrics represent aggregate information from all sessions in a time bucket b. Equations 1–4 describe how each metric is calculated.

$$R_b = \frac{\sum_{s=1}^{total\_unique\_sessions_b} estimated\_rebuffering}{bucket\_duration_b * total\_unique\_sessions_b} \qquad (1)$$

Table 1. Definitions of metrics used for QoE score.

Metric	Definition
R_b	Average estimated rebuffering ratio in bucket b
T_b	Average time taken to serve request in bucket b
B_b	Average bitrate drops in bucket b
A_b	Average requests per session in bucket b

$$T_b = \frac{\sum_{s=1}^{total\_unique\_sessions_b} time\_taken}{total\_unique\_sessions_b} \tag{2}$$

$$B_b = \frac{\sum_{s=1}^{total\_unique\_sessions_b} number\_of\_bitrate\_drops}{total\_unique\_sessions_b} \tag{3}$$

$$A_b = \frac{total\_requests_b}{total\_unique\_sessions_b} \tag{4}$$

We track these metrics individually and calculate a derived anomaly indicator score as well. We represent the QoE score at a given time bucket as a combination of R_b, T_b, B_b, A_b (Eq. 5). We note that it is possible to add more dimensions to our analysis to update the granularity of QoE score.

$$qoe\_score_b = R_b * T_b * B_b * A_b \tag{5}$$

Lower values are better for each dimension of QoE score. For example, a good video stream should have lower estimated rebuffers, less time taken to server requests, lower number of bitrate drops, etc. therefore *higher values of the QoE score represent anomalies*. Having a single metric to track QoE anomalies provides operational simplicity and a quick litmus test if further analysis is needed. A single metric also simplifies automated anomaly detection and alerting, since standard techniques such as tracking changes (more than 3 standard deviations), cosine similarity, etc. can be easily used.

In this paper, we normalize the value of QoE score between 0 and 1 for comparison with other monitoring metrics, by dividing each calculated value by the maximum QoE score seen in a given time window. However, SSQoE tracks the raw QoE score values and does not rely on this normalization; we simply do this for easier representation and comparison of the results.

Detailed Algorithm to Extract Session Info

In Algorithm 1 we describe how SSQoE calculates the estimated rebuffering along with the other metrics. For the sake of simplicity we present this method as one procedure but our implementation comprises of optimizations that enable us to perform such analysis at scale and at different granularities, e.g. for different CDN customers, ASNs, user agents, etc. For each session, we extract all requests (r_s) seen in CDN logs. We initialize arrays d_s, tt_s, Δt_s, b_s to keep track of rebuffer durations per request, time taken values per request, inter-arrival times between

---

Algorithm 1. Extract Session Info

1: **procedure** EXTRACTSESSIONINFO(s)
2:    $r_s \leftarrow$ *Requests for session s sorted by time*
3:    $d_s \leftarrow array[]$ ▷ //Initialize array to store rebuffering duration for every timestamp seen in current bucket
4:    $tt_s \leftarrow array[]$ ▷ //Initialize array to store time taken to serve request
5:    $\Delta t_s \leftarrow array[]$ ▷ //Initialize array to store inter-arrival times
6:    $b_s \leftarrow array[]$ ▷ //Initialize array to track bitrate changes
7:    $bsize_s \leftarrow 0$ ▷ //Initialize variable to track estimated video length in client player buffer
8:    **for** each request r_{si} in r_s **do**
9:        $seg_s \leftarrow$ *Get segment ID from* r_{si} *URL*
10:       $b_{s_i} \leftarrow comp(b_{s_i}, b_{s_{(i-1)}})$ ▷ //Track bitrate changes
11:       **if** seg_s *was requested before for session s* **then**
12:           *Ignore duplicate requests for same* seg_s
13:       $vlen_{si} \leftarrow len(seg_s)$
14:       $tt_{s_i} \leftarrow$ *time taken to serve the request* r_{si}
15:       **if** $i > 0$ **then**
16:           $t_i \leftarrow$ *timestamp of request* r_{si}
17:           $\Delta t_i \leftarrow t_i - t_{(i-1)}$
18:           $bsize_s \leftarrow bsize_s - \Delta t_i$ ▷ //Remove the time difference between requests from estimated buffer length
19:           **if** $bsize_s$ ¡ 0 **then**
20:               $d_{s_{t_i}} \leftarrow abs(bsize_s)$ ▷ //Player rebuffered same amount as the gap detected in estimated buffer length
21:               $bsize_s \leftarrow 0$ ▷ //Reset buffer length
22:       $bsize_s \leftarrow bsize_s + vlen_{si}$
23:       $tt_{s_i} \leftarrow moving\_average(tt_{s_{(i-1)}}, tt_{s_i})$
24:    **return** d_s, tt_s, b_s

---

subsequent requests, and bitrate changes per request for session s (Steps 1–6). Duplicate requests are ignored, since from the server's perspective same amount of video will be available in the player buffer for two duplicate requests. For each unique request received, for the session in current time bucket, we extract the session ID, compare change in the bitrate from the previous request and finally subtract the time difference between the current and previous request time from our estimated client buffer, *bsize* (Steps 7–18). This describes the duration of video that the client has already consumed. If a subsequent request of a session does not arrive on time, *bsize* falls below zero, indicating a rebuffering event (Steps 19–24). We extract all these metrics per session to be aggregated next.

Global Deployment

As mentioned in the previous paragraph, while the methodology can be described as standalone process running on a server, our implementation of SSQoE leverages the global scale of the CDN. Figure 5 describes an overview of our global deployment. An edge service consumes CDN access logs for a given video provider (a new instance is launched per video provider/customer). Each edge video QoE

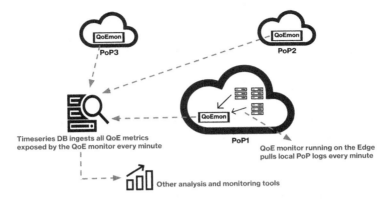

Fig. 5. Distributed log processing for live server-side QoE monitoring.

service only consumes logs for the past one minute from the same PoP as itself, calculates the QoE score and exposes these metrics to a time-series monitoring service at the CDN. Performing this computation at the edge locally per PoP achieves two goals: 1) Get the QoE score as close to real-time as possible, which is most beneficial for live streams, and 2) Achieve redundancy. Operations at one PoP does not affect the QoE monitoring service at another PoP. This provides resiliency in how we capture per PoP QoE anomalies.

5 Validation

In order to validate the methodology used by SSQoE we employ testbed consisting of a server and client that we control, in order to compare the rebuffering reported directly by the client to that measured by SSQoE using server-side logs. We then also perform a detailed comparison between two weeks worth of client-side beacon rebuffering data obtained from a large live sports video streaming provider and the QoE estimates derived using SSQoE on the CDN during same time period.

5.1 Testbed Evaluation

Testbed Setup. For the controlled experiment, we use Nginx as a streaming video server, compiled with the RTMP module [6] to enable HLS live streaming. For the client, we instrument a Javascript HLS video player [4] that we extended with the ability to log timestamps and durations of rebuffering events, as well as timestamps of video segment requests and download durations. The client runs on a local machine while the server is hosted on a cloud VM, with approximately 20ms mean RTT between the two.

We use a 1200-second video that consists of 100 segments. We export the player logs and analyze them to establish the ground truth for the timings of player events like segment download, playback, and rebuffering. On the server

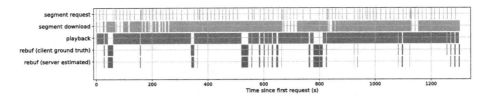

Fig. 6. Testbed evaluation. Comparison of Server-side estimated rebuffering with client reported rebuffering.

side, we export logs that contain request timestamps, request URL and segment duration. We then feed that information to the QoE algorithm in order to estimate rebuffering events and their durations, and we compare that to the ground truth reported from the client logs. During each experiment run we induce artificial network bottleneck using `tc` [5], with inter-arrival times of the throttling events and their durations drawn from a Poisson distribution.

Validation Results

Figure 6 visualizes a single experiment run. The top four rows plot the timestamps and durations of events (request, download, playback and rebuffering) as reported from the client, representing the ground truth. The last row is the output of the QoE estimation based on the server-side logs. The estimated client rebuffering events plotted on that row align well with the client-reported rebuffering events on the row above it, showing that the algorithm detected both the segments for which rebuffering occurred, as well as the corresponding rebuffering durations for the session. The total rebuffering duration reported by the client was 120.8 s and the server estimated 111.3 s of rebuffering (7.9% error).

To evaluate the accuracy of our method over multiple runs, we repeat the experiment 10 times such that the client downloaded 1000 segments (large enough sample to produce meaningful results) and measure the accuracy of detecting rebuffering duration. First we calculate total rebuffer duration as reported by the client and estimated by our method. We calculate error as the absolute difference between rebuffer durations as reported by the two methods. In this test the median error across all the runs was 8.1%. This aligns with our previous single-run error (7.9%) indicating the method's consistency.

In the Fig. 6 we can visualize that rebuffering was detected at the same time by the server and the client. To confirm same is true for our experiment with many runs we evaluate if the rebuffering was seen for the exact same segment by both server and client. Out of 1000 segments across all runs combined (200 minutes of playback time), 121 segments were reported by the client to suffer rebuffering. The algorithm estimated rebuffering in 107 segments, with 3 false positives (segments for which rebuffering was detected, but did not occur) and 17 false negatives (segments for which rebuffering happened but was not detected). There were 104 true positives (segments for which rebuffering happened and it was detected), providing 85.95% accuracy (precision).

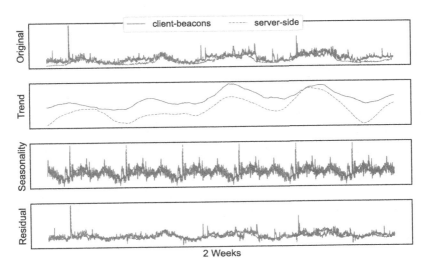

Fig. 7. Time-series decomposition analysis of client-side beacon reported rebuffering vs server-side rebuffer estimation for a large video provider over two weeks. Server-side QoE is able to track both general trend and instantaneous spikes.

5.2 Comparison with Client Beacon Data

As stated in Sect. 2, video providers often use client-side beacons to evaluate video and CDN performance. In order for SSQoE to provide value, it is important that its QoE estimations match the trends of rebuffering ratio reported by such client-side beacons. To validate this, we obtain two weeks of client-side data from a large video provider for which we deployed SSQoE, and compare the results.

Time-series Seasonality Decomposition
Time-series data is composed of systemic components (lower order trends that repeat) and non-systemic components (higher order fluctuations that are local or instantaneous). SSQoE aims to capture both components, i.e. both the general trend of rebuffering as well as large instantaneous anomalies. Therefore, we decompose the client beacon and the SSQoE score time-series into the following three components:

Trend: Lowest component, changes very slowly over long time period (days)
Seasonality: Predictable repeating component, captures local change (hours)
Residual: Anomalous instantaneous component, not predictable (minutes)

Figure 7 (top) shows the original time-series for client-side beacon data and server-side QoE score. To simplify comparison, we normalize each dataset between 0 and 1 as described in Sect. 4. We observe that the two datasets match in overall trends with a *Spearman correlation of 0.7*, and server-side QoE score (SSQoE) matches large anomalies in the client-side beacon data. However, we note that in these original signals there are a few spikes seen in beacon data that are not obvious in the QoE score data. We also note that there is a large amount of noise (local fluctuations) in both datasets.

We use a standard additive model to decompose the two time-series such that *original = trend + seasonality + residual*, as described in [17]. This well established model quickly provides us an ability to analyze the data at different granularities. Figure 7 also plots these three sub-components, which, combined, compose the original time series. We analyze each component separately to evaluate the precision, recall, and F1 score of SSQoE. We detect anomalies in each component using a sliding window, where a datapoint is marked as anomalous if it is greater than three standard deviations ($> 3\sigma$) compared to past 5 minutes. For each anomaly in the client beacon data we check if the QoE score data also captured an anomaly in the same 5-minute window. If it did, we count that as a true positive, otherwise we flag that as a false negative. Similarly, if we detect an anomaly in QoE score data but no anomaly is reported in the same 5-minute window in the beacon data, we count that as a false positive.

Table 2. For each sub-component, server-side QoE shows high precision values. Server-side QoE tracking is accurate for detecting large instantaneous spikes and long term trend but some local short term fluctuations could be missed.

	Precision	Recall	F1 score
Trend	1	1	1
Seasonality	1	0.57	0.72
Residual	0.89	0.76	0.82

Table 2 shows the results of our precision/recall analysis for each time-series component. The Trend sub-component is expected to be stable and slow changing, and thus anomalies are easily caught. SSQoE captures the trend of the client beacon data accurately. For the Seasonality and Residual component, we get high precision (1 and 0.89) indicating the QoE score is highly accurate in detecting anomalies for local changes (minutes or hours level granularity). Recall is 0.57 for the Seasonality component and 0.76 for the Residual component, indicating that the QoE score can have some false negatives for anomalies that are short lived.

6 Video Performance Monitoring at the CDN

This section presents results from using SSQoE to measure video performance at the CDN. We first demonstrate how per-PoP analysis can aid in fast detection and response to incidents by showing how we used SSQoE to measure streaming performance for the Superbowl LIV event while delivering millions of live streams.

We then explore ways that the measured QoE score can provide additional insight to those gained by existing approaches. CDNs employ a variety of server and network based performance analysis systems to detect and resolve performance issues [12,26]. In Sect. 6.2 and 6.3 we show examples where server and network metrics were not sufficient during anomalies and how SSQoE exposed the impact of the issues on client-perceived QoE.

6.1   Using Server-Side Video QoE

Region-Wise Performance Evaluation. One challenge with client beacon based reporting, even in cases where access to such data is available to the CDN operators, is that it is not always possible to map the reported problems to the CDN region (PoP) that might be the root cause of a degraded client experience. This problem is much more pronounced for a large anycast-based network such as ours where the decisions regarding which PoP a client talks to is largely decided by the BGP policies. Since SSQoE is implemented on the server-side, it allows to easily perform PoP-level breakdown which can reveal regional anomalies that can happen only in a handful of PoPs.

Superbowl LIV
During the live streaming of Superbowl LIV, along with several other performance monitoring tools, we used SSQoE to measure the performance of the stream delivery. We detected short lived spikes in the QoE score which matched beacon-reported rebuffering ratios. More interestingly, mid-way into the game, the QoE score for the Seattle PoP started trending upwards. Figure 8 shows the normalized QoE score for several PoPs[1]. This trend was not exposed by third-party beacon data used for monitoring performance. We confirmed that this was not a false positive, and were able to identify the root cause of this issue: cache servers hit CPU limits, inflating the time it took to serve the video asset. While a large impact was observed at 02:00 UTC on Feb. 3rd (client reported problems to the NOC[2]), SSQoE actually reported spikes in the QoE score earlier than that. As a result SSQoE reduced the time to take action during one of the largest online streaming events in the US. This example emphasizes the ability of SSQoE to detect problems that might even be missed by client-side beacon metrics. This can enable CDN operators to pinpoint issues in the CDN infrastructure proactively and without any external dependencies.

QoE by User Agents
As shown in Sect. 3, it is possible to evaluate the performance of a video stream over various dimensions using the time taken to serve the requests. Here, we analyze the QoE grouped by user agent. In Fig. 9 we show QoE scores for the most popular browser/operating systems that are observed in the CDN access logs. Chrome on Windows 7 was the user agent with the highest QoE score, which translates to more rebuffering. While the exact version number of Chrome is not

---

[1] For visualization simplicity in the figures, each PoP is represented by the city/metro name it is located in.

[2] Network Operations Center (NOC) is responsible for 24×7 monitoring of global CDN performance and respond to customer incidents.

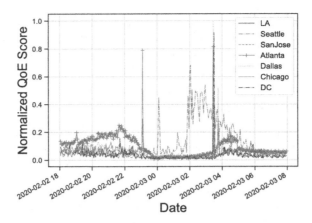

Fig. 8. Normalized QoE scores during Superbowl 2020 per PoP. Spike in the QoE score of Seattle PoP due to CPU bottleneck could be easily identified (3rd 02:00 UTC). Other rebuffering spikes were also accurately caught at several PoPs.

shown in the figure, we note that this is an older version of Chrome (74). We also carefully acknowledge that lower performance of this browser/OS combination might also be an artifact of the device CPU/memory since older devices running these older versions of browsers and OSes also tend to have older specifications.

6.2   QoE vs Server Metrics

In this section we look at QoE scores in the context of CDN performance metrics. One of the metrics tracked in order to monitor CDN health is the ratio of total number of server-side errors (HTTP code 5xx) to the total number of requests, defined as the *error ratio*. Under normal operations, this error ratio is under 0.3%. The baseline behavior of this metric can differ at different PoPs based on current conditions, which can introduce noise to the metric.

Monitoring the error ratio is useful to understand performance of the CDN and origin cache performance for cache-fill. If a large number of users request for the same video segment (e.g. during a popular live event) and if the error ratio is high, many clients can take a performance hit. However, we argue that QoE score can be a better metric for tracking such impact. By looking at the error ratio, it is hard to estimate how long the impact of missing segments lasted, or what the intensity of the impact was i.e., how many concurrent users suffered. Moreover, video players are designed to buffer segments a few seconds ahead of current play time, hence a small ephemeral spike in error ratio may not always affect the video playback.

Figure 10 shows SSQoE scores and error ratios from a North American PoP. In this case, for a few hours the video provider origin had performance issues and returned 5xx responses. During such events it is operationally difficult to evaluate the actual impact on end users based on HTTP errors alone. In Fig. 10 we see

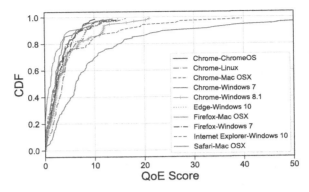

Fig. 9. CDF of QoE Scores by top user agents. Older browsers/OSes often perform worse.

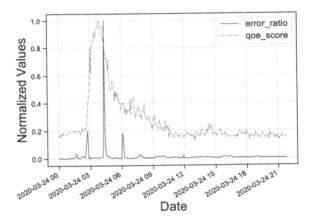

Fig. 10. QoE score compared to HTTP error ratio. QoE score provides a picture of user impact during origin server performance problems than the error ratio.

a correlated spike in error ratio and the QoE score. However, we observe that error spikes were more instantaneous (once a content is available at the origin, the error ratio subsides). In contrast, the QoE score was increased for a few hours after the last spike in the error ratio, indicating availability but degraded origin server performance. Several mitigation steps were taken to alleviate this problem. In this case, monitoring the QoE score instead of error ratio provided a more accurate picture on the intensity of the impact. This also emphasizes the SSQoE's ability to track performance issues whose root cause lies in early steps of the live video streaming pipeline (Fig. 1).

6.3 QoE vs Network Metrics

A common practice in performance monitoring at content providers is to monitor the RTT and retransmits towards clients. This information is then used to infer problems in connectivity either at the client ISP, transit provider, or at the CDN itself. Systems such as *BlameIt* [19] operate in such fashion. Network metrics, however, do not capture a complete view of the media delivery stack. In our experience, other factors (as described in Sects. 2 and 3) can cause client level impacts and lead to rebuffering.

To demonstrate this, we show the QoE score vs average RTTs and average retransmits for a 2-day period from a North American PoP in Figure 11. One of the transit providers for this PoP faced a connectivity issue during this period. As shown in the figure, the RTT and retransmit aggregates did not fluctuate much. However, we clearly see a spike in the QoE score around the time connectivity issue was reported (starting at 20:00 UTC on the 17th). Due to fallback routes and other network-layer load balancing it is possible that network layer issues get masked, but client sessions resetting or suffering playback issues are captured by the QoE score.

Wireless ISPs

SSQoE measurements also enable analysis by ISP. This adds value for operational monitoring by providing an additional dimension to compare and evaluate performance. Nowadays users consume large volumes of video content on their mobile phone over wireless networks. It is common practice to monitor network metrics towards such wireless carrier ISPs by tracking RTTs and retransmits. Here, we evaluate whether lower RTT translates to lower rebuffering. In Fig. 12a we plot the average RTTs from one of the CDN's North American PoPs towards the top three wireless carriers in the U.S. over 8 days. We normalize these values between 0 and 1, where maximum RTT across the ISPs is set to 1. The RTTs profiles for the three wireless carriers are different at this PoP, making it a good candidate to evaluate if lower RTTs lead to less rebuffering. Since we are trying to eliminate the network impact, we only look at estimated rebuffering captured using the method described in Sect. 4.

Interestingly, we note that Wireless ISP 1 has the lowest rebuffering but the 2nd highest RTT. We also note that the distribution of estimated rebuffering is similar for wireless ISPs 2 and 3 even though their RTT profiles vary. This indicates that network metrics do not necessarily capture user perceived experience.

The above analysis shows how SSQoE can be used to profile ISPs based on QoE scores. Categorizing ISPs by performance in video delivery can help identify providers which are persistently under-performing, and can help drive traffic engineering decisions during large live streaming events.

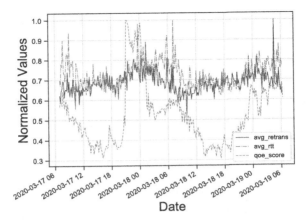

Fig. 11. QoE score compared to RTT and retransmits. A transit provider connectivity problem, from 17th 20:00 to 18th 01:00, is better captured using the QoE score.

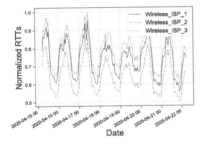
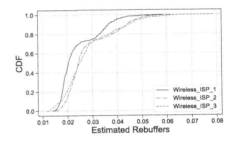

(a) Normalized RTTs for 3 largest wireless carriers in the U.S from a North American PoP. Each ISP has a unique RTT profile.

(b) CDF of estimated rebuffers used in QoE calculations. Wireless ISP 1 shows lowest rebuffering but has 2nd highest RTT measurement (left).

Fig. 12. RTT vs QoE for U.S wireless carriers.

7   Discussion

There are some aspects of video content delivery that this paper does not cover in detail and must be kept in mind while deploying such method.

Variable Segment Size and Quality

A common practice to deliver large files is to chunk the file. Here the original file (could be a few GBs) is broken into similarly sized chunks (in the order of MBs). Each chunk is treated as a separate content asset. In such cases, one video segment request from the client can map to more than one chunk. Care needs to be taken to account for flow completion times of each chunk as well as add only the corresponding video segment duration to buffer estimation algorithm (described in Sect. 4) that the chunk represents. Note that subsequent requests from the client can be of different quality therefore video duration of chunks in subsequent requests can vary.

Estimation During Fewer Video Sessions

While the proposed method detects rebuffering on a per-session granularity, we note that relying on this signal when the number of sessions is too few may lead to noise. We aggregate the estimated rebuffering for all sessions that lie in the current time bin and draw aggregated average value, therefore, it is imperative that there are enough data points where the average is a reliable representative value. Too few data points result in averages sensitive to outliers.

We perform our analysis using a minimum of 50 sessions per minute, a threshold which showed empirical evidence in tracking meaningful rebuffering ratios. We have designed SSQoE with CDN delivery and performance-based decisions in mind. We do not focus on all client behavior metrics that video providers might want to track from their players, such as video start up failures, ad engagement metrics, protocol performance level A/B testing like QUIC vs TCP clients, etc. At present, these analyses are not supported by our system.

Impacts of user Interactions with the Video Stream

It is possible that user actions such as pausing, switching from WiFi to LTE, etc. can impact buffer occupancy and lead to estimation inaccuracies. SSQoE score is by design an aggregate metric that combines the performance (rebuffer estimations, time taken to download segments, etc.) of all the sessions in a time window. It is highly unlikely that a large fraction of viewers pause the video or otherwise introduce similar user behavior at the same time. Thus on a large scale, individual session inaccuracies become negligible. The aggregate signal represents how performance looks on average for many users that are e.g. in the same ASN or that connect to the same PoP. Future work can quantify and account for this small fraction of error margin in SSQoE.

Change Management

The QoE score's ability to track user level impacts due to degraded server side performance such as CPU bottlenecks (Fig. 8) or origin server issues (Fig. 10) makes it a good candidate for change/configuration management. During a recent update to the cache management software at the CDN, a bug caused degraded I/O performance. The impact this bug caused on live video streams was captured by our methodology where the QoE score spiked up by 3 times its baseline value. Thanks to our automated detection, our site-reliability team could proactively work on rolling back the change. We are working towards integrating QoE score into the CDN's ML-based monitoring service.

Other Considerations

We do not make any protocol assumptions while estimating the QoE score. We have tested the feasibility of SSQoE for HLS and DASH with success. It is possible, however, that future protocols that support low latency streaming such as WebRTC might need to be evaluated to determine the efficacy of SSQoE.

Ethical considerations are kept in mind while designing proposed method. We do not track or expose anything more than what is already captured in the

CDN access logs. We only track the performance of the video stream by looking at the meta information. The content segments remain encrypted (HTTPS).

8   Related Work

Measuring video performance and evaluating QoE has been studied from many angles. To the best of our knowledge our work is the first to propose a pure server-side client player buffer estimation and show its feasibility at a large multi-tenant scale. However, there are several methods that are relevant to our work. Broadly we classify these into three categories based on whether they use QoE for: a) video performance monitoring and characterization of traffic, b) steering traffic at large content providers, or c) evaluating change in network configurations.

Video Performance Monitoring
Poor video performance leads to less user engagement [15,23]. In [7] authors quantify the impact of QoE metrics in user engagement during a large live OTT streaming event. Specifically, this work points out that bitrate and rebuffering have the most impact on how users engage. The authors propose using PCA and Hampel filter for live detection of QoE impairments. We take insights from this work and build more scalable method that instead of performing resource consuming PCA, estimates the client player behavior to detect rebuffering. In [18], using client-side metrics authors identify that video quality is determined by subset of critical features. Tangential to our server-side scoring mechanism, their methodology provides a QoE prediction scheme that can be deployed on beacon data at scale.

Authors in [11,14,20] address the challenge of detecting QoE in encrypted traffic. As video streaming platforms provide end-to-end encryption, it has become challenging for middle-mile network providers to perform video specific optimizations to specifically target video traffic with the goal of improving QoE. Our work differs from the focus of these papers. SSQoE is designed for the video provider infrastructure (i.e., CDN) where the TLS termination occurs. The CDN can identify unique video traffic, video segments, etc. to perform the proposed QoE estimation. In [22], similar to our work's motivation, authors emphasize that network metrics alone may miss QoE degradation event. Here, the authors propose using user behavior information such as pausing, reducing viewing area as indicators to predict QoE degradation. This differs from our server-side methodology where we do not rely on user metrics. User metrics are often tracked by the video player and in case of 3rd party CDNs they may not be available to estimate QoE.

In [21] use automated tests on the client side to interact with several online services and throttle throughput to monitor video performance. This work focuses on understanding the diversity in how different streaming services operate. Different platforms might optimize their player's ABR behavior for different guarantees of QoE, such has utilizing only limited amount of available bandwidth or compromising bitrate to keep up with live stream. The methods used in this paper revolve around a one time study to understand the landscape of video streaming. It is not designed to be an operational component of a multi-tenant CDN provider. On the other hand, given the diversity in streaming landscape this work motivates the need to perform measurements from the server-side and use a method such has ours that is completely player agnostic. YouTube's video traffic has been studied by many researchers [9,13]. These works differ from ours since they are either aimed at specifically analyzing YouTube's traffic behavior or trying to understand the ISP and CDN caching implications on QoE all using client-side data.

Traffic Management Systems
Recent performance measurement and traffic management systems developed by Google [28], Facebook [26,27], Mircrosoft [12,19] use several measurement schemes to evaluate performance and use that information to either localize faults or pick an alternate route for egress traffic that will lead to better QoE. In particular, `EdgeFabric` [27] and `Espresso` [28] focus on egress steering methodologies. Both of these systems leverage data from the client apps to gain performance insights. `Odin` [12] uses several data sources from both client and server-side along with active measurements for CDN performance evaluation. Although these systems are relevant for measuring performance, they do not explicitly track video performance. A more general approach proposed by Facebook is by tracking `HDratio` [26], which indeed focuses on video performance. The authors propose using the achievement of 2.5Mbps throughput i.e., enough to serve HD content as an indicator to measure performance. Similar to our work, this method also relies on only server-side measurements and can be applied for a multi-tenant environment. However, relying on such hard thresholds in a multi-tenant mixed-workload streaming landscape does not scale well. It is operationally hard to perform different analysis for HD, Ultra-HD, 4K, multiple bitrate qualities using multiple thresholds. Moreover, tracking throughput gives you a red flag on network performance degradation, there is no guarantee that the client player did actually suffer rebuffering. Our estimating buffer algorithm tracks the actual client player buffer therefore every time an event is detected i.e., estimated buffer at client is zero, we know with high accuracy the video has rebuffered. Using throughput based metrics also do not work well for server-side Ad insertion in the video stream. Ads in the middle of the video could be encoded in a lower or higher bitrate in which case a change in throughput is expected and may not necessarily indicate performance degradation. As shown in Sect. 6, our proposed methodology does not suffer from such unintended impacts.

Configuration Evaluation
In [16] authors measure QoE to evaluate network buffer change. Authors in this work attempt to measure the impact on QoE while tuning network buffer in a testbed. However, authors do not measure important user engagement impacting metric such as rebuffering [7]. We agree with the motivation of this work, that QoE impacts of network configurations are largely unknown. We have proposed an easily scalable server-side methodology that we hope will be used by future research on network parameter tunings and evaluate impacts on client player buffer. The proposed methodology is part of our change/configuration

management strategy at the CDN, including for a recent change we made for our network buffer sizes. While the evaluation of that change is out of scope of this work, we note that server-side QoE was able to accurately track the progress of this network change and we encourage other large content providers to include such metric in their change management process as well.

9   Conclusion

With the rise of video streaming applications on the Internet, their ingest, distribution, and performance monitoring has become increasingly complex. Current state of the art monitoring solutions rely on client-side beacons which require considerable instrumentation. Moreover, this beacon data is not easily exposed to multi-tenant third-party CDN providers. This results in cases where CDNs deliver a bulk of the video traffic without proper visibility into client-perceived QoE and performance.

In this paper, we analyzed the video processing pipeline, characterized the video streaming workload on a large scale CDN and derived key features that can be tracked from the server-side to understand client-perceived QoE. We then presented and validated SSQoE, a method for estimating client rebuffering using passive measurements, by analyzing a sequence of requests from CDN access logs to derive a QoE score that represents the health of video stream. Traditional client-side metrics can only reveal the device or last-mile problems. Mapping them to the CDN infrastructure is generally not easy, making client-side beacons less viable for large scale CDN operations. Server-side QoE estimation has been in operation globally on our CDN for the past year. To the best of our knowledge, this is the largest deployment of server-side video monitoring at a commercial CDN. It is currently used for monitoring some of the biggest live news, sports events, conferences, movie releases that millions of users engage with, and it has helped identify issues using the QoE score in near-real-time and correlate performance degradation with other CDN insights during large scale events.

We have explored the possibilities of server-side QoE analytics and invite the industry and academia to collaborate, contribute, and explore more use cases in this direction.

References

1. Adaptive bitrate (ABR). https://en.wikipedia.org/wiki/Adaptive_bitrate_strea ming
2. Conviva platform. https://www.conviva.com/about/
3. FFmpeg utility. https://ffmpeg.org
4. HLS.js player. https://github.com/video-dev/hls.js
5. Linux Traffic Control (TC) utility. https://man7.org/linux/man-pages/man8/tc. 8.html
6. NGINX RTMP. https://github.com/arut/nginx-rtmp-module

7. Ahmed, A., Shafiq, Z., Bedi, H., Khakpour, A.: Suffering from buffering? detecting qoe impairments in live video streams. In: 2017 IEEE 25th International Conference on Network Protocols (ICNP), pp. 1–10 (2017)
8. Ahmed, A., Shafiq, Z., Khakpour, A.: Qoe analysis of a large-scale live video streaming event. In: Proceedings of the 2016 ACM SIGMETRICS International Conference on Measurement and Modeling of Computer Science, SIGMETRICS 2016, pp. 395–396. Association for Computing Machinery, New York (2016)
9. Añorga, J., Arrizabalaga, S., Sedano, B., Goya, J., Alonso-Arce, M., Mendizabal, J.: Analysis of Youtube?s traffic adaptation to dynamic environments. Multimedia Tools Appl. **77**, 7977–8000 (2017). https://doi.org/10.1007/s11042-017-4695-9
10. Böttger, T., Cuadrado, F., Uhlig, S.: Looking for hypergiants in PeeringDB. SIG-COMM Comput. Commun. Rev. **48**(3), 13–19 (2018)
11. Bronzino, F., Schmitt, P., Ayoubi, S., Martins, G., Teixeira, R., Feamster, N.: Inferring streaming video quality from encrypted traffic: practical models and deployment experience. Proc. ACM Meas. Anal. Comput. Syst. **3**(3), 1–25 (2019)
12. Calder, M., et al.: Odin: microsoft's scalable fault-tolerant CDN measurement system. In: USENIX NSDI, April 2018
13. D'Alconzo, A., Casas, P., Fiadino, P., Bar, A., Finamore, A.: Who to blame when YouTube is not working? detecting anomalies in CDN-provisioned services. In: 2014 International Wireless Communications and Mobile Computing Conference (IWCMC), pp. 435–440 (2014)
14. Dimopoulos, G., Leontiadis, I., Barlet-Ros, P., Papagiannaki, K.: Measuring video QoE from encrypted traffic. In: Proceedings of the 2016 Internet Measurement Conference, IMC 2016, pp. 513–526. Association for Computing Machinery, New York (2016)
15. Dobrian, F., et al.: Understanding the impact of video quality on user engagement. Commun. ACM **56**(3), 91–99 (2013)
16. Hohlfeld, O., Pujol, E., Ciucu, F., Feldmann, A., Barford, P.: A QoE perspective on sizing network buffers. In: Proceedings of the 2014 Conference on Internet Measurement Conference, IMC 2014, pp. 333–346. Association for Computing Machinery, New York (2014)
17. Hyndman, R.J., Athanasopoulos, G.: Classical decomposition of time-series data. https://otexts.com/fpp2/classical-decomposition.html
18. Jiang, J., Sekar, V., Milner, H., Shepherd, D., Stoica, I., Zhang, H.: CFA: a practical prediction system for video QoE optimization. In: Proceedings of the 13th USENIX Conference on Networked Systems Design and Implementation, NSDI 2016, pp. 137–150. USENIX Association, USA (2016)
19. Jin, Y., et al.: Zooming in on wide-area latencies to a global cloud provider. In: ACM SIGCOMM, August 2019
20. Khokhar, M.J., Ehlinger, T., Barakat, C.: From network traffic measurements to QoE for internet video. In: 2019 IFIP Networking Conference (IFIP Networking), pp. 1–9 (2019)
21. Licciardello, M., Grüner, M., Singla, A.: Understanding video streaming algorithms in the wild. In: Sperotto, A., Dainotti, A., Stiller, B. (eds.) Passive and Active Measurement. pp, pp. 298–313. Springer International Publishing, Cham (2020). https://doi.org/10.1007/978-3-030-44081-7_18
22. Mok, R.K., Chan, E.W., Luo, X., Chang, R.K.: Inferring the QoE of http video streaming from user-viewing activities. In: Proceedings of the First ACM SIG-COMM Workshop on Measurements up the Stack, W-MUST 2011, pp. 31–36. Association for Computing Machinery, New York (2011)

23. Nam, H., Kim, K., Schulzrinne, H.: QoE matters more than QOS: why people stop watching cat videos. In: IEEE INFOCOM 2016 - The 35th Annual IEEE International Conference on Computer Communications, pp. 1–9 (2016)

24. Richter, P., et al.: A multi-perspective analysis of carrier-grade NAT deployment. In: Proceedings of the 2016 Internet Measurement Conference, IMC 2016, pp. 215–229. Association for Computing Machinery, New York (2016)

25. Rüth, J., Wolsing, K., Wehrle, K., Hohlfeld, O.: Perceiving QUIC: do users notice or even care? arXiv:1910.07729 (2019)

26. Schlinker, B., Cunha, I., Chiu, Y.-C., Sundaresan, S., Katz-Bassett, E.: Internet performance from facebook's edge. In: Proceedings of the Internet Measurement Conference, IMC 2019, pp. 179–194. Association for Computing Machinery, New York (2019)

27. Schlinker, B., et al.: Engineering egress with edge fabric: steering oceans of content to the world. In: Proceedings of the Conference of the ACM Special Interest Group on Data Communication, SIGCOMM 2017, pp. 418–431. Association for Computing Machinery, New York (2017)

28. Yap, K.: et al.: Taking the edge off with espresso: scale, reliability and programmability for global internet peering (2017)

Security II

Routing Loops as Mega Amplifiers for DNS-Based DDoS Attacks

Yevheniya Nosyk[✉], Maciej Korczyński, and Andrzej Duda

CNRS, Grenoble INP, LIG, Univ. Grenoble Alpes, 38000 Grenoble, France
{yevheniya.nosyk,maciej.korczynski,andrzej.duda}@univ-grenoble-alpes.fr

Abstract. DDoS attacks are one of the biggest threats to the modern Internet as their magnitude is constantly increasing. They are highly effective because of the amplification and reflection potential of different Internet protocols. In this paper, we show how a single DNS query triggers a response packet flood to the query source, possibly because of middleboxes located in networks with routing loops. We send DNS A requests to 3 billion routable IPv4 hosts and find 15,909 query destinations from 1,742 autonomous systems that trigger up to 46.7 million repeating responses. We perform traceroute measurements towards destination hosts that resulted in the highest amplification, locate 115 routing loops on the way, and notify corresponding network operators. Finally, we analyze two years of historical scan data and find that such "mega amplifiers" are prevalent. In the worst case, a single DNS A request triggered 655 million responses, all returned to a single host.

Keywords: DDoS · DNS resolvers · Amplification attacks · Reflection attacks · Routing loops

1 Introduction

Distributed Denial-of-Service (DDoS) attacks have become increasingly common and constantly growing in size. One of the largest known attacks against Google services already peaked at 2.54 Tbps and the attack volume is likely to get more important with time [18]. The two main factors that contribute to the effectiveness of DDoS attacks are *reflection* and *amplification*. Attackers use Internet services that satisfy two requirements: respond to their requests (*reflect*) and generate either a large number of responses or a response of a much larger size (*amplify*) towards a victim. Reflection attacks are only effective when compromised hosts (bots) send requests with spoofed IP addresses. Consequently, they need to be located in networks that do not deploy Source Address Validation (SAV), known as Best Current Practice 38 (BCP-38) [22,50], for outgoing traffic.

Several initiatives aim at reducing the possibility of DDoS attacks [1,5,6, 11,27,28,30,34,37,38,46,47,49,55,61], for instance, measurements of the amplification potential of different protocols and notifications of the affected parties. Other non-profit initiatives, such as Shadowserver Foundation [51], provide

O. Hohlfeld et al. (Eds.): PAM 2022, LNCS 13210, pp. 629–644, 2022.
https://doi.org/10.1007/978-3-030-98785-5_28

daily reports to network operators and 132 national Computer Security Incident Response Teams (CSIRTs).

Amplifying services are mostly UDP-based because of their connectionless nature. An attacker sends spoofed requests and the services reflect responses to victims. The most prominent UDP reflectors are NTP and DNS [20, 21], which have been leveraged by several attack vectors [1,6,11,34,46]. Theoretically, the TCP three-way handshake prevents the connection establishment with spoofed hosts because the response of the reflecting service goes to the victim and not to the host launching the attack. Nevertheless, certain TCP implementations are prone to amplification [27,28] and potentially with infinite amplification factors [5].

In the concurrent work, Bock *et al.* [5] located middleboxes inside routing loops by sending a sequence of carefully crafted TCP packets. They even found 19 IP addresses that triggered infinite loops. In our work, we show that a trivial DNS A request is enough to trigger a similar behavior. Moreover, we identify 64 IP addresses triggering possibly infinite amplification. Our methodology consists of probing the whole routable IPv4 address space with DNS A requests to find 15,909 destination addresses from 1,742 autonomous systems (ASes) triggering up to 46.7 million identical response packets. We then run traceroute measurements towards 435 destination hosts that resulted in the highest amplification and identify 115 routing loops involving 35 autonomous systems. We have reported these findings to network operators. Finally, we analyze 2 years of packet traces from our DNS scans in both IPv4 and IPv6 address spaces to find 944,087 requests that triggered repeating responses—397 of them caused more than 1,000 responses and 18 requests caused more than 1 million responses. As an extreme case, one DNS A request triggered 655 *million* responses.

The rest of the paper is organized as follows. Section 2 provides background on DDoS attacks, amplification, and reflection. Section 3 describes the threat model and Sect. 4 introduces the measurement setup. We present scan results and analyze the persistence of the vulnerability in Sect. 5. Section 6 discusses ethical considerations and disclosure. Finally, we present related work in Sect. 7 and conclude in Sect. 8.

2   Background on DDoS Attacks

One of the largest DDoS attacks known to date took place in September 2017 and was reported by Google in October 2020 [18]. Attackers sent spoofed requests to SNMP, CLDAP, and DNS servers that, in turn, sent amplified responses to Google. The reflected traffic peaked at 2.54 Tbps. In February 2020, Amazon Web Services (AWS) reported an attack using hijacked CLDAP servers that generated traffic up to 2.3 Tbps [3]. If measured in requests per second (rps), two prominent attacks happened in 2021: Yandex [45] and Cloudflare [62] reported receiving 21.8 million and 17.2 million rps, respectively. As the Internet grows in terms of computing power, bandwidth, and the number of connected devices, the volume of DDoS attacks becomes increasingly high [18].

A DDoS attack aims to overwhelm the victim service with a tremendous amount of traffic to prevent legitimate clients from using the service. Although an attacker alone may achieve this effect, large-scale attacks usually rely on botnets, networks of compromised machines that receive instructions from the command-and-control (C&C) center (operated by the attacker).

The real danger of DDoS attacks comes from *reflectors* and *amplifiers*. A *reflector* is a machine that accepts a request (with a spoofed source IP address) and sends a response [44]. There are millions of services on the Internet such as web servers or open DNS resolvers that can act as reflectors. Once reflecting services are located, the attacker instructs the botnet under her/his control to start sending requests. Requests with the spoofed source IP addresses of victims are sent to reflectors. As a result, the victim receives all the reflected traffic. Carefully crafted requests can trigger reflectors to send large or numerous responses; such reflectors are called *amplifiers*.

There are several ways to assess the effectiveness of a DDoS attack. We can measure the absolute amount of generated traffic in packets per second (pps), bits per second (bps) or requests per second (rps) [18]. In the case of amplification, another informative metric is the ratio of traffic generated by the amplifier to the traffic needed to trigger the amplifier. Rossow [47] proposed two units of measurement: bandwidth amplification factor (BAF) and packet amplification factor (PAF). BAF divides the size of the packet payload sent from the amplifier to the victim by the size of the packet payload sent from the attacker to the amplifier. Likewise, PAF divides the number of packets sent to the victim by the number of packets sent to the amplifier. In both cases, the higher the value, the more destructive the attack is.

In the remainder of this paper, we use Rossow's [47] packet amplification factor (PAF) metric to assess the amplification potential of DNS queries caught in routing loops. As we only send one DNS request, the PAF is always equal to the number of received responses.

3   Threat Model

Our threat model is an amplified and reflective DDoS attack in which the attacker sends DNS queries. Therefore, we first recall how regular DNS resolution operates. It starts with a client sending its DNS request to a recursive resolver. This entity is capable of following the domain name tree from the root down to the authoritative nameservers of a given domain. Recursive resolvers heavily rely on caching and query prefetching to speed up the resolution process. Whether it succeeds or not, a recursive resolver returns a response packet to the client with one of the defined response codes [35]. Thus, a client expects to receive a single response packet for a single request.

When one is constantly receiving multiple copies of the same packet, there might be some routing anomaly on the way between the sender and the receiver, such as loops. Routing loops are a well-known, old phenomenon, extensively studied in the literature [19,32,43,54,60,63–65]. They fall into two broad categories: transient and persistent. Transient loops appear when topology changes

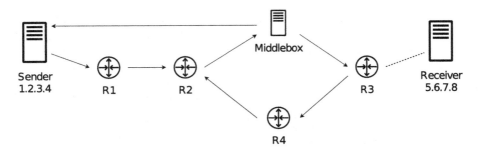

Fig. 1. The sender (1.2.3.4) initiates a request to the receiver (5.6.7.8). The packet travels through R1 and R2 until being caught in the loop involving R2, R3, R4. Although the request never reaches the receiver, the sender receives replies from the middlebox.

and the routing protocol has not yet converged. Such loops do not require manual intervention to be resolved. Persistent loops are likely to be a result of a misconfiguration, such as announcing addresses that are routable but not allocated [32,60]. A packet entering the routing loop is very likely not to reach the destination. Xia *et al.* [60] analyzed the location of routing loops and found that the majority of them involve destination autonomous systems. We report similar findings later in Sect. 5.2. Consequently, the same loops can be triggered from multiple vantage points.

Recently, Bock *et al.* [5] discovered that networking middleboxes (such as firewalls or national censors), when located inside the routing loop, continuously process a request caught in a loop and keep responding to it. Figure 1 illustrates such a setup. The sender (1.2.3.4) sends a request to the receiver (5.6.7.8) via R1 and R2. Somewhere on its way (in transit or at the destination autonomous system), the request packet enters the routing loop between R2, R3, and R4. Each time the packet goes from R2 to R3, it triggers the middlebox to respond to the sender (more precisely, to the host with the source IP address of the packet, which can be spoofed). The receiver (5.6.7.8) never sees the request. Such a looping packet should be dropped when its time-to-live (TTL) reaches 0. However, if the TTL is not decreased for any reason, the packet may loop infinitely (or until a reboot or router failure drops it).

An attacker knowing about the presence of routing loops and middleboxes can achieve two principal goals: saturate links involved in the routing loop and reflect the generated responses. If the loop is located in the destination autonomous system (AS) and the spoofed source IP address belongs to the same AS, such a packet may be dropped at the network edge even before reaching the loop. It happens when SAV for incoming traffic drops the packet from the outside with the source IP belonging to the inner network. However, recent work showed that inbound SAV is not widely deployed [12,23–25].

We have very few assumptions about the capabilities of the attacker. Most importantly, (s)he has to be located in the network that allows outbound spoofing. Thus, DNS packets with spoofed IP addresses can leave the network. Recent

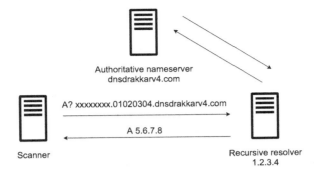

Fig. 2. Measurement setup for the DNS scan. The scanner sends a DNS A request to the recursive resolver (1.2.3.4). The resolver contacts the authoritative nameserver, obtains the response, and returns it to the scanner.

work showed that such misconfigured networks are still not uncommon on the Internet [31,33] and they are publicly listed [8]. The attacker does not have any special hardware or software requirements, because a single DNS packet, occasionally resent, is enough to keep the loop going. Finally, it is not necessary to register a domain name as any existing one can be queried.

4   Internet-Wide Scans

Our measurement technique relies on sending DNS requests to trigger routing loops. In IPv4, we probe all the routable prefixes retrieved from the RouteViews dataset [48], resulting in more than 3 billion individual IP addresses. In IPv6, however, the exhaustive scan of the routable space is not feasible. Instead, we scan more than 445 million hosts from the IPv6 Hitlist Service [17].

Figure 2 shows the measurement setup for the IPv4 scan. We run our experiments on top of the existing measurement infrastructure and use our custom scanner[1] capable of sending DNS packets in bulk [53]. Nevertheless, any other DNS scanner such as zdns,[2] would achieve the same goal. We set up an authoritative nameserver for **dnsdrakkarv4.com** domain name and all its subdomains. We encode the two following pieces of information in each queried domain: a random string (**xxxxxxx** in Fig. 2) and the hexadecimally-encoded IPv4 address of the query target (**01020304** for 1.2.3.4). In IPv6, we encode the target IPv6 address as a network byte order 32-bit integer. The encoded address is used to attribute each domain name to the scanned destination address. As a result, all domain names uniquely identify each sent request. Importantly, we capture all the incoming requests on the authoritative nameserver and all the responses on the scanner.

---

[1] https://github.com/mskwarek/myDig.
[2] https://github.com/zmap/zdns.

Table 1. Repeating responses received on the scanner (October 2021).

Group	Response Count	Destination IP addresses	Destination ASNs	Average PAF	Maximum PAF
2–9 responses	15,511	15,488	1,733	2.1	9
10–254 responses	380	372	21	49.8	246
255 + responses	64	64	5	927,796	46,734,052

We have run our scans from one vantage point. Although we plan to acquire more vantage points at different locations, we later show in Sect. 5 that the great majority of all the routing loops involve destination autonomous systems, so they can be triggered regardless of the measurement vantage point.

5   Scan Results

In this section, we first present the results of the latest Internet-wide IPv4 DNS scan (Sect. 5.1). We next run traceroute measurements towards the biggest amplifiers and identify routing loops (Sect. 5.2). Finally, we present the results of our two-year DNS measurement study in IPv4 and IPv6 (Sect. 5.3).

5.1   Internet Scan

We launched the latest Internet-wide IPv4 DNS scan in October 2021. In total, we sent more than 3 billion DNS A requests (one to each routable IP address) and received 7.6 million responses on the scanner. From each DNS response packet, we retrieve the following fields: the queried domain name (remember that each domain name is globally unique as it encodes the destination IP address to which we send the request), the source IP address of the response (can be the same as the destination IP address or different, in case the destination is a transparent forwarder [40]) and the DNS response code. We refer to each *response* as a three-tuple (*source_IP_address, domain_name, response_code*). Whenever we see a response tuple more than once, we refer to it as a *repeating response*.

Table 1 presents the results. We assign each repeating response to one of the three groups (first column) based on the number of times the response was received. We received 15,955 unique repeating responses in total. The first group (2–9 repeating responses) is the largest one, although the average amplification factor remains low (2.1 packets). Previous work analyzed the queries on root nameservers and found many repeating (with different query IDs) and identical (with same query IDs) requests [9,59]. These were most probably results of configuration errors. Consequently, such repeating requests could produce repeating responses to our scanning host. As suggested by Bock *et al.* [5], responses sent more than 10 times are likely to be triggered by routing loops. If the TTL of the initial request is gradually decreased to 0, such a loop is finite. These responses

Table 2. Top 10 destination organizations (anonymized) in terms of triggered repeating responses.

Rank	Organization type	Country	Response count
1	Telecommunications service provider	PH	59,288,099
2	IT Services	GB	50,265
3	Internet service provider	IN	45,579
4	DNS services	CN	8,042
5	IT services	US	5,390
6	Telecommunications service provider	CN	3,474
7	Internet service provider	CN	1,637
8	Telecommunications service provider	BR	956
9	Telecommunications service provider	IN	695
10	Telecommunications service provider	RU	624

belong to the second group (10–254 repeating responses). Note that in this case, the maximum count of received responses (254 responses) is an overestimation, as we would need to subtract from the maximum TTL (255 hops) the number of hops to reach the amplifier [5]. Finally, the third group (255+ repeating responses) contains the smallest number of response tuples, but the average PAF is very high (927,796 packets). The biggest amplifier seen during this scan triggered 46.7 million responses during 7 h.

We use the CAIDA's AS Rank dataset [7] to map autonomous system numbers (ASNs) to organization names and countries. All the destination autonomous systems originate from 133 countries, mostly from Brazil, India, and the USA. Table 2 presents the top 10 organizations (anonymized) in terms of the number of triggered repeating responses. The number one of the ranking (a Philippine telecommunications service provider) triggered many more responses to our scanning host than any other autonomous system.

We would expect that one DNS A request triggers repeating responses from the same source IP address and of the same DNS response type. In other words, one request triggers one repeating response tuple. Nevertheless, in groups 1 and 2, there are more repeating response tuples (second column of Table 1) than scanned destination IP addresses (third column of Table 1). The reason is that certain DNS requests triggered replies from different IP addresses. In particular, we found 15 destination IPs triggering repeating responses from 2 or more source addresses. Park *et al.* [42] have shown how a single request to the DNS forwarder was processed by 89 different recursive resolvers (as seen on the authoritative nameserver). If such a forwarder is transparent (i.e., it forwards the request without changing the source IP address field), the replies from different recursive resolvers will be returned to the original requester. Consequently, we could cumulate PAFs from all responses triggered by a single request.

The received DNS responses are of five following types (as defined in RFC-1035 [35]): NOERROR (13,797 responses), SERVFAIL (1,684 responses), REFUSED (430 responses), NXDOMAIN (41 responses) and NOTIMP (3 responses). We take a closer look at 345 NOERROR responses from groups 2 and 3. Although this response code signals that the request was completed successfully, the answer section of the DNS packet may have been manipulated. Surprisingly, 76% of these responses did not contain the A record in the answer at all. As for the remaining non-empty responses, we did not detect any manipulation.

If the majority of NOERROR responses are empty, we raise the question of whether the authoritative nameserver for our test domain dnsdrakkarv4.com experienced any significant load from repeating requests. Specifically, we have analyzed 444 repeating responses from groups 2 and 3. As expected, the great majority of domain names (350 domains) were never queried on the authoritative nameserver, which suggests that attackers can safely reuse existing domain names in their queries without domain name operators noticing any abnormal activity.

In the attempt to characterize the devices responsible for response packet amplification, we made an assumption that we might have been dealing with national censors' middleboxes, as suggested by Bock et al. [5]. Censored Planet initiative [10] is constantly measuring the presence of censorship worldwide. More specifically, their Hyperquack [56] project infers application-layer blocking. We checked whether the Hyperquack data contains measurements towards destinations that triggered response floods but we did not find any overlap between the two datasets. We next referred to Tracebox [13] – a middlebox detection software that relies on ICMP time-exceeded replies to check whether the originally sent packet was modified and in which way. We run tracebox towards all the destination IP addresses from groups two and three. We notice modifications (such as unexpected source/destination addresses or ports, checksum, etc.) on the way to each measured host. However, when compared to a random sample of routable IP addresses (that did not trigger any amplification), there are no specific packet modifications that would distinguish the amplifier group from non-amplifiers. Therefore, identifying and characterizing those devices that trigger response floods remains an open question.

5.2 Running Traceroute

The responses from the second and third groups (see Table 1 rows 2 and 3) are likely to be caused by routing loops. One could use the traceroute [29] utility to track the path a packet takes from the source to the destination and check for the presence of loops. Augustin et al. [2] indicated, however, that traceroute does not capture the complete view of the network, often showing anomalies (such as loops) when there is router load balancing in place. To address this limitation, we use Multilevel MDA-Lite Paris Traceroute [57]. This tool relies on the new MDA-Lite algorithm to avoid inferring false links and to give a more accurate view of the path between the measurement server and the destination.

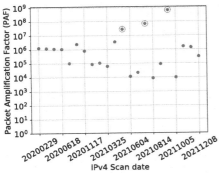

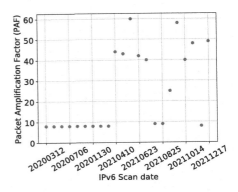

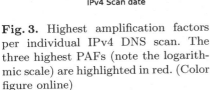

Fig. 3. Highest amplification factors per individual IPv4 DNS scan. The three highest PAFs (note the logarithmic scale) are highlighted in red. (Color figure online)

Fig. 4. Highest amplification factors per individual IPv6 DNS scan.

We trace the path to all 435 *unique* destination IP addresses in groups two and three (see Table 1) immediately after the end of the scan. Notice that certain destination IP addresses form more than one response tuple and, consequently, may appear in multiple groups, which is actually the case for one destination host that belongs to both groups two and three. The great majority of traceroutes (67%) did not reach measured destinations, even though they triggered repeating DNS responses. We found 115 unique loops towards 392 tested hosts. Importantly, Nawrocki *et al.* [39] have shown that roughly 90% of all the DNS DDoS events captured at the IXP used up to 100 amplifiers. Therefore, the discovered 115 loops are sufficient to mount real-world attacks. As for the remaining 43 destination IP addresses, we consider that packets may have encountered transient loops during the scan, which disappeared at the time of the traceroute measurements.

Traceroute loop lengths vary greatly and involve up to 38 interface IP addresses, but most often 2 (39 loops). Interestingly, 6 loops involved reserved IP addresses from private [36] and shared address ranges [58].

Overall, IP addresses involved in 115 routing loops originated from 35 autonomous systems. As for the location, 102 loops involved destination autonomous systems. Consequently, the great majority of all the routing loops could potentially be triggered from different vantage points.

5.3   Longitudinal Analysis

To test whether the threat of response floods is constantly present, we analyzed the results of regular DNS scans that we have been performing since February 2020 (22 IPv4 and 22 IPv6 scans). For each scan, we first identify the response returned the maximum number of times. We plot the highest packet amplification factors for IPv4 in Fig. 3 (note that the y-axis is on a logarithmic scale).

Table 3. Repeating responses received by the scanner between February 2020 and December 2021 (IPv4 and IPv6 combined).

Group	Response count	Destination IP addresses	Destination ASNs	Average PAF	Maximum PAF
2–9 responses	938,606	690,988	21,855	2.3	9
10–254 responses	4,750	2,132	295	40.8	254
255 + responses	731	542	42	1,852,087	655,195,124

There are apparent outliers (highlighted in red): three scans generated 28, 69, and 655 million responses maximum, all triggered by sending one request to hosts in three different autonomous systems. Overall, these biggest response floods lasted between 7 s and 39 h. However, occasionally resent A requests could keep restarting these loops.

We take a closer look at the maximum PAF ever observed. One query to a host from an autonomous system in the Philippines generated 655 million SERVFAIL responses sent during 2 days. It is the same autonomous system that triggered most of the repeated responses during our latest scan. We performed a traceroute measurement towards this destination and found a routing loop involving 9 hosts from two autonomous systems (including the destination AS), 21 hops from the scanner. Note that this particular traceroute was limited to 64 hops. Overall, the maximum PAF per IPv4 scan varies between 8,795 and 655 million, the average maximum is 35 million.

On the other hand, for IPv6, the revealed amplification factors are less impressive. Figure 4 presents PAF for IPv6 (note that the y-axis is now in linear scale). The maximum PAF is 60, thus there are no infinite routing loops (unless the looping packet was dropped early). The average maximum amplification factor is 22. The IPv6 results should be interpreted with caution due to the composition of the IPv6 hitlist [17]. It contains responsive IPv6 addresses, whereas one of the root causes of routing loops is sending packets to announced but not allocated IP space. We performed an additional scan of randomly sampled 50 million IPv6 addresses from each routable/40 IPv6 network but did not trigger any routing loop.

Table 3 presents the same results as Table 1 in Sect. 5.1, but this time aggregated over two years. Similar to our latest scan, the great majority of repeating requests were sent between 2 and 9 times. The average amplification factors remain similar between groups 1 and 2, but the largest revealed amplifier significantly increased the average PAF of group 3. Altogether, the scanner received nearly 1 million repeated responses corresponding to 1.4 billion packets during two years. The destination IP addresses are distributed among 21,804 unique autonomous systems. More than half of autonomous systems in groups two and three appeared during two or more scans. Consequently, the routing loops on the way to these networks were very likely persistent and required a manual fix.

6   Ethical Considerations and Disclosure

Research scans are widespread these days, allowing for quick and efficient discovery of all sorts of vulnerabilities and misconfigurations. Nevertheless, measurement studies require careful planning so that risks are minimized and benefits outweigh potential inconveniences [14]. As there is no mechanism to explicitly request permission to scan each IP address in advance, researchers developed a set of guidelines [15] to inform network operators about the scanning nature and opt-out easily. We follow those guidelines and configure our domain name (and all the subdomains) to point to a web page explaining who we are and what we do. The provided contact email address can be used to opt-out from future scans. In addition, we do not consecutively scan all the hosts of a single network but randomize our input. We received one complaint during the scan and removed 1 autonomous system from the experiment, containing 32k IPv4 addresses.

Discovered routing loops raise a significant threat to networks containing them and those receiving the response flood. We have used the Registration Data Access Protocol (RDAP) [16,41] protocol to find contact information for the IP addresses involved in routing loops and notify the corresponding network administrators. In our emails, we explain how we discovered the vulnerability and the potential consequences.

7   Related Work

The number of open DNS resolvers dropped substantially in recent years – from 17.8 million in 2015 [26] to around 2 million in 2021 [4,25,40,52]. Yet, DNS has been heavily involved in reflection and amplification attacks [20,21]. In their recent work, Nawrocki *et al.* [39] extensively analyzed the whole DNS amplification ecosystem, using data from honeypots, an Internet Exchange Point (IXP), active measurements, and Internet-wide scans. They have shown that DNS-based amplification attacks are even more present than previously thought. Alarmingly, the attackers do not yet fully exploit all the available amplification potential.

One approach to the detection of DNS amplifiers is to craft a single request that will produce a large response. MacFarland *et al.* [34] issued A and ANY requests for 363 million (domain name, authoritative nameserver IP address) pairs to identify amplified responses. They reached a 32.77 amplification factor for ANY type query with EDNS0 enabled. It was later shown that ANY responses for DNSSEC-signed domains can reach the amplification factor of 179 [46].

Another approach is to create one DNS request that will trigger a series of additional lookups. The DNS Unchained attack requests recursive resolvers to follow a long chain of CNAME resource records [6]. Even more destructive is a recently discovered NXNSAttack, which relies on bogus referrals that can overwhelm both recursive resolvers and authoritative nameservers [1].

More generally, the stateless nature of UDP allows many protocols, apart from DNS, to be used for reflection and amplification. Rossow [47] analyzed 14 popular UDP-based protocols with amplification factors between 3.8 (BitTorrent, NetBios) and 4,670 (NTP). The latter, NTP, is infamous for its high DDoS potential and is often seen in real-world attacks [20]. Czyz *et al.* [11] estimated that roughly 2.2 million NTP servers could be misused. Earlier, Kührer *et al.* [27] cooperated with CERTs, NOCs, clearinghouses, and other security organizations worldwide to improve the NTP amplifier landscape.

It was long believed that the three-way handshake prevents TCP from being abused in reflection attacks with spoofed requests. In practice, one can trigger remote servers to retransmit (up to 20 times) unacknowledged SYN/ACK segments before the handshake is completed [27]. Additionally, other types of TCP misconfigurations (such as repeating RST packets or the actual data being transmitted before the handshake is completed) result in an average amplification factor of 112 [28]. Finally, recent work has gone beyond the initial handshake and found how network middleboxes can be used to reflect and amplify TCP traffic towards victims [5].

The method presented in this paper does not require any complex setup or specifically crafted requests to amplify the response. We rely on a trivial UDP packet to trigger routing loops.

8   Conclusions and Future Work

In this paper, we have shown how a single DNS A request can generate a response packet flood. We have scanned all the routable IPv4 address space and found 15,909 end-hosts in 1,742 autonomous systems that triggered the repeating responses with the maximum packet amplification factor of 46.7 million. We have collected traceroute measurements towards the destinations that triggered most responses and found 115 routing loops. We have disclosed our findings to network operators. Overall, having analyzed two years of our DNS scans, we have found 18 query destinations that triggered more than one million responses. The historical data reveals that this phenomenon is not a one-time event. At any instant, an attacker can locate amplifiers with little effort, trigger them, and redirect the generated traffic to a victim.

We foresee three directions for future work. First, we plan to identify and further characterize those devices triggering response packet floods. Second, we intend to perform scans from geographically distributed vantage points. Although we have shown that the majority of loops involve destination autonomous systems, there may be more loops in transit. Finally, we will explore which other query types and protocols can be used to trigger routing loops as easily as DNS.

Acknowledgements. The authors would like to thank Baptiste Jonglez, the reviewers and our shepherd for their valuable and constructive feedback. This work was partially supported by RIPE NCC, Carnot LSI, the Grenoble Alpes Cybersecurity Institute under contract ANR-15-IDEX-02, and by the DiNS project under contract ANR-19-CE25-0009-01.

References

1. Afek, Y., Bremler-Barr, A., Shafir, L.: NXNSAttack: recursive DNS inefficiencies and vulnerabilities. In: 29th USENIX Security Symposium (USENIX Security 20), pp. 631–648. USENIX Association, August 2020
2. Augustin, B., et al.: Avoiding traceroute anomalies with Paris traceroute. In: Proceedings of the 6th ACM SIGCOMM Conference on Internet Measurement, pp. 153–158. IMC 2006. Association for Computing Machinery, New York (2006)
3. AWS Shield: Threat Landscape Report - Q1 (2020). https://aws-shield-tlr.s3.amazonaws.com/2020-Q1_AWS_Shield_TLR.pdf
4. Bayer, J., et al.: Study on Domain Name System (DNS) abuse final report. Tech. rep. (2022)
5. Bock, K., Alaraj, A., Fax, Y., Hurley, K., Wustrow, E., Levin, D.: Weaponizing middleboxes for TCP reflected amplification. In: 30th USENIX Security Symposium (USENIX Security 21), pp. 3345–3361. USENIX Association, August 2021
6. Bushart, J., Rossow, C.: DNS unchained: amplified application-layer DoS attacks against DNS Authoritatives. In: Bailey, M., Holz, T., Stamatogiannakis, M., Ioannidis, S. (eds.) Research in Attacks, Intrusions, and Defenses, pp. 139–160. Springer International Publishing, Cham (2018)
7. CAIDA AS rank (2022). http://as-rank.caida.org/
8. CAIDA: The Spoofer project (2022). https://www.caida.org/projects/spoofer/
9. Castro, S., Wessels, D., Fomenkov, M., Claffy, K.: A day at the root of the Internet. SIGCOMM Comput. Commun. Rev. **38**(5), 41–46 (2008)
10. Censored planet: an Internet-wide, longitudinal censorship observatory (2022). https://censoredplanet.org
11. Czyz, J., Kallitsis, M., Gharaibeh, M., Papadopoulos, C., Bailey, M., Karir, M.: Taming the 800 pound Gorilla: the rise and decline of NTP DDoS attacks. In: Proceedings of the 2014 Conference on Internet Measurement Conference, pp. 435–448. IMC 2014. Association for Computing Machinery, New York (2014)
12. Deccio, C., Hilton, A., Briggs, M., Avery, T., Richardson, R.: Behind closed doors: a network tale of spoofing, intrusion, and false DNS security. In: Proceedings of the ACM Internet Measurement Conference, pp. 65–77. IMC 2020, Association for Computing Machinery, New York (2020)
13. Detal, G., Hesmans, B., Bonaventure, O., Vanaubel, Y., Donnet, B.: Revealing middlebox interference with tracebox. In: Proceedings of the 2013 Conference on Internet Measurement Conference, pp. 1–8. IMC 2013. Association for Computing Machinery, New York (2013)
14. Dittrich, D., Kenneally, E.: The Menlo report: ethical principles guiding information and communication technology research. Tech. rep., U.S. Department of Homeland Security, August 2012
15. Durumeric, Z., Wustrow, E., Halderman, J.A.: ZMap: fast Internet-wide scanning and its security applications. In: USENIX Security Symposium (2013)
16. Gañán, C.: WHOIS sunset? A primer in Registration Data Access Protocol (RDAP) performance. In: Network Traffic Measurement and Analysis Conference, TMA. IFIP (2021)
17. Gasser, O., et al.: Clusters in the expanse: understanding and unbiasing IPv6 hitlists. In: Proceedings of the 2018 Internet Measurement Conference. ACM, New York (2018)
18. Google Cloud: exponential growth in DDoS attack volumes (2020). https://cloud.google.com/blog/products/identity-security/identifying-and-protecting-against-the-largest-ddos-attacks

19. Hengartner, U., Moon, S., Mortier, R., Diot, C.: Detection and analysis of routing loops in packet traces. In: Proceedings of the 2nd ACM SIGCOMM Workshop on Internet Measurment, pp. 107–112. IMW 2002. Association for Computing Machinery, New York (2002)

20. Jonker, M., King, A., Krupp, J., Rossow, C., Sperotto, A., Dainotti, A.: Millions of targets under attack: a macroscopic characterization of the DoS ecosystem. In: Proceedings of the Internet Measurement Conference, pp. 100–113. IMC 2017. Association for Computing Machinery, New York (2017)

21. Kopp, D., Dietzel, C., Hohlfeld, O.: DDoS never dies? An IXP perspective on DDoS amplification attacks. In: Hohlfeld, O., Lutu, A., Levin, D. (eds.) PAM 2021. LNCS, vol. 12671, pp. 284–301. Springer, Cham (2021). https://doi.org/10.1007/978-3-030-72582-2_17

22. Korczyński, M., Nosyk, Y.: Source address validation. In: Encyclopedia of Cryptography, Security and Privacy, pp. 1–5. Springer, Berlin, Heidelberg (2019). https://doi.org/10.1007/978-3-642-27739-9_1626-1

23. Korczyński, M., Nosyk, Y., Lone, Q., Skwarek, M., Jonglez, B., Duda, A.: Inferring the deployment of inbound source address validation using DNS resolvers. In: Proceedings of the Applied Networking Research Workshop, pp. 9–11. ANRW 2020. Association for Computing Machinery, New York (2020)

24. Korczyński, M., Nosyk, Y., Lone, Q., Skwarek, M., Jonglez, B., Duda, A.: The Closed Resolver Project: measuring the deployment of source address validation of inbound traffic (2020)

25. Korczyński, M., Nosyk, Y., Lone, Q., Skwarek, M., Jonglez, B., Duda, A.: Don't forget to lock the front door! inferring the deployment of source address validation of inbound traffic. In: Sperotto, A., Dainotti, A., Stiller, B. (eds.) PAM 2020. LNCS, vol. 12048, pp. 107–121. Springer, Cham (2020). https://doi.org/10.1007/978-3-030-44081-7_7

26. Kührer, M., Hupperich, T., Bushart, J., Rossow, C., Holz, T.: Going wild: large-scale classification of open DNS resolvers. In: Internet Measurement Conference. ACM (2015)

27. Kührer, M., Hupperich, T., Rossow, C., Holz, T.: Exit from Hell? Reducing the impact of amplification DDoS attacks. In: 23rd USENIX Security Symposium (USENIX Security 14), pp. 111–125. USENIX Association, San Diego, August 2014

28. Kührer, M., Hupperich, T., Rossow, C., Holz, T.: Hell of a handshake: abusing TCP for reflective amplification DDoS attacks. In: 8th USENIX Workshop on Offensive Technologies (WOOT 14). USENIX Association, San Diego, August 2014. https://www.usenix.org/conference/woot14/workshop-program/presentation/kuhrer

29. linux.die.net: traceroute(8) - Linux man page (2022). https://linux.die.net/man/8/traceroute

30. Lone, Q., Frik, A., Luckie, M., Korczyński, M., van Eeten, M., Ganan, C.: Deployment of source address validation by network operators: a randomized control trial. In: Proceedings of the IEEE Security and Privacy (S&P) (2022)

31. Lone, Q., Korczyński, M., Gañán, C., van Eeten, M.: SAVing the Internet: explaining the adoption of source address validation by internet service providers. In: Workshop on the Economics of Information Security (2020)

32. Lone, Q., Luckie, M., Korczyński, M., van Eeten, M.: Using loops observed in traceroute to infer the ability to spoof. In: Kaafar, M.A., Uhlig, S., Amann, J. (eds.) PAM 2017. LNCS, vol. 10176, pp. 229–241. Springer, Cham (2017). https://doi.org/10.1007/978-3-319-54328-4_17

33. Luckie, M., Beverly, R., Koga, R., Keys, K., Kroll, J., claffy, k.: Network hygiene, incentives, and regulation: deployment of source address validation in the Internet. In: Computer and Communications Security Conference (CCS). ACM (2019)
34. MacFarland, D.C., Shue, C.A., Kalafut, A.J.: Characterizing optimal DNS amplification attacks and effective mitigation. In: Mirkovic, J., Liu, Y. (eds.) PAM 2015. LNCS, vol. 8995, pp. 15–27. Springer, Cham (2015). https://doi.org/10.1007/978-3-319-15509-8_2
35. Mockapetris, P.: Domain names - implementation and specification. RFC 1035, November 1987. https://rfc-editor.org/rfc/rfc1035.txt
36. Moskowitz, R., Karrenberg, D., Rekhter, Y., Lear, E., de Groot, G.J.: Address allocation for private internets. RFC 1918, February 1996
37. Moura, G.C.M., Castro, S., Heidemann, J.S., Hardaker, W.: TsuNAME: exploiting misconfiguration and vulnerability to DDOS DNS. In: IMC 2021. ACM Internet Measurement Conference, pp. 398–418. ACM (2021)
38. Moura, G.C.M., et al.: Anycast vs. DDoS: evaluating the November 2015 root DNS event. In: Proceedings of the 2016 ACM on Internet Measurement Conference, pp. 255–270. ACM (2016)
39. Nawrocki, M., Jonker, M., Schmidt, T.C., Wählisch, M.: The far side of DNS amplification: tracing the DDoS attack ecosystem from the Internet core. In: Proceedings of the 2021 Internet Measurement Conference. IMC 2021. Association for Computing Machinery, New York (2021)
40. Nawrocki, M., Koch, M., Schmidt, T.C., Wählisch, M.: Transparent forwarders: an unnoticed component of the open DNS infrastructure. In: Proceedings of CoNEXT 2021. Association for Computing Machinery, New York (2021)
41. Newton, A., Hollenbeck, S.: Registration Data Access Protocol (RDAP) Query Format. RFC 7482, March 2015
42. Park, J., Jang, R., Mohaisen, M., Mohaisen, D.: A large-scale behavioral analysis of the open DNS resolvers on the Internet. IEEE/ACM Trans. Networking, 1–14 (2021)
43. Paxson, V.: End-to-end routing behavior in the Internet. In: Conference Proceedings on Applications, Technologies, Architectures, and Protocols for Computer Communications, pp. 25–38. SIGCOMM 1996, Association for Computing Machinery, New York (1996)
44. Paxson, V.: An analysis of using reflectors for distributed denial-of-service attacks. ACM SIGCOMM Comput. Commun. Rev. **31**(3), 38–47 (2001)
45. Reuters: Russia's Yandex says it repelled biggest DDoS attack in history (2021). https://www.reuters.com/technology/russias-yandex-says-it-repelled-biggest-ddos-attack-history-2021-09-09/
46. van Rijswijk-Deij, R., Sperotto, A., Pras, A.: DNSSEC and its potential for DDoS attacks: a comprehensive measurement study. In: Proceedings of the Fourteenth ACM Internet Measurement Conference, ACM IMC 2014, pp. 449–460. IMC 2014. Association for Computing Machinery, New York (2014)
47. Rossow, C.: Amplification hell: revisiting network protocols for DDoS Abuse. In: Proceedings of the 2014 Network and Distributed System Security Symposium, NDSS (2014)
48. University of Oregon route views project (2022). http://www.routeviews.org/routeviews/
49. Sasaki, T., Ganan, C., Yoshioka, K., Eeten, M., Matsumoto, T.: Pay the piper: DDoS mitigation technique to deter financially-motivated attackers. IEICE Trans. Commun. **103**, 389–404 (2019)

50. Senie, D., Ferguson, P.: Network ingress filtering: defeating denial of service attacks which employ IP source address spoofing. RFC 2827, May 2000. https://rfc-editor.org/rfc/rfc2827.txt

51. The Shadowserver Foundation (2022). https://www.shadowserver.org

52. Shadowserver foundation: open resolver scanning project. https://scan.shadowserver.org/dns. Accessed Dec 2021

53. Skwarek, M., Korczyński, M., Mazurczyk, W., Duda, A.: Characterizing vulnerability of DNS AXFR transfers with global-scale scanning. In: IEEE Security and Privacy Workshops (SPW) (2019)

54. Sridharan, A., Moon, S.B., Diot, C.: On the correlation between route dynamics and routing loops. In: Proceedings of the 3rd ACM SIGCOMM Conference on Internet Measurement, IMC 2003, pp. 285–294. Association for Computing Machinery, New York (2003)

55. van der Toorn, O., Krupp, J., Jonker, M., van Rijswijk-Deij, R., Rossow, C., Sperotto, A.: ANYway: measuring the amplification DDoS potential of domains. In: Proceedings of the International Conference on Network and Service Management (CNSM), pp. 500–508 (2021)

56. VanderSloot, B., McDonald, A., Scott, W., Halderman, J.A., Ensafi, R.: Quack: scalable remote measurement of application-layer censorship. In: USENIX Security Symposium (2018)

57. Vermeulen, K., Strowes, S.D., Fourmaux, O., Friedman, T.: Multilevel MDA-lite Paris traceroute. In: Proceedings of the Internet Measurement Conference 2018, IMC 2018, pp. 29–42. Association for Computing Machinery, New York (2018)

58. Weil, J., Kuarsingh, V., Donley, C., Liljenstolpe, C., Azinger, M.: IANA-reserved IPv4 prefix for shared address space. RFC 6598, April 2012

59. Wessels, D., Fomenkov, M.: Wow, that's a lot of packets. In: Passive and active network measurement workshop (PAM) (2003)

60. Xia, J., Gao, L., Fei, T.: Flooding attacks by exploiting persistent forwarding loops. In: Internet Measurement Conference 2005 (IMC 05). USENIX Association, Berkeley, October 2005

61. Yazdani, R., van Rijswijk-Deij, R., Jonker, M., Sperotto, A.: A matter of degree: characterizing the amplification power of open DNS resolvers. In: Passive and Active Measurement Conference (PAM) (2022)

62. Yoachimik, O.: Cloudflare thwarts 17.2M RPS DDoS attack - the largest ever reported. https://blog.cloudflare.com/cloudflare-thwarts-17-2m-rps-ddos-attack-the-largest-ever-reported/

63. Zhang, M., Zhang, C., Pai, V., Peterson, L., Wang, R.: PlanetSeer: Internet path failure monitoring and characterization in wide-area services. In: 6th Symposium on Operating Systems Design and Implementation (OSDI 04). USENIX Association, San Francisco, December 2004

64. Zhang, S., Liu, Y., Pei, D.: A measurement study on BGP AS Path Looping (BAPL) behavior. In: 2014 23rd International Conference on Computer Communication and Networks (ICCCN), pp. 1–7 (2014)

65. Zhang, Y., Mao, Z.M.: Effective diagnosis of routing disruptions from end systems. In: 5th USENIX Symposium on Networked Systems Design and Implementation (NSDI 08). USENIX Association, San Francisco, April 2008

Quantifying Nations' Exposure to Traffic Observation and Selective Tampering

Alexander Gamero-Garrido[1,2]([✉]), Esteban Carisimo[3], Shuai Hao[4],
Bradley Huffaker[1], Alex C. Snoeren[6], and Alberto Dainotti[1,5]

[1] CAIDA, UC San Diego, La Jolla, USA
[2] Northeastern University, Boston, USA
`a.gamerogarrido@northeastern.edu`
[3] Northwestern University, Evanston, USA
[4] Old Dominion University, Norfolk, USA
[5] Georgia Institute of Technology, Atlanta, USA
[6] UC San Diego, La Jolla, USA

Abstract. Almost all popular Internet services are hosted in a select set
of countries, forcing other nations to rely on international connectivity to
access them. We identify nations where traffic towards a large portion of
the country is serviced by a small number of Autonomous Systems, and,
therefore, may be exposed to observation or selective tampering by these
ASes. We introduce the Country-level Transit Influence (CTI) metric
to quantify the significance of a given AS on the international transit
service of a particular country. By studying the CTI values for the top
ASes in each country, we find that 34 nations have transit ecosystems
that render them particularly exposed, where a single AS is privy to
traffic destined to over 40% of their IP addresses. In the nations where
we are able to validate our findings with in-country operators, our top-
five ASes are 90% accurate on average. In the countries we examine, CTI
reveals two classes of networks frequently play a particularly prominent
role: submarine cable operators and state-owned ASes.

1   Introduction

The goal of this study is to identify instances where a significant fraction of
a country's inbound international traffic is managed by a select few networks.
Such networks are in a position to observe and tamper with a nation's traffic,
as could any third-parties who infiltrate them (*e.g.,* using a phishing attack or
a remote vulnerability exploitation). For instance, observation—of unencrypted
traffic and metadata—may be performed by domestic or foreign actors with the
purpose of conducting surveillance or espionage, respectively. Conversely, selective tampering—for instance, with individual network flows carrying popular-
application traffic—has been reported by actors that are both domestic (e.g.,
government censorship) and foreign (e.g., dis-information campaigns).

Because actual traffic information is difficult to obtain at a global scale, we
instead quantify the fraction of a country's IP addresses exposed to tampering

O. Hohlfeld et al. (Eds.): PAM 2022, LNCS 13210, pp. 645–674, 2022.
https://doi.org/10.1007/978-3-030-98785-5_29

and observation by specific networks. While all IP addresses are clearly not created equal, they facilitate an apples-to-apples comparison across nations, and the ranking of networks influencing a particular country. Traffic towards any given IP address is frequently handled by so-called transit networks, *i.e.,* those who sell connectivity to the rest of the Internet to other, customer networks for a fee; customers include consumer-serving access networks.

These transit networks are often unknown and unaccountable to end users. This opacity may allow both domestic and foreign actors to observe or tamper with traffic—capabilities we term *transit influence*—without facing diplomatic or political backlash from governments, activists or consumer groups. We aim to bring transparency to the public regarding oversized observation and tampering capabilities granted to specific transit networks in a large group of nations.

In order to reveal these crucial, nation-level topological features, we develop the country-level transit influence (CTI) metric. CTI quantifies the transit influence a particular network exerts on a nation's traffic. Studying transit influence requires an analysis of the global routing ecosystem which enables networks to exchange traffic between them. We extract information from the Border Gateway Protocol (BGP), the central system by which networks exchange interconnection information. CTI is based on an analysis of a large compendia of BGP data [8,54] and includes both topological and geographic filters designed to facilitate inference despite incomplete and biased data [25,31,48].

We apply CTI in countries that lack peering facilities such as Internet exchange points (IXPs) at which access networks might connect directly with networks of other nations. In these *transit-dominant* nations, transit networks—often a select few based in geographically distant countries [16,28,32,58]—serve as the dominant form of connectivity to the global Internet. Moreover, the lack of internationally connected, domestic co-location facilities places these nations at further risk of exposure to observation and tampering because popular content is generally hosted abroad [19,26,37,51,60].

We employ a two-stage approach based on a comprehensive set of passive inference and active measurements. First, we identify transit-dominant countries. Countries that are transit dominant may be more exposed to observation and tampering by transit providers than countries where peering agreements are prevalent: the latter can receive some traffic from other countries through such peering agreements and bypass transit providers. Second, we quantify the transit influence of the networks serving each country using the CTI methodology, the central contribution of this study. We validate our findings from both stages with in-country network operators at 123 ASes in 19 countries who each confirm that our results are consistent with their understanding of their country's networks. These discussions, and our analyses showing the metric's stability, lend confidence to our inferences despite the considerable technical challenges in this measurement space.

In addition to releasing our code and data, our contributions include:

1. A new Internet cartography metric that quantifies the transit influence a particular network exerts on a nation's traffic: the country-level transit influence (CTI) metric, which ranges over $[0, 1]$.

2. We apply CTI to infer the most influential transit networks in 75 countries that rely primarily on transit for international connectivity. These countries have, in aggregate, ≈1 billion Internet users (26% of the world [2]). We find that many of these countries have topologies exposing them to observation or tampering: in the median case, the most influential transit network manages traffic towards 35% of the nation's IP addresses.
3. We identify two classes of ASes that are frequently influential: those who operate submarine cables and companies owned by national governments.

Ethical Disclaimer. We acknowledge several ethical implications of our work. Our mass (validation) survey of operators was classified as exempt by our IRB. Our reporting of available paths to repressive countries might trigger government intervention to remove such paths. Another potential issue is the identification of networks that would yield the most expansive observation or tampering capabilities in a country, which is potentially useful information for a malicious actor. We believe most governments and sophisticated attackers already have access to this information, and that our study may lead to mitigation of these concerning topological features; thus, the benefits significantly exceed the risk.

Roadmap. The remainder of this paper is organized as follows. We start in Sect. 2 with a high-level overview of our methodology before describing how we assign nationality to prefixes, ASes, and BGP vantage points (Sect. 3). We introduce the CTI metric in Sect. 4. We apply CTI in 75 countries where international connectivity is predominantly transit and describe our findings in Sect. 5. Then, we discuss in detail how we identified the transit-dominant countries (Sect. 6). We present our validation with operators and stability analyses in Sect. 7. Section 8 discloses some limitations of our study while Sect. 9 compares with prior work. Due to space constraints, we include further details and a flowchart summarizing our full methodology in the appendix. We release the CTI code and datasets at https://github.com/CAIDA/mapkit-cti-code.

2   Approach Overview

Conceptually, international Internet traffic crosses a nation's border at some physical location, likely along a link connecting two routers. For our purposes, we are not interested in the physical topology, but the logical one: in which autonomous system(s) does international traffic enter a nation on its way to access networks in that country (i.e., origin ASes). Topologically, these ASes can have two different types of relationship with the first domestic AS encountered: transit (provider-to-customer or *p2c*) or peering (peer-to-peer or *p2p*). We focus on countries where international connectivity is dominated by transit (p2c) interdomain relationships as they are easier to identify from public data sources.

High-Level Model. We look for evidence of a country's exposure to observation or selective tampering by specific networks. Studying this exposure requires a quantitative model of the reliance of the country's access networks, in aggregate, on specific transit networks. The model must factor in the size of the address space originated by each AS with presence in the country. Intuitively, the greater the share of a country's IP addresses that are served by a particular transit AS, the higher the potential exposure of the nation's inbound traffic to observation or tampering by that AS. The model must then produce a country-level metric of exposure for each transit network serving the nation. To that end, we determine the frequency at which transit networks appear on routes towards the country's IP addresses.

We start our model by building a graph where nodes are ASes and edges are connections between them, weighted by address space. Then, a metric of node prominence on said graph provides a quantitative assessment of how frequently a (transit) node AS_t is traversed when delivering traffic from any given node to edge (origin) nodes. The higher the value of this metric for any AS_t in a given country, the more exposed the transit ecosystem is. At one extreme (most exposed) are countries with a single transit provider (*e.g.*, a legally-mandated monopoly) connecting every network in the country to the rest of the Internet; at the other end are countries with many transit providers, each delivering traffic to a small fraction of the nation's IPs. Note that we do not need complete visibility of the graph (*e.g.*, backup links) to infer potential exposure to observation or tampering, as traffic will likely flow through the links that are visible given capacity constraints on long-haul (incl. international) links [14,44,50,67].

Our technical approach to build this conceptual model using real data uses as inputs a combination of two types of measurements: *(i)* passive, to study AS-level connectivity, and *(ii)* active, to study transit dominance.

AS-Level Connectivity. We rely on two major input sources: BGP paths and prefixes from RouteViews [8] and RIPE RIS [6], and AS relationship inferences from CAIDA. We begin with the 848,242 IPv4 prefixes listed in CAIDA's Prefix-to-Autonomous System mappings derived from RouteViews [22], excluding the 6,861 (0.8%) prefixes with (invalid) length greater than 24, and the 9,275 (1.1%) originated by multiple ASes. We find those prefixes in the 274,520,778 IPv4 AS-level paths observed in BGP table dumps gathered by AS-Rank [1] from RIPE/RouteViews [6,8] during the first five days of March 2020. We consider the set of prefixes and the ASes that originate them on each observed path in combination with the 377,879 inferred AS-level relationships published by CAIDA [5].[1]

Transit Dominance. Because we are focused only on countries where transit—as opposed to peering—is the main form of trans-border connectivity, we use active measurements to identify and exclude nations with evidence of foreign peering, *i.e.*, where an AS that originates addresses geolocated to the

---

[1] In the 75 countries where we study transit influence, no path contained any of: unallocated ASes, loops, poisoned paths (where a non-clique AS is present between two clique ASes, clique being the AS-level core of the Internet inferred by [5]); additionally, all paths towards these countries are seen at least once per day across all five days.

country establishes a peering agreement with another AS primarily based in another country[2]. We conduct a two-week-long active measurement campaign (see Sect. 6.2) in May 2020 to determine which countries are transit dominant based on the business relationship between the "border" ASes traversed by our probe packets while entering the country (as inferred by BdrmapIT [49]).

3   Definitions of Nationality

CTI hinges on the correct nationality assignment for IP address prefixes and BGP monitors. ASes are also assigned a nationality in the transit-dominance analysis. Given the diverse set of information available, we devise distinct methods for each. (We include an analysis of CTI stability given an alternative geolocation input in Sect. 7.) For our purposes, a country is one of the 193 United Nations member states, either of its two permanent non-member observer states, or Antarctica.

Address Prefixes. We first geolocate each IP address in every observed BGP prefix to a country using Netacuity [12]. Then, on a country-by-country basis, we count how many addresses in each prefix are geolocated to that country. If the number is less than 256 (a /24), we round up to 256. If Netacuity does not place any of a prefix's IP addresses in a country, we attempt to find a delegation block from the March 2020 RIR delegation files [7] that covers the entirety of the prefix. If there is one we assign all of the delegated prefix's addresses to the indicated country. Hence, while Netacuity can place a prefix in multiple countries, at most one country will receive addresses through the RIR process, and only if it was not already associated with the prefix through Netacuity. Netacuity accounts for 95.1% of all prefix-to-country mappings, while delegation-derived geolocation accounts for the rest.

A particularly pressing concern with geolocation is the correct assignment of IP addresses belonging to large transit ASes with a presence in many countries. We compute the fraction of a country's address space that is originated by ASes that have at least two thirds of their addresses in that country. In the vast majority of countries, the address space is dominated by ASes that are primarily domestic.

BGP Monitors. As our study is focused on measuring inbound country-level connectivity, we seek to limit our analysis to paths going towards addresses in the target country from a BGP monitor located outside that country. Hence, we confirm the BGP monitor locations listed by RouteViews [59] and RIPE RIS [57] through a set of active measurements. The details of this process are included in Appendix A.

Autonomous Systems. Our transit dominance analysis relies on a concept of AS nationality, which is based on IP geolocation of the AS' originated addresses; for transit providers, we also include the IP addresses originated by direct customers. We classify each autonomous system AS operating in a country C as being *domestic*, $AS \in \mathrm{dom}(C)$, when the AS has at least two thirds of

---

[2] This "nationality" assignment is described in Sect. 3.

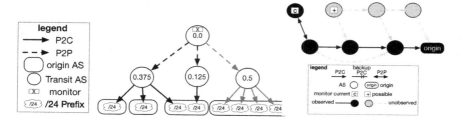

Fig. 1. Example of country-level transit influence.

Fig. 2. Unobserved paths in BGP.

its addresses in the country, and *foreign* otherwise. The vast majority (97.4%) of ASes are classified as domestic in one country, with the remaining small fraction being classified as foreign in every country. In fact, 89.8% of ASes have all of their address in a single country, and 98.6% have a strict majority of addresses in one country.

4   Transit Influence Metric

We define the transit influence $CTI_M(AS, C) \in [0, 1]$ using a set of BGP monitors M as

$$\sum_{m \in M} \left(\frac{w(m)}{|M|} \cdot \sum_{p|\text{onpath}(AS,m,p)} \left(\frac{a(p,C)}{A(C)} \cdot \frac{1}{d(AS,m,p)} \right) \right), \qquad (1)$$

where $w(m)$ is monitor m's weight (Sect. 4.1) among the set of monitors (Sect. 4.2); onpath(AS, m, p) is true if AS is present on a preferred path observed by monitor m to a prefix p, and m is not contained within AS itself (Sect. 4.2); $a(p, C)$ is the number of addresses in prefix p geolocated to country C; $A(C)$ is the total number of IP addresses geolocated to country C; and $d(AS, p, m)$ is the number of AS-level hops between AS and prefix p as viewed by monitor m (Sect. 4.1).

We illustrate CTI's use in Fig. 1, with CTI values for a toy example with three transit ASes and four origin ASes, in a country with eight /24 prefixes: the transit AS on the right has the highest CTI, since it serves the most addresses (half of the country), followed by the transit AS on the left (3/8) and the AS in the center (1/8). Note that the top AS has a CTI of 0, because it hosts the BGP monitor from which the set of routes used in this toy example are learned—hence, onpath(AS_t, m, p) is always false for that AS. Should that AS not be the host of the BGP monitor (or be seen on these routes through another monitor), it would have a CTI of 0.5—transit influence over the entire country as an indirect transit provider (distance 2 from the prefixes).

Note that originating addresses directly does not grant an AS transit influence, as our focus is on identifying ASes that carry traffic to destinations outside of their network.

4.1   CTI Components

We explain the rationale for the various factors in Eq. 1 in the following subsections.

Indirect Transit Discount. As the number of AS-level hops from the origin increases, so too does the likelihood that there exist alternative paths towards the same origin AS of which we have no visibility (*e.g.*, backup links, less-preferred paths). Figure 2 shows this limitation in visibility for a toy example with a single origin AS. There, given the location of BGP monitor C we see the AS-level chain in black, erroneously concluding that the origin AS has a single direct transit provider and two indirect transit providers. In reality, there exists another set of both direct and indirect transit providers (the AS-level chain in light gray). We miss all these paths given that we do not have a monitor in any neighbor of a light-gray AS (such as that marked with a plus sign). In this example we miss backup links of the origin AS, as well as preferred links of the origin's direct transit provider, and a backup link of both indirect transit providers.

As a coarse mechanism aimed at mitigating this limited visibility, we discount the influence of transit providers in proportion to the AS-level distance from the origin: we apply a discount factor as $1/1, 1/2, ..., 1/k$, where k is the number of AS-level hops from the origin AS. In practice, that means we do not discount the measurements of direct transit providers, as there the probability of missing a backup or less-preferred link is lowest. We note that this heuristic yields a conservative estimate of the observation opportunities of an indirect transit provider over traffic flowing towards a country.

Prioritizing AS Diversity. ASes can host more than one BGP monitor. In fact, more than 20 ASes in RIPE RIS and RouteViews host multiple monitors; for instance, AS3257-GTT hosts five. In order to favor a topologically-diverse view (given the available observations), if more than one monitor from the same AS sees an announcement for the same prefix, we discount their observations to limit the influence of monitor ASes with multiple monitors. Formally, the weight for each monitor m's observation of a prefix is $w(m) = 1/n$, where n is the number of BGP monitors in the AS that see an announcement of that prefix.

4.2   Filtering ASes

To correct for the limited, non-uniform coverage of the BGP monitors that collect our table dumps, we apply a number of filters to the set of paths over which we compute CTI.

Provider-Customer AS Filter. BGP monitors by definition collect paths from the AS hosting the monitor to the origin AS. Therefore, we always exclude the AS hosting the BGP monitor from the path to avoid inflating their transit influence. Further, we employ a heuristic that attempts to consider only the portion of the path relevant to the origin prefix, and ignore the portion dictated by the monitor's topological location.

The intuition behind our filter is that, from the perspective of the origin AS, there is a "hill" above it capped by the last observed provider-customer (p2c, *i.e.*, transit) link, with traffic flowing from the hill's peak down towards the origin. The transit AS in that link is the highest point in the path we want to keep, as it directs traffic towards its customer (and its customer's customers, if applicable). After reaching that topological peak, we discard any other AS present in the path. The remaining path would then include the origin AS, its direct or indirect transit provider at the topological peak, and any other ASes appearing between the origin AS and the direct or indirect transit provider. Note that this filter excludes peers of the transit provider at the peak—appearing between the topological peak and the AS hosting the BGP monitor—since we only apply CTI in transit-dominant countries, and therefore these peers are unlikely to be central to the country's connectivity.

Formally, for the analysis presented in this paper, we refine onpath(AS_t, m, p) to be true only if the path observed at monitor m has at least one inferred p2c link where the customer is either the origin of p or closer to it than AS_t, *i.e.*, we discard paths where there is no topological peak from the perspective of the origin. This heuristic discards 0.2% of the paths observed by our monitors. In the median country we discard 0.2% of paths using this filter, with 0.3% being the average case. In all countries we keep over 98.6% of paths.

This filter ensures that at least one AS (the inferred customer of the transit AS) relies on at least one other AS (the inferred transit provider) for transit from and towards the core of the Internet. As we aim to measure transit influence, these business relationships are an important source of information: merely being directly connected to an AS path that reaches the origin AS in a given country does not necessarily make an AS influential; being a direct provider of the origin, or of an AS closer to the origin, lends more confidence to our inference of influence[3].

CTI Outlier Filtering. Finally, we filter BGP-monitor-location noise by removing outlier estimates of transit influence—both overestimates and underestimates resulting from the AS hosting a BGP monitor being topologically too close or too far from the origin AS—to get an accurate assessment of transit influence towards that origin. We implement a filter recently proposed for another AS-topology metric (AS hegemony [31], see Sect. 9). Specifically, we compute the CTI of each transit provider AS_t using BGP monitors from each monitor-hosting AS_h independently, as $CTI_{m(AS_h)}(AS_t, C)$, where $m(AS_h)$ is the set of monitors within AS_h. We determine which potentially-biased AS_h have gathered observations producing $CTI_{m(AS_h)}(AS_t, C)$ values in the bottom and top 10% of all values for that transit provider in that country and disregard all paths observed by monitors hosted in these potentially-biased AS_h. As in [31], we implement

---

[3] Refer to [33] (Sect. 2.1.5 and Sect. 4.2.4) for an extended discussion of the intuition behind the CTI model.

outlier filtering only where we have observations of $CTI_{m(AS_h)}(AS_t, C)$ from 10 or more AS_h, which occurs for 58.4% of transit AS-country pairs in our sample (a single AS can operate in multiple countries).

5   Country-Level Transit

In this section we present the results of applying our CTI metric to the transit ecosystem of 75 countries with little-to-no international peering. (We describe our method for selecting these countries in Sect. 6.) We provide a high-level characterization of the transit ecosystem in each country by comparing the CTI scores of the top-5 ASes ranked by CTI (Sect. 5.1), as well as a set of ASes that appear in the top 5 of many countries (at least 10). Our hypothesis is that these countries show different transit profiles as a consequence of the socioeconomic and geopolitical diversity of the sample: from high exposure to observation, where one AS is the most influential transit provider and others are very marginal, to less exposed countries with an ensemble of ASes with similar values of CTI.

Investigating the companies operating the ASes with high CTI, we find two prominent groups of organizations: submarine cable operators (Sect. 5.2) and state-owned providers (Sect. 5.3). For the former, their operation of physical infrastructure connected to the country may underpin their high transit influence. With regards to state-owned ASes, providing transit may give governments the ability to expand their footprint beyond addresses they originate, e.g., through a state-owned broadband provider. In some cases, state ownership of a transit provider may follow their investment in a submarine cable or landing station, while in others it may reflect the government's intention to enact censorship. We limit our analysis to the discovery of the transit footprint of the state, without delving into the underlying motives.

5.1   CTI Distribution Across Countries

In this subsection we present an overview of the CTI distribution across countries. Countries with a top-heavy distribution of CTI values are particularly exposed to specific networks. Other nations with a more flat distribution signal

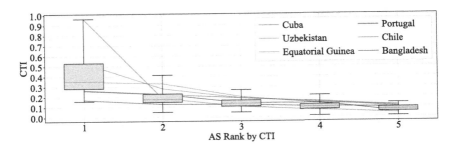

Fig. 3. Boxplot of CTI distributions for the top-5 ASes in each country.

an ecosystem that is less exposed to prominent transit ASes. Figure 3 shows the distribution of CTI values for ASes ranked in the top 5 by CTI in each country. In 51 countries, the top-ranked AS has CTI ≥ 0.3, signaling high exposure to observation and tampering by that specific network.

The distribution of CTI rapidly declines across AS rank, with the median halving from the first to the second position. In 54 countries, CTI declines by over 30% from the top-ranked AS to its successor; the average and median decline across all countries are 50% and 47%. This suggests that in the vast majority of countries in our sample, a single AS is particularly prominent in terms of its capabilities to observe or tamper with traffic.

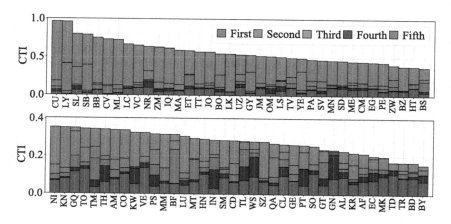

Fig. 4. Overlapping bars showing CTI values of the five top-ranked ASes in the 75 countries we study.

Individual Nations. Results for the full set of countries we study[4] are included in Fig. 4. We discuss several representative cases below.

Most Exposed Countries. Only four countries have a top-ranked AS with a CTI over 0.75: Cuba, Libya, Sierra Leone, and the Solomon Islands (a small island nation). Cuba appears to have the most-exposed transit ecosystem[5], in which the top-ranked AS has CTI of 0.96. Because CTI discounts indirect transit—and the top AS monopolizes observed, direct connectivity—the CTI of Cuba's remaining ASes declines rapidly (81% from the top-ranked AS to the second).

---

[4] Note that multiple ASes may provide transit connectivity to the same prefixes, explaining why the sum of CTI values of top ASes may be greater than 1.

[5] This is consistent with previous work that focused exclusively on Cuba, finding its international connectivity to be constrained [16].

Countries Around the Median. The median of the leftmost bar in Fig. 3 consists of countries that are still considerably exposed to observation and tampering, with CTI values ranging from 0.34 to 0.44, including: Egypt, Equatorial Guinea, Belize and Thailand. In Eq. Guinea, the top-two ASes each have a CTI over 0.3; these ASes have a p2c relationship with each other. Egypt and Belize have more skewed distributions, with a 67–79% decline from the top AS to its successor.

Least Exposed Countries. At the other end of the spectrum in Fig. 4 are five countries where the top-ranked has CTI values under 0.2: Chad, Bangladesh, Belarus, Turkey and North Macedonia. These countries have flatter distributions, with CTI declining at most 21% (or 16% on average) between the top-two ASes. As a result, we find no evidence of these nations being particularly exposed to a single network (unlike most of their peer countries in our sample). India, the country with the most Internet users in our sample, is in the bottom third with a top-AS CTI of 0.29, declining by 27% between the top-2 ASes.

Frequently Top-Ranked ASes. Of the 165 ASes present in Fig. 3, 126 of them are in the top-5 for only one country, with a further 31 ASes in the top-5 of at most 10 countries. There are eight notable exceptions, however: 3356*-Lumen[6] (top-5 in 25 countries), 1299*-Telia (24), 174*-Cogent (24), 6939-HE (18), 5511*-Orange (16), 6762*-T. Italia (14), 23520-C&W (14), and 6453*-Tata (12). Nearly all of these networks (marked with *) are in the inferred clique at the top of the global transit hierarchy [1]. C&W is only present in our analysis for countries in the Caribbean. HE has a very broad footprint, with countries in Africa (7), the Mid. East (3), W. Europe (2), Southeast Asia (2), South Pacific (2) and East/South Asia (1 each).

5.2   Submarine Cable Operators

Submarine cables are known to be an important part of the global Internet infrastructure [15,29,45] and play a role in the top-5 ASes of most countries we study. (Nicaragua, Guatemala, and Guyana are the only three nations where none of the top-5 ASes are associated with the submarine cables landing in the country.)

In this section, for each country, we find the highest-ranked AS by CTI where there is evidence of an institutional connection between the AS and an owner or operator of a submarine cable. We define an AS as a submarine cable operator if we find a direct match between the AS Name, the AS Organization [20], or a corporate parent organization (*e.g.*, CenturyLink for Level3, the Government of Sierra Leone for Sierra Leone Cable Company) and the owners of a submarine cable operator according to TeleGeography [64] and Infrapedia [38]. This process yields submarine cable ASes in 46 countries out of 51 possible, as 17 of the 75 countries are landlocked, and 7 have no submarine cable connectivity according to the operator databases. In three additional countries (Myanmar [4], the Solomon Islands [10], and Congo DRC [43]) only TeleGeography provides an

---

[6] Formerly Level3/CenturyLink.

AS to submarine cable match, which we confirm with information from the cited sources (the operators themselves, the government of Australia, and a submarine cable news source). In the remaining two countries (Thailand [65] and Samoa [63]) where we were not able to find an AS to submarine cable from TeleGeography, we rely on the cited sources (from the operator and a Samoan news outlet) to find a match. Note that only operators of submarine cables who appear as an AS on the BGP path can be identified using this method.

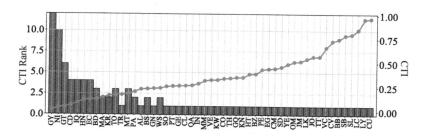

Fig. 5. Orange circles: CTI of top-ranked submarine cable AS. Blue bars: CTI rank of top-ranked submarine cable AS. (Color figure online)

Our findings are shown in Fig. 5, with the CTI of the top cable-owning AS in each of the 51 countries shown as orange circles, and the ordinal ranking of that AS in its country's ecosystem as blue bars. In 36 countries, a submarine cable AS is ranked at the top by CTI, with an average rank of 1.9.

Note that being the top operator by CTI means different things in different countries, as the underlying potential exposure to observation affects the CTI of the top AS. For instance, in Turkey a cable-owning AS ranks first by CTI, but has the lowest CTI among such countries. Said AS (9121-Turk Telecom) has a CTI of 0.17. By contrast, in Cuba and Libya, a submarine cable operator (11960-ETECSA and 37558-LIT) is also ranked first but with CTIs of 0.96 in both cases. As a result, Turkey is much less exposed to a single AS than Cuba and Libya.

We also find regional clusters of high transit influence for the same AS operating a submarine cable, including C&W (formerly Columbus Networks), which is among the top providers in 11 countries in Central America and the Caribbean thanks to its ownership of the ECFS, ARCOS-1 and Fibralink cables. Telecom Italia Sparkle, Telefonica and Bharti Airtel also have an important transit presence in the Mediterranean, Latin America, and South Asia respectively. We release a complete list of submarine cables linked to an AS with high CTI on the paper's repository.

5.3   State-Owned Transit Providers

In more than a third (26) of nations, we find that at least one of the top-5 ASes is state-owned, motivating us to further examine the total influence of a country's government on its Internet connectivity. In particular, we adapt CTI to quantify the influence of state-owned conglomerates—as some nations have more than one state-owned AS—and apply it to the 75 countries in our sample. We use as input a list of ASes that are majority-owned by sovereign states [23]. The list was manually verified and encompasses both access and transit ASes. The dataset includes major telecommunication providers as well as its sibling networks and subsidiaries. Using this list, we find 100 state-owned ASes who operate domestically (*i.e.*, where the state owner and the country of operation are the same) in 41 countries.

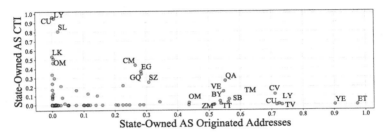

Fig. 6. CTI and fraction of addresses originated by domestic, state-owned ASes in our study.

Influence of State-Owned ASes. Our initial exploration of the influence of state-owned ASes concerns the role each AS plays in the ecosystem of its country, as shown in Fig. 6. We find that state-owned ASes tend to provide either transit or access, usually not a combination of both. (Most points in Fig. 6 line up along an axis, rather than towards the middle.) As a consequence, meaningfully estimating the footprint of the state requires combining the two kinds of influence as well as aggregating data for AS conglomerates. (Two exceptions where a state-owned AS provides both Internet access (*i.e.*, as an origin AS) and serves transit to other ASes are Cameroon and Egypt; in the former, Camtel has both a high CTI (0.44, ranked first) and originates 27% of the country's addresses (second only to Orange Cameroon). Egypt's TE has a CTI of 0.37 and originates 28% of the country's addresses.)

We begin our combined estimation by computing CTI for not just a single AS, but a set of ASes, while not "double counting" influence over the same addresses; *i.e.*, if two of the state's ASes originate and provide transit to the same addresses, we add those addresses to the state's footprint once. We call this derived metric $CTIn$. Intuitively, $CTIn$ reflects the "pure-transit" footprint of the state, crediting only the addresses where state-owned ASes serve exclusively as transit providers. For instance, if AS A and AS B (both of which operate in country C) respectively originate and provide transit to the same /24 prefix, $CTIn$ says that the conglomerate $S_C = \{A, B\}$ does not have transit influence over the /24 prefix. Formally, $CTIn_M(S_c, C) \in [0, 1]$ is calculated as

$$\sum_{m \in M} \left(\frac{w(m)}{|M|} \cdot \sum_{p | \text{onpath}^*(S_c, m, p)} \left(\frac{a(p, C)}{A(C)} \cdot \frac{1}{d^*(S_c, m, p)} \right) \right),$$

which is essentially identical to Eq. 1, except that S_c is a set containing all of the ASes in the state-owned conglomerate of country C; onpath$^*(S_c, m, p)$ is true if onpath(AS_t, m, p) is true for some $AS_t \in S_c$ and p is *not* originated by any AS in S_c; and $d^*(S_c, m, p) = \min_{AS_t \in S_c} d(AS_t, m, p)$, *i.e.*, the AS-level distance from p to the closest AS in the conglomerate.

Finally, we define the total footprint of the state, *i.e.*, addresses that are either originated or for which transit is served by a state-owned AS. The state's footprint $F(C) \in [0, 1]$ is calculated as

$$F(C) = CTIn_M(S_c, C) + \sum_{AS_o \in S_c} \frac{a^*(AS_o, C)}{A(C)},$$

where $a^*(AS_o, C)/A(C)$ is the fraction of addresses in country C originated by AS_o. The first term of the sum is the pure-transit footprint and the second term is the addresses directly originated by the state-owned conglomerate S_c.

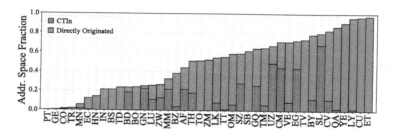

Fig. 7. State-owned originated address space a^* (orange bars), $CTIn$ (blue bars), and state footprint F (bar height) for countries in our study. (Color figure online)

Findings. Figure 7 shows our findings for the state-owned footprint (F, bar height), the originated fraction by state-owned ASes (orange bar), and pure-transit footprint of state-owned ASes ($CTIn$, blue bar). Our results suggest that domestic state influence exists on a spectrum where some countries, such as Ethiopia, Cuba, Libya and Yemen, rely overwhelmingly on the state for the provision of Internet access and (F between 0.90–0.97), whereas others, such as Colombia, Turkey, Mongolia and Ecuador have relatively marginal state-owned enterprises (F between 0.01–0.12).

Regarding the mode of influence that states use, in many countries in Fig. 7, most of the bar height is contributed by the orange portion, meaning that the footprint of the state comes from addresses directly originated. However, in some countries the state punches above its access network weight by deploying an influential transit provider, *i.e.*, those where the bar height is not dominated by the origin contribution in orange.

Table 1. Top countries by $CTIn$.

Country	SL	UZ	CM	EG	SZ	GQ	GN	AF	MM
$CTIn$	0.68	0.49	0.44	0.44	0.28	0.26	0.22	0.21	0.21
F	0.80	0.67	0.71	0.72	0.59	0.64	0.25	0.44	0.32

Pure-Transit Footprint of State-Owned ASes. The countries where pure-transit influence ($CTIn$) is largest (0.2 or more, or pure-transit influence over at least a fifth of the country's addresses) are shown in Table 1. In these countries, all of which are in Africa and Central Asia, providing transit considerably increases the influence of the state. We note that the mere existence of these influential transit ASes does not signal willingness of the state to engage in surveillance or selective tampering, but rather that the government may have opportunities to do so. For instance, Myanmar's state-owned Myanma Posts and Telecommunications (MPT), which is included in our analysis, appears to have been involved in the disruption of the country's Internet service during the recent coup [36].

6   Inferring Transit Dominance

In this section, we describe how we identified the 75 countries that are the focus of the preceding section, *i.e.*, countries where provider-customer transit (p2c) relationships are likely the dominant mode of inbound international connectivity. We start by identifying countries for which public datasets of Internet Exchange Points (IXPs) and Private Colocation facilities (Colo) show no evidence of international peering (Sect. 6.1). Based on this analysis, we conduct an active measurement campaign to confirm the absence of international peering (Sect. 6.2). This second stage based on traceroutes is necessary because peering datasets are incomplete, particularly when it comes to membership lists at IXPs in developing countries [47]. We consider the prevalence of transit links being used to reach each of our target countries from probes distributed worldwide (Sect. 6.3) in combination with our operator validation (Sect. 7) to select a set of transit-dominant countries.

We define international peering as a (logical) link between two ASes that: *(i)* operate primarily in different countries (Sect. 3), and *(ii)* where that link is not an inferred transit-customer link. We use this definition since we are interested in studying the AS-level routes taken towards each country. We are aware of the limitations of our measurements and analysis, particularly with regards to the location (both topologically and geographically) of our probes; we address the issue further in Sect. 8.

6.1   Constructing a Candidate List

We identify countries where international peering may not be prevalent by evaluating evidence of international peering involving origin ASes present in the country. While domestic peering is very common, our hypothesis is that international peering is still not a frequent occurrence in some countries. We begin with the set of ASes that originate at least 0.05% of addresses in each country. We remove marginal ASes that originate a very small fraction of the country's address space to reduce the scope of our active campaign, as we are limited by RIPE Atlas's system-wide limits on concurrent measurements [55]. This set includes origin ASes that we classified as foreign to that country, but that originate BGP prefixes entirely geolocated in the country. (These ASes originate a marginal fraction of the addresses in the vast majority of countries we study; see Sect. 3.) We look for these origin ASes in CAIDA's IXP dataset (from Oct. 2019 [21]), PeeringDB Colo dataset (from Mar. 1st, 2020 [9]), and inferred AS-Relationships from BGP (Mar. 2020 [5]).

We classify an origin as a *candidate* if the following three conditions are true:

1. the origin AS has no foreign peers in BGP [5];
2. the origin AS is not a member of any IXPs or Colos based in another country [9,21]; and
3. the origin AS is not a member of any IXPs or Colos where any member AS is based in a different country than the origin AS [9,21].

The intuition for each test is as follows. If we observe at least one foreign peer on BGP (1), this origin AS already has the ability to receive some external content from that peer, bypassing transit providers. Therefore, transit providers serving that origin will have fewer capabilities to observe traffic flowing towards it. Further, if an AS is a member of an IXP/Colo in another country (2), or a member of an IXP/Colo where another member is from a different country (3), the origin AS is at least capable of establishing peering relationships with those other ASes.

Figure 8a shows the percentage of a country's address space originated by candidate ASes. We select the top-100 countries as candidates for active measurements. This set includes only countries where at least 25% of addresses are originated by candidate ASes. Our motivation is to actively probe the set of countries where it is most likely that transit providers still play an important role on inbound international connectivity. These 100 countries are colored in Fig. 8b.

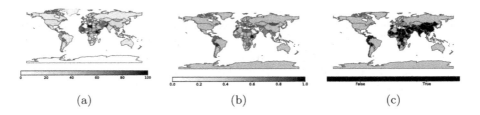

(a)   (b)   (c)

Fig. 8. Non-peering observed perc. on passive datasets 8a, scaled country-level transit fraction in probed countries 8b, and final set, with countries in red excluded 8c. (Color figure online)

6.2   Active Measurement Campaign

We ran a traceroute campaign to the 100 candidate countries for 14 days starting May 2nd, 2020. Additionally, we use all publicly available IPv4 traceroutes on RIPE Atlas during the same period—on the order of several million per hour—in order to opportunistically take advantage of other measurements towards the same ASes. We design our traceroute campaign guided by two constraints. First, we want to select a geographically and topologically diverse set of probes. Second, we have to operate within the rate limits of RIPE Atlas[7], particularly regarding concurrent measurements and credit expenditure.

Within these constraints, we launch ICMP traceroutes[8] from 100 active—shown as "connected" during the previous day [56]—RIPE Atlas probes (located outside any target country) towards a single destination in each AS, twice daily[9]; probing at this frequency gives us 28 opportunities to reach the AS during the two-week period from each vantage point.

We target an IP in a single /24 block for each origin AS in each candidate country by looking for any prefix originated by that AS that is entirely geolocated or delegated within the candidate country (see Sect. 3). Our final dataset is comprised of 33,045,982 traceroutes, including those launched by other RIPE users that meet our constraints. The distribution of the number of traceroutes reaching each country has the following properties: (Min, 25th Pctl., Median, Mean, 75th Pctl., Max) = (36, 13k, 46k, 330k, 250k, 3.3m). That is, the median country received 46k traceroutes. Only three countries received fewer than a thousand traceroutes: Eritrea (667), Nauru (154), and Tuvalu (36).

We use BdrmapIT [49] to translate our traceroutes into AS-level interconnections. BdrmapIT requires a number of external datasets in its operation, which we specify as follows: inferred AS-Level customer cone [48] from Mar. 2020; *AS2Org*, which infers groups of ASes who belong to the same organization[10], from Jan. 2020; and datasets we mention in other sections—prefix-to-Autonomous System mappings (Sect. 2), *PeeringDB* records (Sect. 6.1), and RIR delegation records (Sect. 3). From these traceroutes and external datasets, *BdrmapIT* infers a set of AS-level interconnections and the IP addresses (interfaces) at which they occur. Each interface inferred by *BdrmapIT* has an AS "owner" assignment. We reconstruct the AS-level path observed on the traceroute using such assignments.

6.3   Country-Level Transit Fraction

From the preceding sections we have built a set of AS-level paths taken from the traceroute source to the destination AS. We now need a quantitative analysis

---

[7] Which RIPE Atlas generously relaxed for this study upon direct request.

[8] Using default RIPE Atlas values except number of packets (reduced to 1).

[9] We space traceroutes an hour apart in 800-target IP blocks.

[10] This dataset is published quarterly.

technique to infer the prevalence of transit links on inbound traces towards each country.

To that end, we determine how frequently a transit (p2c) link is traversed when crossing the AS-level national boundary[11] towards an origin AS (AS_o) in a candidate country. We infer the AS-level national boundary as the link between the last foreign AS observed on the AS-level path (starting from the vantage point) and the subsequent AS.

We calculate how frequently, in the inbound traceroutes we process with *BdrmapIT*, the AS-level national border crossing occurs on a transit link for each origin AS. We scale this fraction to take into account the size of the address space originated by each AS using the *country-level transit fraction*:

$$T(C) = \sum_{AS_o, AS_c \in \mathrm{dom}(C)} \sum_{AS_t \notin \mathrm{dom}(C)} \frac{R(AS_o, AS_t, AS_c)}{R(AS_o)} \cdot \frac{a^*(AS_o, C)}{A(C)},$$

where $R(AS_o, AS_t, AS_c)$ is the number of traceroutes destined toward a prefix originated by AS_o that traverse a transit link between a foreign provider AS_t and a domestic customer AS_c in country C; $R(AS_o)$ is the total number of traceroutes where AS_o is the last observed AS; and $a^*(AS_o, C)/A(C)$ is the fraction of country C's address space originated by AS_o. For instance, if an AS originates 50% of the country's origin addresses, and 50% of the traces towards it traverse a foreign transit provider AS, the contribution of that AS to the country-level transit fraction becomes 0.25. Note that AS_c and AS_o are not necessarily the same, as the border crossing may occur at the link between (direct and/or indirect) providers of AS_o.

The values of $T(C)$ for each candidate country are represented in Fig. 8b: countries in darker shades of blue have both a large probed and responsive fraction and a large fraction of traceroutes from outside the country traversing transit providers. The closer the fraction is to 1, the more evidence we have that the country relies on transit providers for its international inbound connectivity.

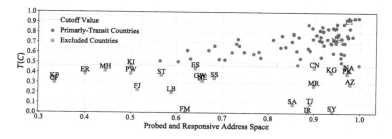

Fig. 9. Country-level transit fractions $T(C)$ for countries in our sample.

---

[11] As defined by our AS Nationality (Sect. 3), not actual political borders.

6.4   Final Selection

Finally, in order to identify a set of primarily-transit countries, we evaluate the values of $T(C)$ across countries, shown in Fig. 9. At one extreme of Fig. 9 and Fig. 8b are countries such as Ethiopia (ET) and Yemen (YE), $T(C) = 0.95$ and 0.7, respectively, where all available evidence points towards transit links as the main inbound modality. At the other extreme are countries such as Syria (SY) and Iran (IR), $T(C) \leq 0.01$, where we rarely observe AS-level national borders being crossed using transit links.

Outside the upper and lower extremes in Fig. 9, where the decision of whether to include a country in our study is obvious, the middle results (most countries) do not offer clear dividing points. We decided then to set the threshold for $T(C)$ to classify a country as primarily-transit based on our validation with operators (Sect. 7); in particular, we use the value of $T(C)$ for Sudan (0.48) as a lower bound, which is the lowest $T(C)$ in any country that we were able to confirm relies on transit links for its inbound connectivity. The final countries in our CTI study are shown in a blue-white spectrum in Fig. 8c and as blue circles in Fig. 9, 75 of the 100 candidates. Countries in red are excluded from further analysis, as at this time we lack sufficient evidence to support that they are primarily using transit providers for inbound connectivity.

7   Stability and Validation

In this section, we discuss the findings of our stability analyses, validation with operators, and a calculation of transit influence at the organization level.

7.1   Stability

Temporal Stability. We apply our CTI methodology to a set of BGP paths from Feb. 2020 and Apr. 2020 and compare the results to those presented in Sect. 5 (from Mar. 2020). Specifically, we compute the absolute value of the difference in CTI across successive months for transit ASes listed in each country. The results are shown in Table 2. We find that the CTI values are relatively stable across these months.

Table 2. CTI temporal stability analyses.

Type	Compared sets	25th ptile.	Mean	Median	75th ptile
Temporal	Feb. & Mar. 2020	0.00000	0.00190	0.00001	0.00016
All ASes	Mar. & Apr. 2020	0.00000	0.00156	0.00001	0.00017

Stability to Changes in Geolocation Input. In order to assess the potential fragility of our study to inaccuracies in geolocation, we also applied our CTI methodology using MaxMind [3] and computed the absolute value of the difference in CTI scores produced with each location database. The output of this analysis is (25th perc.,mean,median,75th perc.) = 0.00000, 0.00104, 0.00002, 0.00017, suggesting CTI is relatively stable across these geolocation inputs.

7.2   Operator Validation

We discussed our findings with employees or contractors of two types of organizations: commercial network operators and non-profits who conduct networking research (universities, registrars, and non-commercial network operators). Additionally, we describe the results of our discussions follwing a mass email request to ASes with prefixes geolocated in countries in our study. Discussions with all of these organizations are anonymized. Our findings are largely consistent with each operator's view of the transit ecosystem of the countries discussed with them.

The results of our discussion of CTI findings with 6 operators in 6 countries[12] are shown in Table 3. Our CTI operator discussions consist of a confirmation of the AS set we identified as being most influential in their countries. Overall, operators confirm that the vast majority of ASes we identify are among the most influential in their nations. We also summarize our discussions with: *(i)* operators regarding our inferences of transit-dominant countries, *(ii)* ASes with prefixes geolocated to these countries. Regarding *(i)* 10 operators in 9 countries[13] confirmed that their nations are primarily transit[14].

Regarding *(ii)* we sent a mass email request to the WHOIS **abuse** address registered by ASes that had prefixes geolocated in 10 countries[15] (with IRB approval): BO, CO, VE, CM, BD, GT, CL, HN, SV and ZW[16]. We received 111 responses in 9 of these countries (all but ZW). Of these, 107 confirmed they operate primarily in the country that we geolocated their prefixes to[17]. Additionally, 108 were willing to discuss which type of business relationship dominated their inbound international traffic: 83 stated that transit relationships are the primary modality.

---

[12] We sent a set of ASes produced before updating our CTI methodology to its current form, which explains the "unconfirmed" column; the "top" ASes were defined as the country's top 12, unless any of those ASes had a marginal CTI score.

[13] CO, ET, CD, LS, SZ, ZW, VE, SD and CM.

[14] Sample, anonymized operator response: "Sudan is characterized by the traditional IP transit model. There is a domestic IXP, which serves five ISPs and [redacted AS Name]'s DNS nodes, but there are no foreign network operators present here. Furthermore, until recently, only two ISPs held gateway licenses (*i.e.,* were licensed to provide external connectivity to Sudan)."

[15] We only contacted ASes who had ≥ 1% of their addresses in the country. Since this survey took place in 2021, we use the addresses geolocated in Jan. of that year.

[16] Selected as a mix of large & small (by #ASes) EN- and ES-speaking countries.

[17] In 3 cases, they stated that they operate in multiple countries.

Table 3. CTI operator validation in 6 countries: CO, ET, ZW, SD, CD and CM.

AS-country pairs	#Confirmed	#Rejected	#Unconfirmed	Total #ASes
Top 5 ASes	27 (90%)	1 (3%)	2 (7%)	30
All top ASes	45 (79%)	7 (12%)	5 (9%)	57

7.3 Organization-Level Transit Influence

In some instances, multiple ASes may be operated by the same organization. We identified 323 instances where multiple ASes belonging the same organization (as of Jul. 2020 [20]) have $CTI > 0$ in a given country. We compute an upper bound of the organization's transit influence (in each country) by summing the CTI of component ASes. We find that 270 org-country pairs—an organization operating in a country—have marginal influence, with the CTI sum under 0.05 (218 were under 0.01).

For the remaining 53 organization-country pairs, we compute the contribution to the CTI sum of the highest-ranked AS in each organization. We separate these into three groups: *(i)* In 36 org-country pairs, the top AS contributes at least 90% of the CTI sum (98% on average). In these 36 cases, then, a single AS is responsible for the vast majority of the organization's transit influence. *(ii)* In 7 org-country pairs, the contribution to the CTI sum of the additional ASes—other than the top AS—in the organization is between 0.01–0.04 (between 11–29% of the CTI sum), or 0.02 on average. Therefore, the change in CTI as a result of their inclusion is relatively marginal.

(iii) In the remaining 10 org-country pairs, only 4 have a CTI sum greater than 0.1. For these, we compute the $CTIn$ of the organization to determine the contribution of the top AS in each organization (rather than a lower bound). In all 4 cases, the top AS contributes 61% or more of the organization's $CTIn$ (country-org, perc. of $CTIn$): VE-Lumen (87% of 0.16), SZ-Orange (61% of 0.14), WS-Lumen (73% of 0.30), and TV-Internap (62% of 0.11). Three of these countries are either a microstate (SZ) or a small island nation (WS and TV). The last instance, in Venezuela, is likely a consequence of the merger of two large companies: AS3356 (Level 3) and AS3549 (Global Crossing) [41].

8 Limitations

At a high level, CTI assumes all ASes and IP addresses are equivalent, which is certainly not the case. At the AS level, it is possible that one, dominant AS provides stronger security than a multitude of smaller ASes with tighter budgets. From the perspective of an attacker, though, a single AS having high CTI creates an opportunity; in the case of sophisticated attackers such as nation-states, the possibility of infiltration of any network cannot be discarded, but compromising many ASes simultaneously—in order to observe traffic towards countries where no AS has high CTI—may be more challenging. As such, ASes with very high

CTI still present a concerningly large observation footprint, regardless of their level of security against infiltration[18].

Similarly, IP addresses can represent vastly different entities. Both access and transit ASes may deploy carrier-grade network access translation (CGNAT) [53]. Since our model treats all routed IPs equally, it does not currently take into account the number of hosts multiplexing a single IP address. We leave this to future work, but note that an additional weight may be added to CTI: one that scales up the number of IP addresses in a given prefix by the number of hosts—or the number of "eyeballs"—connected to those IPs, on aggregate. Even within a given network, however, individual hosts are unlikely to be equally important as some (e.g., those belonging to governmental organizations or power-grid operators) may have more sensitive traffic. Conversely, some networks might not even actually use all their IP addresses—although the latter issue is likely less of a concern in the countries we have studied as their allocation of IPv4 addresses tends to be constrained [24].

In addition to this fundamental conceptual limitation, there are a variety of technical details that could have out-sized impact on our conclusions:

Incomplete BGP data. We acknowledge that the BGP paths we observe and use to compute CTI are incomplete given the location of BGP monitors. Given the serious implications for countries that appear highly exposed to external observation and selective tampering by an AS, we argue that it is important to study such exposure with available data. Further, we note that there are two important factors aiding the credibility of our CTI findings: *(i)* our validation with network operators, who have confirmed that the set of transit ASes identified in their countries is largely consistent with their own understanding of the country's routing ecosystem. *(ii)* There is greater visibility over p2c links in the AS-level topology [25,48], which enables our analysis as we are studying exposure to observation or selective tampering by transit ASes, in particular.

Despite these mitigating factors, we recognize that BGP incompleteness may impact the accuracy of CTI findings. We leave to future work an analysis of CTI's sensitivity to changes in the BGP input (which would further mitigate concerns with BGP incompleteness), *e.g.,* the addition or removal of BGP monitors, or the addition or removal of ASes who feed into each monitor. Finally, we note that CTI incorporates an outlier filter (Sect. 4.2 and Sect. 9.1) which has been shown as robust to changes in BGP input monitors [31].

Traffic. We use a country's geolocated IP(v4) addresses as a proxy for the nation's traffic, as this is a limited resource that is necessary to connect any device to the Internet. IP addresses are often used as a proxy for traffic, *e.g.,* in [61], and previous work has found strong correlations between number of IP addresses observed in BGP and traffic volume for ASes that provide either access or transit service [47]. An AS that serves a larger number of IP addresses would consequently have more capabilities for traffic observation, either of a larger share of potential devices, or of traffic that is more sensitive in nature.

---

[18] Recall that CTI studies exposure to *inbound* traffic observation or selective tampering, which is unaffected by potentially asymmetric AS paths.

Additionally, we do not study direct peering with cloud/content providers, who are responsible for large volumes of user-destined traffic. In addition to p2p links with access or transit networks, these content providers may have in-network caches in the countries we study. These caches may be placed in the access network itself, in the influential transit providers we have identified, or elsewhere [17]. Content providers are large and complex distributed systems, employing sophisticated load balancing [27], routing, and DNS [62] techniques. Given these complexities, we leave to future work an evaluation of the impact on CTI of direct peering with cloud/content providers, and in-network cache placements.

Imperfect geolocation. A potential source of inaccuracy is IP geolocation, as assigning prefixes to a geographic area is challenging and the commercial providers who sell such information use proprietary methods. We have mitigated these concerns by calculating CTI using two commercial providers (Sect. 3), and find that the metric remains stable. We have also limited our analysis to the country level, where geolocation is more accurate than at finer granularities [18, 35,52]. Further, while determining the location of prefixes originated by large transit providers with a global presence is problematic because of its dynamic nature and wide geographic spread, most networks are much smaller and will have limited geographic presence beyond their primary country of operation [69] (where most or all of their addresses will be located).

IPv6. Finally, we note that although our model has so far only been applied to IPv4 addresses—a reasonable scope given that IPv6 deployment is far from wide in many developing regions, including Africa [13,46]—the code libraries and software tools we have used are compatible with IPv6, enabling future research in this area.

Inferring Primarily-Transit Countries. Any active campaign launched using publicly available infrastructure will be limited in its effectiveness to reveal peering links by the location of vantage points (VPs) from which the traceroutes are launched. Our campaign is no exception: our VPs are located in a small subset of the world's ASes, and primarily in Europe and North America. However, we argue that our measurements form a sufficient basis to infer that, in the countries we have identified, foreign peering is rare, since: *(i)* we discussed our findings with operators in 12% of these countries, all of whom have confirmed that their nation relies primarily on transit providers to receive traffic from other countries since foreign peering there is rare to nonexistent; *(ii)* while our measurements are launched primarily from the U.S. and Europe, these regions do serve as important content sources and transit hubs (incl. for intracontinental traffic) for countries in Latin America, the Caribbean and Africa [16,30,32,34,40], where most of the nations we have identified are located.

9   Related Work

Several previous studies have focused on country-level routing, both for the identification of topological bottlenecks [42,58] and to evaluate the impact of specific countries' ASes on routes towards other countries [39]. All of these studies have used delegation data to map an entire AS to a country; these inferences are prone to inaccuracies when compared with more accurate and granular data such as IP-level geolocation, as important transit ASes may span multiple or many countries, or operate in a country different from their registration.

Previous work focused on the topologies of specific countries (Germany [66] and China [68]) and relied on country-specific methods and data sets that do not generalize to automatic inference of AS influence in any given country. Fanou *et al.* [28] studied the interdomain connectivity of intracontinental paths in Africa, using a large traceroute campaign (rather than BGP paths).

CAIDA's AS Rank [48] is another topological metric developed to characterize the customer footprint of an AS on the global routing system. It does not try to capture the capabilities for observation of a transit AS for traffic flowing towards a country; we developed the CTI metric to try to do so.

9.1   National Chokepoint Potential and Hegemony

In this subsection, we describe differences between CTI and two closely related metrics, *National Chokepoint Potential (NCP)* [42] and *Hegemony* [31].

NCP. Leyba *et al.* [42] identified topological bottlenecks, a framework that would also help in quantifying exposure to observation (as CTI aims to address), but with some methodological differences, including: they identify transnational links towards each country using delegation records, and they define bottleneck ASes as those serving the most paths (rather than IP addresses). Further, both CTI and Leyba *et al.* [42] have as a goal the identification of international inbound—and, in their case, also outbound—*chokepoints* (*i.e.,* topological bottlenecks) in each country, based on actual (CTI) or simulated (NCP) BGP paths towards each origin AS. However, their work does not try to capture the fraction of the country's addresses served by a transit provider, but rather the fraction of paths that a border AS (*i.e.,* an AS which is registered to the same country as the origin, but which has a neighbor that is registered to another country) may be able to intercept. Our work is more narrowly focused on the specific case of a transit provider serving traffic towards a transit-dominant country, taking into account the address space of the direct or indirect customers. Conceptually, weighting by paths enhances the influence—or potential, in Leyba *et al.*'s terminology—of ASes frequently serving a broad share of the country's networks, whereas weighting by IPs yields higher influence to ASes frequently serving a large fraction of the country's end hosts.

Hegemony. Our country-level transit influence metric is perhaps most similar to Hegemony [31]. Both metrics aim to identify the transit ASes that are most prevalent on paths towards origin ASes, weighted by the IP address space they serve. Hegemony can be applied either to the global AS-level graph, or to a "Local graph: ... made only from AS paths with the same origin AS" [31]. The latter application is closest to CTI, as this analysis is limited to paths reaching a single origin AS; indeed, we use some of Hegemony local's filtering techniques in our analysis (Sect. 4.2). The applicability of (local-graph) Hegemony to the problem of revealing which transit ASes have observation capabilities over traffic flowing towards a specific country—the issue addressed by CTI—is limited, as Hegemony is a metric of centrality of transit ASes on a specific origin AS (not a country).

We build a country-level alternative metric based on Hegemony [31] and compare CTI to it. The reason for the comparison is to determine if CTI is too aggressive in its filters, discarding too much input data. For that purpose, we build a benchmark using Hegemony local, a metric of centrality of any AS (including both transit providers and peers) on paths towards a single origin. Hegemony consists mostly of a single filter on input BGP data, making it an appropriate benchmark. This benchmark was not trivial to build, as Hegemony local produces a bilateral metric of influence between a transit AS and an origin AS on the global topology. While Hegemony is concerned with extracting the most accurate estimate of centrality on an existing graph, and not with estimating country-level inbound route diversity as CTI, it is possible to build a metric that serves a similar purpose as CTI, which we call *country-level Hegemony* (*CLH*) as

$$CLH(AS_t, C) \in [0,1] = \sum_{AS_o \in (C)} H(AS_t, AS_o) \cdot \frac{a^*(AS_o, C)}{A(C)},$$

where $H(AS_t, AS_o)$ is the Hegemony score of AS_t on AS_o during the same period[19] in March 2020 when we applied CTI, (all the other terms have been previously introduced in Eq. 6.3).

We computed the absolute value of the difference between CTI and CLH for each AS-coutry pair. The output of this analysis is (25th perc.,mean,median,75th perc.) = 0.00000, 0.00104, 0.00002, 0.00017, suggesting that both metrics tend to agree about the country-level influence of marginal ASes (the vast majority of AS-country pairs). Therefore, we find no evidence that the heuristics of CTI introduce unnecessary noise to our analysis because, on aggregate, a country-level alternative based on Hegemony—which excludes considerably fewer BGP monitors than CTI does—tends to agree with CTI's assessment. The metrics do diverge on their assessment of ASes that CTI has identified as influential (CTI ≥ 0.1), with an avg. difference between the metrics in those cases of 0.07.

10   Conclusions and Future Work

In this work we tackled the issue of quantifying the exposure of a country's traffic to observation or tampering by specific ASes. The Country-Level Transit Influence (CTI) metric we developed aims to overcome several challenges with making such inferences using BGP data. We apply this metric in a set of—potentially at-risk—countries where transit provider-customer relationships are still the dominant inbound modality for international traffic; we identified these

---

[19] As Hegemony is published in 15 min intervals [11], we take the 5-day average score.

nations using both passive and active measurements. We applied CTI in these 75 countries and found that the median nation has 35% of their IP addresses served by a single transit AS.

In the future, we would like to develop measurement and analysis techniques that can be applied to study the exposure of countries that are not primarily served by transit providers, but rather by a dense mesh of bilateral and multilateral peering agreements, including those involving cloud providers and CDNs.

Acknowledgements. We thank our shepherd Amreesh Phokeer and the anonymous reviewers for their insightful comments, and Amogh Dhamdhere and kc claffy for providing generous feedback. We are grateful to the network operators who enabled our validation efforts. This work was partly funded by the National Science Foundation (NSF), Grant No. CNS 1705024. Author Gamero-Garrido was supported in part by the Microsoft Research Dissertation Grant (2019) and Northeastern University's Future Faculty Fellowship (2021).

A   BGP Monitor Location and CTI Process Diagram

A.1   BGP Monitor Location

We begin with the 685 monitors in RIPE and RouteViews. We discard (91) monitors aggregated at multi-hop collectors and monitors that are not full-feed, so we are left with 350 monitors in 209 ASes. We determine the location of each full-feed BGP monitor as follows. First, we find the locations of RouteViews and RIPE RIS BGP collectors. We build a first set of locations by finding RIPE Atlas probes co-located at Internet Exchange Points (IXPs), by searching the list of peers for the IXP name, and assign that probe to the country where the (single-location) IXP is present, *e.g.,* BGP RRC01 – LINX/LONAP, London, United Kingdom. We confirm the BGP monitor location by running `ping` measurements from RIPE Atlas probes hosted at the IXP to the BGP monitor's IP address, and conclude that the BGP monitor is in the same city as the IXP if the RTT is lower than 5 ms. For the remaining BGP monitors we look for available RIPE Atlas probes in the ASes that peer with the same BGP collector, and similarly run `ping` measurements towards both the BGP monitor's IP address and a RIPE Atlas probe located in the same city as the one listed for the monitor. We conclude that the BGP monitor and RIPE Atlas probe are in the same city if both sets of RTTs are under 5 ms.

We exclude 118 monitors at this stage because there is no available RIPE Atlas probe hosted at the IXP (in the city where the monitor is listed) nor at any of the other peers of the collector aggregating announcements from the BGP monitor. We discard remote peers from our set, those that have `ping` RTTs higher than 30 ms from the RIPE Atlas probe in the BGP monitor's listed city. For monitors with an RTT between 5–30 ms, we infer them to be at the listed location if we get confirmation using DNS records—*i.e.,* we find a geographical hint such as a three-letter city or airport code, or the full name of the city, using a reverse lookup with the BGP monitor's IP address—or a matching country of the BGP monitor's `peer_asn` record in the RIPE RIS or RouteViews collector list [57,59]. Our final set M has 214 monitors in 145 ASes and 19 countries. We quantify the aggregate impact of all of our filters, including the exclusion of certain BGP monitors per country, in Sect. 9.1, given an alternative metric built using previous research [31].

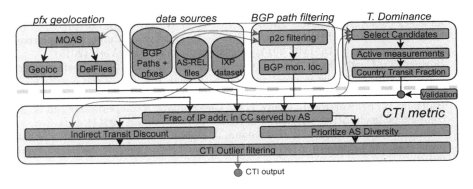

Fig. 10. Process diagram showing input sources and analyses that produce our model of AS-level connectivity, the CTI metric.

A.2   CTI Process Diagram

We show a process diagram of our methodology in Fig. 10. There, our transit-dominance country selection is shown in the top right corner, while the remaining blocks on the top row refer to CTI inputs and preprocessing steps. Finally, the bottom row shows the core components of the CTI metric.

References

1. As rank: about. https://asrank.caida.org/about. Accessed May 2021
2. Internet users - the world factbook. https://www.cia.gov/the-world-factbook/field/internet-users/country-comparison. Accessed May 2021
3. Maxmind geolocation data (2020). https://www.maxmind.com/en/geoip2-services-and-databases
4. MPT, China Unicom plan international cable to boost internet connectivity (2013). https://www.submarinenetworks.com/news/mpt-china-unicom-plan-international-cable-to-boost-internet-connectivity
5. CAIDA AS-relationships (2019). http://data.caida.org/datasets/as-relationships/
6. RIPE Routing Information Service (RIS) (2019). https://www.ripe.net/analyse/internet-measurements/routing-information-service-ris
7. RIR delegation files (2019). https://ftp.ripe.net/pub/stats/ripencc/
8. RouteViews (2019). http://www.routeviews.org/routeviews/
9. CAIDA's PeeringDB dumps (2020). `data.caida.org/datasets/peeringdb/`

10. Coral Sea cable system (2020). www.coralseacablesystem.com.au/about/
11. Hegemony API (2020). https://ihr.iijlab.net/ihr/api/hegemony/
12. Netacuity (2020). http://info.digitalelement.com/
13. Agbaraji, E., Opara, F., Aririguzo, M.: Ipv6 deployment status, the situation in Africa and way out. IJAET **2**(1), 315 (2012)
14. Akella, A., Seshan, S., Shaikh, A.: An empirical evaluation of wide-area internet bottlenecks. In: IMC, pp. 101–114 (2003)
15. Bischof, Z.S., Fontugne, R., Bustamante, F.E.: Untangling the world-wide mesh of undersea cables. In: HotNets 2018, pp. 78–84. ACM, New York (2018)
16. Bischof, Z.S., Rula, J.P., Bustamante, F.E.: In and out of Cuba: Characterizing Cuba's connectivity. In: IMC 2015, pp. 487–493. ACM, New York (2015)
17. Böttger, T., Cuadrado, F., Tyson, G., Castro, I., Uhlig, S.: Open connect everywhere: a glimpse at the internet ecosystem through the lens of the Netflix CDN. SIGCOMM Comput. Commun. Rev. **48**(1), 28–34 (2018)
18. Huffaker, B., Fomenkov, M., Claffy, K.C.: Geocompare: a comparison of public and commercial geolocation databases. CAIDA Technical report (2011)
19. Cai, X., Rey, M., Xuecai, C., Heidemann, J., Johnh, C., Niksun, W.W.: A holistic framework for bridging physical threats to user QOE USC/ISI Technical report (2013)
20. CAIDA. AS2Org (2020). https://www.caida.org/research/topology/as2org/
21. CAIDA. CAIDA IXP dataset (2020). https://www.caida.org/data/ixps/
22. CAIDA. Routeviews Prefix-to-AS mappings (pfx2as) for IPv4 and IPv6 (2020). http://data.caida.org/datasets/routing/routeviews-prefix2as/
23. Carisimo, E., Gamero-Garrido, A., Snoeren, A.C., Dainotti, A.: Identifying ASes of state-owned internet operators. In: IMC 2021. ACM, New York (2021)
24. Dainotti, A., et al.: Lost in space: improving inference of IPv4 address space utilization, October 2014
25. Dhamdhere, A., Dovrolis, C.: Ten years in the evoultion of the internet ecosystem. In: ACM Internet Measurement Conference (IMC) (2008)
26. Edmundson, A., Ensafi, R., Feamster, N., Rexford, J.: Nation-state hegemony in internet routing. In: COMPASS 2018. ACM, New York (2018)
27. Fan, X., Katz-Bassett, E., Heidemann, J.: Assessing affinity between users and CDN sites. In: Steiner, M., Barlet-Ros, P., Bonaventure, O. (eds.) TMA 2015. LNCS, vol. 9053, pp. 95–110. Springer, Cham (2015). https://doi.org/10.1007/978-3-319-17172-2_7
28. Fanou, R., Francois, P., Aben, E.: On the diversity of interdomain routing in Africa. In: Mirkovic, J., Liu, Y. (eds.) PAM 2015. LNCS, vol. 8995, pp. 41–54. Springer, Cham (2015). https://doi.org/10.1007/978-3-319-15509-8_4
29. Fanou, R., Huffaker, B., Mok, R., Claffy, K.C.: Unintended consequences: effects of submarine cable deployment on internet routing. In: Sperotto, A., Dainotti, A., Stiller, B. (eds.) PAM 2020. LNCS, vol. 12048, pp. 211–227. Springer, Cham (2020). https://doi.org/10.1007/978-3-030-44081-7_13
30. Fanou, R., Valera, F., Francois, P., Dhamdhere, A.: Reshaping the african internet: from scattered islands to a connected continent. Comput. Commun. **113**, 25–42 (2017)
31. Fontugne, R., Shah, A., Aben, E.: The (Thin) bridges of AS connectivity: measuring dependency using AS hegemony. In: Beverly, R., Smaragdakis, G., Feldmann, A. (eds.) PAM 2018. LNCS, vol. 10771, pp. 216–227. Springer, Cham (2018). https://doi.org/10.1007/978-3-319-76481-8_16
32. Galperin, H.: Connectivity in Latin America and the Caribbean: the role of internet exchange points (2013)

33. Gamero-Garrido, A.: Transit influence of autonomous systems: country-specific exposure of internet traffic. Ph.D. thesis, UC San Diego (2021)
34. Garcia, G.: Why Miami is Latin America's center of interconnection - interconnections - the Equinix blog. https://blog.equinix.com/blog/2018/05/01/why-miami-is-latin-americas-center-of-interconnection/. May 2018
35. Gharaibeh, M., Shah, A., Huffaker, B., Zhang, H., Ensafi, R., Papadopoulos, C.: A look at router geolocation in public and commercial databases. In: IMC (2017)
36. Giles, C.: Myanmar coup: how the military disrupted the internet-BBC news. https://www.bbc.com/news/world-asia-55889565. Accessed 02 May2021
37. Gupta, A., Calder, M., Feamster, N., Chetty, M., Calandro, E., Katz-Bassett, E.: Peering at the internet's frontier: a first look at ISP interconnectivity in Africa. In: Faloutsos, M., Kuzmanovic, A. (eds.) PAM 2014. LNCS, vol. 8362, pp. 204–213. Springer, Cham (2014). https://doi.org/10.1007/978-3-319-04918-2_20
38. Infrapedia. Infrapedia (2020). https://www.infrapedia.com/app
39. Karlin, J., Forrest, S., Rexford, J.: Nation-state routing: censorship, wiretapping, and BGP. In: CoRR (2009). http://arxiv.org/abs/cs/0608082
40. Kiedanski, D., Grampín, E.: Understanding Latin America ipv6 connectivity: a preliminary exploration. In: SCCC, pp. 1–6, (2017)
41. Level 3 completes acquisition of global crossing (2011). https://www.lightreading.com/ethernet-ip/ethernet-services/level-3-completes-acquisition-of-global-crossing/d/d-id/690402?
42. Leyba, K.G., Edwards, B., Freeman, C., Crandall, J.R., Forrest, S.: Borders and gateways: measuring and analyzing national AS chokepoints. In: COMPASS (2019)
43. Liquid Telecom. Network (2020). https://www.liquidtelecom.com/about-us/our_network
44. Liu, J., Peng, W., Yang, Y., Huang, Z.: A delay-based analysis of multiple bottleneck links of End-to-End paths in the internet. In: Sun, Z., Deng, Z. (eds.) Proceedings of 2013 Chinese Intelligent Automation Conference. Lecture Notes in Electrical Engineering, Springer, Berlin, Heidelberg (2013). https://doi.org/10.1007/978-3-642-38466-0_11
45. Liu, S., Bischof, Z.S., Madan, I., Chan, P.K., Bustamante, F.E.: Out of sight, not out of mind: a user-view on the criticality of the submarine cable network. In: IMC 2020, pp. 194–200. ACM, New York (2020)
46. Livadariu, I., Elmokashfi, A., Dhamdhere, A.: Measuring IPv6 adoption in Africa. In: Odumuyiwa, V., Adegboyega, O., Uwadia, C. (eds.) AFRICOMM 2017. Lecture Notes of the Institute for Computer Sciences, Social Informatics and Telecommunications Engineering, Springer, Cham (2018). https://doi.org/10.1007/978-3-319-98827-6_32
47. Lodhi, A., Larson, N., Dhamdhere, A., Dovrolis, C., Claffy, K.: Using PeeringDB to understand the peering ecosystem. In: ACM CCR (2014)
48. Luckie, M., Huffaker, B., Dhamdhere, A., Giotsas, V., Claffy, K.: AS relationships, customer cones, and validation. In: ACM IMC (2013)
49. Marder, A., Luckie, M., Dhamdhere, A., Huffaker, B., Smith, J., Claffy, K.: Pushing the boundaries with bdrmapIT: mapping router ownership at internet scale. In: Internet Measurement Conference (IMC), pp. 56–69, November 2018
50. Mauldin, A.: Is your planned submarine cable doomed? (2019). https://blog.telegeography.com/is-your-planned-submarine-cable-doomed
51. Mbaye, B., Gueye, A., Banse, D., Diop, A.: Africa's online access: what data is getting accessed and where it is hosted? In: Bassioni, G., Kebe, C.M.F., Gueye, A., Ndiaye, A. (eds.) InterSol 2019. LNICST, vol. 296, pp. 50–61. Springer, Cham (2019). https://doi.org/10.1007/978-3-030-34863-2_5

52. Poese, I., Uhlig, S., Kaafar, M.A., Donnet, B., Gueye, B.: IP geolocation databases: unreliable? SIGCOMM CCR **41**(2), 53–56 (2011)
53. Richter, P., et al.: A multi-perspective analysis of carrier-grade NAT deployment. In: IMC 2016, pp. 215–229. ACM, New York (2016)
54. RIPE NCC. Probes (2020). https://atlas.ripe.net/probes/
55. RIPE NCC. RIPE Atlas - user-defined measurements (2020). https://atlas.ripe.net/docs/udm/
56. RIPE NCC. RIPE Atlas Probe Archive (2020). https://ftp.ripe.net/ripe/atlas/probes/archive/
57. RIPE NCC. RIS - RIPE network coordination center (2020). http://www.ris.ripe.net/peerlist/all.shtml
58. Roberts, H., Larochelle, D., Faris, R., John, P.: Mapping local internet control. Tech Report, Berkman Center, Harvard University (2011)
59. RouteViews. Collectors - RouteViews (2020). http://www.routeviews.org/routeviews/index.php/collectors/
60. Shah, A., Fontugne, R., Papadopoulos, C.: Towards characterizing international routing detours. In: AINTEC 2016, pp. 17–24. ACM, New York (2016)
61. Soldo, F., Metwally, A.: Traffic anomaly detection based on the IP size distribution. In: 2012 Proceedings IEEE INFOCOM, pp. 2005–2013 (2012)
62. Su, A.-J., Choffnes, D.R., Kuzmanovic, A., Bustamante, F.E.: Drafting behind Akamai (travelocity-based detouring). In: ACM CCR. ACM, New York (2006)
63. Talanei. ASH Cable buys bandwidth from TUI Samoa (2020). https://www.talanei.com/2018/05/10/ash-cable-buys-bandwidth-from-tui-samoa/
64. TeleGeography. Submarine Cable Map (2020). www.submarinecablemap.com
65. TOT Public Company Limited. TOT: International Submarine Cable (2020). https://www.boi.go.th/upload/content/tot_5d254fe992f21.pdf
66. Wählisch, M., Schmidt, T.C., de Brün, M., Häberlen, T.: Exposing a nation-centric view on the German internet – a change in perspective on AS-level. In: Taft, N., Ricciato, F. (eds.) PAM 2012. LNCS, vol. 7192, pp. 200–210. Springer, Heidelberg (2012). https://doi.org/10.1007/978-3-642-28537-0_20
67. Zeitoun, A., Chuah, C.-N., Bhattacharyya, S., Diot, C.: An as-level study of internet path delay characteristics. In: IEEE Global Telecommunications Conference, 2004. GLOBECOM 2004, vol. 3, pp. 1480–1484 (2004)
68. Zhou, S., Zhang, G., Zhang, G.: Chinese internet AS-level topology. IET Commun. **2**(1) (2007)
69. Zhuo, R., Huffaker, B., Claffy, K., Greenstein, S.: The impact of the general data protection regulation on internet interconnection. Telecommun. Policy **45**(2) (2021)

Longitudinal Study of Internet-Facing OpenSSH Update Patterns

Jonathan Codi West[✉] and Tyler Moore

School of Cyber Studies, The University of Tulsa, Tulsa, OK, USA
{codiwest,tyler-moore}@utulsa.edu

Abstract. Keeping server software patched and up-to-date is a never-ending struggle for system administrators that is crucial for security. Nevertheless, we know little about how well or how consistently software updates are applied over time across the Internet. We shed light on software update behavior on publicly addressable networks by utilizing Internet-wide scans of OpenSSH banners. We primarily focus on OpenSSH banners which contain patch-level information in order to map accurate release dates. We augment this view by tracking which software security backports fix vulnerabilities in older OpenSSH versions. We find that the availability of backports, not CVE announcements or upstream software updates, trigger rapid updates. Unfortunately, we also determine that the lag in publishing backports (if they are published at all) combined with the steady cadence of new vulnerability reports ensures that most of the time, the vast majority of machines are vulnerable to at least one CVE. Additionally, we observe that major cloud hosting providers are consistently faster to apply patches.

1 Introduction

One of the pillars of cybersecurity hygiene is updating software regularly. When vulnerabilities are identified, developers issue security patches to seal the hole. While much progress has been made in improving the update process for end users, patching server-side systems can still be difficult. Unpatched systems in turn offer an opportunity for attackers to exploit vulnerabilities that lead to compromise.

Despite the importance of patching, we do not know very much about the patching practices at Internet scale. In this paper, we measure software outdatedness on the publicly-facing IPv4 address space. We demonstrate that naïve approaches to measure outdatedness through publicly-announced version information paints too negative a picture of patching in the enterprise.

We hone in on "backports", patches applied by operating system distributors to fix older software versions, to get a more accurate picture. One positive conclusion is that backports are rapidly applied by many, and therefore software is often more up-to-date than what can be inferred by looking at the version information alone. Nonetheless, we uncover significant concerns. For the case of

O. Hohlfeld et al. (Eds.): PAM 2022, LNCS 13210, pp. 675–689, 2022.
https://doi.org/10.1007/978-3-030-98785-5_30

OpenSSH backports on Ubuntu, we determined that around 25% of CVEs had no backport issued. During most of the 2015–2019 period under investigation, all servers were vulnerable to at least one CVE, often more. Moreover, at any given time between 40–80% of machines that could apply a backport to fix a CVE have not yet done so.

We review our approach to data collection in Sect. 2. We then set out to iteratively refine our definition of software outdatedness and patching levels in Sect. 3. In Sect. 4 we explicitly connect software outdatedness to software vulnerabilities for the case of OpenSSH software running on Ubuntu. We discuss limitations in Sect. 5, followed by Related Work before concluding in Sect. 7.

2 Data Collection Methodology

We utilize Censys [2] to acquire open ports and service banner data across the entire IPv4 address space. Censys keeps historical data, and thus we download several snapshots between 2017 and 2020, which contain banners for the services listed in Table 1. After narrowing the scope to just OpenSSH banners, we downloaded weekly snapshots of the entire IPv4 address space that have SSH banners. These weekly snapshots range from October 2015, which was the earliest we found SSH banners on Censys, through December 2020, although more recent data is planned for future work.

We gather software version release dates of several popular Internet-facing software packages from Github [5] and their respective websites and changelogs where available. As will be explained in Sect. 3.2, security patch release and superseded dates for the OpenSSH software package running on the Ubuntu or Debian Linux distributions are gathered from Launchpad [6]. We acquired OpenSSH patch data dating back to OpenSSH 1.3.8 on Ubuntu Warty (4.10) in 2005.

We gather announced IPv4 address space for several cloud service providers, namely Amazon AWS, Azure Cloud, and Google Cloud. The announced address spaces for these providers are mapped to the IPv4 addresses gathered from Censys. Additionally, we use MaxMind's GeoIP2 dataset [4] and Bureau van Dijk's Orbis [9] resource to identify company ownership for IPv4 CIDR blocks.

2.1 Ethical Considerations

We did not perform active or passive scanning of Internet hosts in our data collection. We chose to use pre-existing data and not perform unnecessary scans.

3 Measuring Software Outdatedness

We iteratively build a more sophisticated and accurate measurement of software outdatedness and apply it to the data gathered.

Table 1. Software versions inferred from banner, with example banner text.

Port	Software	Example Banner
80, 443	Apache2	`Apache/2.4.16 (Unix) OpenSSL/1.0.1e-fips`
80, 443	NGINX	`nginx/1.10.3 (Ubuntu)`
21	Bftpd	`bftpd 2.2`
21	FileZilla Server	`FileZilla 0.9.47`
21	Proftpd	`ProFTPD 1.3.4a`
21	Vsftpd	`vsftpd 3.0.2`
22	OpenSSH	`SSH-2.0-OpenSSH_6.7p1 Debian-5+deb8u4`

3.1 First Cut: Base Software Version

We initially explored banner data for over a dozen ports from Censys based on data availability of those ports over time and their perceived popularity. Some of these ports run software that present version information in the banner. This version information may be parsed out and then mapped to the release dates gathered from GitHub and their respective websites. Table 1 displays which software had release dates gathered.

The software release dates are mapped to each IP address with version info. To give an initial impression of the age of Internet software, we subtract a given software version's publish date from the Censys snapshot date to compute the *days since release* for that software version. But this does not really measure outdatedness, since software only becomes out of date once a newer version is released. Hence, to track software freshness, we calculate the difference between the snapshot date and when a given software version was *superseded* by a newer version. The days superseded metric more accurately conveys how long the server owner waited to upgrade and is therefore responsible for running outdated software. If a software version is at the latest version at the date of the snapshot, then days superseded is set to 0.

For the services in Table 1, we compare the distribution of days superseded among ports. Figure 1 shows CDFs for each port using the 2020-08-08 snapshot. We see that the software on these ports tends to be rather old. It is reasonable that port 80 and port 443 have very similar curves given that they run the same software, although port 443 is running on roughly half of the number of IPs that port 80 runs on. Port 443 also has a slight edge in running more recently released software versions. OpenSSH on port 22 lags behind port 80 and 443 for the first three years and then follows a similar curve. The biggest difference is that Port 21 (FTP) is running much older software than the other three ports.

3.2 Second Cut: Integrating Security Patches

Using the superseded date of the base software version, gives a rather incomplete view of the age of Internet software. Basing software patch levels entirely on the

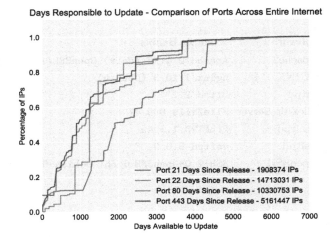

Fig. 1. Comparison of days superseded for the various services in Table 1.

software version information alone may be misleading as it ignores common security practice. Some operating systems will "backport" security patches into older versions of a given software without changing the base version number (referred to hereon as the *upstream* version number or upstream patch). In these cases, software may appear to be quite old when looking at the superseded date of the upstream version number even though the security patches are more recent and may fix vulnerabilities which were present in that upstream version.

It is often the case that security patch level information is hidden to all but those with access to the system, which is unfortunate in the case of external measurement via the Internet. Fortunately, we have identified one case where we can reliably observe the presence of backports. In OpenSSH, the security patch version is shown in some banners depending on the configuration of the host operating system, including the popular Ubuntu and Debian Linux distributions. See the example of the following Ubuntu OpenSSH banner string:

```
SSH-2.0-OpenSSH_7.6p1 Ubuntu-4ubuntu0.3
```

In this banner, the base version of OpenSSH is 7.6p1, which was released on 2017-10-03 according to [5]. Comparatively, the patch level is 7.6p1-4ubuntu0.3, which was released on 2019-03-04 according to Launchpad [7]. Coincidentally, we can infer the operating system version of this machine because this security patch version is only found on Ubuntu Bionic (18.04). All banners on Launchpad refer to a specific backport. While usually unique, the same banner is occasionally used for an LTS release and concurrent development release of Ubuntu. We considered patches in the release, updates, and security channels/pockets on Launchpad. Out of 286 entries examined from 2005 to 2020, 30 were duplicated across two releases. In those cases, the only discernible difference is the date when the patch was published on its respective release. Consequently, we use the patch release date of the LTS version of Ubuntu if it differs. While spoofing these banners is possible, we expect it to be rare since doing so requires editing and compiling the OpenSSH source code. Any edited banners that do not exactly match an Ubuntu backport banner are excluded from that portion of the analysis.

Clearly, these patches can be mapped to a much later release date than initially inferred from looking at the upstream OpenSSH version alone. Figure 3a compares the "days superseded" of the Ubuntu security patch level (green line) to the upstream OpenSSH version level (orange line). Now the picture is not only more accurate, it is also a much better outlook from a security perspective. Around 80% of the Ubuntu OpenSSH servers immediately apply patches. If one simply judged software freshness based on the OpenSSH version, 80% of servers would be considered more than three years outdated.

From this analysis, we conclude that the picture of server software updates is not as bad as it is often portrayed. We are not out of the woods, though, because 20% of OpenSSH servers are slow to patch. That is a non-trivial number of servers. Moreover, more work needs to be done to connect the application of OpenSSH patches to the presence of software vulnerabilities, which we undertake in the next section.

Focusing on OpenSSH banners with security patch information does limit the number of IP addresses that can be used for measurement. In the case of Fig. 3a, which is based on the 2020-08-08 snapshot of Censys, we are using roughly one-third of the total OpenSSH IPs for the Ubuntu security patch measurement. For reference, this same snapshot has a total of 132 million IP addresses, and about 17.6 million of those have port 22 open, 14.7 million of which run OpenSSH. Of these 14.7 million, 4.8 million run Ubuntu, and therefore have accurate backport information. Figure 2 demonstrates the coverage of OpenSSH that the Ubuntu distribution provides. Debian and Raspbian also provide patch information in the banner and could be analyzed in future work. While RedHat Enterprise Linux and its relatives make extensive use of backports [10], they regrettably do not provide patch information in the banner and thus fall into the unknown category with other distributions. For the remainder of this work, we narrow our focus where OpenSSH backported security patch information is visible, namely servers running Ubuntu Linux.

3.3 Do Cloud-Hosted Servers Update Faster?

We next consider whether large cloud providers exhibit different updating behavior compared to the rest of the Internet. We consider three major hosting providers, Amazon Web Services (specifically EC2), Azure Cloud, and Google Cloud. We map their IP addresses based on the publicly announced netblocks each share.

Figure 3b uses OpenSSH patch superseded dates on Ubuntu to compare cloud providers and the remainder of the Internet. Overall, we see that all three cloud providers have relatively similar patch level distributions and that the remainder of the Internet lags behind. These cloud providers collectively account for around

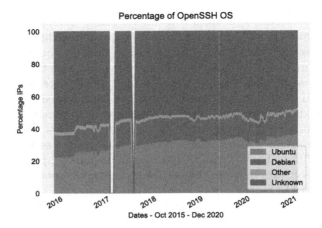

Fig. 2. Coverage of OpenSSH by operating system over time.

one third of all hosted Ubuntu OpenSSH servers, so their improved performance does make a difference overall.

4 How Vulnerable is Outdated Software?

Now that the software patch level of OpenSSH can be more accurately deduced, we look at the distribution of CVEs for OpenSSH over time to test if CVEs influence patch speed. We have collected additional snapshots from Censys which range from late 2015 through 2020 on a nearly weekly basis and contain SSH banners for the entire IPv4 address space collected by Censys. We parse every SSH banner and map to a backported patch version where applicable.

We examined CVEs announced between August 2015 and the end of 2019. For each of these 27 CVEs, we create a mapping of which backported patches are affected by which CVEs. For this mapping, we start by checking which upstream versions are affected by each CVE from the National Vulnerability Database [8]. If the upstream OpenSSH version of a given security patch is not affected by a CVE, then that patch version is not considered to be affected either. For security patches where the upstream version is affected by a given CVE, we inspect the changelog text for that patch, available on Launchpad [7], to see whether either that patch or a previous patch in its tree claim to fix that CVE.

Table 2 reports the CVEs with initial publish dates, the earliest upstream patch date, and earliest Ubuntu backport patch date (if one is available). We also compute the lag between when a given CVE was announced and when it was patched in the upstream or backported fix. In the cases where the lag for the OpenSSH fix is negative, the CVE affected older versions but not the most recent one released at that time. In the few cases where the Ubuntu backport lag is negative, the CVE appeared as fixed in the changelog before the official publish date on the NVD website.

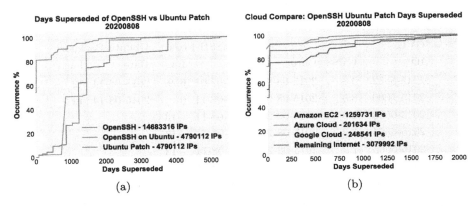

Fig. 3. (a) Comparison of days superseded for OpenSSH servers overall, on Ubuntu (upstream version) and Ubuntu (backport version). (b) Days superseded for OpenSSH Ubuntu servers running on major cloud service providers using backport information.

We note that 7 of the 27 CVEs are not fixed in any backports, so the only way to eliminate these vulnerabilities is to manually update the OpenSSH software to a newer upstream version. One CVE (2016-8858) was disputed in the community whether it was even a vulnerability. No backport was issued.

We utilize the mapping of CVEs to vulnerable Ubuntu backports in order to compute the number OpenSSH servers that are vulnerable and not vulnerable to each CVE for each Censys snapshot within 2015 and 2019. We then combine these over time to show the total number of IPs which are and are not vulnerable to a given CVE over time. An example of this for CVE-2016-10009 is shown in Fig. 4. For this figure, the blue line represents the number of IP addresses which are vulnerable to CVE-2016-10009 over time, while the orange line is the number of IPs which are not vulnerable. The sum of the orange and blue lines at a given point on the x-axis is equal to the number of servers on that Censys snapshot which are running OpenSSH on Ubuntu with a security patch available on Launchpad. The noise in the table is related to the number of IP addresses Censys scanned at each point in time. The number of Ubuntu servers that Censys scans generally increases over time, aside from the sharp drop in early 2016 which might be attributed to large providers opting out of Censys scanning [3]. The gaps in the lines show where no scan data was available from Censys. Several snapshots between 2016 and 2018 contain significantly fewer IP addresses than adjacent snapshots, but we chose not to omit these scans from the plots because they accurately reflect variations in how much scanning Censys completed at those points in time. These dips should be ignored when drawing conclusions.

Table 2. OpenSSH CVEs released during period of study

CVE			OpenSSH Fixed		Ubuntu Backport	
ID	CVSS	Date	Date	Lag	Date	Lag
2015-5352	4.3	2015-08-02	2017-07-01	699	2015-08-14	12
2015-5600	8.5	2015-08-02	2015-08-11	9	2015-08-14	12
2015-6563	1.9	2015-08-24	2015-08-11	−13		
2015-6564	6.9	2015-08-24	2015-08-11	−13		
2015-6565	7.2	2015-08-24	2015-08-11	−13		
2015-8325	7.2	2016-04-30	2016-08-01	93	2016-04-15	−15
2016-0777	4	2016-01-14	2016-01-14	0	2016-01-14	0
2016-0778	4.6	2016-01-14	2016-01-14	0	2016-01-14	0
2016-1907	5	2016-01-19	2016-01-14	−5	2016-05-09	111
2016-1908	7.5	2017-04-11	2016-02-29	−407	2016-05-09	−337
2016-3115	5.5	2016-03-22	2016-03-10	−12	2016-05-09	48
2016-6210	4.3	2017-02-13	2016-08-01	−196	2016-08-15	−182
2016-6515	7.8	2016-08-07	2016-08-01	−6	2016-08-15	8
2016-8858	7.8	2016-12-09	2016-12-19	10	(disputed)	
2016-10009	7.5	2017-01-04	2016-12-19	−16	2018-01-22	383
2016-10010	6.9	2017-01-04	2016-12-19	−16	2018-01-22	383
2016-10011	2.1	2017-01-04	2016-12-19	−16	2018-01-22	383
2016-10012	7.2	2017-01-04	2016-12-19	−16	2018-01-22	383
2016-10708	5	2018-01-21	2016-12-19	−398	2018-11-06	289
2017-15906	5	2017-10-25	2017-10-03	−22	2018-01-22	89
2018-15473	5	2018-08-17	2018-08-24	7	2018-11-06	81
2018-15919	5	2018-08-28	2018-10-19	52		
2018-20685	2.6	2019-01-10	2019-04-17	97	2019-01-22	12
2019-6109	4	2019-01-31	2019-04-17	76	2019-02-07	7
2019-6110	4	2019-01-31	2019-04-17	76		
2019-6111	5.8	2019-01-31	2019-04-17	76	2019-02-07	7
2019-16905	7.8	2019-10-09	2019-10-09	0		
			Median	−5		12

We observe that the near simultaneous publication of the CVE and upstream patch has very little impact on the deployment of vulnerable servers. The steady increase in vulnerable OpenSSH servers continues for slightly more than one year until the Ubuntu backport is published, at which point the patch is rapidly applied to more than one million machines, followed by a steady linear increase in the subsequent months and years. From this one example, at least, it appears that the availability of backports is by far the dominant factor in applying updates to eliminate software vulnerabilities.

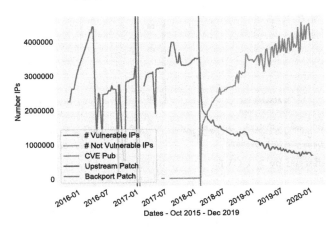

Fig. 4. Number of IP addresses that are affected by CVE-2016-10009 over time

We analyzed the plots of all 27 CVEs (available in Appendix A) to see if the same trend held true. We see that many IP addresses patch very quickly as soon as a backported patch for a CVE is released, although some never patch. For the CVEs that do not have a security backport (with the darker backgrounds), the results are less predictable. Often, the number of vulnerable servers naturally goes down over time as users update their software for other reasons (e.g., CVE-2015-6563). In other cases, the number of vulnerable servers continues to increase well after the CVE was published (e.g., CVE-2018-15919).

Another consistent finding from inspecting the graphs is that the publication of the CVE and upstream patch is *not* the catalyst for updates. Rather, it is consistently the backport that sparks an uptick in patches to plug vulnerabilities.

We now collapse back down from the 27 individual plots in Appendix A that capture exposure to individual CVEs to a single, aggregated view of the presence of vulnerabilities in OpenSSH over time. Ultimately, what matters from a security perspective is whether systems have any unpatched vulnerabilities present.

We start by calculating the fraction of Ubuntu OpenSSH servers throughout the Internet which are affected by at least one published CVE. We see in Fig. 5a that almost all OpenSSH servers are affected by at least one CVE throughout the time of our measurement, saving a small percentage that quickly updated in late 2016. Given that not all CVEs received a backported patch in Ubuntu, this result is perhaps inevitable, but it is alarming nonetheless.

To account for this, we construct additional measures that focus only on the 20 CVEs which have an associated Ubuntu backport. Figure 5b again plots the percentage of Ubuntu OpenSSH servers that affected by one or more vulnerabilities with an available backport patch. The percentages here are a bit better, falling to around 60% of hosts vulnerable to at least one CVE before new vul-

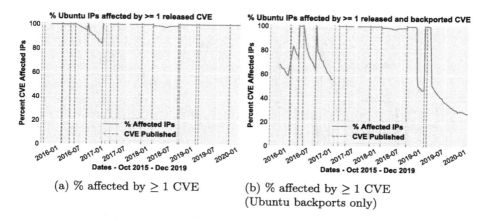

(a) % affected by ≥ 1 CVE

(b) % affected by ≥ 1 CVE
(Ubuntu backports only)

Fig. 5. Fraction of Ubuntu OpenSSH servers with vulnerabilities over time.

nerabilities are published, rendering all hosts vulnerable until a backport can be issued. Note that for two years in 2016 to 2018 new CVEs were consistently published before backports to the older CVEs were disseminated. The largest reason for this is that several CVEs were released in 2016 which did not receive a patch until 2018, so in the meantime, every LTS version of Ubuntu that was stuck on the upstream OpenSSH version without a security backport was vulnerable. At that point, the only way to not be vulnerable to those CVEs would be to install a fixed upstream version of OpenSSH directly. From the above plots, we can see that no matter how quickly one applies security backports, there is still a chance that the server is vulnerable to at least one CVE.

One could argue that the measurements in the previous graphs are "unfair" to system administrators because their servers will remain vulnerable even if they follow best practice and apply security patches as soon as the backports are published. To distinguish between those making a best effort and those simply not applying available security patches, Fig. 7a instead plots the percentage of machines which have not applied all available CVE-related backport patches. This can be interpreted as the fraction of machines responsible to patch a vulnerability that have not done so.

Here, the findings are better, but still quite discouraging. The green dashed vertical lines here indicate when the backport patch is published. Hence, when a new patch is published, the percentage who can apply the patch but have not jumps to 100, before rapidly diminishing. We can see that during periods when relatively few backports are issued, the population can catch up, with the unpatched share falling to nearly 20% at one point in early 2018. However, we can also see that in other cases, when there are multiple backports issued in a row, the servers cannot keep up with applying all of the patches. Hence, an increasing frequency of distributing backports can in fact make it harder for systems to maintain security.

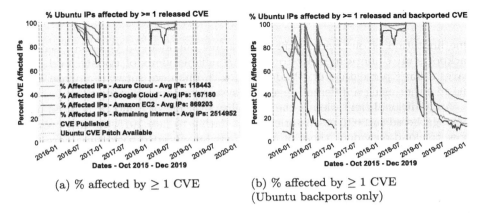

(a) % affected by ≥ 1 CVE

(b) % affected by ≥ 1 CVE
(Ubuntu backports only)

Fig. 6. Fraction of Ubuntu OpenSSH servers with vulnerabilities over time split by cloud provider.

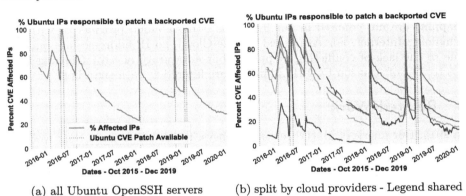

(a) all Ubuntu OpenSSH servers

(b) split by cloud providers - Legend shared
with Figure 6a

Fig. 7. Fraction of Ubuntu OpenSSH servers which are fully patched with available patches that fix vulnerabilities over time.

We utilize the previous method for distinguishing cloud providers from the remainder of the Internet for Figs. 6a, 6b, and 7b. Once again, machines running on one of the three main cloud providers are generally patched faster than the remainder of the Internet. While all perform better, a greater percentage of machines on Google Cloud is consistently patched and not vulnerable to CVEs. We also note that where the cloud providers do best is in rapidly applying backports when they become available. They do not appear to upgrade systems by applying upstream patches, which is shown in the similarly poor performance in Fig. 6a. Even when hosted in the cloud, most machines are vulnerable to at least one vulnerability most of the time.

5   Limitations

One limitation of our work is that we narrow our focus to OpenSSH security backports on Ubuntu in order to obtain a reliable views of update level. This leaves a large percentage of IP addresses with unknown software update levels due to either using a different operating system or Linux distribution.

An additional limitation is the reliability of using of cloud IP address mappings gathered in 2021 on historical data dating to late 2015. As more servers move to cloud providers, those providers may have needed to acquire more IPv4 addresses over the years, causing the IP mappings to not be constant over time. We attempt to account for this by comparing the cloud IP mappings to 10 historical snapshots of MaxMind's GeoIP dataset [4] spanning from July 2015 to January 2020 at roughly six month intervals. For each Censys snapshot date, the nearest GeoIP mapping is compared to the given cloud provider's announced mapping from 2021. For example, with Amazon EC2, we verify that "amazon" is in the GeoIP mapping. A similar pattern is followed for Google and Microsoft. IP addresses that conflict with the organizations listed in the nearest GeoIP mapping are not counted in our figures as either a cloud provider or with the remaining Internet. For Azure and Google Cloud, no IP addresses are omitted due to the lack of conflicting mappings, but an average of 3.6% (ranging from 1% to 5%) of Amazon EC2 IP addresses are filtered at each snapshot.

6   Related Work

In 2015, Durumeric et al. [12] released Censys, which builds upon their work on fast Internet scanning with Zmap in [14]. Censys scans the Internet using Zmap and Zgrab and stores the information in a database. The Internet-wide scan data can be queried by researchers through either their web frontend or through Google BigQuery [1]. Historical Censys data can be queried as well from Google BigQuery. We utilize Censys extensively for this work through researcher access on Google BigQuery.

The empirical measurement of security patches and vulnerabilities is highly relevant to our work. Durumeric et al. [13] follow the release and subsequent patching of the Heartbleed vulnerability. Li and Paxson [15] analyzed thousands of security patches in the National Vulnerability Database [8]. An interesting finding is the difference in the time from when a CVE ID is publicly disclosed and when it appears in the NVD database. This disparity helps explain how a Ubuntu backport can fix a vulnerability that was not "published" until later (see Fig. 2).

O'Hare [17] utilizes Censys and Shodan to identify vulnerabilities on Internet-wide scans. The possibility of backporting security patches to fix CVEs is mentioned, but it does not seem that steps were taken to account for this. Demir et al. [11] analyze 5.6M websites and discussed the update behavior of many types of HTTP(S)-related software (port 80 and 443) and libraries. It also discusses the implications of CVSS scores to updates. It does not appear to consider security backports of server software, which is a focus of our study.

Several researchers have used surveys and interviews to better understand the update process of system administrators, which is relevant to our work in that it can provide explanations for why software updates are applied or not. Li et al. [16] conducted over 100 surveys and 17 qualitative interviews with system administrators and outline what they found to be the 5 stages of the system administrator update process. Similarly, Tiefenau et al. [18] conducted 7 qualitative interviews and 67 online surveys. Both Li et al. and Tiefenau et al. discuss the obstacles that delay or prevent system administrators from applying updates. They also demonstrate the variance in how system administrators approach updates. While most agree on the necessity of timely updates for the sake of security, a minority did not.

7   Concluding Remarks

Despite its importance for cybersecurity, measuring the extent to which software is up-to-date at Internet scale has not often been attempted. One reason why is that it is often hard to construct an accurate picture with external measurements. In this paper, we have demonstrated that simple approaches to measuring outdatedness based on version information appearing in publicly observable banners often fall short. Instead, we have shown that by focusing on the special cases where we can observe the presence of backports, we can construct a more accurate global measurement for the case of the 4 million-plus servers running OpenSSH on Ubuntu Linux.

We find that these backports do in fact trigger the application of security patches for a significant fraction of the population, much more than vulnerability announcements or updates directly from the software developer. We also observe that when backports are not created, these vulnerabilities tend to remain unfixed for most of the population. Moreover, the frequency of introducing new vulnerabilities has ensured that most servers remain vulnerable most of the time. While we have also presented evidence that cloud providers do a better job, it is not enough to keep hosts running on those platforms from being consistently laden with unpatched vulnerabilities.

Acknowledgments. This research was supported by the Air Force Research Laboratory (AFRL) under agreement number FA8750-19-1-0152. The U.S. Government is authorized to reproduce and distribute reprints for Governmental purposes notwithstanding any copyright notation thereon. The views and conclusions contained herein are those of the authors and should not be interpreted as necessarily representing the official policies or endorsements, either expressed or implied, of AFRL or the U.S. Government.

A   Appendix A Plots of Ubuntu IPs Affected by CVEs

Below are the plots (similar to Fig. 4 of vulnerable Ubuntu IPs per CVE within the October 2015 through December 2019 measurement period ordered sequentially by vulnerability publication date. Plots with a darker background do not have a backport on Ubuntu.

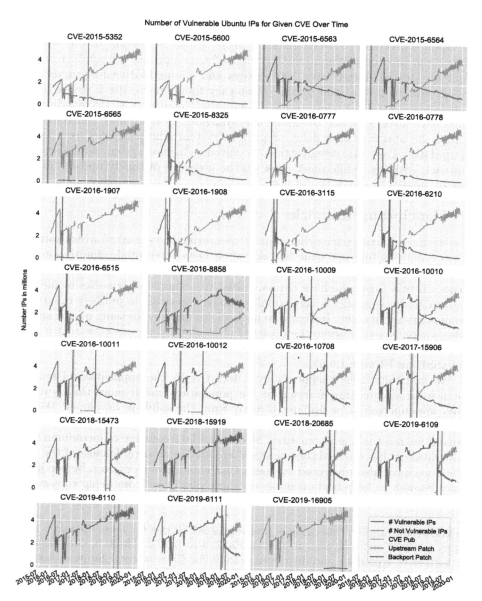

Number of Vulnerable Ubuntu IPs for Given CVE Over Time

References

1. BigQuery: Cloud Data Warehouse. https://cloud.google.com/bigquery
2. Censys. https://censys.io/
3. Censys Opt Out. https://support.censys.io/hc/en-us/articles/360043177092-Opt-Out-of-Scanning
4. GeoIP® Databases & Services: Industry Leading IP Intelligence—xMind. https://www.maxmind.com/en/geoip2-services-and-databases

5. GitHub. https://github.com/
6. Launchpad. https://launchpad.net/index.html
7. Launchpad: Publishing history: Openssh package : Ubuntu. https://launchpad.net/ubuntu/+source/openssh/+publishinghistory
8. NVD. https://nvd.nist.gov/
9. Orbis—Compare Private Company Data—Bureau van Dijk. https://www.bvdinfo.com/en-us/our-products/data/international/orbis
10. What is backporting, and how does it apply to RHEL and other Red Hat products? https://www.redhat.com/en/blog/what-backporting-and-how-does-it-apply-rhel-and-other-red-hat-products
11. Demir, N., Urban, T., Wittek, K., Pohlmann, N.: Our (in)secure web: understanding update behavior of websites and its impact on security. In: Hohlfeld, O., Lutu, A., Levin, D. (eds.) PAM 2021. LNCS, vol. 12671, pp. 76–92. Springer, Cham (2021). https://doi.org/10.1007/978-3-030-72582-2_5
12. Durumeric, Z., Adrian, D., Mirian, A., Bailey, M., Halderman, J.A.: A search engine backed by internet-wide scanning. In: Proceedings of the 22nd ACM SIGSAC Conference on Computer and Communications Security - CCS '15, pp. 542–553. ACM Press, Denver (2015). http://dl.acm.org/citation.cfm?doid=2810103.2813703
13. Durumeric, Z., et al.: The matter of heartbleed. In: Proceedings of the 2014 Conference on Internet Measurement Conference, IMC '14, pp. 475–488. Association for Computing Machinery, New York (2014). https://doi.org/10.1145/2663716.2663755
14. Durumeric, Z., Wustrow, E., Halderman, J.A.: ZMap: fast internet-wide scanning and its security applications. In: 22nd USENIX Security Symposium (USENIX Security 13). USENIX Association, Washington, D.C. (2013). https://www.usenix.org/conference/usenixsecurity13/technical-sessions/paper/durumeric
15. Li, F., Paxson, V.: A large-scale empirical study of security patches. In: Proceedings of the 2017 ACM SIGSAC Conference on Computer and Communications Security, CCS '17, pp. 2201–2215, Association for Computing Machinery, New York (2017). https://doi.org/10.1145/3133956.3134072
16. Li, F., Rogers, L., Mathur, A., Malkin, N., Chetty, M.: Keepers of the machines: examining how system administrators manage software updates, p. 16 (2019)
17. O'Hare, J., Macfarlane, R., Lo, O.: Identifying vulnerabilities using internet-wide scanning data. In: 2019 IEEE 12th International Conference on Global Security, Safety and Sustainability (ICGS3), pp. 1–10. IEEE, London, United Kingdom (2019). https://doi.org/10.1109/ICGS3.2019.8688018. https://ieeexplore.ieee.org/document/8688018/
18. Tiefenau, C., Häring, M., Krombholz, K., von Zezschwitz, E.: Security, availability, and multiple information sources: exploring update behavior of system administrators. In: Sixteenth Symposium on Usable Privacy and Security (SOUPS 2020), pp. 239–258 (2020). https://www.usenix.org/conference/soups2020/presentation/tiefenau

Author Index